T0284889

TILAK

TILAK

The Empire's Biggest Enemy

Vaibhav Purandare

VINTAGE

An imprint of Penguin Random House

VINTAGE

Vintage is an imprint of the Penguin Random House group of companies
whose addresses can be found at global.penguinrandomhouse.com

Published by Penguin Random House India Pvt. Ltd
4th Floor, Capital Tower 1, MG Road,
Gurugram 122 002, Haryana, India

First published in Vintage by Penguin Random House India 2024

Copyright © Vaibhav Purandare 2024

Photographs courtesy *Lokmanya* (a photobiography),
Lokmanya Tilak Vichar Manch, Pune, 2014

10 9 8 7 6 5 4 3 2 1

The views and opinions expressed in this book are the author's own and the
facts are as reported by him which have been verified to the extent possible,
and the publishers are not in any way liable for the same.

Please note that no part of this book may be used or reproduced in any manner
for the purpose of training artificial intelligence technologies or systems.

ISBN 9780670095513

Typeset in Adobe Caslon Pro by MAP Systems, Bengaluru, India
Printed at Thomson Press India Ltd, New Delhi

www.penguin.co.in

For Vedant and Vardaan,
my nephews

Contents

Introduction

Before Mahatma Gandhi, there was Bal Gangadhar Tilak.

If Gandhi got the infinitely great Indian masses behind him in the freedom movement, Tilak was the one who got the vast majority of the Indian people involved—and seriously invested—in the fight for liberation in the first place. Without the solid base built by Tilak, Gandhi would have had no mass movement to build on and carry forward. Tilak made the first major cracks in the British Raj's imposing structure, and the punch he packed in smashing its walls paved the way for the Mahatma and his apostles like Jawaharlal Nehru, Sardar Patel and Subhas Chandra Bose to walk through and deliver on the dream of complete freedom.

It's hard to fully understand and make sense of the Indian struggle for political independence without taking an extremely close and searching look at this man, who laid the foundational stones for self-assertion against the Empire. And it would be impossible to comprehend the real nature of the Empire's relentless repression, ruthless authoritarianism and repeated attempts to bulldoze legitimate Indian aspirations without examining the myriad ways in which it sought to nail Tilak, who was the most articulate voice of those aspirations for an entire era.

The strange thing is that Tilak has not been a subject for several biographers. For a man who was the most popular Indian of his time and the mobilizer of an entire colonized population, he has been ludicrously overlooked and his story and its significance by and large unrecognized. During his centenary in 1956, when India was still in the first flush of freedom, a flurry of books came out; after that, he joined many others, including Patel and Bose, in being relegated securely to the background, his life either devolved into clichés around his famous slogan of 'Swaraj is my birthright' or into a blur of dates in the manner of India's terrifically soporific textbooks.

It's necessary to remove that blur to throw light on the critical and vastly under-examined pre-Gandhi phase of the Indian national movement and to see how Tilak faced off against the Raj and kept going on despite being directly targeted, prosecuted and punished over and over again on charges of trying to overthrow the Empire.

Tilak's life had four broad phases. The first, of twenty-eight years from his birth in 1856 to 1884, was marked by his obsession with mathematics and swimming (both, in time, stuck with him for his entire life) and the development of a deep love for education and of an ardent public consciousness, which resulted in him tying up with the brilliant Marathi essayist Vishnushastri Chiplunkar and close friend Gopal Ganesh Agarkar to set up a school and college that would impart national education. In this same period, when Indians were getting used to the printing presses and daily and weekly publications, came his two newspapers, the *Kesari* in Marathi and *Mahratta* in English. Tilak shaped both his papers into remarkably effective vehicles of political propaganda when such advocacy methods were not well-developed on Indian soil. The third aspect of this growth was the formation, on his initiative, of the Deccan Education Society as the institutional framework for what was for Tilak a profoundly desired academic life.

Politics was intricately blended with the kind of activities he had initiated, and Tilak's politics took off in a big way in the second phase of his life, beginning with conflicts with his colleagues Gopal Krishna Gokhale and Agarkar within the Deccan Education Society and then inside the big tent of the Indian National Congress. This second phase, which spanned from 1885 to 1897, was of dramatic change—Tilak exited the Deccan Education Society after serious differences with his associates and plunged completely into public and political life. At the same time, going by his instincts and predilections, he embraced culture and religion, seeing them in a traditionalist society as essential and critical parts for the construction of public unity. He launched and built two powerful public festivals, one dedicated to Lord Ganesh and the other to the Maratha hero Chhatrapati Shivaji Maharaj, thus roping in farmers, artisans, and the lettered few as well as the unlettered majority for a variety of causes linked to nation-building such as cultural regeneration, industrial progress and the cultivation of the popular political psyche. This phase reached its apogee in 1897 when the British government booked him on charges of sedition and he was convicted and sentenced to one-and-a-half years in prison.

From 1897 to 1907, Tilak's popularity grew phenomenally across undivided India. It was in this third phase of his life that he established himself as the pre-eminent leader of the people's fight for emancipation. His championing of the campaign of 'boycott, Swadeshi and national education' in the wake of the Viceroy G. N. Curzon's plan to partition Bengal saw him outstrip Gokhale and others as the representative of the more combative and uncompromising wing of the Congress, a development that resulted in the famous Surat split of the Congress in 1907. By this time Tilak was being celebrated as 'Maharaj' after 'Shivaji Maharaj' from Pune to Pondicherry, Lahore to Lucknow and Calcutta to Calicut; just as importantly, he was being hailed as the 'Lokmanya', the one revered by the people. Naturally, the Raj cracked down against him, booking him for sedition once again and inaugurating the fourth phase of his life by packing him off to a prison in Mandalay, Burma, for six years when he was already fifty-two years old and diabetic. When that phase ended in 1914 and the fifth and final phase began, Tilak was the freedom movement's unchallenged leader and senior statesman. Gokhale, Pherozeshah Mehta and others had given way to him in terms of both popular appeal and respect; his return to the Congress was inevitable; and he was not only in control of the premier nationalist organization but in a position to decide the course of the Indian people's agitation more or less unimpeded by rivals in his peer group. In this phase came Tilak's 'Home Rule' campaign which spread far and wide, further increasing his fame and enhancing his reputation and incentivizing the Raj even more to portray him as the root cause of its troubles, a point Justice Rowlatt made at considerable length in his report by labelling Tilak as 'the father of Indian unrest'. During this fraught period, Tilak also took a bold step by spearheading the Lucknow Pact which delineated the new political arrangement between the Hindus and Muslims at a time when the Raj was fomenting Hindu–Muslim tensions. The pact attracted controversy but did not diminish his status, and with his leadership intact, Tilak made a fresh, daring move of diplomacy in 1918 by donating 2000 pounds to the British Labour Party to seek its support for the Indian cause, a move that bore fruit well after he died in 1920. It was no coincidence that on the very day Tilak died, Gandhi launched his non-cooperation movement, taking up the mantle of leadership directly from him.

If his political life was dramatic, Tilak's personal life had plenty of ups and downs. Apart from serious fights with his closest friends and colleagues, there were tragedies like the death of his eldest son, which shook him deeply, and then the passing on of his wife when he was locked up in a prison in Burma. There were legal wrangles with associates, ex-associates and their kin, wrangles which not only sapped his energy but caused him enormous anguish and hurt. Many of these were plain ego fights too, showing how people imbued with the noblest of motives are human just like all of us. And while the sword of criminal prosecution always hung heavily over his head—which the Indian population did not see as a sword but as a crown of sorts, making him, in the words of one scholar, 'the uncrowned king of the freedom struggle'[1]—there was also plenty of defamation to deal with, personal as well as political.

Above all, Tilak was a fascinating figure, a man whose life and personality had a transformative impact. In what way?

Tilak was born a year before the great 1857 Revolt, and after that revolt was crushed, the voice of Indians was for the next few decades extremely faint and feeble. The Indian National Congress in its first two decades, and its luminaries like Mahadev Govind Ranade, R.C. Dutt, Badruddin Tyabji, Pherozeshah Mehta and others who spoke for the indigenous population no doubt displayed grave concern for their fellow compatriots. But they were the elite, and their language and positioning were of the elitist. With their distance from the masses, they sounded aloof and impersonal, their prose was buttoned-up, their discussions were filled with verbiage and their representation of their people's concerns could be the dilution of those concerns to the extent of dismissing them by eulogizing the Empire. While the first president of the Congress, W.C. Bonnerjee, was more an Englishman than an Indian, 'almost ridiculed' political activism and in the words of B.C. Pal 'never appreciated the labours' of a nationalist like Surendranath Banerjee, even the grand old man of Indian politics, Dadabhai Naoroji, who had spoken of how Britain had drained India of its wealth, wanted India to grow under the Raj's control and went on to become a member of the British Parliament.[2] Truly these leaders held up the Empire as the dispenser of genuine justice, believed in its so-called fairness and appealed to what they termed as the British sense of evenhandedness. Several among these luminaries even referred to British rule as 'divine providence', God's gift to the Indian people.

Single-handedly, Tilak changed the very manner of communication with the colonial rulers. Through his newspapers, which became the mouthpieces of the silenced Indian, he chronicled the slights and insults suffered daily by the people from an exploitative and rapacious administration. Through his leadership of the Congress nationally and his straight confrontation with the Moderate Wing in it, he emerged as direct and outspoken. And through his work in the social and community sphere, he spoke equally clearly—starting and helming the public celebrations of the Ganesh and Shivaji festivals from 1893 and 1896 onwards respectively, he ensured that the growing national feeling for freedom flourished in India's, and Hinduism's, own cultural milieu; he transmitted his enthusiasm to the masses and marshalled them to fight for their rights, and he made the distinction between the style of his wing of the Congress—which came to be known as the Extremist Wing—and of the rival Moderate Wing stick, thus obliterating the Congress's status as little more than a debating society. He threw out the prose of 'prayers' and 'petitions' and introduced the notion of rights—a notion that the majority of Indians, subjugated and seriously short on confidence after the 1857 Revolt, had either lost sight of or simply not been awakened to. The British Empire did its utmost to crush the souls and spirits of an enslaved people and told them they were introducing them, for the first time, to the world of civilization. They portrayed them as backward 'heathens', incapable of looking after themselves and perpetually in need of outside control and of the British 'civilising mission'. If they so much as dared to show signs of growing a spine, the Raj would come down on them like a load of bricks to drag them back into the jaws of helpless subjugation. It is in this context that Tilak's declaration of 'Swaraj is my birthright and I will have it' was revolutionary: it came out during the glory years of the Empire when it was believed the sun would never set on the British Empire; it ranged far beyond the leap of the political advancement that other fellow nationalists had envisaged up until then, and it was offered as the definitive antidote to the takeover by the Raj of an ancient land in the eastern part of the world, the wholesale plunder of its resources and the wanton crushing of its inhabitants.

Tilak so offended the Raj with his plucky and forthright politics that it flagged him as the prime example of its own stringent applicability of the dreaded sedition law. The sedition case slapped against him in 1897, after two young revolutionaries from Pune had assassinated a couple of British officials, was only the second case of the 1870 law being applied, and the most high-profile one at that. Convicted and sentenced to 18 months in prison in that case, Tilak was booked once again in 1908 and this time packed off to Mandalay to serve a six-year prison term. In between, he was threatened with a slew of other civil and criminal charges, and in one particular case related to Tilak's personal dispute, the Raj actually got its own prosecutor to argue in court against him, unprecedentedly misusing state power in a matter of purely private litigation to try and ruin an uncompromising rebel. Undeterred, Tilak fought on but could never really stay away from the clutches of the law. His legal harassment for close to four decades, his arraignment in various courts on a series of charges, and his conviction in both 1897 and 1908 for having written Marathi articles which were not understood by the jurors even though the whole thrust of arguments in these cases was over the phrasing of sentences and the use of imagery and vocabulary are classic illustrations of the workings of the colonial judiciary and of the whole criminal justice system which made a mockery of fairness while claiming all along that it was in truth bringing the rule of law to a land that didn't know a thing about it.

And at a time when the Empire posited an India where civilization had never been invented at all, Tilak presented a powerfully robust cultural argument for the country and its people. This was one of his most substantive and lasting contributions. From Thomas Babington Macaulay's Minute of 1835, the British were determined to destroy Indian self-esteem and to create an educated elite that would not merely carry out clerical works and keep up their administration but be English in mind, body and spirit. Tilak saw much in India's past that was laudable, much that deserved to be cherished, protected and promoted, and much that was worthy of emulation even as India worked her way towards industrial growth of the Western kind. He wrote three books in all, all dealing with the subject, and his masterpiece was the third one, the *Gita Rahasya*, which offered a radical interpretation of the Bhagavad Gita as the advisor of relentless and selfless action even after the attainment of personal enlightenment, spiritual tranquillity and equanimity. Through his public talks and speeches, his patriotic newspaper writings and his continuous research, Tilak spoke eloquently for the depth and richness of Indian culture and heritage, not as a jingoistic enthusiast but as someone who could plumb the depths of the oldest Sanskrit texts in the language in which they were originally written and analyse them with the seriousness and gravitas of a scholar. His rediscovery of Indian culture and the Hindu classical texts proved to be in that age the bold excavation of a submerged and sunk national esteem, filling Indian hearts with the giddy potential of peering into a foreseeable future in the light of their past, unapologetic, unafraid and unfazed. One thread that ran especially through his voluminous newspaper writings was of a fabulous sense of satire, as much a sign of his cultural aplomb as of an imperturbable confidence in what he was saying.

Tilak was, at the same time, a paradox. He pushed the bounds of political progress aggressively, but socially he was conservative and positioned himself strongly against the social reformers during the Age of Consent Act controversy of 1891 and on various issues related to legislation on societal and religious customs. In terms of caste, he started as almost inflexible in supporting the caste hierarchy and moved gradually towards a policy of openness, but mostly only in words, for when it came to actions, he retraced his steps back to his original conservatism from time to time. If only he had demonstrated a greater will to bridge the caste gap, the divide that later deepened in western India, and as a result, in the rest of India—for western India was a pioneer in the anti-caste movement—between the Brahmans and the non-Brahman movement could have been closed and several subsequent caste conflicts avoided. But Tilak's participating and getting enmeshed in the inner cultural tensions of his era, showing that he was after all a man of his times, constitutes a chapter in itself of India's social and cultural history.

Paradoxically again, unlike the social reformers, Tilak communicated brilliantly with the masses across caste categories and got them directly involved in political agitation. Under his leadership, they felt they could fight for their future and the future of their families. When he was sentenced to six years in jail in 1908, thousands of mill workers in Mumbai went on strike for six days—a majority of them were non-Brahmans and included a large percentage of Marathas, apart from Ramoshis, Kolis and others. The Moderates, who called themselves 'liberals', taunted Tilak saying he was the leader of the '*telis*' (oil grinders) and '*tambolis*' (betel-leaf sellers),[3] two of the so-called lower castes, and he held up their taunts, born of elite disparagement of the common population, as prized medals and flaunted them with pride, winning ever greater goodwill among the voiceless and the neglected.

In any case, paradox or no paradox, Tilak never shied away from controversy. Quite the opposite: he delighted in being a controversialist. In all his quarrels, disputes and conflicts, he was pugnacious, defiantly pugilistic and quintessentially the argumentative Indian.

The story of his conflict with his kindred spirit, the social reformer Agarkar, is among the many things in this biography that show his penchant for controversy. This book reveals how, despite the mythology circulated over their falling-out, that it was the result of ideological differences through the decade of the 1880s—with Tilak representing tradition-bound Hindu society and Agarkar championing iconoclastic reformism—the truth is that it had both its origins and its denouement in very, very petty fights over money and control that broke out in the Deccan Education Society, the educational institution that Tilak and Agarkar founded in 1884. Tilak's clash with Gokhale, first at the micro level in Pune's institutions and then at the macro level in the Indian National Congress, on the other hand, was deeply political and ideological and shows the progression of the two chief conflicting currents in the Indian nationalist imagination of that period. Tilak triumphed over Gokhale and Gokhale's mentor Pherozeshah Mehta by dint of his will, his steel and his energetic activism through which he drew the masses into the fold of political agitation. Gokhale's mash-up of a limited endorsement of British 'benevolent despotism' and political accommodation under the aegis of Empire was no match for Tilak's stylish snark, his mastery of political evisceration, his catchy editorial headlines like 'Has the government lost its head?' and 'To run a government is not to be vindictive' and his edgy, appealing vulnerability that put him invariably within the grasp of Raj-enacted legislation and its vindictive punitive actions.

It was singularly Tilak's personality that led to the dramatic Congress split of 1907 in Lucknow. That ouster of Tilak's group marked a substantial shift in the national mood in the direction of aggressive anti-Raj activity, compelling the Raj to put it on record in 1907 and 1908 that Tilak was its greatest enemy. It was during this era that the trio of 'Lal, Bal and Pal', the other two being B.C. Pal and Lala Lajpat Rai, began to be hailed across India. While Tilak was always, even as part of this trio, the pre-eminent leader, very quickly he was left carrying the torch of the assertive group of Indian nationalists entirely on his own. Both Lal and Pal went abroad towards the end of the first decade of the twentieth century and stayed there for long periods; Pal, in fact, considerably softened his stand towards the Raj. The one leader who could have quickly risen in stature and perhaps have stood shoulder to shoulder with Tilak was Aurobindo Ghose, 16 years younger than the Lokmanya and part of a revolutionary group from Bengal. Aurobindo openly questioned the nomenclature given to the rival groups in the Congress. Tilak's group, to which Aurobindo belonged, was being called 'Extremist', while Gokhale, Mehta and others comprised the 'Moderates,' terms from the Raj era that are still universally applied during any discussion of the Indian freedom struggle, including in this book for their longtime association with the two ideologically disparate sections of the Congress. Aurobindo said the two groups should instead be called 'Nationalist' and 'Loyalist' respectively, though he suggested a third, in-between category of 'Moderates' that would include the likes of Dadabhai Naoroji and Surendranath Banerjee.[4] There was nothing 'extreme' in what Tilak and his group were demanding, he said. How could the call for political emancipation be 'extremist'? And, similarly, the argument went, a majority of the 'Moderates' were actually 'loyalists' because they stood for upholding the Empire, not challenging it or parting ways with it. But Aurobindo was in a sense chased away, into French-ruled Pondicherry by the Raj, which was in pursuit of him, and there he took up spirituality, giving up politics altogether.

When Aurobindo disappeared from the movement in 1909, Tilak was in Mandalay. Tilak's big shift after his release from there in 1914 towards greater accommodation and ultimately in the direction of championing the Lucknow Pact, though termed by several as his move toward moderation, was equally an element of his controversial self, willing to take chances if he felt those chances could result in positive outcomes. Tilak was not anti-Muslim, and Muslims participated in both the Ganesh and Shivaji festivals that he had started. Yet, during the

1893 Hindu–Muslim riots in various parts of the Bombay Presidency, including Mumbai, he had stood solidly by the Hindu community, blaming the Muslims for triggering the violence and not seeking to create any equivalence for the sake of being deemed acceptable by both sections. He was certainly not in favour of separate electorates which Minto and Morley introduced through the 1909 reforms, thus opening the door further to communal conflict. But when it appeared that the Lucknow Pact could possibly lead to Hindu–Muslim unity, he agreed to provide full support to it at the risk of accepting separate electorates for Muslims. The separate electorates had already been made available from 1909 onwards, and Tilak reckoned that if the Congress could forge an agreement with the Muslim League, the fight in India, which had a strong Muslim population with present-day Pakistan and Bangladesh also in it, would become a two-pronged one, of Indians versus the Raj, instead of a three-sided one which benefited the Raj. Without a doubt, it was his last-ditch attempt to bring about a Hindu-Muslim understanding, and he believed that with a young, supportive and suitably deferential Mohammed Ali Jinnah on his side, he could possibly control the trajectory of Muslim sectarian politics and not allow it to become a thorn in the side of Indian unity despite the Aligarh Anglo-Mohammedan Oriental College founder Syed Ahmed Khan's assertion of 1888 that the Hindus and Muslims constituted separate nations. His big gamble failed. Not only did the Pact not have the desired consequences, but after Tilak's death, Jinnah grew distant from the Gandhi-led Congress, with disastrous consequences for the Hindu–Muslim accord and the oneness of India. The debate over the Lucknow agreement has continued to this day, with fingers sometimes pointed at Tilak for providing scope to Islamist separatism which culminated in the Partition in 1947 though it was in no way the sole or determining factor in the matter of the League's intransigence or its push for self-determination. It has been conclusively proven that a number of factors, from Jinnah's turn to Islamist politics to the genie let out of the bottle by the Congress support for the Khilafat movement and the aggressive campaign in favour of Pakistan carried out in the northern parts and especially in the United Provinces, led to an avowedly Islamic State being carved out of India. But to have not taken the big risk would not have been Tilak's personality at all.

Tilak's links with the Indian political revolutionaries have been another subject for intense speculation, and the suspense over his role continues. By arguing that a sense of helplessness in the Indian population and the complete absence of proper constitutional and grievance redressal mechanisms were responsible for certain revolutionary acts, Tilak became, in the eyes of the colonizers, an active encourager and supporter of armed insurrectionists, and his invocation of the great deeds of Shivaji Maharaj and other Indian icons led to him being specifically designated as agent provocateur and to the filing of an array of criminal cases against him. Similarly, after his death, he has been connected to all manner of revolutionary activities by his admirers and also by some of his critics. While his admirers have often suggested that his was the invisible hand behind almost all acts of armed resistance, his critics have done pretty much the same, but with a different motive in mind—of implicating him in what they believe were some unjustifiable actions. The truth is more complex than that. About several revolutionary actions, Tilak was very much aware, and his links with the planners are easily traceable. For example, his links with Aurobindo Ghose of the Bengal group were undeniable; he had an excellent rapport with Pandit Shyamji Krishnaverma of Kathiawar, who set up the India House in London which turned into a hub of revolutionary activity; and it was Tilak who recommended to Krishnavarma in the year 1905 that he should award a scholarship to a young man from Nasik called Vinayak Damodar Savarkar who wanted to study law in the British capital. Savarkar had formed his secret group in the year 1900, and with the kind of prominence he had achieved in student circles in Pune as a student at Fergusson College and the manner in which youngsters flocked to Tilak for advice on pretty much everything and especially on political matters, it is unlikely Tilak was unaware of what Savarkar was up to. And yet, there are plenty of cases where the most conclusive remark I could make as a biographer is that 'it is likely he knew' or 'unlikely he knew.' Where such is the case, I have made it abundantly clear, disregarding the mythologies that have been created. One of my conclusions, which may surprise several readers familiar with the revolutionary movement and especially those brought up on stories circulated across Maharashtra, is that Tilak had no role to play in the act of the Chapekar brothers who killed two British officials in 1897 although he was aware of, and indirectly backed, some other activities of secret groups during the same period.

Interestingly, Tilak hardly ever wanted to come out openly in support of groups that believed in armed resistance because he was determined to do mass politics and saw massive potential in such politics for the fulfilment of Indian hopes and aspirations. He also sincerely believed that isolated acts of armed insurrection could not on their own help India realise its goal of freedom and famously told his associates that if even forty per cent of people were ready to carry out an armed revolt, he would be willing to lead them.[5] What he meant by this was that if such a revolt had even a forty to fifty per cent chance of succeeding, he would back it by providing the remaining fifty per cent of aggressive push on his own. But he didn't really see it happening without a lot of preparation beforehand.[6] For him, it was important to stay in the political mainstream and to lead India's paramount political representative group, the Congress, which he felt was a strong enough vehicle to bring about India's political revolution and its progress towards becoming a nation-state. Thus, despite his sometimes direct and sometimes indirect support for armed resistance, and despite the fact that politically his standing among the people only rose with the perception that he was backing the armed rebels, he never placed an inordinate amount of hope or energy behind violent action. Tilak took risks but those that appeared workable indeed; not where failure and frustration were guaranteed. He sympathized with the selfless, sacrificing revolutionaries, explained their acts as those of the hapless and the despairing when many others simply denounced and disowned them altogether, but he felt that the efficacy of their efforts would be limited given the existing circumstances and failure and the frittering away of energies and lives were the only certainties. The concept of non-violence did not come in the way at all. As one of his aides, Gangadharrao Deshpande of Belgaum said, there was no violence versus non-violence debate at the time, and no one had then imagined non-violence could be the way forward.[7] It was more a question of realism, and Tilak worked all his life to fulfil the Indian dream of freedom as a pragmatist politician.

On this pragmatic yet dreamy man, there are a whole lot of primary sources which I have looked deeply into. Writings, speeches, debates, dialogue, letters, correspondence—Tilak's life was all in the public eye, and the contemporary accounts are full of it. Some of his battles in the press, especially the ones he fought against the British editors of British-owned Indian newspapers, were legendary, and they constitute the early golden age of Indian journalism. The Raj was following him throughout his life, and its own records are full of his words and actions and the Empire's assessments of, and fears about, those words and actions. There was a decades-long wait after he died in 1920 for the Raj's records to become public. But they have been for several decades now, and I have mined them for this biography. Accounts of friends and foes alike are very rich, and I have drawn from these too. Tilak's letters and correspondence from Mandalay I found particularly engrossing because despite his political outspokenness, Tilak hardly ever bared his private soul, especially where his close ones were concerned. As a man of his times, he believed in withholding his sentiment in a kind of stoic firmness and deliberate non-expression of familial tenderness. His entire reserve against self-revelation in this regard collapsed in the prison in Burma, and the family man, with his countless anxieties, came to the fore. That deeply personal Tilak is as much a part of this book as the fervently political one.

Tilak is a man whose life India must know really well in order to understand how it got to be where it is, for so many of the debates about Indian politics, history, culture and civilization draw so much from his own contributions, and his own contests, with his rivals. Very importantly, if Gandhian non-violence represented one potent strand of the anti-colonial struggle and the armed revolutionaries the other, Tilak, with his own non-cooperation and his own militant form of nationalism, straddled both these worlds in his life, wrenching the Indian National Congress away from its ivory-tower elitism and making all of India realize that the movement for political liberation simply could not go forward if the people—the ones for whom freedom was being sought and whose rights were being sought to be upheld—were not an intrinsic part of it and wholly involved in it. Tilak was a man of the 'lok' or people, by the people, and for the people; according to his critics, often excessively so. But there was complete consensus on the title that would suit him best: Lokmanya.

Chapter 1

A Boy Known as 'The Devil' and 'Blunt'

Bal Gangadhar Tilak and Mohandas Karamchand Gandhi, the two pre-eminent leaders of the Indian freedom movement, became known—during their lifetime as well as in their afterlife in the public consciousness—more by the honorifics given to them by the Indian people than by their actual names. Indeed, they were defined, and are still defined, by those popular titles, 'Mahatma' or 'the great soul' in Gandhi's case and 'Lokmanya' or 'the one revered by the people' in Tilak's. Yet, Mohandas, as Gandhi's first name goes, was at least the genuine name his parents had given him at birth. Tilak is known by his first name Bal, has been immortalized as Bal Gangadhar Tilak, and is recognized as the leading member of the famous 'Lal, Bal, Pal' troika (the other two being Lala Lajpat Rai and Bipin Chandra Pal) of the anti-colonial movement. But Bal was not what his parents had chosen for him. They actually named him Keshav, after his great-grandfather and after the *kulaswamini*, or family goddess, Lakshmi-Keshav in the coastal Konkan region. But 'Bal', a simple term of endearment for him which meant 'child' and which was often commonly used to address children in Marathi-speaking homes in the Deccan region, caught on and stuck, turning eventually into the formal name Tilak himself preferred over the original Keshav.[1] Several of his friends and acquaintances, though, weren't so comfortable calling him 'Bal' after he had grown up and acquired a name and reputation for himself. They found a way out, zeroing in on the name 'Balwantrao', where 'Bal' itself was retained but in a way that the full name Balwant, with the suffix 'rao' at the end, appeared weighty enough for a man of his standing and was deemed acceptable for both the private and public sphere. Thus,

1

Balwantrao was what Tilak was, until the end of his life, for most of his close friends, aides and followers.

So much fussing over the name was perhaps not so inappropriate in the case of a man who was, by his own admission, incredibly fussy about certain subjects, one of which was mathematics. Tilak was deeply involved with mathematics and was famously impatient with those who understood neither the subject nor its 'significance', as he saw it. He had a placard posted at his door, saying, 'Those who don't understand math need not enter.' As his latest biographer, I'm fortunate that I live over a hundred years at a distance; if I'd been around during his lifetime and had approached him for an interview, I'd have stood automatically disqualified on this ground.

The preoccupation with numbers ran in the family. For long, the Tilak household of Marathi-speaking Brahmans had held *khoti* rights in Chikhalgaon in Ratnagiri district on India's western coast. In the eighteenth and nineteenth centuries, a *khot* constituted one of the crucial cogs in the wheel of local revenue administration. He (invariably, it was a man) was given land grants, for all intents and purposes hereditary, by the government to settle populations, bring land under cultivation and collecting rent from peasants. He had to submit the amount thus gathered to the authorities and also stand as guarantor for the khoti land's assessed revenue for the year. Tilak's father, Gangadhar, had a starting balance of around Rs 250 in a year in the mid-1860s as the village rent collector and a teacher's job in a government school to boot, which initially brought him a salary of Rs 5 a month and gradually, Rs 15 and Rs 25 per month,[2] a decent sum for those times. He also did some moneylending, albeit on a very minor scale. There were periods of struggle and even of uncertainty and scarcity as the khoti finances dwindled in years of poor rainfall, failed crops and meagre collection of rent, and anxieties gradually increased as the Tilak family grew in size and family disputes over the property resulted in a protracted legal battle lasting three decades. Despite all of these difficulties, in a land of incredible poverty, the reality was that a khot's income was more than what the vast majority of families could afford, though it turned out to be not always a blessing. At a key moment in his emerging years, when differences between leading members of the Deccan Education

Society of Poona resulted in an ugly public spat, Bal Gangadhar Tilak faced repeated barbs from some of his closest colleagues for his not-so-precarious financial condition, and some associates took friendly jibes at other times even if there was no provocation for doing so.[3]

Importantly, the subject Gangadhar-*pant* (as he was known, with 'pant' being an honorific like 'rao') taught was mathematics, and a book on trigonometry he wrote in 1854 had won a handsome prize of Rs 200 from the Bombay Presidency government.[4] He mastered and taught Sanskrit as well, and the son took to both subjects naturally and went on to stamp his own authority on either and especially on Sanskrit, whose texts he parsed to write all three of his books: *Arctic Home in the Vedas*, *The Orion* and *Gita Rahasya*.

Gangadhar-pant and his wife, Parvati, had four children, three of them girls. The first child, a daughter named Kashi, was born in 1846. The last child, a boy, Bal Gangadhar Tilak, was born in the family village of Chikhalgaon exactly a decade later, on 23 July 1856. The air all across the land was still at the time; it was, in truth, the calm before the storm. Ten months after the boy's birth, the great Indian Revolt of 1857 broke out across the northern and eastern parts of the Indian subcontinent, with Nana Saheb, the adopted son of the last Peshwa ruler of the Maratha Confederacy, leading the Indian rebels in Kanpur or 'Cawnpore' as the British called it.

The Peshwas were Chitpavan Brahmans, also known as Konkanastha Brahmans or those from the coastal Konkan belt. So were the Tilaks. Opportunities for Chitpavans had opened up during Peshwa rule, and among those to benefit was the Lokmanya's great-grandfather, Keshav. Apart from his ancestral lands, the Peshwas gave him charge of nearby Anjanwel in the Konkan, but after the Peshwa rule collapsed in 1818, he gave it up and returned to Chikhalgaon. Tilak's grandfather Ramchandra was born in 1802, and he and his wife Ramabai had their first child, Tilak's father Gangadhar, in 1820. They had two other children after him, a son called Govind and a daughter, Dwarka. Ramachandra had taken up work with the British East India Company's survey department. But in 1837, Tilak's grandmother Ramabai died of cholera, and his grandfather, in a bid to turn into a renunciate, moved first to Chitrakoot, where one of the Peshwa families had settled, and from there to Benaras, thrusting on the eldest son the responsibility of looking after his younger siblings.[5] Gangadhar had initially studied in a Marathi school in the Konkan and then moved to Poona to start his English education at a school there. Ramachandra's departure to Chitrakoot forced him to give up his English education before he had made much headway, return to Chikhalgaon and join the education department to supplement the family's khoti income.

Starting as a school teacher, Gangadhar went on to become assistant deputy inspector in the Bombay Presidency's education department and for his command of Sanskrit earned the title of 'shastri' and the respect of his friend, fellow Ratnagiri resident and one of the foremost scholars of Indic studies, R. G. Bhandarkar. In addition to his award-winning text on trigonometry, he wrote books on the history of England, arithmetic and Marathi grammar, which were incorporated by the provincial government into the school curriculum, and his career path eventually brought him a transfer to Poona. Bal was ten years old at the time, and the shift was beneficial for him, for the one-time capital of the Peshwas in the Deccan was a far bigger centre of education than the comparatively massively under-developed Ratnagiri. A smattering of Sanskrit *shlokas* and verses he had already learnt early on in childhood, with his Sanskrit teacher–father cheerfully gifting him one *anna* for every verse he memorized, and the elementary stuff in maths had come pretty easily to him. When he was six years old, he had been enrolled in the local Marathi school in Ratnagiri; at the age of ten, he joined what was known as the City School in Poona.

But just when things were looking up somewhat, there occurred twin tragedies for the family in quick succession. The first was the death of Tilak's mother in 1866, the very year in which they had shifted to Poona. And the second was the substantial losses suffered by his father in what turned out to be just one of many cases of fraud involving Arthur Crawford, a high-ranking British official. Crawford was the collector of Ratnagiri and had floated the Ratnagiri Saw Mill Company. Like scores of other Indians, Gangadhar-pant had bought shares of the company worth Rs 1000. Like the other investors, he also got a decent 9 per cent interest for a while, but it dried up pretty quickly, and in a few years,

Crawford declared the company was running into losses and faced bankruptcy. In October 1870, Gangadhar wrote an imploring letter to Crawford, saying he needed his money back as he wanted to use some of it for his son Bal's marriage which, he said, he had 'already put off for two years' because the funds had got stuck. In a telling line about the conventions of the era in Indian society, Gangadhar told Crawford, 'People are ridiculing me because my son isn't married yet, and I can hardly bear it.'[6] Tilak was then all of fourteen years old!

The money never returned. Nevertheless, Gangadhar, through his income, had the means to conduct his son's marriage in 1871. At the age of fifteen, Bal Gangadhar Tilak was married to a ten-year-old Chitpavan girl called Tapi of the Bal family from Dapoli in the Konkan, the same region the Tilaks came from. After marriage, Tapi was renamed Satyabhama. Gangadhar-pant had prepared the horoscope of his son immediately after his birth, and according to it, the boy was destined to marry twice. Tilak belied the forecast; he never married again.

The boy's studies also continued uninterrupted. After his primary schooling, Tilak joined the Poona high school in 1869 and began studying English, among other things. As a student, he was self-willed, stubborn and uncompromising, something his mid-nineteenth century teachers—used to caning their pupils liberally and unaccountably—found quite unacceptable. After he became the pre-eminent leader of the Indian freedom struggle, a story spread far and wide about his childhood, where he had been incorrectly blamed by one of his teachers for eating groundnuts and dropping groundnut peel on the floor of the classroom. Told to clean things up, Tilak declared, 'I haven't eaten the nuts, and I won't clear the mess,' and stormed out of the classroom.[7] If the class teacher asked him to come forward and write the correct answer to a mathematical riddle he had set forth on the blackboard, Tilak would often give out his reply without stirring from his own bench, saying it was unnecessary to walk across and put it down in writing; and in his answer papers for his examinations, he developed a habit of writing out solutions only to the toughest mathematical questions,[8] reasoning that if he could provide the right answers to those, surely his teacher could figure out that the rest *had* to be correct?

The exhilaration of clearing high school in 1872 was destroyed for Tilak by the sudden death of his father. Barely six years earlier, he had lost his mother, and now, when he was only sixteen years old, the caring Gangadhar-pant too was gone, a victim of oedema or swelling caused by fluid accumulated in the body's tissues.[9] The blow was massive, but Tilak never wrote or spoke about what must have been its deep impact, except for mentioning it in a letter he wrote to his nephew and sons from Mandalay jail at the time of his wife's death in 1912. All his life, he took a decidedly stoic approach and made it a point not to display his personal emotions during moments of tragedy. Perhaps the only time anyone ever saw him in an emotionally weak moment was when an acquaintance came knocking at his door one day in his forties. Tilak had lost one of his sons, Vishwanath, only some months earlier, and when the outsider knocked, he heard Tilak, who was deeply engrossed in his work of writing, calling out reflexively to his (departed) son to open the door. After a few moments which the acquaintance obviously spent in a perplexed and disturbed state of mind over what he had just heard, the Lokmanya was himself at the door, and there was not a single tear coming down his cheeks, only the look on his face of a shattered man trying his best to conceal his real feelings.[10]

Thankfully for the teenaged Tilak, his uncle Govind and aunt Gopika stepped in after his father's death and took care of him. Gangadhar-pant had left funds for the son's academic pursuits, and Tilak himself was determined to press on with his education.

In 1873, Tilak got admission to the Deccan College in Poona, which at the time was the only college in the Marathi-speaking regions outside of Bombay. Here, within six months, he moved in as a resident in the students' hostel, his very young wife staying with his uncle and aunt in the same city. In the first year, Tilak made a conscious decision to prioritize his physical fitness over studies. From his childhood, he had been thin and rather weak, and the brilliant sparkle in his eye was often dimmed by scaly eczema patches on his head.[11] By the time he reached college, he had a small head, reedy limbs and a slightly protruding tummy—a combination that nearly spelt malnutrition, though Bal didn't have any background of poverty.[12] Moreover, while Tilak looked much too frail, his wife appeared healthier in comparison, and Tilak had to face ridicule from his college mates in this regard.[13] So, preferring to bunk classes after the mandatory attendance was recorded in the morning, he practically spent all of his days either in the gym, where he displayed a predilection for *kusti*, or wrestling, or in the waters of the river which ran not very far from the college. His daily wrestling opponent and companion was a college mate, Daji Abaji Khare, with whom he'd go on to form a bond of deep friendship. The two were also each other's punching bags in the genuine sense of the term: as hardly any bags were available then for anyone to practise, Tilak targeted his friend's shoulders and forearms instead, and the friend did likewise with him.[14] While Tilak enjoyed rowing boats, it was swimming he loved the most; for hours, he liked to simply float. This passion he sustained almost all through his life: whenever an opportunity arose during his hectic political career, he'd take a dip, and colleagues who attended a Congress session with him in Benaras later recalled how he swam a considerable distance in the Ganga almost effortlessly. Swimming was also a sport where he was sharply observant about what children and youngsters around him were doing and handed out tips to them liberally.[15] But he seems to have completely stayed away from tennis and especially from cricket, a sport the British Raj was claiming to use to instil the values of Empire in the 'natives'.

With so much exercise, Tilak started eating better, though he had to digest failure in his final exams—a result of his total neglect of first-year studies. Not that the red-lined mark sheet put him down in any way; he didn't really care, at that point. Earlier a consumer mostly of rice, dal and curd and little else, he now took to most of the green-light foods, making wheat, grain, cereals, milk and above all vegetables an essential part of his intake.[16]

The results were soon apparent. By the end of the year, Tilak was lean but strong and wiry like an athlete, or better still for him, like a talented swimmer. He felt active and superbly energetic. And he came across as a strapping teenager in the classic *Deccani* Maharashtrian attire of the period he had adopted: a light, longish, flowing robe of *khadi*, or homespun cloth, with strings on its side, with a *sadra*, or shirt of soft cotton, tucked away inside, an *angawastra* flung across the shoulder, a dhoti and red chappals. On his head, he wore a red *pagdi*, or turban, commonly known as the *Puneri* pagdi, but without any lace end; and when he took it off, he displayed a clean-shaven head, with a traditional Brahman's tuft of hair at the back.[17] Nothing dimmed the bright eyes any more.

In the second year, he was much less casual about his studies, though it didn't mean any targeted pursuit of marks or distinction. What he focused on was his own method of doing things, and so long as he thought he was getting it right, all was okay with his academic world. For instance, he had as a part of his syllabus a textbook on the lives of Mary, Queen of Scots, and Elizabeth I. He pretty much put the prescribed textbook aside and consulted a number of books on the remarkable rivalry between the two queens, making copious notes on the intrigues of sixteenth-century English and Scottish politics, notes which apparently stood the test of time and proved useful to the next few generations of students as well.[18] He preserved most of his notebooks very well, and quite a few were found intact well over a quarter of a century after he had left school and college; one of them carried passages his college professor had asked students to translate from English to Sanskrit, and another contained a Sanskrit verse of three *shlokas* composed by the young Tilak. His uncle was worried by his disregard for accumulating marks and for obtaining scholarships, but the uncle's own annual books of accounts revealed that Tilak, in his second and third year in college, was the recipient of a junior scholarship of Rs 10 every month.[19]

More than the classroom lectures, Tilak enjoyed his daily walks around the college's campus, which was situated not in the heart of the busy town but at one end of it, providing tranquillity and fresh air. Neither early to bed nor early to rise, Tilak would go on his walks mostly in the evenings. They weren't purposeful walks but completely desultory, and they'd go on till 10 pm, which by the standards of Poona's nocturnal languor of the time was unpardonably late. While on these walks, Tilak didn't miss any chance of finding scapegoats for fun. On occasions, college mates who'd want to wind up early would find the doors to their hostel rooms bolted from the inside after Tilak had scaled a low wall in the corridor in the dark to get in and out through the windows. On other occasions, those who relied on what was termed then as 'patent medicines'—touted as quick-fix solutions to many medical problems but innately harmful because of ingredients like opium and tar in an era of poor governmental regulation and equally poor medical knowledge— would find they'd gone missing. Tilak's retort to those who'd accuse him of hiding them was 'join me in the gym instead'. One fellow student was in the habit of strewing flowers all across his bed before going off to sleep. If for a moment he slipped out before retiring for the night, Tilak would see to it that the flowers were scattered across the floor instead and the student robbed of his bed of roses.

About his own habits, however, he was totally unyielding. For his meals, he would sit down on the floor of the mess in a silk dhoti in the orthodox Brahman style. No matter how bitterly cold it got in the winter, he wore the silk dhoti for lunch and dinner. And his manner of learning remained as keenly and strongly individualistic as it had been during his school years. He read widely and well, but exactly what he wanted, especially in Sanskrit, history and religious literature; the syllabus was for him neither a constraint nor a spur for further exploration. If a teacher was not particularly impressive, he was often first off the block to say so. One of his Sanskrit instructors was the German Indologist Franz Kielhorn, a scholar of considerable repute who'd worked at Oxford with Monier Williams on the creation of a Sanskrit dictionary and who corresponded regularly with the Sanskrit scholar Max Müller. Kielhorn also wrote, while working as professor of Oriental languages at Deccan College from the mid-1860s until 1881, *A Grammar of the Sanskrit Language*, which was published by the Department of Public Instruction, Bombay; and he helped to trace and examine many ancient 'palm-leaf' Sanskrit manuscripts gathered from across the Bombay Presidency and added them to the local government's collection.[20] Tilak routinely skipped his lectures, prompting Kielhorn to ask him one day why he didn't attend. Simple, the professor had nothing to add to his knowledge of the subject, Tilak replied.[21] Another professor was George William Forrest. He had studied at Oxford and the Inner Temple and counted history and English literature among his areas of specialization; the son of a British official who had fought in Delhi during the 1857 Revolt, he wrote *the History of the Indian Mutiny* in three volumes, apart from books on Warren Hastings and Robert Clive.[22] In Deccan College, he was for some reason appointed as professor of mathematics, and most students felt he was a little out of his depth. They wrote to the principal asking for a replacement, with their signatures forming a neat circle so that no one could detect the initiator of the campaign. The clever little stratagem had been thought up by Tilak along with his friend, Daji Abaji Khare.[23] Tilak was also firm about supporting some of his teachers who, according to him, drew unfair criticism from certain quarters. One of the most outstanding professors at Deccan College during this period was Shridhar Ganesh Jinsiwale. A man of near-encyclopaedic learning, Jinsiwale had come up the hard way. His family was originally from Sankur near Ahmednagar, so the family name was Sankurkar; sometime in the eighteenth century, one of his forebears was appointed head of *jinsi* or artillery in the Gwalior state of the Shindes or Scindias, and the new name 'Jinsiwale' stuck. A family dispute over property brought his parents back to Ahmednagar, and by the time the case was decided—against Jinsiwale's parents—their situation had turned from one of affluence to poverty. Born in 1852, Shridhar Jinsiwale was from an early age crazy about reading and education. In the evenings, he'd burn a stack of dry leaves and read in the light of the fire or go as close to the lights in a neighbour's house as possible or, if nothing else worked, he'd sit by the steps of a mosque in the neighbourhood and read with the support of the streetlamp placed there by the local civic body. It was while he was sitting by the mosque's steps one evening that he was spotted by a local teacher, Wamanrao Paranjpe, who took him under his wing and backed his education. Jinsiwale was a complete maverick. He could speak on most subjects for a couple of hours at a stretch without consulting notes, and his lectures invariably drew a full house. But he could sometimes digress, and such was his quirkiness that no amount of reminding that he should return to the main topic helped. The result was that what would for the most part be a fascinating talk would tip into a wearisome one. Jinsiwale was also often attacked for his socially conservative views. But Tilak, who hardly ever followed Jinsiwale's diktat of transcribing whatever it was that he was telling his students, nevertheless saw him as an exemplar where both learning and teaching were concerned. Jinsiwale's chief flaw, according to many of his contemporaries, was that he never really wrote down anything, so he left behind no writings, yet he was a force to reckon with in public life in the Deccan in the last three decades of the nineteenth century, and Tilak was certainly among those who endorsed the view put forward by one of Jinsiwale's students, the sociologist N.G. Chapekar, that what the masterful Marathi essayist Vishnushastri Chiplunkar did in that era through his writings, Jinsiwale did through his public talks—light the spark of self-respect among the young generation.[24]

For his candid talk and assertive manner and for never hedging evasively about anything, Tilak was soon nicknamed 'the Devil' and 'Blunt' by his college mates.[25] On the whole, he was also popular among the 100-odd students then studying at Deccan College. Though quite a few of them had been at the receiving end because of his never-play-it-safely-down-the-middle approach, they saw him as essentially gentle, helpful and forthcoming. Proof of it they saw with their own eyes, on the campus. When one of Tilak's friends, an MA student surnamed Marathe, fell seriously ill and the doctor said he needed full-time care, it was Tilak who stepped up and looked after him day and night. Unfortunately, the friend died, and at his funeral, there was an odd moment: one of his legs jutted out all of a sudden while the rest of the body, placed on the funeral pyre, was being consumed by fire. Most watchers hesitated, but not Tilak. He stepped forward and placed the leg gently and carefully back on to the pyre, with grief but also with determination that the final rites should be properly conducted for his dear friend.[26]

Besides, both the students and teachers at Deccan College knew that despite his scepticism about some of the instructors, Tilak felt a real attachment to the institution. For just one single term of six months, he shifted to the Elphinstone College of Bombay but was disappointed by the math teacher there, a certain Professor Hawthornwaite. On the other hand, Deccan College had the brilliant Kero Waman Chhatre. A self-taught man, Chhatre was a favourite of all students because he combined scholarship with humility; for Tilak in particular, his rigour and method of teaching kept the mind's mathematical machine humming happily. Chhatre was, in addition, fascinated with astronomy and on several nights, he'd stay back on the college campus to give students a glimpse of the stars and planets with his telescope. Tilak was among the first and most enthusiastic to line up for a close view; with Chhatre's help, he scanned star images and made mental and written notes of star fields in an era before photography and later, TV cameras and computers made all of it unnecessary. Later, when writing his book, *The Orion* on the antiquity of the Vedas, Tilak took an astronomical view of things and underlined stellar constellations, inspired no doubt by the knowledge of the night sky he'd gained in Chhatre's company. Chhatre was so well-regarded that in spite of his extremely limited knowledge of the English language, he was appointed acting principal by the Deccan College authorities for a while during the temporary absence of the incumbent.[27] Tilak looked up to him all through his years at the college and beyond, and Chhatre sincerely and openly nourished the hope that Tilak would carry forward his own work in the area of mathematics. Tilak would have been very happy to do that; he said later, as a matter of fact, that if India were a free country, he'd have spent all his life teaching mathematics.[28] But other things beckoned. Among them were degrees in the arts and, importantly, the law.

Tilak cleared his bachelor of arts (BA) exam in 1876 with first-class honours and enrolled for the LLB course, which he completed three years later, in 1879.[29] What most likely made him pursue a degree in law was the personality and influence of Vishwanath Narayan Mandlik, a family friend of the Tilaks and, just like the Tilak family, a khot or holder of land grants. Mandlik came from the same district in the Konkan as the Tilaks and had acquired a reputation as a lawyer in the Bombay High Court and as a councillor in the Bombay Municipal Corporation; he held positions, besides, on the provincial council and the Central viceregal council. Mandlik routinely called on Tilak's father Gangadhar-pant at their home, and after Gangadhar-pant's death, Tilak continued to make visits every now and then to Mandlik's place.[30] Mandlik's example, and possibly his word, had an impact, and Tilak, along with Mohandas K. Gandhi, became one of the earliest leading luminaries of India's freedom struggle to study law; among the others who soon followed suit were V.D. Savarkar, Jawaharlal Nehru, Vallabhbhai Patel and the crusader against caste inequities, B.R. Ambedkar. For the law degree too, Tilak followed his preferred pattern of studying. Asked to go through John D. Mayne's book on Hindu law, he examined some of the chief sources of authority on the subject such as the works of Manu, Yajnavalkya and Vijnaneshwara in the Sanskrit original before reading the recommended text in English.[31]

It was while he was studying for his law degree that Tilak met, on the premises of his college, a young student exactly his own age. Very slightly built, lanky, fair-skinned and light-eyed, Gopal Ganesh Agarkar was looking to get a BA degree and was, like Tilak, staying at the college hostel. Soon, as Tilak got talking to him, he discovered that the two of them had been born only nine days apart—Tilak on 23 July and Agarkar on 14 July in 1856. This small coincidence might have given them an early feeling of affinity, apart from the fact that Agarkar was, like Tilak, a Chitpavan Brahman with family roots in the coastal Konkan. Other than that, their young lives up until that point were a study in contrast. Tilak hadn't seen poverty, but Agarkar had been born into a life of penury in the small, backward village of Tembhu in Karad near Satara in Maharashtra. Both his parents had severe asthma and could barely work; it was his mother's side of the family, and specifically his maternal uncle, a resident of Karad, who financially supported them all. Though the maternal uncle's family was hardly well off, prospects in Karad were better than in Tembhu village, so the parents moved Gopal to the uncle's home and a school there as soon as they could. His education was the only hope for the family's emergence from poverty and its fight against asthma, which the little boy too had unfortunately developed early in childhood. Yet the school in Karad could help him clear only the first three years of English education. It did not offer classes beyond that; to study further, he'd have to go elsewhere. For a while he went to a relative's place in Ratnagiri, walking a distance of 240 kilometres from Karad to get there, but this relative, though financially secure, was petty and unwilling to lend a helping hand. Unhappily, Gopal returned to Karad and began to earn some money by working, at the age of thirteen, as a clerk in the office of the local *mamledar* or revenue collector and doing a stint as a compounder in the local clinic. Fortunately, he got a chance to go to Akola in Warhad in northern Maharashtra with his maternal aunt when she was on one of her family visits there, and he decided the place had the kind of educational facilities which would allow him to clear his matriculation exams. Once he had cleared those exams, the question of 'what next' arose again. This time, his teachers stepped in and pooled Rs 60 so that he could go to Deccan College, and he started scrimping and saving at every point so that life on the Poona campus would be bearable and could bear some fruit. To get some money of his own, he began securing scholarships, contributing to local newspapers and aiming at prizes at elocution contests.[32] Tilak had hardly had any of these difficulties, and if his concern was wearing the silk dhoti at lunch and dinner in the orthodox fashion, Agarkar's challenge was to use the solitary piece of *sadra,* or cotton shirt, that he had, day in and day out—his way of doing that was to wash it late every night and wear it once it had dried up adequately by morning.

However different their material circumstances were, Tilak and Agarkar realized soon that their wavelengths were quite similar. Wavelength did not mean a matching worldview. Far from it. Brought up in the discomforting lap of indigence, Agarkar had little respect for traditions, customs and rituals; Tilak, on the other hand, as seen from his insistence on wearing a certain attire at meals, was a bit of a stickler for these and saw age-old customs as being important. Agarkar had deep literary and poetic sensibilities and was a big admirer of William Shakespeare and Percy Shelley; at the same time, he was profoundly influenced by the rational political philosophy of the West and especially of John Stuart Mill and Herbert Spencer. Tilak had his own paradoxical young personality: he loved the cold logic of mathematics and was quite taken by astronomy, physics and chemistry, yet his religious convictions were strong and his reliance on Sanskrit classics had as much to do with his beliefs as his approach as a linguist and grammarian.[33] And while Tilak loved sitting up late at night to read, Agarkar dreaded the nights, especially cold ones which could bring on bad bouts of coughing. Together, however, they began to spend a lot of time discussing a variety of things and taking long walks on the green campus. If Tilak spoke of stars and constellations, then Agarkar could be relied upon to state categorically that there was no grand design behind it all, whatever the religious-minded felt about it. And if Agarkar emphasized the utilitarian approach, Tilak was sure to reply that human beings didn't live by bread and utilitarianism alone. In some respects, there was agreement too, as in the keen acknowledgement that their professor Kero Laxman Chhatre had no equal among his peers. Hardly a worshipper of men, Agarkar described Chhatre as a 'Mahatma'; he fell at his feet the day Chhatre retired from the college and, in his own words, 'cried a lot'.[34]

The animated exchanges of Tilak and Agarkar included good-natured ribbing; there was fun, there were quips and there were laughs. Above all, despite the divergence of views on a number of topics, they felt they had the same inner urges and pulls. A majority of students at Deccan College nursed ambitions of obtaining lucrative government jobs and postings after getting their degrees. Tilak and Agarkar weren't among them. Each one of the two composed a chorus of distinctive tunes in their heads, only to find that their harmonies were somehow automatically turning into a chorus of one. At the core was emerging a single voice, an epochal ensemble, and it pushed against what they were seeing around them—ignorance, the lack of a broad public consciousness, and the overwhelming presence of imperial rule speckled with racialized violence, subjugation, oppression and injustice. They were going to take their scrutiny of the situation and examine it against what they saw as a panorama of misrule.

Chapter 2

'Like Bullocks Whipped Around'

On 3 July 1879, the year in which Tilak cleared his law degree
exams, the Governor of Bombay, Richard Temple, sat down to
write a letter to the Viceroy of India, Lord Lytton. The intent of the
letter was to explicitly warn the viceroy about a particular community of
Brahmans in western India. These were the Chitpavan Brahmans, the
group to which Tilak belonged. Temple believed that for British rule,
in particular, they were a distinctly threatening type.

'There is one class among the Brahmins,' he stated, 'who indirectly
foment all troubles,' no matter who appeared to be at the forefront of
such troubles; and 'they are, or have been, 'in' with every row in the
Deccan.' They were, in his decided opinion, incorrigible: their approach
towards the British Empire resulted not from any of the government's
policies or actions; rather, it was caused 'by British Rule *even* at its best'.[1]

Why were the Chitpavan Brahmans such serious suspects in
Temple's eyes?

The British East India Company became the principal political
power in India in the first two decades of the nineteenth century after
subduing the last of the Peshwas or prime ministers of the Maratha
Raj, Bajirao II, and other elements of the Maratha Confederacy such
as the Shindes, Holkars and Bhosles who were spread across western
and central India. The Peshwas had been at the helm of Maratha power
for most of the eighteenth century and had taken it to the height of its
success. They were all Chitpavan Brahmans. 'Chitpavan' was the term
used for Marathi-speaking Brahmans from the Konkan coastal corridor;
they were otherwise and more commonly known as Konkanastha

Brahmans, literally those from the Konkan; the other categories of Maharashtrian Brahmans were the Deshasthas, those from the *desh* or Deccan plateau, and the Karade, those from Karad in south-western Maharashtra. The term had its origins in a popular legend about how the community came into being. According to the legend, Parshurama, an *avatar* of Lord Vishnu, had reclaimed the western Indian coast from the sea, forming the forty to fifty-kilometre-wide Konkan strip that separates the seafront from the ghats and mountains inland. Aeons ago, the story goes, on a particularly stormy night, a ship boasting of a crew of fourteen fair-skinned and light-eyed men, all experienced mariners, hit a spot along the Ratnagiri coast, and the tempest swept away all of the sailors, flinging them upon the shoreline. In the morning, their bodies lying ashore were discovered by the swarthy occupants of the coastline, who built a pyre of resinous wood to cremate them. But just as the flames went up, Parshurama appeared miraculously on the scene and raised all fourteen of the shipwreck victims from the dead, purifying them in the process of all worldly blemishes. Their life breathed into them anew, they came to be known as the Chitpavans, '*chit*' being their corpses on the pyre as in '*chita*' and '*pavan*' signifying the purifying purge; another version has it that the 'chit' is actually '*chitta*,' which means 'soul' in Marathi and Sanskrit, making them 'soul purified' rather than 'pyre purified'.[2]

The Brahmans were the elite in a rigidly caste-driven society, but even among the elite, there had long been a hierarchy: the Deshasthas were the most privileged and considered the most educated and employable, perhaps because the Deccan plateau was much less inhospitable than the perennially semi-dank Konkan with its treacherous rivers, streams and woods, and it was they who had held the top positions in the realm of the sacred and the material. The rise of the Peshwas changed all that: the Chitpavans or Konkanasthas got on top thanks to their fellow caste men who were in charge, acquiring premier slots in the political and revenue administration and parallelly growing in stature in the priesthood stakes. So, when the Peshwa regime officially came crashing down in 1818—unofficially, the last Peshwa had sounded the death knell for his own reign fifteen years earlier, in 1803, by placing himself under the protection of the East India Company—the Chitpavans easily had the most to lose.

Quickly enough thereafter, they also had the most to gain, as did the other Brahmans too, if they chose to. Over the next few decades, the British aggressively brought in institutes of Western education with English as the language of instruction, in keeping with the 'Minute on Indian Education' tabled in 1835 by the chief law member of the Governor-General's executive council Thomas Babington Macaulay, so that they could train Indians to take up jobs in the lower and middle rungs of the administration they were building up after having given up all pretensions of pure trade.[3] As members of the social elite, the Brahmans were expected to enrol before anybody else, and the Chitpavans did finally, along with the Deshasthas and Karades in western India, but not before they had demonstrated much less alacrity than the *bhadralok* of Bengal; it was only in the second half of the nineteenth century that they took up western education in truly significant numbers. Even after they embraced Western educational and administrative institutions, the Company and its senior officials never really believed in the loyalty of the Chitpavans. They were convinced that the Maharashtrian Brahmans in general and the Chitpavans in particular were smarting under the loss of Maratha rule and would inflame sentiment and trigger a bid to throw out the Company at the earliest available opportunity.

The East India Company had appointed Mountstuart Elphinstone as its first commissioner of the Deccan immediately after the end of Peshwa rule in 1818; a year later, he was made governor of the Bombay Presidency as a whole, which included the Deccan. Son of a peer from Scotland, Elphinstone had joined the Company in 1795, and after serving initially in Benaras, had worked in the principalities of Gwalior and Berar. For a couple of years from 1801, he had been assistant to the British Resident at the Peshwa's Court, and in 1810 he was brought back to Poona, after stints elsewhere, as the new Resident. He reported to his bosses in his role as governor that the Maratha Brahmans were 'intriguing, lying, corrupt, licentious and unprincipled' and when in power, 'coolly unfeeling and systematically oppressive'. Now 'generally discontented,' he remarked, they were 'only restrained by fear from being treasonable and treacherous'. And as a warning about their intentions, he ascribed warrior qualities to several of them. 'The military Brahmins,' he wrote, 'combine part of the character of Mahratta soldiers with that of their own caste.'[4]

Very early on, Elphinstone discovered 'a plot' to 'murder the Europeans and restore the Peshwa' in which a few Brahmans 'were the chief conspirators'. The plotters were caught, and Elphinstone 'ordered the ringleaders to be blown from the cannon's mouth'.[5] Between 1818 and 1857 there were other, very small and occasional rebellions by various groups, which were put down relatively easily. However, the big Revolt of 1857 deeply reinforced British suspicions. Among the uprising's key leaders were three Maratha Brahmans: Dhondu Pant Nana Saheb, heir to the last Peshwa who had been deposed and exiled from Poona to Bithoor in the north; Rani Laxmibai, wife of the Maratha maharaja Gangadhar Rao Newalkar of Jhansi who also had the Maharashtrian 'Tambe' for her maiden surname; and Tatya Tope, Nana Saheb's artillery specialist. Nana Saheb gained notoriety among the British as the biggest villain of the rebellion because of his massacre in Kanpur of members of the British garrison when they were getting on to their boats in the Ganga and the killing of over a hundred imprisoned British women and children. 'Few names are more conspicuous in the annals of crime than that of Nana Sahib,' wrote two British chroniclers.[6]

A direct fallout of the troika's role in the *sipahi* revolt was the exclusion of Marathas from the army of British-ruled India. Once the 1857 uprising was crushed, the British crown folded up the East India Company and took over its territories in India, marking the launch in 1858 of what came to be known as the British Raj. Among the early things the Raj did was to draw up a list of 'martial races' for recruitment into the government's army. The Marathas were kept out of the list, along with the people of Oudh (Awadh or Ayodhya region) and Bengal, because the province of Oudh was at the heart of the sepoy stir and the Bengal Army (which comprised not just those from present-day Bengal but a huge number from Awadh and the United Provinces and from Orissa and the other eastern parts which were then part of the large Bengal province) had been a recalcitrant force.

The Raj made its rule increasingly powerful over the next decade and a half. It introduced laws such as the Indian Penal Code, for tackling crime, and the Code for Civil Procedure, for replacing faith-based religious rules other than those for marriage and inheritance. It created the Executive Council, a five-member white-men-only cabinet of the viceroy, who was to be the crown's top representative on Indian soil, and the Legislative Council, an extension of the cabinet with six to twelve additional members in all—apart from the five white officials from the Executive Council, the others in the other law-making body could be 'British or Indian'.[7] The Indian bit, though, remained for the most part on paper, as it did in the early decades of the Indian Civil Service, the bureaucratic machine that would control the administration. Indians were nowhere close to the top posts; if they held posts on the Legislative Council, their role was purely recommendatory, and they had no powers to make any decisions; and Indian judges were not even allowed to try white-skinned Europeans outside of the main cities and towns.[8] The more tightly the Raj held the reins, the more weakened the Indian population appeared, without any basic rights and without the spirit of mobilization any more alive or active.

The Raj's law-making spree was accompanied by a core, two-pronged strategy: the creation of a new, 'educated class' of Indians immersed in Western educational and political customs who would do all kinds of clerical governmental jobs at the lowest, low and middle levels, and the granting of a voice, adequately limited, to this elite, so that they collaborated either as part of the state machinery or as influential critics who did not allow people's views to stray in the direction of revolt or insurrection.

And if someone strayed or was simply perceived to be going out of line, they would face the criminal laws which had been specifically designed to put down and suppress a subject population.

In the 1850s and 1860s, there sprang up a number of local groups of Indians of a political or quasi-political nature, among them the British Indian Association of Calcutta, the Deccan Association of Poona and the Bombay Association of the island city on the west coast. Occasionally these organizations did raise niggling doubts in the minds of British officials, but on the whole their model temperance and their mild petitions and representations to the authorities on giving greater representation to Indians on the Councils and in government and their near-pious appeals for police, administrative and judicial reforms were innocuous enough not to create any sense of alarm. Almost all these groups were led by the landed and business elite, in other words by those with vested interests—even if they could boast of individuals who commanded wide respect such as Rabindranath Tagore's father Debendranath of the Calcutta group and Dadabhai Naoroji of the Bombay Association—and their submission to British authority seemed sincere; their regional character and often fractious nature reassured the Raj further. Yet the British never took their eye off these groups, particularly the ones in western India, an area they believed needed watchful observation. And when an organization called the Poona Sarvajanik Sabha began its activities in the capital city of the Peshwas in 1870, the British felt that politically minded Indians might have turned a corner.

All through the 1870s, the Sarvajanik Sabha (People's Association) pushed the hitherto extremely narrow boundaries of political activity and political representation. Its founder, the noted Poona lawyer Ganesh Vasudev Joshi, popularly known as Sarvajanik Kaka (People's Uncle), pioneered the idea of Swadeshi in manufacturing and purchasing, setting up local stores and co-operatives. Under its intellectual guide, the brilliant judicial officer Mahadev Govind Ranade, the Sabha pursued an investigation into the condition of Deccan's farmers and the nature of land taxation and assembled a mass of evidence and testimony from villagers and village officials, calling for the administration to take urgent corrective measures in a period that saw frequent famines. It highlighted the steep revenue rates, the indifferent responses of district officials, rural displacement caused by the failure of crops from 1873 and the undercounting of deaths, especially after the big famine of 1876–77.[9]

While placing its faith in British rule, the Sabha sought to aggressively broaden the nature of popular representation on the governor's legislative council: of six Indians on it, four represented the city of Bombay (now Bombay), which had a population of seven lakh, and only one represented the wider, rural Deccan region and the big-sized Bombay Presidency which also included most of Gujarat. The Sabha suggested Bombay City and the other Marathi-speaking regions in the western parts should have two members each, one should be from the southern Maratha country, one from Gujarat, and other sections of society, such as the 'Mahomedan community,' must also get a nominee.[10] What made it speak for so wide a swathe of society was the fact that the Sarvajanik Sabha had laid down a condition for each of its members—they had to carry letters of representation from at least fifty people, which gave them the authority to represent them all. So at a time when Poona had an adult population of nearly 65,000, the Sabha had ninety-five members at its very first meeting in April 1870, speaking for 6000 adults (men), and the following year, it had 141 members acting on behalf of 17,000 adults or 26 per cent of the town's adult population.[11]

Political organization at this level, which included not only the educated elite but unlettered peasants, was worrying for the Raj, and especially so because both Joshi and Ranade were Maratha Brahmans—the first a Deshasthas and the second a Chitpavan. In what became known as the Deccan riots of 1875, several farmer groups turned violent and obliterated records of debts put together by local village moneylenders, making the Raj deduce that the Sabha might have had a hand behind the destruction. With Ranade directing most of the Sabha's actions, he was initially spied upon and in 1878 was transferred from his position as a judge in Poona to Nasik. The transfer was ordered by the Governor, Richard Temple.[12] That same year, a thirty-three-year-old Maratha Brahman, Vasudeo Balwant Phadke, who worked in the local government's military accounts department, left his family and entered the forests of the Deccan to build an army. The next year, he and his men raided villages around Poona, declaring that 'unless the salaries of imperial bureaucrats were cut and the money redistributed to poor peasants, Europeans would be attacked and assassinated'.[13] Phadke was caught in July 1879 and after a trial, transported to Aden (where he died soon of an illness), but one British judge wrote that even in largely middle-class Poona, 'sympathy was on the side of the accused'.[14]

It was in the light of Phadke's rebellion that Temple wrote to Viceroy Lytton in July 1879 about the Maharashtrian Brahmans. Spelling out what he believed these elements were ultimately aiming at, he told the viceroy:[15]

Like as the Mahrattas under Brahminical guidance once beat the Mahomedan conquerors bit by bit so the Chitpavans imagine that some day more or less remote, the British shall be made to retire into that darkness where the Mughals have retired.

Convinced about the invisible hand of the Sarvajanik Sabha in all the troubles in the Deccan, Temple stated in the same letter:[16]

The conduct of the association of landholders called the Surva-Janik-Sabha has long been . . . regarded with suspicion – which suspicion continues. Although the Society may not be directly connected with recent events, yet its wires are believed to be pulled by men tainted with the views described in this letter.

Of equal alarm to Temple and other upholders of imperial domination were the activities of the native Marathi press during the decade that was drawing to a close. The Marathi press had proliferated, but without showing the kind of obsequiousness the Raj expected of it. Not inaccurately, the British establishment saw its approach as the result of the growth of education among the natives. Education of the Western kind had been imparted in order to create a class of clerks and other collaborators, and indeed that class had been created, but not everyone who went to school and college and obtained degrees wanted to be part of that category.

When, during the initial years of the Company's rule in the Deccan, British administrators were wondering whether to bring in English education straightaway or first allow for education in Marathi and Sanskrit, the traditional languages of learning, Bombay governor Mountstuart Elphinstone had chosen to start with Sanskrit, the language of India's ancient past. Elphinstone was as authoritarian as any other British governor but in a paternalistic way. So, when the question of whether the Company should continue the handing out of the money the Peshwas annually gave as a '*dakshina*', or gift, to Brahman priests arose, Elphinstone diverted a part of the 'dakshina' for setting up a Sanskrit school in Poona's Vishrambaug Wada, formerly the palace of the Peshwas in the heart of the city, in a quarter known as the Shaniwar Peth.[17]

Smartly, his successors launched English classes at the school in 1842, and a quarter of a century later, in 1868, the Deccan College emerged as an offshoot of the same institution.[18] The English school survived as the Government High School; slowly but surely, the Sanskrit division was sidelined and gradually forgotten as English increasingly became the language of administration, and Marathi too appeared to lag.

The Deccan College of Poona and the Elphinstone College of Bombay were the first higher education institutions to come under the aegis of the University of Bombay, which was formed in 1859, exactly twenty years before Tilak cleared his LLB exams. Initially, the Deccan College functioned at the Vishrambaug premises but by the time Tilak joined it, it had moved to a 'magnificent new edifice beyond the Bund',[19] the 'bund' being a mini dam on the Mula river that ran through the city. In 1856, an English schoolteacher in his mid-twenties, Edwin Arnold, who would later become famous for his poem 'The Light of Asia', was appointed principal of Deccan College, and he thought highly of the talent there. 'Among my native teachers,' he wrote, 'were some very capable men like Krishna Shastri Chiploonkur and Kero Punt, with minds as receptive as could be found in Oxford or Cambridge.'[20] Kero Punt, of course, as mentioned earlier, eventually went on to become Tilak's favourite teacher, and Chiplunkar's son Vishnushastri in particular would leave an indelible stamp on the Maharashtrian consciousness with his writings, with Tilak as one of his countless admirers and associates. 'Among my students too,' stated Arnold, proudly, 'were brilliant young men, who might have distinguished themselves in the front rank at our universities.'[21]

By the time Tilak cleared his law exams in 1879, the University had expanded quite a bit: it had close to 3,00,000 students, with eight colleges and almost 5000 schools.[22] The Bombay governor was the chancellor of the University, and with Tilak among those who collected their law degrees, governor Richard Temple at the convocation ceremony clearly enunciated the aims of British education. 'I should consider the success of natives as civil administrators to be the truest test of that combined mental and moral training which our education seeks to give,' Temple said.[23]

Tilak, at least, was looking elsewhere for his own mental and moral training. He no doubt appreciated the method and qualities of Western education, but Temple's claim of the British ruling class's mental and moral superiority didn't cut any ice with him. He looked instead at Vishnushastri Chiplunkar, the son of Krishna Shastri whom Edwin Arnold had considered during his tenure as Deccan College principal to be one of his top teachers. Vishnushastri Chiplunkar was a literary figure of prodigious talent, and through his scintillating writings in Marathi, he sharply questioned the Raj's establishment wisdom mouthed by Temple and other senior officials. For Tilak and several other students at Deccan College, Vishnushastri showed a sense of confidence. For the British, he showed the Indians' rising appetite for confrontation.

Vishnushastri ran a monthly magazine called the *Nibandhmala* (A Garland of Essays), in which he assailed all those who argued that the Hindu religion, and broadly India's various traditional faiths, were incompatible with modernity. In the previous few decades, a number of Hindu and Maharashtrian reformers had made such assertions, including the essayist Gopal Hari Deshmukh, who had won much acclaim as 'Lokahitawadi' or 'One who propounds what is good for the people', and Vishnushastri's own father Krishna Shastri, who was a reformist. Vishnushastri maintained that there was nothing innately wrong or harmful about Indian religion and Indian culture, as most of the reformists were trying to say. He stated that custom and modernity were not binary categories and that although changes and adjustments were necessary to make Indian society stronger and the English language was a source of tremendous knowledge, there was no need really to throw the baby out with the bath water. Indians could cherish their culture and traditions and build on them, and the wholesale adoption of Western education and ideals and complete rejection of the Indian way of life was in his view preposterous and suicidal.[24]

Tilak saw that Chiplunkar's self-assurance went well beyond what Ranade was saying, and he liked the fact that the essayist was quite unapologetic about it. So did many other students at Deccan College. One of them was V.K. Rajwade, a scholar who went on to become an authority on the history of the Marathas. Rajwade recollected later that

'Mr Ranade, whose name has been beyond doubt the name of a saint to me, was then no hero of mine. Along with others I, too, enjoyed the ridicule poured on him by our teacher, Chiplunkar . . . He (Chiplunkar) poured ridicule on the Prarthana Samaj, the Brahmo Samaj, in fact on every Samaj that interfered in the slightest degree with the time-honoured customs of his beloved India . . . The appearance of his monthly essay was eagerly awaited and when the essay did make its appearance, it was avidly devoured . . . It was the outburst of patriotism in the Nibandhamala that appealed to every heart.'[25]

The account of a Russian visitor, Ivan Pavlovich Minayeff, to the Deccan College around this time is highly illuminating. It shows how Tilak and other youngsters were viewing the scenario around them in the aftermath of Phadke's revolt and the various things which were working on their minds.

Minayeff was a Russian Indologist known especially for his research on Buddhism. Days after he had arrived in Poona early in 1880, three students at the college told him they 'agreed with the emancipatory aims' of Phadke. Though the means he had adopted were 'stupid', they felt, the ends were 'noble'. They had attended court during Phadke's trial and, Minayeff believed, may have been among those who had shouted '*Phadke Ki Jai* (Victory to Phadke!)!' When Minayeff went around the students' hostel, the boarders showed him an album. 'Among the notables was Phadke.'[26]

In their talks with the Russian, the students voiced direct criticism of the colonial regime. Their principal complaints were that Indians were denied higher posts and forced to pay unreasonably steep taxes, the wealth of the country was making its way to England, and any expression of discontent was not merely frowned upon but punished with legal action.

The poor suffered the most on account of high rates of taxation, they said that these rates had gone up to four English shillings per person. A village barber who didn't earn even three rupees a month had to pay much more in taxes. Land taxes too were high, and payment had to be made in the currency and 'not with the yields of nature.' Even salt was taxed, and it indeed represented one of the harshest measures of indirect taxation; in the early 1880s, this rate was raised by 25 per cent. The tax was levied on salt manufactured in India and also on that imported from outside. And there was a prohibition on manufacturing salt from seawater and even on exploiting the forests by gathering leaves and brushwood. Indians who wanted to do business or professional work or manage an industry weren't spared either. The Raj had brought in the Licence Act, first in 1867 and subsequently in 1878, which taxed anyone wishing to conduct any of these activities, and those hardest hit by it were artisans and small traders and merchants.

On Indian wealth flowing into England, the students sounded deeply aggrieved. The groundwork for their argument in this regard had been laid in the Deccan region even before the Parsi businessman and leader Dadabhai Naoroji articulated his 'drain' theory in 1867, saying that 50 per cent of the revenue earned by the British government in India was finding its way to England.[27]

The Marathi press was born in the year 1832 when the scholar, journalist and educationist Bal Shastri Jambhekar launched a bilingual newspaper—a part of it in Marathi and another part in English—called *Bombay Durpun*. Jambhekar was one of the early products of western education and spoke of trying to 'spread liberal sentiments in matters of religion and politics', but his idea of 'native improvement' essentially meant social reform carried out from within Hindu society without any finger-pointing at the nature and character of the East India Company's rule. If anything, Jambhekar was an admirer of the Company's first Bombay governor, Mountstuart Elphinstone, and saw merit in what the so-called mercantile firm was doing.[28] One of his students, Bhaskar Pandurang Tarkhadkar, thought exactly the opposite.

Born in Bombay in 1816 and Naoroji's senior at the Elphinstone Institution which later became Elphinstone College, Tarkhadkar was one among three brilliant siblings; one of his brothers, Dadoba Pandurang, was so much of an authority on Marathi grammar that the surname 'Tarkhadkar' is to Marathi what 'Wren and Martin' have been to English; and the other, Atmaram, was one of the founders of the reformist Prarthana Samaj, which was to western India what the Brahmo Samaj was to Bengal.

Early in July 1841, Bhaskar Tarkhadkar saw a note put out by the editor of *Bombay Gazette* inviting readers to write about their grievances against British rule. The 'Gazette' was a pro-Company paper, but for a brief period in 1841, it had an editor, George Buist, who cared for the 'natives'. In response to Buist's call, Tarkhadkar wrote eight long letters from the end of July 1841 until the November-end that year, under the pseudonym 'A Hindoo.' The letters sought to demolish the notion of 'divine providence' which the British promoted, and their Indian admirers entertained, about the Company's rule.

'Nothing has drained India so much of its wealth as your trade,' Tarkhadkar wrote in one of his letters, published by *Bombay Gazette* on 20 August 1841. 'If you were half so honest as you say you are, or had you a tenth part of the regard which you vauntingly say you have for the welfare of India, you would not have persuaded yourself that all the raw materials produced in the country should be sent to England for manufacturing them into articles and be brought back again here for sale. Were cotton cloth manufactured here, how much cheaper we could get it than we now do, and how much India had been relieved from its present reduced state?' In order to ensure handsome sales throughout India of cloth manufactured in England, he told the British, they had 'established a very high duty on the country cloth and made yours free of charge!' In 1838, the British had launched their 'unethical' first war in Afghanistan and had almost simultaneously started an 'unwarranted' opium war against China, for which they had used Indian money, he stated. What of the British claim that they were spending resources on educating Indians? 'The present little donations,' the British were handing out 'out of the immense revenues of India' for the education of Indians, wrote Tarkhadkar, were 'ridiculously trifling'. And exclaiming 'woe be to you and your Government' and 'would to God you had not come to India,' he laid out his verdict—the government of the British was 'the most bitter curse India has ever been visited with' because 'India has been got hold of by a race of demons who would never be satisfied with until they have despoiled her of all her precious things and reduced all her sons and daughters to total beggary.'[29]

This was a spectacularly acerbic attack for its times, for it came well before the 1857 Revolt and at a time when Indian confidence was at an all-time low. Two other fellow Maharashtrians and contemporaries of Tarkhadkar mounted similar verbal assaults on the British—Bhau Mahajan, who studied alongside Dadabhai Naoroji at Elphinstone Institution and who started his own newspaper, *Prabhakar*, in October 1841, and Ramkrishna Vishwanath, who wrote in 1843 'the first book on Indian history and political economy to be attempted in Marathi'.

Naoroji, of course, gave a further and fuller exposition of the 'drain' theory by citing facts and figures, but when he articulated it for the first time at a gathering of the East India Association in London in May 1867, he acknowledged the role of Tarkhadkar and the two others. 'More than 20 years earlier,' he said, 'a small band of Hindu students and thoughtful gentlemen used to meet secretly to discuss the effects of British rule upon India. The home charge and the transfer of capital from India to England in various shapes, and the exclusion of the children of the country from any share or voice in the administration of their own country, formed the chief burden of their complaint.'[30]

Tarkhadkar's attack on the British thus not only anticipated Naoroji's theory but foreshadowed Tilak's later eviscerating critique of the Raj.

By the time the students at Deccan College had their conversation with the Russian visitor in 1879, several decades had passed since the 'drain' had begun, and a lot more wealth had been taken away to England even as India continued to be bedevilled by famine and the decline of indigenous industry in much the same way it had during Tarkhadkar's times. In fact, by this time the British had started a Second Afghan War, and the students complained that the Raj was keeping the truth and not giving the Indians full information about the conflict. One of the professors at the college was Kashinath Telang; he too spoke to the Russian at length. A lawyer, teacher and author of historical and philological works who later went on to become a legislator, Bombay High Court judge and president of the Asiatic Society of Bombay, Telang was described by Minayeff as 'very nice' and a 'very young and handsome' man. Telang told the Russian that the Afghan War was 'senseless, there was no necessity for starting it, and above all, India would be saddled with the cost'. Another teacher said the government had already frittered away the 'famine funds' in the Afghan War. After the severe famines between 1876 and 1878, the Raj had created what it called the 'Famine Insurance Grant' to fund work in famine-stricken areas. Though contribution to this fund was capped at 15 million rupees, it was being collected by hiking tax rates, and perception was growing that it was all going to the North-West borders. Minayeff observed that the removal of import duty was also hurting the Indians. Between 1874 and 1879, the Raj had, with the clear motive of benefiting British manufacturers, greatly slashed and partly abolished import duty on a number of goods, and in 1879 in particular, duty on several manufactured cotton articles was removed. This affected not only the Indian owners of textile mills but also the poor, 'depriving them of their means of livelihood.'[31] And the local hero M.G. Ranade himself, in two public addresses delivered in Poona in 1872–73, had spoken of how British competition was ruining Indian industry and making the countryside poorer. Ranade had, in the usual style of the moderate Sarvajanik Sabha, balanced this criticism with a description of the often 'unproductive' ways of the Indians, urging his compatriots to bring about their own economic revival, but the message had sunk in to the extent that Vasudev Balwant Phadke during his trial mentioned Ranade's twin lectures as his sources of inspiration which led him to stage an armed revolt.[32]

Evidently, the British argument about how they were modernizing India's physical infrastructure and bringing her into the industrial age was no longer working as effectively as it did even a decade earlier. After crushing the armed Revolt in 1858, the British had begun a raft of works, building roads, steamships, a network of railways and lines for telegraphic communication, saying they wanted to 'improve a society they believed was backward'. Yet, the reality, as British historian Jon Wilson has pointed out, was that the construction spree had taken off as 'little more than the limited British attempt to shore up their shaky grip on power', and imperial bureaucrats such as the Bombay Governor of the 1860s Bartle Frere saw it 'not as a means for economic or social transformation but as 'a vehicle to project British power and character'.[33] The purpose of the works was two-fold: if yet another revolt of a similar scale broke out, dispatching police units and armed forces to crush it would be far speedier, and if more British-manufactured goods and commodities were being brought in and sold across the land and raw materials from within India were taken out to the English shores, then their movement would be much swifter and more profitable to the British governmental and industrial establishment. Frere boasted that the railways would 'quadruple the available military strength of India', and the top officials argued that all works to be undertaken 'needed to be profitable in a pecuniary point of view' to the Raj'.[34]

Indians had at the very least, slowly started seeing through it all. The evidence was building up all around. For example, people in the Deccan could see that neither the building of the railways nor the new irrigation systems had prevented 'some of the world's worst famines,' which occurred in India in the 1870s and later in the 1890s. 'Millions died' in these famine years, and when the famine of 1876 broke out, 10,000 of the 67,000 residents of Indapur, a town situated to the east of Poona, were forced to leave.[35]

To add to such injury, there were racial insults and blatant racial discrimination. Russian Indologist Minayeff has given a crisp account of an incident in which he found himself involved:

At 1 o'clock today I went to the Deccan College. Examined Jain manuscripts. I chose one and wanted to get a copy of the same, this gave rise to a curious talk with the Principal Mr [R. J.] Oxenham. He insisted that I should approach Dr. [J. G.] Buhler [who was an Austrian Sanskrit scholar in service of the British and engaged as professor of Oriental Languages in Mumbai and Pune from 1863 to 1880] for materials about the Jains and when I observed that I could have the very same materials from native scholars, he vehemently disputed it. [H. J.] Dastoor [assistant professor of Oriental Languages], who was present at the discussion, did not at all like Oxenham's remark.[36]

For Tilak, a law student of the same institution where this incident occurred, it was thus important that Chiplunkar in his *Nibandhmala* was saying it like it was. Ranade was taking care not to start and stay on an adversarial footing by highlighting the so-called virtues of the Empire; Chiplunkar was doing nothing of that sort. It was true that Chiplunkar demonstrated a high appreciation for certain aspects of Western society, among them the almost universal regard for history, the progress in the various sciences and in technology, and the richness of European and English literature and poetry. In one of his essays, he wrote of how, in English, literary criticism had been honed into an art form, something the Indians hadn't managed until then despite the wealth of their own poetic texts. But he was not in thrall to the Empire, unlike many scholars of his generation. He saw it as a vehicle of oppression and a destructive force for India's self-identity. 'We have completely lost our freedoms under British rule,' he wrote. Contending that the people of India had been robbed of their sense of self as the result of various assaults by the British on their persons and their psyche, Chiplunkar said they were being 'treated like bullocks who were being whipped around' and made to do their owners' bidding. 'We have no rights, and the British think that they can do what they want with wealth they get from India and that we should be grateful with whatever little crumbs are thrown our way, no matter how we are treated.' Chiplunkar especially objected to the Raj's 'civilizing mission,' asking how it was that the British had the temerity to say all the time that the Indians were good for nothing and incapable of managing their own affairs. 'Our civilization has been around for 3,000-4,000 years, and our people built states, established laws and codes, developed skills, mastered the arts and made much progress in material and spiritual thinking. Were these all gifts given to us by the English people? Where exactly were [Robert] Clive and [Arthur] Wellesley *saheb* when our King Porus took on the mighty Alexander in the Punjab? Where were Macaulay's ancestors when Panini wrote his rules of grammar? All this was far into the past, but more recently . . . had our Shivaji Maharaj, who challenged an Empire and built the glorious edifice of Maratha rule, taken 'strategy' as some kind of loan from the British?' He wanted the British to stop telling the Indians that they were 'uncivilized' and that if were not for the arrival of the imperialists, they would have remained 'brutes'; if the Britishers had not come in, he asserted, there was in fact the distinct possibility that the people of the land would have been in a far better position.[37]

Tilak and Agarkar keenly followed and appreciated Chiplunkar's writings. Sometime after 1879, word got around in Poona that Chiplunkar was thinking of giving up his job as a teacher in state-run schools and starting a school of his own. This bit of news piqued Tilak's curiosity, and in September of that year, the two friends set out to meet Chiplunkar at his residence.

Why were they heading there? Tilak, in his last year of LLB., and Agarkar, about to sit for his final MA exams, had determined not to get a government job. The tumult in the Deccan had had an impact on their minds, and as mentioned earlier, they would, in their incessant rounds of the college premises, have lively discussions and debates on public issues, including on the nature of the British Raj and ways to improve the condition of the Indian people. Tilak looked up to Ranade, because he believed Ranade had set the ball of action rolling in Maharashtra at a time when the western Deccan lay 'stone-cold and motionless'. Now, Chiplunkar was promising to go further. Both Ranade and Chiplunkar held government jobs, but Chiplunkar was planning to quit and branch out on his own, in service of his own people instead of the Raj. Tilak's impulse to join him in this endeavour was extremely strong, as was that of Agarkar.

A letter written by Agarkar to his mother conveys the intensity of their feeling:

> You may be hoping that with your son about to appear for important exams, he will soon get a job that brings him a handsome salary and your efforts in raising him would be finally rewarded. But I want to make it clear to you right away: Without hankering for any big wealth or for any comforts, I am going to be satisfied with subsistence-level pay and dedicate all my time to the betterment of people.

When Tilak and Agarkar told Chiplunkar what was on their minds, he was obviously delighted. He wrote to his younger brother Laxman on 13 September 1879:

> The memorable 1st of October is approaching. I shall enjoy the pleasure of kicking off my chains [of government service] that day. Mr Agarkar (going for M.A.), Mr. Tilak (going for L.L.B.), Mr. Bhagwat and Karandikar (appearing for B.A.), have tendered proposals for joining me in the enterprise. This they have done of their own accord. We have settled 1st of January for the hoisting of the

standard. Such a battery must carry the High School instantaneously before it.[38]

The night was cold when the young Tilak and Agarkar walked back from Chiplunkar's home to their hostel rooms in the college, and there was a strong wind blowing. It was no ordinary wind; it was a wind of change, and it would transform the nature of Indians' protest and fight against the Raj.

Chapter 3

School of Infamous Scribblers

As 1 January 1880, the planned date for inaugurating their new school, drew near, Tilak and Chiplunkar experienced a major shake-up that threatened to undo their enterprise even before it had begun. Chiplunkar was happy that four bright and educated young men were going to join forces with him to establish a private educational institution that would match those set up by the government in quality and at the same time differ from state-run schools in the kind of education it offered by focusing on the idea of a national consciousness that drew from India's culture and heritage. On the day of the launch at the Morobadada Fadnis Wada premises in the Budhwar Peth locality of Poona, three of the original core team were nowhere to be seen. Two of them, Bhagwat and Karandikar, had backtracked abruptly, presumably out of fear of a hostile reaction from the Raj. Agarkar, on the other hand, had deferred his involvement: he had failed his final year MA exam, and he wanted to clear it before he came in. Thus, it was Tilak and Chiplunkar who did the opening on their own.

But despite the initial hiccup, this opening partnership blossomed, and an entire team was eventually built, counting among its members Gopal Krishna Gokhale, the man Gandhi would call his mentor. Tilak himself laid a very solid ground for reaching great heights in his career. Few people get to build even a single institution in their early years in public life. Tilak got to build four in his first decade, from 1880 to 1890—a school, two powerful newspapers, and a college. He joined a fifth institution, the Indian National Congress, which he later turned almost single-handedly into the vehicle of a mass movement for India's liberation. With his writings in one of his papers, the Marathi language

Kesari, in particular, he blazed a trail that ignited Indian minds and aspirations and transformed the very manner in which a subjugated people communicated and interacted with their racially minded colonial oppressors.

Many people gleefully predicted the quick demise of the school, Chiplunkar said later. First, there was the apparent incongruity in the aim of the institution and the medium of its instruction. It was going to be called the New English School, and the principal language of teaching was going to be English though it was more accurately bilingual as Marathi was also going to be taught simultaneously. Tilak and Chiplunkar were committed to building up the self-respect of Indians, and Tilak openly said they were troubled by the state of the country and saw that education alone could turn things around. In the same breath, both the founders wanted Indian languages to grow and come into their own. Sceptics saw the adoption of the colonizers' language as incompatible with the idea of inspiring national self-confidence, though Marathi was going to be taught from Class 1 to 3 and Sanskrit from Class 4 to 6 along with English.

Soon afterwards, the school's founders made it clear, while presenting their views before the Education Commission, the local governing body for education headed by the official William Wilson Hunter, that they had started a 'private English school' for four reasons.[1] One, popular demand for English education was high, and Chiplunkar in particular saw English as 'the milk of the tigress', a language of empowerment because of the vast streams of information and knowledge it contained. Two, they aimed to stop what they termed as the 'de-nationalization' of Indians studying in English schools by running such schools themselves and imparting lessons that didn't merely glorify the British, their history and their culture; secondary education, especially, they felt, 'checked the free growth of national character through the operation of the monotonously uniform system of instruction conducted upon English models and English tastes . . . and the adoption of textbooks like Morris' history, the tenor of which was to magnify British influence and British power and to lower and degrade Indian men and manners'. Three, they wanted to actually end the 'suppression of vernaculars as media of instruction' by steadily placing Indian languages at par with English in these schools so that knowledge could be diffused like the 'Despatch of 1854' had stated, 'through the medium of the English language and the vernacular languages of India together'. Four, they 'confidently hoped' they would be able to take control of government high schools 'within 8 to 10 years' so that education would be in the hands of 'natives' if the government was willing to help them by introducing 'a more liberal and less interfering' system of grants-in-aid. Essentially, they wanted to enter the system to change the system. A tall order.

Students at the time matriculated if they cleared Class 7, and the New English School would have classes leading up to matriculation; in the final year, while English of course would be a subject, out of Marathi and Sanskrit the students could choose one for their 'second language' paper. Also, in keeping with their aim of giving equal importance to Indian languages, the use of the local language was going to be made wherever possible, ensuring a possible hybrid language model. For example, one of the textbooks for students in Class 6 was going to be K.L. Chhatre's 'Physics', which was in Marathi.

But even if the school tried to stay afloat somehow, the critics asked, where were the funds going to come from? No government grants would be available, and as far as donors were concerned, would there be enough who contributed adequately over a period of time? In this respect, the founders even appeared to have scored a self-goal before starting. They had decided to adopt a version of the Jesuitical principle of public service, where they would do everything for the institution but take only the bare minimum pay to keep body and soul intact. There would be no religious teachings, however, though the founders were Hindus, so unlike Jesuit institutions, there was little hope of generating a lot of funds from faith-based institutions. And the school's motto was 'making education affordable and easier', which meant charging lower fees than government-run schools, making the build-up of finances harder. So, while the Poona High School, the biggest state-run school in the city, charged Re 1 as the fee for the first three years, the New English School would charge 12 annas; for Classes 4 and 5, the two schools would charge Rs 2 and Rs 1.5 respectively, and for Classes 6 and 7 the fees would be Rs 3 and Rs 2 respectively. As it turned out, Tilak and Chiplunkar didn't take any salary in the first year at all. How long was such an arrangement based on altruistic idealism going to last?

We have evidence that some months into the school's launch, Tilak himself may have been on his guard. In May 1880, he applied, as a qualified lawyer, for the position of a sub-judge despite his and Agarkar's early resolve not to take up a government job. Why did he do that? Was he, as one of his biographers has suggested, concerned about whether he would get along with Chiplunkar, who was after all regarded as a maverick? Was his morale affected by the absence of his close friend Agarkar? Or was he pushed into applying by his uncle, who had looked after him since his parents' passing, and who was keen that Bal take up a government job? Or was it purely a flicker of uncertainty about the school's future? Though Tilak never really explained what lay behind it, the fourth reason sounds plausible, or it may have been the jumbling together of all, or most, of the questions. The truth is that Tilak did waver, even if it was for a moment. Soon he recovered and stuck to his original resolve of being with the school. If he hadn't, it's unlikely he'd have got the title of 'Lokmanya' and it's highly unlikely this biography, or any other on his life, would have been written. On such small turns can the course of an entire life change.

Tilak was soon in a position to put the momentary flicker of doubt behind him. Within months of the school beginning its classes, curiosity about it began to grow in and around Poona, and there was much talk about the youth, sincerity, vigour and energy of the founders and teachers. While Tilak began teaching his two favourite subjects, mathematics and Sanskrit, Chiplunkar took lessons in English and Marathi. Soon they were joined by Mahadev Ballal Namjoshi. He was an extraordinary character: he hadn't got a varsity degree, but he was intelligent and taught history and geography, and his greatest skill was to act as an organizer, manager and an envoy of sorts for the fledgling institution, spreading word about it among various stakeholders in Poona's society and gathering goodwill. A superb catch by the school that year was the Sanskrit scholar Waman Shivram Apte; he had won virtually every prize and scholarship worth its name during his student years and was also known to be a 'born teacher'. The founders were so happy to have him that they straight away appointed him as school superintendent, while Chiplunkar kept the role of headmaster. Apte justified his appointment by helping one of the students, Bhaskar Ramchandra Arte, to win for the school in its very first year one of two coveted Sanskrit scholarships offered by the university.

On the first day of the school, it had thirty-five students; by the end of December 1880, it had 336. Many parents and guardians had shifted their wards either from government-run schools or other private ones. From the first year, 70–75 per cent of its students who sat for the matriculation exams were successful; in the fourth year—1884—by which time the total number of students had crossed 1,000, the pass percentage was 89 per cent, higher than in any school—state-run or private—in the Bombay Presidency. The success was beyond all expectations, and it was in part because Tilak and the other instructors—his dear friend Agarkar had joined him in the second year—were imbued with a missionary spirit of sorts.

So driven was the bunch that many of them independently wrote fresh textbooks with a view to changing learning for the better. Tilak wrote a book on mechanics in the inaugural academic year; Apte brought out a *Guide to Sanskrit Composition* which became a mini-classic in its own right; Agarkar wrote a book on grammar; and after Gokhale joined in 1886, he too penned a work on algebra which earned much respect. Teaching styles were varied and perhaps added to the overall appeal. Chiplunkar would start on a subject and then meander into a vast, digressive realm of unrelated topics; Tilak would stick to the point and the syllabus in an engaging fashion, though he would frustrate students sometimes by refusing to write down difficult sums on the blackboard, preferring to solve them orally for his pupils instead; Agarkar was quiet, solid and rational in his approach; and Namjoshi's sheer enthusiasm was infectious and made up for what he might have lacked in pedagogical skills in comparison with the other men around.

By no means was Tilak well-known across Poona when he started as a teacher, but he was looked upon as a promising young man who had won a first-class at his master's exams and a good law degree. His passion and discipline in teaching, his authority in math and Sanskrit, and the excellent growth of the school resulted in his reputation slowly building up.

Gradually and steadily, funds and other resources too started coming in for the school. Baba Gokhale, who used to run a private school in

Poona which had by 1880 folded up, was the first to make a gift of 'a few good wall maps and a few blackboards amounting in value to about Rs 10'. Four gentlemen from Berar, which was then part of Hyderabad State, donated Rs 1200 for the purchase of books and setting up of a library; several others, among them the doyen of Marathi theatre B.P. Kirloskar, donated books; the much-respected M.G. Ranade gave Rs 50 for scholarships; K.T. Telang, the Sanskrit scholar whom the Russian Indologist I.P. Minayeff had recently met at the Deccan College, gifted Rs 50 for buying lab apparatus; and Jaysingrao Ghatge, the regent of the princely state of Kolhapur and chief of Kagal, announced an endowment of Rs 500 for a prize to be given to the school's topper in the matriculation exams.

Soon the Bombay government was compelled to grant recognition to the school for its achievements. The head of the Education Commission, W.W. Hunter, visited the school on 8 September 1882 and said he could 'with certainty affirm that throughout the whole of India I have not yet witnessed a single institution of this nature which can be compared with this establishment. This institution, though not receiving any aid from government, can rival and compete with success, not only with the Government High Schools in this country, but may compare favourably with the schools of other countries also'.[2] And the Bombay governor James Fergusson contributed Rs 1250 for the foundation of a prize, saying that 'within a few years it has achieved a standard of excellence comparable to institutions more highly favoured' and that 'it would not only be unjust to it but discreditable to ourselves were we not to extend to it a helping hand, and gain for ourselves some portion of the credit that the promoters have achieved for themselves'.[3] Fergusson's patronage came in the year 1884 and also ensured his status as patron of the Deccan Education Society that Tilak and Agarkar were then setting up. But before that, the two close friends had taken a major step beyond the school in any case.

Tilak and Chiplunkar had started out with a focus on school education all right, yet they had in mind the broader objective of public education beyond classrooms and syllabi. One afternoon in December 1880, the core team of the New English School—Tilak, Chiplunkar, Namjoshi, Apte and the soon-to-join-after-his-MA-results Agarkar—

had gathered for lunch at Apte's residence. They were all relieved that the school had struck roots despite all odds, and discussion naturally veered after some desultory talk to 'what next'. Chiplunkar was still running his *Nibandhmala* (it would close in 1882), but it was a monthly, and he batted in favour of something more immediate and newspaper-like, if not a daily. As mentioned in the previous chapter, the Marathi regions had taken enthusiastically to the press, and the school's top brass agreed that papers were fast emerging as reliable sources of information and could be used as both educators and watchdogs—to impart learning to the people as well as to highlight their issues and grievances under foreign domination.

To start a regular publication was also going to be an act of daring because of what had happened over the past couple of decades and especially in the past few years. The clause on sedition had been part of the original Indian Penal Code drafted by Macaulay, but when the Raj chose to introduce the legislation in 1860, the section was for the time being kept on ice because the Viceroy Charles Canning, known as Lord Canning, thought it might be construed as an attack on the press. Ten years on, the IPC was amended, and the clause duly introduced. The British government nevertheless still remained wary of the press and especially of the Indian language press; a British official had famously commented, in a post-1857 report, that if newspapers in the North Western provinces had been carefully studied in 1856–57, 'the rebellion could have been anticipated and prevented'.[4] In an age where public rallies could not be big because there was no electronic equipment that could carry a speaker's voice afar and where other forms of technology were simply not available, the press had become an important tool in the hands of Indians to disseminate information and voice their opinions and concerns and even criticisms of the government. The hardline imperialists resented this, and one such hardliner, Edward Lytton or Lord Lytton, who took over as viceroy in 1876, brought in the Vernacular Press Act in 1878 to gag the native language press as the government came under fire for its policies during a string of devastating famines. Under this law, any district magistrate or police commissioner could seize the printing press, paper and any other material of a publication that carried 'objectionable' and 'seditious' content.[5] Worse, no printer or publisher who faced such action could move a court against the confiscation, a fact that exposed as hollow the British claim that they had brought in 'the rule of law' in the subcontinent. The Act's chief target was the *Amrita Bazar Patrika* of Bengal, which niftily got around it by transforming overnight from a bilingual English-and-Bengali weekly to a purely English one.[6] Criticisms mounted, and in just a couple of years the government in Britain and viceroy in India too changed: William Gladstone, as the new British premier, sent George Ripon, known as Lord Ripon, to oversee Indian affairs, and Ripon repealed the much-criticised Act in 1881. At the time the core group of the New English School was meeting at Apte's home, the debate over the 'gagging' Act, as it was called, was at its height.

The consensus that emerged from the discussion was to launch two weekly papers, one in Marathi and the other in English. The Marathi paper would be called 'Kesari' or 'The Lion', and the English one would be titled *Mahratta*, the eighteenth- and nineteenth-century English style of spelling the word 'Maratha'. G.G. Agarkar would be the editor of the *Kesari*, and B. G. Tilak would be at the helm of the *Mahratta*. The official declaration made by the founding group of the publications' objectives was the understatement of the century: apart from dealing with regular subjects, the two weeklies, they said, would contain essays on the condition of the populace, book reviews and a summation of political happenings in Britain and elsewhere abroad.[7] In reality, the *Kesari* and *Mahratta*, standing masthead to masthead, would be extremely potent weapons in the arsenal of a society seeking redress and justice against a system of racialized repression and violence, and though Tilak started out editing the *Mahratta* and only later took over as editor of the *Kesari*, he wrote in the Marathi paper with the fervour of a man passionately seeking the freedoms of his people, his unrelenting voice pulling down the ivory tower of elitist isolation which had placed constraints on the drive towards liberation and unleashing the power of the masses in pursuing that national objective.

One of the first campaigns carried out by the papers put the concerns of the Indian people at the centre of the narrative, albeit indirectly. At the same time, as a result of their campaign, Tilak and his friend Agarkar found themselves entangled in a major controversy.

This first big controversy of Tilak's career revolved around the alleged mistreatment of the native Kolhapur prince at the hands of the British-appointed and British-controlled administrator.

To understand why the issue gained traction and generated a strong reaction, it's important to know how the population in the Deccan viewed the rulers of the local principalities and harboured questions in their minds about developments in the recent past.

When the British had carved up the Peshwa's dominions for themselves, they had also truncated the size of many of the Maratha principalities, subsuming entire regions into Company territory. Among those hit hardest were the states of Satara and Kolhapur, both of which were ruled by descendants of Chhatrapati Shivaji. The Shivaji factor meant people of the Marathi regions had a particularly soft spot for these two states which, post 1818, had been reduced to barely a few districts. In the 1830s, the Company had fabricated charges against the Raja of Satara, Pratap Singh, accusing him of fomenting a conspiracy against the British. Some conscientious British officials were aghast: the British resident or chief overseeing official in Satara in 1836, Colonel Lodwick, admitted later that the accusers 'bore false testimony', 'deeply regretted' his part in the affair and told the Company's Court of Directors in a letter how he was prodded by the then Bombay governor Robert Grant to 'decoy and entrap the Raja in a plot against the British government'.[8] Some people close to the Raja too were recruited by the Company to do the dirty job; one of their chief collaborators was Balaji Pant Natoo, the first assistant of the local British resident (a 'resident' was the Raj's chief political agent in every princely state who indirectly held the reins of administration with other officials under his charge). In September 1839 the British handed over to the Raja a horribly self-incriminating letter in exchange for allowing him to stay on as the ruler, obviously as their puppet. Pratap Singh was a man of self-respect, and he refused to sign, preferring to lose his power instead. He was deposed immediately and sent off to Benaras, where he died in 1847; his not-so-capable brother Appa Saheb, who was willing to do the Company's bidding and was propped up by the local intriguer Natoo, was pronounced the new ruler. The dethroning left a bitter aftertaste for the local population, and its memory rankled.

Satara was also a classic case of how, unlike the impression the British sought to create (and successfully created especially for future generations, ensuring it lasted long and decades into India's independence), all the native Indian princely rulers were not wastrels or delinquents. Some rulers were good, some were bad; some resisted reforms, some welcomed and even championed them; some were perfect invertebrates, and some others had at least a semblance of a spine. The reality was more nuanced, and in the period this book is about, the local Indian populace certainly saw it as being much more nuanced than the British portrayal made it out to be.

If Satara was an episode that stuck out, decades later, the case of the ruler of Baroda, Malharrao Gaekwad, became another acute sore point. Malharrao, it was agreed overall, was hardly an ideal ruler or well-inclined towards positive administrative changes, yet he was removed by the British in 1875 arbitrarily. First, he was accused of maladministration, and soon afterwards, he was arrested on the bizarre charge of attempting to poison a local British resident. A special six-member tribunal was set up to try his case. It comprised three Europeans, all of whom pronounced him guilty, and three Indians, all of whom declared his innocence. The three-all outcome resulted not in his acquittal but his instant removal, something that the Indian people and particularly those in the Deccan with their history and memories of the Maratha Confederacy saw as unfair and autocratic.[9]

The Baroda case was fresh in people's minds and a wider debate on British intervention in the native states was thus being rigorously conducted at the time the *Kesari* and *Mahratta* began to roll off the printing press. The *Mahratta* was the first of the two weekly papers to be launched, on Sunday, 2 January 1881; the *Kesari* came out two days later, on Tuesday, 4 January; and it was decided that from then on, the two papers would be brought out every Sunday and Tuesday respectively.[10] The inaugural edition of the *Mahratta* put out a list of 'evils of the British administration'. Tilak mentioned, among these evils, exorbitant taxes, decimation of local industry, the Vernacular Press Act (which was repealed only the following year) and the Arms Act; like the Press Act, the Arms Act had been introduced by Lytton in 1878, and it was openly discriminatory, stipulating that Indians could not possess weapons without first obtaining a licence but Europeans could.[11]

Equally prominently, he pointed to another problematic area on this list: the 'elimination of the native aristocracy' and 'the destruction of native municipal and judicial institutions'. He declared firmly that 'our policy would always be for the uninterfered continuation of' the native Indian states and 'to shield the Native Princes from uncalled-for interference on the part of the politicals (Raj's political agents)'. Yes, he was all in favour of administrative improvements, he wrote, but 'if [the new viceroy] Lord Ripon is serious in his purpose of reforming the government of Native Chiefs, he must first set about reforming the Political Agents, and try to give constitutional government to the Native States'.[12]

Such early and bold strokes helped the two papers gain a foothold in an arena that was getting increasingly populated with growth in literacy and education. The Bombay Presidency had about seventy newspapers in all during this period. Among the leading provincial Marathi voices were the *Dnyan Prakash*, founded in 1849 by Krishnaji Trimbak Ranade, and the *Indu Prakash*, founded in 1862 by M.G. Ranade. While both these papers were edited by Brahmans, the top paper which championed the cause of the so-called non-Brahman classes was the Marathi *Deenbandhu* edited by Narayanrao Meghaji Lokhande. Parsi writer and poet Behramji Malbari had recently bought an English language paper, *Indian Spectator*, in which he had decided to push the case for social reform; and the British had English language dailies like the *Times of India* and *Bombay Gazette*, with their white or Anglo–Indian proprietors and editors, to bat for them in the region. The native princes, as part of a 'Native Association' they had formed in the 1850s, had started their own English journal, called the *Native Public Opinion*, but it had closed soon after, having failed to garner readership. Mahadev Ballal Namjoshi, who had joined the New English School as a teacher, had also started in 1879 an English daily called *Deccan Star*; at the time of launching their two weeklies, the Chiplunkar–Tilak–Agarkar trio subsumed it into the *Mahratta*, and Chiplunkar bought the printing press that Namjoshi owned in Poona for his own brand new publications.[13]

They were soon making their mark: the *Mahratta* under Tilak began to be read seriously as a prominent 'organ of educated public opinion in Maharashtra' (defined here as the broader Marathi-speaking regions and not the state that came into being in 1960), and the *Kesari*, which focused more on imparting 'public education', became stiff competition for the other regional language publications.[14] In just a couple of years, *Kesari* became the largest-selling Marathi paper, and by 1884 it had a circulation of 4350,[15] which was significant for a weekly of that era; its other Marathi competitors were still to get to the 4000-mark, plus each issue was supposed to have been read not just by one person but either read aloud in groups or by entire families. By 1884, though, the real founder Chiplunkar was not alive to check those circulation figures. Just a year after the papers had taken off, he died in February 1882. His death came as a big blow for Tilak and Agarkar, who looked upon him as their mentor. But they had not enough time to grieve; they were, in the same month, in serious legal trouble.

They had openly accused the *karbharee*, or native administrator, of the state of Kolhapur, Mahadeo Vasudev Barve, of doing his damnedest to brand the young local ruling prince as 'insane' and therefore mentally unfit to rule, so that he could, in collusion with the dowager queen Sakwarbai, foist a more compliant ruler on the people of that province. And a furious Barve had, in turn, filed a case of criminal defamation against Tilak and Agarkar, which meant, under the provisions of the Indian Penal Code, that if they were held guilty, they could be sent to prison.

In 1870, the Raja of Kolhapur, Rajaram Maharaj, had been in the seat of power for barely four years when he died suddenly, at the young age of 20, in Florence during a visit to Italy. The same year, before the young raja's death, Barve was appointed karbharee of Kolhapur. The karbharee was, in Barve's own words, 'personal assistant to the Political Agent' of Kolhapur, but he was in fact the chief local administrator, the hands-on man in-charge. The raja had two wives but no children, so the question of adoption arose. Barve deposed in court that the surviving queens, Laxmibai and Sakwarbai (also known as Sakhubai), were allowed to adopt from among 'some six or nine boys proposed of the Khanwat branch of the Bhonsla (Bhosle) family, which was founded by Shivajee'.[16] Narayan Rao was the boy they picked. He was only '8 or 9 years old', and he was duly adopted and given the title of Chhatrapati Shivaji the Fourth on 23 October 1871.

Sometime in 1879, people whispered on the streets of Kolhapur that the prince, now in his late teens, had started behaving oddly. While some jumped to the conclusion that he was losing his sanity because of ill-treatment at the hands of the karbharee, others were convinced there was nothing wrong with him but the theory of 'insanity' was simply a ploy by the administrator and the queen Sakwarbai, who by now wanted to adopt more of a 'yes man' than Narayan Rao, to oust him from the *gaddi*.

Barve immediately came under a cloud of suspicion, especially owing to his record. He had served the British loyally, having joined the government's education department in 1856 and having been appointed, in 1865, deputy collector and magistrate at Belgaum before being sent to Kolhapur. He had already been known for some time as 'Rao Bahadur' or 'His Honour', a title that many government servants obtained in recognition of their service to the Raj; in June 1881, he had also been made a Companion of the Order of the Indian Empire or C.I.E.[17] Administrators of native states seen as being loyal to the Raj were increasingly at the receiving end of criticism from those Indians who saw these states as the remaining symbols of native freedom and their rulers as 'representatives and custodians of social, political and cultural traditions of the land'.[18] Tilak himself had hit out through the columns of his paper at the *diwan* of Baroda, T. Madhavrao, for his alleged 'weak-kneed surrender of the rights and interests of the State to the British government'.[19]

Plus, if anyone could be seen to be influencing the prince's conduct the most, it had to be Barve. 'The whole of the work of the administration relating to the state passed through my hands. All preparatory work of the administration passed under my signature, and final orders were taken under the political agent's signature,' he himself said. How scrupulously he stuck to his job as told by him by his British masters was also well-known. To cite an example: the natural parents of the adopted boy were Dinkarrao and Radhabai. Because he was a child, they were allowed to live with him 'at the palace for about a year after his adoption'. But they were eventually removed from the palace because 'Mr Hammick of the Civil Service, who was the guardian of the Maharaja at the time . . . found that their presence interfered to a certain extent with the education and proper discipline of the young Maharaja'. The guardian sent a report to the political agent, and orders given by the political agent for their removal were carried out by Barve.[20]

The assistant political agent of the time, Edward Cox, went a step ahead in underlining the authority that Barve enjoyed. 'There was no doubt that he (Barve) possessed more power and influence at Kolhapur than the Political Agent (Colonel Schneider),' wrote Cox. 'The latter officer (Schneider) often drove about in a fine carriage and pair, and the people in the streets saluted him respectfully enough' but 'Mahdu Rao, following him in a humble little tonga, received the most obsequious tokens of obeisance'.[21]

As news spread that the young prince had been taken to Rajkot, Mahabaleshwar, Poona, Bellary, Madras, Ootacamund, Kunnur, Trichinopoly, Tanjore and Pondicherry for possible recovery and that he had been examined in Bombay by 'Dr Patrick Murphy' and 'Drs 'Hunter and Cook', who were about to confirm that he had 'melancholia accompanied by delusions', the Marathi papers, led by the *Indu Prakash* of Bombay and including the *Mahratta* and *Kesari*, opened campaigns in support of the raja and against Barve in particular.[22] On 24 November 1881, the residents of Poona held a public meeting, with the noted scholar Gopalrao Deshmukh, better known as 'Lokahitawadi' for his writings for public enlightenment, in the chair. Speakers at the meeting accused Barve of coercion, ill-treatment, placing the raja under fetters and conspiracy and demanded that he be replaced immediately. Initially, along with the *Indu Prakash* of Bombay, papers like the *Dynan Prakash* and *Native Opinion* of Poona were more vociferous than Tilak and Agarkar in denouncing the karbharee. 'Does the Indian Penal Code not apply to the Rao Bahadur (Barve)?' asked one of them.[23]

The *Mahratta* on 27 November 1881 referred to the Kolhapur prince as 'an Indian Hamlet, persecuted by the Claudius of a *karbharee*' and alleged that Barve, the queen Sakwarbai, the newly-appointed guardian of the prince, Cox, and the Private warder or personal attendant Green were hell-bent on establishing that the raja was 'mad'.[24] Soon afterwards, there appeared exposes in the form of three letters reproduced in the *Dynan Prakash* which were purportedly written by Barve and which were apparently proof of the plot he was hatching in collusion with the raja's adoptive mother and the others.[25] After that the letters were published by the *Mahratta* and *Kesari* with scathing comments against Barve, and the *Kesari* even dared him in an editorial—written neither by Agarkar nor by Tilak but by Waman Shivram Apte—'to prove his innocence in a court of law'.[26] What Tilak and Agarkar certainly did was to write to the Bombay government, along with editors of other publications, seeking a thorough probe into the matter. They declared that they were openly siding with three people who had lent weight to the allegations: the adopted boy's natural mother, Radhabai, and her lawyers Nana Bhide and Keshav Bakhle.

Accepting *Kesari*'s 'dare', Barve sued for defamation, not in Kolhapur and not in Poona but in Bombay because he was convinced he would get better legal advice there.[27] Arraigned as accused were Tilak, Agarkar and the editor of *Dynan Prakash*, Waman Ranade, along with Radhabai and her two lawyers. The moment the case was filed, the difficulty of fighting it appeared to have occurred to the two young editors, for Agarkar wrote in the *Kesari* appealing to all those who had the national interest and the interests of the native states at heart and those who did not countenance injustice to help liberally considering the legal expenses were going to be 'extraordinary'.[28] The response was highly encouraging: a Defence Fund was launched by the residents of Poona, and among the earliest contributors were students of the New English School and Deccan College, who between them raised Rs 200.[29]

The whole case turned on whether the letters purportedly written by Barve were genuine or not. They turned out to be forgeries, and the editor of *Dynan Prakash*, which had published them before Tilak and Agarkar reproduced them in their own papers, struggled to establish their provenance. Tilak had partly relied on those letters and partly on the depositions of some eminent persons, among them the chief of Kolhapur's neighbouring Kagal province, Abasaheb Kagalkar. A well-known Sardar and part of the elite circle of rulers in the region, Kagalkar, according to Tilak's close aide and biographer N.C. Kelkar and the Marathi scholar Y.D. Phadke, compelled him to burn certain letters in his possession which pointed to Kagalkar's involvement in the whole business.[30] While most of the persons cited by Tilak never turned up in court, Kagalkar's name on the list of defence witnesses turned out to be especially ironic. Not only did he not depose in favour of Tilak and Agarkar, but with the raja quickly and duly certified as 'insane', the Bombay government in March 1882 passed a resolution appointing Kagalkar as Regent who would take care of the state with assistance from Barve and two others till a replacement for the prince was found or the incumbent's sanity restored and with it, his position.[31]

The case was committed to the sessions court in Bombay and then to the Bombay High Court. Tilak and Agarkar were represented by two bright lawyers, Pherozeshah Mehta and K.T. Telang, and Barve had the government's top law officer, advocate-general B. Lang, on his side, along with the lawyer J.D. Inverarity.

Barve's lawyer Inverarity strongly assailed the argument made by Telang in Tilak's defence that he had been justified in making allegations against Barve 'when he saw that other native papers which had been publishing them since the year 1879 had not been prosecuted'. Inverarity said Barve had taken no notice of charges made against him for some time on the advice of the political agent Colonel Schneider, who believed that if proceedings were initiated, the name of the prince 'would be unnecessarily dragged through the dirt'. It was 'imprudent', he said, on Tilak's part to have concluded that because the charges had passed unnoticed for some time, they must be true.[32]

Nothing worked in favour of the young journalists, and after Nana Bhide became the first to be held guilty by the court and after the editor of *Dynan Prakash* issued an unconditional apology, so did the editors of the *Mahratta* and *Kesari*. Addressing Barve, Tilak and Agarkar stated:

> We feel it our duty to tender to you our unqualified and unreserved apology for the statements concerning you that appeared in our articles and petition (to the government, which was signed by Tilak). Those statements were based on information (which we at the time honestly believed to be true) supplied to us by persons whom we had at that time no reason to doubt, namely, Sadashiv Pandurang (Nana) Bhide and Waman Govind Ranade, to be in your handwriting, a fact which was also assured (of) by Vinayak Raghunath Kele, Hari Anant Gabale, and Kashiram Shivprasad that they would be able to prove conclusively. The facts elicited during the inquiry into Sadashiv Bhide's case have satisfied us that the information and letters were alike untrue . . . We feel that we have done you grave injustice, and that we offer you but very imperfect reparation in thus absolutely and

unreservedly withdrawing all imputations against you . . . We can
assure you that we never were, and are not, actuated by any feelings of
personal animosity towards you . . . [33]

If Tilak felt that such a comprehensive apology would work and
persuade Barve not to pursue the case any further, that hope was crushed.
Barve's lawyer, Inverarity, argued in the high court that the articles
'casting imputations upon Mr Barve' were published before the forged
letters were found; the 'apology was not sent until after the conviction
of Nana Bhide in respect of the three letters'; and 'these newspaper
editors persisted in their allegations . . . until the last moment, and
they offered to withdraw them only when they saw a halter round their
neck'. The lawyer further said that during the preliminary proceedings
in the magistrate's court itself, it was clear that Mr Barve was innocent,
but instead of apologizing at that time, 'the case against Mr Barve was
pressed with great pertinacity; and he was cross-examined in a most
offensive manner . . . After conducting himself in this manner, the
accused (Tilak), with his colleague (Agarkar), came forward at the very
last moment . . . with their apology'. [34]

   To many, this sounded like a determined and insistent prosecutorial
side. To most Indians who were following the case, however, it sounded
more a statement of intent from the British bureaucracy, made
emphatically to two young and up-coming editors who had shown signs
of having a mind of their own.

   On 17 July 1882, Tilak and Agarkar were held guilty by Justice F.L.
Latham of the Bombay High Court based on a special all-European
jury's findings and convicted of defaming Barve. They were sentenced
each to four months' imprisonment, the judge observing that 'they
had not acted with any malice, but were guilty of a want of due care
and caution in making serious charges'. [35] 'I acquit you of malignity,
but I can't of recklessness,' he stressed. [36] Tilak actually had two cases
against him: the one he faced in common with Agarkar, and the other
specifically filed by Barve against the *Mahratta* and Tilak as its editor.
The punishment for him in the second case—where the charges were
exactly similar—was pronounced at the same time and was identical to
the one in the first, and both sentences were to run concurrently. He
would be spending four months in jail in all.

The two editors were driven to the Dongri prison in Byculla. There, they were kept in a 13x13 cell, where mosquitoes and little creepy crawlies were in abundant supply. The food in jail was barely edible, and the young Agarkar, who was an asthmatic, found the going especially tough. His tummy simply couldn't take it, and Tilak put in a request to the jail superintendent asking that he be allowed to take that part of the food in Agarkar's plate which was unpalatable to his friend and pass on that portion from his own which Agarkar wouldn't mind eating. The nights weren't easy to pass because of the bugs, and Tilak and Agarkar spent hours discussing their lives, their aims, and where they had gone right and wrong so far and what they needed to do to get most things going for them in the future. Among the questions they debated was: how had they not seen the legal peril for them in the Kolhapur affair beforehand?

Agarkar badly sought writing materials at least; he loved to write and believed he could spend some of the jail time usefully if he could get hold of them. A month into the prison term the request was granted for both, and Agarkar made the fullest use of it, translating Hamlet—which the *Mahratta* had quoted in the Kolhapur case, with disastrous consequences—into Marathi and writing a short, thirty-page account of their days in prison, which was later published in book form. Interestingly, for someone who eventually became immortal as a writer and editor, the young Tilak wasn't a natural writer and took to writing when he usually ran out of other, more favoured lawyerly options like public speaking or debating. On the whole, the stay in the cell took a toll on the health of both: Tilak lost ten kilograms and Agarkar, much thinner and weaker anyway, seven kilograms.[37]

While Tilak and Agarkar were incarcerated, eminent citizens led by W. Wordsworth, a history and political economy professor who had taken over as principal of Elphinstone College in 1880, and the Poona-based lawyer V.N. Mandlik signed a petition asking the then Bombay governor James Fergusson to commute their sentence. On the one hand the British-owned papers such as the *Times of India* and *Bombay Gazette* thought the punishment appropriate, and the *Gazette* commented that 'the sentences were severe, but they were well-deserved' and would 'meet with general approval'; and on the other, the native papers, the Marathi ones and also the Gujarati and Parsi publications such as the 'Gujarati',

'Jame Jamshed' and 'Rast Goftar' were united in saying the sentencing was unusually harsh and the two editors should have been let off with a warning.[38] The native papers also pointed to what they felt were serious anomalies in the case: the main doctor, Patrick Murphy, who had looked after the Kolhapur prince, had admitted in court that 'it was necessary to whip the Raja of Kolhapur', pointing to the state the prince had been reduced to; many members of the jury had apparently conducted themselves as if they had presumed guilt rather than innocence; and worse, Justice Latham who delivered the ruling had earlier appeared as a lawyer for Barve in a case but had not thought it fit to recuse himself.[39]

As the government ignored both the petition and the native press commentary, the *Deenbandhu*, the paper of the non-Brahmans which took inspiration from the pioneering anti-caste agitator Jotiba Phule, advocated the idea of giving the young editors a massive welcome on their release from jail by placing them in a 'rath' (chariot) and taking them all around town. The *Deenbandhu* and another non-Brahman paper of the time, *Shri Shivaji*, were seeing the episode through a Brahman versus non-Brahman lens—according to this lens, Barve was a Chitpavan Brahman, and the raja was a Maratha by caste, and Tilak and Agarkar had taken up for the Maratha raja. This positioning overlooked the basic truth that Tilak and Agarkar, whom Barve had sent to jail when he could very well have sent them off with a word of caution for their supposed editorial indiscretions, were like him Chitpavan Brahmans, but the sentiment of honouring the imprisoned duo showed signs of being widely welcomed.

Tilak and Agarkar didn't like the idea at all. They were released not after four months or about 120 days but after 101 days owing to their good conduct in prison. Two days before their release, they issued a statement in the *Kesari* saying they were opposed to any big reception 'because they hadn't yet done anything that deserved such an honour, and it was gratifying enough for them to know that people had expressed a desire to welcome them to freedom in this manner'. The '*Deenbandhu* and others should take note of our statement,' they urged.

Yet, things were beyond them. On the morning of 26 October 1882, the day of discharge from Dongri, a substantial crowd had gathered outside the prison. The non-Brahmans egged on by *Deenbandhu* were of course there, but so were the Brahmans, and members of various communities, besides. According to the Poona pro-Brahman paper *Native Opinion,* 'except for the Europeans, Eurasians and Parsis, people of every community were present'. Many of them held garlands and flowers; others were carrying *pedhas* (sweets), *paan-supari,* often distributed among men at auspicious functions at the time, or *attar* (perfume), again meant for happy occasions. The British-owned *Times of India* had, like *Bombay Gazette,* welcomed Tilak and Agarkar's imprisonment. Reporting on their release, it wrote:

> A carriage and pair was driven into the jail compound, and Messrs Tilak and Agarkar having taken their seats in it were driven out on the public road where they were welcomed by upwards of a thousand people. They were then decorated with garlands, flowers being also strewn over them. Munsi Shaik Hoosein Joonakur having presented them with an address, they were accompanied to Girgaum, behind the bungalow of the late Hon. Morarjee Goculdas, where some more garlands were put round them; speeches were also delivered. In the evening they were entertained at Byculla, and at 8 p. m. to-day, an address is to be presented to them at the Madhav Bagh, Cowasjee Patel Tank.[40]

The *Native Opinion* reported:

> People had assembled on both sides of the streets to look at Tilak and Agarkar. Those in their homes looked out from their windows, and some stood atop the steps of shops to take a peek . . . Many expressed their happiness by donating alms to beggars . . . and among those who made speeches were Jews, Hindus and Muslims.[41]

When Tilak and Agarkar left for Poona, a group of forty students from the Deccan College went forward to the Kirkee station, which was en route, to greet them in advance, and a much bigger crowd waited for them at the Poona railway station. A series of functions followed, of which two were more notable than the rest: on the evening of their arrival into the city, they were given a reception under the aegis of the Sarvajanik Sabha, and at another place, they were honoured by the leader of the non-Brahman castes, Jotiba Phule.

The young Kolhapur prince's story had a terrible ending. Already branded as 'insane', he was taken to Ahmednagar from Kolhapur and kept there under the watch of his British guardians. At the end of December 1883, news emerged that the prince had suddenly died, after some sort of fracas with his minder, Private Green. According to the official version put out by the raja's new guardian, a certain Mr Birch, a seven-member coroner's jury had concluded that 'no one has killed the Rajah intentionally', and 'no one has held him with intent to hurt or assault him'. The jury said the young prince 'threw bolts against Green's shoulders, and Green, thinking that the Rajah would assault him, tried to make him sit on a chair by holding him. Their legs were accidentally entangled in a chair, and the Rajah fell, and 'we think it was this fall,' the doctor says, that brought about death.' The acting civil surgeon of Ahmednagar, a certain Dr Tatham, reported that 'the cause of the Maharajah's death was rupture of the spleen, which was enlarged'.[42]

Most people in the Deccan felt the explanation did not wash, and the local English magistrate, Mr Jopp, felt similarly and sent a report to the Bombay government, casting blame on Green. The government promptly gave Green a clean chit, saying the death had been purely accidental. The *Native Opinion* wrote, in response, that 'Mr Green is really lucky. When there is a row between white people and the brown population, the whites are generally lucky.'[43] The matter had aroused sentiments even in Bengal, and the *Amrita Bazar Patrika* accused the government of a cover-up. It wrote, scathingly:

> To speak plainly, the evident desire of the Government would seem to be to hush up matters . . . Political considerations require that there must be no public trial in a case like this, and that Green must be supported, either guilty or innocent. That is, no doubt, the view of the Government, for, according to the Government view, a public trial or a conviction of Green would give rise to a political feeling in the country. It is not safe to permit the growth of such feelings, and therefore it is expedient to suppress the matter and nip it in the bud. This is the consideration, we fancy, which guides our eminently moral Government.[44]

Like the Calcutta paper of the Ghose brothers wrote about the raja's death, the people of the Deccan were convinced that the manner in which Tilak and Agarkar had been prosecuted and jailed for over a hundred days for defamation showed the desire of the British government to hush things up. The overall response of the Indian and Maharashtrian educated elites, the press and the masses showed that Barve was seen as little more than a political instrument used by the Raj, and that however much Barve may have tried to project Tilak as a villain, in the eyes of the local populace, the young editor of the *Mahratta*, along with fellow editor Agarkar, had emerged as something of a hero and had for the first time entered the public spotlight.

In British eyes, though, Tilak had already become something of a villain. Edward Cox, the assistant political agent who had also been accused by Tilak in the Kolhapur case, described him angrily as 'a most mischievous newspaper editor' and dubbed the *Mahratta* as a 'vile rag'. Tilak, he wrote, had 'worked himself into a state of frenzy' and 'published scandalous falsehoods,' which Cox found 'intensely annoying'. Cox's memoirs show he hardly ever held himself back from demonstrating racial contempt for Indians. About his first meeting with the young prince of Kolhapur, he wrote, 'He (the raja) was about eighteen, dreadfully ugly, and intensely melancholy . . . He was an appalling specimen of humanity.' About Tilak too, his own anger drove him to frenzied expression. He stated baldly that 'if any man could wish to have his knife into someone, I might be pardoned for wanting to have mine into Tilak'.[45]

Unlike in the Kolhapur case of the prince's death, nothing had been left to guesswork, proof of substantiation or the imagination. A Britisher had said it in so many words—he wanted his knife into Tilak.

Chapter 4

'Mud of Acrimony and Abuse'

On the afternoon of 5 February 1887, Bal Gangadhar Tilak's walk was a little brisker than usual. He was on his way to the office of the Deccan Education Society. A little over a year after he and Agarkar had emerged from Dongri prison, the Society had been formed to provide an institutional framework for their educational activities, a framework that was needed because they had decided to get into the sphere of higher education by starting a college. Now both the New English School and the college, called the Fergusson College, were up and running nicely, and Tilak was running slightly late for a meeting of the Society's ten life members where all the top decisions were made about the two institutions.

It was a relatively young crowd that filled the room as Tilak made his way in and took his seat. Tilak and Agarkar were both thirty years old; a bright, round-faced and bespectacled man who had been included in the elite decision-making body just the previous year, Gopal Krishna Gokhale, was only twenty-one; and the other seven too were in the age group of twenty to forty.

Discussions had gotten underway well before Tilak walked in, and Agarkar had raised, with a quiet urgency, the matter of salaries of all the ten life members, the ensemble cast that ran the school and college administration. He wanted the monthly salary of each one of them to be hiked by Rs 5. As Tilak joined in, he was told everyone was in favour of the proposal, and only his vote needed to be taken. 'Not a little surprised,' Tilak introduced a powerfully discordant note in what had so far appeared a humming ensemble of 'yes'. He voiced an emphatic 'no', and an extremely bitter exchange followed.[1] Tilak was insistent that their entire work, from the time they had launched the school in 1881, was predicated on the principle of Jesuitical self-denial, and Agarkar argued it was time for them all to get a bit realistic if they wanted to keep body and soul together and work with the same energy and enthusiasm they had shown all along. The more the arguments stretched, the uglier it got. Some others joined Tilak in opposing Agarkar, and as soon as their side had secured the majority, Agarkar's proposal was negatived and jettisoned. Many of those present at the meeting, including Tilak, wrote of the unpleasantness of it all, but cryptically. Not a single one of the participants gave out the exact words which were uttered. Yet the consensus was that there were quite a few low blows.

Things needn't have gone that way. But they had, and not all of a sudden but gradually, over a couple of years. Despite the good beginning.

It had been a rousing start, really, to a new innings when the college was opened. Right from the start, Tilak had set his sights beyond a school, and his own style of mostly oral teaching was more attuned to the demands of higher learning. Moreover, Tilak's idea, and the idea of all his mates working at the school, was to build a network of educational institutions under the aegis of a corporate, trust-like entity. Such an entity would help with management and with garnering of adequate funds as donors could be shown there was an organizational basis to what the founders were doing. That is how the Deccan Education Society was formed.

On 21 October 1884, V.S. Apte issued an appeal on behalf of the school management to 'sympathisers of private education' to gather at 'Gadre's Wada, Shanwar Peth, Poona, on Friday, the 24th instant at 8.30 a.m. precisely for the formation of the proposed Society and appointment of the Council and Trustees'.

Owing to the school's success, a number of notables turned up. Among them was the senior British official William Wedderburn, who had held a number of important posts in the Bombay government; he would, in later years, become president of the Indian National Congress and be known as a sympathizer of the Indian people. M.G. Ranade was there, and so was the Sanskritist,

R.G. Bhandarkar. If their names lent weight to what Tilak and his associates were doing, so did the association of the then Bombay governor, James Fergusson.

Fergusson was a slow mover in the matter of political and administrative reforms, and for that, he was criticized in the pages of *Kesari* and *Mahratta* in their early years. But he had been supportive of private education, and the papers and their editors had noted the backing he had provided to their own educational endeavours. He had made a personal donation of Rs 1250 to the New English School; he had presided over its annual prize distribution function in February 1884; and he had praised it generously, saying its standards were 'comparable to those of institutions more highly favoured'.[2] Tilak and his friends reckoned their Society would benefit if Fergusson's name came to be linked to the college they were setting up: at the least, it would guarantee that the official bureaucracy, which looked up to Fergusson, would not take the first opportunity to create trouble. The governor consented to lend his name, and the foundation stone of Fergusson College was laid, by Fergusson himself, on 5 March 1885. His patronage had brought with it results immediately. Recognizing that Gadre's Wada would be too cramped if it were to accommodate the school and college, Fergusson and his Bombay government decided to give the Society one of the big buildings in Poona it had taken into its possession—the Faraskhana and a garden attached to it, called the Budhwar Wada Garden. For some reason that site didn't work, and some years later the college was given another spot in the same city, where it still stands; the foundation stone originally laid by Fergusson was dug up and promptly planted in the new place.

The Society appointed seven 'life members' at the time of its formation to take all its big decisions. Of these, Tilak and Agarkar were the leading duo. When differences first began to emerge at the end of the year 1885, the original seven were in place. In 1886, two more, one of them Gokhale, joined, and the following year one more life member was added, making it a total of ten.

The three principal characters at the heart of the battle were Tilak, Agarkar and Gokhale. Tilak represented one side and Agarkar and Gokhale, in alliance, the other; the remaining seven members played supporting roles, siding with one faction or the other depending on individual predilections. What happened between them determined the course of the tense rivalry that Tilak and Gokhale would harbour in later years as they led the twin principal national currents of Indian politics, the Extremist and Moderate wings of the Indian National Congress. Tilak decided to quit the Deccan Education Society in the wake of the conflict, a decision that had a massive impact on India's anti-colonial struggle. His heart was set upon the educational institutions, and he himself baulked at any activity carried out by any of the core team members outside of the school and college; his resignation took his energies completely in the direction of the freedom movement and had ramifications for the way Indians would fight their colonial rulers.

The first rumblings were over how the two weekly papers were to be run. People were reading them, but not in numbers that would make them independent of the school and college's economic support. In August 1885, the manager of the Aryabhushan Press, Ganpatrao Sohoni (not part of the Society's ten-member core group), pointed out the difficulty of running the press single-handedly, saying everyone was showing neglect; the frail health of Madhavrao Namjoshi, who had been assigned key responsibilities, meant he couldn't devote time or effort; and the papers themselves were in poor health as everyone was so caught up with school and college work. Could someone please step in and assist him, he asked.[3]

The core team's consensus choice was Tilak. He would not only manage the press but as a steady stream of articles was necessary, it was decided that he would write one weekly piece each for the Marathi and English papers and a short column for the *Mahratta* besides. For two pieces of editorial comment either publication required for each issue, their respective editors, Tilak and Agarkar, were made to commit; they both drew a nominal salary for their editorial tasks anyway; in case they were unavailable, someone else from the core group would be commissioned to write, without pay. Agarkar suggested the editors be not paid for their writing at all because the publications were bleeding and they, together with the Aryabhushan Press, owed about Rs 800 to the school and college which they had taken as a loan; it was only the success of the educational institutions that had kept the papers somehow afloat. In a clear jibe at Tilak, who was at least in this period rather reluctant to write, Agarkar said he had 'no desire to take up the editorial work of others' just because he had been given a salaried position at the papers.[4]

If Agarkar sounded finicky in this case, he sounded finickier still when he shot down a suggestion made by Tilak in March 1886 to grant a loan from the Education Society's coffers for the Aryabhushan Press. Agarkar was the Society's treasurer for most of 1886. A majority of the life members okayed the loan, but Agarkar said no. The money was finally granted, but not without Agarkar acquiring for himself a major concession: 'to satisfy Mr Agarkar', the life members passed a resolution stipulating no loans would be given in future if there was no unanimity among the decision-makers.[5]

Most biographers of Tilak have put forward the theory that it was the proposal for a salary hike that triggered the big row within the Society. They are mistaken. In Agarkar's view, which was very accurate in this case, it was with the issue of granting a loan to the press and Agarkar's insistence on 'the consent of all' in the future that the upward spiral of conflict began.[6]

Soon afterwards, in June 1886, Namjoshi asked for a loan of Rs 300 from the Society. The Society's records are filled with many of the life members asking for loans or an advance against salaries from time to time and the loans or advances being granted without much protest. The only two life members who were financially in a stable position were Tilak and Vasudeo Kelkar; after 1885, Kelkar even generously agreed to shoulder responsibility for the two papers' wobbly finances. The others were in a precarious position, and the monthly salary of Rs 40 was often not nearly enough; they all got an additional Rs 35 each per month in a lump sum at the end of the year when the government grants came through. But the grants began only a couple of years after the college's formation, and the amount was often insufficient for those already scraping the bottom. Agarkar and Waman Shivram Apte were among those whose needs were greatest. Both had poor health, but astonishingly, these two were the only ones—apart from the reasonably self-sufficient Tilak and Kelkar—to not solicit any loans or advances until after Tilak's exit from the institution in 1890. Apte had been orphaned in childhood and was a self-made educator; considering his background of poverty, both Tilak and Agarkar had allowed him from the beginning to take up book-writing projects to supplement his meagre earnings. Agarkar was a chronic asthmatic. His son, born in 1885, had a delicate disposition; and Agarkar's parents and younger brother too were dependent on him. He knew fully well how family dependency could weigh down a person. And yet, when Namjoshi asked for money for a wedding in the family, both Agarkar and Tilak rejected his plea, deeming the reason 'unsatisfactory'.[7]

Then Agarkar made a stunning reversal of position. Some months after Namjoshi's plea, it was Gokhale's turn to request a loan. Agarkar this time not only 'proposed the loan himself' but advocated that Gokhale's case be made 'an exception to the rule passed on 3 April 1886 that no loan should be advanced without the unanimous consent of all'.[8] Tilak was appalled at what he saw as partisan behaviour, but Gokhale, most probably seeing the mood in the group, withdrew his request, and the matter rested there for the moment, albeit not without the atmosphere getting further soured.

It was amid these growing disagreements that Agarkar proposed a salary hike of Rs 5 per month, saying the finances of the Society had improved. Tilak said the reasoning was problematic, besides the fact that the account-keepers didn't quite agree the finances were so good. He said he wouldn't lose out if he agreed, but his objection was 'to the principle of increasing pay because finance permitted it'. The existing salary, he declared, was 'enough for our purposes', and 'so long as we got decent maintenance, prosperity of the finance was no ground for increase in salary, at least not so long as the society was not properly endowed'. The principle of providing a gratuity to anyone in need had been agreed upon at the launch of the institution, and Tilak 'proposed to the members to allow Mr. Agarkar a gratuity according to our rules if he had special causes of expenditure at the time'.[9]

In the tense discussion that ensued, Tilak emphasized the founding principles. Their mission, he argued, had been 'to establish an educational institution at Poona after the model of missionary societies for the purpose of making English education indigenous by placing it on a popular basis'. To do that, they had 'voluntarily consented' to 'form ourselves into a society of Indian Jesuits,' he said, reminding everyone that 'it was our determination to devote ourselves to the work accepting only bare maintenance'. Since the term 'bare maintenance' was rather vague, he spelt out what the original founders'—meaning his, Agarkar's and Chiplunkar's—idea of it exactly was. 'Our highest estimate,' he said, 'never rose higher than Rs 75 per mensem [month],' something they had mentioned in a letter sent to a Poona gentleman in 1879. Tilak stressed that 'I have always believed' and 'still believe that our mission is to be content with bare maintenance and to devote all our resources, gains and time to the institution'.[10]

The last part of the sentence was Tilak's statement against doing any 'outside work', which was increasingly becoming another point of contention within the Society. Tilak was of the opinion that such work affected commitment to the core job, while those in favour, like Agarkar, felt they could do it without their work at the institution getting impacted in any way. Most of the outside work was really an attempt to augment their not-so-adequate income, and it was neither entrepreneurial in nature, nor did it involve financial profit or speculation: the life members were either writing books or teaching and were thus engaged in an intellectual and educational activity whose rewards, at best, were modest. Yet Tilak rallied against moonlighting, which he saw as coming in the way of the 'mission'.

Clearly, Tilak believed their sacrifice—a word he used several times in his eventual resignation letter—gave them a moral authority their work would much benefit from.

Agarkar, on the other hand, felt it was 'more than doubtful whether the Jesuitical organization has done more good than harm to the civilization and the world' and was convinced 'therefore no body can imitate its discipline without making important modifications in it'. His contention was that

No Jesuit is a married man; no Jesuit has private property, nor is he allowed to make any; the Jesuits have a common mess, and they lodge in a common house. Above all, they are a religious body in which free thought is strictly forbidden.[11]

As far as private work was concerned, Agarkar said he concurred with the view of a fellow life member, with whom he had discussed the matter, that 'members of our Body must be allowed perfect freedom, provided they show no lack or neglect in discharging the duties assigned to them by the Body in connection with its institutions'. He had no objection to the framing of 'the most stringent rules' for 'proper discharge of those duties, but beyond securing that object, any further restriction would simply prove ruinous to the Body' and convert it, if it were given the power to approve every little bit of private work, into 'a most frightful court of Inquisition producing disgust about it in the mind of every member'.[12]

Tilak later described the heated discussion as having thrown up 'the mud of acrimony and abuse' and said, 'Mr Agarkar's feelings were so roused' that it 'ended in a disgraceful squabble', making the 'day memorable in the history of our internal relations'.[13]

According to Tilak, many members were convinced by his arguments about working in mission mode, and as a result, Agarkar, who 'perceived his majority was lost . . . charged me with defying the authority of the majority and thus arrogating wisdom to myself'. Within a few days, allegedly Tilak, Agarkar and Gokhale resorted to subterfuge, ostensibly seeking to bring in by-laws to 'better regulate' the Society's meetings but in reality, 'as Mr Namjoshi (Tilak's ally in this episode) has observed,' to 'gag' the members and 'prevent plain and outspoken discussion'. Tilak was so upset by the turn of events that a fortnight after the acrimonious exchange, he wrote to the Society's secretary that 'under the present tension of feeling it has become practically impossible for me to devote my heart and time to the ordinary school and college work' and that the questions under consideration should therefore be immediately decided. This led to a few 'confidential meetings', but instead of a solution being worked out, they produced 'more rancour and bitterness.' Tilak claimed a 'reasonable' compromise on the pay issue was within sight: it was proposed that 'the question of raising pay should not be taken up until there was a clear balance of Rs 35,000 and that the salary should never exceed Rs 100 per mensem', a figure which he said he and Agarkar had believed to be good during their initial discussions on starting a school in 1879 and which they had apparently resolved not to approach in any case in the early days. But no settlement could be reached even on this, and Tilak alleged 'Mr Gokhale went so far as to declare that in his opinion it was not desirable to tie down our hands in this way.'[14]

Accusing his factional rivals of violating core values, Tilak added, bitingly:

> My feelings towards the apostates and their followers are such that propriety alone prevents me from recording them here as emphatically as I wish.[15]

Agarkar didn't take Tilak's decide-or-I-resign letter well. He hit back, stating that 'some of us . . . have determined . . . to set at naught the rules and to force their hobbies upon the rest, trying to cow down opposition by threatening to leave the body. I am sorry I am unable to put up with such self-assertion and disposition of such men who would move heaven and earth to pose themselves before the body and the world as most disinterested patriots.'[16]

Cut to the quick by use of the word 'apostates', Apte joined Agarkar in slamming Tilak. He wrote, 'Tilak should not think that other members don't know what sacrifice is all about . . . He doesn't need reminding that just like him, there are others in the society who have sacrificed their personal interests . . . To label those who suggest changes as apostates is an unwarranted and unforgivable kind of breach of conduct.'[17]

Things went further downhill quickly. The maths results of the majority of Class 6 students at New English School had not been good for the years 1885 and 1886. Agarkar attributed the low scores to the random teaching style of their instructor, Tilak, who wrote nothing on the blackboard, and suggested he be asked to teach English or some other subject instead. His proposal was to come up for discussion at the Society's formal meeting on 24 September 1887. Hours before that meeting, an informal one was held at Agarkar's home, in which he and Tilak had an unpleasant quarrel over the subject. Tilak later wrote that Agarkar was so incensed, he asked him to 'get out' of his house.[18] And if it was Tilak who had said on the previous occasion that he could not devote himself to work if things continued in this manner, it was now Agarkar's turn to state it would be better for him to stay out till things cooled; Agarkar even skipped some meetings of the Society, but then got back into the thick of it.[19]

The next flashpoint, again over money, occurred the following year. In December 1888, the ruler of Indore, Shivaji Maharaj Holkar, was on a visit to Poona. Holkar had excellent relations with Agarkar in particular, and to appreciate his and Tilak's work, he had given the Deccan Education Society the Holkar Wada (an old palace) owned by the family on lease at a nominal rate to conduct classes. When some officials of the Holkar state in 1888 moved to take the premises back from the Society, Agarkar informed the Holkar ruler of the developments, and Shivaji Maharaj promptly went beyond extending the lease: he handed over the place to the Society altogether. During his stay in Poona, the Holkar czar invited Tilak and Agarkar for a meeting and handed them a purse of Rs 700 as appreciation for the work they were doing as editors; he wanted them to share Rs 350 each; as noted earlier, the *Kesari* and *Mahratta* editors had often batted for the princely states and had even endured a term in prison.[20]

Before they met him, Tilak and Agarkar had an inkling of what was on offer. Holkar had, just a few days ago, invited them for a felicitation function he was organizing in Poona for several editors, where he wanted to honour them as well. Tilak and Agarkar had skipped the function, determined not to compromise their position as editors. So, it was decided between them that if Holkar offered anything during the private meeting, he should be told the purse should not be given to them as editors but to the Deccan Education Society. When Holkar presented the purse on the morning of 20 December 1888, Tilak and Agarkar made their condition clear, and Holkar consented. Tilak and Agarkar decided that even if Holkar wished that they should divide Rs 700 between the two of them, the total amount would be split equally among all the core group members of the Society.[21]

On their return, Agarkar himself handed over the purse to the clerk of the Society. Later the same day, Agarkar found out Holkar was putting together a list of Poona-based authors whose books he intended to purchase. Holkar really looked up to Agarkar; when there had been problems between him and his father Tukojirao, the father had asked Agarkar to intercede with the young man on his behalf, and the prince had heeded the word of the editor. Obviously, Agarkar was optimistic the man would buy his books and sent word to him about two books he had recently written: *Vikar Vilasit*, a play, and *Vakya Mimansa*, a work on Marathi syntax. As expected, Holkar immediately offered to buy copies of *Vakya Mimansa*. But Agarkar was not to be paid separately for the books. The Maharaj told his aide-de-camp, a certain Mr Gupte, that of the Rs 700 he had gifted to Tilak and Agarkar, Rs 400 should be given to Agarkar alone for copies of his book, and the remaining Rs 300 should be divided among all the ten members of the Society.[22] This meant Agarkar would in addition get Rs 30 as his share of the remaining Rs 300.

Mistrust between Tilak and Agarkar ran so deep that Tilak at once suspected his comrade of arranging things so in an underhand way with his admirer, Holkar. Tilak drafted a reply to be sent to Holkar's aide-de-camp, stating that he had understood from their conversation that the Maharaj had given them Rs 700 for their work, and he had communicated this to the Society's fellow members and the total amount had already been divided among all the members.

Almost every Tilak biographer has pilloried him for saying the amount stood already divided. Yet the truth is that while Tilak did send out a reply to Holkar's aide-de-camp on his own, he hadn't done it behind Agarkar's back. He sent another copy of the draft across to Agarkar, with a note. It said, 'Please see if you are okay with this reply to Gupte. If Holkar wants to honour you for your efforts in writing a book, I feel he should give you a purse separately for that. If you agree with what I have written, please replace the "I" in my letter with "We", and please send across the final draft for me to sign.'[23]

Simultaneously, Tilak wrote to the Society's secretary Trimbakrao Joshi directing him not to give 'a single paisa of the seven hundred rupees received from Holkar Maharaj to anyone without letting me know in advance.'[24]

Agarkar, whose health was in any case precarious, was deeply hurt. First, he enquired with Trimbakrao Joshi what had happened to the money. Joshi told him Tilak had instructed him to credit the full sum to the Society's account. This upset Agarkar further. He thought Tilak just wanted to make sure he got nothing. He wrote back to Tilak:

> This is perhaps the last time I am writing a personal letter to you. From the way you, out of your malice and spite against me, sent off letters to Gupte and Trimbakrao and asked Trimbakrao to credit Rs 700 to the Society's account, it is clear what a rotten heart you have.

I can provide enough evidence to back my statement. But let me say straightaway that please don't think I am upset over the obstacles you have created in my getting Rs 400. I am fully aware it's not a sum that will last me a lifetime. I have never had a desire to earn anything beyond a subsistence-level amount. Except you and perhaps one or two others, this is not something I need to clarify to people who know me.

In recent times, ever since it became apparent that my son's growth would not take place as naturally as it should, I have been feeling I should keep at least a thousand rupees aside for him and for my wife. My own health is in very poor shape. There is no knowing when death will come to me . . . Of late I have been wondering whether the Society will, as agreed upon, indeed give Rs 10 as pension to my wife and son if I die . . . That is why I have been trying to make some provision for my wife and son . . . You are in excellent health. And you have some money and property left behind by your father. Perhaps that is the reason you are unable to understand my concern and anxiety on this score. For the provision I want to make for my family, I intend to work hard. I am going to write 2-3 books, and I feel they will sell well. I hadn't even imagined I would get Rs 400 from Holkar. I'm not even counting it in now. If at all I get it, I am going to give the sum to my parents so that they can undertake a yatra to Kashi that they have set their hearts on. Only yesterday, you said no one will let go of money that's unexpectedly pushed into his pockets by someone. (But) I showed willingness to accept the money only after I realized that Holkar Maharaj wants to acknowledge my contribution to literature . . . Holkar Maharaj invited me after going through my book 'Vakya Mimansa', saying he wanted to give me robes of honour for my contribution to the mother tongue. And he did give me robes of honour. I know you have a habit of denouncing anyone who goes ahead of you. You always feel others should progress only up to the point you have reached, or perhaps not even come up to the point where you are. But I am not going to accept any kind of criticism from you for having received robes of honour. For you yourself had in the past accepted such robes from him, that too not because you were receiving an honour yourself but as a representative of the Deccan Education Society! . . .

I am ashamed to be your colleague. Did you think I was going to run away with the money? Did you think I would take the money from Trimbakrao without the board's approval? . . . Only you can stoop so low. Only you can think I would pocket the money without the Society's nod. You have inflicted as deep a wound as you possibly could on my soul. From now on, it will be better if, except for the work we do together for the Deccan Education Society, we treat one another as strangers.[25]

Agarkar also described Tilak's letter to the Society's secretary Trimbakrao Joshi as 'meanness of the grossest kind – a meanness of which you alone could be capable'.[26]

Tilak clarified his position. 'I was doing my duty,' he replied. 'I thought that all I should do was to direct Trimbakrao to retain the money with him until the matter was decided by the board.'[27] Conciliatory though these lines sounded, they came mixed with biting sarcasm. While speaking of only having done his duty, Tilak remarked, 'Your own conception of duty is higher than mine. That is why, on one occasion, even after the Society's board had passed a resolution, you had refused to release money from the Society fund for the Aryabhushan Press.'[28] Tilak also bluntly maintained that Agarkar had been 'unwise' in the first place to ask Holkar for a 'favour, especially after having loudly stressed that we were not going to pursue our individual interests'. The whole thing had flared up because of Agarkar himself, Tilak wrote.[29]

Agarkar made up his mind. He was not going to touch any of the money given by Holkar. Not after Tilak had blamed him for pursuing self-interest. He wrote once again to Tilak, accusing him, as he had done earlier during the dispute over salaries, of grandstanding:

Play what tricks you like with words, and try to cover as much as you like your mean, despotic, and selfish conduct under a cloak of Jesuitical casuistry or legal sophistry . . . I can well understand your disinterestedness and your anxiety to secure the money for the board, when I remember that during our conversation in the vehicle (horse cart) you expressed your perfect willingness to accept the money for

private use if the Maharaj only allowed us to make Namjoshi and
Apte and perhaps one more of the members to be partners in it!

He added:

No amount of plain writing can set right a person whose one business
all along has been self-glorification at the cost of honesty, unity,
friendship, public duty, and several other social virtues.[30]

Tilak was extremely disturbed by the charges. 'So vitriolic was the
language in that letter of Agarkar,' he said later, 'that I found it
unbearable, and I sent him an open postcard immediately to stop this
shameful correspondence between us.'[31]

In January 1889, Tilak asked for a semester's leave from his teaching
responsibilities. He needed time to think; the rate at which things were
going, he said, a break was a must, and he was going to resign from the
institution altogether if tensions did not ease during this period. Was he
issuing a threat so that others would backtrack? Surely, Tilak hoped his
absence for a while would convince many of the members of the futility
of the worsening conflict and the costs to be paid for losing so energetic
and committed a founder. He also hoped time spent outside would heal
his wounds.[32] Yet he was determined to leave if ties didn't show signs of
improving. Proof of his determination was that in this six-month break
itself, he wrote out the text of his final resignation, which he submitted
at last in 1890.

Immediately after he resumed his teaching work in June 1889, a
new issue cropped up. The Society had to appoint a superintendent, and
Tilak and Agarkar clashed over who it should be, ultimately agreeing
to accept Mahadev Shivram Gole as the compromise nominee. Still
unhappy over it, Tilak said 'it was not my desire to work under such
circumstances' and voiced afresh his wish to quit.[33] The core team
worked out a new compromise formula: the post of superintendent
itself, which hadn't been in place for long, would go. And Tilak stayed
back. For the moment.

The last straw from Tilak's point of view came the following year.
The point at dispute was 'outside work', which had proved contentious
earlier too. Gokhale was offered the job of secretary of the Poona
Sarvajanik Sabha. It was honorary work, and he took it up as he was

going to be able to discharge his responsibilities at the Deccan Education Society at the same time.

Tilak objected to 'such divergences of our energies' and said the idea was 'inconsistent' with the Society's aims. 'Allowing such definite engagement outside the Body' would be 'carrying the principle of private work too far', especially when 'even government did not allow its servants to do anything else,' he pointed out. 'The secretaryship' of the Sarvajanik Sabha, Tilak declared, 'was offered to me before, but I declined to accept it as long as I was connected to the Body', and 'Mr Gokhale could do the same'. Besides, he added, there was ample scope for Gokhale's energies in his duties as professor of English literature, and if Fergusson College wanted to compete with other colleges, 'we must at least show that we were not behind in reading work'.[34] The implication was that Gokhale could very well devote his free time to reading.

A meeting of all the life members had been called on 11 October, and in it, Tilak hoped to bring in, through his aide Vasudev Kelkar, a motion on Gokhale's apparent moonlighting which could be put to vote. The meeting got delayed by three days over what seemed a minor thing, but it appeared to have irritated Tilak quite a bit. Gokhale had taken to the game of cricket, introduced in India by the British who had invented it. That year, 1890, Lord Harris was appointed governor of Bombay, and he tried to promote cricket among the 'natives', not really to involve them in the sport in a healthy way but because he believed it would help the Empire in its so-called 'civilizing mission', a pretend cause that combined racism, contempt and perfect nonsense. Gokhale had begun playing in the matches organized in Bombay and Poona by Harris between the Europeans and the 'natives', and one such game, in which he was keen to put on his white flannels, was scheduled for 11 October. He said he would be unavailable for the meeting that day. His was not the only reason the meeting was put off; a couple of other members had cried off, but Tilak felt Gokhale was trying to avoid a confrontation and also prioritizing the wrong things. Tilak didn't like cricket at all: he saw it as an alien sport, and his way of dismissing it was to derisively call it a sport of 'ball and a wooden plank' and of 'ball and a *dandu*' (*danda* in Hindi or stick).[35]

The meeting was convened on 14 October 1890, and a majority of life members backed a resolution saying Gokhale's work at Sarvajanik Sabha was not consistent with his duties at the Society.

Whether to stick on with the Sabha or not was nevertheless left to Gokhale. Agarkar at this point pulled out his trump card; at least seven of the ten life members did some outside work, Tilak and himself included, he said, so why shouldn't the same resolution apply to them all? The result was that a 'vote of censure' was passed against Tilak, Agarkar and five others. Voting took place for each member separately. The others, meaning Agarkar and his camp, didn't mind at all. Tilak, however, felt personally targeted for having pursued the twin issues of salaries and outside work. Believing 'it was impossible to pull on any longer', he passed on a short letter of resignation to the Society secretary while voting on the matter of some other members was still in progress. Gokhale then offered to resign himself. 'I want to say that if my withdrawal from the Body can induce Mr. Tilak to remain, I hereby offer my resignation as a life member,' he said.[36] Tilak would not be persuaded to stay back, however, so Gokhale's offer was declined.

A couple of months later, Tilak submitted a detailed thirty-three-page statement on his reasons for resigning. Here again, the last bit of exchange on internal matters was ugly. Tilak accused the majority of his colleagues of being unscrupulous, claiming they had been 'prepared to show cooked-up accounts to suit' the grant-in-aid rules when they 'apprehended that the grant would be reduced according to the new rules by a few thousands'.[37] The Society took note of the charges and dismissed them as being groundless.[38]

Tilak noted in his statement that the Society had strayed from its essential principles and termed the new members in particular as opportunistic:

> They believe that the life membership of the Deccan Education Society is a good start for a beginner in Poona and that if one has energy and ambition, he can use it as a stepping stone for personal distinction and gain.[39]

Speaking of how 'incompatibility of views' had resulted in the 'rupture', Tilak hinted, with a tone of regret, that the Society should have set a higher bar for entry:

It is now useless to speculate what would have been the result if more care and rigidity had been observed with respect to admissions of life members into the Body, or if the constitution had been less liberal or representative than it is or if the principles of the Body had been put down as articles of faith and members required to observe them or else withdraw from the Body, or if there had been one amongst us who, by virtue of his personal character, could have commanded respect and admiration from the rest, thus exercising an effectual control over all. It is also idle to discuss what would have been the consequences had the Body been all composed of friends brought up in the same traditions and actuated all along by the same desires and motives. As a matter of fact we have chosen to come together on a secular basis and that too of equality, all or nearly all, when the Body was formed, being of the same college standing.[40]

Tilak owned up to some of his personal shortcomings which had contributed to the discord and conflict:

I am deeply conscious of my faults which, I know, have given at times reason to some of my colleagues to be offended with me. The chief fault that I am aware of in me is my manner of expressing myself in strong and cutting language. I am, I think, never violent in the beginning, but being a man of very strong feelings, I often fall into the error of giving sharp and stinging replies when aroused and of being unsparing in my criticism. And sharp words do cause an amount of mischief. But I can assure . . . that I spoke strongly because I felt strongly for the interest of the institution . . . I am quite free to confess that I may have been at times led into strength of expression quite unwarranted by the exigencies of the occasion.[41]

Tilak said he had decided to quit 'only after a great struggle with my own feelings'. The next line showed that he was truly heartbroken. 'In fact,' he said, 'I am now giving up my life's ideal.'[42]

Tilak's 'life's ideal' was to work in the arena of education. But he was going to move henceforth in a different direction—a direction that would impact the course of his country's struggle for freedom.

It is amazing how a life can unfold. It was a conflict filled with abuse, invective, and all sorts of nasty charges exchanged between truly gifted and meritorious individuals like Tilak, Agarkar and Gokhale that led to the denouement in the Society. It showed that at the bottom, they were, as humans, capable of inflicting massive blows on each other, sometimes on very petty issues.

One of the chief myths mainstreamed about Tilak and Agarkar is that they fell apart over ideological issues. Indeed, their ideological differences ballooned over time, and the next chapter will look at their many significant exchanges over social and political issues in detail. Yet they were fully aware, from their college days, that they had varying thoughts on different issues, had, in Tilak's words, 'different temperaments',[43] and they had gotten together despite that and stuck to their viewpoints even as they built the twin institutions of the New English School and the Fergusson College.

At best, it could be said that their ideological outlook would have eventually and inevitably resulted in separation if the fight in the Society had not erupted and come to a boil.

Both Tilak and Agarkar expressed contrasting opinions in the early years of the *Kesari* and *Mahratta* as editors, and when the first major social issues—of female education and change in marriage laws—emerged in 1884 and 1887 respectively (which, again, we will deal with in the next chapter), they stood on opposite sides without their personal relationship getting into the area of bitterness. Agarkar was in the habit of expressing radical views for those times, and he often chafed at restrictions placed on him because *Kesari* was the voice of so many members and was inextricably linked to the Society as a whole. Various people started writing for both papers on various issues without a byline in the initial days. That could confuse readers about whether a particular view was of the publication or an individual editor and writer. When this issue of contrasting perspectives arose, Tilak, Agarkar and the others decided on a policy early on that if anyone was keen to express particularly strong views on a subject, they should put their names to the piece.[44] Agarkar did it for some time. But he always had to keep in mind that the *Kesari* represented so many others. Seeing that he could not express several of his opinions in the

Kesari or *Mahratta* without making it appear they were the views of all concerned with those papers, and since Tilak and Kelkar had taken over management of both dailies in any case after the mid-1880s—the debate over the papers then too was over how to manage them and what their relation would be with the Society—following Agarkar's own reluctance, Agarkar started his own paper, the *Sudharak,* or Reformer, in 1888. His paper would give him much more leeway, and importantly much more space, to lay out his worldview. He continued his journalism there independent of other members of the Society, except for his friend Gokhale, who joined him from the beginning as editor of the English section of *Sudharak*. Other than Gokhale, every other life member of the Deccan Education Society sided with Tilak on social issues, so Agarkar saw this development as unavoidable and even after resigning as editor of *Kesari* wrote a few pieces for the paper under his byline.[45]

Apart from the fact that neither Tilak nor Agarkar ever said that their partnership had come to an end because of their respective ideological orientations, the reality is their estrangement was over other issues such as money and management of the Deccan Education Society. Both got personal, pugilistic, and often petty. And were enmeshed in an extremely messy factional dispute. Tilak was not at all off the mark when he said in his resignation statement that 'party feeling led to jealousies', which eventually 'ripened into rancour', and thus 'instead of different temperaments harmoniously blended by solemn obligations', they stood 'divided in aims and pursuits, estranged by conflicting passions and interests and wearied by simplicity and rigidity of conduct'.[46]

The negative vote against Tilak had censured him for outside work he had undertaken. What, exactly, was the nature of this work? One was the handling of the papers and the press. That, Tilak argued, was 'originally . . . the work of all' and 'when it ceased to be so, I was expressly allowed to connect myself with it'.[47] The other two components of the work were his involvement, as a legal mind, in a campaign linked to a corruption scam that had broken out at the time, and his entry into a new and apparently promising group of Indians, the Indian National Congress. Tilak insisted both components were temporary in nature, and he had taken these up during his break from the Society from January 1889 to June 1889, a period when he was thinking of resigning. He conceded he hadn't given up the work after his return to the Society in June 1889, but that, too, according to him, was because he 'did not regard the settlement [within the Society] as final' and because the work was 'temporary'.[48]

In the end, his involvement with the Congress would turn out to be anything but transient. And the graft case in itself raised a massive stink across British-ruled India. It was no small matter.

Chapter 5

The Crawford Corruption Scandal

A rthur Travers Crawford was a name familiar to most people, literate or unlettered, in the Bombay Presidency from the 1860s to the 1890s. A man with a prominent forehead, broad shoulders and a walrus moustache, he was one of the most high-profile British officials in the region, having served as the first municipal commissioner of the city of Bombay in the 1860s and as revenue commissioner elsewhere. He was known for his charm and his competence. As his career steadily progressed, by the 1880s, he was also increasingly getting to be known among the 'natives', as the British Raj called the local population, for his corrupt ways.

Tilak's family could actually claim to have experienced his style of working firsthand. When Bal was in school in the 1860s, his father Gangadhar-pant had put some money in a sawmill floated by Crawford, who was then commissioner of the southern division, which included Bal's birthplace Chikhalgaon and the wider Ratnagiri district. The mill had made huge losses soon thereafter and shut, resulting in investors losing whatever they had staked. There was no way of knowing if that was a genuine case of an enterprise going bankrupt, and the Tilaks appeared not to hold it against Crawford; Bal's own memory of the episode was faint. But with time, in hushed tones, in the streets and bazaars, word spread that Crawford was not above board.

By mid-1886, a time when Arthur Crawford was posted as revenue commissioner of the Central division of Bombay Presidency, the whispers could no longer be ignored. Complaints were made publicly that Crawford was busy knocking money off his subordinates, and a local Marathi paper, *Poona Vaibhav*, wrote two articles, one in

August that year and another in February 1887, stating that offices in the civilian administration were being 'obtained according to the *nazrana* [payment] offered', just as 'during the Mughal era'; the paper also provided guesses of what the going rates for various positions might be.[1] The Bombay government demanded proof or an apology, and the editor published an apology.[2]

Before long, an Indian official in the agriculture department came forward with a written complaint of corruption and land grab against Crawford, and an upright British official reporting to Crawford sought a transfer citing murky dealings in the revenue department. And the scam unravelled. It emerged that Crawford had an extensive network of agents who collected payments and bribes on his behalf from '*mamlatdars*' in the revenue administration in order to give them choice postings or promotions and transfers.

Who were the 'mamlatdars'? The Bombay Presidency was big, one of three Presidencies the British had formed on their takeover of Indian territories, the other two being Calcutta and Madras. Its central division had six districts: Khandesh, Nasik, Ahmednagar, Poona, Satara and Solapur. Every district was divided into a number of local areas. While the '*patil*' was the revenue affairs head for a village, tasked with assessing revenue and collecting it, and the '*deshmukh*' was chief for an entire district, the '*mamlatdars*' were 'chief officers entrusted with local revenue administration of a taluka' or tehsil, which was a sub-division of a district comprising several villages.[3] From the times of Maratha rule, the mamlatdars had liaised with the village patils and fixed the revenue to be collected for the entire taluka, and it was often only if the patil and mamlatdar disagreed that the deshmukh stepped in. Thus, mamlatdars played a very vital role in the administration. In addition, they were arbiters in local disputes, including certain kinds of criminal acts. When the British took over, they adopted the model but changed the mode of remuneration from a share of the revenue pie to fixed and standardized pay and got them to follow established civil service regulations. The British also formed different grades for mamlatdars, with both salaries and powers increasing as the officials went up from one grade to another.[4] The appointment of mamlatdars, who were all Indians without exception, was wholly in the hands of the commissioner of a division, and they were promoted, demoted, transferred or retained at a particular spot at his 'sole discretion'.[5]

Crawford had in all seventy-six mamlatdars under him in the central division, and he was forcing most of them to pay in order to build up or salvage their careers.[6] Crawford was easily among the global pioneers of the work-from-home model, for he preferred to spend most of his day working out of his bungalow at Kirkee in Poona instead of his office in the same city, which was the administrative centre of the central division.[7] He was also in the habit of throwing extravagant parties at his Kirkee bungalow on the weekends.[8] When the complaints against him were made, it was revealed that it was on the veranda of this very bungalow that he would meet aspiring or existing mamlatdars seeking promotions, transfers or retentions and promise them what they wanted in exchange for money. A local man called Hanmantrao Raghavendra, who was not a government employee, was Crawford's chief agent or middleman; he finalized all the 'deals' on Crawford's behalf and arranged his meetings with those who were told to pay. Typically, once a deal was fixed, Hanmantrao would call the extorted party to Poona and ask it to wait on the veranda of Crawford's bungalow. Hanmantrao would then go inside and come out with Crawford, who in turn would look at the favour obtainer and say crisply, with an imperial sense of authority, 'I will do everything for you.'[9]

With the scandal breaking out, the Bombay Presidency government, led by Lord Reay, decided to set up a commission of inquiry. But there was a fundamental question about how the probe would proceed.

How were the mamlatdars expected to speak out against Crawford or give evidence of his system of extorting bribes? They would implicate themselves if they did that and invite action. And if Crawford was ultimately not nailed by the British system of justice, he could unleash the full force of his vindictiveness against these subordinates, another reason for them to tread warily.

The Bombay government figured that the only way to get the mamlatdars to come forward was to assure them they would not be punished. In the middle of the year 1888, Crawford was suspended, Hanmantrao was arrested on the basis of the agriculture department official's complaint which named him, and the Bombay government promised immunity from prosecution to all those who offered evidence and testimony.

A British government Act of 1850, which authorized Presidency regimes to set up a special commission to put on trial government officials 'by those of appropriate rank', was invoked, and what came to be known as the Crawford Commission was established. It had three members, all from outside the Bombay Presidency in the interests of fairness: Arthur Wilson, a sitting judge of the Calcutta High Court, James Quinton, a senior public services commission official in the North-West Provinces, and Robert Crosthwaite, judicial commissioner for the Central Provinces.[10]

While the Crawford Commission sat in Poona for its hearings, the agent Hanmantrao was tried separately after his arrest by a district magistrate. And their cases went in two widely different directions.

Hanmantrao's trial in the Poona district court lasted barely a month: it began in August 1888 and ended in September with the verdict of 'guilty'. He was sent off to Yerawada jail to serve a prison term of more than a year. Hanmantrao's conviction on charges of corruption was important for the Bombay government. That was the only way it could really catch Crawford; Hanmantrao was the collector of bribes meant for the former. The first step having been taken successfully, the more imperative second step of official action could begin.

The Bombay government had decided to use different laws to bring Hanmantrao and Crawford to book. Hanmantrao was tried under the Indian Penal Code of 1860, but it was going to be unwise to try Crawford similarly. Why? The Indian Penal Code's section on bribery and corruption said the prosecution had to give proof of 'not more than' two acts, both of which ought to have taken place within twelve months of each other.[11] Crawford's corruption spanned a far longer period, and there were many mamlatdars whose testimonies were to be collected, and many acts recorded. Just two acts and a couple of testimonies wouldn't do. The British Government Act of 1850 allowing for a special commission was a better and fairer one to invoke, and the Bombay government, led by the relatively conscientious Reay, went for it.

Yet, just as Hanmantrao's prosecution was launched, the Crawford Commission announced and the terms of indemnity to be granted to the mamlatdars became public, the press which was loyal to the Raj in India and in England rose in seemingly righteous anger. While *Times of India*, which had British owners and editors at the time, led the attack against the Reay regime domestically for having decided to probe a senior British official like Crawford, *The Times* of London was far more aggressive in its denunciation of the government's offer of immunity to the mamlatdars. J.C. Macgregor, the correspondent of *The Times* based in Calcutta, filed a series of despatches in which he expressed horror and disbelief that 'corrupt officials' who had 'trafficked in public appointments' and 'paid illegal gratifications to a public servant' were going to be 'retained in office'.[12]

Macgregor and correspondents and editors of other British-friendly papers were disingenuous in their reporting and commentary. While Macgregor did not once mention for the benefit of his readers in the British capital that the main accused on trial in the case was a British official named Crawford, he and the other British correspondents repeatedly referred to the mamlatdars as 'native judicial officers',[13] indicating clearly what a travesty of justice it was that judicial officers guilty of graft were sought to be protected. In reality, the mamlatdars were principally revenue officials, with auxiliary magisterial functions, and their magisterial powers weren't sweeping ones but exercisable in certain matters only.

As Crawford's trial progressed and more and more mamlatdars testified before the three-member panel, *The Times* of London called for immediate action against the testifying officials. The paper wrote, 'The government's vindication – in some parts even laudatory in tone – of the conduct of these officials, who have publicly admitted their venality and corruption, cannot fail to have a terribly demoralizing effect, unless the evil is stamped out by immediate and resolute action. To palter with the evil is to crystallize it. These men have shown themselves unfit to be retained in the public service in any position of trust.'[14] *Pioneer*, one of the papers on Indian soil loyal to the British, backed this argument and added, 'If Lord Reay is unequal to discharging this unpleasant duty, or refuses to satisfy public opinion in England and India, his resignation would free him from all personal responsibility.'[15]

The press's vociferous campaign demanding the sacking and prosecution of the mamlatdars had its effect. First a judge in the

Bombay High Court made his opinions known on the row, and subsequently, the matter was raised in the House of Commons by some British parliamentarians.

Justice John Jardine of the Bombay High Court spoke out strongly about the retention of the mamlatdars 'despite the fact that the government knew full well about their corruption' and urged the executive branch of the government 'to deal with such corruption'.[16] He referred to a bribery scandal of 1725 in England involving the Earl of Macclesfield, a chancellor who had sold judicial positions. That case had led to the passing of a law, called 'Statutes 5 & 6 of Edward VI', on buying and selling of judicial offices; it looked at a person who had purchased a judicial post as a 'future extortioner', and Jardine said by an Act of Parliament, the statute had been extended to all English colonies.[17] The statute would be referred to again and again to buttress British arguments on the controversy.

In the House of Commons, MPs of contrasting political ideologies came together to pose questions. James M. Maclean of the Conservative Party and Charles Cameron of the Liberals demanded to know if it was true that the 'magistrates' (again the emphasis was on this word) in Bombay had admitted to purchasing their positions and if a Bombay High Court judge had pointed to the 'illegality of retaining those magistrates'.[18] The fact was that Justice Jardine had not pronounced a verdict. He had been hearing a case of an Indian collaborator of Crawford; the collaborator had made certain claims against some witnesses who had pointed fingers at Hanmantrao, and after his claims had been dismissed by the district magistrate, he had moved the high court.[19] During the hearing of the matter, Jardine had made *obiter dictum* remarks, which is basically the airing of opinions by a judge in court; these opinions are neither essential to the case being heard nor legally enforceable, and they certainly cannot be seen as legal precedents. As a matter of fact, Indian opinion perceived the collaborator's case as an attempt 'to intimidate the mamlatdar witnesses at the Crawford trial and thus influence the outcome'.[20] Yet the London *Times* and the Parliamentarians continued to highlight the comments, and Justice Jardine himself kept up his insistence on what he saw as the law indisputably laid down.

Tilak was watching all of this with interest and with concern. He had just turned thirty-one years old when the scam broke out in 1887;

and he had recently taken over the running of both the *Mahratta* and *Kesari* from his colleagues following disputes in the Deccan Education Society.

The Crawford affair caught so much public attention that Tilak noted it had 'eclipsed all other subjects of popular discussion'.[21] In his first comments on the controversy in *Kesari*, he criticised the Raj-aligned papers for their campaign in favour of Crawford and against the Bombay governor Lord Reay. 'It's true that in English too, there are publications like the Bombay Gazette which write prudently,' he stated. However

> The norm is that as soon as any charge is made against a European official, these papers lose their temper. We're not thinking at present about whether Crawford is guilty or not, nor do we have any means of finding out. But if one looks just at the comments being made about Crawford in the bazaars – comments which have reached the ears of European officials often – then one marvels at the audacity, partisanship and obstinacy of these English papers.[22]

Right up front, Tilak brought up an issue which the English dailies had scrupulously held themselves back from mentioning in print. Finding the heat turned up on him, Crawford had tried to escape. He had written misleading notes about committing suicide and, donning 'a false beard, a slouch hat, and a long coat'[23] and looking like a tramp, he had taken a train to Bombay, sitting in the third-class compartment, in order to try and escape to Colombo on a ship and from there to England. But he had been caught by the police in Bombay. And this was not the first time he had tried to flee! He had a history of doing that. As the first-ever civic chief of Bombay in the 1860s, Crawford had initiated several works, especially related to sanitation, for which he had won much praise. But in doing so, he had spent too much money and nearly bankrupted the city's treasury, and it was revealed soon enough that a lot of the costs had to do with the fact that Crawford had handed out contracts to his friends and cronies with whom he had financial ties. Councillors in Bombay demanded that the Presidency government dismiss Crawford, and the Bombay government passed a resolution reproaching him for his 'extreme improvidence and recklessness' and said it could not shut its eyes to the 'culpable disregard exhibited by him . . . as the dispenser of large public revenues'.[24] Thinking that the net was closing in on him, Crawford escaped to England. There was no extradition; he stayed there and after some years, returned to India, again to enjoy a top position. He was straightaway brought back in 1884 as revenue commissioner in Bombay's southern division, after which he moved to the central division.

After he was caught attempting his latest flight, Crawford's partisans argued that he had gone to Bombay in disguise so that he could move the courts to get his case heard by the magistrate's court rather than a probe panel. Tilak referred to Crawford's 'previous pattern of behaviour' and said that in view of that, 'who will say that when he donned a false beard and went off in a third-class train compartment, he was not trying to run away?'[25]

Crawford's sympathizers had also been claiming that he was on his way to becoming the victim of a conspiracy hatched against him by the 'natives' and by some of his rival British officials. To this, Tilak responded that 'if only this trial had been against a native official and if our papers had made even one-hundredth of the noise the English papers are making, the English press would have dubbed all the native papers and in fact all natives as seditious'.[26] There was no option but to try Crawford before a commission and not under the IPC, Tilak said, because there weren't just one or two allegations against him but 'at least 20-25 cases'.[27] Crawford's supporters and the English papers were 'heaping abuse' on Bombay governor Lord Reay for having initiated a probe, wrote Tilak. He himself, however, thought Reay had shown 'notable courage', even if it had to be acknowledged that it was only after 'the government was left with no choice' by a whistleblowing 'native' official that it had initiated an Inquiry.[28]

American scholar Stanley Wolpert in his comparative study of Tilak and Gokhale wrote that Tilak's approach in this controversy contrasted totally with that of Gokhale. While Tilak, Wolpert indicated, had zero faith in the British, Gokhale appealed to what he perceived as the British sense of justice. At this particular point, though, things were a little more complicated. Gokhale indeed did show faith in, and appeal to, the Raj's sense of fair play on the mamlatdar issue, but the archives show that Tilak too, at this juncture, had made a distinction between the Raj as a whole and the Bombay government led by Reay, and he had placed a lot

of genuine belief in Lord Reay taking the probe to a logical conclusion.
'If all officials had been as clean as Lord Reay, many poor mamlatdars
would not have entered the morass of unethical practices in the first
place,' he stated confidently. He was certain, he said, that the 'courage
Reay had exhibited in exposing a scandal that had been an open secret
for two decades was of a kind that could hardly be matched.' Further
demonstrating his trust in the course of action directed by the 'just and
impartial' Reay, Tilak urged mamlatdars to step forward, without fear,
to tell their stories of extortion and also lauded the young generation
of mamlatdars, without whose initiative he said such a murky scandal
'would never have to come to light for many more years'.[29]

Tilak's faith was quickly undermined. Two blows came for the
Indian side, one after the other. In the first, Crawford was given a
clean chit by the inquiry commission and thirty-two corruption
charges against him were rejected as baseless even though close to
forty mamlatdars had offered their testimonies. He was held guilty,
nevertheless, of taking loans from his subordinates. Loans? But the
outcry wasn't over loans taken by Crawford at all, said Tilak. The
'real nature of the loans', of course, was a different matter, he stressed,
hinting that some of these were indirect extortion, but far graver were
the direct charges of corruption. 'Loans can be legitimate and can be
obtained by clean people,' Tilak argued. The miracle wasn't so much
that Crawford had taken many loans in two or three years, but that he
had 'extorted Rs 14,000 from the poor in a single month'.[30]

Crawford was compulsorily retired, and his name was taken off the
list of Bombay civil servants in March 1889. The Indians saw this as
nothing but a reluctantly handed rap on the knuckles, for he was going
to receive a pension and all other retirement benefits, and he had been
freed of any taint on his name.

The second shocker was that the blanket immunity granted to the
mamlatdars was revoked. As the clamour for action against these Indian
officials grew after Crawford was pronounced innocent, the secretary
of state for India Viscount Cross—Britain's highest official for Indian
affairs, stationed in London and part of the British Parliament—stepped
in and directed that the mamlatdars who had offered testimonies be
placed in two separate categories. Those who had purchased offices
voluntarily would be fired, though they would be kept immune from

suits and prosecution in keeping with the promise made by the Reay government, and only those who had paid under 'extreme duress'[31] would be retained.

How were the authorities going to determine which mamlatdars had paid on their own and who among them were victims of a shakedown, asked Tilak. The probe hadn't been conducted with this aspect in mind, and when the system of bribery was so deeply entrenched, as it was in this case, possibly many would have paid simply because they knew that was the only way things worked if they wished to protect their elementary rights, he pointed out.[32]

The case of Yashwant Ballal Tambe illustrated the system's workings. Tambe was a mamlatdar in Nasik. He was due for promotion, but five others were promoted before him. He was also transferred to places which did not have good weather. As further harassment, he was demoted from grade 3 to 4 (mamlatdars were placed in various grades) and was forced to refund to the government a major part of his salary for two months. Because he 'still held out against paying', he was threatened with another transfer to Peint, which was among the unhealthiest of spots. Fed up and aware of how money was known to do the trick, he wrote to G.V. Deshmukh, a sub-agent of Crawford's, and sent him Rs 500. After that too, someone very junior was promoted ahead of him by Crawford. Tambe later complained that before the Crawford commission, he was 'only allowed to give direct answers to direct questions without any opportunity to explain his actions', so he didn't really get to talk about the circumstances in which he had paid.[33]

Intensifying his campaign in the Kesari, Tilak said the government must honour its word given to mamlatdars as 'the government neither has enough evidence to determine things either way, nor does it have so much time on hand'. The government has no right to touch the mamlatdars without whose cooperation it wouldn't have been able to investigate the scandal, he emphasized, adding that besmirching their name now was tantamount to freeing the guilty and punishing the innocent. And he put forward a pointed question: if Crawford was not punished for corruption, how could the mamlatdars be?[34]

That question pretty much summed things up, because if Crawford, according to the commission, had not taken any bribes, how could the mamlatdars be held guilty of paying them? To Hanmantrao, perhaps?

But Hanmantrao's case was separate, and the mamlatdars had sworn they had met Crawford after Hanmantrao had acted as the go-between. It didn't make sense unless, as Tilak alleged, the government was differentiating between 'a white official' and 'natives'.[35]

Yet, swiftly, action was initiated against thirty-eight mamlatdars. Eight mamlatdars were sacked, and the other thirty were suspended for periods ranging from one to fifteen years. Yashwant Ballal Tambe, who had spoken about how the holding back of promotion, repeated transfers, a demotion and threats of further transfers had made him pay up, was among those dismissed from service. In a petition he wrote to the government, Tambe mentioned that 'great injustice' had been done to him and others like him who 'sprang to the assistance of the government's effort to end the regime of corruption, had risked everything' and got 'a most disgraceful dismissal from the service' and earned 'the contempt of their more foresighted brother officers' who had not come forward to testify.[36]

Headlining his editorial 'Is this justice?', Tilak remarked that:

The all-powerful God does not like the tiger or other wild beasts as sacrificial offerings. He likes innocuous chickens and goats instead. With this belief, thousands of speechless and weak animals are being killed in the name of God in our country. In our Bombay Presidency, at the end of the nineteenth century, English officials who call themselves progressive and sensible are also doing exactly that.

Asserting that the Raj's actions had nothing to do with 'right or wrong' and everything to do with 'whites and non-whites', he noted:

People of previous generations always used to warn us that we should not be taken in by English glitziness and promises delivered using extravagant, beautiful and high-sounding words. On the outside everything looked fine, but Ram (as in God) alone knew what was going on underneath. There was a massive gap between word and deed. So we were told to deal with them with cunning and shrewdness. When the rulers and the ruled are of different races, religions and principles, this is going to happen . . . The Crawford episode is proof that this is true. He is white, and so is the government. If not here, certainly in England, someone will stand by him and set him free. Then people of the same community as Crawford won't hesitate for a moment to take their anger out against your witnesses.[37]

Retaining his praise for Lord Reay, Tilak said it was the Bombay governor's qualities which had reinforced his belief in the dictum 'Satyameva Jayate' or 'the truth shall prevail'.[38] But Viscount Cross, the secretary of state, he believed, had committed 'massive injustice and a massive crime'. And about Lord Lansdowne, the Viceroy of India who pressed the Bombay government to act quickly on the secretary of state's orders, Tilak remarked caustically that 'his sight appears to have been impaired either by his zeal to implement the directives of London or the fog of racial pride in Simla', the hilly region in northern India where the viceroy had his palatial summer residence.[39]

As Viscount Cross ruled further that the Bombay government had exceeded the scope of its powers by holding out the promise of immunity to mamlatdars and a bill was proposed to be passed in the Viceroy's Council, the Central cabinet of sorts in British India, limiting the terms of immunity, a number of representative groups of Indians protested against the unfairness of it all. Here, Tilak stood out for his acerbic comments. For instance, the Bombay Presidency Association sent a signed statement to the viceroy. The group included luminaries like the Parsi councillor and Bombay leader Pherozeshah Mehta, the lawyer K.T. Telang and Parsi businessman and politician Dinshaw Wacha and was known for its faith in the justness of British rule. While all of them wrote[40] that Cross had not questioned the validity of the promise of immunity when it was first reported to London, Tilak was cutting in his criticism. 'Lord Cross,' he pointed out, 'says the promise of the Bombay government is illegal. What I want to ask him is, was he sleeping all these days?'[41]

Tilak stood out in another respect when the Poona Sarvajanik Sabha held a public meeting on the issue on 1 September 1889. This was most probably Tilak's first-ever address at a public rally, and he deployed his legal knowledge to full effect in a bid to turn the British argument about the correct course of the law in the mamlatdar case on its head.

Was the pledge given by the Bombay governor truly ultra vires, as Lord Cross and the Raj claimed it was? And was it right to cancel the pledge? Centring his argument around these two questions, Tilak referred to Justice John Jardine's comments which the British regime was relying on. Jardine had cited the 1752 impeachment trial of Lord Macclesfield and declared that the related clause in the Statute of Edward VI had been extended to India by Statute 40 of George III, C. 126, in 1809. According to this clause, Jardine said, corrupt officials or those buying their posts stood disqualified from holding a government position.

Tilak went into the Macclesfield case and said it was similar to the controversy surrounding the mamlatdars. As chancellor in the 1720s, Macclesfield had appointed juniors called 'masters of the rolls', whose job it was to act as 'trustees of the estates of widows, orphans, the mentally ill, and children'. All these estates kept their money with the masters of the rolls. Over several years, Macclesfield took bribes to hand out these positions, and the appointees in turn stole the funds of the various estates to recover the bribe money they had offered. This was a loot of the poor, and Tilak said there were 'Hanmantraos' even at that time, who acted as the middlemen.

Drawing further parallels, Tilak observed that just as in the Crawford case, it was hard to get the masters of the rolls to give evidence against Macclesfield. The only way out was a guarantee of immunity. So, the House of Commons passed a bill stating the masters of the rolls were protected against action or prosecution as mentioned under the Act of King Edward VI. It was after the Act, called the Statute 11 of George I, C. 2, was cleared that the masters gave testimony and Macclesfield was convicted, though it was true that the statute was later rendered obsolete and was repealed by the British Parliament in 1864.

For Tilak, the Act was a precedent in parliamentary legislation, and he insisted that it 'fully justifies the Government of Bombay in giving indemnity under similar circumstances'. If the law of King Edward VI was not applicable in the Macclesfield case which Jardine was going on about, why should it be applicable in the mamlatdar row, he asked. The masters of the rolls, 'serving under a man of their own race and civilization', had agreed to testify only after Parliament had passed an Act giving them protection, he stated. The mamlatdars, on the other hand, had not insisted on any such Act. They had believed in the word of a British governor, and they had been 'sacrificed'. If the masters of the rolls who had purchased their positions were seen as victims of extortion, how could the mamlatdars be perceived as anything else?

Tilak had obviously come for the meeting prepared. The government was seeking to create two categories of mamlatdars, those who had paid voluntarily and those who paid under pressure. But had the Statute of Edward VI made any such distinction? It hadn't, he said, and all masters of the rolls had been retained in their positions. At the most, Tilak suggested, Jardine could have insisted on the passing of a law for the indemnity in the current case to be legally protected, nothing else.

Gokhale and the chairman of the Sarvajanik Sabha's public meeting, R.B. Krishnaji Laxman Nulkar, also spoke on the occasion and criticized the government's targeting of the mamlatdars. Gokhale hit out at *The Times* of London in particular and asked whether the British officials who had also been aware of Crawford's corruption but who had preferred to stay silent were 'morally superior' to the mamlatdars who had imperilled their careers to expose the scam.

However, as the US diplomat and scholar Michael D. Metelits has written in his meticulous study of the Crawford scandal, while the others spoke more in abstract terms of justice, Tilak drew attention to concrete terms of the law.[42] Thus, if Justice Jardine of the Bombay High Court quoted the Macclesfield case, Tilak quoted the same case back to the British to refute their own claims and arguments on the mamlatdar controversy. It was an example of a combatant using the adversary's own tool to saw away at the opposing side with sharp-minded analysis and aplomb.

This meeting marked Tilak's public political debut, and the Crawford scam in itself turned out to be his first real brush with the Raj and its system.

Right from the moment the scandal broke, Tilak had feared, despite his appreciation for Lord Reay's actions, that it could turn against the Indians. When the investigation was underway, he had mentioned a recent case where a British official had gotten away scot-free and wondered if the same would happen here too.

The case he was referring to was a sex scandal of 1885 involving a British civil servant, G.D.H. Wilson. A British political agent in the native state of Cambay in Gujarat, which was then part of the Bombay Presidency, Wilson was accused of asking the diwan, or chief minister of the province, to get his daughter to provide 'sexual favours' to him. A special commission was formed, under the same Act 37 of 1850 under which Crawford was later tried, and Wilson was held guilty. Lord Reay accepted the commission's report and sent it to Viscount Cross for approval. Wilson then went to London and appealed to Lord Cross, who in turn asked the then Chancellor Lord Salisbury for his view. Salisbury found the commission's findings against Wilson unacceptable, and Lord Cross promptly rejected the report. Wilson was pronounced innocent though he was immediately compulsorily retired with a pension.[43]

Crawford's case proved Tilak's apprehensions true because its outcome turned out to be almost exactly the same two years later, with the difference that unlike Wilson, Crawford wasn't even held guilty of the main charge against him.

It's surprising that almost all of Tilak's previous biographers have given relatively short shrift to this entire episode and that it hasn't got the sort of close attention it deserves. The Crawford scandal and its result played a significant role in shaping Tilak's political convictions against the Raj. He was convinced that the system the British had established in India was essentially unjust and unfair. The British were in the habit of repeatedly claiming that they had brought the rule of law to an entire sub-continent. What Tilak saw was that beneath the veneer of a proper legal mechanism was a system of racial randomness and oppression. With his learning and reading of Sanskrit texts from early childhood, Tilak in any case did not doubt that the land the British had colonized was not one of heathens and ignorant people, whatever the coloniser's depictions of it might be, and that its value rested in its social, cultural and political orders. What things carried value and what didn't, he and his friends and opponents would often endlessly argue about and agree or vehemently disagree on, yet the fallout of the Crawford scam made him firm in his view that British imperialism meant tyranny and injustice and that India, and its people had to forge their own destiny. The scandal left a permanent mark on Tilak's mind.

Tilak had done most of his public and press advocacy for the mamlatdars during his semester break from the Deccan Education Society and later during other breaks while the internal fight of the Society's members intensified. During this period, he and Gokhale also attended the first Provincial Conference of the Indian National Congress in Poona. This, in 1888, was Tilak's entry on to the Congress platform, and a low-profile one it was for someone who would eventually dominate the organization. The Congress had been formed in 1885 as a national group that would give voice to Indian views and represent Indian concerns before the Empire. Three years after its founding, the Congress decided it needed to take its message and programme across the provinces, so the three presidencies of Bombay, Calcutta and Madras were picked for local conferences, which came to be known in the annual Congress calendar as Provincial Conferences. Though Tilak attended the inaugural conference held in Poona as a part of the Bombay Presidency, it was Gokhale who was more prominent at the session. The Bombay leaders of the Congress like Dinshaw Wacha were unhappy that Poona's Congressmen had not taken them into confidence while organizing the meet, and he complained in a letter to Dadabhai Naoroji in this regard. Bombay's leaders were placated somehow by Gokhale's speech. Reflecting the views of the Bombay Congress mandarins, most of whom believed in the essential goodness of British intentions, Gokhale expressed confidence that if the Indians put forward their positions clearly and in detail before England, they would definitely get justice.

The next year, 1889, Tilak and Gokhale travelled to Bombay together for the fourth annual session of the Indian National Congress. Here, Tilak made his presence felt on the Congress dais for the first time. He moved an amendment to a resolution on the reform of the Viceroy's Council and made a plea for allowing members of the Provincial Councils to elect members of the Viceroy's Council. It was supported by Gokhale but ultimately not cleared. The consolation for Tilak was that he was chosen to be on the subjects committee for the next year's Congress session. The official Congress report on the 1889 session described the then thirty-three-year-old B.G. Tilak as 'one of the ten gentlemen connected with the Fergusson College, Poona, who deliberately putting aside the prizes that the learned professions offer to such men, have settled down on the smallest pittance on which they can support themselves and their families to promote by their personal exertions the education of their countrymen'. Tilak had put forth the amendment which he sought to introduce 'ably', the report noted.

Compared to the enormous heat and dust raised by the Crawford scandal, the Congress session was a staid affair. The staidness appeared restricted to the tent of the Congress, though. Outside, there was a veritable storm brewing on the cultural front, and Tilak was getting ready to ride it as the foremost champion of one of the two warring camps.

Chapter 6

Faith, Culture and Controversy

On 26 June 1885, a letter published in the pages of the *Times of India* created ripples across the Bombay Presidency. The letter writer, a woman, had not revealed her name. She had identified herself only as 'A Hindu Lady' and had dwelt at length on what she described as the 'evil customs' in Hindu society of infant marriage and enforced widowhood. The 'wicked practice' of 'early marriage has destroyed the happiness of my life', she declared, urging the British government in India to bring in a law abolishing both infant and early marriages. If the Raj didn't act, 'our people' wouldn't do it 'for centuries', she said. By 'our people', she meant principally the men, who had framed the laws. They had given themselves the right to marry and remarry as many times as they wanted and to enjoy the fullest mental and physical freedoms; they could study, work, do whatever they liked. A woman, on the other hand, had every freedom curtailed by the custom of early marriage, and once she was widowed, things got worse, she stressed.[1]

In demanding a law, the 'lady' was extending her support publicly for the proposal for such a legislation mooted by Behramji Malbari, a Parsi journalist and activist, just the previous year. Malbari's proposal had triggered a controversy. Among Poona's legal luminaries, M.G. Ranade supported him, K.T. Telang spoke out against him, and within the group of the idealist young educationists who had just formed the Deccan Education Society, Agarkar was virtually alone in backing him.

Tilak was strongly opposed to any such legislation. The question in this debate was not simply whether early marriage should be discontinued but equally whether legislative intervention was required. Thus, while Hindu society in the past few decades of the nineteenth century had begun to get divided into the traditionalists and the reformers, many of the reformers too calibrated their views carefully during this controversy, wondering if a law would do the trick or societal opinion needed to be moulded first. In many ways, Tilak was a man of his times. He was not reform-minded when it came to marital traditions. In this phase of his career, however, he said he was 'not opposed to change' but insisted nothing should be thrust upon society unless it was prepared to accept it. He kept up his 'not opposed' claim throughout the debate, which raged for almost seven years, while at the same time upholding the traditional roles enjoined upon men and women by Hindu religious and social customs.

The Hindu lady's letter fuelled the fires of the controversy. One reason for it was that a long-suffering woman from within the community was describing her ordeal, and the fact that she preferred to remain anonymous added to the curiosity about her case. The second had to do with the platform she had chosen. In the nineteenth century, newspapers were the only game in town and for most people, the solitary source of information and debate, and the *Times of India* was the chief English and English-run daily in the Bombay Presidency. The third reason was that its reach and influence apart, *The Times*' British editors had further highlighted the woman's letter by writing an editorial comment on the issue the same day and in the same edition in which the letter was published. Not surprisingly, the paper spoke openly for a law.

On 19 September, *The Times* published a second letter by the 'Hindu lady'. In this, she focused more on the aspect of enforced widowhood and, lambasting the Hindu 'shastris' for imposing a life of wretchedness on women who lost their husbands, asserted that '[T]he Hindu widow – unbeloved of God and despised of man – a social pariah and a domestic drudge, must continue for centuries together to bear her hard portion and pine in solitude till the pressure of legislation or the influence of foreign civilization comes to her help.' Like the previous letter, this one was accompanied by an editorial comment lauding the woman's stand and assuring the Hindus that 'if the Hindus will themselves take up this part of the question . . . we can promise them the support and sympathy of the English community, from the viceroy downwards'.[2]

The same morning on which these views were carried in the paper, the case of a Hindu woman called Rukhmabai came up for hearing in the Bombay High Court.

Born in 1864 to Jayantibai and Janardhan Pandurang, Rukhmabai had lost her father when she was just two-and-a-half years old. As widow marriage was allowed in her community, which she said belonged to 'the second class of castes', her mother in 1871 married Sakharam Arjun, 'a celebrated doctor in Bombay'. Dr Sakharam 'proved an unusually kind stepfather to me,' Rukhmabai said later, and 'he protected and loved me as his own child.' When she was 11 years old, she was married to Dadaji Bhikaji, a seventeen-year-old boy who was the kin of her stepfather. That was an era in which Hindu girls were married off as early as at the age of four or five, so Rukhmabai said her age (eleven) was 'rather beyond the limit' of the then 'marriageable limit' for girls. The bridegroom's side agreed to her stepfather's conditions that the girl would stay at her parents' place until Dadaji studied and became 'a good man'. Until then, Rukhmabai's parents would provide for him. But, according to her, he had abandoned his studies, fallen into bad company and ruined his health. 'Attacked with consumption (tuberculosis),' he had been confined to his bed for three years but had later somehow recovered, she noted.[3]

She, on the contrary, had grown up learning some amount of English even though she hadn't been to school after the age of eleven and hadn't completed her Marathi studies. Right from childhood, Rukhmabai said, 'being of much reserved disposition', she had a 'great liking for study' and 'a great disgust for married life'. And 'the habits of the man to whom I had been given in marriage added more to my natural distaste for married life'.[4] Eventually, she refused to go to her husband's home, despite the husband putting in many requests. In March 1884, Dadaji filed a suit in the high court 'for restitution of conjugal rights'. Rukhmabai responded by saying she wouldn't go to him as he was poor and could not 'provide her lodging, maintenance and clothing'. He also had poor health, so she could not 'safely live with him'. While these were 'contingent reasons', there was moreover a matter of principle for her. She said the marriage was invalid because she was only eleven when it took place and had not arrived at 'years of discretion'. There was no consent, so the marriage couldn't be binding, she argued.[5]

Justice Robert Hill Pinhey of the Bombay High Court, hearing the case, was evidently morally appalled by what Rukhmabai was being made to go through. The hearing had started on a Saturday. After it had resumed on Monday, Dadaji's lawyer completed his argument. The moment the advocate–general, a Britisher called F.L. Latham, stood up to speak on Rukhmabai's behalf, Justice Pinhey stopped him. 'I think I need not trouble you as I am prepared to dispose of the case at once,' he pronounced. The marriage had happened eleven years ago, Rukhmabai was twenty-two now, and she and Dadaji had 'never cohabited', he said. The judge ruled that he would not force Rukhmabai to go to Dadaji's house 'in order that he may consummate the marriage arranged for her during her helpless infancy'. He remarked that Dadaji 'should not have tried to recover her person, as if she had been a horse or a bullock'.[6]

The verdict sounds inarguably good from a twenty-first-century point of view. It became hugely controversial, however, at the time, causing polarization between those in favour and those against. Tilak clashed with the champions of the court order, a clash that marked the beginning of his claim as the upholder of long-held traditions and the opponent of those purportedly seeking to topple the broader Hindu way of life by chipping away at it, step by step. The Rukhmabai controversy, entangled with the issue of Malbari's proposals on abolishing infant and early marriage, was followed by four other similar raging social rows— over the Age of Consent, over schools for girls, over consumption of food and tea by Hindus at a Church institution and over a woman reformist's proselytization campaign. In each of these, Tilak took particularly vehement stands. In fact, these controversies were absolutely central to his emergence as the darling of the masses and represented the socio–cultural route to his becoming the 'Lokmanya' or the one 'revered by the people'. As these issues got enmeshed with the nature of the British regime in India, they burnished his image as a staunch foe of that dispensation and lent enormously powerful social armour to the political battle he would wage against it.

Tilak positioned himself unabashedly as a cultural traditionalist, though, as mentioned earlier, he often contradicted himself by saying he was a believer in change but wished it to come through society and not by way of legislation, that too enforced by a foreign ruler. Tilak's defenders point to his 'let change happen' comments to argue

he was no cultural conservative and was merely adopting a strategy
to counter the Raj whose courts' rulings, it was feared, would have
serious implications for Indian society and specifically for Hindu
society. It is wholly true that Tilak used these controversies to make
the political point that legislative interference was unacceptable.
His concerns, nonetheless, were unmistakably as much social and
cultural as they were political. Tilak's decriers, on the other hand,
survey these controversies and brand him as a stuck-in-the-past
conservative.

The truth is slightly more nuanced than what either side would
have us believe. Tilak made statements that appeared totally retrograde.
He tied himself up in knots at times when he attempted to claim he
was pro-change. There is no reason to agree with him or defend him on
any of these counts. What is important is to know the tensions roiling
British–Indian relations on the twin issues of law and society at the
time and how these tensions were reflected in the responses coming in
from both sides. Without knowing these, there's no way we can even
understand why the Rukhmabai case, for instance, attracted so much
controversy to begin with.

The denigration of Hinduism was one of the core elements
of British policy in India. While other faiths like Islam, Sikhism,
Buddhism and Jainism were also reviled, Hinduism was naturally
the prime target because the majority of Indians followed its tenets,
and English officials with their sense of racial superiority, believed
undermining it would help consolidate their control over the land
and crush the confidence of the 'natives'. They consistently portrayed
Hindu society as a cesspool of superstition and ignorance and
placed Hindus beyond the pale of culture and civilization. And they
advocated the spread of Western values through Western education
and the propagation of Christianity, increasingly from 1813, when the
Charter Act laid the ground for setting up the Church of England in
India and gave Christian missionaries a free hand on Indian territory.
Gradually the Indians were convinced that the British government
and the Church operated as part of an alliance against India, Hindus
and Hinduism.

Macaulay had neatly summed up the British approach in his Minute
of 1835. Declaring that 'a single shelf of a good European library was
worth the whole native literature of India',[7] he had commented:

All the historical information which has been collected from all the books written in the Sanskrit language is less valuable than what may be found in the most paltry abridgements used at preparatory schools in England . . . The question now before us is simply whether, when it is in our power to teach the English language, we shall teach languages in which . . . there are no books on any subject which deserve to be compared to our own . . . whether, when we can patronize sound philosophy and true history, we shall countenance at the public expense medical doctrines which would disgrace an English farrier, astronomy which would move laughter in girls at an English boarding school, history abounding with kings thirty feet high and reigns 30,000 years long, and geography made up of seas of treacle and rivers of butter.[8]

Macaulay believed that the people of the land were 'idolators, blindly attached to doctrines and rites which . . . are in the highest degree pernicious'. At the same time, he wrote to his father enthusiastically that 'western education and ethics' would ultimately 'lead Hindus to embrace Christianity' and 'there will not be a single idolator among the respectable classes in Bengal thirty years hence.' Because 'every young Brahmin who learns geography in our colleges learns to smile at the Hindoo mythology' and 'no Hindoo, who has received an English education, ever remains sincerely attached to his religion'.[9]

Another long-serving British official, Charles Trevelyan, had pronounced proudly in 1838, 'Hinduism is not a religion which will bear examination. It is so entirely destitute of anything like evidence and is identified with so many gross immoralities and physical absurdities, that it gives way at once before the light of European science. Mahommedanism is made of tougher materials; yet, even a Mahommedan youth who has received an English education is a very different person from one who has been taught according to the perfect manner of the law of his father.' Almost five decades later, Trevelyan was still passionately rubbishing Hinduism. In an address, he said:

'Hinduism is the only remaining great system of idolatry; and of all the religions which mankind have invented for themselves, it has gone furthest in deifying human vice . . . From murder to petty larceny, every crime has its patron in the Hindu Pantheon . . . You now see

what the world would become if Hinduism generally prevailed. The
wonder is how human society can subsist at all under such a religion.
The truth is that human nature is better than Hinduism, and the kind
and affectionate dispositions implanted in us by [the Christian] God
cannot be entirely effaced even by the worst of false religions.'

What gave him confidence was the belief that 'the grammar and
spelling-book suffice to destroy the Hindu religion' and that 'a
generation is growing up which repudiates idols.'[10]

Richard Temple, one of the seniormost officials in the Bombay
Presidency, was a hater, especially of Deccani and within that group,
Chitpavan Brahmans like Tilak, as mentioned in an earlier chapter.
Temple stated plainly in a public address in London in 1883 that
'India presents the greatest of all fields for missionary exertion' and
'in respect to our moral responsibilities before God and man, India is
a country which of all others we are bound to enlighten with eternal
truth'. His confidence stemmed from his belief that 'the religions in
India – the old-established religions – are each of them waning and
declining towards their ultimate fall. Buddhism is effete. Hinduism
is gradually breaking up, like the clouds before the advancing sun.
Muhammadanism, no doubt, will hold out much longer for this reason
– that it has a much more rational foundation than either Buddhism or
Hinduism . . . Hinduism is still the religion of the million, no doubt,
but only of the uneducated million. It is no longer the religion of the
educated Hindu. It is no longer the religion of those who have either
theoretical enlightenment or practical knowledge. It is being gradually
dissipated, like the mist.'[11]

This had been the pattern of much of the British commentary,
official or non-official, right through the nineteenth century, and
as Trevelyan's and Temple's cases showed, it had not changed until
the decade in which Rukhmabai's controversy arose. Racism, racial
oppression and denunciations of Hinduism—to the extent of denying
the basic humanity of its adherents and rejecting in totality the culture
and heritage of the faith—went together.

Thus, Rukhmabai's may have appeared a fairly straightforward case,
but in keeping with the well-established pattern, the British and Anglo–
Indian press, while celebrating the verdict in her favour, enthusiastically

portrayed British law in India as emancipatory and condemned Hindu practices as being regressive. *Times of India*, where the 'Hindu lady' had aired her grievances —it was eventually revealed that the lady was Rukhmabai herself—wrote that 'the Hindu marriage laws are as unjust as they are unnatural. But a distinct step in advance has been gained by Mr Justice Pinhey's decision . . . And for the first time, so far as we remember, in India, the law distinctly refuses to be made the instrument of this personal degradation.'[12] Both *Times of India* and *Pioneer*, which, published from the then imperial capital Calcutta, was even more of an official mouthpiece of the Raj establishment, urged Indian reformers to use Pinhey's judgement to change Hindu marriage customs. *Pioneer* recommended that 'the next step would be to establish the argument that a woman who cannot be compelled by law to accept the position of a wife is not a wife in the legal sense, and that, therefore, should her so-called husband die, she cannot become a widow'.[13] This went well beyond what Rukhmabai was saying. Rukhmabai herself had not questioned her position as Dadaji's legally wedded wife. She had argued she had been married without her consent and did not want to go to her husband; she had not sought approval to annul the marriage or to be free to marry someone else. *Civil and Military Gazette*, another British organ published from Lahore, wrote that 'in the matter of jealous Hindus who bite off the noses of their mistresses, it cannot be denied that he has most notably helped forward the cause of social reform'.[14] And *Indian Daily News*, yet another British-run paper, stated that 'European sympathy is naturally on the side of the Judge's decision', maintained that the judgment was 'thoroughly' in keeping with 'European notions of justice and equity', and concluded that 'the case points very clearly to the necessity for legislative interference in the matter of infant marriage.'[15]

For a majority of Indians and especially Hindus, these comments came not merely as an encouragement to the British legal machinery to regulate their social and religious matters but as a firm push for further legislation. The *Native Opinion*, a paper edited by V.N. Mandlik, lawyer and Tilak's family friend, remarked, 'Mr Justice Pinhey has tried to legislate and not to interpret the existing laws; and when a judge attempts to do so then there is an end to all stability. The single decision of Mr Justice Pinhey will convulse the whole community. Husbands and wives would be deprived of all their rights under the Hindu Law and Mr Justice Pinhey will have done all this in the Court-house and not in the Council-chamber.'[16]

Here, Mandlik's paper was getting into the classic theory of how the judiciary was supposed to interpret the laws as framed by the legislature, not make them.

Tilak got into elucidating the other points. Mandlik had stated that wives would be deprived of their rights too. How? Tilak noted in the *Mahratta* that Hindu wives' right to maintenance and financial security was under threat. 'Where a man possessed of property has married a girl of eight or nine, and died before consummation of marriage, it would be dangerous to hold that the infant widow was not entitled to her husband's property, because the marriage contract had not been completed.'[17] And who was saying that the marriage contract had not been completed? Justice Pinhey himself, according to Tilak; because he had held the view that 'among Hindus the performance of the marriage ceremony is merely a contract which might be set aside before consummation'. Pinhey's reading of the Hindu laws was wrong, contended Tilak. 'A Hindu marriage, once entered, can never be dissolved . . . It is merely a principle of the English law, English custom that Mr Justice Pinhey had consulted in the present case.'[18] Tilak wasn't saying 'A Hindu marriage, once contracted'; he was deploying his legal acumen to use the term 'entered (into)', just in case the word 'contract' raised the prospect of its dissolubility.

The message was explicit: the British could not be trusted when it came to Indian laws. And what were the British doing tinkering with Indian social and religious laws anyway, which the Queen of Britain had promised not to touch with her proclamation of 1858? Hadn't the 1857 Revolt been triggered by rumours of army cartridges being smeared with cow fat, abhorrent to the Hindus who revered the cow, and with pig fat, abhorrent to the Muslims whose faith forbade them from consuming food of this animal considered unclean? 'The court's work is not to see if laws governing society for ages should be reformed. Its duty is to implement the laws as they exist,' Tilak underlined.[19]

Soon Dadaji appealed against Pinhey's verdict in the Bombay High Court itself, and the order was overturned by the judge who heard the plea. Rukhmabai was ordered to go to her husband's home; if she didn't, the high court said this time in a tone completely opposite to the one Justice Pinhey had adopted, she would have to go to jail for six months.

Commenting on the fresh verdict, Tilak took a swipe at Rukhmabai's supporters. Her ardent backers included German philologist and Sanskrit scholar Max Müller. A razor-sharp master of satire, Tilak had taken over the *Kesari* early in 1887, though Agarkar's name was formally taken off the print line only towards the end of that year. Once Tilak assumed charge, he converted it into a paper that had the raciness of a tabloid and the depth of a broadsheet. One of his great gifts as a journalist and editor was his conversational style of addressing his readers. He broke from the established pattern of using slightly heavy prose and came up with iconic headlines and catchphrases which stood the test of time. The Rukhmabai episode produced some of the earliest examples of his biting satire. In March 1887, Tilak addressed Max Müller as the 'Moksh Muller' of the reformist group and referred to Justice Pinhey, whose verdict had been overturned, as 'Maharshi' Pinhey', and in one place, even as 'Pinhey-*charya*' of what he termed the Kali Yuga, the third of the Yugas or ages in Hindu traditions which represents the ascent of evil.[20]

With Rukhmabai, Tilak eschewed satire and was more direct in his criticism. He accepted that,

> It is extremely important that our women make progress. But the only thing I want to tell our fake reformists is that such progress cannot be brought about by someone uninformed and full of half-baked ideas like Rukhmabai.

On Rukhmabai not having consented to her marriage, Tilak said:

> Thousands of men live happily with their wives who still haven't reached their years of discretion. Is it not surprising then that a woman who herself lacks any sense of discrimination should tell the court her husband is not fit for her? Isn't it more surprising still that our reformers should take up cudgels for her and raise such a big hue and cry? Even among the English, a married woman,

regardless of whether her marriage has been consummated or not, cannot simply claim the right to separation by saying she doesn't like her husband (this was legally true at the time); if such a case had been filed in England, the woman would have been exposed to ridicule.[21]

Didn't consent matter altogether, then? 'It's not a bad thing at all that a marriage should take place with the consent of both man and woman,' Tilak said. But, according to him:

If we only see the kind of rifts that take place between people who have married with mutual consent, we have reason to wonder whether changing our age-old practices makes any sense. Clearly there's no need to change things. So why is there so much fuss over this? And even if it were conceded that change is needed, it's not the high court's business to think about whether traditional practices should be overhauled . . . The recent high court order, which says that a woman cannot reject her husband so long as society accepts a marriage is sanctified once the seven *pheras* are over, is correct. And suppose the courts do pass an order that our marriages aren't legal if there's no consent, then how many children living today would be termed as legal? Who would even follow such an order? We don't look at high court orders while fixing our marriages. So viewed from various angles, the recent high court verdict is in keeping with Hindu shastras. If some time in the future, after our reformers' long efforts, our customs of marriage get altered, it's a different matter altogether.[22]

Tilak however disagreed with the second part of the court's order ruling that Rukhmabai should be sent to prison if she doesn't agree to go to her husband. Rukhmabai herself had defiantly said that she would still not go back to Dadaji, never mind if she were placed in fetters. Tilak declared it would be wrong to imprison her 'needlessly' and equally wrong to give the court power over any punitive aspect of marital jurisdiction. 'If we argue courts have no business to intervene, then how do we accept this either?' he asked.[23]

He wasn't yet done with targeting Rukhmabai and the reformers, however. In a subsequent editorial in *Kesari*, he compared her to

Shikhandi of Mahabharata, who had been used by the Pandavas as a cover to vanquish the grand old man of the Kuru clan, Bhishma:

> Just as the Pandavas had placed Shikhandi in the forefront to be able to win against Pitamaha (an honorific for Bhishma) in the Mahabharata, our reformers put forward Rukhmabai and using her as a shield, fired their guns at our ancient religion in order to undermine it. They had strong hopes of winning, but unfortunately for them, their plan didn't succeed.[24]

Rukhmabai's spirit remained indomitable despite such criticism, and she would not budge from her position of risking imprisonment. Finally, and quite soon, Dadaji gave up all hope of getting her back.

But there had been recognition by the various parties, including the reformers, that Dadaji too in a way had been a victim in this episode. One of the Anglo-Indian papers, *Indian Daily News*, wrote that 'the fact can scarcely be conveniently be put out of sight that the man also has a grievance. He is saddled with a wife who is not a wife . . . not in the sense that she is a burden upon him . . . but in the sense that she is still legally his wife. Mr Justice Pinhey's (original) judgement, though it debars him from access to his wife, does not sever the marriage tie. So if the young wife is a victim of the unfortunate marriage custom of the country, the husband is only a degree less a victim.'[25] Mandlik's tradition-minded *Native Opinion*, on the other hand, had not liked the fact that Rukhmabai had mentioned Dadaji's poverty as one of the reasons she didn't want to enter his household, though Pinhey had clarified his order rejecting the husband's suit was not based on grounds of poverty and ill-health cited by her. *Native Opinion* wrote:

> Now as to the allegation of the husband's inability to maintain . . . The inability to maintain is a relative term and can be used in almost every case. What may be competence to one may be poverty to another, and if such an indefinite definition were held good in such suits society would be sorely disarranged.'

On the 'dislike' she had voiced for her husband too, the paper stated 'there is only one case in which a wife can resist her husband's claim to conjugal rights and that is in the case of cruelty which involved danger or fear of danger to her person by the violence of the husband.'[26]

Rukhmabai's supporters such as Professor William Wordsworth of Deccan College advised her that for the case to end altogether, there would have to be some compromise. Wordsworth, along with K.T. Telang and a few others had formed a 'Rukhmabai Rescue Committee' to help her legally. (Just how sensitive the matter was for Hindu society at the time was partly revealed by developments within the committee. Telang was a keen member, but the moment some of Rukhmabai's well-wishers demanded that the Viceroy's Council legislate on the matter, he made a public statement opposing any such move and said he would protest if anyone tried to push through 'other aims' in the guise of fighting for Rukhmabai.) The committee was aware that Dadaji had spent a lot of money on the court case and got pushed further into poverty. Rukhmabai's side decided to compensate him for the expenses incurred, on the condition that he would not insist any more on the implementation of the court's order about sending her to jail. He agreed and got Rs 2000 as legal costs, and thus the matter ended in July 1888.

In less than a year, Dadaji got married a second time. He was simply not destined for marital happiness, however, for he died just a few years thereafter. Rukhmabai went on to have a truly remarkable life. Months after the legal imbroglio ended, she left for England to study medicine. There, she acquired two medical degrees but could not enrol for an MD in London because the local university did not take in women for that course. Heading to Brussels in Belgium, she earned her MD degree there in 1895 and, coming back to her homeland, served for close to three decades as a doctor in Bombay, Rajkot, Surat and some other places. She died in 1955, aged eighty-nine.[27]

The Marathi scholar Y.D. Phadke correctly points out that there was one course of action Rukhmabai could have taken to get out of an unwanted marriage immediately.[28] Conversion to Christianity offered her an escape. It would have effectively terminated her matrimonial ties with Dadaji, nullified his legal battle, and given her the liberty to get into a new marital relationship. A periodical in England, *Saturday Review*, had suggested she take this option, but she didn't.

Another Hindu woman at the time, though, enthusiastically embraced Christianity and engendered a storm of protest by exposing herself to the charge of being involved in religious proselytization. Her name was Ramabai Dongre, and she was much better known as Pandita Ramabai. Tilak was the first to raise multiple red flags in relation to her activities, and he led a campaign against her up until the point she was forced into a defensive position and almost became a shunned figure for the mainstream Hindu community.

Born in 1858 in Karnataka, where her father's Chitpavan Brahman family had moved a few generations ago, Ramabai saw early on the vicissitudes of life. Her father, Anant Dongre, was a Sanskrit scholar and had earned the title of shastri, a master of sacred texts. He had seen tremendous prosperity and, at one point, had Rs 1,75,000 because of his intelligent buying of shares at the time of Bombay's financial growth in the 1860s. Once that growth, caused by the American Civil War which led England's textile mills to turn to India for cotton purchases, had vanished, so did Anant shastri's fortunes. Contrary to convention, Anant Shastri had taught Sanskrit to his wife Lakshmi, and it was the mother who taught young Rama the language. According to Ramabai's biographer Meera Kosambi, Ramabai could recite from memory 12,000 Sanskrit shlokas by the time she had turned twelve years old.

The sudden death of her parents one after the other in 1874 pushed Ramabai and her brother Shrinivas deeper into poverty. They travelled a great deal for livelihood, preaching the puranas in their role as Brahmans in various places, including northern and eastern India. In Bengal, Ramabai's reputation reached the ears of the local Sanskrit masters, and she was subjected to an examination by the top scholars at the Senate House of the University of Calcutta. Convinced that her command of the language was prodigious, they gave her the title of 'Pandita', which stuck. In that province, she joined the Brahmo Samaj, the reformist monotheistic order, and met a young Bengali lawyer, Bipin Behari Das Medhavi, who was part of that order. He wooed her, they married in mid-1880 against the wishes of his family which opposed the inter-caste marriage, and soon they had a daughter, Manorama. But in 1882, cholera claimed her husband's life, and Ramabai, with her little daughter, moved to Maharashtra.

She had spent only a year earlier in the region during her father's wanderings but had identified herself as a Maharashtrian always despite having lived elsewhere. Her parents had spoken Marathi at home and had taught her the language, and she was also into reading Marathi books and newspapers. In the early 1880s, Maharashtra's reformers like M.G. Ranade and others of the Prarthana Samaj, which was, in a sense, the regional avatar of Calcutta's Brahmo Samaj, invited her to the western parts, and she chose Poona as her base in 1882. There, she soon became a well-known personality, forming the Arya Mahila Samaj for women's uplift and being called upon by the Education Commission led by W.W. Hunter, which was reviewing the education system, to testify as a witness. Her interactions with British officials, with the English teacher Miss Hurford of the Zenana Mission located on the city's eastern fringes, and with Sister Eleanor and Sister Geraldine of the Anglican Community of St Mary the Virgin (CSMV), a Christian group with a Poona chapter, convinced her of the need to study further. She was keen on medicine, and the nuns of CSMV helped her to actuate the desire; the group's headquarters near Oxford agreed to take her in, provided she would teach Indian languages to their India-bound nuns.

Before she left Indian shores, Ramabai had got a word of caution from one of her friends in Poona, the young and brilliant Kashibai Kanitkar, who went on to become one of the pioneering women writers in the Marathi language. Kashibai had felt that the nuns Eleanor and Geraldine had won Ramabai over with ease, and the influence of the CSMV would induce her to convert to Christianity. Ramabai's response was to promise Kashibai that she would never do such a thing. In September 1883, Ramabai broke that promise and was baptized by the founder of the CSMV, Canon Butler, in the parish church at Wantage near Oxford. Her witness at the ceremony was Sister Geraldine. The Anglican Church also ensured she did not get to study medicine; it laid out for her a future as a teacher, which she accepted, and got her enrolled at the Cheltenham Ladies College. Her conversion caused much rueful comment among Indian commentators, including the reformers. They expressed sadness over the development but hoped she would continue her studies and not alienate herself fully from her homeland.

After she had spent three years in England, Ramabai got in December 1885 a letter from the Woman's Medical College of Pennsylvania inviting her to a function at which degrees were to be awarded to women. Among the recipients was going to be Ramabai's cousin, Anandibai Joshi, who became India's very first woman doctor. Ramabai happily went to America and was soon being called to address public gatherings because of her scholarship and now, her hold over English too. Backed by the president of the Woman's Christian Temperance Union, she extended her originally intended three-month stay in the US to nearly three years, addressing audiences in Philadelphia, Boston, Washington, DC and many other places.

On her return to India in February 1889, Ramabai chose to settle in Bombay and opened close to Girgaum Chowpatty the Sharada Sadan, a residential and educational facility for high-caste Hindu women, especially widows. She had raised funds for the Sharada Sadan from donors in the US, who had promised her between $5000 and $15,000 every year for a decade. In addition, the Ramabai Association she had formed during her stay in Boston in the state of Massachusetts 'for the purpose of assisting in the education of child widows in India' had collected $36,285 from contributors across the US and Canada. If all of this created concerns in Hindu society that the Church may be bankrolling her, she made it clear on the occasion of the facility's opening that it would be secular and her aim would not be to convert women to Christianity. Her statement was bolstered by the support she received from the likes of Ranade, N.G. Chandavarkar and G.G. Agarkar, who hailed her efforts at women's liberation at a time when Hindu widows were condemned to live a life of social isolation, barred from auspicious familial, social and cultural ceremonies and forced to cut their hair completely. Tilak's *Kesari* too initially bought into the theory. Praising Ramabai, the paper wrote on 12 February 1889:

It is a marvellous deed to collect thousands of rupees in a foreign land by begging on behalf of people of an alien religion and of alien tradition and customs. The fact that this was accomplished by a weak, unsupported woman through her firm resolve, courteousness, and other laudable traits makes us pity our menfolk, and also makes us feel proud that such an extraordinary woman was born in our midst. By our misfortune she has been somewhat alienated through her religious conversion, which is sad indeed.[29]

Three months on, *Kesari* was still showering praise on her, saying, 'Today our society is in great need of women like Panditabai. Her pure conduct, mature thinking and deeply ingrained concern for the uplift of her compatriots will impress upon the minds of our people the beneficial effects of good education.' The paper reiterated 'it is our misfortune that Panditabai has changed her religion' but was categorical that 'it will not be proper to dissociate from her for this reason alone.' It was 'to her credit that she did not discard her patriotism along with her religion', it stated, adding 'It is obvious from her conduct thus far and from the thoughts she has expressed in public that she has not undertaken this task for the propagation of Christianity. Therefore, it will be self-destructive to harbour suspicions about her, keep a distance from her, and refuse to help her cause.'[30]

Soon, Ramabai shifted the Sharada Sadan to Poona, where conservatism was far more deep-rooted than in Bombay. There had been murmurs in Bombay itself that the Sadan might be involved in proselytization; these grew after it moved to Poona. Tilak himself began to have serious doubts about the real motive of Ramabai and veered around quickly to the view that her Sadan was more an instrument of the Church than of women's education and emancipation. He got into a war of words with his friend Agarkar, who had by this time started his own weekly, the *Sudharak,* or Reformer. It was a bilingual publication, like many others of the time; Agarkar supervised and edited the Marathi section, and Gopal Krishna Gokhale looked after the English part.

Tilak said in the *Kesari* that Ramabai had formed a local advisory board (comprising Ranade, Bhandarkar and C.N. Bhat) to guide the Sadan's workings, but she had been acting pretty much on her own without seeking their counsel. He accused her of having given up the principle of religious neutrality and of goading the Sadan's girls to give up idol worship and embrace the Church. Further, he claimed that the funds flowing in from the US had 'an ulterior religious motive' and told his readers that 'we should regard this as a school for evangelization and conduct ourselves towards the Pandita as we do towards the missionaries'. Not sparing Ranade either, Tilak wrote he would hold the esteemed judge responsible if any of the women in 'Pandita Ramabai's Mission House for Widows' got converted.

Agarkar labelled Tilak and other opponents of Ramabai as 'biased', 'malicious' and people with a 'clouded vision' who were 'persecuting' an 'innocent institution' because they were 'envious' of its founder's feat. Alleging that Tilak was 'possessed by the devil of public appeasement', Agarkar said Ramabai's idea really was to be no longer dependent on foreign funds after a decade, and 'this precluded a Christianising agenda.'[31] Ramabai had indeed expressed her hope at the opening ceremony of the Sadan that it would be 'self-supporting'[32] after ten years, and Agarkar had full faith in her words.

Escalating criticism soon turned into a crisis for Ramabai. Tilak got hold of a report carried by the *Christian Weekly* of New York in December 1889 on the Sadan's activities. The report said, 'At present there are seven young widows in the Sharada-Sadan, two of whom have expressed their love of Christianity. They regularly attend the daily prayers with Ramabai. The institution gives full freedom of faith and that this freedom has done no harm to anybody suggests that the Sadan is clearly a Christian institute.'[33] If a *Boston Herald* report of 29 August 1889 quoting Ramabai during her years in the US were to be believed, then she had identified herself fully with proselytization activities even before she returned to India. The Boston daily had reported that Ramabai had said 'privately when in this country that the greatest difficulty in missionary work in India was not that the Hindus were not ready to become Christians, but that the missionaries were so unwilling to recognize anything good in the Hindoo faith, and so ready to flout out against it . . . that it made the Hindoo people too angry to even entertain the Christian creed.'[34]

Tilak went to town citing the report, and his protests carried deep resonance across Hindu society. Right through the nineteenth century, Hindus had had considerable worries about missionary activities, and the New York paper's report, highlighted by *Kesari*, confirmed their worst suspicions. *Kesari* went still further by carrying a signed letter by one of Ramabai's kinswomen, Krishnabai, who worked in the Sadan. Krishnabai had written, 'Hindu girls were not allowed to observe their religious rites and festivals in the Sadan. Nor were they allowed to visit Hindu temples.'[35] The public wave of criticism was so forceful that all three members of the advisory board handed in their resignation letters to the Ramabai Association in Boston. The *Kesari* published Ranade and Bhandarkar's joint letter. Implicating Ramabai even more, their letter read:

> We have reasons to believe that many of the girls are induced to attend Ramabai's private prayers regularly, and read the Bible, and that Christian doctrines are taught to them. Pandita Ramabai has also shown her active missionary tendencies by asking the parents and guardians of girls to allow them to attend her prayers and, in one case at least, to become Christians themselves; and we are assured that two of the girls have declared to their elders that they have accepted Christ. Such a departure from the original understanding cannot fail in our opinion to shake the stability of the Institute and alienate public sympathy from this work. We are sorry our individual remonstrances with Pandita Ramabai have proved of no avail. If the Sadan is to be conducted as an avowed proselytizing institute we must disavow all connection with it.[36]

Agarkar had, with his belief in Ramabai's noble motives, sent his maternal cousin Venu Namjoshi to live and study at the Sadan. He was a rationalist and far more progressive in his thinking than Ranade and Chandavarkar, but he was totally opposed to the Church's proselytization campaign. He was left embarrassed at the denouement of the Ramabai episode, especially owing to the attack he had mounted on Tilak. Disapproving of what was going on at the Sadan, Agarkar withdrew his cousin Venu from the institution immediately and brought her home.[37]

The revelations severely damaged Ramabai's standing in western India and alienated her from the main current of Hindu society altogether. Soon, she moved out of Poona, setting up the Mukti (Salvation) Mission in Kedgaon, about seventy kilometres to the southeast of Poona. With all the Sharada Sadan inmates shifted there, she now ran an openly 'church-dominated settlement of more than 2000 people' spread over a 100-acre plot she had purchased.[38]

Tilak did not relent on his verbal attacks on Ramabai, however. Rather, emboldened by the success of his expose against her, he described her as a 'benevolent tigress in sheep's clothing'[39] and a 'female padre [padrin-bai in Marathi]' working to 'set afire the ancient religion of her compatriots with the help of foreigners'. Had she done something similar in the political sphere, she'd have been held guilty of treason and got due penalty, 'but Hindus take a liberal view of religious matters and so Ramabai was saved,' he remarked.[40] With his characteristic satirical touch, he suggested she remove the 'taint of the title "Pandita" that she's got because of Hinduism and assume the prefix "Reverenda" instead.'[41]

In another battle cry, Tilak made a public statement in the *Kesari* that if the guardians of the women living at Ramabai's institution wished to withdraw them from the Sadan, the women would be given admission to the Female High School which had been started in Poona in 1883 and their fees paid for by some noted personalities. (The earlier advisory board members also offered to fund the girls' education at the Female High School, and some girls did indeed make the shift).[42]

Tilak's batting for entry into the Female High School was slightly ironic. With its founders, who were of the reformist school, he had expressed serious differences. These were not about the setting up of the school. Tilak repeatedly said he favoured female education, and he in fact sent his daughter to study in the same school for girls whose educational curriculum and policies he criticised. Yet he argued that women did not need the same kind of education as men. In doing so, he came across as a real social conservative. He said reformers 'ought not to sprint a 100 years ahead of society' and any changes to be made 'must take society along'. His principal argument in this regard was that Indian women grew up very differently from those in the West. In England and some other countries, they married late and started working and supporting their families before they got married, he said. In India, on the other hand, girls got married before reaching puberty and handled family responsibilities.

'Even in England this kind of education has been given to women for only the past 20-25 years. Then why are we in such a hurry? If we start marrying in adulthood, if our joint family system breaks down, and if our middle-class families start saving some money (which they aren't able to at the moment), then girls emerging from high school with an English education will have value. All we need at present are women not tired of their religion and familial responsibilities who can read and write a bit. If a school is going to have the opposite effect, we don't need it. If someone thinks girls can do some amount of household work at their parents' or in-laws' place and get education in the 2-3 hours that they will still get in the day – education that is appropriate for *stree dharma* and Hindu *dharma* – then such education is achievable. But a school that brings girls of different faiths together and gives them Anglicized education, just like boys, from 11 am to 5 pm, will be useful only either to the ultra-rich or orphaned girls who need to take up some work to support themselves. Women falling in the middle bracket will get nothing from such a school; in fact, it will land them in trouble. Many people will say that if we want to bring in adult marriages . . . then such Anglicized education for women will help. But this belief is bereft of thought. The Prarthana Samaj is proof of what happens if, in areas where reform is necessary, you take several steps ahead. The same can be said about the female school.'

What he was saying was that the monotheistic Prarthana Samaj had failed to bring about any reform in society. His recommendation was: 'First introduce female education of the kind that's digestible for society. Thereafter, gradually make improvements in keeping with society's proclivities. You can then achieve your desirable aim.'[43] In another essay, he maintained it was the shape in which the 'high school' idea was being put forward which he found unworkable: it would catch women unawares at the very time they were about to get married and take them neither here nor there; there had been primary girls schools in Poona which had been doing quite fine for long, and they would suffice for the time being unless the reformists wanted to cater to just a thin sliver of society.[44] Did that mean he did not want higher schooling for women? No, he said, he very much wanted education for girls above the primary level and recognized the need for a new institution for that, but it would have to be an institution more attuned to the women's needs, not European-style education.[45]

Suggesting that Indian society be permitted to go through its own stages, and also to underline that he genuinely backed further schooling, Tilak said:

In England, in order to do independent work, women expect to get higher education and go on to work, like men, as lawyers, doctors, editors and clerks. It's not at all my case that our women shouldn't do such independent work and get out of their status as slaves to their men. But this is something that will take a hundred years or a thousand . . . We haven't a doubt that in 2-3 or 5-10 centuries, our women will be independent and pursue their own professions or businesses, emerge from the slavery of marriage to get time for themselves, and with both men and women educated and industrious, our nation will be prosperous and make progress. Our only question is: What do we do to improve the present condition of our women and what education is best for that?

Still, anchoring himself in contemporary societal mores, he noted that 'the in-laws' house is a workshop for a girl's education. Without pulling her out of this workshop, if she can be given useful and liberal education in consonance with her own *dharma* (implying a set of principles here rather than faith), we want that education. If such an arrangement is made and some girl wants western education, it will be good to provide it to her. But the first arrangement cannot be sacrificed for the second.'[46]

Though maintaining he was not against secondary school female education, Tilak was here being largely, if not entirely, status quoist; he was almost baulking at the changes being suggested. At the same time, he had got his daughter enrolled in the same school and was allowing her to pursue education. Did this indicate a mismatch between speech and conduct? His critics certainly thought him duplicitous.[47]

Yet he was absolutely clear that what he was seeking was the political unity of the people. For him, social reforms were secondary, and political freedom came first. In a piece in 1886 headlined 'What comes first? Political or social?' he had set out unambiguously that the 'petty-minded British . . . did not like the political pursuits of the Indian people' for obvious reasons and lectured the Indians constantly on the need to remove social ills in their country. But 'there was no need to lay down lives for social reforms; once political improvements started happening, social reform would automatically take place, sometimes in lockstep with political reform and sometimes just a few steps behind.'[48] Once independence from the Raj was achieved, all other changes could be made. To win independence, political action was a must, and for that action to be effectual, the majority of the country's population needed to put up a united front. Social reform was not an issue that united society, it divided it into at least two separate camps, if not more than two owing to small and sometimes subtle yet significant differences between groups largely in agreement over most matters.

He was also extremely transparently eyeing a leadership role in Indian society, which was evident from his actions in the field of education and his anger at not being able to have the final say in affairs of the Deccan Education Society, in his involvement from 1888–1889 onwards with the Indian National Congress, in his advocacy for a native province to the extent of spending a term in prison, and his mobilization of the Indian mamlatdars who were getting the rough end of the stick in the Crawford scandal.

By opposing most of the drastic social changes proposed by the reformist class, Tilak demonstrated he was of the same wavelength as the majority of the indigenous population; in sending his daughter to Poona's high school for girls, he put into practice his individual beliefs, not worrying about the opprobrium he might attract because he had plenty of confidence in his own personal magnetism and ability to win over people; and in making suitably reformist noises, he also indicated to that faction that he represented their strand of thinking adequately enough for them to accept and embrace his own primary goal of freedom first.

Tilak wanted to be all things to all people, and in time, that's exactly what he became—the chief representative of all of them, and the foremost voice for all of them. In short, the Lokmanya, the one chosen and regarded as a leader, not by this camp or that, but by the 'lok' (people) as a whole.

His family life too was fairly settled by now for him to focus more and more on public life. In 1871, he had married the then fifteen-year-old Tapi, whose family, like his own, hailed from the Konkan. He gave her a new name: Satyabhama. She was fair-complexioned, broad-shouldered, and had a big face and a sharp nose. Within a year of their marriage, Tilak's father died, and the couple came to live with Tilak's uncle Govindrao's family in Poona. At the time of her marriage, Satyabhama was unlettered. Govindrao's sons went to school, however, and in their house, Satyabhama used their textbooks to acquire a preliminary understanding of the Devanagari alphabet. Gradually, and wholly unassisted, she taught herself enough to be able to somehow read her husband's paper, *Kesari*.

Satyabhama was cast in the traditional mould. Quiet, conscientious about her domestic responsibilities and keen that the husband should not be saddled with any familial headaches but be free to concentrate on outside work, she lived the life of a simple homemaker right from the early days of their marriage. From all accounts, the husband and wife got on extremely comfortably, and Tilak's later references to her in his letters from Mandalay prison—his only public expressions of his feelings for her—make it clear that there was between them a genuine love. The late nineteenth century, though, was not a time when husband and wife even spoke to one another in the presence of outsiders, let alone demonstrate any affection. So friends, acquaintances and visitors were not privy to their exchanges. But a few of Tilak's friends and associates who saw Satyabhama fairly regularly in the house recorded their impressions. One of them wrote that Satyabhama's clothes bore the mark of utter simplicity. There was no brocade, no chintz, 'and on the rare occasions she wore silk, it was of the least expensive kind'. Her demeanour was similarly simple. She rarely left home; her conversations were mainly restricted to the husband and family members; and she did all the cooking and cleaning on her own. Unlike many other women of her era, she was not really into listening to a lot of stories from religious texts, and her visits to religious shrines were few and far between.[49] Yet there is no doubt that she was religious-minded in her own way. During the time Tilak taught in the New English School, the family lived in a house in Poona's Narayan Peth. In this locality of Brahmans, plenty of young priests subsisting on *dakshina*, or alms, and food given by neighbours would go around collecting it in the afternoons. Not everyone was welcoming, later recalled Ramkrishna Sane, then a young priest pursuing his education who later went on to become an official in the public works department. If Satyabhama heard their cries from outside, Sane wrote, she would immediately come out on to the verandah, check how many young Brahmans were waiting, and then rush inside and emerge with food for all. Once she had dropped the food into their laps, she would do a humble namaskar to them all. If he made a lot of progress in later years it was thanks in large part to the food she gave him, remembered Sane.[50]

Satyabhama gave birth to their first child in 1880, a girl who was named Krishna and came to be known as Krishna-bai. It was this eldest daughter whom Tilak enrolled in the female high school. Subsequently, a son was born but he died in his infancy and very little is known about him; one more child died very early. In 1883, another boy, Vishwanath, was born, and in 1889 another daughter named Durga, followed by Mathubai (a girl) in 1891 and two more sons Ramachandra (1894) and Shridhar (1896). Thus, Satyabhama bore him eight children in all, six of whom—three boys and three girls—survived into adulthood.

Though mostly calm, 'mother could get short-tempered at times. But because our father too had a short fuse, she would curb her own anger', wrote the eldest daughter later.[51]

In the female high school Krishnabai studied in, the girls were taught Level 1 of English when they reached Class 4 with Marathi as the primary language of instruction. When she reached Class 4, Tilak met her school administrators and arranged for her to skip the English Level 1 classes and study mathematics or Sanskrit instead during those periods. This, Krishnabai reminisced afterwards, was because girls were usually married by the age of twelve in those days, and if they were taught in both Marathi and English, the perception was that many ended up not knowing either of the languages really well. Tilak wanted the eldest daughter to get a good grip on Marathi before she started on English and told her school instructors so. 'For that, many in my school would call him eccentric and would criticize him,' the daughter recalled later.[52]

When Krishnabai cleared her final-year exams at the female high school, Agarkar congratulated her publicly in his paper *Sudharak*, as much to bruise the ego of her traditionalist father as to convey his genuine wishes.[53]

Krishnabai and the eldest son Vishwanath, who read up to Class 3 (English) at home and was then enrolled in the New English School, had taken to reading. The elder daughter in particular read not only *Kesari* that her father edited but also Agarkar's *Sudharak*, mostly agreeing with the latter publication which advocated female emancipation. But Tilak did not permit the children to read plays and novels. 'If he saw us with a book of plays in our hands, he would take it away and scold us, saying little children should not be reading plays,' said the daughter.[54] At the same time, Tilak did not stint on providing information and knowledge inputs to his children, whether it was about worldly matters or mythological. Often in Indian homes, it was the mother who read the sacred texts to children, but there is no record of Satyabhama doing that. Instead, it was Tilak, according to his youngest daughter Mathubai, who told all the children stories from the Mahabharata and also quoted the Manusmruti to them. 'He would get completely absorbed in the narration of the stories,' Mathubai said later.[55] According to Tilak's amanuensis A.V. Kulkarni, Mathubai in fact had been taught the 'Savitri-geet, Rukmini-geet, Sita-geet', among other things, and Tilak had got her to read several stories from the Ramayana and Mahabharata.[56]

Subsequently, the Tilak family moved to Sardar Vinchurkar's Wada in Poona and from there to Gaikwad Wada in the year 1905. There, Tilak constructed the still-primitive kitchen the way Satyabhama wanted it to be, and specially put up a tulsi plant in the courtyard. But in their other home, a weekend or summer retreat of sorts, which they bought afterwards on top of Sinhagad Fort in the vicinity of Poona, Satyabhama did not have it easy. Drinking water was not readily available there. Recollecting her travails, one of Satyabhama's sons wrote that she would have to walk 200 metres to bring drinking water from there two or three times a day.[57] She was clear that that duty fell on her, and not on anyone else.

* * *

Tilak was very happy with the outcome of his campaign against Pandita Ramabai. So, it was with a sense of confidence that he framed his response to the Age of Consent law proposed by the British government in 1890. The law generated a controversy bigger than that over the lives of Rukhmabai and Ramabai, and it enabled Tilak to further establish his credentials as the spokesperson for the vast majority of the Hindu community.

Behramji Merwanji Malbari, the Parsi editor and reformist, had initiated in 1884 a campaign for an end to early marriage by publishing two sets of notes, titled Infant Marriage in India and Enforced Widowhood in India. When he petitioned the then viceroy, Lord

Ripon, to enact a law prohibiting early marriage, Ripon had made what one scholar called a 'qualified refusal', saying his policy was to uphold 'customs [that] are sanctioned by the general opinion of the society in which they prevail' but he could take a fresh look at the policy if and when 'the sentiment and opinion of the community' was in favour of such a law.[58]

Malbari reinvigorated his campaign in 1890 after the death the previous year of an eleven-year-old girl, Phulmani Bai of Calcutta, from injuries sustained during sexual intercourse with her husband Hari Mohan Maithi. The husband was tried for rape but was acquitted by the sessions court on the grounds that, apart from the fact that the law did not recognize marital rape, the girl was eleven years old, and the age of consent was ten, fixed through the Criminal Law Amendment Act of 1860. Maithi was subsequently held guilty under Section 338 of the Indian Penal Code for 'causing grievous hurt by act endangering life' and sentenced to one year's rigorous imprisonment, which Malbari called a 'predictable' and mild punishment.[59]

The Parsi editor travelled to London towards the end of the decade and met the Secretary of State for India, Viscount Cross, to push for legislation in this regard. Cross ordered the viceroy to publish a draft bill and solicit public opinion on the subject. The bill envisaged increasing the minimum age for sexual intercourse for girls from ten years to twelve. Any flouting of this rule would be a penal offence and specifically invite the charge of rape under the Indian Penal Code. The bill sought to introduce two more provisions: freedom for a girl if married as an infant, to dissolve the marriage on becoming a major, and a legal prohibition for men to move court for restitution of conjugal rights if a girl were married early (as in Rukhmabai's case) and didn't want to go to her husband afterwards.

Tilak was extremely upset with Malbari for nudging the London government over Hindu social and religious customs. He complained bitterly that the Parsi editor had gone to England ostensibly to restore his health but had instead been busy lobbying there for legislative meddling. Tilak felt Malbari had no business to poke his nose into Hindu affairs to such an extent. The Hindus were grateful to him for having raised awareness on the issue from 1884 onwards, but to campaign so aggressively for a law was going too far, he said. Once again Tilak deployed his weapon of choice, satire, making a reference to the Parsi man's heavily accented Marathi. 'Saara deshbhar bom karun sorla [Raised a big hue and cry all across the country]', Tilak wrote, deliberately bringing in the word 'bom' which Parsis often used for loud noise, and 'sorla' in place of the correct Marathi usage 'sodla' to indicate their amusing twist of the tongue. When the 'bom' didn't work in India at all, Malbari had left for London to work his wiles, Tilak alleged.[60]

Early marriages were bad, Tilak agreed. But 'education and not legislation' was the answer, he insisted. A law would make a foreign government the arbiter on social and religious customs, demolishing the religious liberty of a people who had already lost their political liberty. Tilak made two legalistic suggestions if at all the bill were to be converted into law. The first was to make attainment of puberty the legal age for the consummation of marriage, not twelve years, which he termed as arbitrary. This was in keeping with what the orthodox Brahman shastris were arguing: they quoted the religious texts as saying a marriage should be consummated within sixteen days of the bride's reaching puberty, and if this happened before a girl turned twelve and she were not married under the new legislative framework, the rule of the shastras would stand violated. Tilak's second suggestion was to apply the legislation only to those who backed it. Once the reform-minded started following the new rules and education led to awareness, the people would follow suit, he said.[61]

Moreover, Tilak sensed the widespread opposition to the bill from within the Hindu community and believed that if a campaign were to be inaugurated against it, a great deal of grassroots-level mobilization was possible.

Giving the way social, cultural and faith-based issues had been coming to the fore in the past few years, he had already been preparing to position himself as the prime upholder of tradition and the Hindu ethos. Just before Malbari's travel to London, Tilak had headed to the United Provinces in the North for a symbolic dip in the Ganga.

The British authorities had begun to keep a close watch on Tilak by this time. A police inspector, Mr Brewin, from the Bombay government's 'political and secret department' sent this despatch to his bosses:

Up to this period of his life, Tilak paid little attention to the customs of caste. Knowing, however, that he would want the support of all orthodox Brahmans in the struggle he was about to engage in, he determined to conform to all his caste usages, so that it might not be alleged against him that he was unfit to champion their cause. With this object in mind, he proceeded to Allahabad and performed the ceremony of shaving his moustache and bathing in the Ganges. Having thus conformed to what he had long neglected, he returned to Poona and prepared for the struggle.[62]

The Australian scholar Richard Cashman accurately notes that for Tilak, religion was about practice and not so much about sentiment. His approach differed significantly from Gandhi's *bhakti* or devotion in this respect.[63] The dip in the holy waters, for the man who loved to swim, was the first public display of praxis philosophy.

A series of meetings were held by various Hindu groups across the Bombay Presidency and across British-ruled India to protest against the Age of Consent bill, and Tilak's *Kesari* gave them wide publicity. The reformist faction too held its own meetings, but the crowds at the traditionalist Hindus' meets were considerably bigger. For example, a meeting at the Tulsibaug in Poona organized by the orthodox section in October 1890 attracted a crowd of 5000, while the pro-law group's gatherings could muster not more than 200 at the most.[64]

Tilak especially promoted the public meeting held at Tulsibaug in Poona. Several of his emerging lieutenants were among the organizers. One was Wasudeo Ganesh Joshi, affectionately called Wasu-*kaka* Joshi. Born in a rich moneylender's family from Satara, he was a successful businessman. He had been the manager of the Chitrashala Press which had originally published Vishnushastri Chiplunkar's *Nibandhamala*, and in subsequent years, he assisted Tilak in publishing his papers. Another was Kashinath Nilkanth Khasgiwale. He came from a fief-holding family and was therefore called a sardar. He sold horses and was a member of the Poona Cow Protection Society. Khasgiwale was also the patron of one of the most militantly orthodox members of the Hindu party, Balwant Ramchandra Natu aka Balasaheb Natu. Natu, who too was among the Tulsibaug meet's organizers, vehemently opposed the slightest tweaking of Hindu religious practices, funded pilgrims' visits to Kashi, advocated for cow protection groups and generally prided himself on being ultra-orthodox. His younger brother Ramchandra Natu had set up a gymnasium to teach Hindu youngsters riding and fencing, and among the gym's members were the Chapekar brothers who'd later assassinate British officials. The ultra-conservative Balasaheb Natu was not exactly one of Tilak's lieutenants, unlike Joshi, Khasgiwale and some others, but Tilak didn't mind an association with him at this point in time at all.[65]

To coincide with the Tulsibaug meeting, Tilak suddenly floated eight of his own draft proposals. They were: 1) no girl should be married till she turns sixteen years old; 2) no boy should be married before he is twenty years of age; 3) men aged over forty should be legally barred from marrying; 4) if at all men over forty wanted to marry, they'd have to marry a widow; 5) prohibit consumption of liquor (a habit Indians believed they had ingrained owing to British influence); 6) end the practice of dowry; 7) give one-tenth of your income to public interest initiatives; and 8) no widow should be made to cut off her hair.[66]

Tilak's idea in making these proposals, which went well beyond the demands of the proposed bill, was evidently to checkmate the reformers. And while placing them for consideration, he was not demanding they be made legally enforceable for all of society. He said those in favour of reforms in Hindu society should adopt these measures voluntarily, commit to the government in writing that they would stick to them and focus on their implementation. Their initiatives would set a precedent and once they worked, would be an example for the rest of society to follow.

At a meeting held at the Joshi Hall in Poona, Tilak spoke in detail on these proposals, saying he was open to allowing some flexibility such as bringing down the marriageable age for girls from sixteen to fourteen or raising the legal bar for men to marry from age forty to forty-five. What of the *shastric* rule that marriages be consummated within sixteen days of a girl attaining puberty? Tilak suggested a *shanti puja* held at the time of marriage would eliminate all religious obstacles that might arise in this regard. Tilak was a very close reader of the shastras, so it was hard even for the orthodox to challenge him on dharmic injunctions and ways to get around them. If his draft proposals were accepted by the progressives, it would actually end the whole debate over the Age of Consent bill, he claimed.

The meeting at which he made these remarks was of noted citizens of Poona and not just of the conservatives. M.G. Ranade was slated to speak after Tilak. He said, 'The controversy we're seeing isn't new. Just as Mr. Tilak has been thinking over the matter for the past 4-5 years, so have some people done 6-7 years ago in places like Gujarat and Madras. Some groups there accepted proposals similar to the ones put forward by Tilak, but after some time, their resolve to implement them weakened, and the groups came apart . . . We too have been trying to get signatures along these lines for the past one-and-a-half years. From the numbers we've got, I feel there will be very few who will sign up to Tilak's proposals.'[67]

Tilak had put Ranade, the elder statesman of sorts in Poona, on the defensive.

Another meeting addressed by Tilak in Poona was large, reported the Bombay political department's officials. It was called for 'adopting a petition to government asking them not to interfere with the long-established habits and customs of the Brahmins by legislation'. On this occasion, Tilak 'publicly denounced Mr Malbari's suggestions as absurd and as involving an interference with the Hindu religion,' the Raj's reporter recorded.[68] At what the *Deccan Herald* described as a 'monster meeting' held outside Poona's iconic Peshwai monument, the Shaniwar Wada, Tilak protested that the Raj was making a departure from its avowed policy of 1858 that it would not intrude into faith-based issues and added that it was 'a question of great constitutional importance whether the promises of the Queen-Empress are to be violated for the purpose of forcing reform in purely domestic matters on millions of unwilling people'.[69]

When the reformist camp called a meeting on 25 February 1891, violence broke out. Massive crowds began to push in at the entrance to the venue, Krida Bhuvan in Poona, at the appointed hour, and once a crowd of over a thousand people had gotten in, there was complete chaos: chairs were thrown around and uprooted, and lanterns were broken. The reformers had to take shelter in a house nearby, which was part of the same premises and where proceedings of the meeting were within earshot, and lock themselves in. Interestingly, Tilak and his aide Mahadev Ballal Namjoshi had been sitting in the same house all along. 'The police, not keeping order, allowed the mob to come in, and some supporters of the Bill were assaulted,' wrote *Times of India*. 'The house was besieged, and stones and earth thrown into it. It was then closed.' The British-run *Times* alleged that Tilak had done nothing to stop the violence despite an appeal from the police, suggesting the attack had taken place at Tilak's behest. 'After a while a police jemadar came in and told Mr. Tilak to tell the mob to disperse,' the paper reported, noting that 'Mr. Tilak said nothing. The jemadar came in again with Mr. Abasaheb Paranjpye [a maths scholar and educationist and one of Pune's esteemed residents], saying the mob would disperse if Mr. Tilak told them. Mr. Tilak said, 'Why should I take the responsibility?' All this while the mob was shouting for Mr. Tilak. Things were in this state, when the District Superintendent of Police, Major Macpherson, came there and dispersed the mob in five minutes.'[70]

Tilak's solicitors sent a letter to the British-run newspaper, saying its description of the meeting 'conveys a very false impression as to what took place' at the Poona meeting, and 'was calculated to injure' Tilak's reputation. They explained that 'Mr. Tilak had no connection whatever with the mob or the mobbing that took place. It is true that the police jemedar (jamadar or officer) asked him to tell the mob to disperse, but Mr. Tilak told the jemedar that he was in no way responsible for the action of the mob, and that he was as powerless as any other person to disperse the mob, and by interfering and undertaking upon himself the duties of the police he would only expose himself to great risk of personal injury. Mr. Tilak at the time thought the request made to him to disperse the mob was part of a trick on the part of someone to make him appear responsible for the riotous proceedings.'[71]

Gokhale argued in the *Sudharak* that Tilak couldn't evade responsibility altogether. He wrote:

Mr Tilak's presence in Mr. Kelkar's house during the time of the meeting was a very unfortunate incident and betokened a lamentable error of judgment on that gentleman's part, [since] Mr. Tilak is the leader of that section of the Poona people who have taken up an attitude of uncompromising hostility to the Scoble Bill. He had

become recently a kind of demigod to the orthodox community of
this place, and we think he knows this. He should have seen that his
presence in the Krida Bhuvan, even as a mere unsympathetic spectator
of the meeting, was sure to encourage the mob in its unsympathetic
(approach) toward the meeting.[72]

Gokhale's description of Tilak as 'leader' and 'demigod of the orthodox'
was meant as criticism, but it might well have come as music to the
ears of Tilak's band of followers which, according to Gokhale's own
statement, was growing.

Tilak's anti-legislation campaign picked up momentum and,
going beyond the borders of the Bombay Presidency, carried itself
across Bengal and Madras as well. When one of the Raj's Indian Civil
Service administrators, Romesh Chunder Dutt of Bengal, echoed the
traditionalist view that the law would 'interfere with religion and create
deep discontent among the people of India', there was much surprise
in the British bureaucracy. Two reformers from Maharashtra, R.G.
Bhandarkar and K.T. Telang, both Sanskrit scholars in their own right,
contested Dutt's claim and asserted the law would in no way violate
Hindu scriptures. Tilak said he 'could not understand' their position.
'Every writer of note on Hindoo law', whether it was 'Raghunandana,
Kamalakar, Vijnaneshwar, Anantdev and a host of other equally
well-known authorities' had 'laid down in explicit terms that the first
attainment of 'a certain well-known physical condition' is the proper
period . . . for the consummation of marriage', he argued. Telang had
quoted the shastras and specifically Manu, the ancient Hindu lawgiver,
in support of legislative intervention. Citing Manu's line that 'a sovereign
who conquers a country should make authoritative the lawful customs of
the inhabitants', Telang had suggested the word 'lawful' meant customs
'the conqueror thinks to be worthy of adoption'. Tilak questioned this
interpretation and cited other *smriti* texts. Devala, he said, 'lays down
that a conqueror should give legislative effect to what the subjects
consider as their custom, for, says he, it is the law of the land'. Brihaspati
too 'directs that the king should recognize the subjects' customs as they
are, or else it creates discontent'. According to Tilak, Manu too meant
it the same way when he used the word 'lawful', and 'not in the sense in
which Mr. Telang understands the word'. Bringing in his favourite note

of sarcasm, Tilak said there were 'a thousand other places where' Telang and Bhandarkar could 'show the skill of their argument. The subject of Dharma Shastra is not one of them. You are not told to find new discoveries in Dharma Shastra, and you are not asked to bring 'good tidings' (a reference to the activities of Christian missionaries) out of them. If you don't know how to interpret the shastras correctly, then at least try to remain silent.' The 1858 proclamation of zero meddling in people's faith was 'in strict keeping with that suggested by Manu and other sacred writers on Hindu law', Tilak concluded.[73]

What if someone didn't have faith in the shastras? That was fine, Tilak said, but that was no reason to bring in a law and to not show respect to the feelings of others. 'Mr. Telang probably knows,' he pointed out, 'that the (Indian) National Congress does not hold its sittings on Sundays in deference to the feelings of Christian delegates, though we Hindus may have no faith in it, nay, might regard it almost ridiculous.'[74]

Despite the massive opposition campaign, the Raj pressed ahead with the legislation, and the bill on the Age of Consent was passed by the Viceroy's Council on 19 March 1891. The law member (minister) of the Council, Andrew R. Scoble, who tabled the bill, noted that he would rather 'be wrong with Professor Bhandarkar, Mr. Justice Telang and Diwan Bahadur Raghunath Rao, than be right with Pandit Sasadhar and Professor Tilak'.

Tilak nevertheless found the campaign hugely beneficial to him. He had shored up his popularity among the various sects in the Hindu community, endeared himself to millions of the devout, impressed the wider Hindu community, including those who disagreed with him, with this thorough knowledge of the sacred texts, and put up a spirited fight against the British government. He had come to be increasingly recognized as someone who could be trusted to resist the Raj on Indian terms and without showing the slightest willingness to cede ground to a foreign establishment.

He also got a golden opportunity during this nationwide controversy to show the reformers in a very poor light. Gopalrao Joshee, the husband of Anandibai Joshee, India's first woman doctor, was one of Poona's famous eccentrics. He loved to put people in a spot by occasionally playing tricks. Soon after the Age of Consent law was passed, he organized a lecture by a clergy member, Reverend Luke Rivington,

at a Christian missionary home run in the city known as the Panch
Howd Mission. Almost all of Poona's eminences were invited, and fifty
people turned up, including Tilak, Ranade, Gokhale, the historian V.K.
Rajwade, the dramatist Govind Ballal Deval, Tilak's aides Wasu-kaka
Joshi and Vasudeo Kelkar and others. After the lecture, the invitees were
taken to an area where refreshments were served. Tilak and many others
took tea and biscuits there before they left the missionary home.

The next day, the conservative *Poona Vaibhav* published, thanks to
their 'source', the inviter Gopalrao Joshee himself, a list of those who had
partaken of tea and biscuits. Why had it done it? It sounds astonishing
and atrocious today, but it was, at the time, a journalistic mini scoop
of sorts. There was an orthodox Hindu injunction against consuming
anything at a Mission Home. The conservatives raised howls of protest,
meetings were held across Poona, and some of them approached the
Shankaracharya, one of the contemporary Hindu lawmakers, to get a
ruling against the so-called violators of shastras. Tilak too came under
a fierce attack. For the orthodox wing, it was especially odd that he
should have committed such a 'wrong'. Hadn't he just set himself up as
a champion of the Hindu cause? The hardliner Balasaheb Natu, who
had accepted Tilak's leadership during the Age of Consent row, now
openly called for his excommunication. The overall consensus among
conservatives was that the 'violators' should be socially boycotted.[75] The
priesthood refused to perform basic pujas and rites at Tilak's home,
forcing him to call in on one occasion pundits from outside Poona.
Agarkar too hit out at his now nearly estranged friend, labelling Tilak
as 'neither conservative nor reformist' and likened him to 'a bat hanging
upside down', whose status was 'nowhere'.[76]

Tilak pulled out the Hindu scriptures once again and, citing them,
made a counterstrike. 'There was no sin in taking tea, from anybody,'
he declared defiantly.[77] He had no desire to alienate the followers
he had begun to gather, though. To placate them, he was willing to
go through the minor penance ceremony that the Hindu shastris
wanted the 'violators' to go through to avoid excommunication. It
involved the giving of *dakshina* or gifts to some Brahman priests. He
underwent the so-called penance. Surprisingly, the avowed reformist
M.G. Ranade too went through the ceremony, without a murmur
of protest, and faced a wave of criticism from those who thought he

had, with that single act of his, 'crushed the social reform movement.' Ranade's wife Ramabai too felt he had made a big mistake and confessed later to having entertained 'bitter thoughts' for a while about the husband on his kowtowing to the priests.[78] Agarkar, a bigger radical than Ranade, also messed things up for himself. He remarked in his paper *Sudharak* that Tilak didn't mind taking tea from the hands of a Mohammedan and a Parsi mess man when he was at the railway station. Since this was made in the nature of an accusation, it went down quite badly as it revealed that the so-called progressives were not immune to the orthodox customs and prejudices they were blaming the conservatives for. What exactly was Agarkar doing targeting Tilak for consuming tea given to him by members of other faiths—considered unacceptable only by the orthodox—except undermining a liberal outlook and extending the principle of untouchability to people of other religions? Tilak of course had no qualms about stoutly denying Agarkar's statement and threatened to sue, forcing Agarkar to publish an apology.[79]

For Tilak, the whole preposterous storm-in-a-teacup worked out positively. He had held his ground even against the shastris and the Shankaracharya on a matter he thought fit and had agreed to the small penance only after asserting he had done no wrong. The reformists, on the other hand, and Ranade in particular, whom Tilak was evidently seeking to supplant as the No. 1 social eminence of Poona, were seen to have capitulated all too easily to the religious hardliners and to not practise what they were preaching. In the public perception, they became identified as people with double standards, while Tilak stood out as a man with a spine.

Moreover, the direction in which Tilak was taking his social and cultural agitations was incredibly important because it ultimately determined the future of the Indian freedom movement.

From the beginning, there were two broad currents among the Indians on the idea of political advancement. One was represented by Ranade and later by his protégé, Gokhale. Ranade believed in the innate goodness of the British people and believed that 'in God's providence Britain had been entrusted with a great mission in India'. He stated that 'the sole rationale of British rule in India is its capacity and its providential purpose of fostering the political education of the country on the largest scale in civil and public activities'. At the worst of times, writes his biographer, he stuck to his conviction that 'the good sense and innate justice of the British character would acknowledge the rightness of India's claims.'[80] Echoing his views, Gokhale wrote, 'I have the profoundest faith in the honour of the British Nation, and if only we keep it well informed of all that passes here, I am persuaded all cause of complaint will sooner or later be removed.'[81]

When the Indian National Congress was formed, this was the dominant strain of Indian political thought. All constitutional advances in India were supposed to happen in close cooperation with the British authorities, and the nature of communication with the Raj government was not merely amicable but routinely deferential. This group, comprising the English-educated elite who looked up to the mores and practices of the foreign rulers, came to be known as the Moderates. Their principal method of working with the British government was to make polite written representations and earnest requests and to generally eschew the path of agitation. If at all an agitation was launched, it was with the attempt to put pressure on the government no doubt, but it was hardly ever adversarial in nature, certainly not so in the first two decades of the Congress.

Tilak represented a sharply contrasting outlook. As early as 1881, the year in which he became editor of the *Mahratta*, he had spoken of self-rule. That very year, the Sarvajanik Sabha had in its journal published a piece, unsigned but most probably written by Ranade, urging the people of Poona to voluntarily commit to increasing the age at which they married off their children. The view had found echoes in Britain, with some Englishmen insisting on framing a law in this regard. Tilak had opposed these voices and suggested how Indians could work towards self-government in the wake of these demands. 'If we want that we should be proficient in the art of self-government,' he noted, 'the first qualification we should show is the ability to manage our own business among ourselves, and particularly that business which will be better regulated by ourselves than by the passing of an act or a resolution . . . Let our people, therefore, form associations, frame rules and restraints for themselves and do all they can to check the evils of this evil custom.'[82] This was an opening declaration of sorts, almost a decade before the Age of Consent controversy ballooned, that a foreign power should not thrust social and religious laws on Indians but leave it to them to regulate their customs. Later, implicating the pro-reformists almost as much as the Raj, Tilak highlighted the apparent absurdity of foreigners dictating laws, stating that 'in English society many evil cases of divorce come before the court. On the basis of these, Professor Jinsiwale openly stated that the marriage system of the English people must be very faulty. For this statement Professor Jinsiwale was very much criticized by those very people (the reformers), yet they make a statement condemning our entire country because of a few examples of rape committed on small girls, and they ask us to apply to the government to change the law. What better proof is there of our emasculation?'[83]

Tilak saw the Raj as intrinsically an abomination, its officials as mean, crooked, corrupt and casually cruel, and its colonial methods of ruling over the Indians as fundamentally unjust, tyrannical and exploitative. At every stage he was encountering the Raj—whether in the matter of the Crawford corruption scandal or the matter of Indian societal customs—and finding it hostile and impervious to what he saw as justice. He was not for imploring the Raj and its bureaucracy. He was for a firm push against it. As changing times brought in officials like the patronizing Lord Harris, who took over as governor of Bombay in 1890 after the relatively genial Lord Reay, and Lord Dufferin (after Lord Ripon, neutralizer of his predecessor Lytton's press-gagging legislation) who, as viceroy at the time of the Congress's birth, called it a 'microscopic minority',[84] Tilak advocated a line of resistance as against one of least resistance offered by the Moderates. Unlike the Moderates, who felt gradual changes were welcome, Tilak wanted to accelerate the pace of political transformation. The Moderates sought allowances and indulgences; Tilak spoke of rights. He embraced, endorsed, and took the path of agitation. And his conviction was that requests and 'prayers' made in written representations would not take the Indian people far. What they needed was a form of protest. Powerful and robust protest, so that the Raj could feel the heat. The Western-educated elite were, in his view, ineffectual in that they, with their undying faith in the British people and their system, elicited condescending responses from the likes of Viceroy Dufferin. The power of the masses had to be mobilized for any substantive and meaningful political change to materialize. Tilak realized that both the Congress and the educated elite needed the ordinary people to be solidly behind them if their work was to produce results. Demands to the British government must go not just from Congress conclaves but from 'every province, district, city, in fact from every village', he said. Further, it was 'foolish for the educated people' of India', he made plain, 'to consider themselves to be a class apart from the people. They would have to 'sink or swim with the people'.[85]

Tilak was mobilizing the people with his protests. Soon, he would find more productive means of getting them together and in the process pose a serious challenge to the Moderate wing within the Congress.

Chapter 7

One Riot, Two Festivals

Much heartened by the response he got during the Age of Consent controversy, Tilak realized acutely the need to build on it. Fortunately for him, the matter of earning a livelihood had been settled to his satisfaction within a year or two after his exit from the Deccan Education Society in 1890. To be economically self-sufficient, Tilak had started a law class in Poona, and it had attracted a good amount of students who wished to appear for the high court pleader's exams. Tilak taught law himself in his by-now widely discussed de-personalized style, gazing down at the ground while addressing his students, momentarily looking up if a student asked him a question and then proceeding once again to contemplate the floor while coming up with an answer. Despite the style, students found his lectures absorbing, and on one occasion, the jurist M.G. Ranade quietly slipped into his class and sat at the back, taking in Tilak's exposition of Hindu law, and at the end of the lecture praised him for his command of the subject. Head securely down, Tilak had missed Ranade's presence in the class all through.

Tilak had also started, along with a friend, a ginning factory in Latur, which was then part of the Nizam-ruled Hyderabad state, and it had taken off steadily, with the friend playing a hands-on role.[1]

Tilak was obsessed with public life, and with these two sources of income fixed, he felt he could focus on it the way he wanted. The magnitude of the back-to-back Rukhmabai, Ramabai and early marriage legislation rows had stirred in his mind the idea of giving his social and cultural work more of a mass character. He saw religion as a solid ground on which to base his social, cultural and political agenda.

Tilak had already created a positive impression in the minds of Hindus with his sound knowledge of the shastras. With his massive interest in the ancient texts and penchant for scholarship, he now moved to establish himself as an authority on these. Spurred by Lord Krishna's statement in the Mahabharata that he was 'the Margashirsha of the months', Tilak had started thinking about whether the Vedas, Hinduism's oldest texts, could be dated accurately by a close examination of what lay within these texts. Professor Friedrich Max Müller, the German Indologist, had done his own study on the subject and said in the early 1880s that 'for the study of man, or if you like, for a study of Aryan humanity, there is nothing in the world equal in importance with' the Vedas.[2] Max Müller had said the Vedas could be dated back to 1200 BC. Tilak, referring to what he termed as astronomical data in the texts, came to the conclusion that 'the traditions recorded in the Rigveda unmistakably point to a period *not later* [italics Tilak's own] than 4000 B.C., when the vernal equinox was in Orion, or, in other words, when the Dog-star (or the Dog as we have it in the Rigveda) commenced the equinoctial year'.[3] His findings were published as his first book, *Orion: Or Researches into the Antiquity of the Vedas*, in 1893, and while there was much praise, there was much criticism as well, with several scholars disputing his discoveries. On the whole, however, his ambition was applauded, and so was his approach which relied on research and deduction, the sole methods, in the absence of later scientific and technological innovations, for making informed guesses about ancient calendars.[4] He later wrote a sequel to the book, which we will look at in a subsequent chapter.

What helped to crystallize Tilak's thinking on the use of religion for popular mobilization was the explosion of communal violence, first in Gujarat and then in Bombay, Poona and towns across the Deccan.

In the last week of July 1893, Muslims on their way to a riverbank to carry out immersions of *tazias* (images of tombs of Prophet Muhammad's martyred grandsons) on the occasion of Muharram rioted in the village of Veraval in Prabhas Patan in Kathiawar, which was part of the princely state of Junagadh. The Hindus had originally opposed the spot, Kharijal, which the Muslims wanted for the immersion, but the local British police had overruled Hindu objections and granted permission. According to wire reports later published by the Anglo–Indian dailies, the Muslims were aware that the water body lay outside the town and knew the height of the town gates. Yet, the pro-British wire correspondents reported, 'they intentionally made their tazias this time higher than usual'. The ruler of Junagadh was a Muslim, and 'for preserving peace', his durbar asked the local administration to make special arrangements 'by digging under the gates'. Once they had passed outside the town gates, the Muslims, who had assembled in big numbers, 'left the road marked out for them, and broke through the police cordon'. When the superintendent of police, who was present at the spot, tried to intervene, he was 'pelted with stones' even as the crowds 'rushed suddenly with the *tazias* to the road leading to the Hindoos' sacred place of Dehotsarg'. There, they 'entered the Hindoo temples and struck the monks therein with lathis and hatchets. They then polluted and set fire to these temples' and 'poured kerosine oil on some monks and burned them alive'. Eleven Hindus were killed and twenty wounded; and two Muslims sustained injuries, but the authorities said the community had 'not yet produced them before the police'. 'This was totally an unprovoked attack,' the Ango–Indian papers reported, 'though not altogether unexpected as there existed ill-feeling between the Mahomedans and Hindus for the last two years'. The local doctor, his assistant, a vaccinator and a jailor, who were all proceeding to carry out an inquest, were also killed on the way.[5]

Junagadh, though a principality, was one of many within the Bombay Presidency. In fact, the Bombay Presidency was so big, going up to Sindh in the north and the southern parts of the Deccan on the other side, that more than 50 per cent of India's princely states at this point in time were located within it.[6] Following the riot in Prabhas Patan, the Gujarati Hindus of Bombay held a series of meetings to condemn the violence and put together a fund for the assistance of those affected. Muslims in the city held their meetings and set up a committee to coordinate help for those from the community who had been injured and to assist those who faced criminal charges in court.

In the afternoon of 11 August, the violence reached Bombay. At 1 p.m., a large number of Muslims emerged from their Friday prayers at the Juma Masjid, the chief mosque in the city, and raising cries of 'deen, deen', rushed in the direction of the Hanuman lane, at the entrance to which was a Hanuman temple. When the police tried to stop them, wrote the British-run daily *Bombay Gazette*, 'they used tiles and stones as missiles, injuring several policemen and many Hindus'. Soon the rioting spread across the city, and Hindus were attacked everywhere, on the streets, in the bylanes, and even in the tram cars in the city.[7] The next morning, the Hindus, mainly the Maharashtrian mill workers in the city, retaliated, and the papers reported 'hand-to-hand' fights in some places. To stem the violence, the police had to call in the military, and by the time it was all over, eighty people were dead, 530 hurt and 1505 arrested. The *Gazette* wrote that the riots 'have assumed proportions unparalleled in their magnitude and alarming in their gravity' and 'wholly eclipsed the memory of the serious riots which took place between the Parsees and the Mahomedans in this city in 1851 and 1874'.[8]

Initial reports pointed to the rival meetings held by the Hindu and Muslim groups in the city over the Patan incidents as the reason for the rioting. Some reports also said the Muslims had objected to Hindus playing music outside the Juma Masjid some days before the violence broke out, but the British-run *Gazette* said there was no basis to this accusation as no Hindu procession with music had gone past the Masjid in recent times.[9]

Soon, the acting police commissioner of Bombay, R.H. Vincent, blamed the cow protection groups of Bombay for the violence. The first such group had been founded in 1887. Led by the Parsi mill owner Dinshaw Petit, it had mostly Gujaratis as its members. A second organization was set up in 1893, and it was headed by Lakhmidas Khimji, a Gujarati mill owner. Vincent's statement was supported by the city's municipal chief, H. Acworth, and in his report to London at the end of August 1893, the Bombay governor Harris wrote that 'undoubtedly the Mahomedans have been annoyed' by the work of the cow protection societies.[10]

Tilak aggressively countered the British government's allegation that the cow protection groups had created conditions for an outbreak of violence. In an editorial in the *Kesari*, he called the theory 'meaningless' and an 'excuse' for the government's 'overall lack to preparedness' to tackle the situation.[11] Tilak suggested that cow slaughter and the sensitivities of Hindus and Muslims on the issue might have resulted in riots in India's northern parts, but the Raj was needlessly extending the parallel to the Deccan and the south. He wrote:

We haven't heard anywhere that the Muslims have been robbed of their food ever since the agitation for cow protection began . . . In north Hindustan, the Muslims may be dominant in many parts, but in our regions, that has never been the case. The history of Maharashtra before the arrival of the British shows how the Marathas had acquired a *sanad* (legal authority) for cow protection from the *badshah* of Delhi himself. If such an arrangement was in place between Hindus and Muslims during Muslim rule, then why the Muslims should be provoked into attacking Hindus here on the issue of cow protection today is beyond us.[12]

Despite what it was saying in public and in its public reports, the Bombay government conceded in a secret despatch to the Secretary of State of India that the cow protection groups hadn't led to the flare-up. The despatch referred also to the previous Muslim-Parsi riots of 1873 and stated, 'On both occasions (1873 and 1893), the first resort to violence must be laid at the door of the Mohammedan community, and on both occasions, the scene of outbreak was the neighbourhood of the Jama Masjid . . . Mr. Vincent (police commissioner) lays the blame primarily at the door of the cow-protection societies in Bombay and elsewhere . . . but it is to be observed that while the cow-protection movement has undoubtedly been pushed of late with growing vigour, the movement itself is not a new one. We hesitate to adopt the opinion that the cow-protection movement is the principal cause of these riots.'[13]

Tilak was hard on the Muslims in his own analysis of the violence. He commented:

Many argue that the meetings held by Hindus in Mumbai to raise funds for victims of the Prabhas Patan riots made the Muslims angry. I fail to understand this argument. The Hindus had, by organizing meetings, not resolved to rush towards or raid or attack the Muslims. It is everyone's duty to help the victims and the shelterless, and with this idea in mind, the Gujaratis of Mumbai had held meetings so that assistance could go out to the Prabhas Patan sufferers. If the Muslims are incensed by such meetings, the blame lies squarely with them. The Hindus had done no wrong by holding the meetings, and so

long as their conduct was lawful, the Muslims had no reason to feel
bad about it. The Muslims too had organized meetings to help their
co-religionists [in Prabhas Patan] and collected a lot of subscriptions.
So if, after both sides had held their rival meetings, the Muslims
mounted an attack on the Hindus, then it is right to cast all the blame
on the Muslims alone. It's truly baffling that Muslims should attack
the Hindus deliberately and without any reason.[14]

Tilak accused the British government in both *Kesari* and *Mahratta* of
purposely inciting the Muslims against the Hindus, noting that:

> The Muslims think the government is scared of them and so in case a
> riot breaks out, it will not side with the Hindus. Whether their belief
> is correct or not is not really the question. But the fact that it exists
> is beyond a shadow of doubt, and Lord Harris's refusal to meet [the
> president of one of the cow protection groups] Lakhmidas Khimji
> the other day [after the Mumbai riots] and other such examples
> help to confirm the belief. It's not good for the health of society
> overall that the belief that the government is afraid of a particular
> community and shows it excessive favours should gain ground . . . No
> sane person would like to see enmity between Hindus and Muslims
> and for them to attack each other . . . If the Muslims have grown
> arrogant, then the principal reason for it is the instigation on the part
> of the government . . . If the British government and its officials don't
> encourage the Muslims unnecessarily and out of fear, riots will not
> happen at least in these [Deccani] regions . . . We [in the Deccan]
> have never lived by the sufferance of the Muslims . . . The Hindus,
> and at least the Marathas, have not been so emasculated that they
> will take things lying down if they're attacked by rioters . . . Many
> government officials attempt to incite the Muslims, thinking that
> if Hindu-Muslim relations remain bitter, the British government
> would benefit. Senior officials like Lord Harris should stop such
> attempts and if a riot breaks out even after that, they should take
> action against those who initiate the violence.[15]

By stating that 'those who initiate the violence' should face action, Tilak was pointing a finger at the Muslims. Just as aggressively, he absolved the Hindus of all blame:

> If the Hindus of Mumbai are furious, it's for reasons of self-defence, not owing to religious fanaticism and thoughtlessness as in the case of the Muslims. They waited for a day, and when the police failed to protect them, they took it upon themselves to retaliate against the rioters. It is clear the Hindus were not first provoked into violence, and if the government had rendered help in time, no Hindu would have thought of engaging in a fight. Even now, if the government vows that it will protect the Hindus and punish the Muslim rioters for their wanton violence, the Hindus will happily backtrack.[16]

Unlike Tilak, the Moderates of Poona and Bombay blamed neither the government nor the Muslims. They saw the riot in Bombay as 'the unfortunate outburst of passions of the lower-class Hindus and Muslims for which no person or community was entirely to blame'. They stressed the importance of working for 'communal harmony', and leaders of both communities held a joint public rally in Bombay, which was chaired by Governor Harris. The Hindu and Muslim leaders also marched through the city's thoroughfares to put up a united front.[17] Similarly, Harris made an appeal to leaders of both communities on the floor of the Provincial Legislative Council to promote peace.

Tilak noted that there was no point in talking to people who were in no way connected to the rioters. 'There isn't a single representative of Mumbai's Muslims in the Council, and to make the Hindus quiet, you don't need Mr. [Pherozeshah] Mehta, Mr. Jhaverilal or Mr. Setalvad.' Similarly, leaders like the Congress stalwart Badruddin Tayabji and the reform-seeking Social Conference luminary R.M. Sayani couldn't do much by themselves. What Tilak wanted was for the Hindu and Muslim leaders not to talk among themselves and show their own unity but to communicate with their own community members, so that 'the Arabs, the Siddis . . . the mill workers'—in short, the ones referred to by the reformers as 'lower-class' and by Tilak as 'ignoramuses' on both sides—could be persuaded to stop the madness. More than anything else, he argued, all obstacles to Hindu–Muslim amity in western India would be removed if the government took 'firm action in time' and was 'neutral' and 'did not unnecessarily goad the Muslims'.[18]

The bottom line, Tilak argued, was that there were three sides to this conflict, not two. 'Just as there is a Hindu and a Muslim party, so there is a government party,' he said. He agreed Hindus and Muslims had certain contradictory religious beliefs; for example, Hindus saw the cow as holy, the Muslims ate beef, and Hindus were into idol worship while Muslims were iconoclastic. That was no reason for them to be in conflict. They could live peacefully alongside each other, he felt, provided the government allowed people of both faiths to observe their social and religious festivals without hindrance and the government handed out the punishment to any side that encroached on the other's practices. So 'if the Muslims turn violent because the Hindus put a vermillion mark on their heads, install idols and worship the cow and do pooja of the *naag* (snake) [on Naag Panchami], the government must take action against them. Similarly, if the Hindus, on account of their reverence for the cow, enter a Muslim *mohalla* and try to rescue a cow from the butcher at the local abattoir, they too must be punished'.[19]

Just in case the Muslims still had any doubts, Tilak said he 'hated communal riots' and had absolutely 'no desire to hurt the feelings of his Muslim countrymen'. Nevertheless, departing again from the stance of the Moderates, he added, indirectly urging the Hindus to build and maintain their own strength, that 'friendship and good relations can exist only between people of equal strength'.[20]

The British Raj and Tilak's critics among his compatriots found three reasons to view these statements with great concern. One was his uncompromisingly Hindu line. In the minds of many Indians who genuinely cared for Hindu–Muslim solidarity, it sparked fears of worsening inter-community bitterness, because Tilak was popular and his appeal among the Hindus was growing. The British, and especially the orthodox elements in the Muslim community, were worried on account of the possibility of Tilak mobilizing the majority. If such mobilization occurred, then the Raj could no longer be so secure, nor could the inflexibility of the orthodox among the Muslims go unchallenged. The second reason was his appeal to involve everyone in important conversations about Hindu–Muslim relations, and particularly the ordinary, powerless and largely unlettered people because he firmly believed it was they who were either going to hold the peace and promote harmony or break it. Such an approach made the reformers uncomfortable: it openly questioned their status as the educated elite who determined things and took the big decisions; it exposed their ivory-tower existence and alienation from the masses; and it put the onus on them to start a dialogue within their own community groups, and with sections they had almost totally stayed away from. For the British in particular, this call to speak to the lowest of the low was truly subversive. What if the voiceless millions realized their real power and acted in unison, with a common purpose? Here lay Tilak's unique vision of leadership, the fact that made him the 'Lokmanya'. Nothing could happen without the masses and everything was possible with them marching in lockstep, he contended. The British were absolutely right in sensing this danger he represented. And the third reason was equally concerning for the British rulers. By accusing them of encouraging the Muslims and being partisan, Tilak was powerfully hurling at them the accusation of 'divide and rule'—an accusation that would well and truly stick.

In September, Tilak and the orthodox Hindus of Poona decided to organize a public meeting to discuss the communal riots and let the Bombay government know of public sentiment in this regard. Both Ranade and Gokhale thought the gathering undesirable as it could exacerbate tensions. But Tilak went ahead, and *Kesari* reported that 7000 people attended the rally, making it 'the largest municipal gathering since the Age of Consent agitation'.[21]

As an immediate reaction to the communal conflict, Tilak came up with the idea of giving the traditional annual celebration of the Ganesh festival among the Hindus a new purpose.

For generations, Maharashtrians in the Deccan had had a tradition of getting clay Ganpati idols at their home during the annual festival dedicated to the son of the Hindu goddess Parvati and Lord Shiva. After one-and-a-half, five, seven or ten days, they would carry the domestic idols to the local river for immersion. Often an entire village headed to the river or local water body in a single-line procession, with members of the many families clashing cymbals and singing devotional hymns and songs. The Ganpati festival had acquired colossal prestige, especially during the era of the Peshwas, who patronized the worship

of the deity like no other rulers had done before them. After the end
of the Peshwa rule, however, the celebrations had lost quite a bit of
their lustre, though devout families had continued religiously with the
annual tradition.

The orthodox sections of the Hindus, and Tilak himself, had noticed
that a number of Hindus used to participate annually in the Muharram
processions of the Muslims and even lend music to those gatherings.
Tilak decided to make the celebration of the Ganeshotsav *sarvajanik*,
or public. What this meant was that while families continued their
traditions, each village and unit within the village, individual areas or
markets in towns and even lanes and by-lanes could install their own
Ganpati idols. A group of citizens and volunteers drawn from the area
would organize the festival and manage the details, and the familial
bond through the medium of religion would extend to a societal bond.
The orthodox sections of Hindus in Poona and Bombay had already, in
the wake of the communal rioting in Prabhas Patan and Bombay, asked
the Hindus not to participate in the Muharram processions. Extremely
importantly for Tilak, the energies of the same Hindu youngsters could
be channelled to make the public celebration of the Ganpati festival a
success. Once they were weaned away, the Ganpati processions could
become a far bigger counterweight to the Muharram marches, and
Hindu music bands too would not have to seek patronage elsewhere.

One of the longest-standing myths about the life of Tilak is that
the Sarvajanik Ganeshotsav he launched was targeted exclusively at the
British Raj. The truth is that the festival was a straight response to the
communal rupture between the Hindus and Muslims in a year of riots.
Naturally, if Hindu unity looked achievable even up to a point and faith
helped people to solidify societal ties, it was going to be a potential
headache for the British, and certainly, once the communal tempers had
calmed, Lord Ganpati was smartly conscripted by Tilak for the cause
of political unity and the anti-colonial movement of Indians by way of
organizing talks and lectures on political issues and embedding cultural
motifs and symbols on to the popular consciousness. But at the very
start, it was a festival born out of a deeply sectarian clash.

Not exactly coincidentally, the first public celebration of the Ganpati
festival took place not in Poona but in Bombay, the city which had just
witnessed communal riots. The Keshavji Naik Chawl in Girgaum was

a cluster of Maharashtrian Brahman households; the families there got together and brought in a community idol for the first time, just days after Tilak's mammoth public meeting on the Hindu–Muslim conflict in September in Poona. Quickly, the festival grew in size and character, with large idols installed in *mandaps* or nicely decorated pavilions, *melas* or local groups taking charge of the festivities, and subscriptions collected from neighbourhoods to fund the fest.

Initially many of the verses and songs, often sung impromptu during the processions, targeted the Muharram proceedings. For instance, a part of one verse went like this:

Oh! Why have you abandoned today the Hindu religion? How have you forgotten Ganpati, Shiva and Maruti? What have you gained by worshipping the tabuts?[22]

Another one declared:

Give up the dolas [tabuts] . . . Chintamani is our deity Celebrate this festival with pride What will not be achieved if we act unitedly? Let the wicked know.[23]

One late night in 1894, the second year of the festival, Tilak's follower Balasaheb Natu was leading a procession near the Daruwala Bridge in Poona. The procession passed by a mosque, without any breach of public order, at 11 p.m. On their way back after the immersions, Natu and his band were still playing music, which the police asked them to stop when they reached the neighbourhood of the mosque. Momentarily the crowd obliged but when they were close to the mosque 'the whole mela sent up a shout of defiance', reported the then superintendent of police. The Muslims inside 'dashed out' and a riot ensued, in which one Muslim was killed.[24]

Natu and thirteen other Hindus were put on trial, and the Poona sessions court acquitted them after just three days of hearing. The judge, a Britisher named Mr Jacobs, said the police 'had no authority to order the playing of music to be stopped in the neighbourhood of the masjid' and called 'the police directions given to that end not reasonable' as 'playing music was not an illegal act.' Further, the judge said, 'it was not proved that religious worship was going on' inside the mosque 'but it appeared the Mahomedans' pretence of assembling for worship was really to lay in wait for the Hindus.' 'Rioting was committed by Mahomedans,' the judge concluded.[25]

Following this verdict, several of the British-owned papers advised the Hindus that they should, as a matter of courtesy, not play music outside mosques to help keep the peace. Tilak was absolutely aghast and said these papers were demonstrating their bias by giving lectures only to one side. He also claimed that apart from the fact that it was against the law, their suggestion was tantamount to encouraging Muslims to resort to violence.[26]

Likewise, when the reformists found fault with the Sarvajanik Ganesh festival, Tilak hit out at them. Agarkar's *Sudharak* wrote that despite all the claims about the Ganesh festival, it did not have a national character. It was the Muharram that was truly national, it said, because both Hindus and Muslims were a part of it. Other critics alleged that the public Ganpati celebrations were nothing but a pure imitation of the Muharram festival and mere entertainment.[27]

Tilak responded that not only did the Brahmans and Marathas, the latter in particular, put together the Ganpati festival beautifully, but various sections such as the *salis* (weavers) *malis* (gardeners), *rangaaris* (dyers or painters), *sutars* (carpenters), *kumbhars* (potters), *sonars* (goldsmiths) and *wanis* (traders and merchants), among others, had made it their own.[28] This was borne out by evidence. The Bombay Police, for instance, wrote that the seven Ganpati groups that organized the festival in Yeola, a town near Nasik, in 1896, were composed of '(1) Brahmans and Gujaratis, (2) Marathas, (3) Salis (weavers) and Khatris, (4) Vanis (traders) and Khatris, (5) Sonars (goldsmiths) and Darjis (tailors), (6) Pardeshis (foreigners) and (7) Rangaris (dyers) and Sonars.'[29] Yeola was one of the several places in the Deccan that witnessed communal riots between 1893 and 1895, and Tilak made it a point of going there and taking stock of the post-riot situation.

What was more, once the outburst following the riots died down and communal fervour reduced and Tilak's statements were no longer seen as being tinged with a pro-Hindu streak, Muslims in some places started participating in the festival along with the Hindus. The bilingual English-Gujarati paper *Rast Goftar*, published from Bombay, reported in 1896 that 'the most noticeable feature' of the celebrations in Solapur that year was that 'local Mohammedans freely mixed with the Hindus in doing honour to Ganapati', and in Nasik, Hindus and Muslims carried the idol together for immersion, with a Muslim at the head of the procession.[30]

On whether the festival had copied Muharram, Tilak said 'even if it is perceived' that it had, its promoters had reason to feel proud of it, for 'at least they had given a new turn and shape to an old tradition and not just come up with new gimmicks' unlike the reformers.[31] He also pointed out that 'those who say the procession of Ganpati is an imitation of the tabuts of Muslims have not seen the *bhajan mandalis* on the occasion of Ekadashi in the months of Ashadh and Kartik. The playing of *lezim*, the beating of large drums and such other things are observed in every fair'.[32] And wasn't the Prarthana Samaj, the hive of the reformist faction, itself an imitation of the Christian Church, he asked.[33]

On the charge of the music bands and processions making the fest pure entertainment, Tilak's retort was that not all entertainment was bad, and it was often necessary. 'Hindus of all sects worship Ganpati,' he said, 'and if the ceremony of conducting the God to the water bodies became public, it would be a recreation without trouble and would help achieve harmony among various sections of the Hindu community . . . Religious thought and devotion may be possible even in solitude, yet demonstration and eclat are essential to the awakening of the masses.'[34]

In some of the processions, the participants had narrated verses critical of the reformers, and followers of the reformist leaders protested these 'attacks on men who were revered by many people'. To this, Tilak said piquantly, 'What's the point in protesting against the criticism of the reformers' . . . '*andi* [eggs in Marathi] and brandy' culture? Aren't these reformers the same people who, without knowing a single word of the Sanskrit language, proceed in a blasé manner to attack our rishis of the past who are revered by the people?'[35]

Tilak scoffed at what he saw as the elitism of the educated class and told them festivals could be used to spread social and political ideas. He insisted that 'this work will not be as strenuous and expensive as the work of the Congress' and that 'educated people can achieve results through these national festivals which it would be impossible for the

Congress to achieve. Why shouldn't we convert the large religious festivals into mass political rallies? Will it not be possible for political activities to enter the humblest cottages of the villages through such means?' Indeed, by involving the masses in festivals and rallies, he was gathering together the ordinary people so they could be the driving force for the movement for liberation. For reformers like Ranade he had an additional message: 'Instead of singing devotional songs in the Prarthana Samaj, it would be better if people, such as judges, would describe the importance of bhakti in the Ganpati festival hall.'[36]

For the political ideas that needed disseminating, Tilak very soon zeroed in on Chhatrapati Shivaji Maharaj as the political icon to hold up.

The personality of Shivaji Maharaj, founder of an independent Maratha state and scourge of the Mughal Emperor Aurangzeb in the seventeenth century, was inextricably tied up with the identities of the people in the Deccan. He was the uber hero, the exemplar, and the gold standard for political action.

Without really intending to, a Britisher who visited Raigad in the early 1880s had engendered discussion on the state of Shivaji's forts. In 1883, James Douglas, an Englishman, walked up the Raigad Fort, which was Shivaji's capital and where he had been coronated, and wrote that 'its interior (was) a mass of weeds'. About the Jagadeeshwar or Shiva temple atop the fort, Douglas said there were 'trees growing up through the pavement of its *dhurumsalla* (dharamshala); its temple (was) foul and dishonoured; and its god cast down to the ground'. This 'god' was not the main idol but the image of *nandi* or 'the sacred bull', which had 'toppled over and was lying on its back'. Douglas concluded, 'No man now cares for Seevajee. Overall those wide domains, which once owned him lord and master . . . not one man now contributes a rupee or keep or repair the tomb (he meant *samadhi*, the place where the Chhatrapati's funeral pyre had been lit and where a memorial structure had been built subsequently) of the founder of the Mahratta Empire.'[37]

The movement for reviving the memory of the Maratha hero had actually begun in the Deccan within a couple of decades of the fall of the Peshwa rule. G.H. Deshmukh, popularly known as Lokahitawadi, wrote a series of instructive articles on social, educational and political reform which eventually became famous as the '*Shatapatre*' or 'A Hundred Letters'. In one of his pieces titled 'Rajyadharma' and written in 1848, he made a distinction between 'mutiny and revolution' and said Shivaji's establishment of a state was a political revolution. Lokahitawadi also said the Marathas had lost their political power to the British because they lacked a leader like Shivaji.[38] James Grant Duff, a British official and resident of Satara, had written a history of the Marathas in 1826. N.J. Kirtane, a student of Deccan College, presented a critical paper on Duff's work in 1868 and emphasized the need to write Maratha history from the point of view of the Indians.[39] Jotiba Govindrao Phule, the well-known social reformer, went beyond what Lokahitawadi and Kirtane were saying. He wrote in 1869 a *powada,* or ballad, on Shivaji which said, '[T]he ryots were happy because Shivaji provided them with new laws, took care of the ordinary people, and none was neglected.' Phule, who declared he was writing the ballad for 'those on the lowest ladder of a caste-ridden Maharashtrian society' and had deliberately eschewed heavy Sanskrit words for that reason, was looking at Shivaji from the people's point of view and depicting him as the hero of the masses.[40] In that sense, Phule presaged what Tilak did later. Soon, Marathi newspapers and periodicals in the 1870s were writing about Chhatrapati Shivaji regularly and publishing extracts from some of the old Marathi *bakhars* which were still in the public domain. Most of them, including the Peshwa diaries, had been put under lock and key by the British government after the takeover of the Maratha territories. Ranade and Telang began at the end of that decade a movement to get the government to make the Peshwa diaries available so that people could know their own history; the movement soon grew massively in the Deccan and thanks to the unyielding efforts of V.K. Rajwade, who joined the Deccan College in 1884 and graduated in 1891, and many others, resulted in the Raj ultimately throwing open the archives. At around the same time as Ranade and Telang began their work on Maratha history, the rebel Wasudev Balwant Phadke styled himself 'the Second Shivaji' and before his eventual capture by the British hid with his group for a while at Shivaji's famous Sinhagad Fort near Poona.

James Douglas had, after noting his disappointment during his Raigad visit, made a plea to the Bombay government. 'The British government conserves the architectural remains of Tudor and Stewart. Will not the Bombay government do as much for the tomb, the temple and the arch of Seevajee? A few crumbs that fall from the archaeological bureau of Western India would suffice to keep in repair memorials of a dashing and most romantic period.'[41]

Ranade called a public meeting in Poona of sardars and influential citizens to take up the cause of the Shivaji memorial, and the Bombay government led by Lord Reay in April 1885 made an annual grant of five rupees for maintenance of the samadhi. Around this time, biographies of the Chhatrapati and plays on his life began to be produced in the Marathi-speaking regions. Ranade himself wrote a series of articles on the Maratha power in 1893, and the following year, the scholar R.P. Karkaria gave a lecture on the Shivaji versus Afzal Khan episode at the Royal Asiatic Society of Bombay and spoke of how Shivaji was fully justified in killing the Bijapur general. The lecture created a mini sensation, spurring further interest, and early in 1895, the *Native Opinion* reiterated Douglas's complaint about the state of Shivaji's samadhi.[42]

Taking the cue, Tilak stepped forward to champion the cause of the memorial. Quite provocatively, he said, 'It is useless to blame the government for neglecting the shrine. It is the business of the people of Maharashtra to take the opportunity to vindicate the name of Shivaji. It would be highly creditable to those generous and grateful descendants of the Maharaja who opened their purses for contributing to the fund of the insignificant Lord Harris, if they renovated the shrine of Shivaji.'[43] Harris had just retired as governor that year, and in calling him 'insignificant', Tilak was attacking him as well as asking Shivaji's descendants to step up. In another piece, he asked, 'Should we not hang our heads in shame that a foreigner should tell us about our duty to Shivaji?'[44]

Tilak proposed that a fund be set up to repair and restore Shivaji's memorial and began to publish in *Kesari* the names of contributors, however small the amounts they came up with. 'Every pai (one-third of a penny) would be acknowledged in the Kesari,' Tilak made plain.[45] A student with no source of income sent in two annas, and Tilak praised him in the *Kesari* of 30 April 1895 for his 'spirit to work for Swarajya (self-rule, the idea embodied by Shivaji)'.[46] Other papers in Poona too picked up the campaign, and it gained enough momentum in a couple of months for Tilak to organize a meeting, jointly with Senapati Dabhade of Talegaon, at the Hira Baug in Poona on 30 May 1895. A number of princes and local chieftains attended, and it was resolved to raise a fund for repairing the samadhi, build a *chhatri* or umbrella on it and to set up a committee to oversee this task, with Tilak as its working secretary. 'One of the resolutions was seconded by a Muslim.'[47] Among the members of the committee were not only Tilak's followers such as Khasgiwale and Balasaheb Natu but three chiefs (one of Ichalkaranji near Kolhapur and two from Kurundwadi), some sardars, G.K. Gokhale of the Ranade group and Gangaram Bhau Mhaske, a big Maratha promoter of the education of non-Brahmans.[48]

This was an achievement in itself. People across social groups were involved from the beginning, taking Tilak's success beyond that of the Ganapati festival. So impressed was the pro-reform *Sudharak* that its correspondent reported that 'never in the history of Poona was there ever seen, since the advent of British rule, the like of the Hira Baug meeting.' More and more people were being mobilized for what would eventually be political action in the cause of national freedom. The *Indu Prakash* exulted that 'no surer sign of raising the national spirit can be seen.'[49] By November that year, the fund had gathered Rs 11,000, with the single biggest contribution of Rs 1000 coming from the Maratha ruler of Baroda, Sayajirao Gaekwad.[50]

To give things a more institutional character, Tilak launched the annual celebration of the Shivaji festival on the Chhatrapati's birth anniversary in 1896. With a significant bunch of followers, Tilak reached the base of the Raigad fort the evening before the celebrations, which were due on 15 April. He had already appealed to the locals of Mahad, the area in which the fort stands, to make the event big, and many of them had joined in. Everyone expected to climb up early the next morning. But Tilak, after his evening meal, said he'd go straight away. Those around him decided to go along. Immediately, a number of flaming torches were organized, mostly by the locals of Mahad, and a biggish group began its ascent. The pathway wasn't easy; Raigad had been neglected for long, and in some places, the passes were narrow. Yet scores of people moved up in a single file in the dark, with individuals carrying torches placed between every four or five persons. Shivram Mahadev Paranjpe, an evocative chronicler, editor of the *Kaal* and a keen follower of Tilak, wrote that it brought up in everyone's mind a picture of how Chhatrapati Shivaji must have climbed the fort in the seventeenth century with his loyal Mavale (soldiers). The spirit got into them all, and there were cries of 'Shivaji Maharaj Ki Jai' and 'Tilak Maharaj Ki Jai'.[51] For a very, very long time after this, and in fact even after he had obtained the title of 'Lokmanya', Tilak during his lifetime was commonly referred to as 'Tilak Maharaj' by those who saw him as their hero.

The 'spirit' was exactly Tilak's idea. He said his notion wasn't that people should imitate exactly what Shivaji had done in the seventeenth century. Those were different times. But it was the spirit Shivaji Maharaj had fostered that needed imbibing, he said. Most importantly, 'if there was a single iconic figure who had the love, affection and respect of all castes and all social groups in Maharashtra, it was Chhatrapati Shivaji. So, to maintain differences such as "Brahmans and Marathas" and "Brahmans and Prabhus" in the festival would be absolutely wrong'. Shivaji had given the people a national identity, he stressed, and it was this identity that must be focused on.[52] In later editions of the festival, he pointed out Shivaji was not anti-Muslim and had never insulted the Islamic faith but had fought against Mughal rule and against Aurangzeb for the protection of his faith and society.[53]

Tilak was by now getting to be an increasingly well-known Congress figure as well. Ranade's followers still comprised the totally dominant group, and in it, the emerging star was undoubtedly Gokhale. Yet Tilak had made his presence felt with his force of personality, his various agitations on controversial issues, and his bold stands which indicated he was trying to set up his own party within the Congress fold. By 1895, Tilak had gained enough traction to be 'elected', in keeping with the elective principle introduced by the Raj in 1892 in the provincial councils, to the Bombay Legislative Council. It was the municipalities which 'elected' members to the Council; there was no direct election with the people voting.[54] Tilak was picked by the Poona municipal body to be its representative in the Council. Now he would get an inside view of the functioning of the legislatures and the administration.

The Congress was to hold its annual session in December 1895 in Poona, and with his public profile growing, Tilak asked the president that year, the Bengali leader Surendranath Banerjea, to speak at a public meeting he was organizing to mark six months of the Shivaji movement.

A massive crowd of 15,000 turned up. Tilak said people had contributed Rs 15,000 to the Shivaji memorial fund so far, and he was not asking for funds from the Congress leaders and delegates but support for the cause from across the country.

Surveying the size of the crowd, which he described as 'vast, enthusiastic and unparalleled', Banerjea said in his speech that the thing that occurred to him at the sight was, 'What may not be expected from the organizers of a movement like this in the cause of national advancement and progress? We are all – I think I may say the members of the National Congress are all – in strict sympathy with this movement, the object of which is to commemorate the memory of the greatest Hindu hero of modern times.' Pointing to the portrait of Shivaji put up by the organizers, he told the gathering, 'Standing face to face in the presence of that picture . . . may we not imbibe from him a similar ardour to march forward in the constitutional battle which has for its object the political emancipation of our people? This Shivaji movement calls forth the sympathy of the entire country.'[55] Pandit Madan Mohan Malviya, the Congress leader from Allahabad, said 'people were not efficiently governed' by the rulers of Shivaji's times, and Shivaji had given them 'peace and order'.[56]

Tilak's repeated appeals, the effect they were having, and the endorsement by the national Congress leadership worried the British government. Though Banerjea had used the term 'political emancipation' in his speech, it did not mean at this point in time complete freedom from the Raj or even dominion status under the umbrella of the Raj. India's top political leaders and representatives had somewhat mild political ambitions like more seats in the councils, Central and provincial, greater constitutional progress, including more of a say in decision-making and administrative matters, and on the whole, an extension of their rights, which they themselves—definitely the Moderates—even hesitated from terming as 'rights', preferring the word 'concessions' instead. And though Tilak himself was often speaking about 'self-rule', he was careful at this point not to antagonize the Raj and was part of the national Congress current, albeit hoping, as his activities indicated, to take things in a different direction in the future. At the launch of the Shivaji festival at Raigad, Tilak even thanked the Bombay government for the permissions it had granted and he said more than once that the government should be fair because that was how it would be looked up to and well-regarded by the masses. He was also now a member of the provincial Council, and in his own small way, was working inside the system.

Still, the government reckoned that his actions betrayed his real motives. And it was convinced these motives weren't pro-Raj. Its first instinct was to try and neutralize the Shivaji movement. S.W. Egerby, the secretary to the Bombay government, suggested it would be 'worth Government's while to spend a few hundred rupees in doing up Shivaji's tomb and generally showing that to respect Shivaji is not synonymous with being 'against the Government'. . . If it is simply a Congress and seditious scheme, the Government (can) come in and spoil the whole campaign and take the taste out of it.'[57] There was also a claim by another official, John Nugent, which was more wishful thinking than fact, that 'the entire agitation is purely a Brahmin move. The Marathas have held aloof'.[58] In fact, Marathas were major contributors to the Shivaji fund, and many of the meetings held in various parts of the state—Thane, Satara, Solapur, Kolaba, Ahmednagar, Nasik, Ratnagiri, Bombay and Belgaum—to spread the word about the memorial subscription were presided over by Marathas, among them Narayan Meghaji Lokhande, who was like Jotiba Phule one of the pioneers and champions of the neglected and the poor.[59] The tempo gained by these meetings finally grew so much that the chief secretary to the Bombay government, E.C.K. Olliwant, considered issuing a circular warning government servants not to participate in the 'political or quasi-political movement'. The collector of Solapur, W.T. Morison, backed this view in May 1897, noting that 'at meetings held in upcountry towns and villages, the President or one of the speakers is generally a pensioned subordinate judge, mamlatdar or clerk' who didn't think twice before criticizing the government.[60]

One of the reasons the government was worried was Tilak's growing appeals to the Muslims too to participate in his movements, whether it was the Shivaji or Ganpati festivals, and the drifting in of the Muslims, in small numbers but nonetheless real and voluntary drifting-in. The British had registered the fact that while Tilak criticized Muslims at times for what he felt was their riotous and inappropriate conduct and for inflicting violence on the Hindus, one thing he never did was attack the Muslim faith or its tenets. He even said, to emphasize that the holding up of Shivaji as an icon was not an act against Muslims and to indicate he wasn't seeking Hindu supremacy, that the next Shivaji to emerge from among the Indians might even be a Muslim.

The great Indian Revolt of 1857 had happened with Hindus and Muslims acting in unison. After that, and after stamping out the 1820s-born Wahhabi movement of the Islamicists in North-West India by the 1870s, the British had worked to try and broaden the differences between the two communities which existed owing to the history of Islamic invasions and Islamic rule in the subcontinent from the eleventh century onwards. If there were periods of relative peace, there were equally periods of conflict and religious tensions, even religious oppression, most recently during Aurangzeb's rule a couple of centuries ago. As Mughal Emperor, he had put in place discriminatory policies against the Hindus and demolished some of the major Hindu temples. Since the arrival of the British, the Hindus had taken quickly to Western education, but the Muslims largely resisted it, accentuating the differences. 'By the start of the 1880s,' wrote a couple of chroniclers, 'there were 36,686 Hindus studying in English high schools' across India 'but only 363 Muslims'.[61] Similarly, if 3155 Hindus possessed university degrees at this point in time, the Muslims had just fifty-seven graduates among them in all of India.[62]

An important consequence of their lagging behind was that when the Indian National Congress, which boasted chiefly of the educated Indian elite in its early years, was formed in 1885, only two of the seventy-two delegates to the first Congress session were Muslim. The next year, of the total 430-plus delegates, just thirty-three were Muslim, and by 1895, when the Congress session saw 784 delegates coming to Poona, only fifty-four were Muslims.[63]

Ironically, a prominent leader of the Muslims who actually pushed for Western education proved to be instrumental in them continuing to keep their distance from the Congress. The Congress was, for all its perceived flaws, a genuinely representative body of Indians, but the Muslims stayed at its fringes, in minuscule numbers. Born in 1817, Syed Ahmed Khan, hailing from a Delhi family that had served the Mughal Empire as senior functionaries, became a junior judge in the courts set up by the British. Stationed in Bijnor near Meerut in northern India, he refused to come to the assistance of the Indians in the 1857 uprising, opting to save the local British collector called Shakespeare from being massacred by the rebels. He wrote a book called *The Loyal Muhammadans of India* to put to rest any British concerns over alleged Muhammadan intransigence and urged his fellow Muslims to do three things urgently: (1) get over the fact that they had lost their power over Hindustan, (2) take up western education, and (3) stay miles away from politics. In 1870, Syed Ahmed was knighted for his services to the British Empire, was made a member of the Viceroy's Imperial Legislative Council thereafter, and in 1885, he established the Muhammadan Anglo-Oriental College at Aligarh. In the Viceroy's Council, he spoke out against the policy of elections, arguing that in a place like India, elected bodies—which the Congress wholly favoured—would mean 'the rule of the majority' or Hindus. He didn't want 'a game of dice, in which one man had four dice and the other only one'. Syed Ahmed went on to say in 1888 that 'the Hindus and Muslims were two different nations even though they drank from the same well and breathed the air from the same city'.[64] His reference to representative democracy as 'a game of dice' was the earliest contention that if the Hindus had four votes, the Muslims couldn't just have one simply because they were in a minority; it was the launch of the claim for separate electorates, where one Muslim vote would have the weight of more than one Hindu vote. And his talk about the two religious groups being separate nations was the first ever public articulation of the two-nation theory which was to result in India's division later.

The British had things going their way in the mid-1890s, though they were always anxious about the prospect of a Revolt. They were alert to the fact that Tilak was making a bit of a stir. Would he go beyond his twin festivals? Would he be able to mobilize Hindus any further? With his increasing mass appeal, could he emerge powerful in any way within the Congress? And could he succeed in pulling Muslims into the mainstream of the National Congress?

There were no definite answers to these questions just yet. But the British didn't really want to wait for the answers to emerge, this way or that. They'd much rather fix things earlier. So, they set out to find a pretext to rein in Tilak.

Chapter 8

'Sedition-Monger'

Tilak had hardly been on speaking terms with Agarkar ever since their conflict in the Deccan Education Society had turned into a full-blown one. After Tilak's resignation in 1890, the connection was severed almost altogether, and in the next few years, their clashing positions on a variety of issues and their harsh remarks against each other, which were not at all infrequent, exacerbated the divide.

The lowest point was reached in the wake of the communal riots of 1893. When Tilak had, along with M.B. Namjoshi, taken the lead in organizing a rally of the Hindus in September following the violence in Prabhas Patan and Bombay, three top leaders of the liberal and reformist faction—Pherozeshah Mehta, Ranade and Gokhale—had urged him not to go ahead. Ranade believed the meeting could precipitate tensions, and Mehta urged Tilak to wait until the government took some action against the rioters. Tilak hit out at Ranade, saying his opposition was motivated by his desire to be appointed as judge at the Bombay High Court. About Gokhale, he was still more scathing, calling him 'impetuous' and 'thoughtless'. Tilak also pointed to what he believed were Gokhale's double standards: the bespectacled young man had written an anonymous letter to *Times of India* in which he had rubbished the police commissioner Vincent and civic chief Acworth's claim that the work of the cow protection groups had sparked the riot, and yet he was opposed to a meeting in which the Hindu community could present its side publicly.[1]

Agarkar hadn't opposed the meeting, and his views on Hindu–Muslim relations differed from those of Tilak, but only somewhat. Much like Tilak, Agarkar, states his biographer, believed that the

155

Muslims were 'inherently courageous, had a staunch pride in their faith and were fanatical'. He saw the 'differing belief systems, practices, languages and history of the Hindus and Muslims as being at the root of the long-term Hindu-Muslim discord'. It would take a long time for the communities to be friendly, but slowly an element of friendliness was seeping in, he felt. Like Tilak, Agarkar too accused the Muslims of being the ones who 'started violent conflicts'. Where he differed from Tilak was in that he did not see governmental incitement as the cause of the riots. For Agarkar, it was the core cause of the discord that was still holding and inflaming tensions from time to time.[2]

Agarkar was stung by Tilak's criticism of Mehta, Ranade and Gokhale, however, and wrote a belligerent article after Tilak had held his September meeting, which surpassed the size of the meet held by the orthodox wing during the Age of Consent row. In *Sudharak*, Agarkar described the meeting as a 'flop' and called Tilak 'abusive, vindictive, and lowly' and added that 'people were shunning him like he were a leper'.[3] When it was pointed out to him that Tilak had actually gathered a good crowd, Agarkar exploded, 'What are these people puffed up about? The fact that some schoolchildren, *telis* (oil sellers) and *tambolis* (betel-leaf sellers) . . . came together outside the Shaniwarwada? Such crowds turn up also to see a monkey's rope-trick or a *tamasha* or a *dahi-handi* event or just at the Wednesday and Sunday bazaars!' Tilak 'didn't have the brains to achieve *lokmanya-ta* [wide acceptance and popularity],' Agarkar claimed.[4]

The reformists had of late started speaking of Tilak in derisive and dismissive terms as a leader of the '*telis*' and '*tambolis*'. With his once-upon-a-time dear friend Agarkar too chipping in, Tilak held it up as a badge of honour, almost as a medal. He was proud to be in communication with the masses, the common people, the workers, the farmers and the mill hands. He turned an intended brickbat into his most prized bouquet and proudly pronounced himself as the champion of the masses all through his life and career, ultimately proving Agarkar wrong that he could never be 'lokmanya'.

Referring to Tilak as 'inhuman', Agarkar had also claimed in his piece that Tilak would not mind ruining institutions like the Deccan Education Society, the Sarvajanik Sabha, the Provincial Conference, the Social Conference and the Indian National Congress in order to serve his own interests.[5] This charge appeared to have hurt Tilak more than anything else, because in his response to Agarkar, Tilak focused almost exclusively on it. He said it was Agarkar's own 'selfishness, self-centred approach, prejudice, hatred, jealousy and pettiness' that had led to the rift in the Deccan Education Society. Tilak said that 'if those who left the Society had wanted to harm it, it's not as if they couldn't have done that. But that was not their way'. He further said that by making 'foolish' remarks that he would harm the Congress, the Sabha and the various conferences, Agarkar had demonstrated how 'obstinate' and 'malicious' he was.[6]

Evidently the two were heaping abuse on each other. What was put out through the pages of *Sudharak* and *Kesari* after the Bombay riots wasn't a debate or discussion between two editors, nor was it a simple airing of differences. This was personal. It was humongous bitterness that two genuinely close friends, who had had a sour falling-out, were displaying in full public view. If Gokhale said something rude to Tilak or if Jinsiwale or Namjoshi of Tilak's group similarly targeted Agarkar, it wouldn't go so deep. Here it had, and after that, all communication came to a close.

Until the middle of 1895. Agarkar had been wracked by ill health, and his condition had progressively worsened, with a badly damaged liver adding to his severe asthma problems. By mid-1895 Agarkar was bedridden, and talk in Poona's circles was that he wouldn't live for long. Agarkar had three children—two sons and an infant daughter—and he was worried about their future, even though two of his well-to-do Maharashtrian friends had promised to take care of them and also provide for his wife Yashoda if they ran out of money that the family would get as a result of Agarkar's accumulated dues at the Deccan Education Society and as pension.

As soon as Tilak got to know of Agarkar's precarious condition, he proceeded to his home to meet him. For both of them, there was much to think about. In that era, in the first place, life expectancy hardly went beyond thirty-five or forty. Besides, four people they had very closely worked with in their educational institutions had died already. While Chiplunkar died in 1882, Waman Shivram Apte had passed on thereafter. In 1894, Narayan Krishna Dharap, who had mostly sided with Tilak in the fights within the Society, died of a brain illness. And then, in May 1895, Vasudeorao Kelkar, who helped Tilak run the *Kesari* after he had taken it over, passed away suddenly. The oldest at the time of death was Dharap, and he was just forty-three.[7]

The face-to-face encounter of the estranged friends turned out to be exceedingly awkward. Tilak sat in a chair by Agarkar's bed, and common courtesies followed. To the usual questions about the illness, medicines and family, Agarkar replied mostly by way of monosyllables, and when Tilak tried to extend the conversation, it became clear to him that Agarkar wasn't keen at all. Both fell silent for a while; and after some time, Agarkar, who was lying flat on the bed, turned his head around, facing away towards the wall. Tilak got the message and left.[8]

Was it that Agarkar couldn't go on owing to his illness and had therefore to put an end to the conversation? Agarkar dispelled any such assumption the same evening. Soon after Tilak's exit, Sitaram Deodhar, who used to write *Sudharak*'s editorials in Agarkar's absence, trooped in to consult him on what next to write about. Bringing up the subject of Tilak's visit, a disturbed-looking Agarkar told him, 'A person who's ill feels horrible when someone who has ill-feeling in his mind shows affection in his talk. Tilak sat here shedding false tears. The moment I saw him, my mind was unsettled by thoughts of all the unpleasant things that had happened between the two of us. And I said to myself, the sooner he leaves, the better.'[9]

Just days after that, on the morning of 17 June 1895, Agarkar died. He was just 39.

Kesari was due for publication the next morning. On his return from the funeral, Tilak began dictating Agarkar's obituary to his amanuensis. Tilak would routinely dictate his editorials, and he was in the habit of speaking a little more loudly than someone normally does as he had developed a small hearing defect in his youth. He also very routinely asked his amanuensis if he was done with writing down a sentence so he could get on with the next. On this occasion, his voice was subdued and downcast, and no questions were asked of the amanuensis.[10]

Tilak noted in the obituary that he was beside himself with grief and dismay. Memories of the happy and sorrowful moments he and Agarkar had shared during their intimate association had come flooding to him, and he wondered how he was going to put together his thoughts on paper. But he was doing so as he had to do his 'final duty by Agarkar', he said. Agarkar was among the very few persons who had dreamt and resolved to set up the New English School and a college in Poona, and he had given his best years to the task from 1879 onwards, Tilak stated. According to Tilak, it was normal for people to study and then start earning their livelihood and once they had hung up their boots, to get their children to start earning so that the livelihood concerns of future generations could be taken care of. But Agarkar had given the full bloom of his youth to society despite having come from a background of straitened family circumstances. How many people did that, when they knew that that way lay a lifetime of uncertainty, a precarious livelihood, poverty, physical discomfort, neglect and even calumny? That made Agarkar special, he said. Agarkar and he (Tilak) had resolved in their youth to work for society, and to that end, the two of them had, 'with oneness of spirit, worked at home, outside home and even in prison.' When they had just about started their public work, at a very young age, Tilak and Agarkar had together spent a total of 101 days in the Dongri prison after being held guilty of defamation in the Kolhapur regent's case. Of two men who had had one goal in mind and had worked relentlessly towards it together for ten to twelve years undaunted by difficulties, one had gone, Tilak lamented. Much worse for him was that he had to do the distressing duty of informing the *Kesari*'s readers of his friend's passing, he pointed out.[11]

What about their deep differences? Indeed, several of their differences had come to the fore in the past five-six years, Tilak pointed out, but so shocking and upsetting was the nature of death that such 'minor things' had receded from memory; instead, what came overpoweringly and 'again and again' to his mind, emphasized Tilak, was the recollection of what they had done together, and it made him disorientated.[12]

Tilak's voice was also tinged unmistakably with regret. He felt he 'ought to have told' Agarkar while he was still alive that he was a man of extraordinary courage who had embraced a life of immense difficulty for the sake of society. Similarly, he was kicking himself for never having told Agarkar that if the native papers had acquired importance recently, it had had so much to do with Agarkar's intelligence and brilliantly sardonic writings.[13]

Things, alas, had been left unsaid, and a deeply cherished friendship had, for quite some time, been dead.

Barely a month after Agarkar's death, Tilak's relations with Ranade and Gokhale, never so close to start with, took a serious turn for the worse. The resultant rift proved to be a glaring preview of the massive national political development that was to come about twelve years later—the split within the Congress.

The annual general meeting of the Poona Sarvajanik Sabha, the political group guided and nurtured by Ranade since its inception in 1870, was scheduled for 14 July 1895. Just the previous year, something disconcerting for Ranade and Gokhale's dominant faction within the Sabha had happened after the Poona riot near a masjid. Tilak had prevailed upon members of the Sabha to submit a memorandum to the government that said a blanket ban on music by processionists was not the right solution to objections raised by a group at a religious shrine. The best way to uphold the feelings of the objectors was 'not by banning all music at all times . . . but loud music . . . which might hamper prayer during the prescribed hours of prayer'.[14]

Ranade, who totally disapproved of the congregational aspect of Ganpati, was not expected to approve of such a memorandum. Nor were the Muslim members of the Sabha; they quit immediately. When the annual general meeting of 1895 came around, their seats had to be filled. Tilak got his supporters to join in, and his bloc succeeded in winning a majority of seats on the Sabha's thirty-six-member managing committee. Though Gokhale was elected one of the secretaries, the Ranade-led faction found itself outnumbered for the first time. Gokhale wanted to quit but was persuaded by Ranade and Mehta, who often decided his moves, to stay on till the annual Congress session had taken place.[15] That year's Congress session, significantly, was going to be held in December in Poona.

The build-up to that session was tenser. Two years after the formation of the Indian National Congress, Ranade had in 1887 started organizing the National Social Conference in the same pavilion as the national political organization. This conference was for and by the reformist wing. First, the Congress would have its session, and once that ended, the Social Conference would meet the following day. Though the two organizations were not directly connected, the idea was that those who were working in the area of social reform would find it convenient to meet at the same time and at the same place, since in any case, a majority of delegates of the Congress were proponents of social reform.

Tilak, who was joint secretary of the panel appointed to make arrangements for the Poona Congress, called for a separation of the two conclaves. His argument was that convening the Social Conference in the same pavilion was unfair to those Congress delegates who did not follow the creed of its organizers and also to the majority of the Indian population, which wasn't with the pro-reforms pack. Such a thing 'is very likely to make the Congress itself unpopular', wrote his English paper, the *Mahratta*.[16]

The reformers decided to consult the various provincial Congress committees, hoping to get the majority to concur with them. But the verdict was indecisive, and Ranade was not keen on an open confrontation with Tilak's faction ahead of the Congress session. He backtracked, agreeing to hold the Social Conference elsewhere in the city. The win was a significant one for Tilak and truly anticipated the showdown that was to come in Surat in 1907. The bosses in the Bombay Congress, nevertheless, were extremely upset. The Congress unit in the Presidency was ruled by the likes of Pherozeshah Mehta and Dinshaw Wacha, for whom Ranade was a respected equal and Gokhale a brilliant understudy. To get back at Tilak, Mehta and company appointed more secretaries to the Congress's reception and arrangements panel; one of them was Gokhale. Tilak's response was to resign promptly from the committee. Gokhale indeed entered the limelight at the Congress session. With the reception committee's head, Moreshwar Bhide indisposed, the Bombay Congress mandarins got him to read the welcome address to delegates who had come in from across India.[17] During the session, Tilak for his part achieved success outside the Congress pandal by getting Surendranath Banerjea and Madan Mohan Malviya to address a meeting on the Shivaji memorial.

Ranade, who had taken a few steps back before the Congress session to maintain party unity, didn't want to stay in the Poona Sarvajanik Sabha after the fracas. He formed a new and parallel organization called the Deccan Sabha, which he said would speak for 'moderate and liberal opinion'. Tilak asked what Ranade was trying to say. Did he imply that

Tilak and his friends were immoderate and illiberal? Terming Ranade as 'Kautilya' and 'mean', Tilak characterized the Deccan Sabha as a '*pinjrapole* [stable] of Rao Bahadurs (a title bestowed on well-placed government servants and assorted Raj loyalists by the government)'. The Deccan Sabha proved ineffective with its very mild politics of being, like the previous avatar of the Poona Sabha, a mediator between the ruler and the ruled and went totally quiescent following Ranade's death in 1901.[18] Times were changing, and Tilak's more assertive approach was finding takers.

The Bombay government of course wasn't going to humour the Poona Sabha if it was led by Tilak. It soon got what it saw as an opportunity to crack down on it.

Signs of famine in the Deccan had been apparent at the time of the Poona Congress, and some farmers had placed the picture of an emaciated peasant outside the party pavilion to highlight their grievances. Speaking on a resolution on the matter, Tilak had said at the Congress that in some cases, land revenue assessment by the authorities had seen mammoth and unreasonable hikes. The situation got worse as the rains played truant in 1896. Tilak called for instant implementation of the Famine Relief Code introduced during a similar crisis in 1876. Sections of the Code stipulated that if total crop output was 'less than five annas in a rupee' or less than 25 per cent, collection of land revenue would, with the district collector's nod, be suspended or remissions granted. The Relief Code had not been introduced with any alacrity in 1876 but only after the 1875 Deccan agrarian riots, and twenty years later, the Raj showed no urgency in enforcing its provisions, disregarding appeals from Indians to announce in the official gazette about its application. In response, Tilak came up with the argument that the Code was already in the statute book, and it was time farmers demanded their rights. Most of the peasantry did not speak of rights, and the government presented whatever relief it offered as largesse. A majority of farmers didn't even know what relief measures the law contained for them. With his new-found control over the Sarvajanik Sabha, Tilak sent its agents across the Deccan and the wider Bombay Presidency to create awareness about the relief provisions and got the Famine Relief Code translated and not only printed it in the *Kesari* but published it in the form of booklets. Copies of the booklet, along with other handbills containing similar useful information, were sent to administrative offices for distribution to the farmers, and agents of the Sabha themselves handed over copies to villagers they met in various parts. When it became amply clear to him that the government still wasn't thinking of not collecting land revenue for the season, Tilak wrote a piece appealing to ordinary farmers not to pay if it entailed taking a loan for the purpose. A miffed government looked closely at the piece, but the usage 'if you have to incur debt' precluded action on the grounds of asking people to violate the law.[19]

Famine was unfortunately not a new thing in India, but Tilak sought a departure from the sense of fatalistic resignation the Indian people displayed. He wanted them to push, and still further push the government. Some years ago, the Raj had set up a special famine relief fund for use exactly in such situations. Why was that lying unused in the State treasury, Tilak asked. It was 'the people's money', he argued, and 'when their own money is with the government, why should they die of hunger?'[20] Once again, putting the conditional 'if' to good use, he reminded the farm population, 'If conditions as laid down in the Famine Code prevail in any district, then obviously there is no need for the peasants to pay the land tax, at least not for this year.' He had got to know that in some places, officials were forcibly collecting land tax though conditions were unmistakably of famine there. 'We warn them that their action is wrong and illegal. They must remember that it is clearly stated in the Famine Code that "the peasants'" cattle and land must not be auctioned to collect government dues.'[21]

Beyond criticizing the state machinery, Tilak made a positive contribution. Short of food, large swathes of the rural population had rushed to the bigger towns, and places like Poona, Panvel, Junnar, Kalyan, Nasik, Ahmednagar and Solapur, among others, had turned into camps for the displaced. At some of the spots, desperate villagers ransacked shops for food materials. Tilak asked them, 'Why loot the bazaars? Go to the collector and ask him to give you work and food. That's his duty.'[22] Further, aware that such ransacking would only worsen the situation by bringing in the element of internal strife, he gathered provisions and got the Sabha's volunteers to head to the villages for distribution so that hordes did not rush to the towns. By successfully appealing to some local bankers and grain traders, he collected funds and corn for setting up community kitchens in many of the affected areas and made arrangements for free meals.[23]

Tilak travelled widely through the Deccan, speaking to farmers and villagers and attempting to infuse hope in them. And not only did he witness signs of hope and strengthen his bond with them, but one of his biographers wrote that 'in a sense, the famine of 1896 largely decided the ultimate course of Tilak's career' in that it was a lesson in the centrality of the farmer in Indian life. Tilak's idea of the route to political emancipation at any rate became clearer. He said, 'The country's emancipation can only be achieved by removing the clouds of lethargy and indifference which have been hanging over the peasant, who is the soul of India. We must remove these clouds, and for that we must completely identify ourselves with the peasant – we must feel that he is ours and we are his.'[24]

Attacks on the Tilak-led Sabha were mounted by the Anglo–Indian press for what they described as his 'no-rent campaign'. They hated his contention that British rule was one of the causes of the famine as 'Indian trade was monopolized by Britain', the pressure on land 'increased' and agriculture 'made unproductive'. Tilak wrote in the *Kesari* that 'it is true that lack of rain causes famine, but it is also true that the people of India have not the strength to fight the evil. The poverty of India is wholly due to the present rule. India is being bled till only the skeleton remains'.[25]

The defiant acts of Tilak and his aides galled the pro-government press and the authorities all the more. One of the Sabha's secretaries, Achyut Sathe, was booked and arrested for holding a public meeting of peasants in a village without permission. Just as Sathe was addressing villagers in Chikhalwade in Thane district, the assistant collector arrived at the spot with a team of armed police, hoping to instil fear of a shooting. Sathe told the assembled crowd not to be scared by the presence of the armed cops. 'The more you are terrorized, the more you will be suppressed,' he said.[26]

Tilak was in Calcutta for the 1896 annual Congress session when Sathe was arrested. He rushed to Poona for his defence and the evening before the case came up in court, addressed a public rally. Tilak understood the importance of the case; it was the first in which a member of the Sabha was being tried merely for alerting villagers about provisions of the Famine Relief Code. Tilak declared, 'If Sathe is to be prosecuted for enlightening people about their legal rights, they (government) must prosecute me, and many times for that matter, because I have been doing exactly that, day in and day out.'[27] In response to the intimidatory tactics, Tilak wrote an editorial and provocatively headlined it 'Monster meeting of *rayats* within close range of loaded guns.' Remarking that government officers were 'out to terrorize people in order to squeeze out land revenue from helpless peasants', he warned them that such actions were against the law and the wishes of the Queen and asked the people to be 'prepared to die rather than give in'. Tilak admonished the Indian members of the civilian administration, who were the Raj's collaborators, asking them 'not to forget they were Indians first and civil servants afterwards' and 'must not put in false reports to please their British superiors'. He asked the people to expose 'such toadying officials'.[28]

In addition to Sathe, three other Sabha agents were prosecuted for distributing a handbill purportedly aimed at getting farmers to resist the authority of public servants. When two of these volunteers were being tried before a magistrate's court in Pen near Panvel in the coastal Konkan belt, the tent housing the court was surrounded by hundreds of farmers shouting slogans of 'Tilak Maharaj Ki Jai!' Despite police appeals, the crowd did not quieten, so the magistrate, named Mr Brook, looked at Tilak, who was present in court, and requested him to help. Tilak went out of the tent, and in a minute, the crowd had fallen silent.[29] Sathe and the three others were subsequently acquitted.[30]

Before long, a pretext was at hand for the authorities to act against the Tilak-led Sabha. One of the handbills prepared and circulated by a member of Tilak's group in Dharwad in the southern Deccan contained a factually incorrect statement that the local commissioner had ordered remission. The member acknowledged his mistake, but for the government, it wasn't nearly enough.[31] The governor's executive council, the cabinet of the Bombay government, passed a resolution that the Poona Sarvajanik Sabha had ceased to be recognized as a body 'which has any claim to address government on questions of policy'. On the de-recognition, Tilak wrote in the *Mahratta* that whether to favourably consider a petition or not was up to the government, 'but that does not preclude anyone from addressing government on questions of public policy. The Sabha was not created by a government resolution and it cannot be abolished by it'.[32]

After the Congress session of 1896 in Calcutta, Tilak suggested the national organization should be far stronger in its advocacy of people's rights. 'For the last twelve years,' he wrote:

> We have been shouting ourselves hoarse, desiring that the government should hear us. But our shouting has no more affected the government than the sound of a gnat. Our rulers disbelieve our statements or profess to do so. Let us now try to force our grievances into their ears by strong constitutional means. We must give the best political education possible to the ignorant villagers. We must meet them on terms of equality, teach them their rights and show how to fight constitutionally. Then only will the government realise that to despise the Congress is to despise the Indian nation. Then only will the efforts of the Congress leaders be crowned with success. Such a work will require a large body of able and single-minded workers, to whom politics would not mean some holiday recreation, but an every-day duty to be performed with the strictest regularity and utmost capacity.[33]

The British-controlled papers found such language particularly unacceptable given that Tilak was a member of the Provincial Legislative Council. They had campaigned against his election in 1895 itself when he was a candidate from the Presidency's central division and faced a nominee of the Ranade faction. When he still won, the *Bombay Gazette* had described him as 'a rabid journalist and a discredited agitator' and called upon the governor to veto his election. Tilak knew that the Indian Councils Act of 1892 had not really empowered the Indians. They had no decision-making powers on the councils and could only make recommendations, and as mentioned earlier, an Indian's election could be nullified by the governor. Yet he had first entered the Poona municipality as a councillor in 1895 and the same year entered the Provincial Council, thinking they were platforms that could nonetheless be used to speak up. Though the

Council met for just eight days in its two-year term and worked for less than thirty-six hours, Tilak on its floor took the opportunity to sharply criticize the government's taxation policy, saying that though the government's collection had gone up considerably, hardly anything had been passed on to the people and for development of the province. In 1897, Tilak's two-year term ended, and he stood for re-election and won again. His Anglo–Indian critics were infuriated, but what they did not know yet was that Tilak's second term was not going to last long beyond a month. He would soon have to quit both from the Council and the Poona municipality.[34]

Bubonic plague struck in 1897, and it made the previous year's famine appear a little less unforgiving. The city of Bombay was the first to be hit in October 1896, and the scourge reached Pune in about four months. In a little over three weeks, 400 people were dead. The British Raj enacted the Epidemic Diseases Act, 1897, granting itself emergency powers to search people and their homes and belongings, segregate those afflicted and detain those who didn't cooperate or blocked government measures.

George Hamilton, the Secretary of State for India, wrote to the viceroy, Lord Elgin, to tell him the government should do everything to stamp out the epidemic and not hesitate to take certain steps due to concerns over the Indian people's social and religious susceptibilities. Elgin told Hamilton not to worry on that score.[35] For the Poona region, the Bombay government formed a three-member Plague Committee to decide and oversee emergency operations. On paper, the panel was well-balanced: its head, William Charles Rand, was a member of the elite Indian Civil Service, and of its two other members, one—C.R. Phillipps—was a military officer, and the other—W.W.O. Beveridge—was a doctor.

Lord Sandhurst, who had replaced Harris as Bombay governor in 1895, invited the top community and party leaders of Poona to inform them of the stringent steps required and sought their cooperation.[36] Tilak was among those called, and he was fully in agreement with the governor that measures such as searches and segregation might appear exacting, but there was no other way to tackle the outbreak. Of those raising fears of oppressive steps, he was initially critical and tried to reassure the people, writing in his paper:

It is important the government knows where the disease is located. For this, there must be a house-to-house search every two-three days. Men must be appointed for this work. There are rumours that these men will oppress people, but they are baseless. Searches are made so that patients should not be hidden in the house, as at present. Force will be used only if attempts are made to hide the patient, otherwise the governor has given strict orders not to molest the people in any way. There is a strict rule that no male servant will touch a woman; for this, a lady doctor will be appointed. The governor has issued instructions to workers not to enter any part of the house and pollute the Gods or hurt the people's religious sentiments.[37]

People had started panicking and leaving Poona in droves. Tilak urged them to stay and assist the Plague Committee.[38] But the gradual outflow of the relatively well-off continued, mostly the poor remained, and within Poona, complaints began to emerge, day after day, about the Plague Committee's excesses. Rand began ominously, by getting around 300 military personnel to build a cordon around two of the city's chief neighbourhoods, Shukrawar Peth and Budhwar Peth, early on a March morning as he launched his inspection campaign. Both British and Indian soldiers were involved, the British soldiers carrying out searches and the Indian ones disinfecting homes, shops and localities. British soldiers entered prayer rooms with their shoes on—an act of sacrilege in most Indian homes. They were accused of casting away idols and other images, forcing open metal safes and cash boxes and carrying away stuff with impunity, and torching beds, cupboards and other belongings of those who were infected or suspect cases and even setting on fire books, including account books, and sewing machines.[39] Both men and women were manhandled, and the locals complained that women were molested.[40]

Gokhale was visiting England at the time to depose on behalf of the Deccan Sabha before the Royal Commission on Indian Expenditure. He told a correspondent of the *Manchester Guardian* that he had seen the outrages before he had left his hometown, and subsequent letters from his Poona friends had established that the horrors had continued. 'Women were dragged into the streets and stripped for inspection, under the pretext that there was not light enough in the houses, and my correspondents, whose word I can trust absolutely, report the violation of two women, one of whom is said afterwards to have committed suicide rather than survive her shame,' Gokhale said. A number of petitions were sent to Rand, including a joint one by the Hindus and Muslims whose relations had been on the edge in the past few years due to riots, but they had gone unheeded. 'Difficult and delicate duties which in Bombay were assigned to native soldiers were in Poona assigned to British soldiers and were kept in their hands in spite of repeated protests from Hindus and Mohammedans alike,' he said, explaining why similar grievances had not been voiced in the island city of Bombay. Tilak was part of a deputation to Rand. That deputation was 'snubbed', Gokhale told the *Manchester Guardian*.[41]

Tilak's papers highlighted the atrocities, as did every Indian publication in the Deccan. *Dynan Prakash*, a daily that Tilak described as Ranade's mouthpiece, accused Rand of simply laughing off complaints and dismissing them as false and alleged he was behaving 'like the Sultan of Turkey'.[42] Tilak asked bluntly, 'What people on earth, however docile, will continue to submit to this sort of mad temper?'[43]

By the end of May, though, the plague appeared to have mostly receded from the limits of Poona, the relief measures came to a standstill, and a sense of normality returned. Families who had left the city too came back. On the anniversary of Chhatrapati Shivaji's coronation in June, Tilak and his aides hosted that year's Shivaji 'utsav' in Poona; the festival was usually held on Shivaji's birth anniversary, but that had been skipped in the previous months because of the plague. The coronation day was on 13 June, and the festival was held over three days, from 12 to 14 June. S.M. Paranjpe, Professor G.S. Jinsiwale, and Professor C.G. Bhanu addressed the participants on the occasion, and Tilak of course made the final speech. A poem was also recited by a young man. *Kesari*'s 15 June issue carried reports of the proceedings, and the poem which had been recited, titled 'Shivaji's Utterances', was published in the same edition.[44]

Exactly a week afterwards, in the afternoon of 22 June 1897, Tilak walked into the precincts of Ganeshkhind, the Poona residence of the governor, for a gathering of European officials and 'some Native gentlemen' that Lord Sandhurst had organized to mark the sixtieth anniversary of Queen Victoria's reign. The guest list mentioned 'the

Hon'ble B. G. Tilak, Member of the Governor's Legislative Council'. Late evening there was a banquet and a reception, and the celebrations ended with fireworks display in the night. Sometime after midnight, a number of horse carriages left the gates of the governor's residence. One of them was occupied by W.C. Rand. It had travelled only some hundred yards when, on the dark and secluded route, someone suddenly climbed on to the carriage from behind and fired shots at Rand with a pistol. In the carriage that followed Rand's was seated Lt O.E. Ayerst, an official in the commissariat department, with his wife by his side. Another assailant climbed onto the spring of his carriage and shot Ayerst through the head. He died immediately, and Rand succumbed after a few days' struggle in a hospital.[45]

The killings reverberated across the Empire, both in England and India and renewed in the minds of the Raj's senior officials fears of an 1857-like uprising. The finger of suspicion was immediately pointed towards the 'Poona Brahmins'—objects of deep distrust and always seen as conspiratorial. The conservative *Daily Mail* of London wrote, 'Poona of course has long been notorious as the hotbed of Southern Indian fanaticism; a town and district where the mutinous, semi-educated Brahmin walked at large, and freely propagated in newspaper and bazaar his faith in the liberation and regeneration of India on high-caste lines.'[46] Pinning all the blame on the 'Poona editor', the *Mail* warned the British government that 'assassination by the pen may, in the long run, prove to be more formidable to British rule in India than assassination by the sword'.[47] *Morning Post* termed the killings 'the outcome and the expression of seditious and bitter feelings . . . inspired mainly by the vernacular press'.[48]

Secretary of State for India Hamilton had telegraphed Governor Sandhurst the morning after the shootings, asking if he linked them 'to the incendiary tone of the press.'[49] Only two days later, the second Indian to become a member of the British Parliament, Mancherjee Bhownaggree, asked Hamilton in the House of Commons 'under what circumstances these diabolical acts were committed'. Bhownaggree was a Parsi from Bombay who had been elected as Conservative Party MP from Bethnal Green in 1895, and he was widely seen as a Tory pawn to act as a counter to Dadabhai Naoroji. The attackers had still not been caught, Hamilton said, 'but with regard to Mr.

Rand', owing to the 'success which had attended his operations in stamping out the plague, he was subjected to most violent attacks in the vernacular press'.[50]

Official discussions veered towards whether a clampdown on the Poona papers was necessary and whether stricter laws had to be put in place. But the viceroy, Lord Elgin, noted in a telegram to Hamilton that governor Sandhurst 'has such ample military and police resources . . . that he can enforce anything which he thinks necessary, while in the Regulation of 1827 he has summary powers of arrest and imprisonment which . . . probably exceed those of the Czar of Russia'.[51]

Sandhurst immediately brought into Poona 'a punitive police force of 50 Europeans and 150 Natives', a third successive blow for the city's residents who were yet to recover from the disasters of the famine and the plague.[52] A curfew-like situation was in place, and CID agents were crawling around the city; one of them had knocked at Tilak's door hours after Rand and Ayerst were shot, ostensibly to inform him of the outrages but in reality to scrutinize his reaction. An award of Rs 20,000 was announced to anyone who'd provide information on the killers, and the district collector and chief magistrate, R. A. Lamb, sent out a strongly worded warning to the residents of Poona. At a citizens' meet, Lamb expressed 'surprise and regret that that no expressions of abhorrence of the crime had emanated from Poona'. Referring to 'the cowardly disloyalty of a secret band of conspirators', he called upon people 'not to be content with passively bewailing this blow' but to 'hold up to universal condemnation' the 'deeds of the sedition-mongers and murderers' and 'to render impossible the existence of persons whose watchword was strife, whose tongues were full of hypocrisy, and whose deeds were red with blood'. There was a tendency, he said, to 'misuse the liberty allowed under British rule and to mislead the generation now growing up with crude, impracticable notions of political independence'. The vernacular press 'had been teeming with thinly veiled sedition' which, Lamb claimed, had produced 'sinister effects' such as 'the extravagant history of Sivaji now being taught to the young'. Asking those who were 'loyal' to 'take such measures towards those found sowing the seeds of disorder as might minimize the necessity of extraordinary measures on the part of the government', Lamb clarified that 'the extent and application of these extraordinary measures would depend mainly on themselves'. The onus thus was placed on the people, and Lamb further stressed that 'the government had power and resources and would use them'.[53]

Tilak's daring work as editor had already set him apart from his contemporaries in the vernacular press. His public activities and increasing following had made him stand out still more. As Poona's cup of woes brimmed over with the punitive police swarming around and the frantic manhunt launched for Rand and Ayerst's killers and Lamb's stern words filled the local population with apprehension, two successive issues of *Kesari* that rolled off the presses carried caustic editorials whose headlines are as widely known today in western India as they were when they were originally published. Tilak's first headline was the terse, fearless and dramatic '*Sarkarche dokey thikanavar aahey kai* [Has the government lost its head?]'. The second one defined the people's restlessness in direct terms, declaring '*Rajya karney mhanje sud ugavney navhey* [To rule is not to be vindictive]'.

Tilak's initial reaction to the shootings had been to publicly deplore them and ask the people of Poona to cooperate with the police in their probe. So, when he asked stormily if the government had lost its head, he said, many readers of *Kesari* were likely to ask him instead if he had lost his own. But he was going to explain himself. There was no reason for the government to issue severe threats to the people through the district collector when it had in any case resolved to spend Rs 2.75 lakh to bring in more cops into Poona in the next two years, he said. It was 'wrong and sheer madness' to say that youngsters who had obtained modern education and people who organized the Shivaji festival and ran Marathi papers were behind the atrocious acts, and that if they were not reined in, the result would be disaster. 'Why just Pune, the whole region could be made desolate and bleak by the government by firing from canons and using its limitless powers. But by putting it nearly in so many words, Mr. Lamb has demonstrated his arrogance and conceit,' Tilak wrote. 'It's hard to get 5 or 25 Brahmans together in Pune to get any good work done. What to speak of unspeakable crimes? But is the government going to give any thought to this? It is behaving like an elephant gone wild, trampling on everything in sight. It has lost its mind.' On the same day that Rand and Ayerst were shot, a European had been killed in Punjab, but the government had not spelled out the word sedition. Tilak said, 'It's wrong for the government to think that conspiracies are being secretly hatched in Pune or that secret societies are at work here. Hang those who have carried out the killings. That will be good and satisfying for us. But why the government should spare the criminal and hang those doing good work is beyond us.' To punish all the people of the city in which an official had been killed was 'brutal and cold-blooded', he argued, and added that holding an entire populace at gunpoint was akin to wreaking vengeance.[54]

However pungent Tilak's twin editorials might have been, his speech at the Shivaji festival on 13 June—that is, nine days before the shootings—was momentarily under greater scrutiny in the pro-British papers. *Times of India*'s attention had been drawn to it before Rand's killing by a correspondent who wrote in using the pseudonym 'Justice'. In his letter, which *The Times* published on 19 June—that is, three days before the Poona killings—'Justice' had written:

> The words used by Mr. Tilak at the second day of the Sivaji festival . . . are so important that . . . I enclose them in the original Marathi from Mr. Tilak's paper, the Kesari, of which the following is a literal translation:
> "He (Sivaji) murdered Afzul Khan with good intentions and for the good of the people. *If robbers entered our house and if our wrists possessed no strength to drive them out, we should without hesitation lock them in and burn them alive.* The Mlenchas have got no parchment (authorizing them) to rule India and the Maharaja (Sivaji) endeavoured to drive them out of his native country."
> The italics are mine. Comment on these words is superfluous. I may, however, state what is well known (is) that the word mlenchas means those who are outside the pale of Hinduism, and is applicable equally to Mahomedans and Christians.
> June 16.   JUSTICE.[55]

Two days after the Poona killings, *Times of India* wrote an editorial calling Tilak's nomination for a second time to the Governor's Executive Council (or the Provincial Legislative Council) 'a grave error'.[56] How did the question of nomination come in when the elective principle had been brought in? The truth is, the elective element had been introduced only indirectly in a 'constitutional compromise' that specified the government would 'nominate' to the Council 'non-official members elected by an enfranchised elite.'[57] If the governor refused to nominate or cancelled the nomination, the so-called election had little meaning. *The Times* wrote that Tilak had made 'a scandalous attempt to bring the viceroy under popular hatred and contempt', which was 'a plain mark of disaffection towards the chief personage in the State' and 'plain proof that the person responsible for it was unworthy of the confidence of government'. 'A more recent pronouncement of Mr. Tilak's, which is translated in a letter' the paper had carried, 'points as unmistakably to the same conclusion', it said.[58]

On June 28, the paper published another letter, written under the pseudonym 'Shackles', which quoted Tilak's editorial comments on Rand's anti-plague measures in *Kesari* and insinuated that Tilak was linked to the killings of Rand and Ayerst. 'Shackles' went on to say that if only the government had invoked the section on sedition in the Indian Penal Code when the Poona press was targeting it, 'the conspiracy to murder . . . would probably have never been organized'.[59] The next day, an editorial in the paper headlined 'The Sivaji cult' alleged that 'self-interested intriguers have converted the (Shivaji) movement into one which they hope will cause hindrance to British rule'.[60]

Tilak sent a detailed rejoinder to the paper, saying:

Your continued malicious remarks about me and the journals published by me compel me to write this letter. I do not expect any praise from you, but I believed the Times, under its present editorship, would at least be fair; but your recent articles have more than disappointed me . . . The shocking tragedy at Poona, which we all deplore, may have obscured your judgement. But I have little to do with your motives. What I want to show is that you have entirely misrepresented my position . . . I should have attributed it to your ignorance of the language in which the Kesari is published, as well as of what was going on in the city at the time (of the plague), had I not perceived a deliberate intention in your writing, as well as those of 'Shackles' and 'Justice', to pervert and misrepresent obvious facts at a time when they think they can do greatest mischief by each representation.

After outlining how he had backed the government's anti-plague measures and called upon the people to support them, Tilak spoke of how he had thrown himself into the work of fighting the plague by implementing the relief steps himself while asking Poona's residents to do the same:

> I was not satisfied simply with taunting or advising the leaders to organize *peth* (area) committees. I myself went (with other friends whose work I may once for all here state I do not wish to under-rate in any way by stating what I did personally) into a number of *peths* and tried to establish such committees, but found that it was not possible to do so, as most of the leading men had gone out of the town. As regards the Hindu Plague Hospital [which Tilak had set up with funds from donors], I think I can claim a considerable share of the credit of starting and maintaining it in good order. I used to visit it twice a day, going into the different wards and making inquiries about the patients. Then as regards the segregation camp, it was soon found that the persons taken there were being greatly inconvenienced by being required to cook their own food, and that though the Plague Committee paid two annas per head per day to the poor, it was not sufficient to purchase a day's provision. Here again I, along with other friends, had to work hard to establish a kitchen, where two regular meals were given for two annas to anyone in the segregation camp. The loss, which came to about one and a half anna per head per day, was met from subscriptions raised for that purpose. In short, I tried to do all that was possible for me to make the plague measures acceptable to the people, and everything that was done was done with the knowledge and consent of the chairman of the Plague Committee.

Tilak pointed out that:

> If this is sedition, then the Anglo-Indian vocabulary must be more comprehensive than the common English (one) . . . It was my firm conviction that stringent sanitary measures would do considerable good . . . and I have not only expressed this conviction in the papers, but have done as much as a single citizen of my position could do to practically show how people should help themselves and not blame the Plague Committee for everything.

However, he added:

> Unlike yourselves I could not shut up my eyes to complaints and
> grievances, which from personal knowledge I was convinced were
> real and well-founded. I, along with other friends, was the first to
> bring them to the notice of the Plague Committee, but I regret to
> say that the Committee, from whatever cause, never took any serious
> notice of them. I know a number of cases where persons were wrongly
> sent to the segregation camp or plague hospital, or their property was
> wantonly destroyed; and if the papers which I publish, along with
> others, loudly complained about these grievances, it was because the
> Plague Committee could not, or would not, redress them. You and
> your correspondents, I know, hold the opinion that the complaints
> were unfounded. But my personal experience is otherwise, and
> I still hold that the Plague Committee could have executed the task
> equally well in a far more conciliatory manner. If we could make
> the segregation camp a little more comfortable by having a kitchen
> therein, the Plague Committee could have certainly done better . . .
> It is a sheer mistake to believe that the native papers have excited
> the feeling of dissatisfaction . . . The Press accepted the principle,
> but complained about the unnecessary harshness in its execution
> . . . The Bombay government itself anticipated dissatisfaction,
> scavengers' strikes or riots if plague measures were stringently carried
> out (vide Plague Blue Book), and it so telegraphed to the Secretary
> of State. If you blame the native press now you must equally blame
> the Government of Bombay for openly recording their fears in a
> telegram which is now as much known to the public as anything
> said in the native press. Anglo-Indian journalists like yourselves can,
> I know, be hardly induced to take the right view of the question. But
> still I must state what I honestly believe to be the case, viz., that the
> unnecessary stringency of the plague measures, and not the writings
> in the native press, are responsible for the feelings of dissatisfaction
> referred to by you.

Accusing the paper of making reckless charges, Tilak concluded that:

> It is extremely foolish to ignore all the work done by individuals, and
> the good sense and the patience of a community as a whole, simply

because a fanatic took it into his head to perpetrate a horrible deed, which . . . all of us equally deplore. Further discussion must, I think, be reserved for cooler times, when we shall be ready to look at men and things with unjaundiced eyes.[61]

Times of India nevertheless took its unrelenting campaign against Tilak forward and advised the government to slap sedition cases against the editor of *Kesari* and other editors of the native papers. About Tilak, it made clear its opinion that 'whatever he may say, his disaffection for the government is not superficial and temporary but very deep and of a permanent nature'.[62]

The papers in Britain could scarcely believe that such a man as B.G. Tilak was being allowed to operate freely in India and, horror of horrors, had found a seat not once but twice in the legislature. *Morning Post* characterized him as 'one of the most dangerous forces in India' who 'for years' had used his journal 'to spread the basest fabrications concerning British officials'. He had 'produced an outbreak of disorder and insolence', and now that his 'deliberate policy' had 'borne its natural fruit – outrage – he is reported to have been promoted by those same officials to a position of some honour.' Since 'the native', *Post* wrote condescendingly of Indians, 'cannot possibly understand what is popularly described as an "enlightened policy"' and 'force appeals to him and, at least, he pays it the tribute of his respect', such a reward for Tilak would 'inevitably' give rise to the belief 'that Britain is afraid, and that he has been speaking something near the truth in his continual slanders against the rulers of his country'. More so, 'he will be looked at as one who has intimidated the Government of India, and so his influence for evil will be increased enormously'. What was the right approach, then? 'Tilak in prison for sedition-mongering would have formed a vastly more instructive object-lesson to the people of India', the paper suggested.[63]

While the mild-mannered and liberal *Guardian* named Tilak's two papers as among those which had brought 'vile and reckless charges' against officials engaged in plague duty, the bearer of imperialistic pride, *The Times* of London, cautioned the government that there had been no major change 'in the tone of the native press since the Poona murders' and that 'the worst possible effect will be produced if a policy of inaction be persisted in'.[64] An anonymous letter writer to the London *Times*, who called himself 'Scrutatus', referred to the allegations against plague officials made by Gokhale in the British capital and challenged him to 'either offer proof of them or confess that the only authority for them is the vague impersonal statements of the vile papers edited by Mr. Tilak and other of Mr Gokhlee's (sic) personal friends'.[65]

In the third week of July 1897, Mancherjee Bhownaggree stood up to speak in the House of Commons. *Guardian* reported that he was, 'on rising, loudly cheered', and proceeded to ask the secretary of state for India, Hamilton, 'if he was aware that in the last two years an annual celebration to stir up disaffection against England among the natives of India had been set on foot under the designation of the Shivajee Accession ceremony'. Such a ceremony had taken place the previous month in Poona, he said, and 'one Professor (S.M.) Paranjpe' had 'delivered a discourse' whose 'substance' was that 'in discontent lies the root of prosperity.' On the same occasion, the Parsi Tory MP said, '[A] man named (G. S.) Jinsiwale stated that Shivaji's ruling passion was a terrible disgust at the humiliation of his country and religion by aliens – that was, the British – and added that he did not see why the saying of the revolutionists in France that they were not murdering men but simply removing the thorns in their way, should not be made applicable to the Deccan.' Was Hamilton aware, asked Bhownaggree, that 'Gungadhar Tilak . . . presided at the celebration and made a speech in which he counselled the murder of Europeans and (said) that the *mlecchas* – that was, the British – had no charter from God to rule India?' And had any steps been taken by the local authorities to stop such 'incitement' to 'actions as led to the assassinations of Mr Rand and Lt Ayerst within a week of the Shivajee celebration?' Hamilton replied that he knew of the recently started festival and had read reports of speeches which he said 'accord with the description given of them' by the MP, and whether they constituted incitement or not was something the governments of India and Bombay were now looking at.[66]

A month passed. The killers of Rand and Ayerst had not been found. In the last week of July, Tilak proceeded to Bombay for work on a booklet he wished to bring out on the anti-plague measures. He was staying at the home of his lawyer friend Daji Abaji Khare in Girgaum, in the southern part of the city. At 10 p.m. on 27 July 1897, there was a knock at Khare's door. The police had come for his guest. Late in the night, Tilak was arrested on charges of sedition for the comments he had made at the Shivaji festival in Poona, which were published in the *Kesari* on 15 June. He was taken straight to the Esplanade Police Court *chowkie*, where he was kept in a room till the next morning.[67] The authorities had chosen the hour of arrest carefully to prevent any public disorder or possible mobilization. Khare, a lawyer, reached the residence of the chief presidency magistrate before midnight to seek bail for Tilak, but it was declined. From there, Khare went to the police court chowkie to tell his friend about the rejection of bail. According to a story since widely circulated, Tilak was fast asleep and had to be woken up. When Khare told him that the magistrate had been a disappointment, Tilak retorted, 'Why wake me up for this? You could have told me in the morning.'[68]

The office of the *Kesari* was searched in Poona, and several books and papers were seized. The printer of the Aryabhushan Press, Keshavrao Bal, was taken into custody. Similarly, the Natu brothers Balasaheb and Tatyasaheb, were arrested from their Poona residence at dawn and deported from Poona.[69] Though the government cited Tilak's speech reproduced by *Kesari* as seditious in order to take him into custody, it strongly suspected he had had a role to play in the Poona killings. A letter sent by Sandhurst to Hamilton almost immediately after Tilak's arrest showed the Raj's motivations. The Bombay governor informed the secretary of state of India, 'We have arrested Balwantrao Ramchandra (Balasaheb) Natu and Hari Ramchandra (Tatyasaheb) Natu. Along with Tilak, these two brothers are pillars of the group that is generally known to express and propagate seditious views. The native gentlemen of Poona are unanimous in thinking that the Natu brothers have had a hand in the murders. Our officials think that if these three people are taken out of Poona, there is a possibility of the government getting important information about the murders.'[70]

Tilak was taken to the police court the following afternoon, where 'Mr. Russell' of the law firm Messrs Russell and Deshpande, instructed by M. R. Bodas, made a formal application for his release on bail. It was rejected. The police felt vindicated in having chosen a particular hour for Tilak's arrest: at the police court, the Reuters correspondent reported, 'there was a large crowd . . . and unusual excitement prevailed.'[71]

The same day, a Reuters correspondent met a superannuated British official, Lepel Griffin, for an interview. Griffin had served as secretary of the Punjab and earned fame for his diplomacy with the Afghans during the Afghan war of the late 1870s. He was later appointed the governor-general's agent in central India and worked closely with several princely states. Though retired in 1889, he was consulted often by other officials and interviewed by the British press over Indian affairs. When the Reuters man pressed into his hand a telegram containing news of Tilak's arrest, Griffin looked at it and said, 'I rejoice.'[72] He might have been speaking for most former and sitting officials of the Raj.

The next day, Tilak's lawyers filed a bail plea in the Bombay High Court. M.G. Ranade had by now been appointed a judge in the high court, and a bench that included him and Justice Parsons refused bail. The case was then committed to the sessions in the high court where, early in August, the Parsi lawyer Dinshaw D. Davar, appearing for Tilak, applied to Justice Badruddin Tyabji for bail.

Just like Ranade, Tyabji had been a prominent activist and leader. If the first president of the Indian National Congress, the Calcutta lawyer W.C. Bonnerjee, had been a Hindu and the second, Naoroji, a Parsi, Tyabji, a Muslim of the Shiite Khoja sect, became the third president of the Congress at Madras in 1887. He was a liberal and went on to become India's first Muslim judge in the high courts. Granting bail to Tilak, Tyabji said, 'I cannot believe that a gentleman in Tilak's position would not be forthcoming at the trial . . . The ends of justice might be defeated if I refused to grant bail, for it is just possible that if he is imprisoned for a month, it might be ultimately found that he was not guilty.'[73]

Once out on bail, Tilak went home to Poona, where he got a disconcerting bit of news which couldn't have boded well for him given the legal tangle he'd found himself in. Only a few days ago, Gokhale had landed on Bombay's shores. He had been facing tremendous pressure in England to substantiate the charges he had levelled against the Plague Committee at a meeting in London. Gokhale had responded that he had got the information from reliable correspondents who had written letters to him from home, but the British press and large sections of Britain's political class insisted he produce proof in particular of the allegation that a woman had been violated and had preferred to end her life than lead a life of shame. It wasn't easy to produce proof, and

Gokhale's entreaties to friends revealed that nothing legally admissible could be found, especially because hardly any witnesses were expected to come forward for fear of the authorities' wrath. Giving up all hope and genuinely dejected and downcast, Gokhale on his return home offered a 'full retraction' and 'unqualified apology' and withdrew all the accusations he had made. Tilak was very upset. Such backpedalling could discredit the several complaints people had about the Plague Committee's atrocities, he felt. His paper, *Mahratta*, also wondered why Gokhale had issued an apology for all the charges when he could have, in the absence of irrefutable evidence, only withdrawn the one about a woman being violated, which seemed to be the sole issue of contention among the vocal Britons. In view of his approaching trial, Tilak also made a cutting reference to Gokhale in a letter to Motilal Ghose, founder of the Calcutta newspaper *Amrita Bazar Patrika*: 'I think in me they [government] will not find a *kutcha* (weak and raw) reed as they did in Professor Gokhale.'[74]

Tilak's trial began on 8 September 1897 and lasted six days. L.P. Pugh of the Calcutta Bar was on his way to England from Bombay. Tilak's friend Motilal Ghose asked Pugh to lead the defence for the *Kesari* editor, proprietor and publisher. Pugh was accompanied by W. Garth, who also belonged to the Calcutta bar. And there was Davar, of course, who continued to appear for Tilak.

At the same time, a public fund was set up by Tilak's well-wishers. According to a secret report prepared by the Bombay government, the total contributions to it added up to Rs 40,000. Motilal Ghose, president of the first Congress session W.C. Bonnerjee and poet Rabindranath Tagore instituted their own fund in Calcutta and put together Rs 16,768 and 8 annas, to be precise. Most contributors were unwilling to reveal their names, so the first subscription entry simply said, 'By cash received from XYZ – Rs 500.'[75]

The prosecution was carried out by Advocate–General Basil Lang before the court of Justice Arthur Strachey. The jury for the case had nine members: six Europeans and three Indians (two Hindus and a Parsi).

The prosecutor-in-chief started his arguments by reading aloud Section 124A of the Indian Penal Code or IPC. This clause on sedition had been introduced in the IPC in 1870, and the first case to be tried under it, twenty-one years later, was that of Jogendra Chunder Bose, editor of the Bengali periodical *Bangobasi*. Bose was booked in 1891 after he criticized the government's proposed Age of Consent Act. There was no conviction; in the absence of a unanimous verdict, the Calcutta High Court had let him off. Tilak was only the second Indian to be booked for sedition.

Lang spelt out what the section said, a definition that was to prove vital in view of the turn the case eventually took. Who was a seditionist? 'Whoever, by words either spoken or intended to be read, or by signs, or by visible representation, or otherwise, excites or attempts to excite feelings of disaffection to the Government established by law in British India,' the clause said. If held guilty, what punishment would such a person get? 'Transportation for life, or for any term to which fine may be added or with imprisonment for a term which may extend to three years, in which fine may be added, or with fine.' The section had an explanation annexed to it, which said, 'Such disapprobation of the measure of the Government as is compatible with a disposition to render obedience to the lawful authority of the Government and to support the lawful authority of the Government against unlawful attempts to subvert or resist that authority is not disaffection. Therefore the making of comments on the measures of Government with the intention of exciting only this species of disapprobation is not an offence within this clause.'

Two specific charges were laid out against Tilak. The first was that he had published in the *Kesari* of 15 June 1897 the report on the Shivaji festival meeting and a poem 'Shivaji's Utterances', which 'excited feelings of disaffection' against the Raj. And the second was that he had 'attempted' to create such disaffection.[76]

What were the objectionable lines the prosecution was citing? While S. M. Paranjpe, who was the young editor of the Marathi paper *Kaal*, had drawn parallels between the past of the Mahabharata and the present, Jinsiwale had said Shivaji was superior to Caesar and Napoleon as he was not actuated by self-ambition but by service to his country. Professor Bhanu had waded into the Shivaji-Afzal Khan controversy, which was very much alive in the public sphere ever since R.P. Karkaria had raised the issue in 1894; Professor Bain of the Deccan College had also recently, like Karkaria, testified that Shivaji was justified in killing the Bijapur general. Bhanu strongly attacked the English historians who had sought to blame the Maratha hero and produced facts and quotes from historical documents to back his argument.[77] Tilak, referring to Bhanu's speech, had said:

> Was this act of Maharaj (of killing Afzal Khan) good or bad? This question should not be viewed from the standpoint of the Penal Code or the Smritis of Manu or Yagnavalkya or the principles of morality laid down in the Western and Eastern ethical systems. The laws which bind society are for common men like you and I . . . These principles fail in their scope to reach the pedestal of great men.

Tilak had then gone on to say which principles actually applied, in his opinion:

> Did Shivaji commit a sin in killing Afzal Khan? The answer to this question can be found in the Mahabharata itself. Shrimat Krishna's teaching in the Gita calls for the killing even of one's teachers and kin. No blame at all attaches to a person if he is doing deeds without being actuated by a desire to reap the fruits of his actions. Shri Shivaji Maharaj did not commit the deed for personal motives. He killed Afzulkhan from disinterested motives for the public good. If thieves enter a house and we have not sufficient strength in our wrists to drive them out, we should without hesitation shut them up and burn them alive. God has not granted the *mlecchas* (foreigners) a copper plate (*sanad* or charter) to rule India. Shivaji was not guilty of coveting what belonged to others, because he strove to drive them out from the land of his birth. Don't circumscribe your vision like a frog in a well. Get out of the Penal Code, enter the sublime sphere of the Bhagawad Gita, and consider the achievements of great men.[78]

In the same speech, Tilak had powerfully supported Bhanu's declaration that 'every Mahratta, every Hindu, must rejoice at the Shivaji celebration. We are all striving to regain our lost independence, and this terrible load is to be lifted up by us all with joint efforts'.[79]

The poem 'Shivaji's Utterances' had an imaginary speech delivered by Chhatrapati Shivaji. It quoted him as saying, 'I delivered the country by establishing Swarajya and by saving religion . . . Alas! I now see with my own eyes the ruin of my country . . . There was a time when no one raised his eyes towards our women. If someone did, a thousand sharp swords leapt out of their scabbards instantly. But now, the demons are dragging away Lakshmi violently by the hand and by persecution . . . How do you tolerate it?'[80]

A 'letter to the editor', written by someone who had identified himself as 'Ganesh', was in addition cited by the prosecution as proof that the paper produced incendiary material. Mentioning the great deeds of Lord Ram, the hero of the Hindu epic Ramayana, the letter had said Shivaji had followed the example of the great prince and expressed the desire that a Shivaji be born in the new era.[81]

The prosecution argued that the language of the articles and the poem was such that it 'can only be intended to excite disaffection . . . and to seek to overthrow British rule'. Lang alleged that Tilak and his printer, Keshavrao Bal, were 'inciting' people to 'imitate the example of Shivaji' and comparing 'the state of the country as it was in Shivaji's time with what it is now' to 'impress upon their countrymen how justifiable it would be for them to overthrow the Government, as it is at present established.'[82]

Lang claimed one of the *Kesari* articles in relation to which charges had been framed 'contained a clear attempt to justify political assassination' and said it was 'significant' that Rand and Ayerst were killed 'within a week of publication of these articles.' He 'could not produce evidence to show the murders were caused directly by the publication of these articles', but added that 'it would be for the jury to form an opinion as to the probable effect of publishing such articles at a time when much excitement and distress existed in consequence of the famine and plague and the measures which the government had been obliged to take.'[83]

The first witness to take the stand was Mirza Abbas Ali Baig, the 'Oriental translator' for the government. Tilak, with his exceptional hold over the Marathi language, questioned Baig's translations from the original Marathi to English, and the judge even asked Tilak 'to explain some expressions'. At one point, Justice Strachey had the matter of translations very much on his mind. Mid-way through the trial proceedings he told Advocate-General Lang, 'There is one question on which I like to take time to consider. It is with reference to some of these translations; there has been a good deal of dispute about the meaning of some of these words. In a matter of this kind, it is extremely difficult for the jury, who are not Marathi scholars, and for me also, to say what is the proper rendering of these passages. And I think I should consider the matter fully between this (today) and tomorrow whether or not I should myself call a witness who is an expert in Marathi, to give an opinion as to some of these passages.' Yet, the following morning, Justice Strachey decided he wasn't going to call in a Marathi expert but would allow the trial to proceed.[84]

Still, the debate over the language continued. Lang told the judge and jury, 'They have [in Bhanu's speech] this significant sentence, that in the times of Shivaji 'a thousand swords would have leapt from their scabbards.' That does not look like passive redress, and then immediately before the words 'get that addressed' the people of this country are stigmatized as eunuchs, because they have endured this sort of thing. Do you think, gentlemen, that the drift of the person who has stigmatized the people as eunuchs is merely to suggest to the persons who read these articles that they are to apply to the proper authorities by representation for the redress of their grievances?'

Tilak's lawyer Pugh asked the judge if the accused could be allowed to sit right behind him, so he might take directions from him if needed while making his arguments. The judge gave his approval, and Tilak emerged from the dock and took a chair behind as Pugh stood up to speak.[85]

Pugh referred to the line about 'dragging away Lakshmi by the hand'. For 'hand,' *Kesari* had used the word '*kar*', which could also mean 'taxes' in Marathi. Pugh said, 'There you have "The foreigners are teasingly and forcibly dragging Lakshmi by the hand." If you look at the Anglo-Indian papers . . . you will find there are heart-rending complaints increasing . . . with regard to the expenditure on the war on the North-West frontier. You remember also that at the time of the Chitral Expedition (a military expedition of 1895 by the British to relieve the besieged fort of Chitral beyond the North-West Frontier) many of the very prominent Englishmen said . . . rightly or wrongly: 'You are spending money here which the country cannot spare . . . and which the country will never be able to stand' . . . the Advocate General has admitted that it is not seditious to say 'India is getting poor'. How is it then sedition if you say, 'Lakshmi is being dragged by the hand.' I do not care whether it is translated 'by the hand' or 'by imposition of taxes'. With regard to the income-tax there is unanimous discontent amongst Anglo-Indians and natives at the present day . . . In other countries you will find these complaints about taxation. You are perfectly familiar with this at home, but no one is ever charged with sedition for blaming the Government in spending money out of the country for the purpose of foreign warfare.'[86]

The defence side contended that the case ought to have been heard in Poona, where *Kesari* was published and printed, and not in Bombay. The language of the courts in Poona was Marathi, so they were best equipped to try the matter, it said. 'You have this extraordinary position,' Pugh said, addressing the judge and jury. 'The majority of you, the gentlemen of the jury, do not know Marathi. The learned judge has told us that he does not know Marathi.'[87]

Addressing the jury after the arguments of the prosecution and defence were over, Justice Strachey first explained why his court indeed had the jurisdiction to try the case. '*Kesari*,' he said, 'has a considerable circulation, having six or seven thousand subscribers, not only in Poona, but in many other places, including Bombay. This particular issue of the 15th June . . . was sent by post from the office at Poona to the subscribers in Bombay and elsewhere. So the paper's publication extended to Bombay. Sending the newspaper by post . . . constitutes in law the publication in Bombay or any other place to which it is so sent.'[88] And even if a Poona court were to hear the case, the judge said, 'it would have been tried only by a judge, assisted by assessors. But the assessors' verdict is not in any way binding upon the judge, and if the case had been tried there, there would have been an appeal to this Court . . . This would have been very inconvenient, and it was desirable to have the trial at a more convenient place. Besides, Poona was in a state of excitement. Here we have a calmer atmosphere. This is a most important case. It is the second case of its kind that has been brought before a jury in India, and the first in this Presidency.'[89]

The judge then told the members of the jury how he thought they ought to address the linguistic tangle and interpret the meaning of the articles. They must address the question of Tilak's intent, he said, and they must use their own judgement as well. As a matter of fact, he suggested, it would be tricky to get caught up in the intricacies of the words too much:

> What is the intention that the articles themselves convey to your minds? In considering this, you must first ask yourselves what would be the natural and probable effect of reading such articles in the minds of the readers of the Kesari, to whom they were addressed? Read these articles, and ask yourselves how the ordinary readers of the Kesari would probably feel when reading them. Would the feeling produced be one of hatred to the government, or would it be simply one of interest in a poem and a historical discussion about Shivaji and Afzul Khan and so forth? . . . It would be idle and absurd to ask yourselves what would be the effect of these articles upon the minds of persons reading them in a London drawing room or in the Yacht Club in Bombay; but what you have to consider is their effect, not upon Englishmen or Parsis or even many cultivated and philosophic Hindus, but upon the readers of the Kesari among whom they are circulated and read – Hindus, Marathas, inhabitants of the Deccan and the Konkan. And you have to consider . . . the state of things existing . . . in June 1897, when these articles were disseminated among them.
>
> Then you have to look at the standing and the position of the prisoner Tilak. He is a man of influence and importance among the people . . .
>
> But in the next place, in judging of the intention of the accused, you must be guided not only by your estimate of the effect of the articles upon the minds of their readers, but also by your common sense, your knowledge of the world, your understanding of the meaning of words, and your experience of the way in which a man writes when he is animated by a particular feeling. Read the articles, and ask yourselves, as men of the world, whether they impress you on the whole as a mere poem and a historical discussion without disloyal purpose or as attacks on the British government under the disguise of a poem and historical discussion. It may not be easy to express the difference in words; but the difference in tone and spirit and general drift between a writer who is trying to stir up ill-will and one who is not, is generally unmistakeable . . . You can form a pretty accurate

notion of what a man is driving at, or what he wants to convey, from a perusal of the writing, and can generally tell whether the writing is inspired by good-will or is meant to create ill-will. It is not very difficult to distinguish between the language of hostility and the language of loyalty . . . If the object of a publication is really seditious, it does not matter what form it takes . . . A poem, an allegory, a drama, a philosophical or historical discussion, may be used for the purpose of exciting disaffection, just as much as direct attacks upon the government. You have to look through the form and look to the real object; you have to consider whether the form of a poem or discussion is genuine, or whether it has been adopted merely to disguise the real seditious intention of the writer . . . It would be a great mistake to let the decision of this case turn upon mere verbal niceties of translation or discussions as to the best English equivalents of particular Marathi terms. We must look at these articles, not as grammarians and philologists might do, but as the ordinary readers of the *Kesari* would look at them – readers who are impressed not by verbal refinements but by the broad general drift of an article.[90]

Having indicated the broad sense of direction, as it were, Justice Strachey proceeded to explain what exactly constituted the crime of sedition. His reading of the provision turned out to be dreadfully and dangerously easy. 'Disaffection means simply the absence of affection,' he declared. 'It means hatred, enmity, dislike, hostility, contempt, and every form of ill-will to the government. Disloyalty is perhaps the best general term comprehending every possible form of bad feeling to the government. It means everything that indicates hostility to government . . . You will observe that the amount or intensity of the disaffection is absolutely immaterial except perhaps in dealing with the question of punishment; if a man excites or attempts to excite feelings of disaffection, great or small, he is guilty under the section. In the next place, it is absolutely immaterial whether any feelings of disaffection have been excited or not by the publication.'[91]

At 5 p.m. on 14 September 1897, the jury retired for deliberations. They emerged forty minutes later, to say there had been no unanimity, but a majority verdict was in place. All six Europeans had pronounced Tilak guilty; the three Indian members of the jury said he was not guilty. The judge accepted the majority verdict.

The clerk of the Crown stood up and, addressing the man in the dock, said, 'Tilak, you have been found guilty . . . Have you anything to say why judgement should not be passed upon you?'

Tilak said:

In spite of that verdict I still maintain I am innocent, and for this reason: I think the verdict has been arrived at owing to the misunderstanding of certain Marathi texts. In fact, there was not a single intelligent Mahratta gentleman put into the witness box by the prosecution. It seems to have been lost sight of, and not pressed on the attention of the jury, but whatever it is, I still hold that the writings themselves are not seditious. They were not written with any seditious intention, and were not likely to produce that effect, and I do not think they have produced that effect on the readers of the Kesari, or would produce on any intelligent Mahratta readers.[92]

The judge noted:

Tilak, you have been found guilty of attempting to excite feelings of disaffection to the British government established by law. And I agree with that verdict. I do not think any reasonable and fair man applying his mind to these articles could doubt that in publishing them, you have been animated by a feeling of disloyalty and disaffection . . . and that you attempted to inspire those feelings in your readers.

On the sentencing, the judge said:

I may state at once that I do not intend to pass on you the maximum sentence allowed by law, or anything like that sentence. In my opinion the maximum sentence ought to be reserved for the worst possible offender under that section. Although I take a serious view of your offence, I do not take such a serious view of it as that.

Strachey explained what he was going to consider when deciding on the quantum of punishment:

> I take into account that this is the very first prosecution under this section in the Presidency and the second in India. The section under which you have been convicted has been allowed to remain for a considerable time almost as a dead letter, and I think you and others like you may have been emboldened by this to think that there was no kind of writing in which you might not indulge with impunity. I shall also take into account and will attach still more weight to the fact that, at all events for a considerable period, you did good work in connection with the plague and attempted to enforce a reasonable policy upon your countrymen. To that extent you cooperated with the government . . . not long before you published these articles . . .
>
> But on the other hand, I must take into account certain other facts which are not in your favour. You are not an ordinary obscure editor and publisher, but you are one of the leading members of your community; and a man of influence – many of your people look for their guidance to you – a man of intelligence, a man of remarkable ability and energy, who might under other circumstances have been a useful force in the State. Instead of adopting that course which would have brought you credit, you have allowed yourself to publish articles of this kind which, if persisted in, could only bring misfortune upon the people.
>
> I must also take into account that a man like you must know that, at such a time as this, it behoves everyone, especially persons of influence, to be careful as to how they address the people in regard to their relations with the British government.[93]

The judge convicted Tilak and sentenced him to eighteen months of rigorous imprisonment; Keshavrao Bal was declared not guilty and let off. As a result of his conviction, Tilak also lost his position as a member of the Provincial Legislative Council and the Poona municipality.

There was massive curiosity across India about which way the trial would go, and in the evening the verdict was to come in, significant crowds had gathered around newspaper offices in various cities and towns. In Madras, the people who had massed around the office of *The Hindu* got impatient and left for the telegraph office, where they found a bigger crowd had turned up.[94] In Poona, wrote *Dynan Prakash*, the mouthpiece of the reformers, 'many people, with a pardonable religious belief, too near suspicion, had observed a fast the previous day (Monday) expecting the verdict would be declared that day, and continued without food the whole of the next, praying all the while for a favourable result'.[95]

Describing the popular reaction to the verdict, *The Hindu* wrote, 'The conviction of Mr Tilak has cast a gloom over the whole country.' There was 'intense grief' and 'a sense of humiliation', the paper said, and 'the policy of reaction, which for some time the enemies of the Indian people have been urging, has triumphed'.[96] The Allahabad-based paper, *Advocate*, said the judgement had created a 'sensation . . . throughout the length and breadth of India' and noted that the trial had 'made his (Tilak's) name a household word,' and 'every Indian who reads newspapers, or keeps himself in any way in touch with public opinion feels strongly for him . . . while there are thousands, nay, lakhs . . . who consider him a martyr to his country'.[97] *Native Opinion* of Bombay said that 'government at once have raised Mr. Tilak very high in public estimation by setting all their machinery in motion in order to send him to prison. Mr. Tilak in prison is now a much greater man than he ever was before.'[98]

In Calcutta, three papers—the *Amrita Bazar Patrika*, the *Bengalee* and the *Indian Mirror*—had black borders on their front pages of 25 September 1897 as a mark of solidarity and protest, and *The Hindu* suggested that newspapers carry, for one day, no matter other than the portrait of Tilak. In Lucknow, students of a college walked into their classes with black bands around their arms; in Bombay, groups that held Dussehra processions decided to cancel their annual fest; and in Poona, workers at the Poona Cotton and Silk Manufacturing Company skipped their employer's Dussehra function.[99]

Justice Strachey's startling interpretation of the sedition law came in for considerable criticism, and not just from Indian commentators. Perhaps the pithiest and most acute attack came much later, from the British official John Simon, who was to himself become infamous in India over a Commission he would head in the late 1920s. Simon said Strachey's definition of 'disaffection' was akin to saying 'disease' was the 'absence of ease'.[100] The Indian newspapers and journals said his definition was so detrimental to the freedom of the press that it had made gagging legislation of the kind Lytton had introduced in the 1870s to throttle the vernacular papers totally unnecessary.[101]

An application filed in the Bombay High Court on Tilak's behalf to allow him to appeal to the Privy Council naturally focused on Strachey's exposition of the law, which according to Tilak's papers had 'misdirected' and 'prejudiced' the jury.[102] The *Kesari* remarked defiantly that 'The legislature which introduced the section in the Penal Code had not the least idea that it was capable of bearing such an absurd and mischievous meaning . . . As a wretched critic makes himself ridiculous by . . . distorting a poet's words . . . so the judge who extracts such a meaning from the words of legislators as they never dreamt of, equally becomes the laughing-stock of the world.'[103]

There was also the question of constitution of the jury. In the Raj, Englishmen and Englishwomen had the right to be tried by a predominantly European jury. Not so the Indians. *Kesari* called this 'a very serious defect in the existing law', and so long as it was not removed, 'all talk of equality of law between the rulers and the ruled is mere hypocrisy'.[104] The *Champion*, a pro-native paper from Bombay, alleged that '[T]he European element (in the jury) must have been (in spite of warnings from the bench and the bar) swayed by the rancorous and racial attacks to which Mr. Tilak was subjected by the whole Anglo-Indian press.' In particular, it said, 'the part played by *Times of India* was little short of that of a quasi-prosecutor'.[105]

As expected, *Times of India* welcomed the verdict, saying it 'carries a lesson . . . which every good citizen must hope will not be lost on the followers and imitators of the *Kesari*'.[106] But it was not just the Anglo-Indian papers that were targeting Tilak. *Rast Goftar*, an Anglo–Gujarati paper run by the Raj loyalists among the Parsis and a section of Muslims, praised Strachey and wrote that Tilak:

> 'should congratulate himself that he has escaped with but a light punishment. It was better for the learned judge to err on the side of leniency than enlist the sympathies of people in favour of the convict by undue severity. Already the moral effect of this conviction all over the country is almost magical. The most reckless swashbucklers

of Native journalism are beginning to be conscious of a feeling of responsibility . . . We believe in a healthy and honest criticism of the *measures* of government . . . But such criticism is one thing and the constant vilipending and abuse of government that Hindu, and particularly Brahmin, journalism has indulged in with absolute impunity, is another. We could sincerely wish that after this conviction the Deccani Brahmin would see the folly of hankering after lost power and would become a loyal and honest citizen. But will the leopard change his spots or the Deccani Brahmin his nature?'[107]

Tilak's appeal was rejected by a full high court bench of Chief Justice Charles Farran and Justices Candy and Strachey. The bench termed Justice Strachey's interpretation of the word 'disaffection' as erroneous but asserted the jury couldn't have been misled by it—without, of course, determining from the jury what exactly had led or misled it.[108]

In November of that year, H.H. Asquith, who later became Prime Minister of Britain, approached the Privy Council with an appeal, but it was not allowed.[109]

Subsequently, editors of three other Marathi papers—the *Poona Vaibhav, Modavritta* and *Pratod*—were booked for allegedly inflammatory writings.[110]

Tilak was first taken to the Dongri jail in Bombay, where he and Agarkar had been imprisoned for 101 days exactly a decade-and-a-half earlier. Now Agarkar was dead, and Tilak was on his own. The Raj did not distinguish between political prisoners and common criminals at the time, so he got exactly the kind of food, facilities (or the lack of these) and work that someone with a criminal record did. He was asked to pick oakum or separate fibres from old ropes. Prisoners were made to sit in groups to do this work, and he became a part of one such group. The inmates had a truly hard time: no one was allowed to utter a word or move or sit an inch outside the line while working; if they did, the jailer hurled abuses at them, and if he were in a foul mood, even beat them up or gave them solitary imprisonment for some time as punishment. Tilak was not subjected to such treatment, but the terrible conditions overall quickly got to him.

The food was of poor quality, and as a vegetarian, Tilak had his own taboos about it. He had the dry bhakri served to him, but because he ate nothing with onions in it, he never consumed the dal. There was neither milk nor ghee, both part of this regular diet. The result was that in just two months, he lost over eleven kilograms, dropping from over fifty-eight kilograms to forty-seven, got dark circles under his eyes, and his lips turned an unhealthy black.

Visitors to the jail carried information about his condition outside, and the native papers drew attention to it, forcing the government to shift him after three months to the Byculla House of Correction. Meanwhile, his supporters, led by a Bangalore-based lawyer called S.S. Setlur, wrote to the Howard Association in London which was known to champion the cause of prisoners and push for jail reforms. The Association wrote to the secretary of state for India. As a result of its representation, the surgeon general of prisons was sent in to examine Tilak. He recommended some milk and ghee, and while things improved after that, by the time of his release, Tilak hadn't regained much weight: he was only fifty kilograms.

That was because the Byculla prison was almost as bad as the Dongri one. Like in Dongri, there wasn't enough water; there were periods, Tilak said later, when prisoners didn't get to cleanse themselves or have a bath for a fortnight or, in some cases, a month. There were hardly any facilities to wash clothes, and irritated prisoners had to spend a lot of time scratching and fighting bug bites. The Indian inmates weren't allowed to sleep inside their own cells but in a long line, on the floor, in the barracks. In the night, the dust on the floor and the insets crawling around were ruinous to health. Worse, the blankets the prisoners were given were coarse and uncomfortable, and mosquitoes whirred around the ears all night and stung uninhibitedly. 'It was so dark it was hard even to catch them, and there was no option of going off to sleep anywhere else,' Tilak said. Unsurprisingly, the blankets stayed largely unwashed; when a fresh outbreak of plague was reported in Bombay in 1898, Tilak suggested to the prison authorities that they be cleaned with carbolic acid. The outbreak, and rising concerns about his health on the outside, prompted the authorities to shift him to Yerawada prison in Poona. Here, things changed quite a bit for the better; he had a raised stone slab for a bed in his own cell; he no longer had to do coir matting but was asked to dye yarn; and though he was not allowed newspapers and journals, he got the books on religion and philosophy he wanted and was permitted to use a lamp for three hours in the night. He used the time to research the Vedas with a fresh intensity, and among the people who sent him their own books was Max Müller, himself a Veda scholar. Tilak said that he chiefly studied the Rig Veda and the many commentaries on it, and it was in this prison while he was studying it that he concluded that the 'Aryans' had their origins in a place 'where a night lasted a couple of months'. He deduced that the North Pole was the original home of the Aryans, and from there they had travelled to the southern parts of the world. 'The findings of astronomers support my theory, but I didn't get an adequate number of books in jail,' Tilak said after emerging from prison. 'I still have to consult many works, and when I do, it is possible I might change my mind. But at the moment, I am convinced about it,' he added. He did not eventually change his mind, and as a sequel to *Orion*, later wrote the *Arctic Home in the Vedas* in support of the theory he had developed. The thesis of the Aryans having come in from the North has since been powerfully challenged, though it still has its adherents across the globe.[111]

Representations for Tilak's release had been sent to the Raj from the moment he had stepped inside prison. They picked momentum in 1898 after he had already spent several months as an ordinary prisoner. One of the petitions was signed by two British parliamentarians—the Scottish jurist and Liberal Party member William Hunter and his party colleague W.S. Caine (who, along with, William Wedderburn had set up the India Parliamentary Committee in 1893 to press for Indian political and judicial reform)—and Dadabhai Naoroji and Max Muller, among others. It did not defend Tilak or say he was innocent but asked for clemency for him.

In a letter to the Liberal–Unionist politician and writer John Lubbock, Max Muller explained why he had signed the plea:

> My interest in Tilak is certainly that of a Sanskrit scholar, for though I do not agree with the arguments put forward in his *Orion, or Researches into the Antiquity of the Vedas* (Bombay, 1893), I cannot help feeling sorry that we should lose the benefit of his labours. I sent him my edition of the Rig-Veda, but I am told now that he is not allowed to read even his Bible and Prayer-book in prison. You see, from the wording of the petition, that we do not question the justice

of the sentence . . . But the warning has now been given, and none
too soon, though I do not believe that there is any sedition lurking in
India at present, not even in the hearts of such men as Tilak.[112]

Many of the papers which had lambasted Tilak and were convinced
of his seditious thinking too started publishing letters from readers
asking for his release, and the general consensus among officials
of the Raj seemed to be that the government could prevent him
from becoming a bigger figure in the eyes of his people if he were
released before completion of his sentence. He was thus released on
7 September 1898, almost exactly a year after he had been convicted
and sentenced, and when there were six more months for his prison
term to end.

The release, nonetheless, was not without conditions. The
government had asked Tilak to promise that (1) he would neither
countenance nor take part, directly or indirectly, in any demonstration
relating to his release, conviction or sentence, and (2) he would do
nothing by act, speech or writing to excite disaffection against the
government.[113] Tilak didn't mind the first condition but was worried
the second could curb his political activities. He agreed after he'd added
an amendment of his own, saying he was okay with the conditions on
the 'understanding that by the "act, speech or writing" referred to in
the second condition is meant such act, speech or writing as may be
pronounced by a court of law to constitute an offence under the Indian
Penal Code'. Should he 'fail to fulfil those conditions or any portion
of them', he said, 'the Governor of Bombay in Council may cancel the
remission of my punishment', and 'I may be . . . remanded to undergo
the unexpired portion of my original sentence.'[114]

Tilak walked out of prison at 9 p.m., and as the news spread quickly
across Poona and Bombay, lamps and festive lights were lit outside
many homes; the following morning, crackers were burst, and the odd
home had a silk sari and a brass pot hung together outside it, a symbol
of joyous celebration usually seen across the Deccan at the start of the
Maharashtrian new year. It was an indicator of new beginnings.

Numberless telegrams and letters flowed in. One of these was from
Romesh Chunder Dutt, an ICS officer who had just the previous year,
after several stints in the administration, been appointed professor

of Indian history at University College, London. Dutt was also instrumental, along with Naoroji, in expounding the 'drain of wealth' theory and took up for Indians in the British capital. Lauding Tilak for his 'courage and power of suffering', he wrote, 'I do not doubt that the effect of your example will be permanent. Your endeavours will never go in vain. They are bound to bear fruit. Your hardships will lead the nation to victory.'[115] Another message, from W.S. Caine, an advocate of Indian causes in London, said, 'I am aware of the religious tendency of your mind. And hence you will not disagree when I say that the hardships of man tend to make his life perfect. You are coming out from your ordeal of jail life with a fuller and brighter lustre. It was inevitable, in the circumstances, that some leading personality should fall victim to the government's wrath. You will be proud that you, of all others, got that distinction. The future historian of India will record your achievements in the proper place, and posterity will ever be justly grateful . . .'.[116]

When Tilak returned home, his nephew Dhondopant Vidwans, a young man whom he had recently appointed his manager, noticed that he was in bad shape. Tilak had become 'a skeleton – eyes sunken deep, cheeks pallid and pinched, and gait unsteady'. Keen on a change of atmosphere to improve his health, Tilak chose to go to Sinhagad. Sinhagad is one of Chhatrapati Shivaji's most famous forts. Located close to Poona, it was a tranquil spot amid the Sahyadri mountains, with refreshing, clean air. As mentioned earlier in this book, at this retreat, Tilak had got for himself a dwelling he went to whenever he wanted a break from the hectic life of the city and the plains. Tilak rested there for two full months before returning to the ferment of Poona.

The ferment largely had to do with the trial and hanging, earlier that year, of Damodar Chapekar and his brother Balkrishna, the men who had actually shot Rand and Ayerst. For months, police officers of the Raj had struggled to find the killers. But in October 1897, a man called Ganesh Shankar Dravid, one of the collaborators of the Chapekar brothers who had masterminded the killings, ratted on them. Dravid had been put behind bars in an unrelated case, and he squealed in order to secure an early release and also to bag the Rs 20,000 award the government had announced for information on the assassins. Damodar Chapekar was sentenced to death in February 1898 and hanged in April. His brother Balkrishna, meanwhile, had fled to

Hyderabad but was caught and hanged in May. The youngest of the Chapekar brothers, Wasudeo, was still absconding. Enraged by what he saw as Dravid's betrayal, he knocked one evening in February 1899 on the door of Dravid's house in Poona and called Ganesh Shankar Dravid and his brother out on the pretext that a British police officer was waiting outside to have a word with them. Once they were out, he asked them to accompany him to the corner of the street, where he said the official was standing. And, walking a step behind them, he shot both in the back, as revenge for his siblings' hangings. Wasudeo Chapekar was then himself put on trial and hanged in May 1899.[117]

Was Tilak the real mastermind of the Poona killings? This was a question hotly debated at the time, though he himself had deplored the killings and denounced the killers as 'fanatics', and it continues to be raised and debated intermittently to this day. Were the Chapekars connected to him in any way? And who really were these brothers who had shot two British officials in the dead of night?

The theory of Tilak's association with the Chapekars has primarily rested on three accounts. One is by D.B. Bhide, who was part of the gymnasium culture in Poona at the time. He wrote in his autobiography, published in 1957—ten years after India's Independence—that 'Damodar (Chapekar) took Lokmanya's nod.' The second is a story told by Damodar's associate Krishnarao Sathe, again post-Independence. According to it, the morning after the twin killings, Damodar Chapekar sent a message to Tilak via Sathe, saying indirectly and tactfully, 'The Ganpati of Ganeshkhind has issued His benediction.'[118] And the third is the revelation, yet again post-freedom, by Tilak's aide S.V. Bapat, that Tilak had helped Balkrishna Chapekar to stay out of the police net by sending a message to Keshavrao Koratkar of Hyderabad asking him to take care of Balkrishna while he was in hiding there.[119]

Damodar Chapekar's autobiography, written in prison, tells a different story. Unlike many other self-justifying accounts, it is considered largely reliable. Damodar Chapekar was born in Chinchwad on the outskirts of Poona in a Chitpavan Brahman family of *kirtankars*. He had to give up his education early because of the family's precarious economic condition. But he and his brothers were deeply religious, and many enthusiastic and religious youths of the time were part of a *talim* or gymnasium tradition Poona had developed during this period.

Brahmans were as much a part of the talims as people of other castes (the orthodox Natu brothers were part of the same talim culture), and many of these youths were driven by a fervour to drive out the British. The example of the 1857 Revolt was before them, and more recently, so was the armed rebellion of Wasudeo Balwant Phadke. In religious terms, the Chapekars were revivalist and ultra-orthodox, and to pursue both their faith-based and political objectives, they had formed a secret 'Chapekar Club' in the mid-1890s. They practised their drills near the Parvati hill in Poona and prayed to Lord Hanuman, known in Maharashtra as 'Maruti'. They tried to mobilize people for their cause, but not many people of their own age were willing to join. Disappointed, they decided to focus on younger and more impressionable minds, and one of the things they did was to go 'wherever schoolboys played cricket' and begin their 'exhortations to create in their minds a dislike for cricket and a taste for native games'. Thus, they gathered about 150 schoolboys, but the club soon broke up over differences.[120]

At this point, the Chapekar brothers decided to take matters into their own hands. They could just about tolerate the Congress, though they saw its founder A.O. Home as nothing but a 'British agent' and the Congress itself as a forum for 'eating, drinking, recreation and a profusion of tall talk and nothing more'.[121] What they absolutely hated was the reformists' Social Conference; they called it the 'chandalin [she-devil],' and when the Congress met in Poona, they had even made an abortive bid to burn the pandal in which the Social Conference had taken place.[122] And though they themselves participated in the Shivaji festival that Tilak had started, Damodar wrote, 'My brother and myself do not at all like this festival. Such undertakings as involved a great deal of talk highly exasperated us.'[123]

Of Tilak himself, Damodar Chapekar had a very poor opinion. One day, Damodar had gone to the Anandodbhav auditorium in Poona to listen to a lecture delivered there annually. Tilak was presiding over the session. Damodar wrote that when Tilak's lawyer friend Daji Abaji Khare got up to speak on Shivaji, 'the cow protector', he 'flew into a rage', because Khare was apparently someone 'who ate beef in company with Muhammadans'. Damodar tried to get on to the dais to denounce Khare, but he was stopped by the organizers, and Tilak allegedly asked a wrestler to drive Damodar out. Damodar wanted to 'punish' Tilak for this humiliation. He wrote, 'I know many people have a good opinion of Tilak, but they must be devoid of reason.' In his opinion:

> According to the saying, alas, [he is] neither a Hindu nor a Yavan, Tilak is neither a thorough reformer nor is he thoroughly orthodox. For if we were to credit him with devotion to his own religion, (we must remember that) he is a member of the association for the removal of obstacles in the way of widow remarriage. This sanctimonious individual is the dear friend of the beef-eater Daji Abaji Khare (donkey), to whose house he goes occasionally and with whom he takes meals without any hesitation. This worthy individual was ashamed to undergo expiration for eating biscuits (at the Christian Mission Home), but was not ashamed to take tea. Had he consented to have his moustache shaved off in deference to public opinion, would forty generations (of his ancestors) have been consigned to hell? He tried to place himself on a footing of equality with the authors of the Smritis by introducing certain innovations in the marriage ritual. I do not think that anyone has ever seen him performing such pious acts as hearing a *kirtan* or *puran* or visiting a temple. He did many other similar acts which would be disgraceful to any man calling himself religious. I have mentioned (only) some of them. Owing to these acts we have no good opinion of him. We, however, consider him to be a far better man than a reformer. Latterly, he had adopted his manners to the opinions of his community and this had considerably checked his irregular conduct. We hoped that after some time he would be much improved.[124]

Was this an example of deliberate condemnation with a motive to mislead? My own conclusion, after having read Damodar Chapekar's autobiography, is that it wasn't. There's a certain consistency in Chapekar's revelation of his extremely strong likes and dislikes, and his theory about Tilak fits into that and does not stick out as odd. Also, had his verbal attack on Tilak been artificial and untrue and aimed only at protecting Tilak from getting caught or prosecuted in the assassination case, he'd never have given him the benefit of the doubt the way he did in the last three sentences. To cite Tilak's future association with the likes of revolutionaries Vinayak Damodar Savarkar and Aurobindo

Ghose to somehow link him also to the Chapekars' act is to try and read history backwards.

The post-Independence accounts of D.B. Bhide, who said Chapekar took Tilak's nod, and Khanderao Sathe, who said he carried Damodar's message to Tilak saying 'Ganpati has blessed us', have been uncritically accepted by several historians. The reasons for that aren't clear, but it's hard to accept accounts given decades later, that too in the absence of any corroborative evidence. Sathe's line is anyway about something that happened after the killings, and so is the third post-independence account by S.V. Bapat that Tilak asked someone in Hyderabad to look after Balkrishna Chapekar while he was hiding there. So even if these two were to be trusted, at the most we can conclude that it is entirely possible Tilak found out who the attackers were after the assassinations, and he didn't inform the authorities. It would have been problematic for Tilak to do that, given that the authorities were waiting for the flimsiest of pretexts to link him to the killings. The possibility of Tilak having sent a message to Hyderabad for sheltering Balkrishna Chapekar can't altogether be ruled out, of course; he may have wanted to provide cover to a young man who, he felt, had along with his family committed the act to highlight the grievances of a subject people and not for selfish interests. So accessory after the fact? Maybe, though again there's nothing conclusive in that direction. Plotter or someone who had full knowledge of what was being planned by the Chapekar brothers? No.

The thesis of Tilak being at least the direct inspirer of the Chapekars' actions is also ruled out by Damodar's fierce criticism of the man and by the fact that the *Sudharak* and some other native journals had published pieces equally critical of the plague officials as *Kesari*; the Chapekars were innately hostile to British rule and, as mentioned earlier, looked to the 1857 revolutionaries and W.B. Phadke instead as their inspirers. Unconscious and indirect inspirer, then, if not a conscious one? Certainly, and slightly more than the editors of other journals.

At the same time, indeed, Tilak was definitely the inspiration behind several secret groups that proliferated across the Deccan during the last decade of the nineteenth century and the first decade of the twentieth. Savarkar's group, called the Mitra Mela, formed in 1899–1900 drew inspiration from him, and so did the Shivaji Club of Kolhapur, formed even before that. He most likely knew about many, if not most, of their underground activities and even of the support of Sayajirao Gaekwad, the then ruler of Baroda, for such anti-Raj activities and subsequently got to know Aurobindo Ghose, who worked for the Baroda ruler, and the activities of his group from Bengal very well. Interestingly, after all the Chapekar brothers had been caught and Tilak was booked and sentenced, the Tilak-inspired Shivaji Club of Kolhapur in February 1899 put up a poster on the walls of the famous Mahalaxmi temple in that city. In a strange repeat of the 'Jack the Ripper' killings in London a decade earlier, three prostitutes had been the victims of three murderous attacks in Kolhapur at that time. The Shivaji Club's poster read, 'Awake, young men. Take up arms and use them against those who have sent Tilak to prison. It's better to kill the Europeans than the prostitutes! The Chapekars must be freed from prison.'[125]

Tilak's far more direct involvement in a secret revolutionary plot came in what came to be subsequently known as 'the Nepal episode'. This episode started in 1900 and continued almost up to 1905.

Early in the year 1900, Tilak was in Calcutta along with his associate Vasudev Ganesh Joshi alias 'Vasukaka'. There, they were invited to a Bengali language school for girls. The headmistress of this school was known as 'Mataji'. On Tilak and Joshi's arrival there, 'Mataji' started speaking to them in Marathi, and they were taken aback. It turned out she was a Maharashtrian from Thanjavur. Widowed at a young age, she had gone to Nepal for darshan of the 'Pashupateshwar' in Kathmandu. When the then ruler of Nepal, Dheer Samsherjung Bahadur, spotted her, he was entranced by her beauty and implored her to stay in his palace, which she did presumably as his paramour. But the Nepal ruler was killed later, and 'Mataji' moved to Calcutta and started running a school. Her ties to Nepal were intact nonetheless, for in that place the prime minister, Chandra Samsherjung, wielded extraordinary power. 'Mataji' told Tilak and Vasukaka that they should go to Nepal, where she would introduce them to the prime minister and through him to the new ruler so that Nepal's help could be obtained in bringing about an invasion of India and sparking a rebellion within that would overthrow the Raj. Tilak and 'Vasukaka' began their journey from Patna, hoping to enter Nepal as part of groups of Shaivite pilgrims that were allowed free entry into Nepal at the time of Lord Shiva's festival in February. However, the Nepal border had been shut because of the plague, and they were compelled to return to Poona. Tilak then asked 'Vasukaka' and his other associate, K.P. Khadilkar, to proceed to Nepal in April. They were to open there a factory for the production of tiles which would act as a cover for an arms unit and workshop. Four others joined the group soon: Hanmantrao Kulkarni of Jabalpur, who was a member of a revolutionary group from Beed in Maharashtra; one 'Ketkar' from Gwalior who according to one scholar must have been Bhalchandra Ketkar, who knew Tilak well after having lived with Agarkar's family in Poona for his education; and Damu Joshi and Bandopant Ruikar, both from Kolhapur, the last a member of the Shivaji Club. 'Mataji' introduced them to the powers that be in Nepal, and Joshi also obtained a contract from the Nepal maharaja to re-tile the roof of the palace. From Kathmandu, Khadilkar kept doing the rounds of Calcutta where a representative of Crupps, a German arms manufacturer, was based, in an attempt to purchase arms manufacturing equipment from the German firm. The plan was to take the equipment to Kathmandu and produce arms there for use against the Raj. Despite several negotiations with the German firm's agent and a payment apparently of Rs 4500, the machinery did not arrive, with the Indian buyers being told that it would take at least four to five years for it to reach Indian shores. The plot never succeeded, and later 'Vasukaka' left for Japan and the US, while Hanmantrao Kulkarni returned to India after several years, in 1909, to settle in Indore, and Khadilkar came back to Poona to work with Tilak again; the other two members of the group from Kolhapur had returned to their hometown after just a few months' stay in Kathmandu.[126]

Tellingly, just when this plot was being worked out, Tilak wrote a series of nine editorials in *Kesari* in 1902 whose title was Guerilla Warfare. Many of the articles referred to the guerilla tactics used by the Marathas against the Muslim sultanates of the Deccan and the Mughals and noted that the Boers of Southern Africa had recently used similar methods against the British. One of the editorials stated, 'To win big battles a well-trained army is needed, but for guerilla warfare only a gun is needed.' The next few years, as the Nepal plot was still in the works and Japan's technical capabilities were a subject for much discussion along with its triumphant fight against Russia, Tilak in a sense publicly declared that he was looking East for allies, assistance and inspiration. Writing about 'the unity of India, China and Japan', he compared these three Asian peoples to parts of a fan. 'The Hindus are the blades of this fan. The Chinese are the paper covering; and the Japanese are the nail joining the blades,' he wrote.[127] Nepal was meant to be the invisible helping hand, of course, though the plot did not finally come to fruition.

The truth about the Chapekar case, however, is that the British authorities booked Tilak for sedition and cited his articles in the *Kesari* to somehow get to him, an emerging leader of the masses, in the Rand and Ayerst assassination case. They failed in that attempt, for the prosecution could not stack up evidence on that count. And if the Raj believed that sending Tilak to prison would have a chastening effect not only on him but also serve as a warning for other like-minded Indians, his conviction and imprisonment had not quite the desired effect. On the contrary, Tilak's fame spread nationwide, and he was widely regarded as a hero who had stood up to the British. Most importantly, for the post-1857 generation which had been raised in an atmosphere mostly of resignation to political slavery, it made a devastating crack in the image of Indians as largely passive recipients of colonial repression and violence. Tilak's writings and his actions showed he was bold and aggressive, and where he stood out from among the several critical voices which had also found fault with the plague administration was that he was keen on building a people's common consciousness and was totally unafraid of pursuing the politics of mass agitations, mass protests and mass festivals. He wanted to do things on a certain scale, and in his own way, he was demonstrating that it was possible to do things on a particular scale without soft-pedalling issues, without sacrificing an outlook of trenchant criticism towards the rulers and without at the same time deviating from the path of lawful action.

At that fraught and delicate moment, Tilak appeared to have inaugurated a new chapter—a chapter of Indian resistance against the Raj. How far could such resistance go? What shape would it take? Would the chapter proceed forward or be abruptly brought to a close? How was the imperial government going to react in the future? In the same way, as it had after the Rand and Ayerst killings, or differently? And was there a possibility at all of any fresh new chapters of resistance getting added? The questions were tantalizing. And they were being gone into by both sides, the British and the Indian.

Chapter 9

The Raj Goes Fishing

Thrust centre-stage by his trial and imprisonment, Tilak became the subject of very close scrutiny by both his friends and rivals, whether Indian or British, after his release from prison. His ideas, too—on the British administration, on India's political existence, on what the dominant note of national political action should be, on the role of the Congress and his colleagues within it, on India's past, and on its present social, religious and economic set-up—got crystallized. The result was that the period from 1898 to the 1905 controversy over Lord Curzon's plan to partition Bengal came to be defined by an inevitable acceleration of conflict between Tilak and the moderate elements of the Congress led by the Ranade-Gokhale-Mehta troika that then totally dominated the national organization, and equally with the Raj establishment and what Tilak saw as its ultra-loyal, out-to-get-him press.

First off the block, expectedly, were the Conservative papers in Britain and the British-controlled papers in India. They went to town with reports that suggested religious leaders of the Brahman community wanted Tilak to do penance for food cooked by non-Brahmans he must have had in prison. The 'pain of penalty' included the shaving of moustache, which Tilak apparently was unwilling to go through, though he didn't mind other, milder forms of 'prayaschit', they said.[1] The British parliamentarian W.S. Caine, a well-wisher of India, member of the British Committee of Congress and campaigner for Tilak's early release, remarked that the Tory papers were 'full of ribald jeers just now at the reported caste punishment of Tilak'. With pain, Caine said, 'Those of us who care for India and love her people find it hard to defend them when caste rules are severely and narrowly interpreted with regard to Indians like Mr. Tilak who excite our admiration.' Tilak 'has already suffered so unjustly', Caine said, hoping all the talk about caste penalties was 'only a newspaper lie' so that it didn't become hard for him to argue with those like the MP Bhownuggree and Secretary of State Hamilton when they spoke about the Indian people.[2]

A newspaper lie was what it ultimately turned out to be. But the reports ensured that *Times of India*, which like the Raj blamed the Brahmans for every little act of dissent the Indians showed, did a sudden volte face and discovered virtues in the community. 'The Brahmin caste,' it wrote in a comment, 'is not as intolerant as it has become fashionable to take it . . . We depend upon him (Caine) to understand (this) and make it as widely known as possible.' And 'even supposing the great majority of the Brahmin community to be . . . unhesitating in exacting obedience to caste rules from a man like Mr. Tilak whom they have so much felt for and adored, it should be a thing really worthy of the admiration of Sir M. Bhownuggree and Lord George Hamilton.'[3] The logic was simple: Brahmans with Tilak were bad, Brahmans against him were good; and Brahman practices, even retrograde ones, were welcome if they were aimed at Tilak as pain, punishment and embarrassment.

The paper also made a subtle attempt to stir orthodox Brahman hostility against Tilak. It quoted from the *Indian Social Reformer*, mouthpiece of the pro-reform group, on the marriage ceremony of Daji Abaji Khare's daughter to indicate that Tilak continued to flout caste norms. Tilak's lawyer friend Khare had recently married his daughter, 'who is past thirteen, to the second son of Mr. Ganpatrao Pandit of Ahmedabad', it stated. 'Mr. Khare is an England-returned Hindoo, and it is said that while proposing the marriage, he wrote to Mr. Pandit that he would under no circumstances perform any prayaschit. Mr. Pandit replied that that would be just the reason why he would agree to the alliance! A number of people assisted at the marriage, and Mr. Tilak was among them.'[4]

What incensed Tilak greatly was *The Times'* reproduction in November 1899 of an article in the London *Globe* that accused him of plotting the killings of Rand and Ayerst. Stafford Northcote had just been named to replace Sandhurst as Bombay governor, and the *Globe* pointed out that 'for some years past, parts of the Western Presidency have been permeated by seditious conspiracies of a most dangerous sort, and although the ringleaders have seen fit to remain quiet since that arch-plotter, Tilak, was imprisoned, sedition is merely in temporary abeyance. It rests with the new Governor to complete its extermination . . . Happily, Sir Stafford Northcote goes to his important office with much fuller knowledge of the state of affairs than his predecessor possessed until his mind was informed by the campaign of murder which Tilak directed, if he was not its organizer.'[5]

Tilak immediately filed a defamation case against T.J. Bennett, editor and proprietor of *Times of India*, and F.M. Coleman, the paper's managing proprietor and publisher. The case came up before the Esplanade police court, the same court where Tilak had been taken after his arrest. Tilak said the article made several insinuations, but what he took particular exception to was his description as 'arch-plotter' and the line that he had 'directed the campaign of murder, if he was not its actual organizer'. In case *The Times* argued it had simply reproduced a paragraph from another publication and was not responsible for its views, Tilak said the paper was 'under cover and pretence of quoting from an English newspaper' maliciously carrying stuff with the idea of defaming him. He insisted that *Times of India* had 'for a long time' attacked him 'and made all sorts of false aspersions, insinuations, and imputations'.[6]

Was Tilak not convicted for sedition, Chief Presidency Magistrate J. Sanders Slater asked. Tilak had appointed Pherozeshah Mehta as his lawyer, and Mehta, despite the many problems he had with Tilak's politics, had accepted his brief. Yes, said Mehta on Tilak's behalf, he had been convicted, but the charge 'had nothing to do with the Poona murders', and Justice Strachey too had ruled that the murders and the sedition charge were 'entirely distinct'.

An editor with thirty years of journalistic experience, Bennett saw no way out but to apologize. He told the court through his lawyer, an Englishman called Macpherson, that the paper's London correspondent had sent a selection of comments 'from the home (England) press' on Northcote's appointment as governor. They had been 'inserted as received, without, unfortunately, undergoing any revision.' How had that happened? Were there no editorial checks? Bennett said a sub-editor had brought proofs of the matter to be printed to him, with many other columns of proofs, and he had seen the headline for the piece, which only said, 'New Governor of Bombay'. It had 'never occurred to him for one moment', he said, 'that there would be anything objectionable to Mr. Tilak'. The paper carried a clarification that it regretted the inadvertent insertion of statements which were 'unwarranted' and did 'serious injustice to Mr. Tilak'.

That wasn't the end of the matter, though. Bennett said there was 'not the slightest real ground' to suggest, as Tilak had, that 'this defamation is an item in a series of similar articles'. There had been occasions, Bennett said, when he'd 'deemed it right to comment unfavourably on Mr. Tilak's conduct, and these comments all occurred at a period of Mr. Tilak's career, which culminated in an event which to some extent must be deemed to justify everything that has been said'.

The regret was thus not unqualified, but Tilak accepted it, choosing not to pursue the case any further. But he thought it important to explain why he, himself an editor, had directly gone to court instead of first writing to *The Times* editor. He said the previous year, *The Times* had written an article following the arrest of Balkrishna Chapekar, which connected Tilak to political intrigue. On that occasion, Bennett had the next day 'disclaimed all association with the sentiments expressed by the correspondent' and said the report 'in question, by an inadvertence, was not submitted to editorial revision, or this passage would not have appeared'. Yet, as Bennett had admitted, stuff had appeared once again, apparently 'owing to inadvertence'. So was no one checking anything ever at *Times of India* before it went into print, or was it simply an excuse to get out of trouble? Another reason for moving court was that with the kind of insinuations still being made, Tilak said he wanted to take any opportunity 'to come forward and submit himself to any hostile cross-examination to which he can possibly be subjected to on these matters'.[7]

Tilak felt he was facing up to Bennett's attacks the way he ought to. Without his knowing it, though, Gokhale soon got involved in correspondence with Bennett of a nature that Tilak might not have imagined possible. Or perhaps he would have.

The central division's seat on the Bombay Provincial Legislative Council was going to fall vacant in October 1899. An election was necessary. The seat, which gave the chosen member a two-year term, had been created in 1895, and Tilak was the first to be elected to it. He was re-elected in 1897 but was forced to resign after his conviction in September that year. His slot had been filled by Dhondo Shamrao Garud. Now the slot opened again, and Tilak and Gokhale planned to contest, as did the incumbent, Garud. Gokhale suspected Tilak and Garud of having arrived at an understanding that they'd get their loyal voters in their respective local bastions to vote for them and if Garud was elected, he'd vacate the seat for Tilak after six months. Gokhale told one of his aides he had seen letters in Tilak's handwriting which established there was truly such a deal.[8] It was a somewhat odd allegation to make. Even if there were such an understanding, as Gokhale had alleged, it would divide Tilak's and Garud's votes, not merge them. Tilak's stock had shot up considerably after his incarceration, and even his stern critic, Bennett's own publication, had been forced to admit that Tilak's name 'is now on the tip of the tongue of every schoolboy'.[9] Though schoolboys weren't voters, local pressures might have been brought to bear upon the educated elite who were going to vote, and Tilak might have had the edge. So why might Tilak have struck a deal?

The only answer is that he suspected the British government would block his election if he won—by citing his conviction. In which case, he'd rather have his own representative on the Council than his moderate rival, Gokhale. His suspicion turned out to be correct. A little before the poll campaign began, the outgoing Bombay governor, Sandhurst, wrote to the incoming viceroy, Curzon, 'There are rumours that he [Tilak] is going to stand (he is most likely to be successful); should they turn out to be true, I don't think I ought to accept the recommendation. Tilak's seat may be contested by another Brahmin named Gokhale. He and Tilak are bitter opponents and Gokhale was a man who, in England two years ago, told outrageous falsehoods about the soldiers at Poona. Since then he has done everything to redeem his position, and has been one of the most ardent plague workers in Poona.' Curzon on 10 August immediately okayed the idea that Tilak's name should be vetoed if he got elected.[10]

Gokhale knew the election would be closely fought, and the British politician W.S. Caine told him Tilak was a 'most formidable opponent to you'.[11] Unwilling to take chances, Gokhale wrote to TOI editor T.J. Bennett. Bennett liked Gokhale and was lobbying for him 'with the European chairmen of some of the district boards', who were among the voters.[12] Gokhale told the British editor that he shouldn't attack Tilak too much during the election campaign, lest he get public sympathy. In Gokhale's own words:

> It was a very difficult hint to convey. However, I managed after all to express myself as delicately as I could, I explained to him that my prospects were very hopeful, thanked him for his kindly feeling towards myself and then stated that as I was trying to win over to my side men who were, many of them, Mr. Tilak's personal friends, and any attack on Mr. Tilak in my interests was sure to stiffen their backs and add to my difficulties.[13]

One of Gokhale's better biographers, the Marathi scholar Govind Talwalkar, wrote, 'Gokhale made arrangements for his view in this regard to reach Bennett.' Astonishingly, Talwalkar has also made a sweeping statement that 'there was little chance of Tilak getting elected'.[14] Both statements are absolutely baseless; Gokhale himself wrote to Bennett, he didn't simply make 'arrangements' for his view to 'reach' Bennett, and there was every possibility of Tilak winning the election. Gokhale himself wrote about how tough the electoral fight could be; his admiring biographer however chose to see a no-contest.

In the event, realizing his election would mostly likely be scuppered by the government, Tilak withdrew his candidature, urging his supporters to back Garud, and Gokhale won. He didn't win only as a result of Tilak's withdrawal; Gokhale worked very hard in the constituency, touring it widely and soliciting support from the time Tilak was very much in the contest.

But Gokhale's act of writing to Bennett asking him to go soft on Tilak was extraordinary. Where Gokhale crossed the line was in going to the extent of being hand-in-glove with the British and especially with Bennett, whose paper had not only demonized Tilak but carried on a relentless campaign against him until he landed in jail on the charge of sedition. Bennett went after anyone aggressively advocating the Indian cause, and Tilak was his prime target for the gumption he was showing. To have sought his assistance in a poll fight—even in a negative way by asking him not to write about Tilak in case he should win popular support—was an act of collaboration with the colonial system of oppression.

The tussle between Tilak and the group of political moderates had also begun to be increasingly felt at the Congress sessions. Though the Moderates were quite overwhelmingly in the majority, pressure from Tilak's supporters was mounting, and their numbers were steadily growing. The 1897 session had been held in Amravati when Tilak was in jail. There, serious differences had cropped up over whether a resolution should be passed to express disapproval of the government's action against Tilak. The idea was abandoned as those opposed to the resolution prevailed, though Tilak's ordeal featured in the speech of Congress president C. Shankaran Nair; Gokhale too, still reeling under the impact of his apology over allegations he'd made against plague committee officials, was kept away from the podium. However, referring to the happenings in the Deccan, Congress's first president, Surendranath Banerjea, told the delegates, 'For Tilak my heart is full of sympathy. My feelings go forth to him in his prison house. A nation is in tears.'[15]

By the time the next Congress session of December 1898 came along, Tilak was out of jail and recuperating at Sinhagad. Though not fully recovered, he decided to go to the southern city of Madras or Chennai, which was going to host it. Tensions between what had by now emerged as two contrasting streams in the Congress threatened to reach the surface. These streams had already acquired their own distinctive names: one was the *Jahal* (Extremist) wing, with Tilak as its chief ideologue, and the other was the *Nemast* or *Mavaal* (Moderate) section, helmed by Pherozeshah Mehta, Ranade and, increasingly by their disciple, Gokhale. Tilak travelled to Madras in the same train as Ranade and Gokhale, and the contrast in the reception became apparent along the route itself: people of different classes, especially the voiceless masses, crowded at railway stations to greet Tilak, whereas it was chiefly men of rank and position who stood by to doff their hats to Ranade and Gokhale.[16] Mehta stayed away from the session altogether, sparking speculation in the British-friendly press that he wanted to completely avoid any kind of association with Tilak's group. Mehta's biographer has stated that he skipped the Madras Congress 'for various reasons'[17] and not just to avoid Tilak, but a letter by C. Shankar Iyer imploring the Bombay Parsi leader to be there reflected the anxiety that was being felt among the Moderates over the impending tussle with the Extremists and the feared 'takeover' of the Congress by the Tilak faction. Nair wrote to Mehta:

> In smooth waters, the Congress does not, perhaps, need Mr. Bonnerji or you. But if in critical times you are absent, the Congress may drift into the hands of people we may not like. Allow me to remind you of the advice Gladstone gave our delegates, never to allow disloyalty to get the better of us. If you and others like you come here, you may depend upon it, the Congress will listen to us. If it does not, and the Congress does anything savouring of disloyalty . . . it will be time for you and those who think like you, myself for instance, to leave the Congress.[18]

A tribute to Gladstone, quoted by Nair in his letter, became a bone of contention in the meetings of the Congress's subjects committee, the forum that decided issues to be taken up and in which Tilak took a keen interest. Four-time premier of Britain, William E. Gladstone had died in August that year at the age of 88. In the early 1880s, Gladstone as head of the government of Liberals had appointed Lord Ripon as viceroy, when unrest over the Vernacular Press Act was brewing, and asked him 'to give India the benefits and blessings of free institutions'.[19] Ripon had repealed the Act and given a push to Western education. In opposition a decade later, however, Gladstone had taken an imperialist tone and agreed with Conservatives in the House of Commons that Britain's policy on India must be united and go beyond party differences and underlined that Britain's 'task' in India was both 'noble and peculiar'.[20] Tilak objected to the inclusion of the word 'gratitude' by Surendranath Banerjea in a resolution on Gladstone's death. Insisting on replacing it with 'satisfaction', Tilak said the word proposed by Banerjea 'did not sound well' to his 'Maratha ears' and described Gladstone's approach towards India as mere lip service.[21] But the Moderates' view was dominant, and 'gratitude' it remained.

Tilak didn't speak at the session, setting tongues wagging. Had he crumbled? Had he signed some sort of 'gagging' letter? No, Tilak told a correspondent of the *South Indian Post* who asked him about it. 'I did not consent (to speaking) only because once my speech was published, there would be quite an attack of invitations for public speaking which, on account of my indifferent health, I would not be able to cope with.'[22] Tilak nevertheless attended quite a few functions to which he was invited during his stay in Madras, among them a reception given him by T. Ananda Rao, son of the late Dewan of Travancore T. Madhav Rao. Born in a Maratha Deshashta Brahman family from Tanjavur, one of several families that had moved to the Tamil coast when the Marathas established their rule there, Madhav Rao had gained much fame as a reform-minded administrator; apart from Travancore, he had also served as Dewan of Indore and Baroda before he died in 1891.

At the next year's Congress session in Lucknow, a similar debate to the one over Gladstone broke out in the subjects committee, except that the bone of contention this time was Sandhurst and the resolution sought to be adopted was one of condemnation, not praise. Sandhurst, under whose watch Tilak had been booked for sedition, was slated to exit as governor. Tilak moved a resolution condemning Sandhurst for maladministration, and the Moderates, uncomfortable with direct denunciatory attacks against senior British officials, tried to deflect the matter without saying a straightforward no. They argued that the subject was of a provincial nature and that the Congress passed resolutions only on national issues. On these grounds, Tilak's resolution was invalided by the president for the session, Romesh Chunder Dutt. When Tilak pointed out that the Congress had indeed concerned itself with provincial issues earlier and cited examples, Dutt threatened to quit in a huff. Tilak, preferring not to precipitate matters with seniors in the national organization, retraced his steps and withdrew his resolution.[23] It was still early days for the Extremists in the Congress, and despite the fact that the momentum had begun to swing in their favour, Tilak was keen to maintain party unity at that juncture.

So were the Moderates, actually. Their position still pre-eminent, they did not want to take matters in the direction of a split in these early, albeit promising, years for the Extremists. Tilak was thus not the only one who accommodated his intra-party rivals in this phase of his political life; the rivals accommodated him as well. When Tilak placed the resolution on Sandhurst to vote in the Provincial Conference that followed the Congress, its president Gokuldas K. Parekh threatened to resign in much the same way Dutt had at the national-level meet. After a bitter argument, Parekh permitted a resolution to be made a part of the Congress proceedings.[24] It was considerably milder than Tilak had wanted it to be, and Tilak subsequently criticized it, writing that 'Congresses and conferences are not meant for flatterers and such persons who raise memorials to each and every governor, but for those who will not hesitate to voice public opinion in a fearless and temperate manner.'[25] Yet, however reluctantly, Tilak accepted the resolution; and the truth was it did have some semblance of criticism about the way Sandhurst had gone about doing things. Such an approach of mutual accommodation, at least for the moment, allowed the Moderates and Tilak to go their own ways in relative peace, satisfied with the compromise they had struck.

With the relative peace in the Congress still holding, Tilak was free to concentrate on other things, particularly on his own conception of the role of Hinduism and religion in public affairs, politics and India's national psyche. It is crucial to note that for him, bringing religion into politics was not an artifice or an exercise in political expediency; it was an article of faith; and he was convinced that if the role of religion was to mobilize, it was simultaneously to ennoble, to inspire and to set elevated goals. The idea of a secular, non-religious nationalism had simply not struck root anywhere on the sub-continent, and Tilak saw in Hinduism and the idea of Hinduising politics the moorings for a growing Indian nationalist consciousness.

Always desirous of visiting iconic sites linked to his faith, Tilak, after the Madras Congress, went to the Meenakshi temple of Madurai, where the goddess, the consort of Lord Shiva, sits in her royal splendour in a huge temple compound, with a separate temple dedicated to Lord Shiva nearby. A stop in Tanjavur was necessary for him to look at the southern capital of the Marathas, where Shivaji's brother, Vyankoji or Ekoji, had ruled, and so was a look at the magnificent temples, mutts and monuments of Kumbakonam and Tiruchirapalli. And to go to Rameshwaram on the southern shores where, so the legend goes, the hero of the Ramayana consecrated the Shiva *linga* himself, Tilak undertook a journey of nearly ninety miles on a bullock cart. He also went beyond Rameshwaram on a steamer—to Sri Lanka, then known as Ceylon. After the Lucknow Congress the next year, he took another steamer—first to Calcutta, where had a brief stay—and from there to Rangoon and Mandalay in Burma.[26] This steamer was actually booked by Tilak's friend Vishnu Chhatre, who had a circus group. The group was set to visit these places for performances, and Tilak went along. What was Tilak's impression of the circus troupe? Did he talk to its members and see them in action and if he did, did he like it? We don't know because no one left behind a record.

In Ceylon and Burma (now Myanmar), Tilak witnessed a lot of Buddhism. He also saw plenty of social reforms having already been effected on the ground. Both places, however, were in the hands of a foreign power, and Tilak concluded, and declared, that it was proof indeed of his theory that political progress was not linked to social reform. The sight of the incredibly beautiful temples of southern India appeared to have moved him especially. On his return to Poona, he said, 'One cannot have an idea of the ancient grandeur and glory of Hinduism and the temples of the deities without visiting these institutions. Who can say that they are not powerful influences that give substance to the tree of Hinduism and foster the spirit of unity among the Hindus?'[27]

It was while he was commenting on his twin trips that he mentioned, albeit not for the first time, the word Hindutva, by which he meant Hinduness. He said that:

> The common factor in Indian society is the feeling of Hindutva. I do not speak of Muslims and Christians at present as everywhere the majority of our society consists of Hindus. We say that the Hindus of the Punjab, Bengal, Maharashtra, Telangana, and Dravida are one, and the reason for this is only Hindu dharma. There may be different doctrines in the Hindu dharma, but certain principles can be found in common, and because of this alone a sort of feeling that we belong to one religion has remained among people speaking different languages in such a vast country. And this feeling of being one is still alive because in different provinces there are different institutions of the Hindu religion like temples, etc., or famous places of pilgrimage.[28]

Without a doubt, Tilak was looking at Hinduism as an anchor and a glue for the vast majority of the land's population. But even as he was talking of the oneness of Hindus, he was, oddly enough, alienating a major section of the community with his opinions on caste.

A Brahman Hindu of his times, Tilak was a believer in the caste system. In the early 1890s, he argued that 'caste distinctions' were based on the 'principle of division of labour' and, as the Australian scholar Richard Cashman said about Tilak's ideas, on 'mutual interdependence rather than . . . discrimination'. He saw similarities between caste and the trade associations of medieval Europe.[29] Yet while asserting on the one hand that it was only a secular division of duties that separated castes, Tilak on the other said certain castes did not have the religious authority to learn the Vedas. This was a very odd thing to say for someone who was stressing on Hindu unity and for someone who proclaimed, at the Ganpati festival in 1900, that the three common principles of Hindu dharma were 'treating the Vedas as final authority in all matters; seeking God through a variety of paths; and worshipping diverse objects of devotion'.[30]

He made his position more difficult by aligning with those who were opposing in 1890 the right of the prince of Kolhapur, Shahu Maharaj or Shahu Chhatrapati, to perform religious rites with Vedic mantras. The controversial Vedokta episode, as it came to be called, happened in the middle of a murky legal battle over the adoption of a boy in the family of the former rajguru or spiritual preceptor of the Kolhapur raja, in which Tilak got embroiled. In this battle, Shahu Maharaj openly took the side of Tilak's opponents, and that, according to the Marathi scholar Y.D. Phadke, was the reason Tilak stood in opposition to him. Nonetheless, Tilak came out of it looking like he considered the caste hierarchy inflexible. The legal battle in itself was protracted and as it raged, the British government stepped in once again to pin down its opponent, Tilak, and to create a huge amount of trouble for him, engendering a new episode in the Tilak versus Raj saga. But before we get into that, a look at the Vedokta issue which arose at a vital stage in this dispute.

Tilak and Shahu had started extremely well. Tilak had gone to prison for the cause of the Kolhapur state in 1882, and when the state's beleaguered prince had died early and Shahu (son of Kagal's Appasaheb

Ghatge) was adopted and appointed the new prince at the age of just ten, Tilak had warmly welcomed his appointment. When Shahu became a major, he took over the reins of the state from the regent, and Tilak extended his support to him, wishing him 'a long life, courage and wisdom' and writing in *Kesari* that 'it has been the Kolhapur Maharaj's family's resolve to have adequate pride in Hindutva and to work tirelessly and without any expectation of fruits for its advancement'.[31]

Proud of the Maratha tradition, Shahu soon started questioning the dominance of Brahmans, especially Chitpavan Brahmans, in his state's administration. At the time he took charge in 1894, the Kolhapur durbar had seventy-one officials in all, of which sixty were Brahmans; similarly, Shahu had a private staff strength of fifty-two, of which forty-five were Brahmans.[32] He began to place educated members of the Maratha caste in responsible positions. That didn't create any bad blood between him and Tilak at all. Tilak himself was hailing the name of Chhatrapati Shivaji, whose house the Kolhapur state represented, and when, from 1897 onwards, tensions arose between Shahu and the British political agent in his state, J.W. Wray, both the papers run by Tilak sided with the prince and praised his efforts to provide relief to the region's populace during the famine-and-plague crises from 1896 to 1900. Shahu reciprocated in his own way. A band of Tilak's admirers had created a Shivaji Club, one of many local gymnasiums in Kolhapur, and had also carried out a campaign against cow slaughter. Shahu banned cow slaughter in his state and also ensured that members of the Maratha caste and others joined the Club where horse-riding and the use of spears and other weapons of the Shivaji era were taught. In the end, Shahu was a vassal of the British and could take things only so far. Despite backing cow slaughter, he did not encourage the Shivaji Utsav and Ganesh Utsav in his state as both festivals launched by Tilak were being increasingly seen as vehicles used against the British administration. Also, when the Shivaji Club began to attract the suspicion of the British authorities, especially after the Rand and Ayerst murders, local members of other castes gradually deserted it, leaving it to the charge of Brahmans alone.[33]

The cooperation between the two ceased altogether with the adoption case, later known as the Tai Maharaj case and the Vedokta row. Both controversies got hopelessly entangled.

The rajguru of the Kolhapur ruler, Baba Maharaj Pandit, had just before his death named Tilak among four trustees who would look after his properties and help his wife adopt a boy if needed and guide both the boy and the assets until he became a major. While Tilak chose a boy called Jagannath, Baba Maharaj's wife, Tai Maharaj chose after her husband's death a boy of her own choice, Bala Maharaj, and appointed two trustees, Raghupati Pandit and B.M. Nagpurkar. Raghupati was Shahu's friend, so Shahu backed him in the dispute. The Vedokta controversy actually arose in 1899, and for two years, Tilak stayed completely mum on it. It was only after the Tai Maharaj case went to court in 1901, and only after it became clear to him following Bala Maharaj's adoption ceremony in August 1901 that Shahu was opposed to him, that Tilak wrote a couple of editorials in *Kesari* criticizing him in the Vedokta dispute. Until then, Tilak had sent letters to Shahu asking him not to give his consent to what he saw as the wrongful adoption of 1901 and had even met him twice to convince him about his side of the story.[34]

But who was opposed to Shahu using Vedic mantras, and why?

Shahu was deeply religious, had a Shaivic symbol tattooed on one of his hands, and was a stickler for performing religious ceremonies.[35] One morning in October-November 1899, he headed to the banks of the Panchganga River to have his holy bath. The Panchganga, or 'Five Gangas', River runs through Kolhapur, and it is so named because it is formed by four streams getting together, with the fifth stream according to local belief being that of the Saraswati running underneath. When Shahu began his ablutions, a Bombay-based friend accompanying him, reformist Ramshastri Bhagwat who was also known for his knowledge of the sacred texts, pointed out that the priest who stood next to Shahu was reciting mantras from the Puranas and not from the Vedas. The priest's name was Narayan Bhatt. When Shahu asked Bhatt about it, the Brahman said he was doing so because only mantras from the Puranas could be read out for the Shudras. Shahu was emphatic that he was a Kshatriya from the Bhosle family and not a Shudra and was entitled to perform his rituals with Vedic mantras. Yet Narayan Bhatt demurred.[36]

The orthodox Brahmanical conception of the issue was laid out at that time by K.V. Lele, better known as Bhaushastri Lele, editor of *Dharma* magazine published from Wai near Kolhapur. According

Gangadhar Tilak, Tilak's father.

Govindrao Tilak, Tilak's uncle. Tilak lived
with him in Pune; Govindrao was like a father
to him after Gangadhar's death.

With wife Satyabhama.

Tilak and wife with (L to R) their children and grandchildren;
standing at the back is nephew Dhondopant Vidwans, to whom
Tilak wrote a number of letters from Mandalay prison.

Shridhar, youngest son who
later became an associate of
Dr B.R. Ambedkar.

Ramchandra, second son.

Vishwanath, eldest son, who died
young and after whose death
Tilak betrayed rare emotion.

Gaikwad Wada in Pune, where Tilak moved in the mid-1900s; the
Kesari's editorial office was in the adjacent structure at the back.

Tilak's editorial of 12 May 1908 headlined 'Deshache durdaiva' or 'The country's misfortune' landed him in trouble with the Raj.

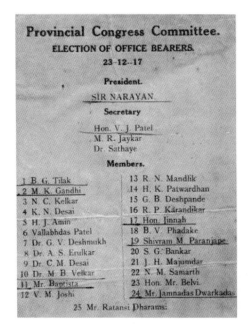

A list of Provincial Congress Committee stalwarts from 1917 which features Tilak and Gandhi.

First issue of *Kesari* that came out on 4 January 1881.

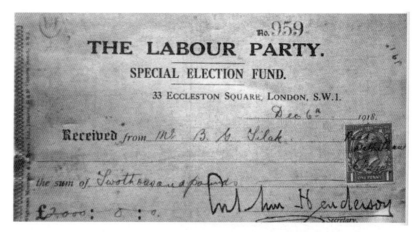

On his visit to England in 1918–1919, Tilak donated 2000 pounds sterling to the British Labour Party in the hope of gaining its support for India's liberation movement.

Gandhi's *Navjeevan* magazine with its cover about Tilak's death in 1920.

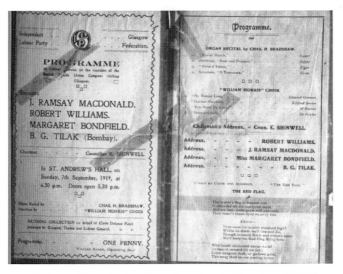

Labour Party invite for a function in London (1919) at which Tilak was a speaker.

Tilak's editorial of 13 July 1897 headlined
'To govern is not to wreak revenge', which
got him booked for sedition.

Gandhi (standing), Tilak and a young Jinnah
(to Tilak's right) at a meeting at Shantaram Chawl in
Girgaum, Bombay some time after Gandhi's return to
India from South Africa early in 1915.

Delegates from Bombay Presidency at the 1890
Congress session in Calcutta; Tilak seated second from left.

The Lal Bal Pal triumvirate.

At the Surat session in 1907 where the Congress split;
to Tilak's right (seated) is Aurobindo Ghose.

The 'Extremist' group at the 1907 Surat Congress session; (standing, L to R) B.S. Munje, Ramaswamy, K. Kunwarji Desai; (sitting) Ajit Singh, Aurobindo Ghose, Tilak and Syed Haider Raza; (seated on the ground) G.S. Khaparde, one of Tilak's closest aides, and Ashwini Kumar.

A piece in the *Illustrated London News*, depicting the violence that broke out in Bombay following Tilak's sentencing in 1908.

Annie Besant and Tilak at a meeting of the
Poona Sarvajanik Sabha, May 1916.

Tilak being welcomed on return from
Delhi meeting with Montagu, 1918.

With members of the British Labour Party, 1919; Tilak seated
third from right; to his left, Sarojini Nadu, Vithalbhai Patel,
G.S. Khaparde and B.C. Pal.

With editor of *Amrita Bazar Patrika* Motilal Ghose,
friend and supporter.

With close
friend and
aide Daji
Abaji Khare.

Tilak's funeral
procession, the
biggest Bombay
had ever seen.

Nehru unveiling Tilak's
portrait in Parliament.

Funeral procession as it reached Girgaum Chowpatty on
1 August 1920; Tilak was cremated on the grounds
of the Chowpatty.

Crowd at Chowpatty for funeral.

to this conception, there were only two castes in the Kali Yuga or modern age: Brahmans and Shudras. The two *varnas* of Kshatriya and Vaishya did not exist, he argued and quoted texts like the Shrimad Bhagvatam, Matsya Purana and Vayu Purana to suggest that because of miscegenation, the dynasty of Ikshvaku, known as the Suryavansha, 'stood to lose its Kshatriyahood after the reign of Sumitra' and the house of the Nandas had similarly ceased to be of the warrior caste 'after the time of Mahanandi, as the one who came after him, Mahapadmapati, was born of a dasi' or slave woman.[37]

This was by no means an unknown thing. Sayajirao Gaekwad, the ruler of Baroda, had been fighting for a full decade against similarly inclined orthodox Brahmans in his own state. Shahu himself was, like almost everyone in that period, a believer in the varna system, but he found the theory patently absurd. Things were made worse for him when a section of Brahmans said that the family of Chhatrapati Shivaji Maharaj was indeed Kshatriya, and the famous priest of Benaras, Gaga Bhatt, who had performed Shivaji's coronation ceremony in 1674, had affirmed that status, but Shahu's position as adoptive son and as being originally from the House of Kagal meant he could not claim the Bhosle family's right to hear Vedic mantras. Shahu's contemporary from Benaras, a famous shastri called Krishnanand Saraswati, used the same logic but came to the opposite conclusion—that Shahu's adoption and entry into the Chhatrapati's Bhosle family automatically entitled him to Kshatriyahood.[38] Some more reasonable people pointed to the introduction of modern schools and said that when education itself was becoming widespread and accessible, there was no point of engaging in such disputes.

Tilak was conservative in his views. Unlike the orthodox, he did not believe the status quo must never be disturbed. But 'if changes were to occur, they must be systemic and gradual', he said, writing two editorials in the *Kesari* on the subject on 22 and 29 October 1901. Further, the change must be such that its usefulness is quickly apparent to people, he argued. The demand for Vedokta did not fall into this category, he felt.

Caste had seeped into the very bones of Hindu society, Tilak declared. Thus, 'even if a Hindu converted to Christianity, he couldn't let go of his caste beliefs'. Chhatrapati Shivaji Maharaj was loved and revered by everyone and was even looked at as an avatar of Lord Shiva, and the priest Gaga Bhatt had fulfilled the wish of every person on Maharashtrian soil by consecrating Shivaji's position as king with a thread ceremony and in keeping with the *shastras*, Tilak noted. But 'though the coronation had taken place with Vedic mantras, there was no evidence that every ritual in that household was done by recitation of Vedic hymns. In fact, given the traditions prevalent in the House of the Maharaj of Satara, it can be seen that the household rituals were carried out with Puranic mantras', Tilak stated, wondering why in that case new-generation Marathas 'whose accomplishments were nowhere near those of Shivaji Maharaj' were insisting on doing things the Vedic way. Vedokta was in his view nothing but 'a fad', and the sooner the Marathas abandoned it, 'particularly in view of tradition, history and past verdicts', the better it would be.

Without in any way disavowing his conservative opinion, Tilak also argued the point from a modern-age point of view. He admitted the modern era was one of individual freedoms, and no one could stop anyone anyway. The Marathas were free to do the Vedokta rites, he said. The only thing was whether it was desirable only because some people had got it into their heads to do so, he asked. How would it make a difference? Even Brahman women could not use Vedic mantras, he pointed out, stressing that 'the respect that Marathas have in Maharashtra is owing to their forefathers' courageous feats, and so long as those qualities of courage, bravery and patriotism are alive in them, that sense of respect can never be reduced'. Moreover, Tilak wanted to know, 'Isn't it wrong for the Marathas to insist on Vedokta *sanskars* when we can see that the Brahmans who get such *sanskars* are in service and the Marathas who conduct Puranic rituals are in the seat of power? For a few thousand years it has been the sign of men (not women) of a certain caste to recite Vedic mantras at the time of religious practices; but history is proof that the respect every caste has earned is not based on such a thing but on the number of action-oriented and accomplished men it produces.'[39]

Resistance from local Brahmans to Shahu's Vedokta wish had built up after the riverside incident. The chief priest, or rajguru, of the state, N.S. alias Appasaheb Rajopadhye, had thrown his weight behind the priest who had defied the raja, and many others followed suit. The state had a tradition of performing a 'shravani' ceremony, which was a thread ceremony held annually. A young Brahman priest officiated at the ceremony with Vedic rites and was ex-communicated by the Brahmavrunda, the caste panchayat of the Brahmans; a powerful body, the panchayat even pronounced itself independent of the Shankaracharya Math that existed in Kolhapur. The next month, Rajopadhye, literally the 'royal priest', skipped attending Shahu's annual Bhadrapad-month rite of honouring the memory of his ancestors, fearing the raja would ask him to do it in keeping with Vedic norms.[40] Shahu's insistence on performing multiple religious ceremonies was a testament to his belief in the faith, and the Brahmans could have taken it as a positive thing given their status as apparent sacerdotal upholders of that faith. Still, a number of Brahmans kept up their resistance, though some others were definitely with Shahu.

Shahu moved immediately to cancel the payments given to the recalcitrant Brahman priests and confiscated the *inams* or hereditary land and revenue grants given to Rajopadhye and some other priests. He argued they had got the inams for performing of religious ceremonies; if they weren't doing their duties, how could the inam grants stay? Further, in an indication of how profound the influence of caste was, he got upset when he heard that the Brahmans were spreading the word that he wanted to get the Vedokta right for all Maratha families. According to his official biographer, Shahu told one of his friends, 'As regards my attempt to pull through other Maratha families, I may say, I have no concern in the matter. Of course, if the Maratha families are really Kshatriyas, I do not know how they can be prevented from putting forth their claims. But the present question is only concerning me and I never asked the Rajopadhye or any other Brahmin to perform Vedic ritual in any other Maratha family.'[41] The scholar of the non-Brahman movement in Western India, Gail Omvedt, has written that 'his (Shahu's) initial position in fact was to state simply that the issue concerned himself only and not other aristocratic Maratha families'.[42] Jotirao Phule's Satyashodhak Samaj backed Shahu's stand, though in reality, in these years at least, Shahu wasn't accommodating everyone, not even all Marathas, let alone the non-Marathas, and furthermore, he was insisting on the 'purity of lineage'[43] and holding the Vedas as highly sacrosanct, whereas Phule and his Satyashodhak Samaj rejected the Vedas altogether. The Satyashodhaks supported Shahu because he was taking on the Brahmans, and if his attacks could weaken the position of Brahmans in any way, the leaders of the non-Brahman movement saw it as a good thing. (In a subsequent phase of his life, after 1913, Shahu became far more accommodating and a part of the broader non-Brahman movement).[44]

Tilak branded Shahu's act of confiscating inams as 'not only improper but unjust' and 'detrimental to the princely state's interests'. He noted, 'Taking away *watans* and *jagirs* is an act of oppression . . . Even when the British government took over in Maharashtra and carried out land settlement, it continued the old *watans* of the *deshpandes* (revenue collection officers at the district level) and *joshis* (priests) . . . If the Maratha princes don't want Brahman priests conducting Puranic rituals, they might as well not call them. But for that reason alone, they cannot, so long as the Brahmans are willing to perform ceremonies according to established custom, cancel their emoluments.'[45] He also made it a point to underline Shahu's status as a vassal, saying, 'If some rulers want to conduct Vedic rites, they are free to do so, but to use one's power to seize *inams* is wrong . . . Even if a king has powers, there are limitations to it. What to say of those who are vassals of the British Raj?'[46] He said it would be good if the rajas didn't bring things to a point where the Brahmans would have to move the British government for justice.[47]

The affected Brahmans appealed to the British political agent, J.W. Wray, against the durbar's decision. When that was shot down and two more consecutive appeals to the Bombay government were rejected on the pretext that the Raj had no desire to intervene in the state's religious affairs, the chief priest Rajopadhye wrote on behalf of the orthodox sect to the new viceroy, Lord Curzon. Curzon's advisors were in favour of sticking to the Bombay government's decision, and the viceroy accepted the view of two of his advisors, V. Gabriel and R. Russell, that the entire Vedokta row was a battle being waged by the Brahmans against the Maharaj with the support of the 'notorious' Tilak.[48]

The British clearly saw the issue as being more than a faith-based one because of Tilak's backing for the orthodox priests. They would, besides, support any crackdown by Shahu against the Brahmans, whom they perceived as conspirators against the Raj. Colonel W.B. Ferris came in as the Raj's new political representative in Kolhapur in 1901. In a letter to Shahu in May 1902, Ferris promised him that if the Chhatrapati took steps 'against Brahmanical oppression, whether it is by Tilak, Gokhale, or anyone else', he and the British government would completely stand by him.[49] The British were happy to fish unobtrusively in Kolhapur's troubled waters, and ultimately, Shahu succeeded in getting the Vedokta right for himself when the Shankaracharya of the Karveer or Kolhapur *peeth* recognized it in 1905 and the Brahmans, who'd been suitably squeezed, acquiesced.

The Raj fished far more freely in the muddy pool of the Tai Maharaj controversy. The case was a peculiar one: it started as essentially a private conflict and quickly transformed into a full-fledged campaign, led by Tilak's domestic detractors and the British government, to destroy his political career and sully his name and reputation. For a matter whose repercussions ideally ought not to have touched public life at all, it haunted Tilak practically for the rest of his life and consumed an inordinate amount of his time and energy. The incredible stress it caused him as its sinister folds opened was the Raj's big success.

Vasudev Hari alias Baba Maharaj Pandit was a resident of Poona. He belonged to the family of the Kolhapur state's rajguru and had been the rajguru himself previously. He had properties not only inside Kolhapur, given to his family as *inams* in the past, but likewise in the Poona, Belgaum and Ratnagiri belts. It was because he and his forebears had served as head priests that he could use the title of 'Maharaj'; he'd also been given the status of a 'first class sardar of the Deccan' by the British government. He and Tilak had first met sometime in 1888, and acquaintance had turned into friendship. Pandit had two daughters by his first marriage; one of them was married to the son of Tilak's friend, the lawyer G.S. Khaparde from Amravati (Khaparde was a man of influence in Berar and the Central Provinces and stood shoulder-to-shoulder with Tilak in his activities). That might have been a factor in the bond becoming strong, apart from the fact that Pandit was, along with Tilak's associates Khasgiwale and the Natu brothers, among the patrons of Poona's local gymnasiums.

After the death of his first wife, the daughter of another sardar, Pandit had married the daughter of a poor bookseller. She was very young and beautiful, and she went by the name of Sakwarbai or Tai Maharaj. When Tai Maharaj, very much in her teens, was pregnant in August 1897, her husband was struck by cholera. His health deteriorated quickly, and word spread that he was unlikely to survive the illness. Tilak had just been released on bail in the sedition case and had returned to Poona from Bombay. On hearing that Pandit was bed-ridden and might not be able to live long, he went to meet his friend.[50]

The bed-ridden Pandit told Tilak he needed to make arrangements for his properties. He was of course hoping his wife would give birth to a son, who'd survive; that would take care of everything because sons were inheritors in a patriarchal society. But he had to account for other possibilities. So, he made a will and made Tilak a trustee. Pandit would appoint three other trustees: his daughter's father-in-law Khaparde and two of his own trusted clerks, S.S. Kumbhojkar and B.M. Nagpurkar. The will, drafted in Marathi, said, 'My wife is expecting a baby. If she gives birth to a daughter, or if a son is born but lives only a short time, then for the purpose of continuing the name of my family, with the consent and consultation of the trustees, a boy shall be placed, as often as may be necessary, for adoption, on the lap of my wife, in accordance with the *shastras*, and the trustees shall, on behalf of that son, carry on the management of my moveable and fixed properties until he attains majority.'[51]

In the same month in which he drafted the will, Baba Maharaj Pandit died. A few months later, Tai Maharaj gave birth to a son, who died in two months. Tilak was behind bars at the time, having been sentenced in the sedition case.

On his release, he was entrusted with the responsibility of implementing Pandit's will. The first thing he discovered was that Pandit had incurred a lot of debt, and the moneylenders were pushing aggressively for repayment. Tilak spent a lot of time clearing some of the debt. Obviously, the need was for austerity given the state of the family's finances, and with the trustees having a decisive say, Tai Maharaj quickly grew deeply resentful of them and especially of Tilak, who was socially the most well-regarded of them all. Why should she require their approval for using or spending her late husband's money, she wondered, like many of those whose departed kin leave fiscal control in the hands of trustees do. The matter of adoption thus came to acquire top priority: if she could adopt a boy of her choice and somehow get rid of the trustees, she'd be free. She, in league with one of the trustees, the clerk Nagpurkar, came up with the plan to adopt Bala Maharaj of Kolhapur, who belonged to a branch of the Pandit family.

Bala Maharaj was four years older than Tai Maharaj; she was fourteen years old, and he was eighteen. So if he were adopted, the son would be older than the mother. But therein lay the nub of it; he was well on his way to going beyond his teen years, therefore the trustees wouldn't be needed for long.

Tilak and Khaparde believed that if Tai Maharaj had her way, their late friend Pandit's family, including Tai Maharaj herself, would soon come to ruin. They zeroed in on a boy called Jagannath from Aurangabad in the Nizam's dominions. Jagannath was from a branch of the same family; it was in fact in the Nidhone village near Aurangabad that the Pandit household had its origins. Jagannath was seven years old, and Tilak felt he was just right. Perhaps in view of Tilak's heavyweight status, Tai Maharaj agreed, and on 18 June 1901, Jagannath was placed on her lap by his biological father in the presence of shastris, local officials and noted citizens and the formal adoption completed. Papers legalizing the process were also duly signed on the spot.[52]

Tilak returned to Poona a much-relieved man. Barely a fortnight afterwards, he was in for a surprise. Tai Maharaj had gone and met H.F. Aston, the district magistrate of Poona. Aston was also the official placed in charge of the Raj's coordination with the rajas and sardars of the Deccan. The chieftains' families needed to keep him informed of all crucial developments. After the Aurangabad adoption, he had been informed of the formal ceremony and the signed papers sent to him. Tai Maharaj in her meeting with Aston told him she had been forced by Tilak to adopt the seven-year-old Jagannath.

At the same time, Tai Maharaj sent a letter to Tilak, saying her signature on the adoption papers should be taken as invalid as she had signed under duress because she had no one to turn to after her husband's death and had been in much trouble and grief. As she had given birth to a son, who had died subsequently, she was the inheritor of his properties, and if at all Tilak felt he had any rights on the basis of her late husband's will, he could try to establish those through the courts. But he should not enter the Pandit house and cause them any trouble.[53]

She then moved to adopt Bala Maharaj, whom she and Nagpurkar had been originally keen on and asked Shahu for approval because the family had got almost all its properties owing to its services for Kolhapur. Tilak wrote three letters to Shahu asking him not to give his nod and instead to allow the trustees to enforce the will. Shahu nonetheless gave his go-ahead to Tai Maharaj.[54] It was after this that Tilak started attacking him on the Vedokta issue.

On 29 July 1901, Tai Maharaj moved court for revocation of the probate granted to Tilak and the other trustees, contending that it was rendered inoperative and void following the birth of her son and adding that the executors were 'unfit to act in the trust'. Aston, an ICS officer and arch-imperialist, was eager to be in the good books of the Bombay government. He had for long cherished a desire to be a judge at the Bombay High Court. He had missed his chances earlier, as others had been picked over him. He didn't want to be left behind again. He revoked the probate given to Tilak and the others in April 1902 and was appointed as high court judge in June of that year.[55] Meanwhile, even before Aston's verdict was in, Tai Maharaj had gone ahead and formally adopted Bala Maharaj in a ceremony in Kolhapur blessed by Shahu. Much to Tilak's chagrin, Shahu immediately transferred Baba Maharaj Pandit's Kolhapur properties in the new adoptive son's name.

Why had Tai Maharaj carried out the ceremony in Kolhapur instead of Poona, where she was based? She had in fact planned to do it in her own home. Hearing that the adoption ritual was going to be quietly carried out late one night, Tilak barged into her home along with Khaparde and others. They got into a face-off with her aides, and Tilak left only after Tai Maharaj's supporters had exited, having chosen in the face of so much resistance to backtrack and temporarily shelve their plan.[56]

Aston, however, was not content with merely revoking the probate. Members of both factions had deposed before him during the hearing of Tai Maharaj's application. While stripping Tilak of all rights as a trustee, Aston ordered the police to file criminal charges against him for intentionally giving false evidence in court, fabricating documents, illegally detaining Tai Maharaj in her home, illegal assembly and rioting.[57] The criminal case against Tilak was committed to the city magistrate.

Tilak was accused of not having been truthful in saying that a boy had been adopted in Aurangabad. He was blamed for restraining Tai Maharaj in her house on the night on which the fracas with her group had happened. And he was to be held to account for attempting to block the adoption of Bala Maharaj. In his ruling, Aston said Tilak had deposed 'with much prevarication, evasion and fencing'.[58]

Tilak was disturbed by such a damaging verdict. His integrity had been questioned. Even when his testimony was on, his friend Khaparde wrote in his diary that Tilak had told him how Aston had 'tried to be nasty, put irrelevant questions and tried to do all he could to introduce into the case before him the question of adoption with a view to pronounce against' the validity of the Aurangabad ceremony.[59] The verdict convinced him of Aston's hostility.

Tilak filed an appeal against the order in the Bombay High Court. And while the court in August 1902 reversed the judgement in the matter of the probate, the criminal proceedings against Tilak were allowed to proceed.[60]

Fighting the British establishment wasn't easy. The Bombay government not only got public prosecutor Vyankat Ramchandra to stand for it but, along with him, engaged a well-known barrister, T.J. Strangman, for a daily fee of Rs 300, a massive amount by the standards of the early twentieth century. Tilak's friend Dadasaheb Karandikar was to argue on his behalf. With Strangman's entry into the case, Tilak also hired an English lawyer called Branson to appear for him for a steep fee of Rs 400 per day. The case dragged on for months, and the costs incurred by Tilak put a severe strain on his finances. He had no option but to eventually let go of Branson's counsel; thus only Karandikar would appear for him, while the other side had two strong lawyers. 'Poor Tilak is very hard up for want of money,' Khaparde wrote in his diary.[61]

Amid these troubles came a devastating tragedy for Tilak. The eldest of his three sons, Vishwanath, who was studying law at Fergusson College, had been struck by fever; the plague was, after all, far from having been totally extinguished. He did not recover. In February 1903, Vishwanath succumbed, snuffing out what the father had seen as the greatest source of hope in his life. Tilak had paid particular attention to Vishwanath's academic progress, teaching Sanskrit and maths to the boy during his school-going days himself. Not only was Vishwanath bent on becoming a legal mind like Tilak, but he had also started writing, much like the father, articles in newspapers. And Tilak would often rib him if he didn't fully understand a particular subject, saying, 'So you're going to run the *Kesari* in the future!'[62] Vishwanath's death came as an enormous blow.

Tilak initially tried to stifle his feelings, telling those who consoled him that 'there was calamity all over and it claimed victims from his house also'.[63] Just days after Vishwanath's death, he had another scare; he learnt that the youngest of his sons too had developed a fever. Still, he tried to be stoic about it, and there was some degree of relief as soon as the boy recovered. Tilak also tried to keep himself busy with his writings. But grief emerged suddenly and without warning. Immersed in the act of writing one day, Tilak heard a knock on his door. Instinctively he called out to Vishwanath to open the door. In a moment, he realized what he had done and stepped out to open the door himself. When his visitor saw him, there was no tear in his eye, merely the expression of a man completely traumatized.

The personal tragedy and the criminal case resulted in Tilak's health breaking down frequently over six months. He picked himself up gradually. If there was any consolation, it was in the fact that he was still getting displays of solidarity from a number of his fellow Indians. One day, news circulated that Tilak was in Bombay and was going to take the 5 p.m. train back to Poona. Khaparde wrote that high school students came in a group and presented an address to the man they regarded as their leader at the railway station. Many others turned up as well. 'So many people assembled on the platform that there was not even standing room. They garlanded him, gave him an address and distributed *pan-supari*, *attar* and flowers,' Khaparde noted.[64] A few months later, Tilak was back in Bombay, and Khaparde accompanied him to Victoria Terminus, from where they took a train back home. 'The ticket collector there,' realizing that here was a close friend of Tilak's, 'showed great interest in me and asked me about the trouble raised up against Tilak. The same was done at Byculla and other stations. I did not know that I was so well known,' stated Khaparde.[65] But he was. He was one of the trustees in the Tai Maharaj case along with Tilak and was getting increasingly known as Tilak's aide and basking overall in the glow of Tilak's popularity. Khaparde also hoped that Tilak would emerge from the legal wrangle a free man. He wrote, 'He (Tilak) is altogether innocent and if things go right, as they are likely to do, he will be saved a great deal of worry and trouble.'[66]

Finally, the special magistrate E. Clements, pronounced his verdict on 2 October 1903. Tilak was convicted of perjury and sentenced to 18 months of rigorous imprisonment. This was the second time he was being given an eighteen-month sentence—after the sedition case. Clements had concluded that the minutes of the Aurangabad meeting had been 'tainted with deceit' and that 'no such adoption [in Aurangabad] took place'. Documents, he said, 'have been fabricated in order to have false documentary evidence to support a false story'. He held that there was 'cogent evidence of the ill-treatment of Tai Maharaj by Mr. Tilak in Poona' and that 'she was taken helpless by Messrs Tilak and Khaparde to Aurangabad' to select boys from that branch for adoption 'against (her) expressed wishes'.[67] His harsh indictment was that Tilak's treatment of Tai Maharaj during her stay in Aurangabad was 'refinement of brutality'.[68]

As soon as the verdict was delivered, Tilak's lawyers applied for bail in the Bombay High Court, and the court immediately released him on bail. But the British authorities hadn't waited for even half an hour, the exact amount of time it took for the high court to admit the plea and grant bail. Within just ten minutes of the magistrate's delivery of judgement, Tilak was taken to Poona's Yerawada jail in an extraordinary hurry. When the high court decision became known, he had, therefore, to be brought back from prison to be released on bail.[69]

Not only had the Raj taken the initiative in fighting the case against Tilak, it had spent more than Rs 40,000 from the Indian exchequer—in more accurate terms, money looted from India—for a top lawyer's fees and more. The Tamil language newspaper *Swadesamitran*, founded by the nationalist G. Subramania Iyer and published from Madras, posed hard questions to the British government:

If Mr. Tilak was actually guilty of perjury, those who suffered loss on account of it should have brought a case against him. For what purpose has the Government undertaken to conduct such a case at a cost of nearly half a lakh of rupees? Does it undertake at its own cost to commit all people guilty of perjury on this earth and conduct the proceedings with the help of its own officers? What can be its motive in having spent the public money for causing so much affliction to such a patriot and well-learned man as Mr. Tilak, who is known for his good disposition?

The Tamil paper proceeded to provide the answer too:

There has been a feeling of hatred for and enmity towards him in the minds of several Anglo-Indian officials since the year 1897, when he was convicted as a traitor . . . His enemies who were waiting for an opportunity to bring him into trouble took advantage of the adoption case.[70]

A Marathi weekly, *Brahmodaya*, declared that 'either Mr. Clements' mind was prejudiced against Tilak or . . . he is unfit for the task of administering justice.' It described the order as 'abuse of power and authority' and commented on Clements' observation that Tilak's witnesses were untrustworthy because they were all Brahmans. 'The Magistrate . . . is certainly a wiseacre,' the paper said. 'He ought to study the Evidence Act. Like Tilak, his opponent was a Brahmin. How was the latter then considered to be trustworthy?' The *Brahmodaya* editor also noted, like the Tamil daily had done, that 'many persons think that some selfish and bureaucratic European officers have of late begun to hate Tilak because he is held in universal esteem for his learning, ability and disinterestedness as a public leader.' But the paper saw reason to 'thank' the magistrate too. It stated, 'History tells us that the persecution of national leaders is an indication that a national revolution is at hand . . . The greater the persecution, the nearer will be the approach of the revolution. Had it not been for Ravana, who threw all the gods into jail, there would have been no incarnation of Rama.'[71]

The *Gujarati* wrote that hardly any Indian believed in the verdict of guilty in any case. 'The public find it difficult to acquiesce in the finding of the magistrate . . . that a public leader of Tilak's position could have committed such a serious criminal offence as perjury.' The *Baroda Vatsal*, from the same region in western India, described Tilak's sentencing as 'a reward for his integrity and disinterested solicitude to carry out the last wishes of his friend.' And the *Gujarati Punch* regretted that 'poor Tilak' seemed to have been 'born at a very unlucky time; it appears to be his lot to suffer persecution at the hands of those inimical to him'.[72]

Tilak appealed against Clements' judgment in the sessions court, and the sessions judge Lucas held him guilty but with extenuating circumstances and reduced the prison term to six months.

Lucas held that Tilak had made a false statement that the valid adoption had been completed in Aurangabad. The process hadn't been completed at all, the judge concluded. But Lucas' judgment gave Tilak a clean chit on several points. He remarked that 'Tilak was a celebrated man on this side of India. He is regarded by a large section of the native community as a hero and a martyr. On the other hand, such a man is bound to have enemies.' The judge observed that 'I do not think that the accused (Tilak) and Khaparde had any interested motives . . . such as love of power or desire for pecuniary benefits.' He also disbelieved Tai Maharaj's claim about unlawful confinement in her own home. 'On the 24th (June) Khaparde returned to Amraoti. From the 24th till the afternoon of 27th June nothing of importance seems to have taken place. It was during this interval that Tai Maharaj states she was confined by Tilak in the small room opening out of the hall in which she received visitors. There is absolutely no corroboration to this statement . . . and I consider it to be highly improbable,' Lucas stated. And even as he discussed the point of why he thought Tilak had made a 'false statement' that Tai Maharaj had placed Jagannath on her lap on 28 June 1901, the judge accused both Tai Maharaj and her supporter Nagpurkar of bearing false witness and Nagpurkar in particular of entertaining 'designs' and being involved in 'machinations.' Declaring that 'men like Nagpurkar . . . will give evidence on whichever side they can see prospects of profit for themselves', the judge said:

> The question then arises: What was his (Tilak's) motive in making this false statement . . . Mr. Clements (the special magistrate) does not come to the definite conclusion that he had any corrupt motive . . . He says "the only alternative is to regard the act of perjury . . . as the demented act of an obstinate man who has been completely defeated by people whom he apparently made the mistake of despising." I think that in saying this Mr. Clements has come somewhere very near the truth.
>
> I believe that in desiring the adoption of Jagonath (sic) the accused's motives were pure and that he foresaw evil consequences to the estate if Nagpurkar succeeded in getting Tai Maharaj to adopt Bala Maharaj. When Bala was ultimately adopted on the 19th August 1901, his mother passed a deed to Tai Maharaj, a perusal of which shows . . . all the management of the estate remained with Tai Maharaj, a young Hindu widow, who was under the thumb of an unscrupulous schemer like Nagpurkar.
>
> Assuming as I do that Tilak really desired the welfare of the Maharaj family and the improvement of the estate he must have been, to say the least, disgusted at the course events had taken and

exasperated at having been outwitted by a man like Nagpurkar. Such feelings would be merely human nature. I am not prepared to say that he had any excuse for deliberately committing perjury, but I do think there are extenuating circumstances in his case, the more so as Nagpurkar and Tai Maharaj have, I am convinced, both of them given false evidence against him before Mr. Clements. Again, to an obstinate and masterful man such as Tilak undoubtedly is, the long punishing examination which he underwent in Mr. Aston's court must have proved a severe trial of temper.[73]

Though the judge was categorical that both Tai Maharaj and Nagpurkar had lied on oath—the very offence Tilak had been convicted for—no action was recommended or taken against them. On the day he delivered his judgement, the district judge's court in Poona 'was crowded, and the sentence came rather as a surprise to a good many', wrote the correspondent of *Times of India*.[74]

What happened immediately after the pronouncement of the judgement brought shock and dismay to many. Tilak was handcuffed like a common criminal and dragged away. Appalled by Tilak's deliberate humiliation, the Bengali newspaper *Pratibhashi* from Calcutta wrote:

We were not prepared for the startling and shameful tidings . . . the news of a distinguished native gentleman of Bombay . . . in the presence of the district judge of Poona, manacled as a common felon . . . Shame upon all the perpetrators of this foul and disgraceful act. What was the necessity of handcuffing Mr. Tilak? Was this through fear of his escaping? Nothing of the kind. It was . . . to gratify the spite of a few government underlings who experienced the delight which the coward always feels in kicking a man who is down.[75]

Down he certainly was, but from Madras, from Calcutta, from Gujarat and from Lahore, Tilak was getting a great deal of support from his compatriots. It was confirmation that he had achieved star status across the four corners of the sub-continent.

The high court bench led by Justice Lawrence Jenkins found Tilak innocent and set aside all the charges, including the main charge of perjury, and the conviction. Tai Maharaj's team was not willing to let the adoption case die, though. Tai Maharaj herself died of a bout of cholera late in 1903, but the civil case was carried forward in the name of her daughter Shantabai and the newly adopted son Bala Maharaj. The civil suit also went in Tilak's favour in 1906, after which an appeal was filed by Shantabai in the Bombay High Court. The high court's verdict went against Tilak, who then appealed to the Privy Council in London. The Privy Council ultimately ruled in Tilak's favour in 1915, yet even after that, the British government delayed executing the Council's order, ensuring that the properties of Baba Maharaj were handed over to Jagannath, not before 1917. That was almost seventeen years after the whole drama had begun and passed through a number of courts, consuming Tilak's time and energy and causing enormous headache and anguish.

The more the case dragged on, the more debt Tilak incurred in fighting it, soliciting assistance from his friends. On the other hand, the rival side was financed throughout by Shahu Maharaj of Kolhapur. Shahu mentioned in a letter written to a British official in 1915 that he had spent a considerable amount of money on the case against Tilak. He remarked in the same letter, written in the wake of the 1915 Privy Council decree, that he would unhesitatingly spend more sums to ensure Tilak did not emerge the winner in the case.[76] The British government and a native prince had joined hands to create as much trouble for Tilak as possible in what in truth was a minor civil suit. Tilak, too, oddly allowed himself to be drawn into the muddle when he could very well have extricated himself from someone else's property dispute right at the beginning and avoided all the annoyance and bother altogether. He gave a golden chance to the Raj to fix him, and it did.

The *Mahratta* wrote, in the wake of the Privy Council's order, that the Tai Maharaj case was one of the 'very few instances in which the extra-long arm of persecution which government possesses, with unlimited resources in men and money behind their back, was put to a worse use by them against individuals'.[77] Another paper characterized the long trajectory of the case as perhaps Tilak's 'longest and most excruciating period of intense mental agony, of bodily disease, of hardships, of another imprisonment and loss of thousands of rupees. His reputation was at stake, his honesty was challenged, and his good faith was called into question'.[78]

The one thing to look forward to for Tilak was his move in 1905 into a new residence, the Gaikwad Wada which he bought from the ruler of Baroda, Sayajirao Gaekwad. It was in the Narayan Peth area of Poona, where he had earlier lived in another house before moving to Vinchurkar Wada afterwards. The Gaikwad Wada land was big, covering 1.25 acres in all, including a sizeable courtyard, though the one-and-a-half-storey house itself was in decrepit condition. A Peshwa-era structure that stood out once upon a time, it had suffered much neglect over the decades. Tilak got some portions of the house repaired and ordered others to be pulled down and built afresh. Designing the new parts himself, he made space for his residence on the eastern side and for the *Kesari* office on the western side. The newspaper office had files of newspapers and periodicals stacked on one side and several scrapbooks besides. It was not possible to keep entire files of all publications, so from certain papers and magazines, articles had been cut out, neatly categorized according to subjects and placed in the scrapbooks so that the editor and editorial staff could refer to them whenever they needed to. On the ground floor, Tilak put in place a big library which, according to his amanuensis A.V. Kulkarni, had 'approximately 10,000 books' housed in '32 cupboards'. Among the prized ones in this lot were the complete private libraries of the late social reformer Gopal Hari Deshmukh and the late Professor Jinsiwale, which Tilak had obtained from their descendants; thus, several rare books and special editions had come into his possession. Tilak's collection as a whole was eclectic: numerous Sanskrit texts as well as translations of the Vedas; *bakhars* or family documents related to Maratha history; works of history in English and Marathi and of poetry, especially of the Marathi poets like Tukaram, Moropant, Vaman Pandit; thirty-five volumes of an encyclopaedia; and a number of handwritten manuscripts besides, including fifteen handwritten volumes of the late M. Namjoshi's encyclopaedic works on the Marathi language.

Apart from the drawing room that belonged to the family, Tilak set aside a biggish drawing room for himself in the house, which he would use a private space for his own reading, writing and personal meetings. It was relatively sparse and had a writing table, a couple of plain chairs, another couple of easy chairs and one or two plain benches with chair-like backs. In this room were also two cupboards filled with books and two shelves. Photography was new in those years, and Tilak had kept pictures of all his family members on the walls and the shelves, apart from memorials and souvenirs obtained during his visits across India and the certificate given to him on his election to the Bombay provincial election in 1895.

When he was at home, Tilak's daily routine was more or less set. He would rise at 6 a.m., but if he'd had a late night, could be up by 7.30 a.m. At 7 a.m. usually he'd check the post and first read his personal mail and then the official one. After that he'd take a close look at the newspapers, and if anything special needed to be noted for his own *Kesari* and *Mahratta* papers, he would mention it to his nephew Dhondopant Vidwans, who had come to stay there and whom Tilak had begun to increasingly rely on for management of the two publications. If some visitors arrived in the morning then he would meet them, else he would go straight to his personal drawing room with a book and read. 'Almost his entire day was spent in writing, reading, contemplation and conversations,' wrote his amanuensis. His wife Satyabhama took care of everything related to the household, so he never interfered in the running of the house except when called to do so in an emergency, which was rare. His clothing was his usual white plain sadra and the dhoti, with the red Pooneri *pagdi* on his head. In the winter Tilak had taken to wearing a woollen sweater, but he wore it under his sadra, not over it; when he was travelling, he sometimes used an overcoat; and sometimes, when he was simply relaxing at home, he took off his pagdi and wore something resembling a Hungarian cap. His one weakness was the 'supari' or betel nut: he would be chewing it practically all day, so in various places across the house were scattered a few very small baskets loaded with 'suparis' and sharp 'adkitta' or supari cutters.[79]

Meanwhile, the Congress was, in Tilak's opinion, plodding on, slowly and often desultorily. He found its 'let's meet once in a year' position absolutely untenable. 'We will not achieve any success in our labours if we croak once a year like a frog,' he said.[80]

What was his recipe then? And what about the fact that the Congress was getting increasingly divided into two camps, the Moderates and the Extremists?

Tilak didn't look kindly at the Moderates at all. He was convinced that if it was the Raj that had booked him for sedition in 1897 for his writings and sentenced him to imprisonment, it couldn't have done so but for the instigation of at least a section of the Moderates. Tilak wrote an editorial in the *Kesari* after his release from prison in 1899. Titled 'Punaschya Hari Om [In the Name of God, Let's Start Afresh]!', he categorically stated that the government relied upon locals to understand the nuances of the Marathi language and 'the inner meaning of the writer', and there was no way it could have interpreted his criticism of the authorities during the plague years in a particular way without 'such slanderers' (among the Moderates) having assisted it enthusiastically.

He stated, acerbically:

> There's a widespread theory that a shy bullock or arrogant elephant doesn't come rampaging at a person or thing unless there's someone who incites it. If we look at this theory, it's natural to feel someone must have poured oil into the fire for the government to look askance at some editors in 1897 . . . When a new school of political moderation was inaugurated in Pune, we had expressed our fears that it would result in such a thing happening. Many people then called us names for saying so, but what has to happen does happen anyway . . . There is nothing so heinous as a Hindu or native distorting the meaning of someone's writing simply because he has a different political point of view and attempting to establish him as a seditionist and then rejoicing when that label sticks to the rival. We are lucky there are only a handful of such people around. But they do exist, and we have no doubt that they're busy with their designs . . . We need to be more careful about these people than about the government . . . An open enemy is one thing, but such people are far more terrible.[81]

At the same time, Tilak believed the only way the national movement could be revived and could go forward after a few years of stasis was through the alienation of those 'handful of trouble-makers' and the coming together of the Moderates and the Extremists. That was indeed possible, according to him. Both sides were convinced that the Indians needed rights, and they could unitedly push for the rights that there was complete consensus about, he suggested. Differences existed everywhere and so did petty people, but just as the fingers of a hand, albeit all different in size, could still work together, so the nationalists had to put their minds and hearts together for the national interest and 'work to fructify the hopes an organization like the Congress has generated in our minds', he said.[82]

His immediate suggestion in the early years of the twentieth century was that Congress should send three of its elder statesmen— Pherozeshah Mehta, Surendranath Banerjea and Ananda Charlu—to England to advance India's interests. The Congress leadership, made up entirely of Moderates, saw this as an attempt to weaken their domestic front so that the Extremists led by Tilak could get hold of the organization and the Congress could be riven into two separate factions. They got the Grand Old Man, Dadabhai Naoroji, to write to Tilak and even to chastise him for apparently running down the Congress. Naoroji wrote to the *Kesari* editor:

> The reason for today's letter is this – the National Congress has become our war weapon in the field of future politics. The National Congress is not perfect today. But gradually we wish to make it stronger. It is understood that through Kesari you are pushing it down. If it is once weakened in this manner and sustains injury, then it will take a long time for us to make repairs. In our struggle against the government we must all be of one heart. Criticism should be friendly and constructive. If Congress is broken then it will be a great disaster to India, and a great triumph for the Anglo-Indian people. Stay in Bombay and place your suggestions before the Subjects Committee, and let all abide by the majority decision.[83]

Tilak responded that Naoroji's 'opinion' was what 'everyone values the most' and pressed his own point:

> I have never been, nor am I in any way against the Congress. Constitutional agitation, I shall be the last person to decry. But I am rather positive and optimistic by temperament, and I think we must push our efforts to their logical extreme. I firmly believe – and let me tell you that you yourself have been the principal cause of this belief – that if we wish to get any rights or privileges we must agitate in England in a missionary spirit. The Anglo-Indians here won't listen to what we say . . . I do not mean to say that the Congress work in India is entirely useless. But I do maintain that without persistent

work in England carried on *by our own men*, mere annual gathering in India would be of no avail.

That being my view I have been urging it upon the attention of our Congress leaders here privately for some years past. What a grand thing it would be, I said, if Sir P. M. Mehta, Mr. Surendra Nath Banerjee or Rai Bahadur Ananda Charlu were to go to England and stay there for some years.[84]

At the 1904 Congress, held in Bombay, the Congress did take a decision to send a couple of its representatives to England. It chose younger faces over the elder statesmen Tilak was suggesting: Gokhale and Lala Lajpat Rai from the Punjab. Gokhale firmly believed that the Indians and the British could work together, and that Indians needed greater representation on the local and national councils and in the civil and other services. Tilak saw very little room for common cause where the British and Indians were concerned. For him, the Britishers were foreign rulers who needed to exit. At the Bombay Congress, he said, 'The Indian Empire is a dead body and a foreign body, and if that foreign body is not assimilated within the British Empire, we shall have to perform a surgical operation and take out that foreign body from the living Empire.' These words of his were followed by cries of 'Hear, hear', something that the Congress chroniclers of the time did not fail to note.[85]

Tilak's words came at the very end of 1904. In 1905, the Indian national movement would enter a brand new phase, in which Tilak's salvos would become more forceful and the Congress considerably more energetic than in its first couple of decades.

Chapter 10

Curzon 'the Serpent'

On 11 August 1898, when Tilak was still behind bars in the sedition case, Lord Curzon, all of thirty-nine years old, was appointed the new Viceroy of India. About him, two of his classmates at Oxford's Balliol College had written what Curzon himself described, in moments of anger, as an 'accursed doggerel'. It went like this:

> My name is George Nathaniel Curzon
> I am a most superior person
> My cheek is pink, my hair is sleek
> I dine at Blenheim once a week

The classmates who composed these lines were superbly perceptive. George Curzon looked down upon his own family, which boasted of having one of the best country houses in England in Derbyshire and could count among its members some of England's MPs of the eighteenth and nineteenth century, even if they weren't political top-rankers. 'My ancestors were a feeble lot,' he said. 'No family could have remained in possession of the same estate since the twelfth century had they manifested the slightest energy or courage.'[1] George himself wanted to go well beyond the estate—to India, specifically. Like the place he had clearly identified, the position he wanted to gain too was specific: he wanted to be the viceroy, he said at a dinner at the House of Commons in 1890.[2] He worked towards it, touring India and the East extensively and after that serving as under-secretary in the India Office and the Foreign Office.

Curzon described himself as an 'imperialist heart and soul' and
announced that his purpose was 'to rivet the British rule more firmly
on to India and to postpone the longed-for day of emancipation'.[3]
At the same time, he underlined that he cared not 'a snap of the
fingers for the tawdry lust of conquest', and he was not among those
who dismissed Indian civilization outright. He quite disliked the
mistreatment of Indians by British officials, particularly those in the
military, and by Britishers in the trading community, who literally got
away with murder or worse. Among these arrogant Britishers, he knew,
were tea planters who ill-treated and assaulted their Indian workers
simply because local magistrates were in their favour, and men in the
army who committed outrages such as rape and got their military
superiors to bury the whole matter. All of this was problematic for
Curzon, and 'the racial pride and the undisciplined passions of the
inferior class of Englishmen' were dangerous in his opinion because
they could put British rule in India in peril. He wished to make
'Britain's administration equitable and her dominion permanent' and
said, proudly, 'I have never wavered in a strict and inflexible justice
between the two races. It is the sole justification and the only stable
foundation for our rule.'[4]

Despite these protests against the maltreatment of Indians, Curzon's
words and actions did not really reflect any equality of treatment. He
said he would not appoint an Indian to his Council because 'in the
entire country there was not an Indian fit for the post'. And when the
British MP William Wedderburn asked him to appoint more Indians
to the Indian Civil Service, Curzon replied that in an emergency, 'the
highly placed native is apt to be unequal to it, does not attract the respect
of his subordinates, European or even Native, and is rather inclined to
abdicate, or to run away'.[5]

Curzon's favourite catchword was 'efficiency', and among the
priorities he set for himself was the building of peace along India's
north-western borders by pacifying the local tribes there. He did so
by creating in 1901 the new North-West Frontier Province, separating
the north-western districts from the Punjab province. He similarly
resolved to expand the country's railway network, another task he
accomplished successfully and announced reforms to the school system
and the police administration.

As Curzon portrayed all of these moves as being driven by a keen desire for India's progress, Tilak was profoundly sceptical. Aware of Curzon's—and the Raj's—suspicion of Russia, he noted that new administrative arrangements along the frontiers were useful merely from the point of view of the Empire's security. As for the railways, Tilak said, it was 'one thing for a country to have its own network and another for traders from one country to build a train network in a foreign land'. And as for the supposed reforms, would they end up crushing the autonomy of private education institutes and result in plum police posts being filled by more Europeans, he wondered.[6]

Curzon soon came up with the idea of a grand durbar in Delhi to mark the accession of the new king Edward VII. Held in 1903, the two-week extravaganza was an ostentatious display of power, with all the princes and other loyalists publicly pledging their allegiance to the British crown. The viceroy's biographer has written that Curzon personally planned all the pageantry, dictating 'the programme of the events', 'the architecture of the arena, the layout of the camps', 'the movement and accommodation of about 1,50,000 people', 'the width of the roads, the placement of the tents, the planting of the flower-beds'.[7] Special camps were set up for important dignitaries, and Curzon's own camp had 2774 people in all.[8]

'Lord Curzon has fulfilled to his heart's content his desire of strutting around the ancient city of Hastinapur (Delhi) astride an elephant!' Tilak remarked, sarcastically. Lord Lytton had, in 1877, held a similar gathering in the same place, Tilak noted, but Curzon 'with his intelligence and cleverness' had outdone that one in its 'ceremonial grandeur', 'boastfulness' and 'imperialistic pride'. British power was already well-entrenched in India, but Curzon wanted to take credit for the Raj reaching its apogee with such a grand durbar, and fortunately for him, he could take all the credit for it, Tilak declared in the *Kesari*. Poor indigenous people like him, Tilak said, nonetheless could not help but wonder why such a 'tamasha' was necessary. He wrote, 'Everyone except those intoxicated with their own power is naturally going to ask: when it was clear to all Indians that Edward VII was going to ascend the throne and be their new sovereign after the death of the Queen (Victoria in 1901), what could possibly be the reason behind declaring such an obvious fact with an exhibition of authority and riches and

with the aid of canons and trumpets?' Tilak said the whole fuss appeared
to have been enacted 'across an area of 40 miles almost to disprove the
notion that the Englishmen were traders focused on their principles
rather than on opulence'. Never one to let go of a cultural argument if he
could make it, Tilak said that in ancient India, rulers had carried out the
rajasuya yagna and other such ceremonial acts, but those were used as
occasions to take stock of the condition of the people and to announce
welfare measures. The Raj could well have announced an exemption for
cultivators from pending payments of agricultural tax, he said. It would
have cost not a rupee more but earned the blessings of the thirty crore
people of India, he added. 'To spend crores on the Delhi durbar is sheer
madness,' Tilak baldly stated. In a direct attack on Curzon, he said that
'the statesmen who wished to demonstrate the so-called permanence of
British rule by spreading the odious smell of imperial garishness were
doing good neither to the Raj nor to the people'.[9]

Early in 1905, during the convocation ceremony of Calcutta
University, Curzon, who was the varsity's chancellor, told the graduating
students superciliously, 'I hope I am making no false or arrogant claim
when I say that the highest ideal of truth is to a large extent a western
conception.'[10] Tilak's retort in *Kesari* was sharp. He wrote, 'If Curzon
only wanted to pour it his bile, he could have done it anywhere after a
suitable dinner-and-drinks session. Why go and puke at the temple of
learning?'[11] Once again, in response to imperialistic pride, he brought
into play his cultural contention. 'If the Christian nations of the West
take pride in upholding the truth,' Tilak wrote, 'then it is because of
the Christian religion born in the East. The truth is all the heroes of
faith, be it Christ, Muhammad, Shri Krishna, Buddha or Confucius,
were born in the East and not a single one was born in the West'.[12]
Curzon had said in the same speech that the Mahabharata eulogized
the truth but allowed for exceptions to be made in certain cases.
'What does he even know of the Mahabharata,' Tilak asked and added
that even if he did, India's ennobling truths had turned bitter in his
bosom, and the viceroy was 'like a serpent who drank milk and spewed
poison'.[13] About Curzon's use of the term 'Oriental diplomacy', Tilak
said that the people could see that this particular catchphrase had come
to the viceroy's mind, but how, then, had he conveniently forgotten
'Perfidious Albion'?[14] An English translation of the French *la perfide*

Albion, Perfidious Albion was a phrase widely used across Europe in the eighteenth and nineteenth centuries to describe Britain as a country that lied, went back on treaties and employed treachery in international affairs. For an editor who had already been held guilty and imprisoned once on charges of sedition, these were extraordinarily bold things to say about the incumbent viceroy and the colonial regime.

As part of his thrust on 'efficiency', Curzon initiated the process of partitioning Bengal. For at least a couple of decades, British officials had felt that the province, in which the then capital of the Raj—Calcutta—stood, was much too big. Apart from Bengal, the regions included in it were Bihar, Orissa and Chhota Nagpur (which covered most of present-day Jharkhand and parts of what is today Chhattisgarh). Its population was 7.85 crore, more than one-fourth of India's total population of about thirty crore. In 1902, Curzon wrote to London advocating a division of Bengal into two separate provinces, East and West Bengal, for the purposes of administrative ease. The Empire's top officials in the British capital were anyway thinking in the same direction. They passed on to him their own file of discussions carried out on the subject thus far, and Curzon, though cut up that they'd shared their file only after he had told them about his intentions, went right ahead.

On 3 December 1903, Curzon made his plan public. A vertical boundary would be drawn, going right down the east of Calcutta; and Assam, which was a small, separate province, would be made a part of East Bengal. West Bengal, which would include Bihar, Orissa and Chhota Nagpur, would have a population of 5.4 crore, and the eastern part would have 3.1 crore people in all. The Hindus of Bengal were outraged: not only were they going to be split into two provinces, but they would also be in a minority in East Bengal, 1.2 crore as against the Muslim majority of 1.8 crore. West Bengal would have a comfortable Hindu majority, yet Bengali speakers would be down to 1.7 crore, with Hindi and Oriya speakers together forming the overwhelming majority (3.7 crore).[15]

Howls of protest arose across Bengal; a number of meetings were held, with town halls, maidans and other venues filled beyond capacity by angry Bengalis; thousands of pamphlets were distributed, and countless petitions were sent to Curzon. He harboured an acute dislike for the Bengali-educated elite and had accused them of bringing in political questions into educational matters when they had complained about his attempt to poke his nose into the higher education system.[16] He privately also held that 'the incurable vice' of the Bengali 'babu' was his 'faculty of rolling out yards and yards of frothy declamation about subjects which he has imperfectly considered, or which he does not fully understand'.[17] So when the Bengalis accused him of adopting a policy of divide and rule, Curzon impatiently brushed it all aside, saying it was 'a calumny so preposterous that it scarcely seems worthy of notice'.[18] Still, a little before the partition was finalized, Curzon went to Dhaka and told the Muslims there that they would have a 'preponderating voice' in the new province and would be able to achieve 'a unity which they have not enjoyed since the days of the old Mussulman Viceroys and Kings'.[19]

Curzon was also sure that the protests would die down soon. His simple theory about the Bengalis was that they 'howl until a thing is settled and then they accept it'.[20] He was proven utterly wrong in this respect. When the partition came into effect on 16 October 1905, the protests grew louder and crossed the borders of Bengal.

Curzon was also convinced that the division of Bengal would weaken the Congress, where the Hindus were in the majority and the Muslims were not very enthusiastic members or participants. He'd be delighted if that happened, for he had written in a confidential note to the Secretary of State in 1901 that he believed 'the Congress is tottering to its fall, and one of my greatest ambitions while in India is to assist it to a peaceful demise'.[21] This reading of his too proved to be altogether fallacious, and the one Indian leader who fully and most effectively used the opportunity offered by the partition of Bengal to breathe new life into the premier political organization of the 'natives' was Bal Gangadhar Tilak.

The Congress had been going through a genuine crisis as it approached the end of two decades of its existence. It was merely drifting along. Its second decade had been worse than the first. At the end of 1903, hardly any province was willing to play host to the next annual session, and the Congress of 1903 saw poor attendance when it met in Madras. Even a comparison with the previous Madras sessions showed how bad things were for the organization that called itself the chief political voice of Indians. The 1894 Congress in Madras had been attended by 1163 delegates, the Madras Congress of 1898 by 614 delegates; in 1903, only 538 showed up. *Hindustan Review* declared it a 'distinct and dismal failure,' and *Amrita Bazar Patrika*, the *Poona Vaibhav* and the *Bengalee*, among many other nationalist papers and leaders, suggested from time to time all through the decade that it might not be a bad idea for the Congress to stop its operations, if only for a while.[22]

Ever since Tilak had been imprisoned in 1897 and Gokhale had turned momentarily despondent after having offered his apology to the British the same year, the Congress had found the going especially difficult. These two were its two most dynamic young leaders, showing the greatest promise of taking over from the previous generation. Though Pherozeshah Mehta's presence still loomed large, the young generation of both the Moderates and the Extremists had become increasingly resentful of his domineering personality. Mehta was a tall leader, a Moderate, but he was elitist in his conception of politics. The poor had hardly any role in his scheme of things, and his extravagant living and excessively personalized style of politics, seeing success as his own rather than as a collective achievement, did not win him a lot of admirers. Yet, as someone who had had four terms as chairman of the Bombay Civic Corporation and three terms as the Bombay Legislative Council's pick on the Imperial Legislative Council, he was unquestionably a political heavyweight and was in a position to dictate terms. There was no doubt that he commanded respect: despite being a believer in the Raj as 'an act of divine providence', he had taken on the Empire on issues of racial discrimination and various unjust pieces of legislation and had also fought for the right of Indians to carry weapons; his own weapon had been taken away from him by a British police constable when he went out with it on the streets of Bombay during the 1874 Parsi–Muslim riots. But his routine dismissal of arguments that did not match his own, even if they came from his own supporters in the Congress, and his contemptuous talk about 'popular movements' meant that respect was mingled with resentment, which gradually grew. It increased considerably as the Congress struggled. In the 1903 Congress, both the Moderates and Extremists opposed Mehta's inflexible approach. In 1904, Gokhale, who often found himself under Mehta's overt or indirect control, cited Japan as an example of a nation that had succeeded because it followed its leaders and suggested obliquely to Congress delegates that Mehta should be followed. Gokhale went to the extent of saying that Indians 'must be prepared to subordinate their judgement to that of' their leaders,' meaning Mehta. Tilak's associates at the same Congress, Lala Murlidhar in particular, nevertheless 'complained bitterly about Pherozeshah . . . carrying everything his own way'.[23]

Tilak, for his part, after coming out of prison, had been caught up in one thing or the other, writing his book on the Vedas and fighting the Tai Maharaj case. Gokhale had slowly worked his way back into prominence, but his voice was heard mainly by the British and a section of the Indian elite and no one else. As one chronicler of the organization wrote, nineteen years after it was founded, 'the Congress had little to show for its existence'. It had 'no money, no permanent organization, no sustained activity. It had failed to find any significant support among the masses and the Muslims. It was a house divided, with little confidence in itself and enjoying the confidence of others. It was ignored or ridiculed by British officials. It received moralistic and condescending lectures on its shortcomings from its British friends.'[24]

Tilak would change all of that.

On 7 August 1905, a mammoth meeting took place at the Calcutta Town Hall to condemn Curzon's move. So many people had turned up that instead of one meeting, three had to be held—one on the first floor of the Town Hall, one on the ground floor and one outside. This was just two months before the partition would take effect. The Bengalis resolved at the meeting that they would boycott British goods if the government went ahead with its plan to split the province. Tilak recognized the potential of the political moment, and the headline he gave for his editorial comment in *Kesari*, 'A Critical Moment!', reflected his thinking. He began in his usual trenchant style, characterizing Curzon as 'a Viceroy who wants to stomp all around Hindustan unimpeded like Ravana', as a 'modern-day Aurangzeb' imposing an unjust reign and as someone who was already 'trampling like a crazed elephant upon the popular sentiment of the Bengalis, treating them as grass'. Popular opinion had been mobilized in the province and that was a good thing, Tilak argued, but more important was to make the mobilization effective. That could be done purely by way of action; protests and meetings weren't enough, he said. Further, he stressed:

We don't need words. We must act. And act with resolve . . .
The government pays absolutely no heed to meetings attended by
thousands or lakhs of people, and if we don't find a way of responding
to this, people will lose faith in popular movements. It is the duty
of leaders to awaken public opinion, but what's the use of such an
awakening if the government can crush public opinion under its feet?
The state of our public opinion is such that waves hitting the shores
would appear somewhat better and more effective. Waves are salty,
so before they are beaten back by the mountains near the shores,
they cut through the edges of the mountains and create crevices. Our
public opinion is so weak that the waves it creates have no effect on
government! The question we have to address therefore is how to
transform the insipid nature of our public sentiment.

The idea of boycott was just right, Tilak asserted, for 'there is no other
way to puncture the government's arrogance than by doing things that
would really hurt'. True, he carried on, 'The government is neglecting
public opinion and treating it like a lotus fiber or grass, but as a poet has
told us, when grass becomes united a rope is formed, and it can even tie
up an elephant.'[25] Tilak finally urged the Congress to give up 'begging'
and stand shoulder-to-shoulder with the people of Bengal. 'Don't look
behind. March right ahead!' he told the masses.[26]

In the same month, August 1905, Curzon resigned, two years into
his second term in office as the viceroy. His quitting had nothing to
do with the protests over Bengal's partition. He got into a conflict
with British India's commander-in-chief Lord Kitchener, who was
unhappy that one of his subordinates and not he, had been made a
military member of the Viceroy's Executive Council. He complained
to the British premier, the king, and the Secretary of State for India,
John Brodrick. Brodrick had been Curzon's schoolmate and his rival
at Oxford, and he sided with Kitchener.[27] Curzon resigned in protest.

While the Indians were relieved to see him go, Tilak saw that the
effects of Curzon's rule would continue to be felt in the future. Seeking
to dispel the impression Curzon had tried to create that he was a friend
of the 'natives,' Tilak said his love for Indians was akin to a cattle-
owner's love for poor animals held by him in captivity. So long as they
had been shorn of their horns and so long as they 'behaved', he was

willing to bestow upon them his 'demonic compassion'. If they started
thinking and deciding for themselves, they were a problem. Tilak did
not begrudge Curzon his genuine qualities. Truly, the outgoing viceroy
was 'energetic, industrious and intelligent.' But so were the 'Asuras' in
ancient Hindu texts, Tilak commented in a scathing assessment of
the imperial statesman in the *Kesari*. And 'what would otherwise be
qualities had turned demonic in his hands owing to his ill-intent, just as
they had in the hands of the Asuras'.

Unfortunately, Tilak wrote, in Curzon's first two years as viceroy,
both the Congress and the Bengali newspapers had showered a
great deal of praise on him, taking at face value his extravagant and
ornamental language when there was no reason to do so; Curzon had
always made it clear that he wanted to 'further entrench British rule in
India and expand it across Asia'. With that aim in mind, he had cracked
down on the population without hesitation, undermined it and 'broken
its limbs'. Curzon had not an iota of sympathy or generosity towards
the people of India, and his record, Tilak pointed out, was ultimately
more disastrous for the people of the country than that of any of his
predecessors. The first disaster of his rule, in fact, had been experienced
by the Bengalis themselves who had commended him excessively in
the early years, Tilak reminded the anti-partition protestors; in the
initial phase of his Viceregal stint itself, Curzon had robbed them of a
degree of administrative autonomy when he had halved the number of
elected members on Calcutta's seventy-five-member municipal council
from fifty to twenty-five and given the 'official' or British members an
unquestionable majority.[28]

Now, however, was the time for people across India to stand by the
Bengalis, who had come up with the accurate means of protest, Tilak
remarked. Gokhale wanted the anti-partition agitation to be confined
to Bengal; Tilak was eager for it to quickly cross that province's borders
and rumble through the sub-continent. The Maharashtrians must
especially back the Bengalis in their efforts, he said. The idea of the
boycott had in India emerged for the first time in Maharashtra, he
argued, and 'there were still people around in Pune who had seen the
homespun cotton shirt and turban of Sarvajanik Kaka' or G.V. Joshi,
one of the Sarvajanik Sabha's pioneers who had attended the 1877
Delhi durbar clad in khadi. Tilak said meetings to show solidarity with

Bengal and to propagate the idea of boycott must be held in every district and taluka. To those sceptical of the efficacy of such a method, he cited the examples of Italy's boycott of Austria in the previous century, the use of the same principle during the American struggle for independence, and China's recent adoption of a similar strategy against America to protest the ill-treatment of Chinese citizens on US soil. Indians did not want to use violent means, he clarified, but if petitions didn't work, the best way to press a point was to exert pressure on the foreign rulers.[29]

When several critics of the boycott pointed out that a sufficient number of products were not manufactured in India to be used as alternatives, Tilak described the practice of shunning British-made items as *bahishkar yoga*. According to him, yoga didn't produce results in a day, but like Krishna had told the doubting Arjuna in the Bhagawad Gita, you had to start practising it straightaway. 'Start buying whatever is available in India. If certain things aren't, buy those from places other than Britain. There too, opt for an Asiatic country like Japan. If certain things aren't available there as well, get them from Germany, France or America. There's scarcely a thing manufactured in Britain that isn't also made in these countries,' he reasoned. Once demand for domestic products rose, so would the supply as production would naturally increase. Money spent on buying domestic products would in turn push up industrialization; with more industries being set up in India, more local employment would be generated. In the interim, a tariff of 10 per cent on imports was necessary so that Indian industry could grow; if only it were enforced, India could produce ninety out of 100 items her people required in just ten years, he contended. On the other hand, if people refrained from buying Indian goods until all 100 of them were manufactured at home, production would never pick up at all. That was simply not how it worked in the arena of economics, he said. He urged the people not to listen to the critics of the boycott who were speaking of the impossibility of buying local goods until they were available in sufficient numbers and accused them of distorting the meaning of the agitation that was under way and of twisting the basic principles of economic theory.[30]

If Indians could thus use economic leverage to voice their political disapproval of Britain's conduct, the boycott agitation could provide the underpinnings of a Swadeshi movement—the country's new arm of political agitation. Tilak called for the establishment of Swadeshi outfits and even helped to set up one such group, the *Bharat Vastu Pracharini Sabha*. To create a favourable environment for the campaign, he toured various parts of Maharashtra, roping in the young and dynamic editor of the *Kaal*, S.M. Paranjpe, to assist him.

At the same time, Tilak envisioned the fusing of the twin ideas of boycott and Swadeshi with a third element—that of national education. Tilak believed the Indians needed to reassess their position on education. He himself had appreciated and accepted the methods and values of western education and had set up a school along the lines of English ones so that a private school could help Indianize education while retaining the best aspects of western systems of learning. Private schools, though, had been undermined and weakened by the policies of the Raj, which had chipped away at their autonomy and their improvements, and more so by the interventionist policies of Lord Curzon, he said. While the likes of Ripon and Reay had been liberal in their approach when the New English School and Fergusson College were started in the first half of the 1880s, Curzon had frowned upon private educational institutes that fostered an independent spirit and forced them to fall in line with the curricula of government-run schools that sought not to embolden and empower but to emasculate. Those who resisted and sought to retain their relative autonomy were punished by withdrawing grants. Tilak could no longer put his faith in the education system brought in and promoted by the British, for the Raj had seen to it that Indians did not come away from it self-reliant, creative, confident and in a position to shape their own future by getting into sync with academic, industrial, scientific and technological advances across the globe. Whatever the British government's declared commitments, its true intent, Tilak openly alleged, was to create conditions favourable for the churning out from schools and colleges of slavish employees for the official machinery, their intellectual growth stunted, their spirit and self-respect dented for purposes of Empire and their creative abilities neutralized.[31]

The solution Tilak proposed was the creation of a parallel education system with the setting up of private national schools and colleges independent of government aid. Such a system would be free of the

shackles of mental slavery imposed by the British system and produce
not mere clerks but individuals with a mind and spirit of their own
and build a community that could pursue its best interests. Tilak cited
the National Council of Education established by Bengali educationists
in November 1905 as an ideal template for this kind of education 'on
national lines and under national control'. He also upheld the idea
propounded by Allahabad's Madan Mohan Malviya of a 'Hindu Vishwa
Vidyalaya', which was at an inception stage and ultimately fructified,
despite Tilak's serious doubts about whether it ever would, in 1916 in
the form of the Banaras Hindu University.[32]

Tilak thus put forward the triumvirate of boycott, Swadeshi and
national education as the mantra for a national awakening.

The response to Tilak's call was heartening, and among the ones
to show early enthusiasm were members of some secret revolutionary
groups in the Deccan. A twenty-two-year-old student at the Fergusson
College, Vinayak Damodar Savarkar, approached Tilak with some of
his friends, seeking permission to organize a bonfire of foreign cloth
in Poona. Born in Bhagur near Nasik in 1883, Vinayak had formed
his own revolutionary group, the Mitra Mela, in Nasik in 1900; it had
been renamed the 'Abhinav Bharat' recently and had attracted a bunch
of youngsters from across the Deccan. Tilak appreciated Savarkar's idea
of a bonfire but set a condition for his nod—the youngsters ought to
be able to collect enough cloth to fill a cart for the impact to be felt.
The bonfire of 8 October 1905 turned out to be 'the highlight of the
western Indian movement'. Savarkar and his friends marched through
the streets of Poona with a cartload of cloth and a music band at the
head of the procession, drawing considerable attention. Tilak joined the
students along the route to the Haveli, a vacant spot near Fergusson
College where the bonfire was supposed to take place. By the time they
reached the spot, the crowd had surged to 5000. And not just clothes,
but umbrellas, pencils, even buttons, were gathered in a heap and set
on fire. A Bombay Police agent, who was watching the proceedings,
reported that Tilak addressed the crowd as the flames went up. Tilak
said that 'although it had been proposed to give the European clothes to
the poor instead of destroying them by fire, still it was not right to do so
from the point of patriotism and religion, as what is bad for one is bad
for all'. Tilak also told the students that 'the boycott had created anxiety

in Lancashire and Manchester', the cotton and cloth-manufacturing centres in Britain, and asked them to be 'resolute thereafter in purchasing Swadeshi articles.' Tilak's lieutenant S.M. Paranjpe, editor of the *Kaal*, enlivened the protest with an act of his own. In the middle of his address to the crowd, he went and picked up a jacket from the pile that the fire still hadn't consumed and looked into its pockets, as if to show he was searching for the money England had looted from India. He then threw the jacket dismissively into the fire, saying that that was where it belonged. Tilak himself deployed his extraordinary capacity for getting ordinary people involved in a stir. After all the speeches had ended, he asked everyone in the crowd to walk around the blaze three times, in keeping with sacred Hindu tradition, and to then apply ashes to their foreheads and take a vow that they would never buy British cloth again. It was all rousing for the young patriots, and the meeting ended with cries of 'Jai Shivaji'.

The pro-British dailies and even mouthpieces of the Moderates like the *Indu Prakash* skewered the protest, and the Fergusson College authorities were particularly upset that the initiative for it had come from one of its students. They expelled Savarkar from the college hostel, compelling him to seek shelter in the house of a family acquaintance. F.G. Selby, principal of the government-run Deccan College, asked if it was proper for students to be involved in such demonstrations. Incensed, Tilak wrote three back-to-back editorials, all headlined 'These are not our gurus!' (Parts 1, 2 and 3) in the *Kesari*. Obviously, a state-run institution like the Deccan College would want to promote mental subjugation, Tilak said, but he was incredulous that a private institution like the Fergusson College had punished a student for being part of a nationwide movement. As one of the founders of Fergusson College, Tilak said its teachers ought to have been participating in the Swadeshi stir themselves in the same way Surendranath Banerjea, as principal of a private college, was giving Swadeshi lessons to his students. Instead, a student had been penalised, he said, and asked why Savarkar had been charged with indiscipline. Tilak wrote, 'We don't send our children to schools and colleges for them to remain untouched by the national movement. The idea is to actually imbue them with the nationalist spirit. When a guru, motivated by selfishness, slavishness or intellectual bankruptcy harasses a student for doing the right thing, he can't be called a guru really, and defying his diktat is not indiscipline.'[33]

The bonfire was a key moment in Savarkar's life. A few months later, having completed his graduation, Savarkar approached Tilak for a letter of recommendation. A London-based Indian patriot, Pandit Shyamji Krishnavarma, was offering scholarships to Indian students, and Savarkar wanted to go to the British capital to study law. Tilak knew Krishnavarma well. Originally from Kathiawar in Gujarat and a scholar of Sanskrit and other languages, Krishnavarma had set up India House, a hostel for Indian students, in London's Highgate, and he edited a journal called the *Indian Sociologist*. He was known for his revolutionary views on the question of India's political liberation and had no patience for the mild ways of the Congress. Tilak wrote to Krishnavarma saying he knew full well that he would be inundated with applications, 'but still, I may state, among the applicants there is one Mr Savarkar from Bombay, who graduated last year and whom I know to be a spirited young man very enthusiastic in the Swadeshi cause, so much so that he had to incur the displeasure of the Fergusson College authorities.'

Savarkar got the scholarship of Rs 2000, and Krishnavarma sent the first instalment of Rs 400 to Tilak so that he could hand it over to the young man. This he did by inviting Savarkar over to dinner. That was the last meeting between the two.[34] Savarkar became a leading political revolutionary in London and was sentenced to two terms of life imprisonment, adding up to fifty years, by the Raj in 1911 and sent to the Andamans or the dreaded Kaala Paani. When Tilak died in 1920, Savarkar was still in the prison at Port Blair.

By the time Curzon left Indian shores in November 1905, Tilak's message of boycott, Swadeshi and national education had reverberated across India. Two of his editorials of August—'A Critical Moment!' and 'National Boycott'—became so widely popular that they were translated into various Indian languages by newspapers in Calcutta, Benaras, Patna, Allahabad and Madras.[35] All the nationalist Bengali papers denounced the partition move, and Surendranath Banerjea's *Bengalee* took the lead in this regard, earning him the sobriquet of 'Surrender-not'. There was some amount of difference between Surendranath's and Tilak's writings, however. Surendranath's prose was stylistic; he appealed to emotion and ticked all the boxes, especially in Bengal, where the people were directly affected. Tilak was the quintessential newspaper man, shooting straight from the hip and speaking in shoutlines. There was nothing oblique or enigmatic about what he was saying. He was boisterously blunt and hard-hitting, impudent in his attacks on imperialism and fierce in his concerns for the well-being of Indians. His writings in the wake of Bengal's partition carried tremendous force, and his unapologetic framing of British rule, albeit not for the first time, as an instrument of racialized oppression enabled him to have a candid conversation with the Indian people about the humiliation they were being subjected to, winning him admirers in Bengal and in every province of British-ruled India. As Tilak came to be recognized as the most vocal proponent of anti-colonial resistance, three prominent and promising leaders of the Congress—Lala Lajpat Rai of Punjab and Bipin Chandra Pal and Aurobindo Ghose of Bengal—gathered around him to form a united front.[36] Afterwards, Aurobindo quit politics and the revolutionary movement to pursue his spiritual interests, but the trio of 'Lal, Bal, Pal', as it came to be popularly known, acquired a formidable reputation as a challenger to British rule.

Interestingly, B.C. Pal was initially not in favour of Tilak's fervently anti-British stand; he stood with the Moderates and looked upon British rule as a 'divine dispensation'. Curzon's actions changed him completely. As Pal later wrote, 'it was Curzon and his Partition plan involving as it did total disregard of the popular will that . . . destroyed our old illusion about British India.'[37]

Lajpat Rai felt that the principles being enunciated by Tilak were not altogether new. Most of them, he said, had been 'tried and with varying success in all parts of the country, but more particularly in the Punjab and Maharashtra before this. The Deccan Education Society and the Poona Fergusson College were the offshoots of the desire to further the cause of education . . . with the underlying motives of quickening the patriotic impulse and the nationalist spirit. Similarly, Swadeshi, co-operative organizations, and private arbitration courts had been thought of and tried'. Other examples he mentioned were Bengal's private colleges started by Vidyasagar, Madras's Pachaipiya College, Punjab's DAV College, Bombay's 'purely Indian industrial and trader organizations,' and co-operative groups such as 'the Punjab National Bank, Bharat Insurance Company and other joint-stock concerns.'

According to him, 'Long before 1905, the Punjab had a network of privately organized, privately financed, unaided schools and other charitable institutions, over which the government had little effective control. Patriotism and philanthropy were the underlying motives of these institutions, but *not politics*'.

What had changed now was that Tilak was calling for all such institutions to acquire a distinctly political nature and to change their focus, which according to Lajpat Rai was earlier 'association and co-operation with government,' to 'independent self-assertion'. Besides, Bengal had stepped in vigorously. 'So far Bengal had been rather backward in the matter of national development on these lines,' wrote Lajpat Rai. 'So when Lord Curzon proclaimed the partition of Bengal, attacked the veracity of the orientals in his Calcutta University convocation speech, and on other occasions called them cowards, windbags, unpractical talkers, and mere frothy patriots, the Bengalis awoke to a consciousness of their weaknesses, and resolved to revenge themselves upon Lord Curzon.'[38]

Effects of the campaign were felt on the ground soon. In various provinces, funds were created, and contributions poured in for starting and promoting indigenous industries. With Tilak's support, activists in Poona had in 1903 established the 'Paisa Fund' to impart agricultural and industrial education to locals and manufacture goods domestically. That fund got a boost. Youths living as far apart as Lahore and Madras or Surat and Bhubaneshwar took oaths renouncing foreign goods. Among the leaders of the movement in the Bombay Presidency, stated a report of the government's intelligence department, was 'Mrs. Ketkar,' Tilak's daughter. In Poona, Muslims joined hands with Hindus to boycott foreign products, and songs in praise of Swadeshi and Japanese goods rent the air during the Ganeshotsav processions in the Deccan. As the response from the city of Bombay, where the Congress's Moderate leadership held fort, was initially poor, Tilak's followers held a meeting there and appealed to people to join in the campaign.[39] Demand for indigenous products itself surged so much that from the Bombay Presidency, 'the mills of Bombay and Ahmedabad . . . sold about 1,00,000 bales of cloth to the Calcutta merchants during August–September 1905 – a sale six months ahead'.[40] Usually, it was in October that the merchants of Manchester signed fresh contracts with traders in Calcutta. In October 1905, not a single contract was signed, giving a boost to local production, especially of handspun cloth.[41]

With so much happening, would the Congress session scheduled at the end of the year in Benaras still continue to be a sort of safe house for the Moderates?

In the run-up to the session, the Congress had sent two of its representatives to England: Gokhale, who was president-elect of the Benaras conclave, and Lajpat Rai. Gokhale, who along with his Punjab colleague held a large number of meetings, especially with Liberal Party leaders, said Indians must be allowed 'a larger voice in . . . their own affairs' and the councils expanded so they were 'more representative of the people'. He appealed to the British 'sense of justice', confident that 'when the whole position is brought home to you, you will rise as one man and put an end to these Russian methods of administration'.[42] But Lajpat Rai, on his return to India, 'frankly told his people that British democracy was too busy with their own affairs to do anything for them', 'the British press was not willing to champion Indian aspirations', and 'it was hard to get a hearing in England'. If Indians 'really cared for their country', Lajpat Rai wrote, 'they would have to strike the blow for freedom themselves'.[43]

Tilak nonetheless lauded Gokhale for his painstaking efforts and felicitated him at a function at Poona's Reay Market for his spirited work in England.

When Tilak arrived in Benaras for the Congress session in the last week of December, he got a hero's welcome. A crowd of 10,000 turned up to receive him at the railway station. They gave him flowers and bouquets, and he gave them, before he proceeded to the venue, the slogan 'Militancy, not mendicancy',[44] setting the mood for what was to come not only at this session but at its subsequent gatherings over the next two years.

Expectedly, the meetings of the subjects committee were 'uproarious' and 'afforded ample evidence of the temper of the people'. On the first night that the panel met in Benaras, said Lajpat Rai, 'it appeared that a split was inevitable.' The Prince and Princess of Wales were to visit India early in 1906, and Gokhale and the other Moderates proposed a resolution welcoming them. Tilak, Lajpat Rai and Motilal Ghose opposed it strenuously, and the proceedings broke up late night with no unanimity on the issue. 'The reception committee and the older leaders were all furious', said Lajpat Rai. They 'threatened all sorts of retributions . . . but the younger men would not listen'. *Times of India* reported that the president of the reception committee, the Benaras pleader Munshi Madhav Lal, thought the observations of Tilak and Lajpat Rai were 'unmannerly,' prompting Tilak to send a letter to the newspaper stating that not only had his views on the resolution been 'totally misrepresented' but that Madhav Lal 'did not say anything in the subjects committee as stated by your correspondent, nor, so far as I know, was he present on the occasion'.[45] The *Times of India* correspondent wrote in response that he stood by his report, and Maneckji Kawasji Patel, a Congress delegate who was present at the meeting, sent a letter to the paper's editor, saying he 'could testify to the truth of the statement made by your correspondent'. A member of the Moderate faction, Patel also stated that Tilak had opposed the resolution 'much to the disgust of sober-minded members of the subjects committee'.[46]

In the morning, the meeting was put off for three hours as Gokhale tried to work out an agreement. He requested Tilak, Lajpat Rai and Ghose not to make their opposition open, and finally, Tilak and the others agreed to abstain when that resolution came up for a vote so that it could be passed.

The second resolution was related to the approval of the boycott agitation, and it proved to be equally contentious. The Moderates refused to allow it to be adopted, but since the Extremists had taken a step back in choosing to abstain on the first resolution, a compromised was reached on the boycott row with Gokhale and his group consenting to a resolution which stated that 'The Congress records its earnest and emphatic protest against the repressive measures . . . adopted by the authorities in Bengal after the people there had been compelled to resort to the boycott of foreign goods as a last resort.'[47] The 'last resort' bit was intended to take the sting out of the resolution.

Gokhale condemned Curzon in his presidential speech, calling him 'Aurangzeb', just as Tilak had done before him. In that sense, the two of them were still speaking in one voice. But unlike Tilak, who gave the idea of boycott an almost religious sanctity, Gokhale said the word boycott 'has got unsavoury associations' and 'conveys to the mind before everything else a vindictive desire to injure another'. Swadeshi he described as 'both a patriotic and an economic movement', but he wasn't so sure about boycott, which in his view was 'bound to rouse angry passions on the other side'.[48] On the contrary, Tilak told the delegates at Benaras that to look at the notion of boycott merely from the prism of Bengal's partition was a mistake. That issue was undoubtedly important, but the term had much wider ramifications and was 'capable of being applied on a national scale for the attainment of Swaraj'.[49] Gokhale's Swaraj was 'self-government within the Empire', and Tilak was for complete political freedom.

A split in the Congress was thus narrowly averted in 1905 with the rival sides making adjustments for one another. The young camp was nonetheless restive and deeply unhappy with the status quo. They chose to hold their own conference within the Congress pandal and established what came to be known as the National Party. This wasn't going to be a separate party but one within the Congress, with its own clear-cut programme.

Tilak was 'received with an ovation' when he stood up to speak at this conference, and as one observer wrote, '[A] new turn was given to Indian politics: the policy of "mendicancy," as the Congress method was derisively called, was henceforth even more seriously assailed.'[50] It was here, Lajpat Rai said later, that Tilak 'gave out the idea of passive resistance'. The passive resistance movement would have two aims: 1) to expose the 'hollowness' of the British claim that they were in India to civilize 'the semi-barbarous native' and 'awaken the Indian people to a sense of their own strength and an appreciation of their own culture'; and 2) 'to create a passionate love of liberty, accompanied by a spirit of sacrifice and readiness to suffer for the cause of the country'.[51] Perhaps because no formal resolutions were passed in this regard, this launch of a new party did not create too much alarm about its programme. Yet Tilak's contribution was incredibly significant in that he became the first leader on Indian soil to speak of resistance of this sort. Gandhi, living in South Africa at the time, had started using 'satyagraha' and non-violent resistance to secure the rights of Indians in that country; Tilak was the first to do so in India, crediting Thoreau and Tolstoy for the inspiration they provided in this regard. Gandhi would, after Tilak's era, of course, take the method to remarkable new heights in India.

Khaparde wrote that the Congress camp was 'nicely laid out', with 'the Ganges flowing close by'. Tilak stayed in the room next to his, and Khaparde recorded in his diary that 'a large number of people came to see him. They worship him like God'.[52]

Beyond the Congress campus, Tilak addressed separate functions in Benaras on two issues: a common language for Indians, and the role of religion in Indian life. One of the elements of the newly inaugurated movement was national education. But India had a multitude of languages and multiple scripts. At a meeting of the Nagari Pracharini Sabha presided over by R.C. Dutt, Tilak said though the ultimate aim was a common language for Indians, a beginning had to be made by zeroing in on 'a common character (script).' He described as 'utterly ridiculous' the suggestion made by some people that Indians adopt the Roman alphabet as the common one. It was 'very defective and entirely unsuited to express the sounds used by us', he said, explaining that 'sometimes a single letter has three or four sounds, sometimes a single sound is represented by two or three letters. Add to it the difficulty of finding Roman characters or letters that would exactly represent the sounds in our languages without the use of any diacritic marks'. Devanagari, he insisted, was the best choice, noting that 'it would be suicidal to go for any other alphabet'. This, of course, was for all the 'Aryan' languages or those derived from Sanskrit. What of the Dravidian languages? Yes, the aim, he said, had to be 'to harmonize' the Devanagari script and the Dravidian or Tamil script, but he felt 'the distinction is not of character, only inasmuch as there are certain sounds in the Dravidian languages which are not to be found in any Aryan language'. Letters had to be devised based on the existing ones so that the script could express all the sounds used in the Sanskrit-based languages and was 'capable of being extended to express the Dravidian sounds without diacritic marks'. 'If we put our heads together it would not be difficult to devise such a character (script),' he said, appealing to all Indians to give up their 'provincial prejudices' and to not solve the question from a purely antiquarian point of view but 'in a business-like and practical manner' and pick the alphabet (Devanagari) 'best suited to represent the different sounds we all use'. Once such a script was ready, the government should be urged to introduce 'in the vernacular schoolbooks of every province a few lessons' from it 'so that the next generation may become familiar with it from its school days,' he said.[53]

Above all, Tilak regarded language as a key component in the forging of national solidarity. He remarked that:

> The first and the most important thing we have to remember is that this movement is not merely for establishing a common character for the Northern India. It is a part and parcel of a larger movement, I may say a National Movement to have a common language for the whole of India; for a common language is an important element of nationality. It is by a common language that you express your thoughts to others, and Manu rightly says that everything is comprehended or proceeded from *vak,* or language. Therefore if you want to draw a nation together there is no force more powerful than to have a common language for all.[54]

At the Bharata Dharma Mahamandala in Benaras, Tilak spoke on the centrality of religion in the life of a nation. 'Religion is an element in nationality,' he maintained. 'The word Dharma means a tie and comes from the root *dhri*, to bear or hold. What is there to hold together? To connect the soul with God, and man with man . . . Hindu religion . . . provides for a moral as well as social tie.' During Vedic times, he said, India was united, but 'that unity has disappeared, bringing on us great degradation and it becomes the duty of the leaders to revive that union.'

Why was that revival necessary? According to him:

> A Hindu of this place is as much a Hindu as the one from Madras or Bombay. You might put on a different dress, speak a different language, but you should remember that the inner sentiments which move you all are the same. The study of the Gita, Ramayana and Mahabharata produce the same ideas throughout the country. Are not these – common allegiance to the Vedas, the Gita and the Ramayana – our common heritage? If we lay stress on it forgetting all the minor differences that exist between different sects, then we

shall . . . before long be able to consolidate all the sects into a mighty
Hindu nation. This ought to be the ambition of every Hindu.

Such a resurgence was possible as Hinduism, Tilak explained, had the
resilience to fight back. Here, he spoke of the period when the faith
had stood in conflict with Buddhism. 'Buddhism flourished and attacks
were made on Hindu religion by Buddhists and Jains,' he said, but 'after
600 years of chaos rose one great leader, Shankaracharya' who 'brought
together all the common philosophical elements of our religion' and
effected a renaissance.

What Tilak said next further suggested that his conception of the
Indian nation was essentially Hindu, but also that owing to what he
saw as its distinctiveness, he viewed Hinduism as the one faith which
would acknowledge and accept all other faiths as being equally true.
Citing Krishna's word in the Gita that he'd assume an avatar and
restore dharma whenever unrighteousness was in the ascendant, Tilak
pointed out that there was no religion except Hinduism which offered
this kind of promise. 'After Muhammad no prophet is promised, and
Jesus Christ comes once forever.' At the same time, truth was 'universal
and catholic', 'not vouchsafed to one only' and 'not confined to any
particular race', he declared and continued that the 'Hindu religion
tolerates all religions' and 'says all religions are based on truth, "you
follow yours, I mine".' Tilak regarded Hinduism as being based
on the 'whole' or 'Sanatan [eternal] truth' and emphasizing its 'very
comprehensive' character, quoted Krishna again as saying that 'the
followers of other religions worship God, though not in a proper form.
Shri Krishna does not say that the followers of other religions would
be doomed to eternal hell. I challenge anybody to point out to me a
similar text from the scriptures of other religions.'

Tilak found two forces arrayed against Hinduism—science and
Christianity. Science, he was convinced, was increasingly 'vindicating
our ancient wisdom'. For example, Hinduism asserted that Chaitanya
(universal consciousness) 'pervades everything'. Jagdish Chandra Bose
had recently shown that this 'strictly . . . Hindu theory,' 'this Vedantic
doctrine is literally true,' he asserted. In terms of the theory of karma
and reincarnation too, he said that a change was coming over the West,
and scholars like the British physicist Oliver Lodge had come round to

the view that 'the soul does not die with the body' (Lodge subsequently published a book called *The Immortality of the Soul*). Christianity, on the other hand, held that 'God gives a new soul each and every time'. So, Tilak implored Hindus to 'take courage and work hard for the final triumph', for if they took advantage of modern science and education, a time would come when 'instead of Christians preaching Christianity here we shall see our preachers preaching Sanatan Dharma all over the world'.[55]

Chapter 11

Split Wide Open

In Bengal, B.G. Tilak had become something of a folk icon. Not only had he attacked Curzon powerfully, he had amplified the province's grievances across the length and breadth of the sub-continent. After Curzon's exit, the Liberal Party had defeated the Conservatives in parliamentary polls in Britain. Yet things had taken a turn for the worse after Bengal's partition. The new Viceroy for India, the Conservative Lord Minto, provided no relief, and Lord Morley, who came in as the Secretary of State, was a major disappointment in spite of his reputation as a Liberal thinker. Morley declared, to the chagrin of Bengal and the rest of India, that the partition was 'a settled fact'.[1] On the ground, the situation had deteriorated seriously. In the freshly-minted Eastern Bengal, Bampfylde Fuller, who had been appointed by Curzon as the lieutenant–governor, had started 'a reign of anti-Hindu administrative terror'.[2] The Raj, which had not consulted or heard the Bengali population nor any of its prominent leaders at the time of carrying out the partition, was now doing not what the Muslim patriots wanted, but what the fanatical elements of the majority Muslim population in the eastern parts had hoped to do. Fuller publicly said that to him, Muslims and Hindus were like his two queens, the first 'favoured' and the second 'neglected'.[3] He banned the singing of 'Bande Mataram', the song from Bankim Chandra Chatterjee's famous novel Anand Math, which had become an anthem of sorts for local patriots, 'and unleashed the punitive police' on 'offenders'. In one case, a house was razed because it had 'Bande Mataram' written on its walls; in another, a schoolboy was whipped in a public square for singing the song; and policemen on the streets were accused of beating 'indiscriminately with their belts' anyone who passed by.[4]

Tilak accused Fuller of 'behaving like a mad dog' and lauded the people of Bengal for the resistance they were putting up. He said Fuller had gotten 'frantic' because he knew that the new arms of the Bengal movement, Swadeshi and boycott, were going to result in the people's triumph and the administration's defeat. To the province he accorded a special status in the fight for liberation, saying it was 'Bengal's destiny to bear the brunt of the attack in India's political struggle.'[5] In April 1906, the police crackdown on a conference organized in Barisal was particularly brutal. Surendranath Banerjea was arrested, and the delegates were assaulted with batons; one of them was thrown into a tank; and Gurkha soldiers assisting the punitive police pillaged the entire town. Applauding Banerjea for his personal courage, Tilak thought there could be a divine meaning in all the suffering and proclaimed that 'this [struggle] alone is our path of progress'.[6] There wasn't a single example in the world of colonialists granting freedom willingly to an enslaved nation, he observed. 'Without difficulty there would be no freedom, just as without night there was no day.'[7]

Tilak was invited in May 1906 to inaugurate the Shivaji Utsav in Bengal. Inspired by Tilak, the festival was started there in 1902 by one of his followers, Sakharam Ganesh Deuskar. A Maharashtrian by birth and Bengali by domicile, Deuskar had created quite a stir in Bengal and impressed the great poet Rabindranath Tagore, among several others. When exactly his family moved to the east is not clear, but Deuskar's father was known to have settled in a place near Deoghar, and Sakharam himself was born there in December 1869. He imbibed lessons on Maratha history and on India's cultural heritage early in childhood, and when he moved to Calcutta in his youth, he earned a reputation for himself as a writer who questioned the theories of imperialism. In the journal *Bharati*, he compiled a collection of letters called 'Aitihasik Patravali' which attracted the attention of Tagore and drew praise from the poet for Shivaji's policies; Tagore also praised Deuskar's essays on Ranade in the journal 'Sahitya'. After launching the Shivaji festival in Bengal, Deuskar wrote a pamphlet 'Shivaji Mahatya [The Greatness of Shivaji]' and in 1905 wrote another piece titled 'Shivajir Diksha [The Initiation of Shivaji]'. Deuskar requested Tagore that he should write a poem on Shivaji, and after he had done that on 27 August 1905, Tagore wrote to his friend Dinesh Chandra Sen the same day, 'Driven by the electrifying pressure of Deuskar, I composed a poem to-day. It is called Shivaji Utsav.' While Deuskar's writings on Shivaji became well-known, his most outstanding work was the book *Desher Katha*, a polemic on how British rule had ruined India. Published in 1904, it made Deuskar massively popular in Bengal, and his popularity, and that of *Desher Katha*, grew further in the wake of Bengal's partition, in due course leading to its proscription by the British authorities.[8] An excellent proof of India's historical amnesia is that S.G. Deuskar is a man not adequately celebrated in the twenty-first century either in Bengal or in Maharashtra.

Bengal was seething; Deuskar's work was drawing attention; and Tilak, besides, got letters of invitation also from Bipin Chandra Pal and his good friend Motilal Ghose of the *Amrita Bazar Patrika*. Of course, he would go. Khaparde and three others accompanied him; and there was also a cook who'd come along. Along the train route, a pattern was by now establishing itself: huge crowds at railway stations, ready with flowers, garlands, tea and fruits. At Nagpur, students greeted Tilak with cries of 'Vande Mataram' and 'Shivaji Maharaj Ki Jai', and so 'sumptuous', according to Khaparde, was the food and the sweets on offer at Dongargada, Raipur and other places that 'our journey became a tour of feasting.' Khaparde went off to sleep after all the eating, and when he woke up as their train was about to enter Calcutta station, he noticed that 'the whole of Howra platform was so full of people that not even an ant could creep in'.[9]

Tilak was practically lifted out of the railway carriage; all the other passengers on the train, Europeans included, were stuck inside their compartments for want of space on the platform; and Tilak's friends too had a hard time getting out and had to be somehow 'piloted' out, along with Tilak, by B.C. Pal to a carriage waiting outside. The fervently enthusiastic crowd sent up 'deafening' slogans of 'Bande Mataram' and 'Shivaji Maharaj Ki Jai', banners were unfurled and drums were played. Youngsters, meanwhile, untied the horses that drew the carriage and held the carriage themselves, asking Tilak to step on to the coach box; they were going to pull the carriage themselves. 'The procession was tremendous' and its progress was slow. Halfway down the Harrison

Road was the ground where a Swadeshi exhibition and the Shivaji festival had been organized together, and Tilak declared both of them open in the presence of Motilal Ghose.[10]

The next day, Tilak spoke at the Shivaji festival. The pro-Raj *Times of India* dismissed his speech at the bottom of page six (of the paper's total eight pages). The report had only four lines, and it did not carry a headline at all, making it clear the paper wished to 'bury' it, as such treatment of reports is known in newspaper parlance. Nonetheless, one of the four lines of the report read, 'Great crowds attended'.[11] The next morning, again, the report was in the same slot, except that it was three lines long, not four, and still headline-less. One of the lines stated, 'Mr Tilak is receiving great attention during the Sivaji festival.'[12] Addressing the crowd on the anniversary of the Maratha hero's coronation, Tilak said, 'The Goddess Kali is the presiding deity in Bengal. The same Goddess was the protector of Shivaji. I am told that some persons objected to the worship of Kali here today. I see no reason, in fact no logical reason, why such objections should be raised. We are all Hindus and idolators and I am not ashamed of the fact.'[13]

The following evening, a crowd of nearly 20,000 turned up to listen to Tilak at a public meeting. He was also photographed, a rare thing for those times. With Motilal Ghose presiding, Tilak said it was 'hopeless' to expect anything from the rulers, and even protests were 'of no avail' as 'the three Ps – pray, please and protest' wouldn't work 'unless backed by solid force'. Targeting Morley, who claimed to have a certain fellow feeling for the Indians, he said the Secretary of State had given 'a strange illustration of his sympathy' during the Bengal crisis by saying he had 'full sympathy' but 'cannot or will not undo partition'. Weren't the laws of the land classic examples of what he was saying, Tilak asked. He explained what he meant: 'Punishment of whipping is provided in the Penal Code and there is another law which provides that the sufferer will be sent to hospital for treatment. If you want that sort of sympathy, Mr. Morley is ready to give it to you.' Maintaining that 'love of nation is one's first duty' and next came 'religion and the government', Tilak said, 'Swadeshi will be our cry forever and by this we will grow in spite of the wishes of the rulers.' And he urged the people of Bengal not to give up the 'partition grievance for the whole of India is at your back'. Their grievance, he added, was 'a cornerstone'; it would be 'the edifice for the regeneration of India'.[14]

At another meeting in Bhawanipur, over 15,000 people were present, and locals took him in a procession to the temple of Kali.[15] On the last day of his stay, the *Bombay Gazette*'s Calcutta correspondent reported that Tilak, 'followed by thousands of Bengalees', was taken in a procession, 'with bands playing and men carrying the portrait of Shivaji, to Prasonno Coomen Tagore's bathing ghat'. After a bath in the Hooghly, a 'gathering was formed up on (the) bank and speeches delivered on the unity of all classes of Hindus by the purifying bath in the waters of the sacred Bhagirathi'.[16] Khaparde termed the scene unique and said the people 'worshipped Tilak like a God', a description he had also earlier made about popular sentiment on the way to Benaras and in Benaras. Some of the worship was transferred to Tilak's friends too. Khaparde wrote in his diary, 'They touched our feet, put the mud of our feet on their heads . . . They literally made a path on the beach with their hand[s], and thousands leapt into (the) water with us.' The same day, Tilak spoke to the Marwari businessmen of Calcutta and brought them around to the Swadeshi movement as, according to Khaparde, 'the Calcutta leaders did not know how to speak to the Marwaris'.[17] On the whole, Tilak's visit was a smashing success, and on the way back, when he made a brief stopover in Nagpur and was taken around the city in a procession, the *Bombay Gazette* reported that women showered flowers on him from their balconies.[18]

Tilak made a second visit to Calcutta that year, in December, for the Congress session was to be held there. A split had barely been avoided the previous year. Would it happen this time? The Moderates' belief in the make-or-break stakes of the 1906 session was strengthened when Aurobindo Ghose, one of the prominent faces from Bengal, suggested that Tilak be chosen as president. Tilak's popularity was at an all-time high; the young and radical wing felt his lead could help the Congress overwhelmingly reject the rigid, cautious stance of the Moderates in favour of a more forceful approach; and more important than anything else was the fact that he had come to be recognized across India as the Raj's biggest enemy.

Born in 1872 in Calcutta and educated at Cambridge, where his father wanted him to study so that he could qualify for the Indian Civil Service, Aurobindo had secured eleventh rank in the ICS exam but had deliberately skipped the horse-riding test, which was a mandatory part of the exam, come back and joined the Baroda state service. In 1893, during his stint with Baroda, he wrote a series of articles in the *Indu Prakash* of Poona attacking the policies of the Congress. Though he believed the Congress was 'a well of living water', he assailed it for being 'organically infirm to the verge of impotence'.[19] From all accounts, he and Tilak met for the first time at the Ahmedabad Congress of 1902. Aurobindo had just joined the Congress and looked up to Tilak, and Tilak was curious to see the man who had castigated the Congress in his writings. They had an hour-long discussion outside the tent where the main Congress event was held. What exactly they discussed on that occasion, we don't know, but they had several common interests—apart from the Indian freedom movement, Aurobindo was, like Tilak, obsessed with India's past and dug deep into its traditions of religion, spirituality and Hindu philosophy. Aurobindo would also occasionally visit Poona, and on one occasion, he had dinner at Tilak's place. Although accustomed to eating meat and fish 'once a day', Aurobindo, according to a biographer, 'found Marathi food too hot and Gujarati food too rich in ghee'. Yet his impression of the food at Tilak's home was different. Tilak and his family served him dal, rice, puri and vegetables, and Aurobindo loved the food for its 'spartan simplicity'.[20]

Much like Tilak, Aurobindo wanted the Congress to be 'a popular body empowered by the fiat of Indian people in its entirety', and he considered Tilak the best man to lead it because 'the Congress movement was for a long time purely occidental in its mind, character and methods, confined to the English-educated few, founded on political rights and interests of the people read in the light of English history and European ideals, but with no roots in the past of the country and in the inner spirit of the nation'.[21] By 1906, Aurobindo was editor of a fiery journal called *Bande Mataram*, and in his opinion, the credit for Indianizing the Congress went entirely to Tilak.[22] His proposal for Tilak as Congress president was endorsed by several provincial party committees, and the Moderates got worried that the party was likely to slip out of their hands. Their counter-move was to propose Dadabhai Naoroji's name for president. Though Naoroji was eighty-one at the time, respect for him went across, and beyond, categories such as Extremist and Moderate. His choice itself showed the Moderates' sharp awareness that their position was tenuous. A few years earlier, when Tilak had called for a more assertive Congress, the Moderates had got Naoroji to write to him to desist from taking a hard line. This time again, through

Naoroji, they sought to stay Tilak's hand. And albeit desperately, they succeeded. Tilak himself had suggested the name of Lala Lajpat Rai for the post of president and had remarked that the Congress needed to be told precisely what Bhima had said to his elder brother, Yudhistira, at a key moment in the Mahabharata: 'Give up your attitude of supplication and demonstrate the character of a Kshatriya.'[23] With Dadabhai's name coming forward, though, he withdrew, and stated ten days before the start of the session that 'Dadabhai can have only one message to give to India – that of Swaraj'[24] and went on to insist that 'Dadabhai is a radical among radicals'.[25] Naoroji's views had truly become more radical than earlier, and he said in his closing address at the Congress session that what India was asking for could be spelled out 'in one word, self-government or Swaraj, like that of the United Kingdom or the colonies'.[26] In the meeting of the subjects committee, again there were bitter arguments as Tilak, Khaparde, B.C. Pal and Aurobindo wanted a resolution extending the call for boycott across India while the Moderates sought to restrict it to Bengal. Finally, a proposal drafted by the Extremists that stated the boycott movement inaugurated in Bengal 'was and is legitimate' was accepted as a compromise.[27] Both sides read in it what they wished to, the Extremists persuading themselves it was part-legitimization of their demand and the Moderates thinking they had little to lose with the words 'across India' not a part of it. Significantly for Tilak and his supporters, resolutions were passed also in favour of two of their other big planks, Swadeshi and national education.

Times of London reacted angrily to the Calcutta session, describing the demand for self-government as 'very pernicious nonsense'. Accusing Naoroji of giving a speech 'as mischievous' as the radical elements 'could desire', the paper said:

> The threatened split between the Extremists – the professed enemies of British rule – and the Moderates has been averted, but averted by the adoption on the part of the Moderates of no small part of the Extremist policy. It is, of course, disguised, but the disguise is too transparent to deceive anybody . . . Mr. Dadabhai Naoroji was chosen to be President as the safest representative of "moderation", and the Extremists appear not to have pressed the candidature of Mr. Tilak, a politician who has been tried and convicted for sedition. They have good reason to be satisfied with the result.[28]

It wasn't the imperialists alone who were unhappy. So was Pherozeshah Mehta. When he met Tilak and Gokhale just before leaving for Bombay, he told Tilak, spitefully, 'You got the boycott resolution passed in Calcutta, but you would not have a chance to do it in Bombay.' At this point, Gokhale interjected, telling his Congress mentor and boss, 'No, Mr. Mehta, there is no forecasting the capacity of this man.'[29] It was not a mere concession of a point. On Gokhale's part, it was an acknowledgement of his rival's extraordinary talents and capabilities.

What this conversation however foretold was an intensifying of conflict between the rival factions, whatever the appearance might have been at the Calcutta session. Keeping in mind the vehemence of the opinions of Tilak and the other anti-imperialists, Gokhale, in a string of public speeches in Allahabad, began a public debate around the theme of constitutional agitation, saying no action should go beyond its bounds. Where's the Constitution, Tilak asked. India had no Constitution, and its government was created by the statutes of the British Parliament, he underlined. And was such a government responsible to the people it ruled over? 'What Mr. Gokhale calls India's Constitution is really the Indian Penal Code,' which laid down what was legal and what wasn't. At the most, Gokhale could insist the IPC should not be violated; 'that would be understandable', though the despotism of India's official bureaucracy meant the laws could be interpreted and applied by it any which way. Tilak clarified that he wasn't suggesting that Indians take to arms or do anything illegal; but, he continued, the more honest thing would have been to tell people to keep their agitation 'legal' and not to use 'futile and misleading' words like 'constitutional'.[30]

As a result of this and similar other statements made by Gokhale, Mehta and others, apprehension grew all through 1907 in the minds of Tilak and the radical elements that the Moderates could walk back on the resolutions on self-government, Swadeshi, boycott and national education passed at the Calcutta Congress. Their worry came amid egregious examples of Raj misrule and suppression. In Bengal, lieutenant–governor Fuller of the 'Muslims are my favourite queen' jibe had resigned, but his successor had continued a similar policy, encouraging pro-partition demonstrations led by the Nawab of Dhaka, Salimulla, and provoking riots in which Hindus were attacked and the assailants, as the then correspondent of *Guardian* recorded, got 'no punishment'. In the Punjab, land assessment rates were significantly hiked, and a couple of Indian editors were prosecuted, resulting in riots by peasants and protests led by Ajit Singh, a nationalist who had started the 'Indian Patriots Association', and Lajpat Rai. The two organized rallies across the province to articulate the grievances of farmers and the broader community. Suddenly, in May 1907, three days ahead of the fiftieth anniversary of the 1857 Revolt, Lajpat Rai was deported from Lahore, and Ajit Singh from Amritsar, to Mandalay in Burma without charge or trial. Two days later, Minto issued a proclamation placing curbs on public meetings in Punjab and Bengal. Tightening the screws further, the Raj's home department released a circular mandating stringent action against students who participated in political protests and brought in the Seditious Meetings Act to deny permission to public meetings.[31]

Meanwhile, Morley and Minto were putting together proposals on reforms, and the Moderates positively pinned their hopes on these. Morley's act of inducting two Indians into his Council in London (K.G. Gupta, an ex-official in Calcutta, and S.H. Bilgrami, Muslim League member and ex-official of the Nizam of Hyderabad) raised their expectations further. Tilak was anything but hopeful: he saw the proposed reforms as another calamity in the making. And he felt the sooner the Indian people interpreted the meaning of boycott beyond the shunning of goods, the better it would be. Boycott everything, he said, including the government, weaving in the idea of non-cooperation without using the term and instead characterizing it as passive resistance. 'The country is ruled by the British because you co-operate with them,' he told the people. 'If you withhold your co-operation the administration must cease to function – I dare say it will collapse.'[32] He was for quickly moving away from Britain; and the Moderates were quite keen on embracing reforms.

Tensions evidently ran high as the annual Congress session drew closer. Psychological warfare had started well before the session itself, with the Moderates succeeding in the provincial conferences in places such as Surat, Raipur and Allahabad in thwarting resolutions of Swadeshi and boycott and also disallowing the singing of Vande Mataram. The annual meet of 1907 was going to be held in Nagpur. In the preceding year, it had been finalized that the president for the next session would be decided by the local reception committee— in this case, Nagpur's—on the basis of a three-fourths majority. The young brigade again wished that Tilak should be president, but neither they nor the Moderates on the Nagpur panel could summon that kind of majority. The panel chairman, Gangadhar Chitnavis, who had for several years represented the Central Provinces on the Viceregal Legislative Council, called a meeting nonetheless, and the radical wing alleged they were purposely not told about it in advance so that Chitnavis and his friends could rush through a resolution determining their own choice for president. Getting wind of the deliberations being held in the city's Town Hall, Extremist agitators forced their way in. Cards were torn, a lot of bitter language flowed on both sides, and the meeting 'had to be dissolved in confusion'. *Times* of London reported that many of the Moderates 'only escaped serious injury by pledging themselves to vote for Mr. Tilak'.[33] The local Nagpur committee finally expressed its inability to hold the December session, and Pherozeshah Mehta succeeded in moving it to Surat. He had tremendous hold in Surat and felt more reasonably confident about a session there; Nagpur was better than Poona or Berar, of course, where Tilak and Khaparde exercised control, but it had not proven as safe as the Moderates thought it might have been; and Lahore was a bad option for them as Lajpat Rai carried much influence there. Still not willing to accept Tilak as president, Mehta's and the Moderates' pick for the post was a Bengali educationist, Dr Rash Behari Ghose.[34] Gokhale spoke for the entire Moderate cohort when he said that Ghose's name would 'keep on our side a considerable body of Bengali delegates, who otherwise may work and vote with the new party'.[35]

Why were the Moderates so resolutely opposed to giving Tilak a chance to be president? All the evidence suggests they thought he was running away with the party. For almost a decade, they had worried about him. For instance, as mentioned earlier in this book, Mehta and Sankaran Nair had not wanted to attend the 1898 session because Tilak, just released from jail, was going to be there. At the start of the new century, it became evident that the popular mood was turning in favour of the radicals. In October 1904, D.E. Wacha had written to Naoroji, Wedderburn and W.C. Bonnerjee to complain that 'evidently he (Tilak) is now for flying his own standard and be the leader of a new party'.[36] On that occasion, the Moderates had got Naoroji to intervene and stop Tilak, but after 1905, it was pretty clear that Congress could not carry on with business as usual. That year, a concerned Gokhale had told his comrades that 'the Bengal Party . . . are claiming Tilak as their leader' and added that 'though we all know that he does not believe in the practicability of their programme, as is his wont, he will do nothing to discourage their belief that he is their leader'.[37] In 1906, Gokhale had written about how B.C. Pal had threatened to pick Tilak against Naoroji for the presidential contest if the 'grand old man' didn't step down,[38] but Tilak himself had precluded a showdown by opting out of the contest. And after the 1906 Congress, the Moderates began to see Tilak as the controlling hand behind everything the Extremists were doing. Tilak's visit to Calcutta had resulted in many of the differences between Pal, Surendranath and Motilal Ghose getting sorted out. Wacha wrote to Gokhale: 'Behind all is Tilak . . . Today Lajpat Rai (whose name was being proposed as president by Tilak) and tomorrow Tilak! Where will the Congress be?' Wacha sounded almost despairing in the same letter, saying that he had 'lost all faith in the honesty of the purpose of Tilak and Co'.[39] Similar sentiments were echoed by the Moderate R.N. Mudholkar to Gokhale. Mudholkar made sarcastic remarks about Tilak, saying to Gokhale, 'What your townsman (Tilak) – the tribune of the people – the new Shivaji – has planned out can be more imagined than discerned.'[40] He had spoken of his own impetuosity too. 'The way Pal and even Tilak write is such as to rouse the ire of sober men. I don't want to conceal that whenever I read their vapourings I lose my patience.' Reluctantly, though, Mudholkar also admitted to Gokhale that 'they (Tilak and the radicals) have one thing which I find utterly lacking in the majority of the adherents of the moderate school. They have more go, more life, more activity. They have obtained a hold over the popular mind.'[41]

This time too, Tilak did what he had done on the previous occasion. He proposed the name of Lajpat Rai and withdrew from the fray. Lajpat Rai had just returned from Mandalay, and what better name to have than a people's leader who had been unjustly deported. For the radicals, it would be some statement to make.[42]

The local Surat unit cleared Rash Behari Ghose's name without any difficulty. As a showdown appeared unavoidable, Tilak landed in Surat four days before start of the session. His side held a string of independent public meetings for three days in the lead-up to the session, with him as the star speaker and Aurobindo as chairperson. Talk of the Congress splitting was on everyone's lips, and Tilak said he did not want any such thing to happen. All the radicals were asking for, he insisted at a meeting of 500 delegates on the eve of Christmas, was that the Congress should not backtrack on its earlier resolutions, for those were real milestones. But if they were watered down, the radicals would oppose the election of the president.

What appeared to tilt things drastically was the apparent discovery the same day of a heading of a new Constitution sought to be framed for the Congress by the Moderates. Word spread in the radicals' camp that it said the Congress's ultimate aim was 'the attainment by India of self-government similar to that enjoyed by the other members of the British Empire'. Other members of the Empire could mean 'Crown Colonies, Dependencies, anything'; such wording would mark a shift from the Calcutta resolution which was categorical in asserting that 'the system of government obtaining in the self-governing British Colonies should be extended to India'.[43]

On the morning of 26 December, which was to be the first day of the three-day session, Tilak, Aurobindo and Khaparde went to Surendranath Banerjea's camp with two proposals: keep the Calcutta resolutions unchanged and, although R.B. Ghose would be president, make a 'graceful allusion' to the fact that the people had wanted Lajpat Rai. If some compromise could be arrived at, they were willing to have talks about that as well. There was some time for discussion between the rival camps still, as the inaugural session's opening, scheduled for 1 p.m., had been put off to 2.30 p.m. by the death of a delegate from Sindh. Surendranath asked the radicals to meet Tribhuvandas Malvi, a Surat man who as head of the reception committee would be in charge of proceedings until the selection of the president was formally accepted by the Congress.[44] When Tilak approached Malvi, he wasn't available. The reason cited was he was 'busy with his daily rituals', and it didn't go down well with Tilak's group.[45]

Accounts of what happened inside the pandal that afternoon and the next vary. But we can rely on points on which there has been consensus. By 2.30 p.m., over 10,000 Congress activists had gathered under the massive tent, 1600 of them delegates. First Malvi spoke, welcoming everyone to his native Surat. Ambalal Desai, former chief justice in the

Baroda state, stood up next to propose R. B. Ghose's name for president. The moment he did that, there were voices of protest and some loud protestations of 'Never'. When Surendranath Banerjea seconded the proposal, the cries became more vociferous, and waving 'scarves, sticks and umbrellas', protesters sprang to their feet. Surendranath still tried speaking, but his voice was drowned out by the crowd on the one hand and by Malvi's frenetic pounding of the bell, calling for restoration of order, on the other. Soon all 1600 people were on their feet, and Malvi suspended the proceedings for the day.

The correspondent of *Guardian*, Henry Nevinson, was in Surat covering the session. He had met Tilak earlier in Poona and spoken to him. After the tumult, he walked over to the nationalists' camp. Tilak had just returned, and as was his habit when he was indoors, he was sitting without his shirt on, 'naked in his cloth'. Both sides were stunned by what had happened. Tilak earnestly hoped that things would be set right the next day.

At around 12.30 p.m. on 27 December, that is, half an hour before proceedings could begin, Tilak wrote a note with a pencil and sent it across to Malvi. The note said he wanted to speak on the president's election after the proposal had been seconded. 'I wish to move an adjournment with a constructive proposal,' he stated. According to Roberts' Rules of Order, the accepted norm for such procedure, he had by notifying the chair earned the right to speak. But once the meeting began, Malvi totally ignored Tilak's note. Surendranath Banerjea seconded the proposal, Motilal Nehru backed it, and the chairman, Malvi, declared it had been carried. As Dr Ghose immediately stood up to make his address, Tilak, who was seated in the front row of the delegates, marched up on to the dais and said he had the right to speak as he had given notice to the chairman. Malvi rejected his claim and asked Ghose to proceed with his address. Tilak would not budge. The *Guardian* correspondent wrote, 'With folded arms, Mr. Tilak faced the audience.' Witnessing the drama unfolding onstage, the unease inside the tent boiled over. Loyalists of both camps sent up raucous shouts of 'We don't want you to speak' and 'Let him speak'. In a moment there was chaos, with members of the rival factions hurling accusations at each other. When a group of Moderate Congress activists threatened to forcibly pull Tilak off the dais, Gokhale stood in the way, 'flinging out both arms to protect him from the threatened onset'. Chairs were anyway flying around in the pandal by now. Someone from the audience hurled a shoe, which first struck Pherozeshah Mehta and ricocheted off him to hit Surendranath. As the descent into disorder was complete, the proceedings were catastrophically brought to a close and the police were called in.[46]

The Indian National Congress had split. Both Tilak and Gokhale were deeply distraught. Tilak tried to stitch the gaping wound in the immediate aftermath, agreeing to accept R.B. Ghose as president and 'promising to work for unity'.[47] Mehta and the old guard would have none of it; they were quite relieved to see the radicals go. The viceroy, Minto, was delighted. He telegraphed Morley, saying, 'The Congress collapse was a great triumph for us.'[48]

Chapter 12

'A Diseased Mind'

Just a week before heading to Surat, Tilak had on 15 December 1907 addressed a meeting of mill workers in Chinchpokli in central Bombay. He had over the previous couple of years made quite a few trips to the city. Its position as an economic hub made it vital for the Swadeshi and boycott movements: it could make or unmake things. Tilak had been the prime mover behind the formation of the Swadeshi Vastu Pracharini Sabha and had in mid-1906 also set up the Bombay Swadeshi Cooperative Stores Ltd with the assistance of some mill owners; the cooperative had a share capital of Rs 2.5 lakh, with Tilak as one of its directors.[1] For the December 1907 meeting, around 5000 people, most of them mill hands, were present,[2] but the Bombay police saw it as different from the other meetings he'd held earlier.

That was because Tilak called for the coming together of the entire mill workforce in the city. The size of that workforce was close to two lakh, which was 'perhaps more in number than all the British Forces in India', the then Bombay police commissioner H.G. Gell wrote in an alarmist tone in a subsequent letter to the secretary to the Bombay government.[3] Tilak told the mill workers, 'If you, who are about two lakhs in number, act in unison and in a spirit of determination, what is there that you cannot accomplish?'[4] If even half of them 'pledged themselves to solemnly support' both the Swadeshi and boycott agitations, as Tilak was imploring them to, they could cause serious damage to the Raj and to the British economy, the Bombay police commissioner reckoned.[5]

Besides, the population of Bombay was around ten lakh at the time, and the prospect of one-fifth of it getting together was dreadful for the regime. Tilak had the reputation to pull it off; not only had he emerged as the undisputed leader of the radical wing nationally, the first chairman of Britain's Labour Party, Keir Hardie, had during his visit to India in September and October 1907 met him in Poona and visited the *Kesari* office. Labour was sympathetic to Indian aspirations, and Hardie had, after touring the country, plainly said that the Raj governed India 'like the Czar runs Russia'.[6] Hardie's visit had fortified Tilak's standing. Henry Nevinson, the *Guardian* correspondent, had also around the same time done an extensive interview with Tilak at his Poona residence, portraying him as the principal voice of an assertive Indian nationalism. Nevinson's coverage had not smacked of imperial bias the way reports of some other English and Anglo–Indian papers did; and that, too, had come as proof of Tilak's rising stock. Things might get out of hand for the Raj and for the Bombay government if he wasn't reined in soon enough.

More concerning for the British was that Tilak seemed to have added one more arrow to his quiver at the Chinchpokli gathering—a campaign against liquor. This campaign was notable for four reasons. One, it could hurt the government financially as excise duty on liquor formed, then as it does now, one of the biggest sources of revenue for a government. Two, it could give his followers an agenda for immediate action and keep them motivated in Congress's conflict-ridden times, for Tilak asked them to 'form picket lines' outside government-licensed liquor shops and plead with prospective customers that they should avoid drinking, which was 'against religion and morality' and 'bad from the viewpoint of the drinker's welfare'.[7] Three, such a campaign, if implemented well, could demonstrate that passive resistance and boycott were both eminently workable methods. And four: it could be a common factor between the Extremists and Moderates as the latter too favoured prohibition and could potentially be the first step towards healing the rift in the organization. Tilak certainly hoped the rift would heal before long: a divided Congress was a greatly weakened outfit.

After the Surat split, Tilak travelled widely through the Deccan, holding up the four Congress resolutions that he would not allow to be thwarted by the Moderates, and promoting the anti-liquor agitation.

On 30 April 1908, Tilak was at his New Party's provincial conference in Dhule near Nasik when two Bengali youngsters, Khudiram Bose and Prafulla Chaki, threw a bomb at a carriage in Bihar's Muzaffarpur, thinking that the district judge Douglas Kingsford was riding in it. Kingsford had earned notoriety for ordering the flogging of Indians for minor offences, but he was not on board. Two Englishwomen were instead, and both died in the explosion. Chaki couldn't live with the realization that he had killed innocent women and took his own life, and Khudiram, who was barely eighteen years old, was hanged. Just a couple of days after the bomb incident, the police unearthed a cache of arms and explosives from a garden house in the Calcutta suburb of Maniktala that belonged to the Ghose brothers Aurobindo and Barindra Kumar. Subsequently, Barindra was sentenced to life imprisonment and sent to the deadly Andamans prison, while Aurobindo was acquitted, eventually.[8]

The pro-imperialist press in England demanded that the revolutionary movement in India be crushed swiftly. Blaming the British government for looking upon 'the most seditious revolutionary speeches and articles as mere harmless ebullitions', *Times* of London suggested that 'if Bengal has been chiefly conspicuous in its resort to destructive methods, the cunning brains that conceived and fostered the movement are probably to be found for the most part in Western India'. It was an unmistakable reference to Tilak and his wing. Mentioning the rival factions of the Indian National Congress, the paper said the organization had 'permitted its precincts to be invaded, and very nearly captured, by men whose political activity has been very far from innocuous,' and insinuated that the Moderates and Extremists had many times 'worked together in somewhat unholy alliance'. Naming names, it stated, 'Mr. Arabinda Ghose may be entirely innocent of the charges now brought against him. What we recall is that he was associated with the conduct of the violent journal Bande Mataram, and was apparently the trusted lieutenant of Mr. Bepin Chandra Pal, who has received the public benedictions of Mr. Surendra Nath Banerjee. Mr. Pal stumped the country in support of Mr. Tilak; and that veteran agitator was alternately cajoled and reviled by the Bombay Moderate leaders.'[9] *Daily Telegraph* of London denounced the Indians racially. Censuring Britons who sympathized with the Indian people, it asked how they could regard self-government as the panacea for all ills 'without consideration of race or history'. The paper commented, 'It matters not to them that self-government is the product of only one branch of the Aryan family, and that it has never taken root among non-Aryans, and has, indeed, only flourished exceedingly with men of Teutonic origin.'[10] Across India, the Anglo-Indian dailies asked the government to 'administer the law with firmness' and 'put a stop to the seditious and inflammatory writings and speeches which are bringing India to the verge of anarchy'.[11]

On his return to Poona from Dhule, Tilak obtained complete information about what had happened in Bengal and perused what papers of different persuasions were saying before offering his comments. On 12 May 1908, he wrote in the *Kesari* that 'the bomb in Muzaffarpur had not been thrown out of hatred for an individual or on the impulse of a malign madman. Even Khudiram is feeling terrible that two innocent women of Mr. Kennedy's family fell victims instead of Mr. Kingsford.' The young Bengali revolutionaries had taken to the ways of the Russian 'nihilists' not out of any selfish interests but owing to the exasperation produced by the uncontrolled, autocratic and irresponsible use of power by the official white class, he said. To those Anglo-Indian papers which asked if the revolutionaries were thinking the Raj would disappear the moment five to ten bombs were hurled, Tilak said that the revolutionaries fully knew that repressive regimes didn't end this way and such acts could in fact invite further repression by way of retribution. But when people's opinions were never taken into account, when they were given no representation and when their demand for the rights of Swaraj was disdainfully dismissed all the time, there would always be a few people who'd find their patience exhausted. 'When all ways of defending or saving itself are extinguished, a deer leaps at the hunter. Similarly, with an entire people feeling that their peaceful movement to obtain political rights is yielding no fruits at all, some young minds have started to turn to desperate measures out of a sense of angry helplessness,' he noted.[12] In another article on 9 June, Tilak's aide Krishnaji Prabhakar Khadilkar, who penned editorial comments in the *Kesari* whenever Tilak himself was too busy to write, expounded on the paper's argument that the granting of political freedom and lifting of repressive ways was the wisest way for the government to deal with the situation and prevent a recurrence. The Raj had taken away the right of Indians to bear arms. But the technology of the bomb had fundamentally altered things, he argued. 'Guns and canons,' he stated, 'may be taken away from a subject people by an Arms Act, and the manufacture of guns and canons without permission of government can be blocked as well. But is it possible to stop the bomb or make it disappear by framing laws or by supervision of officials or by places being overrun by the detective police? The bomb has more the nature of knowledge, it is magic [jadu], it is a sacred formula [mantra], an amulet [todga] . . . It is now beyond a government's powers to keep knowledge of this mantra from a "mathefiru" [someone whose head has turned].'[13]

But the Raj was in the mood for frenzied vengeance. Aurobindo Ghose and four other Bengali journalists were booked. In the Deccan, as a prelude of sorts, the government filed sedition cases against editors of three Marathi papers: the *Hind Swarajya*, *Vihari* and *Arunodaya*. Only days later, a similar case was lodged against S.M. Paranjpe, Tilak's associate, confidant and fiery editor of the *Kaal*. Tilak knew what all of it was leading to. He had to be prepared.

On 11 June, Paranjpe was arrested. That day, Tilak was in Nasik for the thread ceremony of his grandson Gajanan V. Ketkar. From there, he was to head home to Poona, but hearing of the *Kaal* editor's arrest, he left straight for Bombay so he could arrange for Paranjpe's bail. Once Paranjpe was released on bail, Tilak left for Poona but returned to Bombay again in a few days to assist Paranjpe with the legal case. In Bombay, Tilak usually stayed in a room at the Sardar Gruha, a building situated almost bang opposite the Bombay police headquarters; the area where the building stood had ironically been given the name 'Crawford Market' after Arthur Crawford, the former British official earlier accused by Tilak and others of coercing mamlatdars into paying bribes. In the evening of 24 June, Tilak and Paranjpe were engaged in a discussion at Sardar Gruha over the *Kaal* editor's prosecution when, at about 6 p.m., the police came calling. They carried with them an arrest warrant. The warrant had been issued by the presidency magistrate four hours earlier, but the police, who simply had to cross the street from their HQ to reach Tilak, had landed up at Sardar Gruha close to sunset so that it would be hard for him to apply for bail immediately.[14] Tilak was taken in a horse carriage to the Esplanade police station in the vicinity, where he was shown as arrested. He spent the night in the police lock-up.

Tilak was charged with sedition under Section 124 A and with promoting feelings of enmity under Section 153 A of the Indian Penal Code. The morning after his arrest, he was brought before the chief presidency magistrate A.H.S. Aston, where his lawyer, J.D. Davar, applied for bail. J.D. Davar was the son of the lawyer Dinshaw D. Davar who had appeared for Tilak in the 1897 sedition trial. The father had now become a judge of the Bombay High Court, and in a twist of fate, the senior Davar would be the presiding judge for Tilak's trial in this case! In yet another legal coincidence, Aston, who was hearing Tilak's plea for bail, was the magistrate who had earlier in Poona ordered the police to start criminal proceedings against Tilak in what was essentially a civil case between Tilak and Tai Maharaj. Aston rejected his bail plea and remanded him in police custody. Tilak was taken to the Dongri jail, where he had spent time twice earlier, once in 1882 and the second time in 1897.

Soon the case was committed to the Criminal Sessions at the Bombay High Court, with the hearing slated to begin on 2 July. Two articles of the *Kesari* were cited by the police, under Superintendent William Sloane of the CID, to press two separate cases: one involving an editorial of 12 May headlined 'The Country's Misfortune', and the other related to a 9 June editorial headlined 'These Remedies Are Not Lasting'. The first of these was written by Tilak, the second by Khadilkar. Subsequently, six more articles were added by the prosecution to its list of incriminating material: two more from 12 May written by Tilak, and four from 9 June by Khadilkar. As printer and publisher of the *Kesari*, Tilak was responsible for all the content in it. And as editor, he knew he was answerable for every word that was published.

Tilak landing behind bars was a massive relief for the Bombay police chief, H.G. Gell. He had been desperately looking for something to pin on Tilak after the December 1907 meeting Tilak had held with the city's mill workers. 'There are 85 mills in Bombay employing some 100,000 hands, of which at least 50,000 must be able-bodied,' Gell wrote to the secretary of the Bombay government's judicial department. 'Anyone able to enlist the sympathy of so large a number of men must occupy a powerful position and if, intent on disorder, can practically set all authority at defiance. Tilak had no doubt considered this point and for some time before his arrest, had endeavoured to gain them over. The large majority of mill hands are Marathas, and Tilak is a Brahmin, but that did not stand in his way . . . Had he been vouchsafed a longer period of liberty, (he) would no doubt in time have had a large organized body of mill hands at his disposal. Fortunately he was arrested in time.'[15]

The arrest, though, came mixed with serious apprehension about popular reactions. The police commissioner was not at all sanguine, for he reported to the judicial department's secretary that on 29 June, the first time Tilak's case was heard before the chief presidency magistrate, 'large crowds collected outside the court-house, and becoming disorderly, had to be dispersed'. A Swadeshi activist named Kanchan Kumar 'took up a position on the maidan and did much to excite the feelings of the crowd by his harangue'. With the crowd getting dispersed and 'an attempt being made to seize him, he disappeared' but was picked up by cops later. The dispersing crowd, wrote the police commissioner, 'stoned the police' and the 'Europeans who were near at the time, and eight arrests had to be made'. For some time after that, there was no trouble. But after the case was adjourned for the day and the court closed, 'remnants of the unlawful assembly recongregated and commenced to stone isolated Europeans passing along Cruickshank Road'. Among those hurt in the stoning were 'the Venerable the Archdeacon of Bombay and a professor of St. Xavier's College'. Once European police officers and native police arrived on the scene, the 'desultory stone-throwing', stopped, and Gell reported that 'the members of disorder were chased away, not to reappear'.[16]

The same day, the first issue of a new Extremist paper, *Rashtramat*, started in Bombay with Tilak's support, hit the newsstands. 'It was sold in thousands that day by newsboys, tobacconists, etc,' wrote Gell. And 'during the time which elapsed between the committal of the case to the High Court and its trial there . . . all vernacular papers drove a roaring trade, while a great deal of quiet preaching was done' by Tilak's friends and sympathizers 'in chals [chawls] and private places'.[17]

On 2 July, as the hearing began, the first thing Tilak did was to apply for bail in the Bombay High Court. A lanky lawyer with a

longish face and slightly hollowed-out cheeks stood up to mention his
bail plea before Justice Dinshaw D. Davar. His name was Mohammed
Ali Jinnah; he was in his early thirties; and he was a follower of Tilak's.
Born in Karachi either in 1875 or 1876 (there is no unanimity on
his birth year, a mystery many members of the nation he founded
subsequently, especially cricketers, have retained) to a family of
merchants, Mohammed Ali Jinnahbhai had dropped the suffix 'bhai'
from his surname after having studied law in London. In the British
capital itself, he had developed a fascination for politics and had sat
in the visitors' gallery at the House of Commons a number of times
to witness its proceedings. On his return to India, he had enrolled as
a barrister at the Bombay High Court in 1896 and soon thereafter
joined the Congress. He had risen in the ranks gradually, having been
in 1904 chosen as one of two Congressmen (the other being Gokhale)
to go to England and represent India's case before British officials.
Though Lajpat Rai had been finally picked at the last moment in
place of Jinnah for the two-member delegation, Jinnah still had
a promising political career ahead of him. Starting as a follower of
Naoroji, Badruddin Tyabji and Mehta, he had slowly shifted to the
Tilak camp. And when a delegation of Muslims led by the president of
the 1896-birthed Muslim League, Aga Khan, had travelled to Simla
to meet Lord Minto in October 1906 and had asked for separate
electorates for India's Muslims, Jinnah, according to Aga Khan, was
'the only well-known Muslim' to have opposed the League's aims.
Jinnah had then argued that the 'principle of separate electorates was
dividing the nation against itself'.[18]

Jinnah told Judge Davar that Tilak's release was 'absolutely
necessary for the proper conduct of his defence'. Tilak had a good
defence, he said, but he wouldn't be able to instruct his counsel if he
wasn't released on bail. Tilak's case was that translations of the articles
in front of the court were 'incorrect and misleading,' and he 'wanted to
instruct counsel in order to give the spirit in which those articles had
been written.' As a fifty-two-year-old, he also suffered from diabetes
and was under medical treatment for it, Jinnah said. Besides, Tilak was
'a B. A. and LL.B.', 'an author', 'a professor in a college' and 'a member
of the Legislative Council' for some time, and he was 'a well-known
man in the Deccan.' Importantly, Jinnah quoted a judgement of the
former high court judge Badruddin Tyabji in which Tyabji had said

the law on release on bail was tied to securing the attendance of an accused at the trial. 'Was there any suggestion or any shadow of hint that there was any apprehension that Tilak would not come forth to stand his trial?' he asked.[19]

Once Jinnah had finished speaking, the advocate-general or chief law officer of the state, R.E. Branson, stood up to speak. The litany of legal ironies continued: Branson had been Tilak's counsel in the Tai Maharaj case! Barely had Branson said 'I appear . . .' when judge Davar interrupted him, saying, 'I will not trouble you, Mr. Advocate-General.' He had made up his mind. The judge said he had given the question of bail his 'most anxious consideration,' and in view of the wide publicity given to everything said in court, it was 'eminently desirable' that 'nothing should be said before the trial that would in any way prejudice either case for the prosecution or for the accused'. Thus he was rejecting the bail plea without stating the reasons for doing so. He 'thought it would be wise under the present circumstances not to give any reason or enter into a discussion of the considerations weighing with him in refusing the application'.[20]

If this was a peculiar kind of judicial secrecy, the next turn was plainly odd. The prosecution asked for a special jury for the case. Apart from Jinnah, the Bombay-based East Indian activist and barrister Joseph Baptista, a staunch follower of Tilak, was his other counsel. Baptista urged the court not to allow such a plea. The court had two kinds of juries: common and special. In the common pool, the majority of jurors were Indian, and the special pool consisted largely of Europeans. It was vital that Tilak should get a group of jurors who understood Indian languages as the entire matter rested on articles written in Marathi, Baptista said. If a special jury were appointed, then in all probability the European jurors would outnumber the Indians, which wouldn't be fair to Tilak, he said, and the Europeans 'would be handicapped on account of their inability to understand the language'.[21] Justice Davar however permitted a special jury. It had nine members, seven European and two Indians, both Parsis.

When Paranjpe was booked by the police, Tilak had advised him to conduct his own defence in court. For his own trial, Tilak chose to defend himself. Jinnah said after Tilak's death that he was supposed to represent Tilak but there emerged differences between them over how to approach the case, and he withdrew. Tilak wanted the battle lines

to be marked out along a political trajectory; Jinnah, on the other
hand, according to his version, took a strictly legalistic view—of defence
aimed at getting an acquittal. At a public meeting after Tilak's death,
Jinnah disclosed, 'He [Tilak] was determined not so much to secure
his acquittal, but to establish that the Anglo-Indian press was guilty of
defaming India and Indian people, which was as much a libel, and the
government did not take any steps against them. There arose a serious
difference of opinion between him and myself as a counsel, because
I refused to adopt any line, as counsel, except what I considered best
for his defence.'[22] The writer A.G. Noorani, who has written a book
on Tilak and Jinnah's camaraderie, has made the astonishing statement
that 'this unfortunate disagreement was to have a crippling effect on
the defence case.'[23] Why would it have a crippling effect? Would Jinnah
appearing for Tilak have ensured his acquittal? Jinnah had appeared
for Tilak to seek bail, using a strictly legal argument, and Tilak hadn't
got bail. Noorani demonstrates a penchant for exaggerating Jinnah's
role and implies, quite ridiculously, that Tilak's chances got very badly
affected because Jinnah opted out as defence counsel.

Besides, though Tilak was going to conduct his own defence, he
was not without any legal assistance. His own legal credentials aside, he
had at least five lawyers assisting him in the courtroom: Joseph Baptista,
Madhavrao Bodas, Dadasaheb Karandikar, N.C. Kelkar and Bapusaheb
Gandhi. There is no reason to underplay Jinnah's role in this episode.
But there is no reason to overplay it either, as Noorani does.

The trial began on 13 July 1908 with M.R. Jardine, the clerk for the
crown, reading the charges against Tilak. Advocate–General Branson
led the prosecution, along with his team members J.D. Inverarity and
D.B. Binning. Jardine, who would later be more famous as the father
of the English cricket captain Douglas Jardine, asked Tilak, 'Do you
plead guilty or not guilty?' 'I plead not guilty,' said Tilak and added, 'But
I think the words on the articles on which the prosecution rely should
be specified.' The prosecuting team's Inverarity told the judge that as 'a
whole lot of the words are objected to', he wanted to amend the charges
to include 'the whole of the articles'.[24]

Opening the case for the prosecution, Inverarity said Tilak's 12 May
article was 'devoted to stating that the whole cause of this (Muzaffarpur)
outrage is the iniquitous character of the oppressive and tyrannical

rule of the British in this country'. The article spoke of the country's misfortune. What was meant by that, Inverarity questioned and continued that Tilak had ascribed the bomb outrage 'to the perversity of the white official class', by which he was referring to 'the British government'. Citing Tilak's line that 'British rule is entirely governed by self-interest except in so far as it is bounded by the necessity of avoiding exasperating the people of the country,' he characterized it as 'gross libel on the Government of India and of Great Britain.' Similarly, Tilak's repeated assertion in the article that the government desired to benefit their own country at the expense of the Indians was 'defamatory', 'unscrupulous' and 'a direct attack on the government', Inverarity told the court.

The word 'Swarajya' used by Tilak came under the scanner. The official translator had translated it as 'literally one's own rule or self-government', and the *Kesari*, said Inverarity, had its own definition of it, which 'apparently means that whenever the people like to upset the government they are entitled to do so'. Appallingly for the prosecutor, 'the Kesari had on previous occasions warned the government that Russian methods would be imitated by the people of India if they were not careful,' and he had no doubt besides that the Russian methods referred to 'must be the throwing of bombs'. Apparently, representing the thirty crore people of India 'burning with indignation', Tilak, he said, had also stated that 'it is impossible not to expect some of them to commit outrages induced by the oppressive system of government'. Inverarity asked the judge, 'Don't you think this article is intended to convey to the reader that the only thing which comes between the people of India and the blessings of the country is the English rule?'

In the second article of 9 June, Inverarity said, Tilak had pointed out that 'people in other countries have obtained what they want from bomb-throwing' and that 'government cannot prevent the manufacture of bombs, they are easy to make, they only require a few chemicals'. He quoted the line that the bomb 'is a charm, an amulet' to ask how a bomb could become so 'unless it is intended to be used', indicating openly that Tilak was inciting people to violent and subversive actions. Highlighting two paragraphs 'to the effect that British rule is a curse to the country and if that is really the case they must expect to have the same state of affairs in India as in Russia', Inverarity said the writer had referred 'to the murder of the King of Portugal as resulting in having the desired effect'. He asked the court, 'Does it not appear to you that it was a threat to the Government of India and a suggestion to the people of India that British rule cannot be allowed to go on as it is at present?' And why was Tilak 'frequently' alluding 'to the alien rulers being white?' Such words, Inverarity contended, 'can only be intended to stir up racial feeling' by pointing out that 'the white class is acting in India in a manner which is directly hostile to the interests of the natives'. The first article was seditious enough, but the second was of 'extreme hostility to the government', Inverarity said.[25]

The first witness for the prosecution was one of the government's translators, Bhaskar Vishnu Joshi. He had not translated the *Kesari* articles himself, the court translator had, but he vouched for the accuracy of the translations. Tilak cross-examined him on the meaning of several words and on usage, intent on establishing that the articles had in fact been mistranslated. Tilak said that 'in expressing current political ideas, many new words have to be coined in Marathi,' and as the language was fast evolving, words could be erroneously translated. For example, for the word bureaucracy, he had used four synonyms in the same article. And while the prosecution was relying on old lexicons, new meanings were being assigned to words. How could the translators not take that into account?

The prosecution's production of a postcard, titled 'Exhibit K', attracted a considerable amount of attention right through the trial. The morning after Tilak's arrest, the police had searched his home and offices in Poona. One of the things they had recovered was this postcard on which titles of two books on explosives were written. On one side were the titles *Handbook of Modern Explosives*' by M. Eissler, published by Crosby and Lockwood, and *Nitro Explosives* by Gerard Sanford, and on the other side was just written, 'Modern explosives, by Eisler, Crosby and Lockwood'.[26] The dangerous insinuation was that Tilak could be engaged in the manufacture of bombs. The card was passed around the jury. What was it really meant for?

The Raj had recently introduced the Explosives Substances Act, which stipulated that anyone in India who possessed explosives or helped in making or storing them or related material would be transported for fourteen years, and anyone who carried out explosions or even intended to do so would get twenty years of transportation or seven years in jail.[27] Tilak said he wanted to write a detailed, critical piece on the Act's provisions and especially on its definition of an explosive, which included even ordinary kerosene oil. 'It was necessary to collect material to see whether the definition given in the Act tallies with the definition given in the works on explosives,' Tilak explained. 'The only reference book we had there was Encyclopaedia Britannica and that was not enough and naturally the first impulse was to refer to the catalogue to see whether there was any work on explosives.' Tilak showed the judge and the jury the catalogue he had referred to. 'If you will see the card you will find that there is one portion scratched and the names are rewritten with the prices,' he said. Two of the titles were of the same book: *Modern Explosives* was what he had found in the text, and the full title of the book he had got from the general index, which is why it was mentioned twice on the card. The books were mentioned along with names of their authors and publishers. Another thing was that, as inspector Peter Sullivan who conducted the search had said in his cross-examination by Tilak, the police had found the card in Tilak's drawer among the most ordinary papers, so it was not concealed, nor was it intended to be sent to anybody. The article criticizing the provisions of the Explosives Act, which defined the word explosives at length, too, had actually appeared in the *Kesari* of 16 June 1908. 'The whole of the third column and fourth column criticizes the definition of the Act,' Tilak said. And yet, he pointed out, the card 'was carried away as a trophy of the search' so that 'insinuations and innuendos' could be made before the court.[28]

Starting on 13 July, Tilak addressed the jury for six straight days. He produced seventy-one newspaper articles from other newspapers and periodicals across India and England. How were extracts from other people's writings relevant at all, asked the advocate-general. They were, argued Tilak, because the whole point of his own articles was that they were part of a raging debate on the use of the bomb. Why had the Bengali revolutionaries taken to it? What ought to be the Raj's response to their activities? What action would be right, what wrong, and what repressive? And what was the way out if a recurrence had to be prevented? A number of questions were at stake, and his articles represented his viewpoint on 'a perfectly legitimate . . . subject for discussion.'

'Something very extraordinary takes place; something that appeals to you as quite out of the way and public discussion is sure to take place. You must realize what my position was,' he told the jury. 'Am I not entitled to put in a single contribution to the controversy? I have read the views of other people and have taken part in the controversy on a certain incident; I have had to modify my views and where I disagree with them I have had to say so. It is for that reason that the freedom of the press is protected.'

A number of English papers had claimed that the 'true cause' of the explosion in Muzaffarpur was 'the agitation carried out by journalists', others had said 'the Nationalist Party is to blame', and still others had opined that the time had come to 'put a stop to the Congress'. Tilak said that what he had shown through his pieces was that the Anglo–Indian papers were 'referring only to a certain number of links of the chain'. They, and the government, needed to look much deeper. 'If you want to stop the bombs now it will not do to put down the Congress agitation; but you ought to put down the bureaucracy first or reform it. I know that some of you may not like this. That does not matter . . . I know that when bureaucracy is not taken to task they like it; and when we take them to task they do not like it. But we are perfectly justified in putting forward our view.'

Tilak cited the English law and landmark English court rulings to stress the value of freedom of the press and the importance of expressing the opinion of a community through the papers. 'I express my view on public matters of interest frankly; and that would be expressing the views of my community . . . My view was the view of the Marathi-speaking people and of the Hindus everywhere,' he declared. 'When I have done that I have done but my duty. Newspapers . . . stand between arbitrary power and the people, and the press represents public opinion to government and this is particularly necessary in the administration of the country.'

Tilak said he had not become editor and proprietor of a paper only to make money but to discuss public questions. He asserted, 'We have a right to complain if India is to be governed in a completely arbitrary manner . . . Although the bureaucracy may feel the inconvenience of the principle, it is your duty, gentlemen, to stand between us of the press and those people and protect us. You are the guardians of our liberties. I say we want local self-government, local Home Rule, whatever you may call it. Government at once says "there they are; they are discontented and they want a share in the government. They are acting disrespectfully." Is it not derogatory to our self-respect and prestige? And if the matter is to be considered like this and the law of sedition is to be considered so rigidly as this, in every case the accused will be found guilty. We had better not have trials at all.'

Tilak's statement covers ninety-five pages of the account of the trial that was published later that year.[29] He ended his days-long speech by making an appeal to the jury: 'The matter has come to a critical stage; we are in want of help; you can give it to us. I am now on the wrong side of life according to the Indian standard of life. For me it can only be a matter of a few years, but future generations will look to your verdict and see whether you have judged wrong or right. The verdict is likely to be a memorable one in the history of the struggle for the freedom of the Indian press . . . I appeal to you not for myself but in the interest of the cause which I have the honour to represent. It is a cause that is sacred.'[30]

Advocate–General Branson was snarky in his reply. He addressed the jury, saying, 'I think, gentlemen, you may safely leave future generations to look after themselves and in the interests of the present generation not to take up more of its time than is necessary.' It was his duty, he said, 'not to overstate things or over-press the case,' but he regretted that 'I could not shorten your (jury's) tortures in having to listen for five days to Mr. Tilak. I cannot guarantee abstaining from inflicting some torture on you. I can only say . . . I will endeavour to avoid all those faults which Mr. Tilak has been guilty of, the maddening reiteration, saying the same thing over and over again till you must have been sick of it as he must have been himself.' He told the jurors he wouldn't be drawn into any discussion on politics. 'Neither you nor His Lordship, nor I,' he said, 'have anything whatever to do with the politics which have been the source of discussion for the past three days. Kindly remember that. Put the whole of the discussion addressed to you on the question of politics and the position of the parties aside. You have nothing to do with that.'[31]

The section of the Indian Penal Code on sedition, 'the more important one' of the two (the other was related to promotion of enmity) applied against Tilak, was all that mattered in the case, and there was no point in Tilak quoting from English law and from the British jurist Thomas Erskine's judgements,' he said. 'The English law . . . does not apply to this country . . . We have got the Penal Code, you cannot take away from it, and you cannot add to it.' Branson was savage in his attack on Tilak's argument about the freedom of the press. He told the jury, 'You have been told that you are guardians of the press. Fiddlesticks! You are guardians of the press no more than I am. Before God you are guardians of the Penal Code and the Penal Code protects the press. You have been told that you are guardians of the press over and over again, until one really felt inclined to rebel against the doctrine of the liberty of the subject.'[32]

What took the cake during the entire trial of course was the fact that none of the jurors were Marathi speakers even if one or both the Parsi jurors could read the language, a point which Tilak remarked was of the greatest importance in terms of understanding the import of the articles and in their interpretation. He pointed out that where he had written *titkara*, meaning 'disgust', it had been mistranslated as 'hatred', and among a host of other, similar distortions, 'sorrow' had become 'pain', 'perverse' had been used for 'obstinate', and 'violence' for 'indignation'.[33] But Justice Davar had warned the jurors about it: he had told them that though the accused was entitled to point out what he considered as wrong translations and though those on the jury who could follow Marathi could tell their colleagues if the accused's contentions were correct or not, it was for them to judge, 'but you must never resort to outside help'.[34] Men not able to comprehend a word of Marathi were going to pronounce judgement on whether articles written in that language were seditious or not.

Not surprisingly, all seven European jurors held Tilak guilty, while the verdict of the two Parsis was 'not guilty'. Accepting the verdict of the majority, Justice Davar asked Tilak if he had anything to say before the court passed the sentence. What Tilak said has, in Independent India, been inscribed on marble stone outside Courtroom No. 46 of the Bombay High Court:

> All I wish to say is that in spite of the verdict of the jury, I maintain that I am innocent. There are higher Powers that rule the destiny of things and it may be the will of Providence that the cause which I represent may prosper more by my suffering than by my remaining free.[35]

At 9.40 p.m. on 22 July 1908, Justice Davar pronounced Tilak guilty and sentenced him to six years of transportation. For the two charges, Tilak had got three years each, and the sentences were to run consecutively. His previous conviction came to haunt him as well, for there was a third charge brought against Tilak in that connection this time. He had got six months of remission for his previous sentence a decade ago and had been released early on account of his good conduct, on the condition that if ever his conduct was found wanting, he would have to serve the remainder of that prison term. In that regard, Justice Davar told Tilak he did not want to add to his troubles any additional period of imprisonment. 'I therefore fine you Rs 1000,' he said.[36]

On the whole, Davar was scathing in the way he laid out his judgement. He said to Tilak, 'It seems to me that it must be a diseased mind, a most perverted mind that could say that the articles which you have written are legitimate means in political agitation. They are seething with sedition; they preach violence; they speak of murders with approval and the cowardly and atrocious act of committing murders with bombs not only seems to meet with your approval, but you hail the advent of the bomb in India as if something has come to India for its good.' Tilak, as a matter of fact, had called the bomb a 'horrible' thing. Justice Davar further said, 'Your hatred of the ruling class has not disappeared during these ten years. And these [articles] were deliberately and definitely written week by week, not, as you say, on the spur of the moment but a fortnight after that cruel and cowardly outrage had been committed upon two innocent Englishwomen . . . Such journalism is a curse to the country.'[37]

It was raining heavily in Bombay when the sentence was pronounced. Still, a big crowd had gathered outside the court building in anticipation of the verdict. At 10 in the night, Tilak was whisked away by the police through the back gate to a waiting car and driven to the railway station. There, he was put in a special train and taken to Ahmedabad. The next day, 23 July 1908, was going to be his fifty-third birthday; it was also the first day of his six-year sentence, inside Sabarmati jail.

Realizing that their leader had been quietly hauled out through the back door, the crowd got restive. Stones were hurled at the police, injuring one British sergeant, before the gathering was dispersed.

The Bombay police had prepared themselves for such happenings right from the start of the trial. They had anticipated disturbances along the route from Dongri jail to the high court if Tilak were made to travel every day during the trial. So, it had been decided, in consultation with the high court's chief justice, that he would be kept in a temporary lock-up in the high court building itself. It was only on Friday evenings, when a two-day break loomed, that he was taken back to Dongri jail and brought back to the court premises on Monday morning. Plenty of *bandobast* was kept around this temporary lock-up: twelve European officers, twenty-four unarmed 'native officers and men' and ten armed men kept vigil every day from 5.30 p.m., when the court usually closed, till 11.30 a.m., when Tilak was taken to the courtroom. During court proceedings, even more policemen were on guard in and around the court, including thirty mounted officers; in addition, the police chief H.G. Gell recorded that 'a military detachment of one commissioned officer and fifty rank and file' was 'posted in the University Hall'.[38]

In the run-up to the sentencing, in the last few days of the trial, as it became increasingly clear which way it was likely to go, disturbances began to be reported from various parts of the city, but chiefly from 'Girangaon', the village of the mills or the mill workers' belt in Lalbaug and Parel of central Bombay. For example, for two days running while the trial was on, a number of mill workers had tried to assemble near the high court. On 16 July, the Bombay police chief said, workers at 'the Queen and Lakmidas Mills struck work to go and see Tilak's trial', along with '320 employees of four other mills.' On 17 July, 28 mills stopped working, and 'the spirit of unrest seemed to seize' the mill workers, Gell reported. Sporadic incidents of violence took place, with windows being smashed, furniture broken in one or two places, a liquor shop vandalized, and some Europeans passing through Currey Road in the same mill land belt 'mobbed and assaulted'. On 20 July, labourers working in godowns at the Grain Bazar and some cart drivers also struck work, and in some cases, the labourers overturned carts along Frere Road carrying goods belonging to Europeans. The day before Tilak's conviction, the police chief wrote that 'notices in the Marathi language were found pasted up in the water closet of the Maneckji Petit Mills' in Tardeo. 'Why are you asleep? Awake, be ready, and assist your Parel comrades,' the notices read.[39]

The fallout of Tilak's conviction was still more remarkable. All the mill workers in Bombay went on strike for six days—one day for each year that Tilak would have to spend in Mandalay. Every one of Bombay's eighty textile mills was shut. Besides, the grain, cloth, copper and share bazaars remained closed, with some of the Indian traders and merchants also unexpectedly coming out in support of the protesters. Violence, more serious than on the previous days, broke out in various parts of the city, and close to Girgaum Chowpatty, the military had to be called in because 'the whole of Girgaum Road as far as Kandewady was in a state of disorder', and 'large stone slabs had been placed (by protesters) across the tram lines'. The police, wrote the commissioner, were 'severely stoned', and the additional presidency magistrate James McDonald 'received a severe blow from a large stone thrown at him.' The military quickly had to make its presence felt all around the city as violence worsened. 'A crowd of operatives attacked a mill that was still working, police officers who intervened were injured, and eventually the military fired on the mob, killing and wounding several people,' wrote The Times of London. 'A couple of volleys,' the paper noted with dismay, 'has usually sufficed to disperse any Bombay rioters, and to send them scurrying into retreat. On this occasion, the mob showed unusual persistence, and rioting continued.' A crowd succeeded in 'holding up' the Poona mail train at Currey Road and was reinforced by men employed in the railway workshops, with the result that the military was 'compelled to fire down a crowded road "packed with rioters", causing many casualties'. In one particular mill, some European officials were besieged, 'the police who rescued them were stoned, and again had to fire on the rioters'. One morning, on the back of rumours that Governor Clarke was going to pass through Sheikh Memon Street, the busy thoroughfare became the scene of a major demonstration. The protesters 'carried black flags bearing the portrait of Mr. Tilak, and after again stoning the police had to be fired on by the military'.[40] The official count of the dead at the end of it all was fifteen, and over a hundred protesters were wounded, almost forty of them seriously.[41] 'There is no doubt but that the feeling against Europeans was most hostile. Much trouble would have ensued had not the military been posted at different points, throughout the island,' Gell wrote in his official report.[42]

About one thing, the police chief was satisfied. 'Throughout the trouble,' he stated, 'at no point did the Mahomedans join in the disorder, and though strenuous attempts were made by the Hindoos to induce them to join forces, they resisted all attempt. Not a small number of Mahomedans are employed in the mills.' Finally, in his report, Gell provided to his government his personal assessment of Tilak's increasing popularity not just in the Bombay Presidency but elsewhere in India as well. 'Many natives,' he wrote, 'even those who do not belong to the extremist party and who do not think with him, look upon him as a man actuated wholly by his desire to ameliorate the condition of Indians, and respect and admire him. He possesses a personality, and wherever he used to address the people, he gained adherents. But even where he was not personally known his fame spread, especially amongst the working classes . . . By many he is revered and in countless houses pictures of him are hung on the wall.'[43]

The coordinated action by more than one lakh mill workers and other workers across Bombay was extraordinary, for they were in an era in which there were no organized worker unions, and the Russian revolution which galvanized labourers in various parts of the globe, including mill workers in India's commercial capital, was still almost a decade away, though it is true that the 1905 disturbances in Russia had disseminated the idea of strikes. Among those who took particular note of the Bombay protests was the leader of the RSLDP in Russia, Vladimir Lenin, whose party had 'played almost no part in the initial strikes and unrest' in Russia in 1905 although, according to his biographer, 'later, Communist rewriting of history' gave it 'a leading role in the events'.[44] Lenin railed against John Morley, calling him a 'scoundrel' and 'lackey of capitalism', and said that men like him, 'the most liberal and radical personalities of free Britain . . . become regular Genghis Khans when appointed to govern India'. 'But,' he said, 'in India the street is beginning to stand up for its writers and political leaders. The infamous sentence pronounced by the British jackals on the Indian democrat Tilak – he was sentenced to a long term of exile, the question in the British House of Commons the other day revealing that the Indian jurors had declared for acquittal and that the verdict had been passed by the vote of the British jurors! – this revenge against a democrat by the lackeys of the money-bag evoked street demonstrations and a strike in Bombay. In India, too, the proletariat has already developed to conscious political mass struggle – and, that being the case, the Russian-style British regime in India is doomed!'[45] We don't know whether Lenin knew about it or not, but the reality was that while the mill workers had no doubt protested in thousands and not hundreds, a section of the merchants and traders in Bombay, the 'capitalist' class so despised by him, had similarly pitched in.

Without Tilak's actual organizing hand being behind the strike, shutdowns of markets and the protests, his status as leader and his appeal had brought the city's booming industries to a standstill. It had comprehensively demolished the theory that he held iconic status mainly for the Brahmans, for the overwhelming majority of the mill workers were non-Brahmans. And it was proof, above all, that Tilak had mobilized people for mass politics and mass protests in a way previously unimagined in British-ruled India.

Most conservative papers in Britain heartily welcomed the court judgement. 'Well-merited severity,' screamed the *Daily Telegraph* in its headline. 'The sentence is a heavy one for a man 53 years of age,' the paper admitted, but added that 'one has to remember Mr. Tilak's antecedents, his conviction ten years ago, his open preaching of Swaraj doctrines.' The judge presiding over the case was 'himself an Indian,' it said, and the jury 'could hardly be blamed if, in the light of certain obvious facts, they regarded Mr. Tilak's arguments as hollow'.[46] *Observer* was of the view that 'the hand of justice has closed sternly upon Mr. Tilak' and that the translations 'showed the incriminated articles to be full of subtle but virulent treason'.[47] *The Times* of London was full of praise for the Bombay governor, George Clarke. 'The Bombay government,' it observed, 'deserve warm commendation for the vigorous steps they have taken of late for the repression of sedition. Sir George Clarke and his advisors had a plain duty before them, and they did not shrink from it.'[48]

However, British leaders like the Parliamentarian and Congress patron Henry Cotton, the Socialist hero H.M. Hyndman and Labour leader Keir Hardie who were sympathetic to the Indians weighed in with powerful words about the farcical nature of the trial and did not stint on their praise for Tilak.

The dock had been 'illumined' by Tilak, stated Cotton, 'with a burning eloquence and a noble courage which would have earned for him the plaudits of the Empire – if he had not been an Indian'. About the court proceedings, Cotton had quite a bit to say.

'Mr. Justice Davar's impartiality,' he noted, 'may be willingly conceded, although the terrible sentence he has passed may not help some of us to appreciate his sense of proportion. What of the jury however? The articles . . . were written neither in English nor in the mother tongue of the Parsees, but in the Marathi language. There are dozens of Marathi-speaking Hindus on the special jury list of the high court. Why were all such so rigidly excluded from the jury which was made up of seven Englishmen and two Parsis, and which went against the accused . . . in exactly that proportion of seven to two? . . . Mr. Tilak strongly denounced the inaccuracy of the official translations . . . They would, he said, make anything seditious and could only be compared to distorting mirrors. He demanded either new translations or a complete acquittal. He obtained neither, but a verdict of guilty from a jury of whom it is safe to say that seven of the nine were not able to read a single word of the articles in their original Marathi. And what is the result? Prior to his arrest, Mr. Tilak was but the leader of a party. He is now a national party and a popular hero. When he was taken before the magistrate . . . there occurred the most violent display of anti-British feeling that Bombay has known for years. The news of his conviction was followed by the closing of the markets and shops in the so-called 'native quarter.' It may be that independent causes must be sought for the strike of the mill hands and the rioting and bloodshed which have followed so close upon the heels of the trial; but at any rate the coincidence is remarkable . . . Bombay has been thrown into a ferment.'[49]

Cotton also made a remark on the floor of the House of Commons that it was 'suicidal' to prosecute for sedition 'the most influential citizen in the Presidency', prompting *Times* of London to respond angrily that 'it would have been far more suicidal, as well as absolutely cowardly, to have been deterred by fear of disturbances from prosecuting a maleficent agitator'.[50]

Hyndman said any unprejudiced Englishman would conclude that 'if articles of that character are to earn the writer six years' transportation to the Andaman Islands then we may just as well at once state plainly that no free criticism of our rule is to be permitted in India at all. I defy anyone to point to a sentence in Mr. Tilak's articles which incites to bomb-throwing or violence; and I cannot understand how Englishmen, who have always supported peoples struggling for freedom in other countries, and are doing so today in regard to Russians or Turks can resort to such measures of repression as those which Lord Morley and Lord Minto, both nominally Liberals, are applying to India.' Moreover, Hyndman said, he simply couldn't fathom how a verdict of guilty could be reached when the jury had not rendered a unanimous verdict given its composition and given that 'the seven Europeans voted in the majority and the two Indians in the minority'. Was it a verdict 'which justifies a judge, nominated and paid by the foreign rulers, in sentencing the leader of the Indian national party to six years' transportation?' Denouncing the trial as 'utterly contrary to the whole spirit of English equity,' Hyndman called upon his countrymen 'in all our great cities to enter their protests against such shameful deeds being done in their name'.[51]

Keir Hardie, who had met Tilak only the previous year, gave the readers of the 'Labour Leader' an idea of what kind of man he felt had just been convicted:

There is no man in India who has such a hold upon the working class as Mr. Tilak, and the result of this conviction will be more far-reaching than that of any single individual which has yet taken place. I spent three days in his company when visiting Poona less than a year ago. His life history has been a record which marks him out as one of those men of whom most nations are proud. As a scholar he has a worldwide reputation, and was the founder of the Fergusson College where for years he was a professor. He is a man of means, and some years ago resigned his position in the college that he might be free to devote himself to the interests of his people. Since then he has been the leading figure in the advance section of Indian reformers, and was, nominally at least, mainly responsible for the break-up of the Congress at Surat last year. His standing in literature is on a par with that of Tchaikovsky, the Russian who is in prison without trial in Russia, or with our own Alfred Russel Wallace, in science. I mention these things that it may be understood who and what Mr. B. G. Tilak is. The conclusion I formed concerning him was that his temperament had been soured by long, weary years of disappointed waiting, but that whilst he advocated extreme

measures of agitation he would be satisfied with moderate reforms
provided they were genuine and indicated a real desire to improve
the condition of India. His sympathy with the peasantry was intense,
and some of his journals were published in the native vernacular and
circulated extensively throughout the country districts of the Bombay
presidency. This stirring up of the peasantry has been, I believe, the
bedrock of his offence.[52]

Some of the more neutral British dailies too underlined the import of
Tilak's conviction. The *Manchester Guardian* termed it 'the most serious
and sensational step so far taken by the Government of India in the
campaign against sedition', for 'he has a personal following larger and
more devoted than any other popular leader in India commands' and
'his is the astutest brain so far placed at the service of the Nationalist
cause'. Doubtlessly, the paper said, the governor of Bombay George
Clarke 'realized that the government could not consistently prosecute
the smaller fry without striking at the most powerful revolutionary in
the country, a man by comparison with whom such persons as Bepin
Chandra Pal and even Lajpat Rai are inconsiderable'.[53] *Guardian*
disputed the theory that gained ground in several British quarters,
largely on account of a Reuters report, that the mill workers' strike was
unrelated. 'It is impossible to dissociate the serious riots of the past
few days from the proceedings against Mr. Tilak. Reuters calls them
strike riots, but we now know that disturbances began immediately
after the arrest'.[54] *Scotsman* stated, pithily, 'The serious aspect of the
situation is that all Native Bombay, from mill worker to merchant,
seems to sympathize with the convict. The feeling is certainly proof
of the supreme popularity of the man.'[55] *Morning Leader* said very few
people in England were in a position to understand what Tilak's arrest
meant in India. 'His personal power is unapproached by any other
politician in the country; he dominates the Deccan, his own country,
and is adored with a kind of religious fervour by every extremist from
Bombay to the Bay of Bengal . . . His is the mind that conceived,
his the pen that expressed, and his the force that has directed the
extraordinary movement against which the bureaucracy is now calling
up all its resources. Bal Gangadhar Tilak is a Maratha Brahmin –
thinker and fighter in one.'[56]

In India, Aurobindo's *Bande Mataram*, itself under serious attack from the Raj, came up with evocative, literary prose.

'We are after all human and cannot press back our tears when high-souled patriotism is . . . rewarded with a convict's fate in a penal settlement,' it said. 'We all have not the stuff of Tilak in us and cannot but indulge in this human frailty. But the hero has himself left us a spell to secure us against the effect of this fearful act of persecution. The brilliant address to the jury which will for ever enrich our patriotic literature was not meant for his own defence but only to put heart into his countrymen. Where is the Indian, nay, the cultured being who, after reading his address to the jury and watching his conduct in the dock can help exclaiming, "Here was a man, take him for all in all, we shall not look upon his like again." Go Tilak, whither you may be sent to crush your body. Your example will hover around us all unimprisoned and unexiled . . . You have fulfilled your mission . . . You have startled the deep slumber of false opinions, you have thrilled a pang of noble shame through callous consciences. And into the next age, if not into your own you have flashed an epidemic of nobleness. What else have patriots, heroes and martyrs done?'[57]

Amrita Bazar Patrika of Calcutta, another solid supporter of Tilak's, stated in less florid and more straightforward prose that 'if Mr. Tilak were tried in England, and two jurors were in his favour, the presiding judge would not have accepted the verdict of the majority but would have ordered a re-trial; and the accused would not have been convicted till the jury were unanimous. What then could have led Mr. Justice Davar to follow a procedure which no judge in England would venture following?'[58]

Most commentators, whether in India or England, believed it was unlikely that Tilak would come back alive from Mandalay. 'Mr. Tilak is fifty-two. He will never return from the penal settlement to which he has been consigned,' wrote the *Guardian*.[59] The *Indu Prakash* of Bombay felt that the judiciary of the Raj had passed 'an almost death-like sentence on a man of fifty-three, suffering long since from diabetes!'[60] So did Henry Cotton, who said that the Parsi judge had condemned Tilak 'to what is virtually a life sentence'.[61] The *Panjabee* of Lahore wrote that the sentence had practically sealed Tilak's fate, 'because a man of his age suffering from a fatal disease like diabetes cannot be expected to survive it and return to the country after serving his term'.[62]

Tilak himself had a feeling that he would not come back alive from the penal settlement. And reticent though he always might have been about his family attachments, the question definitely on his mind was: What about the family if he never returned? They were not badly off; the presses were doing fairly okay; and the ginning mill in which Tilak had been a partner too had not done badly. Yet he had incurred debts in the Tai Maharaj case which had, after years, still not ended until this point in time after several rounds of litigation. And however promising *Kesari* and *Mahratta* looked to be, how would they fare in his absence? In the best of times, the newspaper business was an unreliable one and hardly a route to prosperity, at least in the early twentieth century in India. Without him as the leading voice of the papers, how would they do? His wife, Satyabhama, carried all the weight of the household responsibilities on her shoulders and did no outside work. His eldest child, Krishnabai (born 1880), was married to V.G. Ketkar, a lawyer from Nasik; the second, Vishwanath (born 1883), had unfortunately died in 1903; the third, Durga (born 1889), was also married, to P.R. Vaidya, a government engineer; and so was the fourth, Mathubai (born 1891), to S.M. Sane, a professor who worked in Lucknow. But the last two of his six children—both boys—were small. Ramchandra, born in 1894, was fourteen years old, and the youngest, Shridhar, born in 1896, was only twelve.

What was going to happen? Was everything truly over for B.G. Tilak?

Chapter 13

The Prisoner of Mandalay

Prison life was strange. It was meant to keep away, conceal, hide, isolate. In many ways, in Tilak's case, it had the opposite effect. For someone so habituated to burying away his intensely personal and familial sentiments, it brought out the soft core and provided a window into his soul, into his deepest emotional and spiritual preoccupations and his passion for an intellectual and philosophic quest which a maddeningly hectic public life was preventing from finding genuine and free expression. If such a quest led to his writing his profoundest and best-known work, the *Gita Rahasya*, in his cell, his correspondence from prison, substantial if not voluminous, peeled away the thickly overlaid layers, one by one, offering fascinating glimpses of how life in the raw and the mundane met life on the emotive and speculative plane, sometimes blending, often colliding, and ultimately producing the effect that made Tilak fallible, feeble and frail on the one hand and incredibly will-driven and focused on the other.

Tilak knew, when he landed in Sabarmati Jail, that he was going to be transported. But where, when and how? No one told him anything for more than two months. The food in the jail didn't agree with him, and in the first ten days his weight went down dramatically, by almost five kgs. The jail authorities weren't so much worried by it as they were suspicious: they felt he may be deliberately eschewing food. So they put him under close surveillance and discovered he wasn't on a hunger strike, after all. They ordered his food changed, and on the jail doctor's advice, he was given two pounds of milk and two ounces of ghee every day, plus white bread in the mornings and rice in the evenings so he could get back some of his lost weight. A month on, he showed some recovery, so they continued with this food regime.[1] Until the night of 12 September 1908.

At eight in the morning of 13 September, a jailer unlocked Tilak's cell. He asked Tilak to come with him to the prison office. Once there, Tilak found out that he was going to leave; all preparations had been made already. Leave for where? When he asked that, he received no reply. Soon, he was taken to a train which, according to him, happened to be just on the other side of the prison walls. Inside the train, there was another prisoner who was going to accompany him to wherever they were taking him. He was a Gujarati Brahman, and he had been assigned the daily work of cooking for Tilak. A police squad got in with the two convicts. It had nine members in all: one European, and eight constables, all of them Muslim. Inside the jail Tilak had had to wear the prison uniform; for the purpose of the journey, he was given back his regular clothes—his dhoti, shirt and the red-coloured pagdi. Once they'd all settled in, the train moved in the direction of Bombay, where a military transport ship named 'Harding' stood bobbing in the waters of the harbour to take Tilak across the Kaala Paani or Black Waters—to Mandalay in Burma. Not that he was told about the final destination even when he got on to the ship. The moment he got on board, Tilak realized the ship was a big one. But his room wouldn't be. It was narrow, dark, and suffocating, one of the little cabins in the hold reserved for keeping unruly and truant sailors in quiet captivity. The hold itself was hot to the point of being furnacey, and its airlessness was acute and oppressive. As a measure of relief, Tilak was allowed to take a walk on the deck for an hour every day, albeit under the vigilant watch of a European police inspector.[2]

It took nine days for the 'Harding' to reach the Rangoon harbour, from where Tilak was again put on a train and taken to the prison. The prison, built along the north-western end of the Mandalay Fort, was a long way off: they left the seafront at 3 p.m. in the afternoon and, covering a distance of over 500 km, reached it at 8 a.m. the next day. Tilak's cell was on the first floor. Twelve by twelve feet in size, it had been 'partitioned off from a bigger room'. Inside the small cell stood a writing table, two chairs—one 'hard' and the other 'canvas'—an iron bedstead and a couple of cupboards for books. There was a compound around the cell, about 130 feet long and thirty feet wide, and a brick wall separated the prison building from the rest of the fort. The cell was usually used to imprison European prisoners, not 'natives', but in Tilak's case, the Raj had made an exception. He was also permitted to walk around the compound whenever he wished to, but no one else could come there except if brought in by the jailer. Every night, a heavy padlock was used to fasten the door of his cell. Tilak described the cell as a 'wooden cage', for all barracks in the Mandalay prison were made of wood.[3]

Indeed, Burma itself was full of wood, and what Tilak had missed along the railway route, as he had been denied a look outside by shuttered windows, was the thick forests, rich in teak. But Burma was a defeated land, and Mandalay, much like the rest of Burma, had the look of a place in swift decay after its occupation by the British. In 1885, the Burmese king Thibaw had been taken prisoner by the British and the country captured. Mandalay had been built as a capital in 1857 by the Burmese monarch and had a palace with a seven-roofed spire, a big fort with a moat built around it, a number of Buddhist stupas and just as many monasteries. Now, all of this suffered from wear and neglect while the barracks of the British army were everywhere. And while the deposed king Thibaw had been exiled to Ratnagiri, the district on the western Indian coast in which Tilak was born, Tilak himself was behind bars in Thibaw's own lost capital.

Back home, news of Tilak's incarceration was deeply distressing for his family and friends. On the very evening of the sentencing, Tilak's aide K.P. Khadilkar had taken the train to Poona from Bombay and reached Gaikwad Wada, Tilak's residence, late in the night. When Tilak's wife Satyabhama emerged to meet Khadilkar, she saw him wiping his tears. According to Khadilkar, she was fully prepared to take the blow and in fact berated him, saying, 'You have come to inform me about the punishment, right? The punishment is not for robbery, sexual misconduct or any heinous crime. He (Tilak) strove for the cause of the people, and the government termed it a crime. So there is no point in being crestfallen. Best to get up and carry on the work.'[4]

For all her stoical expression in public, however, Satyabhama was seriously distraught and devastated. Like Tilak himself, she did not believe he would survive the six years in prison. Like Tilak, she had diabetes, and she was also certain she would herself die while he was away in Mandalay and would never get to see him again. In the event, she survived four years into his prison term, and for those four years, according to her grandson (son of Tilak's eldest daughter Krishnabai) G.V. Ketkar, she did not step out of the house. Her attire too had changed completely. 'All she wore was black bangles and black sarees from rough-hewn cloth. She totally avoided ornaments, wearing only the mangal sutra around her neck. And she ate sparingly and fasted often.' As a prayer for their father's early release, the two boys Ramchandra and Shridhar often recited the 'Vyankatesh stotra' aimed at invoking Lord Venkateshwara. The three daughters, all married, would often visit the house and read the *Kesari* out to their mother, but Satyabhama 'did not pay too much attention to it.' But when the eldest daughter, Krishnabai, recited the Bhakta Vijaya, an eighteenth-century text composed by the Marathi chronicler Mahipati in Ovi verse commending the deeds of the saint-poets of the Bhakti movement, 'she gave it much greater attention'.[5] That was Satyabhama's, and her children's, way of dealing with it; hope and pray for the best, prepare for the worst.

In the meanwhile, the Raj had changed the nature of Tilak's punishment. Transportation meant not only going beyond the Black Waters but rigorous imprisonment, and a man thus sentenced was usually given solitary confinement along with hard labour. While Tilak had been at Sabarmati jail, the government had made it simple imprisonment, so in Mandalay he was not going to be given any work, and his confinement would not exactly be solitary either, for he would have the cook for company. If that was some consolation, the rejection of an appeal in the high court to be able to move the Privy Council was a setback.

So Khaparde left for England within days of Tilak's conviction to make a 'special appeal' directly to the Privy Council and if necessary, the House of Lords. Days after the conviction, Dr V.H. Rutherford, a Liberal Party Parliamentarian, had asked in the House of Commons if Morley would recommend to the British monarch 'to extend his clemency to Tilak in view of the position he holds in the Indian national movement and remit a portion of his sentence, with a view to allaying to some extent the present unrest in India.'[6] Offended, another member of the House, John Rees of Montgomery, asked incredulously if Rutherford thought 'expressions of sympathy in the House with notorious enemies of British rule' were likely to 'allay unrest.' Thomas Buchanan, who was the under secretary, replied it was 'impossible for the Secretary of State to take the action suggested' by Rutherford. Rutherford 'hardly realizes the nature of the charge on which Tilak was convicted and the circumstances of the trial', he said, noting how Tilak had 'exercised his full rights of challenge' against the jury and spoken 'for several days in his defence'. Then, reading Justice Davar's scathing remarks about Tilak's articles in the House, Buchanan said 'writings of such a character cannot fairly be held to fall under the exception made by the Penal Code in favour of "comments expressing disapprobation of the measures or action of the government with a view to obtaining their alteration by lawful means."' He added that the government had 'deliberately instituted these proceedings in a court of law', and for it 'immediately to traverse the verdict of the court or precipitately to set aside its sentence would be to stultify themselves'. When Frederick Mackarness of Berkshire asked during the same discussion in Parliament if the sentence could be appealed against, Buchanan said no appeal in the HC was possible against the sentence as a whole but 'points of law may be reserved for consideration.' However, he said, the judicial committee of the Privy Council permitted an appeal, to be heard by the committee itself, 'in cases where grave and substantial injustice appears to have been done'.[7]

Rutherford, for one, was convinced that grave injustice had been done, because he had had an inkling of things to come at least six months before Tilak's trial had even started. He had visited India soon after Keir Hardie's tour, and his conversation with a Raj bureaucrat had been revealing. 'What do you think of Tilak?' the bureaucrat had asked Rutherford, who carried a reputation for being 'one of the small band of vigilant friends of India in the Commons.'[8] 'I think he is a great patriot, rightly fighting for his country's freedom,' the MP had said. The bureaucrat responded, 'Gokhale and the Moderates we do not fear, but Tilak and the Extremists are a danger to British rule, and we mean to hate Tilak.' Rutherford had known, that instant, that 'fear and vindictiveness mingled in the minds and administration of alien bureaucrats'.[9]

In retrospect, Tilak might have considered the heat in the military transport vessel's hold as necessary preparation for the weather he was going to face in Mandalay. Because, as Subhas Chandra Bose, who was later imprisoned there, wrote, 'We could . . . visualize the conditions under which Lokmanya had to live there several years before. In summer the place was a veritable furnace. The wooden palisading offered no protection either from the heat or the glare, and the tiles overhead only aggravated the discomfort. Dust storms were frequent . . . (and) the heat and dust made a good combination to heighten our physical suffering.' It didn't help that summer 'was the longer season.' It lasted nearly eight to nine months, and rain was scanty and fell usually after significant intervals. Bose said, 'I have hardly experienced such heat in my life. Wet towels wrapped round one's person would dry in no time. Until midnight the air was hot and the place was so close and stuffy that sleep was impossible.' In winter, Bose mentioned, 'The cold was bitter, and the wooden bars equally failed to shut out the cold and the biting blast. In a word, the inmates of the building were entirely at the mercy of the elements.' The result, summer or winter, was that 'hardly any one of us escaped repeated attacks of sore throat, colds and influenza. The atmosphere was so depressing that one would feel overcome with lassitude and sustained intellectual work in that atmosphere was well-nigh impossible'.[10]

The Gujarati prisoner who had accompanied Tilak as his cook returned home in just a month's time, for his sentence had come to an end. He was replaced by a prisoner from Yerawada jail, a Marathi speaker named Vasudeo Kulkarni. He stayed with Tilak in Mandalay for a major part of Tilak's term and went back two years before Tilak himself was released. In his recollections, Kulkarni provided a most vivid and illuminating picture of Tilak's daily life in his prison cell.

Tilak got up very early in the morning, mostly at dawn. Immediately after he had brushed his teeth, he would recite some Sanskrit verses, though Kulkarni does not tell which verses these were. After that, Tilak would meditate for about an hour and a half. 'God alone knows what he contemplated so long,' said the baffled cook. This was followed by tea and some reading and writing. At around 9 am began the daily bathing ritual, for which Kulkarni would try to get stuff ready for him. Tilak was 'embarrassed' by his promptness and once told him, impatiently, 'You are a prisoner. And so am I. You must not make such a fuss over me. I don't like this.' He needed a lot of water for his bath, noticed the cook, and he hated it if anyone touched his body, 'even when he was ill'. Always the bath was with cold water, except in winter. In summer, he bathed twice a day. Once in a week, he got a shave for himself in the mornings. The authorities had asked a fellow prisoner in the other part of the jail premises to come in for this work, and Tilak found that the prisoner hardly knew how to do it, and the instruments he used were quite bad. Tilak asked the prison authorities to arrange for a proper barber. His demand was conceded, but he would have to pay a rupee as the charge every time. Tilak light-heartedly remarked to Kulkarni that even the princes in India didn't have to pay so much to get their beards trimmed. 'But what can I do,' he asked. 'I suffer from diabetes, and if I economize, I might have some serious trouble.'

Tilak's post-bathing ritual was to daub either a pinch of ash or a dash of sandalwood on his forehead. The jail manual of Burma permitted a prisoner serving simple imprisonment to use his own clothes. So Tilak did. Initially, he did not do much by way of chanting mantras except early in the mornings, but gradually, realizing he had much time on his hands, he told the cook that both of them should recite the Gayatri mantra before they took their food. Food normally was rice for one meal, chapati for another, and a small portion of lentils. After the first few weeks, the inspector general of prisons granted permission for fruit to be delivered.

Following lunch, which would happen at around 10 am, Tilak would sit down to work, to read and write. At 1.30 in the afternoon, he took a break with a glass of nimboo paani, or lemon water, which provided some relief from the scorching heat. This was followed by nearly an hour of casual conversation between the political prisoner and the cook, which often turned into a session of storytelling, with Tilak speaking to Kulkarni about the Pandavas and Kauravas from the Mahabharata, Shivaji Maharaj and his soldiers, and the Maharashtrian saints from Eknath to Tukaram. Sometimes he also narrated 'funny stories of the Peshwas and the English,' said Kulkarni. Once their talk was over, Tilak would go back to his work. By 5 p.m. both were supposed to finish their supper, and exactly at 6 p.m., Tilak's cell was locked and opened only twelve hours later. When the locks were put in place, the two of them again spoke for some time, with Tilak continuing some of his stories. Then Tilak sat by the lamp at the table and carried on with his work for some time. When it was time to sleep, he first washed his hands and feet clean and, as in the mornings, sat in a meditative pose for nearly an hour before putting his back on the iron bedstead.[11]

In time, however, the sweltering heat of Mandalay got to him. He started feeling 'extremely uneasy', and 'there were blisters on his body'. Two years into the prison term, his diabetes turned problematic, and he started feeling weak. He took his medicines, but since they didn't help at all, he requested the jail authorities to allow him the diet he had had in Ahmedabad. They agreed, and thus the consumption of rice, wheat and lentils was stopped altogether, and the ration of milk and ghee sanctioned in Sabarmati jail was restarted, with the addition of barley. With the changes in food intake, he got his sugar gradually under control and continued the same diet until his release. Only occasionally, he helped himself to puris made of barley flour and had curd along with that. He liked his curd thick and sour and told Kulkarni, 'I am a Konknya (man from the Konkan). I like sour things.' And when Kulkarni first made plantain bhaji for him, he liked it and told the cook that 'Dhondu [his nephew Dhondopant Vidwans] and my children would love it.'[12]

The children and the family were indeed on his mind all the time. Often the busyness of public and journalistic affairs left him little time to think of his close ones. Now, on the other hand, time was abundant, and to add to it, an incredible amount of uncertainty. Every month, Tilak was allowed to write one letter home and to receive one from home or from close friends. The condition was that he would not write a word on politics or developments occurring on the outside, nor would any of the letters addressed to him contain anything on these subjects. He wrote a number of letters from the prison, either to his trusted nephew Dhondopant Vidwans or to his friend Dadasahab Khaparde, who was campaigning in London for Tilak's release. While the letters to Khaparde had a lot to do with his legal case, the ones to Vidwans brought out the family man as he had never emerged before.

Normally Tilak would have written to his kin in his native Marathi. From Mandalay, though, he wrote all his letters in English so that they would be cleared for shipping by the prison authorities after careful scrutiny and not kept back for translation and the translation's interpretation. His first letter to Vidwans went out on 1 January 1909. Tilak's wife Satyabhama suffered, just like him, from diabetes, and her health had been rather delicate for a while. Tilak asked the nephew to let him know how she was doing. 'Tell her that I am particularly anxious about her health,' he stated, adding that they should try the medicine of one Mr. Pade for her. He told Vidwans that he should let him know what the 'specific gravity of urine' in Satyabhama's case was, for it was a measure of the concentration of particles and the density of urine and a way to evaluate a patient's hydration levels and the functional ability of the kidneys. 'You can test it at home with the Urinometre we have,' he wrote.

Two of his sons were very young. About them, he asked Vidwans, 'How are Rambhau [then 14] and Bapu [the pet name for Sridhar, then 12]? I hope you have done all that I told you about their education. Take special care that they are not neglected on this behalf. This is just the time when both of them should be properly attended to.' He then inquired about his daughters 'Mathu and Durgi' and added that as 'Mr. Sane', one of his sons-in-law and youngest daughter Mathu's husband was in Berlin at the time, he 'should be kept informed about my health.' And there was a common message for the family but especially for the wife. 'Assure my wife and other members of the family that I am really doing well,' he wrote. 'I am more anxious about them than about myself. Let them be assured that after all I may not have to keep up the full period of the sentence awarded, even if the application to the Privy Council be not decided in my favour. You must try to give encouraging accounts to my wife, though she knows how to receive them. Nothing keeps up a man in distress so well as hope and so you must see that this is kept up in her. Give her my message and tell her that I do hope to see her and other members in sound health at not a distant date.'[13]

His queries on account of his wife's frail health and his children's well-being and education were almost relentless. In letter after letter, he asked his nephew to send Satyabhama's medical reports to him or to convey his gratitude to 'Dr. Garde'[14] for the care he took of her. He also put across his own views about her medicine in some detail, saying in one letter, for example, that it was 'better to try SAPTARINGI [a form of medicine]' for her 'in the old fashion, that is by preparing a decoction, like coffee, in hot water as suggested by Keshav Bakhle when he was last in Poona . . . When he tried the tincture last May it was not found as useful as was expected. So it seems that the drug contains some medicinal substances not soluble in alcohol. Consult Dr. Garde who knows everything about the tincture as it was prepared by him. The drug should be powered and then a *tola* or half a *tola* should be put in hold water and taken after a time without straining the liquid, so the whole may act on the system'.[15]

As summer approached, Tilak heard his wife was not doing too well despite the medicines she was taking. He thought it 'very likely' that her condition may worsen in April-May and wrote to Vidwans, 'Tell her that I wish her to go to Sinhagad with children at least for a fortnight. She suffered during the hot season last year and let her for my sake if not hers go to a cool station. Mr. Kavade (his sons' tutor) may go forth with the children so that their studies may not be interrupted . . . Tell my wife that I rather insist upon this for the sake of us all. I know the proposal may not be relished by her in my absence, but there is no help. It may do her some good as we know that (the) climate at Sinhagad always benefits diabetic patients. Her health is a matter of importance to us all. Let me know what is done in the matter.'[16]

Tilak was, at the same time, quite keen on finding out if Khaparde's efforts in the imperial capital were fructifying in any way. His initial letters to him are full of legalese and need not concern us, but Tilak was extremely conscious of the time, energy and costs his dear friend was spending on his case in a faraway country. He told Khaparde to telegraph directly to him about the admission of the appeal in the Privy Council and the final hearing. The telegraphic address, he stated, should be simple: Tilak, Jail Mandalay. 'You need not put "Central" before "Jail" as there is no other jail here. That will save you a word, which costs something like Rs. 3 per word.'

In March 1909, the Privy Council rejected Tilak's plea. Before that, Tilak had asked Khaparde to keep ready 'the second string to the bow', meaning a petition to the British Parliament', perhaps realizing that it may be necessary.[17] The signs of a possible rejection were all there, and the beginning was made by Rufus Issacs, who accepted Tilak's brief as a practising lawyer and took sixty pounds sterling from him as fees before suddenly and unexpectedly pulling out of the case and returning the money to Tilak's representative, Khaparde.[18] Later, Issacs came to India as viceroy in 1921 with the title 'Lord Reading'.

When the Privy Council dismissed his plea, Tilak wrote to Khaparde that 'the judicial door is thus finally closed against me'.[19] He had decided to file a petition in Parliament, but Tilak advised Khaparde not to stay for long in Britain and leave for India by putting the matter from then on 'in the hands of friends and sympathizers.' Tilak remarked, 'You may have done all that a friend can do for me, and you may now leave me to my fate and Providence. Six years is a long time, and many events may happen in the meanwhile, which may, who knows, favour us. But it is no use staying in England for the purpose . . . You have been out of India for nearly 7 months at a great sacrifice, and I cannot ask you to be away any longer.'[20] Clearly, Tilak had started feeling that any relief would be hard to get. In a letter to his nephew in the immediate aftermath of the Privy Council verdict, he said that 'though I am not without hope, I must, you know, be prepared for the worst'. His friends should and would, of course, 'always cherish a hope' that he'd be released 'when the atmosphere cools down', he said and added, thoughts of his wife uppermost in his mind, 'in the case of my wife at least do not destroy this hope, nay, stimulate it if possible'.[21] In his next despatch, he expressed the hope to Vidwans that he'd been 'interpreting' each one of the letters to Satyabhama and the children. 'Tell them to be cheerful,' he underlined. 'Of course the times are adverse to us, but the best way to meet adversity is to quietly submit, waiting for the better times.'[22]

The heat in April was terrible, and Tilak wrote to the nephew, 'I do not know how far I shall be able to stand it, but it will be long before I can get acclimatized to this climate if I do get acclimatized at all.'[23] He was thinking of writing to the Bombay government, asking to be relocated to the penal settlement on the Andaman islands as the weather there would perhaps be slightly more agreeable to him. The request was eventually made, and it was turned down. The cook, Kulkarni, later reminisced that 'a little upset at first,' Tilak then told him 'calmly' that 'it appears to be God's wish that I should die in prison'.[24]

Thoughts of dying were to occupy him even more as time went by, ever so slowly.

Some of his health issues, like a gum infection, might have sounded like small irritants, but medicine in the first decade of the twentieth century, including dental medicine, was far from what it is today. Tilak had suffered from the gum infection before his arrest, but it got much worse in Mandalay despite his recent recourse to 'Calvert's Carbolic tooth powder'. Puss came out of the gums near the upper canine tooth on the right side. He thought it was 'something like' scurvy, a disease that's caused by a bad shortage of Vitamin C and that, if left untreated, can lead to bleeding gums. The tooth powder was 'not enough to cure the disease', he wrote to Vidwans and said, 'Please ask Dr. Garde whether he can prescribe any homeopathic medicine(s) and let me know the names so that I shall try to procure them here through the (jail) superintendent . . . Let him prescribe alternative medicines, so that if one fails I shall take another.'[25] Two other issues he had were hydrocele and dyspepsia. These had persisted but had not yet caused him a great deal of trouble, and his diabetes too was under control, he said, with some relief and hope, in a letter of May 1909.[26] But all of these things needed careful watching, and the longer he stayed in jail, the more unsure Tilak became of what lay ahead.

Every three months, the authorities had decreed, a family member could visit him in Mandalay, and it was Vidwans who had started making the rounds to Mandalay to see him. (On a request, a close friend too could meet him every three months, and Tilak was keen that Khaparde come back so he could visit him in jail.) Early in July 1909, he told Vidwans that when he came to Mandalay next, he should bring along a document for a power of attorney Tilak wanted to grant him. 'It is necessary to have such a power of attorney as the chances of my release appear to be more and more distant,' he wrote with a sense of despair.[27]

The same month, July 1909, witnessed an outbreak of cholera in Mandalay prison. So Tilak, along with most other prisoners, was shifted for a while to a prison in Meiktila, which by train was five hours away to the south-east of Mandalay. Meiktila, Tilak wrote to Khaparde, was an Indian name, a Burmese corruption of the Sanskrit word Mithila, the capital city of Sita's father, King Janaka.[28] Importantly, Tilak drew up his will in Meiktila in his own handwriting. It demonstrated an attentive eye for details about personal money as well as any external funds he may have had with him at that point in time. He estimated the value of his home in Poona, the Gaikwad Wada, which he had purchased from the Baroda ruler for Rs 15,000 some years ago, to be Rs 20,000.[29] He wished to set up a Press Institute as a sort of umbrella organization of which both the *Kesari* and *Mahratta* would be a part.

He desired that a part of the Wada should be given to the Institute and set down instructions on how the affairs of the two papers were to be managed. (N.C. Kelkar was overseeing the *Mahratta*'s editorial part, and K.P. Khadilkar was in charge of the *Kesari* in his absence). Narayan Datar was *Kesari*'s agent in Bombay, and Tilak asked Vidwans 'to manage as best as you can' with him. 'Remember that he has suffered on our account,' he wrote to the nephew with some concern. He also asked the nephew to purchase a 'second hand double demy or double crown' printing machine for the *Mahratta*, saying it would not cost more than Rs 1500. The family had some property in the Konkan, and Tilak asked for one of his relatives, the headmaster of a local school, Sitaram Balkrishna Tilak, to assume charge of it at 'a nominal rent', with the rent agreement made in the name of Tilak's son 'Rambhau' (Ramchandra); Balkrishna, in turn, was told to pay Tilak's aunt, 'Ganga Kaku', regularly. From the 'press accounts', the main source of his income, Tilak wanted Rs 75 to be set aside for his sons every month until they turned twenty-five years old. 'Rs 75 per month for about 10 or 12 years more is certainly not heavy,' he maintained. Tilak ordered his shares in the Yavatmal ginning mill to be sold at their value at the time, which was Rs 7000. Before he left for Mandalay, Tilak had said that the defence fund which had been put together for his legal case should be discontinued. Now, only Rs 2000 from that fund remained in the kitty, and he made it clear that Khaparde ought to be able to manage the legal expenses 'within that sum and not exceed the amount', though he specified at the same time that Khaparde 'be provided with funds for maintaining himself in England till the end of the year 1909'.[30]

One of Tilak's longstanding ambitions was to erect a Chhatri at the memorial of Chhatrapati Shivaji Maharaj at Raigad. He had set up the Shivaji Memorial Fund for that purpose. One of the co-trustees of that fund was Daji Abaji Khare, Tilak's friend and lawyer. Tilak wrote to his nephew, 'Tell Mr. Dajisaheb Khare that my idea is not to make it (the Chhatri) very costly.' The total amount in the fund came to Rs 25,000, and the government was expected to contribute nearly Rs 5,000, so it would be Rs 30,000 in all. 'Of these,' advised Tilak, 'Rs 10,000 must be reserved as funded capital to defray the expenses of puja etc. every year. So the sum available for repairs and the Chhatri will be about Rs 20,000. The first estimate of the work should not therefore exceed Rs 16,000, leaving a margin of Rs 4,000 for excess which is sure to take place. You cannot erect a large architectural edifice with this sum. But a Chhatri like the one at Sinhagad, strong and durable if not showy, can be built at this cost. Let the engineer be told specially that we want a Chhatri that will last at least 200 years.'[31]

The people of Poona had, besides, set up another public fund, known as the Paisa Fund, with Tilak's backing, for the promotion of local industry. 'As I am in jail,' Tilak instructed, 'we cannot keep any balance of the Paisa Fund in our hand'.[32]

Outside of the will, Tilak appeared to be continually and deeply bothered about how his children's education was progressing. He had been noticing some small things for some time, and they were not comforting. Both 'Rambhau (Ramchandra) and Bapu (Shridhar)' . . . 'write a bad hand', he wrote disapprovingly in one of his early letters, 'and it is necessary to pay attention to their handwriting'. About their overall studies, his message to their teacher, a certain Mr Kavade, through his nephew was that 'I do not care much if the progress is slow. What is more important is to cultivate a habit of studying and THOROUGHNESS [Tilak upper-cased the letters] in whatever is taught to them.' In the same letter, Tilak voiced the desire that 'some arrangement should be made to teach English to Mathu (his daughter) up to the Matric standard.'[33] Towards the end of 1909, his other daughter Durga lost her child, though whether it was a case of miscarriage or the death occurred at the time of birth or later, we do not know. 'I am sorry for the loss of Durgi's child,' he wrote with fatherly sadness. 'But such accidents are, as you say, inevitable. If possible she may be brought to Poona for a month or so, and may return to [her in-laws in] Dapoli before May next.'

Early the following year, 1910, Tilak, at least in a limited way, tried to take the direct supervisory approach in relation to his boys, albeit long-distance. He had asked Vidwans to send some dhotis, sadras (white, loose cotton shirts) and shoes to him. Along with that 'I want also to see Rambhau's and Bapu's school progress books,' he said.[34] Evidently, they were not to his satisfaction at all, for in the very next letter he stated that both the boys should be told to 'work harder and keep up their rank in the class within the first ten. Their progress as far as I could see from their progress books was not bright. I expect better from them.'[35] The academic advancement that he expected could not be at the expense of their physical development, Tilak clarified. 'Let them have a small gymnasium – (a) perpendicular post and hand stands (hattis) and clubs jodis – set at home, and engage the services of the old N. E. S. (New English School) gymnasium master for an hour.'[36] In another letter, again demonstrating concern for their overall fitness, he remarked to the nephew, 'I hope you are taking good care of their physic (physique). This is just the time they should gain in height, weight and intelligence, and not singly.'[37]

What resonates in all of Tilak's letters is his tremendous and unshakable faith in his nephew, Dhondopant Vidwans. Vidwans, a young man at the time, was unmistakably Tilak's closest confidant in personal, familial and even in press management matters, just as Khaparde was in handling all his legal issues.

Perhaps the most remarkable piece of Tilak's correspondence in these six years of incarceration is his response to Khaparde's question about whether he would be willing to accept liberty if it were offered on certain conditions, mainly those related to the curbing of his political and public activities. Tilak replied to Khaparde in considerable detail to make his point of view abundantly transparent.

He said that any efforts for relief in his case must be made on three grounds specifically: legal, equity-based and humanitarian. The first one had been tried and hadn't succeeded. The second, the ground of equity, was all about securing trial by an Indian jury, just as Britishers in India were entitled to be tried by a British jury; in this regard, the work Khaparde was doing was just right, he observed and could proceed unhindered. The third ground related to the severity of the sentence, for 'six years for what at least is a dubious article . . . is a savage sentence'. Here again, an appeal definitely could be made, because he had been punished, he noted, 'for the offence of merely publishing certain honest views.'[38] Tilak then wrote:

And now I shall tell you my mind about the acceptance of any conditions. If the conditions are the same as those offered to me in 1898 (about not accepting any felicitations for his release or participating in celebrations or congratulatory functions related to his release) I would not hesitate to accept them. I do not care for demonstrations and such other honours. I would gladly forego them. But once out of jail I must have the same liberty of action as every citizen enjoys, under the law of the land. That was secured to me by the conditions of 1898, and I accepted them in consequence. But I do not think the same conditions would be offered now. They will if offered at all, be harsher now; and I do not see how I can accept them.

I have now nearly completed one year of my punishment, and after five years more I shall be, at any rate, hope to be, amongst you as (a) FREE CITIZEN. Do you think I should surrender the chance, distant as it is, by voluntarily incapacitating me (by the acceptance of the conditions) for any public or political work forever? I am now already 53 years, that is, I shall have completed my 53rd year in July next. If heredity and average of health be any indication of the longevity of a man, I do not hope to live, at best, for more than 10 years more. Of these, 5, say, available for unrestrained public work which, if I accept any conditions of the kind you mention, I shall have to live as a dead man, practically amongst you hereafter. To say the least I do not like that kind of life. It is true that my activity is not confined to politics, and I can do some literary work even if I be prohibited from taking part in politics. I have considered this view fully, and have come to the conclusion that it is inconsistent with all my antecedents. In fact I should be undoing my life's work thereby.

You know I have never lived exclusively for my family (or) for myself alone, but have always endeavoured to do my duty to the public. Now judge what would be the moral effect of my effacing myself from public life, for the sake of (a) few years' personal comfort? In the family matters the most important is the superintendence of the education of my sons; but I think I can leave that to friends like yourself during my imprisonment. I lost my parents (both) at fifteen, and my sons won't be worse in this respect than myself. From these remarks you might think that I might accept a condition imposing restriction(s) on my public activity for a short time, say six months or a year after my release. But I shall rather like to be in the jail for that period than be out a disabled man . . .

So all that I should wish you to do is to exhaust the three methods or the means of securing my release as stated in the opening part of this letter. If the release cannot be secured by any of these means the matter must be dropped. I do not wish for release AT ANY COST, and would pray you not to allow your friendly feeling for me to carry the matter further . . .

I forgot to mention above that while working on the lines mentioned above, the matter may be kept alive by questions in Parliament as suggested by you in one of our letters. If the question is kept up persistently before the eyes of government and the public in this way, it is bound to produce results sooner or later, beneficial to the general cause, if not to myself personally.

Please treat this letter as PRIVATE. With kind regards to your good self and expecting to meet shortly.

I remain,

Yours very sincerely,

BAL GANGADHAR TILAK[39]

This must easily count as one of the most fascinating documents of the Indian freedom movement. As a statement of intent, it was clear-cut and firm; as an example of dogged steadfastness, it was exceptionally strong, and as a declaration of an uncompromising commitment to the ultimate goal of political deliverance, it was fantastically insightful. Tilak had shone in the glare of his indictment in the high court. Now he was further extending his poise and presence as the Indian people's noble defender of liberties.

In the postscript to the letter, Tilak asked Khaparde if he could procure for him, from a second-hand bookseller in the British capital, four volumes of the French philosopher Auguste Comte's Positive Polity and clarified that the word in the title was polity, 'not philosophy'. A publisher in Bombay had told Tilak that the book, 'published by Messrs Longman and Co.', was out of print, but he might be able to get it abroad. 'If you consult Mr. Swinny, the editor of the Positivist Review, who knows me, he will help you in procuring four volumes second hand,' he informed Khaparde.[40]

Tilak was not given any newspapers to read in jail, and periodicals too were banned. Books he could have, but they would undergo close scrutiny from prison authorities before they were handed over. Tilak wrote early on to Vidwans that if he sent across books which had their titles purely in Marathi or Devanagari, they would either not be given to him at all or given only after someone who knew the language had translated the title and the jail superintendent had deemed it to be altogether harmless. And in Burma, it was rather difficult to find people who understood Marathi or Sanskrit and could translate from those languages. Thus, for Marathi and Sanskrit books too, Vidwans must make sure the titles were clearly mentioned in English, Tilak said.

Similarly, whenever Tilak asked the jail officials for paper to do any writing, he was invariably given whole notebooks, with the total number of pages mentioned on the cover, so that if any pages went missing presumably because the prisoner wanted to send any secret messages out, the discovery would be swift and easy. Individual sheets of paper were given to him only to write letters, and their numbers were counted before they were handed over. He was not given any ink to write with, only lead pencils, which were sharpened in advance.[41] Contents of all the letters were checked, and if anything even remotely objectionable according to the authorities was found or if a word or line was considered 'improper', it was either totally blanked out by ink or Tilak was told to write the entire letter all over again, leaving out the censored part.

Nevertheless, Tilak had decided to make some good and productive use of the time available to him. Tilak's letters from Mandalay are filled with names and often entire lists of books, either in the postscript or in the main body, which he wants to be delivered to him. We have seen how, in jail, he demonstrated both vulnerability and resolve. In contrast with the vulnerability and in keeping with the resolve, there was equally an approach to doing the reading and writing that he had always wanted to do and that paucity of time and the frenetic nature of public work hadn't ever given him room for. The total number of books he demanded over six years was in excess of 320. One such list in the postscript to a letter went like this:

1. Brahmasutras (Anandashram edition) in two volumes
2. Bhagavad Gita with Shankara's Bhashya or commentary, One Volume (Anandashram edition)
3. Upanishads – text and translation – all volumes hitherto published by Mr. Mahadev Shastri, B.A. Curator, Palace Library, Mysore
4. (Ernst) Haeckel's Monism
5. (Thomas) Hobbes' Leviathan
   (both 'from Ramchandra Govind & Co.')

6. Sankhya Sutras and Sankhya Karika ('From Jinsiwale's library. I think both have title pages in English')[42]

Tilak had for a long time planned to write a commentary of his own on the Bhagavad Gita, one of Hinduism's sacred texts. In one or two of his public talks previously, he had made a brief and suggestive mention of how almost all those who discussed the Gita spoke of action and renunciation as two opposite poles and how his own study of the Gita thus far had led him to think that it was fundamentally a call to action. These talks were just throat-clearing exercises, where he appeared to give simply an outline and to think, as it were, loudly for himself. He had to look far more profoundly at where his thoughts and reading of the text were ultimately leading him, and he wished to approach the question with an open mind, where his tentative, early and mental sketching-out exercise did not quite determine his conclusion but kept it open to outright cancellation, change or revision. He also needed to look at what the other available texts were saying in this regard. So he determined in prison to examine the various existing commentaries on the subject, to compare the Gita simultaneously with other philosophical and ethical texts, including those from Western philosophy, and to then lay out his personal thesis.

It was altogether impossible to do any real serious writing in the summer months in Mandalay. However, in the winter of 1910, Tilak began writing his book in Marathi, and he completed it in four months, by early March 1911. On 2 March he wrote excitedly to his nephew, 'I have finished what I call the Gita Rahasya, an independent and original book investigating the purpose of (the) Gita and showing how our religious philosophy is applied therein to the solution of the ethical problem. For my view of (the) Gita is that it is a work on ethics – not utilitarian, nor intuitional – but transcendental, somewhat on the lines followed in Green's Prologomena to Ethics.' He had written fifteen chapters in all, and as an appendix, he was going to have a translation of the Gita. He had written over 800 pages; when printed with 'demo octavo (pica type)' technology, the main text, without the appendix, he estimated, would 'fill about 300 or 350 pages'. While the book was based on the Brahma Sutras or Shankaracharya's commentary, the main English authorities for the thesis he was formulating were 'Kant's Critique of Pure Reason' and 'Green's Prologomena', he clarified.[43]

And what was the conclusion he had reached? In short, it was that 'the Gita advocates the performance of action in this world even after the actor has achieved the highest union with the Supreme Deity by Jnana (knowledge) or Bhakti (devotion). This action must be done to keep the world going by the right path of evolution which the Creator has destined the world to follow. In order that the action may not bind the actor, it must be done with the aim of helping His purpose, and without any Attachment to the coming result. This I hold is a lesson of the Gita. Jnana Yoga there is, yes. Bhakti Yoga there is, yes. Who says not? But they are both subservient to the Karma Yoga preached in the Gita. If the Gita was preached to (a) desponding Arjuna to make him ready for the fight – for the Action – how can it be said that the ultimate lesson of the great book is Bhakti or Jnana alone?'

He further said that he had no illusions that he was the first one to speak about Karma Yoga. So many others had done it. Yet it was 'especially true about a book like the Bhagawad Gita' that it 'must not be read devoid of its context', and where he differed 'from almost all commentators,' he pointed out, was in stating unambiguously that 'the Gita enjoins Action even after perfection in Jnana and Bhakti is attained and the Deity is reached through these mediums'.[44] Essentially what he was arguing was that the height of metaphysical contemplation, too, could not be perceived as an end in itself: you had to be very much of this world, in this world, and working for the world.

The book was published in 1915 after Tilak emerged from prison and sent it for printing after cross-checking certain references with some works he had not been able to access in Mandalay. Both Mahatma Gandhi and Aurobindo Ghose described it as a 'monumental' work.[45] Gandhi, who would himself interpret the message of the Gita as one of non-violence, said that Tilak's 'masterwork commentary . . . is unsurpassed and will remain so for a long time to come' and that 'nobody has yet carried on more elaborate research in the questions arising from the Gita and the Vedas'. Speaking on one occasion after Tilak's death, Gandhi referred to the Lokmanya's 'encyclopaedic learning and study' and said that 'his commentary on the Gita will be a more lasting monument to his memory', something which would 'survive even the successful termination of the struggle for Swarajya . . . No one in his lifetime, nor even now, could claim deeper and vaster knowledge of the Shastras than he possessed'.[46] Aurobindo thought that Tilak's book was 'no mere commentary, but an original criticism and presentation of ethical truths'. It took 'the scripture which is perhaps the strongest and most comprehensive production of Indian spirituality and justifies to that spirituality by its own authoritative ancient message – the sense of the importance of life, of action, of human existence, of man's labour for mankind'. This single book sufficiently proved, in Aurobindo's opinion, that 'had he devoted his energies in this direction, he might easily have filled a large place in the history of Marathi literature and in the history of ethical thought, so subtle and comprehensive in its thinking, so great the perfection and satisfying force of its style'.[47]

After finishing the Gita Rahasya, Tilak started work on another text about Vedic Chronology and the Vedang Jyotisha (it was a thin one compared to the previous volume, and he finished it before he left Mandalay). It was an 'enlarged, altered, corrected and developed' edition of one of his previous works, 'Orion,' incorporating 'all that has been said on the subject since 1800 A. D. up to date, that is, for the last 100 or 200 years'. He wished to be as unerring as possible in his estimation of the dates of the Vedas. The changes he had made were major, which was why he was giving it a new name, he said.[48] At the same time, he was working on a mathematical theory of his own on the fundamental principles of the 'infinitesimal calculus' and was trying to learn the German, French and Pali languages all by himself with the help of books ordered and obtained from his nephew.[49]

In the middle of these serious academic matters, real life abruptly intervened once again. He was totally distressed by news of his sons not doing well in their exams and told them that their family was not rich and all it had was education, so they had better focus on their studies and especially on their matriculation exam, which he said was a rather easy one for anyone who bothered to study for just a few hours every day. He gave detailed instructions in writing to their teacher, Mr Kavade, on how each of the subjects they were learning needed to be approached and what changes he must make to his teaching methods to make them far more effective.[50] Since Ramchandra's academic performance seemed poorer than Bapu's (Shridhar's), the anxious father, who had not too long ago spoken of the importance of physical exercise, said that in view of the boy's approaching exams, his physical exercise should be stopped completely 'till December or if he takes any, let it not be more than ten minutes'. Physical exercise, he added, 'interferes with the examination work seriously, even when you do not feel it. So stop it altogether or reduce it to a minimum'.[51]

Tilak had had an attack of influenza in Meiktila, but he had recovered properly soon thereafter. On the whole, his health had somehow kept up despite the increase in sugar levels. His weight too, by mid-1911, was not showing any major fluctuations; attacks of diarrhoea had stopped for at least the past six months; and the 'gum discharge' had been fortunately 'greatly checked by medicine'. He had a new complaint, nonetheless, of 'benumbed fingers', but he mentioned with a degree of hope that 'it is not serious as yet'.[52] About his wife and her chronic diabetes, though, he was extremely concerned. In April and May 1912, he wrote out detailed instructions for the diet she must follow, recommending 'soda bicarbonate' thrice a day, and 'milk and ghee plentifully, as one pound of barley flour is not sufficient to sustain strength'.[53] When he learnt that she wasn't taking any barley, he said he wouldn't insist on it, 'for a pure milk diet is better for diabetes'. But she must, he said, 'take almonds and ghee as much as she can and soda powders' as a 'mere milk diet (without any solids) is sure to increase the quantity of urine'.[54]

On 23 May 1912, Burma was hit by an earthquake. Tilak wrote to Vidwans on 4 June, 'A pagoda and church in the town suffered serious damage, and the jail compound wall, which is 20 ft high and about 4 ft wide at the base cracked from top to bottom in several places. However the houses inside the jail, being of wood, escaped undamaged.' According to Tilak, the shock lasted about two minutes, and he 'ran out of the barrack into the open compound'. Having described the temblor, he again broached the subject of how his wife absolutely had to take the 'soda powder . . . 2 or three times a week at least'. It would not cure diabetes, he maintained, but it could 'prevent the accumulation of acidity in the system, which causes coma or collapse in chronic diabetes. Therefore, whatever be the other medicine used, soda should always be taken'.[55]

Before his letter could reach Vidwans, Tilak got a telegram addressed to him from the nephew. His wife, Satyabhama, had died after going into a diabetic coma. It was all very sudden. Tilak was shocked and totally shaken. He wrote a reply immediately:

Central Jail, Mandalay
8th June 1912

My dear Dhondu,

Your wire was a very great and heavy blow. I am used to take my misfortunes calmly; but I confess that the present shook me considerably. According to the beliefs ingrained in us it is not undesirable that the wife should die before her husband. What grieved me most is my enforced absence from her side at this critical time. But this was to be, I always feared it, and it has at last happened. But I am not going to trouble you further with my sad thoughts. One chapter of my life is closed and I am afraid it won't be long before another will be.

Let her last rites be duly performed and her remains sent to Allahabad or Benaras or any other place she might have desired. Carry out literally all her last wishes, if you have not done so already. The task of looking after the physical and intellectual development of my sons falls on you now with greater responsibility; and I shall be still further grieved if I were to find it not properly attended to. I believe Mathu and Durgi (Tilak's daughters) are still there. They as well as Rambhau must have keenly felt the bereavement especially at a time when I am away. Console them in my name and see that Rambhau and Bapu do not get dejected. Let them remember that I was left an orphan when I was much younger than either of them. Misfortunes should brace us up for greater self-dependence. Both Rambhau and Bapu should therefore take a lesson from this bereavement and if they do that I am sure God will not forsake them. See that their time is not lost in useless grief. The inevitable must be faced boldly.

As regards her things and valuables make a list thereof, and keep them with you under lock and key till my release or till you next hear to the contrary from me, in the meanwhile. Above all face the situation courageously yourself, for there is no one else on whom the children can depend in this critical state. May God help you all, is all that I can wish and pray for from this distant place. With love to children and yourself.

I am yours affectionately,

BAL GANGADHAR TILAK[56]

Tilak also asked the nephew to visit him in Mandalay, 'if possible', in December of that year. If he would indeed visit, could he bring along all of the financial accounts with him, Tilak asked. Why did he want the updated accounts? 'I wish to make a fresh will,' he said.[57]

For his two young sons, Tilak composed a separate note:

It is a great misfortune that you have lost your mother at this time. But it relieves me a bit to know that you are not cowed down by the grief. But what I am most concerned now is about your education and progress. If you now fall behind you will ruin yourself for life. Although you have lost your mother and I am away in this distant place, it is not for you to dabble in home affairs or politics. All our domestic affairs will be duly arranged by Dhondu under my advice. Do not meddle in these things yourself. There will be other people to advise you in different way(s); but do not listen to them. Dhondu will see that you get everything you want; do not disobey him or find fault with his management. Nay, do not think of it. I will see to it myself. Your business now is to study zealously and to do that and nothing else. If anything goes wrong I shall set it right when I am released.[58]

Tilak told his nephew bluntly that 'the only thing' he now cared for was the boys' education.[59] And while he kept on giving, in letter after letter, guidelines and directions about teachers to be appointed, methods of teaching to be adopted, outside assistance to be sought of people like N.C. Kelkar to help with the children's studies, and about 'writing practice', which he prized above everything else in the matter of learning, whether it was English or simple arithmetic, he sent out around the same time a petition to the British monarch seeking an early release. Already on the verge of completing four years in Mandalay, it was as if Tilak, who was otherwise drafting and re-drafting his will from within the walls of the prison, was somehow steeling himself for surviving and living for the sake of his children and their advancement.[60]

His petition to the British monarch cited two things which had unfairly gone against him. King George V had held his durbar in Delhi in 1911, and he had offered clemency to a number of Indian prisoners on the occasion as a goodwill gesture for the Empire's subjects. There had been much talk then that Tilak would be among the prisoners released, for that would count as a really important gesture. But it had not happened. Tilak would later find out that it was George Clarke or Lord Sydenham, the governor of Bombay, who had scuttled the chances of his release at the time of the Delhi durbar.[61] Two of his previous convictions were cited as reasons for the rejection. These were technical reasons, Tilak said, and maintained that but for these, he ought to have ideally been released by this time. The second and automatically disabling factor in his case was the fact that the government had commuted his sentence from a rigorous one to simple imprisonment. The catch was that no prisoner undergoing simple imprisonment, which required no hard labour, was entitled to any sort of remission according to the jail rules.[62] Thus, according to rules, there was no way he could get any remission. It wasn't that he was saying here that the law had been wrongly applied; his argument was that the letter of the law had been followed, the letter which in itself was deeply flawed and made no sense whatever.[63]

Apart from the twin hurdles he had mentioned, there was a third one in Tilak's way. The petition to the monarch who ruled India could not be sent directly by an Indian politician, whatever his standing among the Indian people. Tilak had to send it to the secretary of state, in this case, and it was for the latter to place the plea before the King.[64] John Morley had by this time been succeeded as secretary of state by Robert Milnes, like his predecessor a Liberal politician. Milnes replied to Tilak tersely that he was 'unable to recommend' his release to the monarch. Tilak accurately interpreted the message, noting, 'This means that the Secretary of State has exercised his right of withholding the petition from presentation' to the King. 'There is now not the slightest chance of my early release,' he concluded, pessimistically.[65]

Khaparde's tremendous hard work in London too had not borne
any fruit. Soon after he had reached England in the wake of Tilak's
deportation to Mandalay, he had met Keir Hardie, the leader of the
Labour Party, and had provided him with all the details, including a
copy of the proceedings of Tilak's trial. Hardie wanted to take a
delegation to Morley to discuss Tilak's case, but Morley would not
permit any delegation to see him in this regard. He met Hardie alone,
and they had 'a long chat'. According to Khaparde, Hardie told him
that Morley had said Tilak's prosecution 'was the doing of' Bombay
governor George Clarke and 'if it was interfered with, he (Clarke)
might resign'. Hardie had said this 'in confidence' and 'wished it to
be kept secret', Khaparde wrote in his diary. But when he spoke to
Gokhale, he was told exactly the opposite—that it was Morley who
was not amenable to letting Tilak off. 'This is difficult to reconcile', a
puzzled Khaparde noted in his private diary.[66] A plea was then drafted
by Khaparde himself to Morley on Tilak's behalf, and a sympathetic
British politician, the radical anti-imperialist L.H. Courtney, went to
see Morley in that regard. But Courtney, according to the discussion
Khaparde had with him subsequently, came away 'disappointed' and
found that 'Lord Morley is determined to do nothing. In fact, he is
the father of the repression.'[67] Alerted to the Secretary of State's
open resistance, Khaparde and Tilak's legal advisors such as the
lawyer J.M. Parikh, the constitutional lawyer Wynne and solicitor and
Tilak's Privy Council appeal agent Edward Dalgado decided not
to send the draft to Morley at all and to write directly to the British
monarch instead. He, in turn, referred the matter to the India Office
and therefore to Morley, and the Secretary of State, as Tilak's friends
had feared already, declined to offer any relief.[68]

During his stay in the British capital, Tilak's aide Khaparde found
that he was being spied upon by agents keen to know what he was
up to and who all he was meeting as a representative of the sedition
case convict. Espionage activities picked up significantly after a young
Indian studying in London, Madan Lal Dhingra, shot dead the
Secretary of State's aide-de-camp, William Curzon-Wylie, on 1 July
1909. The alleged mastermind of that killing, V.D. Savarkar, who had
come to London following a recommendation letter from Tilak, was
caught and sentenced to fifty years in prison, unprecedented in terms

of the prison time given to the political revolutionary. Similarly, B.C. Pal and others who were at the time in the imperial capital began to be tailed, and Khaparde, who was staying at the lodgings of a certain Mrs Grave, heard from his hostess one morning that an English gentleman had come to her asking about 'an Indian gentleman living in the house'.[69] Another day, Khaparde was reading papers in the dining room when he heard a knock at the door and Mrs Grave responded to it. Seated in a dark corner, Khaparde wasn't visible to the visitor, who was a detective. Khaparde wrote that the sleuth asked Mrs Grave 'what I was doing, how I was spending my time, who came to see me and things of that kind'. The detective further 'wished to know if there was anything hidden or secret' about the Indian lodger. When Mrs Grave replied in the negative, the detective asked her to keep his conversation with her confidential and not to tell her guest anything about the inquiries he was making. He then left.[70] On a third occasion, Mrs Grave noticed that a man was watching her house from a little distance; he went away only after he realized that his movements had been spotted.[71]

With B.C. Pal, whom Khaparde was meeting quite regularly, the intrusions of the secret service were more direct. A Bengali student, Ashutosh Mitter, was staying at Pal's lodgings along with Pal's young son Niranjan. At the Waterloo railway station one day, Mitter was accosted by some detectives and asked to accompany them to a secluded place. There, according to the account which Khaparde said B.C. Pal had given him, they carried out searches on Mitter's person, 'against his will' and 'without any warrant.'[72] And B.C. Pal's own experience in dealing with secret agents was described by Khaparde as 'very peculiar,' a euphemism he used for an attempted honeytrap. One day, Khaparde saw at B.C. Pal's house a certain Miss Barr. 'She said she belonged to (the) Ramakrishna Paramahansa order,' Khaparde told his diary. 'It appears she called again and sat so long that Bipin Babu had to give her dinner and tea. He politely hinted at her returning to her lodgings but she sat on and ultimately requested that some small room may be given to her. Bipin Babu said there was no room available in the house. Miss (Eva) Willis (who worked for Pal) instinctively suspected the woman. This Miss Barr delayed going and at last Bipin Babu did not know what to do. She on her side seeing him alone, went and embraced him. This opened his eyes and he turned her out.' The Indians concluded she was 'a police spy'.[73]

After exactly two years in London, in September 1910, Khaparde chose to return home and continue any efforts to be made for Tilak's release from Indian soil. He kept up a steady correspondence with Keir Hardie and Ramsay MacDonald of the Labour Party and with the legal experts, apart from other English notables like the poet Wilfrid Scawen Blunt and Indian ones such as Tilak's friend Motilal Ghose. From what his correspondence and replies sent to him reveal, they all expressed a massive regard for Tilak and his role as the chief articulator of Indian political aspirations. In one of his letters, Motilal Ghose, then sixty-five years old, wrote to Khaparde with enormous feeling, 'My heart weeps for Tilak, and I hope I shall live till he comes back.'[74] Ghose told Khaparde that in England, Ramsay MacDonald had 'taken the lead' in lobbying with the British government for Tilak's release.[75] The poet Blunt, who was one of the most vociferous critics of imperialism, told him he had 'spoken to several people about Mr. Tilak' and had pushed Henry Cotton to the extent of getting Cotton to write to the Secretary of State for India. 'But,' he wrote to Khaparde, 'I do not suppose it will have much effect . . . The present government seems to surpass all previous governments in its rigours of repression.'[76] William Wedderburn also wrote to the Secretary of State for Tilak's release and received a reply that was 'not encouraging'.[77] Wedderburn openly bemoaned that for such a long period, 'India should lose the services of his (Tilak's) learning, abilities and influence.'[78] Keir Hardie, who petitioned the Secretary of State after the death of Tilak's wife, asking him to remit 'the remainder of Mr. Tilak's sentence,' received an unequivocal reply, stating, 'In passing sentence of six years' transportation, Sir Dinshaw Davar pointed out that the incriminating articles published in the *Kesari* distinctly spoke with approval of murder and the use of the bomb. The question of shortening Tilak's sentence has been under my consideration on several recent occasions; but having regard to all the circumstances, I see no sufficient grounds for mitigating the course of justice in his case.'[79] The lawyer Edward Dalgado was exasperated and voiced his shock at Tilak's continued incarceration. 'What is the reason for harassing Mr. Tilak? It passes my comprehension,' he said.[80]

On his return to India from London in October 1910, Khaparde as a matter of fact did not go straight home to Nagpur. He went to

Mandalay instead to meet Tilak. On 22 October he held two meetings with Tilak in the presence of the jail superintendent P.K. Tarapore, a Parsi: one in the morning and the second at 2 in the afternoon. They discussed matters of health, the appeal to be made to the Privy Council, and Tilak's wife and children. Tilak's wife was still alive in 1910; she would die two years later. Khaparde, however, had already lost someone very close to him while still in England fighting for Tilak's release: his mother. Tilak did not know of her death at all and told his friend how sorry he was to hear about it. Khaparde left the jail at 4 p.m., and subsequently he wrote that he embraced Tilak both in the morning and the afternoon. 'I resisted hard but eyes would get dim with tears,' wrote the truly devoted friend. Driving through the Mandalay fort, Khaparde also saw parts of the exiled king Thibaw's palace. 'That did not relieve our gloom,' he said.[81]

Interestingly, when Tilak was coming to terms with the fact that he wouldn't get to leave Mandalay until mid-1914, he received one day in the early part of 1913 a letter from an ordinary farmer from Yavatmal in Berar. The farmer's name was Vinayak Indapurkar. He was a *dhangar* or shepherd from a village called Kalamb, and he had sent a letter along with certain documents across to Tilak to seek his advice in a civil case he was fighting related to his land with a family relation. The case had already been through two lower courts, and the cultivator wished to make an appeal in the high court. Tilak replied to him, saying that since he was in prison, there was very little he could do for him without having any oral communication with him. That was important in legal matters. But the farmer, he suggested, could certainly seek the advice of his Amravati friend Khaparde. From the perusal of the papers, Tilak could see what was required for the farmer to do, though. He told him that from the papers it was clear that he had 'failed to give all the evidence required to establish his case in the first court.' Therefore, 'an attempt should be made to have the case sent back for inquiry and further taking of evidence if possible', he suggested, putting it plainly that 'on the evidence on record at present' he did not think the farmer would succeed. Further, he asked Vidwans to pass on his message to the cultivator 'without delay', because the papers had reached him quite late. The prison authorities had waited for three months to translate the farmer's letter from Marathi to English before handing it over to Tilak, and Tilak said 'I am afraid the time within which appeal is allowable is now too short if it has not expired already.'[82]

The solicitousness displayed by Tilak in the dhangar's case stands out because it is so much in contrast with what individuals and ordinary citizens have faced in a free India. In Independent India, several Indian political leaders have, over decades, often dismissed individual and innately personal cases of grievances as too minor and too micro to warrant their time and attention. Tilak was India's biggest political leader, yet he did not see the case of the individual cultivator against his own kin as too insignificant for him to offer his frank advice. Even otherwise, at his Poona residence, Tilak regularly offered suggestions and legal guidance to anyone who came seeking his help.

He did something similar for the cook, Kulkarni, as well. Kulkarni had been sentenced to five years in prison, but when he completed three years of his term, Tilak wrote representations to the Raj for his release and succeeded in getting two years of remission for him. 'I really did not want to leave him, but he pressed me to go home,' Kulkarni said later.[83] Kulkarni said he was particularly upset on his day of departure, but Tilak consoled him and also asked him to go to his residence in Poona. But how would Tilak's family even believe Kulkarni had come straight from Tilak's cell in Mandalay? When the cook expressed this doubt, Tilak gave him a tooth of his which had come out recently (Tilak lost almost five teeth in Mandalay) and asked him to give it to his nephew Dhondopant. Kulkarni did that on his return home and provided details about Tilak's life in jail to his family.[84]

In November 1913, Tilak started writing his book on Vedic Astrology, which would be in English unlike the Gita Rahasya, which was in Marathi. He would complete the book in just two or three months.[85] On 1 January 1914, he wrote to Vidwans, sounding obviously relieved, that 'the year of my release has at last dawned.' His focus understandably was his own health and that of his sons. A few months earlier, he had got some boils on his head. Those were 'diabetic boils,' but they had now disappeared, he said. But he lamented that 'the long time taken in curing is a fair index of the impoverishment of my health, by age and diabetes.' Tilak was fifty-two when he had entered the prison; in his year of release, he would turn fifty-eight. His body was already reacting very differently from the way it did just a few years ago, he told the nephew. 'The ebb of life has set in and it is only with great care and self-restraint in diet that I have been able to keep appearances of health,' he noted and cited an example. 'In the winter of 1910 I could and I did write my book on the Gita in four months, but in the last winter, I could finish only two chapters of Vedic Chronology. Not that the cold in 1913 was greater, but the body has become so much weaker that the cold which was once bracing has now become unbearable.' While Tilak was worried that his son 'Rambhau' was wearing eyeglasses when they were, in his view, not necessary, he was most upset that the other son, Shridhar or 'Bapu', had not restarted his workouts after his exams, even though Tilak had specifically told him to do so. 'It seems that he is trying to humbug me by sham excuses, and knows not that he is deceiving himself,' he communicated angrily to the nephew. He wanted the boy's main thrust to be on push-ups, squats and *malkhamb*. His distrust of British-origin sports came out powerfully in his message. Tennis and cricket were not sufficient to develop muscles, they were only 'good for ladies and gentlemen as recreations', he insisted, asking his son not to pursue those sports but to stick firmly to the exercise regimen he was recommending.[86] Usually the nephew, in his correspondence with the maternal uncle, would also put in what the two sons had to say about any points Tilak may have made, but in the letter from Vidwans that followed, there was no word from either of them. This led an extremely upset and restless father to comment, 'Rambhau and Bapu seem to be dejected by my remarks. But they forget that I criticize them harshly because I want them to improve and I want them to improve because I love them.'[87]

In April, Tilak started packing his books and other stuff. Their total number had come to about 400, and he sent them back home in several boxes in May. What of his manuscripts? The *Gita Rahasya* or 'The Secret of the Gita' in particular was the important one from the prison officials' and government's point of view. Unlike the books in his possession, it could not be sent straight back to Tilak's home, he was told. Officials of the Raj took possession of the manuscript from him. They needed to examine it and decide whether it could indeed be cleared for shipping. The Parsi jail superintendent, P.K. Tarapore, took this responsibility upon himself when the Bombay government made it clear that the manuscript must be looked at closely before being sent ahead. Tarapore did not know how to read Marathi himself, but he would get the work translated by an official translator and check it before giving his opinion.

Usually, according to the jail regulations, a prisoner facing transportation was taken back home two months before his date of release. So when the superintendent of Tilak's jail went up to his cell at 8 in the morning of 8 June and told him to collect all his belongings, Tilak had an inkling of what was going to happen. At one in the afternoon, he was put into a car and taken to the railway station. There, he was asked to board a mail train, inside which a compartment had been reserved for him and his uniformed minders from jail. Tilak had put on his red pagdi. It would not do. He was ordered to wear an ordinary cap until the train reached Rangoon. Every time a station approached, all the windows were pulled down so that no one could see who was inside the compartment. At a station close to Rangoon, the police team disembarked with their prisoner. There, the Rangoon police had been waiting for him from the evening before. They drove Tilak to the harbour and took him on board the military vessel 'Mayo'. Was the ship headed for Calcutta? Or Madras? Or would it go directly to Bombay? Tilak was not told a word about it. 'Neither did I care to make inquiries, as I was quite sure that I was on my way home,' he said later. When he climbed on board, he saw that policemen from Poona were already on the ship: 'police inspector Ring and sergeant Jones, who were European officers', and 'inspector Sadavarte, jamadar Maruti Rao and constable Date', all Indians. On making inquiries, Tilak found out that they had reached the harbour the day before but had not been permitted to step out.[88]

As it turned out, the ship was headed for Madras. To reach Madras from Rangoon, a ship took not more than four or five days. But the Raj had timed the ship's entry into the harbour in view of the fact that it had an important prisoner aboard. Its speed was purposely reduced despite the quietude of the sea waters, and it was allowed entry into the Madras harbour only on the eighth day. Two days were wasted in the waters, Tilak said, and 'except for the inspector, Sadavarte, the entire police party was down with sea-sickness'.[89] Tilak did not suffer from seasickness and had no problems.

In Madras, Tilak was put in a second-class railway compartment, which was attached to the back of the brake van of a mail train, and 'immediately all the doors and windows were shuttered'. Every time the train neared a station, the shutters were religiously pulled down again by the cops. Ordinarily, Tilak and the police team ought to have got off the train at the Poona railway station. Instead, the police ordered the train to be stopped at Hadapsar, a station nearly seven kilometres before Poona. Tilak was told they'd be getting off there, and the Poona district police superintendent was present to escort him home. The station master at Hadapsar, who wondered why the train had made an unscheduled stop at his station, asked Tilak for his ticket as soon as he had deboarded. Tilak pointed to the police officer who stood next to him, and the station master got the explanation necessary.

It was a little past midnight, and two cars had been kept ready outside the railway station. Tilak was put inside one of them and driven out. On the way, he suspected that he might be kept at Poona's Yerawada Jail for a month before being released and sent home, but when the car skipped the turn that vehicles invariably took for the Yerawada jail, all his doubts vanished, and he knew he was on his way home. The guard outside Tilak's residence, the Gaikwad Wada, was dozing on his *charpai*. When he heard the weighty chain at the outside gate make jarring sounds at an unearthly hour, he questioned with unconcealed irritation, without leaving his charpai, 'Who is it?' 'I am Balwantrao Tilak. Open the door,' came the reply. The guard could hardly be blamed if he got more irritated. How could it be Tilak? There was no notice of him coming home, and besides, why would he turn up from faraway Mandalay past midnight? Why did people play such pranks? But then a policeman's voice rang out, and the guard thought it must be a police party out to make a surprise search of the house. When he opened the gate, he was taken completely by surprise. The owner of the house had really turned up suddenly in the dark, entirely without warning. Yet, since there was a police squad accompanying Tilak, the guard wasn't sure if he should let him in. Perplexed, he went inside and woke up Tilak's nephew Dhondopant Vidwans. Vidwans could scarcely believe his eyes. As Tilak moved forward to step into the house, the deputy inspector–general of the CID, Mr Guider, under whose supervision he had reached home, informed him that the government had 'kindly and unconditionally' commuted the remaining part of his sentence and that he was now free. Tilak asked the deputy inspector-general to convey his thanks to the government. And entered his house after a long gap of six years.[90]

Poona was a sleepy city, and after midnight, the weak paraffin lamps along its streets served more to accentuate the dark than to relieve it. Still, somehow, and despite the police having kept it a well-guarded secret, news that Tilak had reached Gaikwad Wada spread almost immediately. It was 17 June, and the rainy season had begun. But one neighbour woke up another, and soon the whole town, as it were, was up. A stream of visitors walked towards Tilak for his 'darshan' after 1 a.m., and a few hundred had succeeded in seeing and meeting him, many of them even in touching his feet, by 4 a.m. It was only after that that he could go to sleep. But people would not let him sleep for long. As daylight enveloped the city, even bigger crowds turned up and took up all the space outside Gaikwad Wada, shouting cries of 'Tilak Maharaj Ki Jai!'[91] An eyewitness observed that the crowds poured in all day. 'The day grew dark and deepened into night, but the huge crowds . . . dwindled not at all, nor did their ardour diminish in the slightest.'[92]

'Sensation at Poona', screamed a headline the next morning in the *Bombay Chronicle*, a new English language paper that had taken to reporting things from an Indian point of view in the western island city. The news of Tilak's release 'has caused great excitement in the city of Poona where crowds of people are going to see him . . . Multitudes crowded into the street leading to his residence to have a glimpse at their old hero . . . and as he descended the stairs great shouts of 'Maharaj Tilak Ki Jai' and much clapping of hands greeted him,' the paper said, adding that 'it is extraordinary that in the rush to merely touch his feet and salaam that no casualty occurred.'[93]

With Tilak thus unable to get any rest at all, his friends decided to host a public reception for him. It was held on 23 June, and over 7000 people attended, garlanding him, doing their namaskars and shouting slogans in his support and support of Indian freedom. For a while the skies opened up, but no one moved and nobody left.[94] If the government had hoped that Tilak would be a man more or less erased from popular memory and the public imagination after such a long absence, those hopes, surely, had been dashed.

Briefly addressing the crowd, Tilak vowed to commit himself afresh to the Indian struggle for political emancipation. Taking a new guard, he said, 'When after six years' absence I returned home and began to renew my acquaintance with the world I found myself in the position of Rip Van Winkle. The authorities kept me in such rigorous seclusion that they seemed to want me to forget the world and be forgotten by it. I cannot tell you how happy I am to see that the people have not forgotten me. I can only assure you all that separation for six long years could not diminish my love for you and that I am ready and willing to serve you in the same manner, in the same relation and in the same capacity as I did before – although I may perhaps have to modify the course a little.'[95]

The declaration set off alarm bells in the colonial establishment all over again. And expectedly, it began to think up new measures with which to keep Tilak firmly in his place and to anticipate what modified course, as he himself had stated, he would take and to respond to it strongly enough in order to thwart his plans. Moreover, there was the additional matter of the manuscript Tilak had written in jail to put its mind to. Should the manuscript be allowed to be released to him at all, considering Tilak's credentials as writer-in-chief of sedition-filled sentiments?

The government had just about framed its initial responses to all of these questions when a major, world-altering event occurred. Both Tilak and the government would have to urgently fashion their reactions to it and orient their actions around it.

Chapter 14

Back Home: Congress,
Home Rule and the Lucknow Pact

A secret agent of the police was keenly watching the proceedings of the meeting held to welcome Tilak back home. The agent sought to dispel the impression that the local hero had been showered with garlands by his admirers. He observed that 'in reality only 12 garlands were actually given, the same garlands being presented several times on behalf of other donors'. With perspicacity, he reported that a clerk in the *Kesari* office 'was responsible for the deception'. He put the size of the crowd at 3000 and said it 'consisted of Brahmins, Marathas, Marwadis, Gujaratis, tailors etc'. Yet 'three-fourth(s) of the audience consisted of school and college boys', a point of botheration for the authorities, 'and there were even 100 ladies in the gallery of Tilak's residence'.[1]

The question for the Raj was: were people still in thrall to Tilak's agenda? The answer to it would tell the government what kind of effect his return to public life was likely to have on the ground and on the behaviour of ardent adherents of the anti-colonial movement.

The government had not at all been slow on the uptake. It had not waited until his release to make an appraisal of the situation. Like any self-respecting colonial administration, its senior officials had taken account of the possible fallout a couple of months before Tilak stepped out of prison. When Tilak had been busy packing his books in the Mandalay cell, the home secretary on behalf of the viceroy had written to the chief secretary of the Bombay government asking for an on-ground report, and the governor had quickly sent across the view that the movement led by Tilak's nationalist party was almost moribund and would take time to revive if revive it did.[2] There was no one on the spot who had been able to rally the party in Tilak's absence. Of course, the man himself was hardly likely to change his stripes, but things were going in the Raj's favour which it could press hard if he and his campaign for Swaraj were to be prevented from jumping back into serious reckoning.

What were these things? The Bombay chief secretary reported to the home secretary that Tilak had 'lost complete touch with developments and popular feeling of the past six years'. The political 'structure which took him 20 strenuous years to build has all but collapsed', and he is left without (a) his most powerful weapon the *Kesari* and the Extremist press, which took its cue from it, by the Press Act of 1910 and (b) the strong appeal of the Ganpati celebrations'.[3]

The Press Act was one of the worst pieces of colonial legislation brought in while Tilak was locked away in prison. It made it mandatory for the printer and publisher of any paper to deposit a security amount of up to Rs 5000 with the authorities. The amount would be forfeited if any 'seditious' or 'objectionable' content were published, and such content was so broadly defined that it brought within its ambit almost every kind of criticism of the government or its officials and even of the Indian princes. If a publication so much as asked people not to co-operate with any repressive measure of government aimed at stamping out revolutionary acts or any perceived threats, it could be acted against. Once security was forfeited, a fresh security of up to Rs 10,000 would be demanded. That in itself was a big enough sum in that age to shut any press. To make things impossible, the Act stated that if any further 'offence' were committed, not only the deposit but the press itself would be forfeited. Morley himself had confessed that the press legislation gave him 'the shivers', yet he was weak enough not to stand up to the pressure of Minto and others and, albeit reluctantly, approved of it, producing a chilling effect on the Indian press as a whole.[4]

The government had already obtained the maximum amount due as security (Rs 5000) from the *Kesari*. As *Kesari* was 'almost his (Tilak's) only financial stay, it is hardly likely that he will take any risks', the government believed.[5] From the *Mahratta*, which 'was never very rabid, chiefly, presumably because it is written in English and the chances of conviction are greater', it had got a security amount of Rs 1000.[6] As long as the Press Act was in force, it would 'deprive Tilak of his most powerful and dangerous weapon', the authorities stated confidently.[7] What the government did not mention was that both the *Kesari* and *Mahratta* had also suffered as the two men who had held charge in Tilak's absence, K.P. Khadilkar for the *Kesari* and N.C. Kelkar for the *Mahratta*, had had a bitter falling out which had resulted in Khadilkar's resignation, though he stayed on as one of Tilak's personal aides.

The Ganpati celebrations too had been 'brought under control' and were 'shorn of most of their objectionable features', the Bombay regime noted.[8] This was largely to do with the Seditious Meetings Act of 1907 which had placed excessive curbs on public gatherings, including social ones; some of its brutal measures had been withdrawn in 1911 but the Act itself was in force as a powerful deterrent.[9] Interest in the Shivaji festival too had 'practically died out', the government felt.[10] For it, an important consequence of the subdued festivals was that 'the secret societies which came into being as a result of the Ganpati and Shivaji celebrations have, on the surface, ceased to exist.'[11] 'Even when the celebrations were in their hey day', the government's confidential note attached to its letter stated, 'it was only Tilak's energy and powerful personality that aroused and riveted popular interest. While in prison in 1897 and during his inactivity the following year, in spite of the activity of his lieutenants S.M. Paranjpe and others, interest in the Shivaji and Ganpati celebrations began to wane and all but died out.'[12] In short, the government was saying: take Tilak out of the equation, and things fall apart for the assertive type of Indian nationalists.

Another factor that would hobble Tilak, the government assured itself, was his domestic worries, for it had information that 'his finances are believed to be in a perilous state'.[13]

With so much going against him, the government thought that 'to younger men (around Tilak) the situation might well appear to be hopeless and the possibilities are that Tilak will not be able to rehabilitate the Extremist movement to anywhere near the force which it commanded prior to his conviction'.[14] And although it acknowledged that it was 'impossible to forecast with any precision what Tilak's movements are likely to be on his release,' it said 'the most reliable information seems to indicate that (i) he will go to England to be present at the hearing by the Privy Council of the appeal in the Tai Maharaj Adoption Case'. Tilak had got an adverse verdict from the Bombay High Court in the case, and he had appealed to the Privy Council in London to clear his name. The other possibility according to the government was that 'he may go to Germany to continue the Sanskrit research projects (one relating to his commentary on the Bhagawad Gita and the other on the Vedic Chronology) he had undertaken in Mandalay jail'. Before proceeding to England or anywhere else, he could, the authorities surmised, stay in Poona for a few months 'to study the present political situation and review his own financial position'.[15]

For all the picture of confidence it painted, the very first action of the government after Tilak's release betrayed uncertainty. Barely five days after hordes had turned up at the function at Gaikwad Wada to welcome Tilak back, the Bombay government issued a confidential circular to all its departments directing them to warn people across categories not to associate themselves in any way with the just-released rebel.

The circular began by stating that as the release of Tilak was bound to 'make a considerable change in the political situation in the Presidency', the district magistrate and Bombay police commissioner 'should closely watch any developments that take place and keep government informed of any movement that may be promoted for expressing sympathy with him or promoting his propaganda'. It made the vigorous declaration that 'until Tilak shows by overt acts that he has altered his views and intends to modify his propaganda, he must be looked upon as an enemy of the British government, and people who associate themselves with him must be considered to be unfriendly.' Maintaining that the government had 'a right to expect' that persons 'who enjoy any favour' at their (government's) hands should not associate themselves with Tilak in any way', the circular called for 'special attention to be directed' at the 'jaghirdars, inamdars, watandars, title holders, government servants of all grades, government pensioners and teachers and persons employed or in connection with recognized educational institutions'. If anyone belonging to these groups paid a visit to Tilak, 'he should be warned, the attitude of government as explained in paragraph 2 above (where Tilak was termed an enemy of the Raj)' must be 'explained' and 'he should be informed that association with Tilak or repeated visits will be looked upon with grave dissatisfaction' and 'marked by such punishment as government may consider suitable'. Similarly, students of recognized educational institutions 'should not be allowed to associate themselves with Tilak in any way or to pay visits at his residence'.[16]

As a kind of pre-emptive action, the government set up two police chowkies on either side of Tilak's residence, where names of all visitors to his house would be recorded. An order was also issued prohibiting anyone from putting up pictures 'of persons convicted of sedition' in public places or 'garlanding' such ex-convicts or their kin in public.[17]

Such curbs were deemed necessary in view of the government's conviction that even if the odds were stacked against him, Tilak was likely to try and stir up trouble. Anticipating Tilak's likely conduct going forward, a team of bureaucrats led by government secretary Lawrence Robertson had remarked in a confidential note that:

> Tilak's hatred of British rule is a part of himself and his past character leaves little hope that he will allow himself to drop into political obscurity. Lt. Feunel who conducted him to Maiktila (prison) in 1909 (when there was an epidemic of cholera in Mandalay jail) stated that Tilak told him that the moment he was released, he would recommence his preaching and teaching against government, only he would be more careful in future in the choice of his words. He has a large hold on the popular imagination and provided his age and health have not deteriorated his initiative, it is possible he may be able to consolidate the nationalist position again.[18]

There was also the factor of his immense popularity to contend with. The reception he had got in Poona had shown his popularity had not diminished. And this factor went well beyond Poona. In Calcutta, for instance, a demonstration was held in the college square to celebrate his release, where national songs were sung and his portrait was displayed, garlanded and decorated. In an all-capital-letters strap given just beneath its headline for a report about the demonstration, the *Evening Standard* of London had quoted one of the speakers as saying, 'ENGLISHMEN TREMBLE AT THE NAME OF TILAK.' Another speaker had emphasized the people's dependence on Tilak's leadership, saying 'political life had been at a low ebb while Tilak was in prison, as was evident from the absence of the leaders, who, instead were busy organizing demonstrations for extending the viceroy's term of office.'[19]

Tilak, in fact, had to take stock of a lot of things. So much had happened in the six years that he had been away. Yet, barely had he surveyed the scene when the First World War broke out in August 1914, making an immediate reaction imperative. Apart from the war, in his reaction, Tilak referred to three important developments that had occurred while he'd been in Mandalay. One was the introduction of the Morley–Minto reforms of 1909, the other was the proliferation of and subsequent crackdown on revolutionary acts against the Raj, and the third was a series of articles written by Valentine Chirol, a correspondent of *The Times*, London, who had alleged that Tilak's had been the invisible guiding hand behind the recent violent attempts by Indian revolutionaries to overthrow British rule.

The Morley–Minto reforms, or what was officially termed as the Indian Councils Act of 1909, saw the expansion of the Central and provincial legislative councils with more representation for Indians on these bodies. The one significant advance was the appointment of an Indian, Satyendra Sinha, as law member (minister) of the Viceroy's Executive Council. The rest of the changes were mostly cosmetic in nature: membership of the Viceroy's Executive Council was up from twenty-five to sixty (apart from the eight ex-officio-members), and while twenty-seven of these members would for the first time be elected, thirty-six would be officials and five would be nominated non-officials, giving the unelected a clear majority. The electoral principle itself was not as sacrosanct as it was being made out to be, for the franchise was limited to property owners, tax-payers and special-interest groups such as the Anglo–Indians, municipal boards, commercial chambers and universities. And while members of both the Central and provincial Houses could discuss and vote on proposed law and budgets, their move, if considered unsuitable by the Raj, could be rejected by the viceroy and his bosses in London. Thus executive power remained effectively out of Indian hands. Most importantly, the reforms had introduced the principle of separate electorates for Muslims, a decision which would have serious ramifications for India's future. Among the earliest Indians to be elected to the Executive Council in 1910 as the reforms took effect were Tilak's rival Gokhale, Motilal Nehru, Surendranath Banerjea and Mohammed Ali Jinnah. Jinnah entered the Council as a Muslim member from Bombay though, at this moment in time, he believed the principle of separate electorates to be divisive and disastrous.[20]

Tilak had in a way declared, in his reply to the felicitation function held for him on 21 June, that he was inclined to take a wait-and-watch approach. 'Many people asked me what I would do next . . . It is necessary to see that the path one wants to tread is clear. There is a Vedic tradition, according to which a person walking through the street sprinkles a little water before stepping forward. I may have to purify my way in a similar manner,' he had said and added, 'It cannot be said today whether the path is sacred and, therefore, I am deliberately keeping silent.' At the outbreak of war, he published a statement in both the *Kesari* and the *Mahratta* spelling out in exact terms what he was saying. It raised plenty of eyebrows not only in government but among his own myriad followers because in it, Tilak declared his allegiance to the Raj.

At the outset, he remarked that his statement was intended 'to remove any possible misunderstanding as to my attitude towards government at this juncture'. Reiterating that he found himself 'very much in the position of Rip Van Winkle returning to his home', Tilak felt that since his emergence from his own time in the wilderness, he had had 'opportunities to fill up the gaps in my information as to what had occurred during my absence'. Notwithstanding negative steps like The Press Act, he said he had not given up 'hope of the country steadily making further progress in the realization of its cherished goal'. The Morley-Minto reforms, he noted, had shown that 'government is fully alive to the necessity of progressive change and desire(s) to associate the people more and more in the work of government'. This, he conceded, 'indicates a marked increase of confidence between the rulers and the ruled and a sustained endeavour to remove popular grievances'. From a public point of view, he thought 'this is a distinct gain; and though it may not be all unalloyed, I confidently hope that in the end the good arising out of the constitutional reforms will abide and prevail, and that which is objectionable will disappear. The view may appear optimistic to some; but it is an article of faith with me, and in my opinion such a belief alone can inspire us to work for the good of our country in co-operation with government'.

In the statement, Tilak made it a point to refer to Chirol's articles, which the British journalist had subsequently published in the form of a book. Chirol had attempted, he said, to interpret his actions and writings 'as a direct and indirect incitement to deeds of violence' or his speeches 'as uttered with the object of subverting British rule in India'. Such insinuations, Tilak said, were made 'at a time when I was not a free citizen to defend myself'. So he was taking 'the first public opportunity to indignantly repudiate these nasty and totally unfounded charges'.

Of course, he clarified, 'I have, like other political workers, my own difficulties with the government as regards certain measures, and to a certain extent even the system of internal administration. But it is absurd on that account to speak of my actions or my attitude as in any way hostile to His Majesty's government. That has never been my wish or my object. I may state once for all that we are trying in India, as the Irish Home Rulers have been doing in Ireland, for a reform of the system of administration and not for the overthrow of government.' About the series of violent actions taken by the revolutionaries, especially from 1908 onwards, Tilak said, 'I have no hesitation in saying that the acts of violence which have been committed in the different parts of India are not only repugnant to me, but have, in my opinion, only unfortunately retarded, to a great extent, the pace of our political progress. Whether looked at from an individual or from a public point of view they deserve, as I have said before on several occasions, to be equally condemned.'

Going further, Tilak observed that 'British rule is conferring inestimable benefit on India not only by its civilized methods of administration but also thereby bringing together the different nationalities and races of India, so that a united nation may grow out of it in course of time.'

He held the view that England had been 'compelled by the action of the German Emperor to take up arms in defence of a weaker State (Belgium), whose frontiers have been violated in defiance of several treaty obligations and of repeated promises of integrity'. Thus:

At such a crisis, it is, I firmly hold, the duty of every Indian, be he great or small, rich or poor, to support and assist His Majesty's government . . . It requires hardly any precedent to support such a course. But if one were needed I would refer to the proceedings of a

public meeting held by the citizens of Poona so far back as 1879-80
in regard to the complications of the Afghan war.[21]

Days later, in a speech delivered in Bombay, Tilak made it known
that though the Morley–Minto reforms had meant 'a further step' in
the path to progress, 'we want the pace at which we are proceeding
much more accelerated'. Many reforms requiring years of toil were still
necessary, 'but this is not the time to press for them'. And 'howsoever
wide be the gulf dividing us from the government in ordinary times, we
must now show that we support the government against the common
foe'. At any rate, he said, 'Nothing is farther from our minds than the
idea that the presence of either the Russian or the German rulers would
be beneficial to us.'[22]

Had the rebel finally been chastened? Had Tilak reversed his
earlier position and turned into a loyalist? For a man who consistently
advocated brave leaps towards Swaraj, why was he expressing satisfaction
with baby steps?

A British official, simply not willing to swallow Tilak's statement,
remarked that Tilak's 'mask was not so strong as to hide his real face'.
The official wrote Tilak claimed he had never supported violence, but
anyone who takes a careful look at his speeches before 1908 will be
convinced that he was all for use of violence. In short, what he was
saying was 'ask for Swaraj, and if you don't get it, obtain it by using
force'. He leaves the actual work of taking such actions to misguided
students. When these students commit dacoities or carry out killings he
pretends not to have anything to do with it and says he has never asked
anyone to use violent methods.'[23]

Yet the statement brought some immediate breather for the
released prisoner. The two police chowkies placed outside his house
were removed, and the noting down of names of all visitors was stopped,
enabling Tilak and those who wished to communicate with him to move
about and interact more freely. The circular terming him 'an enemy of
the British government', though, was not withdrawn; it remained in
place until his death six years later.

The British press in particular took prominent notice of Tilak's
declaration. The well-known journal *Truth*, founded by a Liberal
politician in 1877, wrote that Tilak's speech was 'a more remarkable

event in India than the offers of military support'. Tilak, its editor remarked, 'had just come out of prison, after serving I forget how many years for seditious writing. Almost the first use he made of his liberty was to exhort his countrymen to stand by England steadfastly in this time of peril. Such words, delivered spontaneously at such a moment, denote no small nobility of character as well as loyalty. It seems to me that we ought to have a better use for such a man than to imprison him for many years for speaking his mind too freely about what he considers wrong in our administrative methods'.[24] A commentator for another periodical, the *National Review*, said, 'I, for one, take back many severe things written and said about him during past years. It does not follow that in his case these things were in the least unfounded, but it does follow that the attitude they implied cannot be further maintained. The memory of the past must be blotted out, and Mr. Tilak must be recognized only as the brilliant author of "The Arctic Home of the Vedas" and the patriot who swept aside his own propaganda when confronted with a greater and more insistent call.'[25]

The more plausible explanation for Tilak's stance is that he had made up his mind to react, in a delicate moment for Britain, like a political realist. He sensed the gravity of the situation and reckoned that if the nationalist party acted defiant, the British government would bring the house down on it. Instead, if cooperation were extended in the war as Britain faced a ticking clock, there was the possibility of the Raj being compelled by that one act to lift some of the repressive measures and a likelihood of a softening of ties, which would enable him to regroup his forces, rethink his strategy and bide his time for the right moment to strike and to press India's demands. Veteran friends of India like William Wedderburn certainly thought Britain ought to carry out 'a bold act of statesmanship'. Wedderburn wrote, 'The disarming of the population, the rejection of Indians as volunteers, the withholding of commissions in the Army from Indians, the harsh press laws and laws against public meetings, the refusal to grant free and compulsory primary education [a proposal made by Gokhale during Tilak's years in prison] – all such galling race restrictions are evidence of official distrust, of disbelief in the loyalty of the masses. What is now wanted is a declaration by the highest authority of whole-hearted trust in the Indian people, and this declaration in words must be accompanied by corresponding deeds, by sweeping away the whole fabric of distrust and repression, which is alien to British sentiment and destructive of goodwill among all classes of the Indian people.'[26]

Wedderburn had identified the issues correctly. For, on his own, Tilak, after declaring his allegiance, had underlined the first of the points, seeking that Indians be given commissions in the forces. The refusal of the right to carry arms had been a sore point with Indians; they viewed it as an example of the deliberate weakening of their strength by a foreign ruling power and as a denial of the basic right of self-defence. In calling for re-arming by a grant of commissions, Tilak was echoing the views of an embittered population and especially of communities that prided themselves on their martial past and had therefore purposely been struck off the list of those who could bear arms or join the army. He was also saying Indians must not just be *sipahis* but officers.

To Indians who were wondering if Tilak had started sounding like Gokhale or had at least started mimicking Gokhale's loyalist tics, the *Bombay Chronicle* said no one who knew the career and character of Tilak 'would believe him capable, if he did not honestly think it the right advice to give, of urging every Indian to support the government with all the means in his power'.[27]

Ultimately, what was going to provide a window into Tilak's mind was the actions he would take following his announcement of support in the war. Naturally, his first act was to try and reunite the Congress. He still saw it as an indispensable tool and the only all-India organization capable of pulling its weight as far as the fight for liberation was concerned. He also believed that the fight between the Moderate and Extremist camps, if taken too far, would result in the dissipation of nationalist energies, energies which deserved to be better directed.

But how was the rapprochement of the groups and Tilak's re-entry into the Congress to be brought about? It was here that a foreigner, Annie Besant, came into the picture.

At the age of thirty-six, Annie Besant had in 1893 arrived in India from England to work as a member of the Theosophical Society in Madras. She had initially been a non-believer and a Socialist and had worked closely with the atheist Charles Bradlaugh, who was a supporter of the Indian national movement. Like Bradlaugh, Besant was not in favour of imperialism, but in her first decade in India, she restricted her work to the fields of religion, education and social reform, advocating the upholding of Hindu ideals, which Theosophy had always looked up to, and forming the Central Hindu College for boys in Benaras and some schools for girls. As a Westerner who saw enormous value in Hindu thought and philosophy, she wanted to create a new generation of Indians who were not divorced from their own culture and civilization. Her college would impart colonial education to its students along with the knowledge of classical Sanskrit texts, she resolved.

In 1907, she was chosen president of the Theosophical Society and gained further prominence. Slowly, she gravitated towards Indian politics and in 1913 plunged wholeheartedly into political work. The reasons for her shift were two-fold: a case brought against her by the father of Jiddu Krishnamurti, a boy she had adopted, had led to a loss of esteem for the Theosophists, and she wished to repair her own, and the Society's, reputation, by engaging more deeply with Indian society; and two, in 1912, the Irish Home Rule bill had been introduced in the British Parliament and it was on the verge of becoming legislation, and Besant, who was three-fourths Irish, thought similar autonomy for India intensely desirable. Her initial step was to form 'The Brothers of India', a group whose members had to vow they would work for 'spiritual, educational, social and political progress' under the direction of the Indian National Congress as 'India's best interest would be best served by freedom under the British Crown'.[28]

When Besant asked Congress leaders to take her outfit under their wing, Pherozeshah Mehta and Dadabhai Naoroji demurred, saying Congress had long ago 'foresworn interference in religious, social and educational activities'.[29] The main problem, of course, as they saw it, was religion, whereas Besant believed India had a lot to teach the world in terms of faith and build a society based on its religious richness. But Besant was unfazed and joined the Congress nevertheless. In January 1914, she launched a weekly, *Commonweal*, to promote Indian freedom, and later that same year, bought a local daily, *Madras Standard*, and converted it into *New India*, a paper with as much a national title as a national character. In its first issue, the paper announced India should abandon the pursuit of piecemeal reform and aim for Home Rule instead so that it could be a 'self-governing community in the great Federated Empire'.[30]

Besant went to England in the spring of 1914. Gokhale was there, and the two had several conversations. Gokhale had had a disappointing few years immediately after Tilak's arrest. He had placed much faith in the Morley–Minto reforms and had, instead of opposing the Press Act, enabled its passage by abstaining from voting on it as a member of the Imperial Council. After the Act proved draconian, he tried to dissociate himself from it, but the damage was done. His bill on elementary education too was thrown out by the Viceroy's Legislative Council. He also did not see the communal rift between the Hindus and Muslims healing. When his friend, the poet Sarojini Naidu, voiced the hope that there would be communal harmony in five years, Gokhale told her, 'Child, you are a poet, but you hope too much. It will not come in your life-time or in mine.'[31] By 1912, though, Gokhale was again seeing a tinge of hope in the reforms as he was appointed by the Raj to the Royal Commission set up to study and submit a report on public services in India.

He saw much more hope in a Gujarati lawyer, Mohandas Karamchand Gandhi, fighting for the rights of Indians in South Africa. They had first met in 1896 when the young Gandhi had come to India as a representative of the Natal Congress to secure the support of the Indian National Congress for his struggle. From then on, the two men had written regularly to each other, and at the Lahore Congress in 1909, Gokhale had heaped praise on Gandhi, saying the latter was an Indian whose name could never again be taken in public 'without deep emotion and pride' and exulting that 'a purer, a nobler, a braver and a more exalted spirit has never moved on this earth'.[32] Gandhi called Gokhale his 'guru', and he had been urging the Chitpavan Maharashtrian for long to visit South Africa. In 1912, when Gokhale was in England for the public services commission's work, he decided to stop over in South Africa before going back home. The guru and his disciple met in October 1912 after a long gap, and Gokhale told Gandhi, 'You must return to India in a year.' Gokhale's health had deteriorated a great deal, and he wanted the Gujarati to succeed him as leader of the Congress, albeit, as the US scholar Stanley Wolpert wrote, 'In his emphasis on the use of Indian languages, as in his stress on the multiple boycott, Gandhi was indeed more of a disciple of Tilak and his party's platform than of Gokhale's.'[33]

Gokhale had also realized Gandhi was a mass mobilizer, the kind of leader in the Tilak mould that the Moderates lacked. Besides, over the years, Gokhale had come to believe that the Congress should be reunited and 'an early opportunity' taken 'to heal the breach in public life that had resulted from the split of 1907'.[34] There was no discounting the pragmatic aspect of his desire. The Congress had lost almost all of its vitality ever since the Extremists had exited in 1907. Its annual sessions from 1908 to 1910 were insipid and uninspiring, and in 1911, the *Modern Review* wrote of that year's annual session in Calcutta that there were 'long rows of empty benches in the visitors' gallery'.[35] The next year things got worse, with only 207 delegates attending, nearly 100 of them from Bihar and Bengal alone, and just nine from the Bombay Presidency, including three from Gokhale's Servants of India Society.[36]

With Tilak back and declaring loyalty to the Empire, Gokhale, on his return to India from England in November 1914, felt that the 'early opportunity' he was talking about could now be taken. Encouragingly for him, Besant too was back in India and was declaring her desire to take the initiative for reunification.

On 15 November, Besant wrote to Gokhale, 'Mr. Tilak has formally declared for self-government within the Empire, and has abandoned – he says he never advocated – separation [complete independence]. His followers evidently wish for, and his paper advocates, reunion.'[37] Motilal Ghose too implored Gokhale, writing to him the same day, 'My heart weeps for the motherland . . . I am anxious that you & Tilak should shake hands & embrace each other as brothers . . . I know you bear no malice or ill-will to him . . . Even if you have any cause for offence, you are generous enough to forgive & forget . . . As you are in a more favourable position, it would be a graceful act for you to [make an] advance. If he rejects, the people will blame him & bless you. But I believe he will appreciate your motive . . . The so-called Bengali leaders are now fossils. It is Mahratta intellect and patriotism which must save the country. If you and Tilak make up . . . there is yet hope for India.'[38]

Besant met Tilak at his Poona home on 6 December for the reconciliation talks. Accompanying her was N. Subba Rao Pantalu, who was to be general secretary for the Congress to be held in Madras the following month. 'The result' of the meeting, Tilak wrote to his friend Khaparde, 'was disappointing. We all saw that Sir Ph. Mehta was the chief difficulty in our way. Mrs. Besant thinks that if she approaches Mehta the cause may be spoilt and so Subbarao has gone to Bombay. But I am sure that Mr. Mehta would dispose him off in a few minutes.'[39]

What was the difficulty Mehta was going to pose, according to Tilak? On the face of it, the matter was largely technical. After the Extremists had been ousted from Congress, the Moderate section had modified the party's constitution to ensure no member of Tilak's party could sneak in. Before the Surat split, delegates to Congress's annual sessions could be elected at public meetings. In 1908, the Moderates-only Congress at Allahabad mandated that only members of existing Congress committees—and the existing ones now were only of the Moderates—or of groups affiliated to these committees could be picked as delegates. Gokhale had tried to open the door a wee bit in 1911, suggesting delegates be elected by all public bodies that accepted the Congress creed and methods or by public meetings held under the aegis of these bodies. The subjects committee had quickly endorsed the proposal, but Bombay Congress leaders such as Wacha had shot it down, and Gokhale had refrained from introducing the resolution at the main plenary session. The next winter, when Gokhale was in England, the proposal was ostensibly accepted but the truth was that it was so mauled as to restore the status quo: delegations could be chosen at public meetings, but only those meetings held under the auspices of the existing Congress (Moderate-controlled) committees.[40] Both Tilak and Gokhale believed that if they spoke, some compromise could be worked out. But Mehta was unbending. And importantly, though it all appeared a matter of rules and procedure, the reunification talks ultimately broke down on the issue of methods to be adopted by the Congress.

Besant and Subba Rao had two long meetings with Tilak early in December.[41] There was no time to be wasted. The Congress session was to be held in the last week of the month, and if the Extremists were to be brought into the organization's fold again during the session, any truce had to be worked out as soon as possible.

Subba Rao, however, concluded after a third, solo, meeting with the Extremist leader that 'it is impossible to have a compromise with Mr.

Tilak. He has made it clear that if he and his following come into the Congress again, it means a revival of the old struggle'. What exactly did that mean? Subba Rao wrote to Gokhale:

> In Mr. Tilak's opinion, the present programme of the Congress was of no value. 'They were asking for small reforms,' Tilak said. 'Mr. Gokhale had given two years of his time to the work of the Royal Commission, and the only result of it would possibly be a few more places for our people in the Civil Service.' Mr. Tilak would ask his countrymen to have nothing to do with these. He would make only one demand, namely that for self-government within the Empire.[42]

Gokhale wrote to Bhupendranath Basu, who was to preside over the Madras Congress session, that he was 'shaken' by Tilak's statement of his position to Subba Rao. He further said:

> Mr. Tilak has told Mr. Subba Rao frankly and in unequivocal terms that though he accepts the position laid down in what is known as the Congress creed, viz. that the aim of the Congress is the attainment of self-government within the Empire by constitutional means, he does not believe in the present methods of the Congress which rest on association with government where possible, and opposition to it where necessary. In place of these he wants to substitute the method of opposition to government, pure and simple, within constitutional limits – in other words a policy of Irish obstruction.
>
> We on our side are agitating for a larger and larger share in the government of the country – in the Legislative Councils, on Municipal and Local Boards, in public services and so forth. Mr. Tilak wants to address only one demand to the government here and to the British public in England, viz. for the concession of self-government to India, and till that is conceded, he would urge his countrymen to have nothing to do with either the public services or Legislative Councils and Local and Municipal Boards. And by organizing obstruction to government in every possible direction within the limits of the laws of the land, he hopes to be able to bring the administration to a standstill, and to compel the authorities to capitulate . . .

He has explicitly told Mr. Subba Rao that he gives us fair warning that this is his purpose in seeking re-admission into the Congress fold, and that once he is inside, he will strive first for effecting such changes in the rules as will throw open election of delegates practically to everybody as before 1907 and then for getting the Congress to endorse his programme by securing at its sessions the attendance of a majority of delegates of his way of thinking.[43]

Tilak, on hearing of Gokhale's letter to Basu, wrote to 'my dear Gopalrao' and disputed some of Subba Rao's statements, especially about 'boycott of government' and 'obstructionist methods'. Gokhale replied he had mentioned 'Irish obstruction' but not 'boycott of government'.[44]

Gokhale's immediate response to Tilak's approach was to tell Basu that the question of a compromise must be postponed for another year, and talks could restart at that time if Tilak gave definite assurances.[45]

Soon enough, Gokhale got an opportunity to hear Tilak's views himself at the last ever meeting that took place between them at Tilak's residence, Gaikwad Wada, on 19 December 1914. Gokhale was too weak to climb the stairs, so the two met on the ground floor. According to Gokhale, Tilak 'practically confirmed' what he had said to Subba Rao 'in his conversation with me'. Therefore, Gokhale wrote in a letter to Basu, he had told Tilak 'frankly' that 'it was impossible for me to support the idea of a compromise any more, and that with the views and intentions he entertained, it was best from the standpoint of the interests of the Congress that he should remain outside the body'.[46]

After the meeting, Tilak on climbing up the stairs met his aide Khadilkar. When Khadilkar asked him what Gokhale had said, Tilak answered, 'He says I should not enter the Congress, as I will not agree with the present Congress constitution and with those in the Congress at present.' And what had Tilak replied, the aide asked. Tilak said, 'I told him clearly that the Congress belongs to all. It is not given as a gift to any party. I shall first prepare the country, enter the Congress and capture it.'[47]

In an article soon thereafter in *Kesari*, Tilak laid the blame for failure of the negotiations at the door of the Moderates, especially those from Bombay such as Mehta and Wacha, who, he noted, were opposed to any compromise.[48] In another piece, he directly blamed Gokhale, maintaining that his letter to Basu had wrecked the talks. Referring to the point made by some critics that Gokhale had shown readiness for a truce thinking Tilak had changed his opinions after being shut away in prison, Tilak wrote indignantly, 'These fools [who raised this point] haven't understood that prison can never be a reason for a person to change his views, formed scientifically after full thought.'[49]

Remarking that it was futile to fuel the controversy any further, Tilak remarked that both he and Gokhale didn't have long to live. Tilak had been mentioning his intimations of mortality for a while now, and even when the reunification talks began, Tilak said he had at the most one year to live. Using a Marathi metaphor to indicate he and Gokhale were as good as already on their cremation grounds, Tilak wrote, 'It is no use saying that when Tilak enters the Congress he will capture it. The Congress is national. It does not belong to Tilak or even to Gokhale. It is not any one person who will decide the policy of the Congress. The Congress will decide it as a whole. Therefore every person in the Congress has the right to place his views before it and to get them accepted by the majority. So long as these views are lawful and constitutional, no matter who places them before the Congress and gets them accepted after discussion, he should not be branded as a terrible person out to capture the Congress.' He advised that the Moderates shouldn't pull down others if they couldn't get their own house in order.[50]

Annie Besant was sorely disappointed. She remarked that Tilak's statement to Subba Rao had 'very naturally alarmed some of the Congress leaders, among them Mr. Gokhale, as it opened up an indefinite vista of conflicts'. Urging Tilak in a public statement to make clear what his 'methods' were going to be, she stated, 'If I have been mistaken in my belief that the difference of methods is merely the introduction of a little added vigour and insistence, and not a demand for a fundamental change, then I must regretfully give up any further effort to bring about a union which would not invigorate but would destroy the Congress.' She said it was Tilak's statement of August on his willingness to cooperate with the government which had encouraged her to work for a reunion. 'I am not, therefore, without hope that others may succeed, where I have failed.'[51]

By early 1915, Gokhale was almost bedridden. His health had not been keeping up for years, and now it had taken a bad turn for the worse. He was also caught in the middle, in a sense. On the one hand were Mehta and Wacha, who could barely stand Tilak's audacity. While Gokhale had been working on a truce, Mehta had written to Bhupendranath Basu impatiently and almost contemptuously, 'Let us have done with all inane and slobbery whine about unity where there is really none.'[52] On the other, there was his own inner desire to make peace with and work alongside his fellow Chitpavan, for Gokhale knew Tilak's potential to carry the people's sentiment. Gokhale, though, felt forever beholden to Mehta and company and never stood up to them even if he felt differently or had ideas—such as the 1911 one of making a tweak in the rules to get the Extremists back into the Congress fold—which could be taken forward to achieve positive solutions. He chose to kill his ideas rather than take a stand different from that of Mehta and Wacha, whom he saw as his benefactors.

Gokhale felt aggrieved by the comments made by Tilak in the *Kesari* after their talks fell through. He wrote a letter to Besant recounting his battles with Tilak, stating that 'you say if Tilak tries to give trouble again, we should fight and put him down. But it is not an easy fight – certainly not one to be lightly entered on again'. He admitted that 'the parties are not evenly matched. There is naturally a good volume of anti-foreign feeling – expressed and unexpressed – in the country and it loads the scales heavily on Tilak's side'. Gokhale's own view was that 'we have to ask our own countrymen to be reconciled to foreign domination – even though it be as a transitional arrangement – and our propaganda has to rest on one of its sides on some measure of faith in the sense of justice of British democracy'. But, he noted, 'Tilak has no difficulty in ridiculing the latter as "mendicancy", and denouncing the former as pusillanimous and unpatriotic cringing to the authorities. The number of men who can form a sound political judgement in the country is not large. But you can find any number of unthinking men filled with an honest but vague feeling for the emancipation of the country, ready to follow any plausible leader, whom in their heart of hearts they believe to be wholly against the foreigner.'

Gokhale complained that 'it was with the help of such a following that Tilak captured the Poona Sarvajanik Sabha, the work of Ranade's hands, and destroyed its usefulness in less than twelve months'. What he was referring to was the ban on the Sarvajanik Sabha imposed by the government, allegedly owing to its excesses. 'It was with the help of such a following,' Gokhale continued, 'that he nearly wrecked the Congress at Poona in 1895. And finally it was with the help of such a following that he actually wrecked the Congress at Surat in 1907.'

Besant undoubtedly had raised the issue of why the Moderates were unwilling at least to let Tilak's followers in, and Tilak himself had spoken of how he and his followers were being systematically blocked. Justifying their exclusion, Gokhale wrote, 'Who has ever said that democratic methods can at once be applied today in this ancient land, caste-ridden and priest-ridden for long long centuries? You ask why we should keep the door closed against a large number of men who are not likely to give trouble for the sake of one man who may give trouble? But you cannot ignore the fact that this one man is their foremost leader.'[53]

In the end, Besant told Gokhale not to bother too much. 'You must guard your body for future work, and your life is a thousand times more important than Tilak's presence in, or absence from, the Congress,' she said. Gokhale, in turn, apologized to Besant for writing so extensively to her about Tilak. 'As I said to you personally here the other day, I have no wish to treat Tilak ungenerously. In fact, it goes greatly against my grain to take the line I am often forced to take. But by my bitter experience ranging over nearly 30 years now, I have learnt that not generosity but caution has to be the keynote of our dealings with him.'[54]

Both Gokhale and Besant were convinced that Tilak hadn't, and would not, change his stripes, and Gokhale was clearly conflicted in his reactions to him—at once affirming his fairness towards Tilak and then preferring caution over generosity. The old rivalry was alive and flourishing in the hearts of both the Chitpavans.

On 9 January 1915, Gandhi returned to India. He had left South Africa in July the previous year for England with his wife Kasturba and German friend Hermann Kallenbach and had persuaded Kallenbach, during their sea voyage, to throw his binoculars worth seven pounds into the waters as they was 'not in keeping with the ideal of simplicity'.[55] In England, he and a delegation of the Congress – comprising Bhupendranath Basu, Lajpat Rai, Jinnah and three others – which was present then in the imperial capital had signed a letter addressed to the Secretary of State promising India's cooperation in the war. As part of the promise, Gandhi took a six-week course in first aid in October while Kasturba and Sarojini Naidu learnt to make clothes for soldiers.

Gokhale too had been in London then, and the two met, with Gokhale telling Gandhi, who was sticking to his 'no milk, no cereals, no pulses' diet despite suffering from pleurisy, to stop eschewing these things. Gandhi followed Gokhale's advice, but once the latter returned to India in October, he was back to his 'fruit and nuts, tomatoes and grapes' regime. When Gandhi got on the ship to India, he had bandaged ribs.[56]

On 13 January 1915, a meeting was held at Hirabag at C.P. Tank in Bombay to welcome Gandhi back. The Bombay police's agent was present, and he wrote in the first sentence of his confidential report, 'Mr. Tilak was present, though no formal invitation was sent to him.' It was the first time the two leaders, each of whom defined an era of India's freedom struggle, were meeting. Addressing the gathering of 250 people, Tilak said 'they were only doing their duty in honouring Mr. and Mrs Gandhi as they had fought for the honour of India in a distant land'. He said India ought to produce more men and women' of their 'self-sacrificing spirit'. Gandhi, in turn, said, 'it was a pleasure to meet Mr. Tilak in Bombay' and 'he fully intended to pay his respects to him when he visited Poona'.[57]

On 8 February, Gandhi was in Poona to see his 'guru' Gokhale. Gokhale wanted him to join his Servants of India Society, but most of its members weren't amenable to the idea as they felt Gandhi's methods were very different from those of the Society. So the membership issue was kept in abeyance. It was at this time that Tilak's critical comments on Gokhale on the break-up of reconciliation talks were published in the *Kesari*. Gandhi and Tilak met for the second time under such rather delicate circumstances, when Gandhi's mentor and the firebrand editor of the *Kesari* had had a fresh falling-out and had bitter feelings for each other. Gandhi didn't like anyone making uncharitable remarks about Gokhale. He looked at him thus: 'Sir Pherozeshah Mehta had seemed to me like the Himalayas, Lokmanya Tilak like the ocean. But Gokhale was as the Ganges. The Himalayas was unscalable, and one could not easily launch forth on the sea, but the Ganges invited one to its bosom.'[58]

Gandhi met Tilak at the latter's Gaikwad Wada residence and, according to the account of their exchange left behind by Tilak's grandson Gajanan Ketkar, who was present there, remonstrated with him for the strong criticism of Gokhale in his paper. Tilak told him that for almost a month, the *Dynan Prakash*, a Poona paper which was unofficially

Gokhale's mouthpiece, had been attacking him vituperatively. Gokhale himself had written a piece in the *Dynan Prakash* published on 10 February. Since Tilak's editorial against Gokhale had been headlined 'The Thief Calls Himself a Cop', Gokhale's article's counter-headline to it was 'Yes, The Thief *Truly* Calls Himself a Cop'. In a direct attack on Tilak, Gokhale had written in the piece that 'the roots of the inherent malice and prejudice you see in Maharashtra are buried deep inside Gaikwad Wada'. Gandhi said the *Dynan Prakash* was a far smaller paper than the *Kesari*, which had a wide circulation, hinting that Tilak ought to have ignored the criticism. According to Ketkar, Tilak answered, 'That's why I wrote just one article. Besides, the writing in a newspaper doesn't depend on its circulation.'[59]

Before Gandhi left Poona, Gokhale organized a party in his honour on the Society's premises where only fruits and nuts were served. Gokhale was poorly in health and fainted at the party.[60] A month later, on 19 February 1915, he was dead, after a cardiac arrest, at the age of forty-nine.

Tilak was at his other home atop Sinhagad Fort when he heard the news. He came down at once to the city of Poona and went to Gokhale's residence. When he reached the place for the funeral, a massive crowd had gathered, and they cheered for him. Tilak was quite upset over the cheers. He told the crowd that the time was not for cheers, but for shedding tears. He paid a dazzling tribute to the departed man at the funeral, underlining Gokhale's iconic status which he put above that of everyone else, including himself, as a real Karma Yogi or man of duty and action. 'This diamond of India, this jewel of Maharashtra, this prince of workers is taking eternal rest on the funeral ground,' he said. 'Look at him and try to emulate him. Mr. Gokhale has passed away from our midst, after having satisfactorily performed his duty. Will anyone of you come forward to take his place? Like a triumphant hero, he is passing away, after having made his name immortal. Not only none of you here assembled, but no other citizen in all of India will be able to give such a satisfactory account in the other world of having done his duty to his motherland. Up to this time very few have had the fortune of being able to render an account before God of having done their true duty. I knew Mr. Gokhale from his youth (Tilak was 10 years older to him). He was an ordinary and simple man in the beginning. He was not an inamdar, he was not a jagirdar, he was not a chieftain. He was an ordinary man like all of us here. He rose to such eminence by sheer force of genius, ability and work. Mr. Gokhale is passing away from our midst, but he has left behind him much to emulate. Every one of you ought to place his example before his eyes, and try to fill the gap; and if you will try your best to emulate him in this way, he will feel glad even in the next world.'[61]

When news of Gokhale's passing reached him at Sinhagad, Tilak had been engaged in checking the proofs for his soon-to-be-published book *Gita Rahasya*. Written in pencil, the book's manuscript had been held back by the Raj at the time of Tilak's release from Mandalay. The Bombay government sent it to its Oriental translator, S.M. Bharucha, instructing him to scrutinize it and submit a confidential report on whether it contained anything that might encourage sedition. In all, nine of Tilak's notebooks had been held back, and Bharucha wrote that the manuscript of the Rahasya filled four of these. He stated in his report that 'on the whole the work is free from objectionable matter, and the writer seems to have taken care to exclude all reference to politics or to current topics'.[62] Bharucha further noted, 'What is novel about his (Tilak's) exposition of the Gita is the new interpretation he puts on the teaching of the poem. The traditional interpretation as embodied in the ancient Sanskrit commentaries of Shankara, Ramanuja, Madhav and Vallaba, represents the Gita as being merely a metaphysical treatise in verse and as teaching Vedantic quietism. Mr. Tilak's thesis is that the Gita has little to do with metaphysical theorizing and is in fact a work on practical ethics, urging man to do his duty manfully in this world.' Bharucha's confidential report, which also contained his summary of each of the book's fourteen chapters, was examined by the secretary to the Bombay government L. Robertson, a member of the Governor's Executive Council and the Bombay governor Freeman Thomas, and once the governor gave his all-clear, it was returned to Tilak in August 1914.[63] Tilak got the text composed at the Chitrashala Press and proofread and checked for sources by his aides K.P. Khadilkar and Raghunath Hari Bhagwat, before proofreading it himself. In June 1915, the book was published. His first two books were in English, and this was the first in Marathi. Tilak priced it at three rupees so that it could reach as wide a readership in his native language as possible. The first edition of 6000 copies was sold out in a matter of days, with people queuing at the gates of Gaikwad Wada to get their copy. Discussions on the book were fervent and wide, and according to one chronicler, in Poona in particular, many flaunted a copy either in their hands or on their arms, and if anyone asked, they took a certain pride in saying truthfully or not so truthfully that they were 'on their way to Balwantrao's house to get certain points mentioned in the text cleared'.[64]

The mission of publishing a text that was right after his heart accomplished, Tilak was on to his next: re-entry into the Congress. With Gokhale's death, there was no genuine rival for him from within the Moderates' camp for leadership. Yet Mehta remained stoutly opposed to any reunification. Mehta also knew that the Moderates too, with Gokhale no longer around, could gravitate towards a charismatic figure like Tilak. To prevent Tilak from coming back with a bang, Mehta used his clout to get Bombay city to host the December 1915 Congress session. There, his followers would form an overwhelming majority. To be twice as certain, he got his own acolyte and member of the Viceroy's Executive Council, Satyendra Sinha, to be the president of the session. Sinha saw a conflict between Mehta and Tilak brewing and expressed his inability to preside over the session. Mehta sent him a stern wire, saying 'You dare not refuse.' And Sinha agreed. Weeks before the session, though, Mehta died at the age of seventy. Whatever their divergent political views, Tilak paid him a tribute that is still quoted in honour of Mehta, describing him as 'a lion'.[65]

Sinha was still president of the Congress session, but instead of blocking Tilak's entry now, he enabled the tweaking of the Congress constitution to permit the Extremist leader and his party to return. By this tweak, delegates could be elected 'by a meeting convened under the auspices of any association which is of not less than two years' standing on December 31, 1915 and which has for one of its objects the attainment of self-government within the British Empire by constitutional means.'[66] Tilak was absolutely okay with this clause. Still, the opening of the door wasn't going to be instant. He and his party had to wait for a year to mark their formal comeback. He accepted the compromise happily nonetheless and decided to concentrate his energies in the meanwhile to an idea that had been taking ferment in his mind—the idea of a Home Rule League.

He had first mentioned the idea to his Congress interlocuters during the abortive reunification talks of November–December 1914. The credit for mooting it went to Joseph Baptista, Tilak's lawyer friend. Born in Bombay's Mazagaon in 1864 as part of the city's East Indian Catholic community, Baptista had studied law at Cambridge, where he had in the year of his graduation, 1899, moved a motion against the British Raj's prosecution of editors for sedition. On his return to India, Baptista, while practising law, became an aide of Tilak and suggested to him the formation of an Indian Home Rule League along the lines of the Irish League. Tilak, at that point, was concentrating on the Congress and did not take to it. He suggested it a second time in 1906 as the agitation against Bengal's partition raged, but Tilak was not amenable still. In 1908 Baptista appeared as Tilak's lawyer in the sedition case along with Jinnah to apply for bail. On Tilak's return from Mandalay Baptista broached the subject of a Home Rule League again, and this time Tilak was more than open to the idea. He asked Baptista to raise the issue at the Bombay Provincial Conference of 1915, which he hoped to dominate again to make his comeback into the Congress fold a powerful one.[67]

It also helped that Annie Besant, who had earlier been in talks with Tilak over Congress unity, had been speaking the same language. She had been advocating such a League for India, and in September 1915 she announced her intent to form such a Home Rule League for India. She held a conference in Bombay in the last week of December that year to discuss setting up of the League. At the same time, Tilak held his own meeting on the same subject in Poona. Though he saw Besant as a colleague, he wanted to start a League of his own. Besant had undoubtedly been first off the mark in announcing the League, yet Tilak formed his own League before she did. In April 1916, he formed what came to be known as the Indian Home Rule League; Besant formed hers almost six months later and called it the All India Home Rule League. They decided their leagues would not be rivals but would complement each other and play on their respective strengths, so Tilak would carry out his activities in western India and some other parts of India where his clout was the greatest, and Besant would hold the fort in Madras, the headquarters of her Theosophical Society, and the United Provinces, where she had established the Central Hindu

College. She explained later that she and Tilak had decided to start two separate Home Rule Leagues 'since some of his followers disliked me and some of mine disliked him. We, however, had no quarrel with each other . . . Mr. Tilak presided over one League and I over the other, the two working harmoniously side by side'. Both the Leagues would work in affiliation to the Indian National Congress.[68]

In the final week of December 1915, Tilak wrote a series of articles in the *Kesari* explaining his notion of the Home Rule League. Essentially, it would have the same principles as the Irish model. It would demand a scheme of freedom for India, albeit under the British crown. The Indians would get their own Parliament, their political executive, and the administration would be wholly Indian. But it would not be outside the Empire; the British monarch would remain the head of state, and the Secretary of State for India could look after foreign affairs, though the Secretary of State's Council was no longer necessary and would have to be disbanded as Indians were going to govern themselves.

India would get a Central Assembly, which would be the 'seed' of India's own Parliament, and its members would be elected and would represent all castes and creeds, Tilak explained. The Central Assembly, which in time would become the Indian Parliament, would have complete control over the country's budget and the freedom to frame and approve legislation, and it would give its members the right to ask questions, just like the British Parliament did. Tilak envisaged a high degree of provincial autonomy, with the states regulating their own internal administration for the most part. In British India, there were too many government and nominated officials in the provinces, he felt. Their numbers, and more so their powers, would be significantly curtailed to give the elected bunch a clear majority, and it is these elected representatives who would carry the responsibility of a province's administration on their shoulders. Unlike Gandhi, who preached the idea of the village as a key unit of administration, Tilak didn't want the villages so empowered so soon. Provincial autonomy was more his concern; he wasn't dismissing the idea of the village as the basis for self-governance, it was just that in his eyes it was still not a self-sufficient unit, and once provincial self-governance was obtained, the question of rejuvenation of the villages could be taken up. And 'when all the provinces become to a large extent autonomous the control of the

Central Assembly of the Government of India would be the same as that exercised by the American Congress over its States'. Tilak was thus aiming at a system that combined aspects of the British and American forms of government, significantly without the antiquarian village system having much leeway despite his own abiding pride in India's past. He patently saw 'the village units of old' giving way to a modern constitutional scheme of things.

To allay British concerns about his thinking, Tilak once again reiterated India's loyalty. He nonetheless made a subtle distinction in the nature of India's loyalty that he said the British could expect from now on. Thus far, the relationship between India and England had been akin to that between a loyal servant and master; going forward, it ought to be between one loyal friend and another, he said—a relationship of equals, not of servility. Many said that with a world conflict raging, the time was just not right to press such demands. To them, Tilak said the Indian people didn't want everything at once. They would go 'all the way' to assist the government during the war. 'But just as they were loyal, they were equally eager for Swaraj.' They sought freedom under the Crown not as a present or gift but as a natural right, he said.[69]

Tilak's launch of the Home Rule League led to a gushing, fresh wave of political activity across India. Such a wave was important in view of the fact that for the past several years, the national movement, as was clear from the waning stature and actions of the Congress, had lost most of its verve, its push, its energy, its self-assurance and its confidence to consistently pile on the pressure on the Raj. With Tilak back and Besant propagating her own message as an Irishwoman, things were abuzz.

Not everyone was in agreement or happy. Some of Tilak's followers felt he had mellowed and was sounding more and more like Gokhale. The feeling of one such follower, B.S. Munje of Nagpur, came to the fore at the Provincial Political Conference held in Belgaum in April 1916, on the sidelines of which Tilak inaugurated his Home Rule League. Khaparde, who presided over the conference, made a statement there that the ideal of Swaraj declared in 1906 by Dadabhai Naoroji had been fully embraced by the Extremists; the Moderates, on the other hand, had been lukewarm in their response. Now, the Provincial Conference was also part of Tilak's bid to reconcile with the Moderates. Why then was he so keen on reconciliation, asked Munje.

Tilak had been aware of Munje's unhappiness for a while, and he knew some of his other aides too, such as Vasukaka Joshi, K.P. Khadilkar and Shivrampant Paranjpe, were far from enthusiastic about re-unity at the cost of softening of their agenda. Three months before the Belgaum conference, Tilak had on 8 January 1916 written to Munje to address his doubts. He had told him, 'You know that if you need to take a fort, you first need to make a small crack on the outside and use that crack to enter and capture the fort. There's no wisdom in waiting for the fort's gates to open completely. That would be a mistake . . . It's not good to fight always. First let's get 50% of what we want. The remaining 50% we can get once we're inside.'[70]

At the Belgaum conference, Tilak tried to convince Munje once again. His explanation was that this was the right thing to do at the moment and that if they stayed the course and accepted the compromise being worked out, their wing would dominate the all-India representative organization in only a couple of years. Angered further by the explanation, Munje retorted bluntly to Tilak that it was possible that his own 'avatar' too as a towering figure had ended and it was time for him to be defeated, just as Parshuram and Krishna too had been defeated ultimately. Tilak told him that ultimately, the path he was choosing would prove to be the correct one. But Munje sat through the conference totally unpersuaded and upset.[71] He heard silently as Tilak said in his address that 'the question before them was not one of nationalists and moderates but it was how the two parties could unite to do national work in the interests of their motherland'. Without surrendering their principles, they should speak in a 'united voice' and 'devise the best possible scheme for getting certain rights for the country'. Tilak's resolution was backed by Gandhi, who added nevertheless that though he himself was 'neither a Moderate nor an Extremist',[72] he hoped that when the Nationalists rejoined the Congress they would do so in a spirit of cooperation and not to overthrow the Moderates.[73] Such a remark was sure to rile Munje further about the 'compromise' Tilak was seeking. Just days later, the British-friendly *Times of India* wrote an editorial about the conference. It was alarmist in tone. The paper said the Tilak party's resolution to effect a compromise and re-enter the Congress showed 'it is the intention of these gentlemen that the National Congress should give them the right to carry on an unlimited propagandism, in its name and on its behalf, in furtherance of their political programme'. Though the radical wing had 'modified' its declared programme to accept 'self-government within the British Empire on the model of the self-governing colonies,' *The Times* reported that 'otherwise, there does not seem to be any change in their plan of operations'. As evidence of the group's unchanged habits, the paper quoted the president of the conference, Khaparde, as saying the post-split years had 'proved that the real political instinct was possessed by his friends who embraced the programme of 'national education, Swadeshi, boycott and self-government' propounded by Mr. Tilak'. Terming his statement 'a grotesque distortion of facts', the paper lamented that 'the Bombay school', whom Khaparde in his address had referred to as 'the Congress oligarchy' that had kept the nationalist wing out, had 'unfortunately . . . suffered seriously by the death of its two most distinguished leaders (Gokhale and Mehta). But we should be sorry to think that the wisdom, the moderation and the weight which distinguished them . . . have disappeared from the councils of the Indian National Congress'.[74] The editorial changed Munje's mind. He went up to Tilak and apologized and said he had realized what his leader was doing. Tilak smiled, and there the disagreement ended.[75]

Gradually, the new wave triggered by Tilak's Home Rule League started building up in strength and speed, and Tilak, known to write his editorials in a straightforward idiom, made his message about Home Rule simpler still in his speeches in Belgaum, Ahmednagar and a host of other places. He stuck to his new script, but there were occasions when he pushed the boundaries nonetheless. On one occasion, he said, 'Those who carry on the administration of India, right from the Secretary of State and the Viceroy to the collector and the sepoy, must be changed if their rule is not found to be useful or good to the people of India. To say this is no sedition.' Yet sedition was what the government had begun to smell yet again.

Further, Tilak began speaking of a timeframe for the grant of Swaraj after the war ended. Baptista had already, at the Belgaum conference, spoken on behalf of Tilak when he had asked the Raj to 'now construct a scheme of granting within a definite period Home Rule or self-government to India, including financial autonomy with (1) financial independence, (2) an elective non-official majority in the

Legislative Council and (3) the responsibility of the Executive to the Legislative Council'. Baptista had also argued that 'good government was no substitute for self-government'.[76] Tilak underlined the point in May 1916, saying 'neither Dadabhai (who had spoken of Swaraj) nor the nationalists have subscribed' to the conception 'that Swaraj is not to be realized in the near future and would take a long time – perhaps an age'. That was simply the 'idea of the British bureaucracy which has now been discountenanced even by the Moderates', he said.[77]

The government decided to silence him before things got out of hand. Tilak was going to turn sixty years old on 23 July that year. He had hardly expected to come out of Mandalay prison alive. Yet he had, and as a measure of their gratitude, his followers led by N.C. Kelkar, Daji Abaji Khare, Dadasaheb Karandikar and Gangadharrao Deshpande wanted to collect a purse for him. The target they'd set was Rs 1 lakh, and up until the morning of his birthday, people had donated Rs 85,000 in all. His aides also wanted to conduct some auspicious ceremonies at his home on the occasion, and he agreed. It was while these ceremonies were going on in the pre-noon hours of 23 July that Inspector J.A. Guider, deputy inspector–general of Bombay Police, turned up with the government's own birthday gift—a notice for three of his speeches, delivered in Belgaum and Ahmednagar in May and June. Tilak had to leave the ceremonies midway to go get the notice from the gates of Gaikwad Wada, where the inspector was waiting for him. Guider had lodged a complaint in the court of Poona district magistrate, G.W. Hatch, charging Tilak with 'orally disseminating sedition', and the magistrate had directed a notice to be issued under Sections 108 and 112 of the Criminal Procedure Code calling upon Tilak to 'show cause why he should not be bound over for good behaviour for a period of one year' for 'a sum of Rs 20,000 in his own recognizance (legalese, meaning for himself) and in two sureties of Rs 10,000 each.'[78]

Barrister D. Binning opened the case for the prosecution on 7 August in the magistrate's court, while Jinnah and D.G. Erulkar appeared for Tilak. Binning claimed Tilak's talk of loyalty 'under the guise of an agitation to obtain Home Rule . . . was merely a cloak' to save himself from the long arm of the law. He said Tilak had made a series of allegations in his three speeches and reeled off his purported remarks, one after the other.

According to Binning, Tilak had said 'the British government in India keeps the Indians in continuous bondage or slavery', the government 'look only to their personal advantage and to the benefit of Great Britain', 'the British are not the real government', their government 'is full of conceit and thinks itself perfect', 'the main object of the British government is to fill their aching bellies', the 'intervening collectors and commissioners and other people are not wanted', 'all British rule except a mere nominal sovereignty should be removed at an early moment', 'the British have in the course of fifty years failed to educate India so as to make it fit to rule itself', and 'therefore the British are unfit to rule and must go' and 'the priests of the deity, meaning the British officials and government, must be removed'.

That wasn't all. Tilak had said things about the British plunder of India apparently. Binning quoted him as saying 'the officials here keep back facts from the King-Emperor and hence justice is not done', 'the only reason the Viceroy and other officials get high pay is that India has to pay for it', 'the bureaucracy's or government's first idea is to see that their pay is secured', 'the administration of the British government in India is not in accordance with the wishes of the sovereign', and 'under the Company's regime a letter used to come to the Governor-General as follows -- "So much profit should be paid us this year, realise it and send it to us"', which meant 'this is not a good sort of administration' and 'the Parliament under Queen Victoria' (who'd been dead for fifteen years) did not approve of this system. Further, Tilak had admonished the British by pointing out that 'nobody in India told the government and its servants to come here', 'they were not wanted here,' the government 'will not listen to what you say and redress your grievances', 'their sight is so affected that they do not see defects in themselves', 'this government is no government at all because it evades its responsibility', and for it 'the chief question is that the Indian nation is to be treated like beasts'.[79]

A Maharashtrian sub-inspector of the CID, Trimbak Bhikaji Datre, had taken down notes of Tilak's speeches in Marathi shorthand, and he produced these in court, along with his final transcript. He said ordinarily a person could speak 110 words in a minute, and Tilak spoke about seventy to ninety, and he had taken down 'every word'.[80] An Oriental translator with the government, A.K. Thakur, testified to the correctness of the translations 'except for certain words'.[81] Jinnah objected, asking for specific passages from the text of the speeches in order to establish context and objecting to the translation of the word 'pashu' as 'beasts', but the magistrate thought the case was fit to proceed as the speeches were 'intended to create disaffection against the government' and asked Tilak to enter into the bond of good behaviour for a year.[82]

Times of India pronounced itself satisfied. All through his Home Rule speeches, Tilak had been referring to the British monarch as the 'invisible government' and the British government as the 'visible' one and saying he had no issue with the 'invisible' form of it. *The Times* wrote in a sharply worded editorial that 'the King, as the 'invisible government', is held up to shadowy respect; the King's Government is made the subject of every species of objurgation and abuse. If Mr. Tilak really thought that by employing this subtle distinction he was evading a law with whose meaning he ought to be familiar, then he is far less astute than we thought. The magistrate immediately brushed aside this sophistry.'[83]

Tilak moved the Bombay High Court to challenge the proceedings, realizing the government had been rather clever this time. They hadn't directly booked or arrested him as they had on previous occasions. The bond was intended as a humiliation and also as a gag order so it could effectively nullify his work and movements. It mandated 'good behaviour' for a year, which meant he was going to be kept under very close scrutiny and surveillance, and even a word loosely uttered could get the police to put the fetters on him. Deliberately, the Raj was using a new approach—using the anticipation of action to try and produce fear in him. Film-maker Alfred Hitchcock famously said that the fear was not in the bullet, it was in anticipation of the bullet. The Raj anticipated Hitchcock's film technique (which came much later) in its policy for the colonies and especially for a marked rebel like B. G. Tilak.

In the high court, Jinnah again stood to defend Tilak along with Joseph Baptista and D.G. Erulkar. The prosecution was represented by advocate general M.R. Jardine, father of the future English cricket captain Douglas Jardine of Bodyline notoriety, and N.M. Patwardhan. On the high court bench were Justice Stanley Batchelor and Justice Shah.

The truth about Tilak's speeches was that, as a chronicler has noted, they were 'laced with devastating ridicule, apt proverbs, and telling mythological allusions', and he was 'testing the courts by constantly telling his audiences that it was not seditious to say this or that'. Yet it was equally true that he was continually conscious of the very thin line dividing criticism and sedition under British rule and played at its borders like a skilful lawyer, now touching it, now going tantalizingly close and threatening to cross it, and apparently going past it at times only to return so precipitously in the blink of an eye as to make exact determination and definite conclusion a little tough.

Jinnah argued for a full reading of the three speeches, without any picking out of select lines or passages, and said they were 'nothing but a comment or an expression of disapprobation of the measures of government with a view to obtain their alteration by lawful means.' He said he could point out 'no less than 47 passages' which 'conclusively' showed 'Mr. Tilak never intended to cause disaffection towards government'. He said that the Home Rule League was 'not an unconstitutional organization', and:

> The object of Tilak making the speech was to convince his audience that the Home Rule League was a good thing. He began to tell his audience clearly that he wanted to convince them as to 'what we are asking for? What is the thing that we ought to have?' . . . in order that the audience might become members of the League . . . Mr. Tilak had no particular object in having the intention at this juncture to disseminate sedition.[84]

The court was 'overcrowded' when arguments were on, reported *Bombay Chronicle*.[85]

Justice Batchelor delivered his judgment on 10 November 1916, stating that 'the court's aim is to decide upon the general effect of the speeches as a whole. Probably, the fairest way to ascertain that effect is to read the three speeches from beginning to end quietly and attentively, remembering the arguments and remembering the politically ignorant audience whom Mr. Tilak was addressing. I have so read these speeches not once, but several times, and the impression left on my mind is that on the whole, despite certain passages which are rightly objected to by the prosecution, the general effect would not naturally and probably be to cause disaffection, that is, hostility or enmity or contempt, but rather to create a feeling of disapprobation of the government, for that it delays the transference of political power to the hands of those whom the speaker designates as 'the people'.[86] Since the 'general effect was not shown to exceed the limits of fair criticism', Justice Batchelor said the magistrate's order was being set aside and 'the bonds', if executed, needed to be 'cancelled'.[87]

Importantly, Justice Batchelor held that the magistrate had clearly been 'influenced by Mr. Strachey's interpretation of disaffection, namely that it is the equivalent merely of 'absence of affection'. This construction of the word, the judge noted, 'is opposed to all ordinary English usage'.[88]

The verdict led to not just relief but a great deal of happiness among Indian nationalists, who felt that 'the wrong done by a British judge eighteen years ago in misinterpreting the word 'disaffection,' in Tilak's own case of 1897 which had led to his conviction, had been righted by another British judge.' The *Bombay Chronicle* commented that it was 'amusing' that 'certain journals' had with 'extravagant glee' rushed into 'premature comment' on the magistrate's decision pointing to sedition and had described Tilak's speeches 'in the most extreme language that could be used.' On the magistrate's verdict, the *Times of India* had 'pompously declared' that 'no other conclusion was possible', *Chronicle* said. 'How nonsensical this assertion appears today,' it noted, as the high court had found the political executive 'rushing into a prosecution on grounds which are shown . . . to be quite untenable'.[89]

The overall Indian sentiment was nicely summed up by *Young India*, a journal then edited by Lajpat Rai (which was subsequently, from 1919 onwards, taken over by Gandhi):

A great victory has been won for the cause of free speech; a great victory for the cause of Home Rule which has thus been free from the chains that were sought to be put upon it. Firstly, we must render our tribute to the man, who by his fearless and consistent devotion to the cause of Home Rule for India won this great victory for us and who has at last by the judgment of the High Court . . . cleared himself . . . Mr. Tilak has undergone many sufferings in his country's cause. Those who have known him have known how unjust was the view taken of him by many. He has now been vindicated and is free to continue his work for his country with the whole-hearted zeal that we feel sure he will not allow to be diminished, but will rather increase. He has not been and is not to be silenced. But he has won this victory not for himself alone but for his countrymen at large. It rests with them to carry on the good work and reap the fruits that will ripen from the seeds he had sown.[90]

With his quick lawyerly reflexes, Tilak sensed that the high court judgement carried an incredible amount of potential for India's struggle. So when the Bombay National Union held a meeting in Girgaum after the verdict to congratulate him, he told the gathering that the Home Rule movement had received the stamp of legality, and Indians 'should take advantage of the legality . . . and push on the work of the League to its legitimate end.' He stressed, 'This is the time. Strike the iron while it is hot.' Many people, he said, were prepared to help the Home Rule League with money, but not with their name. Now 'no one need fear call himself a member of the League,' and each one should pitch in as they could, 'pecuniarily, physically or intellectually', and 'enter into more vigorous, more arduous, more constitutional work'. There were people at the time who asked why the Home Rule League was needed when the Congress was around and Tilak's group was soon going to re-enter it. The Congress, he pointed out, 'was only a deliberative body. The resolutions passed there yearly were a mere pious wish. An executive body was wanted to work and hence the need for a Home Rule League'. At the same time, the upcoming Congress was utterly important. 'All the world over, the Colonies and England itself, were preparing for reforms after the war. Why should it not be so in India?' All of India's parties needed to 'meet in the Congress without any differences' and 'formulate and 'settle' the 'scheme for reforms'. At the end of the speech, he said, 'Your work is not finished with this congratulatory meeting, but it begins there.'[91]

Significant gestures were at the same time being made to make Tilak feel at home again inside the Congress tent. One of these came from Gandhi. The Provincial Political Conference of 1916 was held early in October in Ahmedabad, with Jinnah presiding over it. The Moderates there, having still not gotten over the Surat row of 1907, distributed provocative pamphlets against Tilak and the Maharashtrian associates accompanying him. Stepping in, Gandhi circulated a signed statement urging the people of Gujarat to give Tilak a public reception. The result was that thousands turned up at Ahmedabad railway station to welcome Tilak, and a procession was taken out for him through the streets of Ahmedabad, with Tilak and Gandhi seated in the same car.[92] Undoubtedly Tilak felt the absence of some very strong colleagues he'd had not long ago. Two of them stood out: Lajpat Rai and Aurobindo Ghose. Lajpat Rai spent a lot of his time abroad, and Aurobindo had relinquished the life of politics and revolution for one of spirituality. Tilak sent an emissary to Aurobindo and urged him to embrace the hurly-burly of politics again, but he wouldn't budge.[93] Yet Tilak was broadly content with the altered situation in the Congress. The road ahead to Lucknow appeared to have no obstacles.

Among the big questions working on the minds of Congress leaders was the safe distance that a vast majority of Muslims had kept from the organization. Hindus and Muslims had had numerous issues and conflicts for nearly a thousand years following the Islamic invasions, but an extraordinary moment of unity was realized in 1857 at the time of the great rebellion. The Raj, which came into being in the aftermath of that rebellion, played on Hindu–Muslim differences to prevent another such uprising, and it was helped in large part by the refusal of Muslims to show enthusiasm for the Congress which aimed to bring together Indians of different castes and creeds. In previous chapters, we have seen how the numbers of Muslims in the Congress hadn't grown over the years. Regular riots across India in the 1890s had led to a further deterioration in relations, and Tilak had sided with the Hindus in the communal conflagration of 1893 and had launched the Ganpati festival to wean Hindus away from Muharram processions. Ever since, however, he had been at pains to say he wasn't anti-Muslim though he'd never be shy of defending Hindu interests if he saw them being threatened. He had participated in Muharram processions the moment he felt they had ceased to be a source of concern for him and the Hindu community, and he had even said in his lectures on Shivaji that the Maratha hero had fought the Muslims because the rulers were Muslims, not because he was anti-Muslim.

Neither this nor any statement by the other Congress leaders had led to a big breakthrough. Instead, the Muslim League delegation to Minto in 1906 asking for separate representation for the community had succeeded in its aim. The Morley–Minto reforms of 1909 had introduced religion-based reservations. Jinnah had played it both ways at the time: he had strongly opposed such quotas and, once they were granted, taken a quota seat in the Council as Muslim member from Bombay. In 1913, the year in which he joined the Muslim League and the Congress, for which such quotas were anathema earlier, began to show signs of openness on the issue, Jinnah urged the Muslim League to join hands with the Congress and sought Hindu–Muslim unity from the League's platform. He was in a special position, in a way: he was a member of both the Congress and the Muslim League, as such dual memberships were allowed at the time, and also of the legislative council. The conservatives in the Muslim League didn't like the idea he was proposing and shot it down. But the war, and the Congress's shift in its position on quotas, opened up possibilities. Though Jinnah openly backed communal representation in 1915, his image as a secular politician worked in his favour, and he and others began working out details of a Congress-League pact, most famously at Motilal Nehru's Allahabad home in April 1916. Motilal praised Jinnah saying he was 'unlike most Muslims' in that he was 'as nationalist as any of us', and most other Congress leaders too felt he was not swayed by the notion of pan-Islamism.[94] The Balkan wars of 1912 and 1913 in which the Ottoman Empire, for which the Muslims had deep sympathy, lost control of a number of states, and the war in which the Ottomans found themselves further embattled also brought down the Muslim League's defences against a pact with the Congress.

Tilak, like Gokhale, had started out not at all appreciating the idea of separate electorates. But Congress, and Gokhale too before his death in a final statement on reforms he'd prepared at Viceroy Lord Willingdon's behest, had become far more flexible on the prickly issue. The Hindu–Muslim 'entente first began to take shape' at a meeting of the Congress and Muslim League in Bombay in December 1915, and through 1916, much progress had taken place, with proposals drawn up at Motilal Nehru's home in Allahabad in April 1916.[95] Tilak now was seeing magnificent and highly promising vistas on the horizon for India as a result of the war, a future rich with political possibilities. For such a future to be realized in its splendid and marvellously radiant avatar, he was desirous, like Jinnah and some others, that Indians close ranks completely. Tilak saw the contest as a three-cornered one, with the British government, the Hindus (Congress) and Muslims as the three sides. According to him, it was imperative that it should turn into a two-cornered fight, with Indians on the one side and the Raj on the other, for India to grasp the present and get a solid hold on what looked like an eminently close-at-hand future of freedom. So he was ready to give his sanction to what would come to be known as the Lucknow Pact.

Tilak's entire team wanted their return to the Congress to be a jubilant one, so once the formal re-entry into the Congress happened with the Poona Sarvajanik Sabha under Tilak formally affiliating itself with the Congress and its members holding a public meeting to elect delegates, his aides came up with the idea of booking a full train. They did so, giving it the triumphant name of 'Home Rule Special'. Along the way, the train was welcomed by massive crowds at railway stations as it wound its way through the Central Provinces to Lucknow, which was in the United Provinces. Tilak was cheered, garlanded, and hailed as the comeback hero who never should have been left out. Outside the Lucknow railway station, the by-now familiar pattern fell into place: youngsters punctured the tyres of the car he was to be driven in, placed him in a carriage and pulled it all through the town. Among the leading carriage-pullers was Ramprasad Bismil, the composer of the famous 'Sarfaroshi ki tamanna ab hamarein dil mein hain' who'd later be convicted in the mid-1920s Kakori conspiracy case.[96]

Though the broad contours were known, by no means was the Hindu-Muslim pact settled before the start of the plenary session. From the day Tilak arrived in Lucknow, 25 December, a joint committee of the Congress and the Muslim League, sitting in what one newspaper correspondent described as 'the dimly-lit tent of the Subjects Committee', debated the 'settlement' for three days, and the whole thing 'trembled in the balance and more than once a crisis' arose, threatening to derail the talks. Deadlock led to arguments, and there were 'prolonged, always excited, and always intensely difficult negotiations'.[97] The two main sticking points were related to Bengal and the United Provinces. In Bengal, the Muslim demand was 50 per cent seats (from the then existing 10 per cent), and the Hindus were willing to give one-third (33 per cent), and in the United Provinces the Muslims asked for 50 per cent and Hindus offered 25 per cent.

At one point, breakdown seemed inevitable as the communities in the United Provinces looked 'hopelessly unable' to clinch an agreement.[98] But the spirit of optimism was too much in the air and too strong. The Hindus of Bengal showed readiness to concede 40 per cent seats, and the Muslims there agreed, and in the United Provinces, the Muslims finally agreed to accept 30 per cent 'with the proviso that the article in the Congress Constitution by which any question barred by three-fourths of the members of any single community should be excluded, shall be embodied in any scheme of reform while the Mohammedans should stand outside the general electorate'.[99]

The principle of separate electorates meant Muslim legislators would be elected by Muslim voters only, as promised first in 1909 by Minto. But while Minto had given the Muslims a separate vote as well as the right to vote in the general constituencies, in Lucknow, they took the separate vote and gave up their vote in the general constituencies. The upshot for the Muslims was that 'weightage' for their vote was increased substantially. 'Weightage' meant that the value of one Muslim vote was greater than that of a Hindu vote, that is, beyond what their proportion in the population indicated. This was apparently to assuage Muslim concerns about Hindu domination in a dominantly Hindu country. One-third of elected seats to the Council too were given to the Muslims. This too was a gain; earlier, eight of twenty-seven elected seats were given by Minto to Muslims on his Central Council—six from the Muslim electorate and two more if none of the other special constituencies voted them in. And in two provinces where separate Muslim electorates didn't exist earlier—Punjab and the Central Provinces—they were introduced for the first time. In Punjab their representation would be 50 per cent, in the Central Provinces and Madras it would be 15 per cent, in Bihar and Orissa it would be 25 per cent and in Bombay it would be 33 per cent, as at the Centre.[100]

'It cannot be said that the compromise really satisfies each side,' wrote the correspondent for the *Bombay Chronicle*, 'but for the sake of unity and the larger issues at stake, it was accepted.'[101]

C.S. Ranga Iyer, who ran the paper *Advocate* in Lucknow and was present at the subjects committee meeting, wrote that Tilak was 'an interesting study' during the delicate discussions on the political arrangement between Hindus and Muslims. 'When the angry speakers were foaming on all sides he was calm as a rock,' he reported. Pandit Madan Mohan Malviya, he said, was 'very much upset', 'would not reconcile himself to the pact' and assured 'the Hindu Extremists, who invaded his spare hours', that if necessary, he would hold 'a huge demonstration against the Congress if it surrendered to the Muslims'. Yet 'the leader of Maharashtra who was the most religious, the most learned in the Vedas and among the most orthodox of the Hindus, would not listen to any argument against the pact. Not that he was enamoured of it himself but if it would satisfy the Muslims, if it could bring them to the Congress, if it could replace their extra-territorial patriotism by Indian nationalism, the agreement was worth reaching'. Iyer felt 'Tilak's attitude was the deciding factor in the Hindu-Muslim settlement, the last word on the subject so far as the Hindus were concerned'. Malviya, Iyer wrote, ultimately did not carry out any demonstrations. He 'wisely lowered the flag and bent before the gale – though suspecting in his mind that the Muslims would only take the earliest opportunity to ask for more concessions'.[102]

Playing the role of a political realist, Tilak had in April itself told his followers, many of whom weren't happy with the compromises he was making to re-enter the Congress and take it forward, that 'we are ready to make a common cause with any set of men.'[103] When he stood up to address the Congress plenary session after finalization of the pact, he got 'an unprecedented ovation.' His response was, 'I am not foolish enough to think that this reception is given to my humble self. It is given, if I rightly understand, to the principles for which I have been fighting, principles which have been embodied in the resolution I have the honour to support.'[104]

Along with the Hindu-Muslim pact, the Congress had prepared a scheme for constitutional reform. It demanded provincial autonomy in finances and administration and elections for 80 per cent of seats on the Central and Provincial Councils. It wanted resolutions of the Councils to be binding on the Centre and provinces unless they were vetoed by the governor-general or governor, and if passed again by the Councils within a year, to be binding despite the opposition of the governor–general or governor. It suggested foreign affairs and defence be left to the Centre to handle and asked for the same status for India as the one for dominions in any inter-imperial system, with relations of the Secretary of State with the Government of India being similar to those of the colonial secretary with the governments of the dominions.

Tilak, who had on his arrival played on the name of the host city to say the session was bound to bring 'Luck Now,' pointed out, 'I am glad to say I have lived these ten years to see that we are going to put out our voice and shoulders together to push on the scheme of self-government. We are now united in every way in the United Provinces.'

On the Lucknow pact, he was emphatic knowing there was still some amount of scepticism in the air. He declared, 'It has been said that we, Hindus, have yielded too much to our Muslim brethren. I am sure I represent the sense of the Hindu community all over India when I say that we could not have yielded too much. I would not care if the rights of self-government are granted to the Muslim community only. I would not care if they are granted to the Rajputs. I would not care if they are granted to the lower classes of the Hindu population. Then the fight will not be triangular, as at present it is.'[105]

Where Tilak differed from the other Congress leaders was that he sought specific details on the various phases of self-government to be obtained and a deadline for the conceding of Indian aspirations by the Raj. Most mandarins in the organization didn't want to go so far, and Tilak, after pressing the demand for a deadline, shelved it momentarily in the interests of party unity.[106] He was not too happy that his resolution calling upon the Home Rule League and other public groups 'to carry on continuously a vigorous propaganda' for Swaraj was passed only with a great deal of hesitation, with both Jinnah and Malviya voting against it and the Moderates opposing it en bloc.[107] Nevertheless, it was cleared, and he was prepared to take it.

Tilak's backing for the Lucknow Pact which granted separate electorates to the Muslims has to be seen in this overall context. Those romantic about Hindu-Muslim togetherness point to his endorsement of the pact to try and show how he was totally convinced and even idealistic about the idea, and those who see it as chimerical and purely dangerous with the benefit of hindsight—which neither Tilak nor his contemporaries had, with Jinnah in fact positioned as a secularist of sorts—paint him as a sellout. The truth is that like most Indian nationalists, Tilak was superbly buoyant at this moment in Indian political life. He was back in the Congress with his bunch of supporters; his leadership was accepted with no rival able to match him; his declaration of Home Rule had been accorded legitimacy by the courts; an elusive Hindu–Muslim arrangement looked ultimately workable along with a concrete scheme of reforms; and if the opportunities provided by the war and its fallout were to be fully utilized to make that scheme a reality and if that called for some compromise, he was more than ready to make it. Indeed, the moment was a defining one for the Raj as well. How it would look at it was the big question. For Tilak, the point was that regardless of how the Raj looked at it, he had to keep pushing the boundaries of the possible. The time for it was now.

Chapter 15

Towards a Free India

The government would not leave Tilak alone. Not after his status as the Congress's biggest star had been reconfirmed and consolidated at the Lucknow Congress and a scheme of Hindu–Muslim understanding and Indian constitutional reform finalized by the chief representative body of Indians under his leadership.

In the Raj's view, Tilak would use the success of the Congress session to stir up discontent across the country. And he did indeed begin to make the winter of 1916 and early 1917 the winter of India's discontent. From Lucknow, he proceeded to Kanpur, where he spoke to an audience in English about how British rule had sought to destroy the qualities of the Indian character. He went to Calcutta to meet his old friend, Motilal Ghose, and from there, he blazed a trail of Home Rule propaganda in the Central Provinces through Nagpur, Akola, Yavatmal and Murtizapur. When he took stock of things on his return home, the results were satisfactory: more than 3000 people had newly signed up as members of the Home Rule League, and subscription money of over Rs 6000 had been collected.[1]

Showing how it completely distrusted Tilak's protestations of loyalty, the Raj barred him from entering the Punjab. On the one hand, Tilak was asking Indians to join the army and demanding that they be made officers, and in February 1917, he went so far as to say in a public speech in Poona that 'if age and grey hair are no disqualification, I am prepared to stand in the fighting line';[2] on the other, the government was keeping him outside the region from which it was recruiting a majority of soldiers for its war effort. Soon afterwards, Tilak was prohibited from entering Delhi too. Evidently, the Raj believed Tilak had sabotage on his mind, not cooperation.

The other Home Ruler, Annie Besant, became another target of the government. This too, like the repeated actions against Tilak, wasn't surprising. She had emerged as a star in the Congress in her own right, and she was an Irishwoman hailing the Irish rebellion and egging on the Indians to fight for their rights. In June 1917, the Madras government served on her and two of her Home Rule aides, George Arundale and B.P. Wadia, a notice interning them in the province. Besant was first confined in Ooty and then in the town of Coimbatore.

Acerbically, Tilak described Lord Pentland, the Madras governor who had issued the internment order, as 'the greatest friend of the Home Rulers'.[3] And indeed he turned out to be. The action against Besant gave Tilak a new point to hammer the government with and to point out a basic incongruity in its approach; Britain was claiming to fight the war in the name of freedom and democracy, and here it was, denying freedom to Indians and repressing all sorts of political activities.

Tilak launched a full-fledged campaign of protest, comparing Besant's internment to the unjust crackdown of 1908. The sole difference, he said, was that while Bombay and Calcutta were the provinces targeted in 1908, this time the honours had gone to Madras. At a meeting of the All-India Congress Committee on 28 and 29 July, he advocated using the weapon of passive resistance or civil disobedience if the internees weren't freed.[4] He didn't want the resistance movement to be narrowly restricted to the issue of their release, however. He suggested it be based on the principal political point of the Indian demand for Home Rule.[5] He also felt Indians led by the Congress should send a monster petition asking the Secretary of State to grant Home Rule to India.[6] As someone who had been proposing for a while that the Congress should send a deputation to England to press India's demand for Swaraj, Tilak characterized the Madras government's action as the direct consequence of the Congress resolve.[7]

While his various proposals were being sent across to the provincial Congress committees for deliberation, thousands flocked to join the Home Rule movement. One thousand men volunteered to march to the place where Besant had been interned; activists from Gujarat collected signatures of thousands of farmers expressing solidarity with Home

Rule; and prominent leaders who had so far stayed outside the League tent—Jinnah, Malaviya and Surendranath Banerjea—signed up for it.[8]

The government saw the Home Rule movement led and inspired by Tilak acquiring massive momentum in just a little over a year of its formation. At the end of its first year itself, in April–May 1917, Tilak's Home Rule League had 14,000 members with a fund of Rs 16,000; the numbers surged further in the wake of Pentland's policies.[9] India's new viceroy, Lord Chelmsford, who had taken over in 1916 from Lord Hardinge, had sent a message across to the then Secretary of State, Austen Chamberlain, a little before Besant's internment that the Home Rule agitation was 'having a mischievous effect on public feeling throughout the country'. Chelmsford had also written that 'Mrs Besant, Tilak and others are fomenting with great vigour the agitation for immediate Home Rule, and in the absence of any definite announcement by Government of India as to their policy in the matter, it is attracting many of those who hitherto have held less advanced views.'[10] His statement sounded especially true after Besant's internment.

Tilak meanwhile pressed the case harder. He decided to send Joseph Baptista to London to prepare the ground for the Congress deputation that was to go there later. On the evening of 10 July, 'a large and enthusiastic gathering' gave Baptista a farewell dinner before he boarded his ship. One of the specific points on his agenda was to place a habeas corpus petition before the Privy Council for George Arundale.[11] A habeas corpus writ is about 'showing the body' or person and is used when someone's whereabouts are unknown or undisclosed, creating a question mark as to what has happened to that person. Such a plea for Arundale meant it wasn't known where the interned Arundale had been kept, and in what condition he was.

Soon, Austen Chamberlain was replaced by Edwin Montagu as Secretary of State. Montagu had worked under Morley as under-secretary at the Indian Office and was considered an Indian sympathizer, just the kind of profile the Raj was looking for as the troubles mounted in India with the end of the war still not in sight. Immediately after taking charge, Montagu in August declared, 'The policy of His Majesty's Government, with which the Government of India are in complete accord, is that of the increasing association of Indians in every branch of the administration, and the gradual development of self-governing institutions, with a view to the progressive realization of responsible government in India as an integral part of the British Empire.'[12]

The declaration was vague and almost entirely composed of undefined and open-ended terms like 'increasing association of Indians', 'gradual development', 'progressive realization' and 'responsible government'. Yet vague-speak was better than no-speak for the Indians, especially when the new viceroy was being a little cold and, in the words of Jinnah, which he uttered in the presence of Tilak at a Home Rule League function in Bombay in July 1917, 'was maintaining a studied silence in the cloudy regions of Simla when India was stirred to its very depths'.[13] The Indians were actually missing the previous viceroy, Lord Hardinge, who was just then being arraigned in Britain for the Allies' debacle in Mesopotamia in the war in 1916. The Indians were getting increasingly unhappy with the way Britain was fighting the war, and seriously injured Indian soldiers who came back home narrated stories of British indifference to their suffering, to their wounds and their very act of volunteering. As a couple of historians put it, the Indian Army had in 1916 been crushed in Mesopotamia 'by a deadly combination of tough Ottoman troops, disease, and boneheaded military incompetence'.[14] The rout still rankled though the Allies had recovered thereafter, and the British government had formed a royal commission to probe its causes. And Hardinge, under whose watch much of the recruitment had happened in India, was sought to be made the fall guy and was to face a judicial tribunal. The Home Rule League held a meeting in Bombay to voice its support for Hardinge. Why? Hardinge, Tilak said at the meeting, 'was the first Viceroy to say that self-government was a perfectly legitimate ideal'. He 'sympathized with the public, worked for them' and was now looking 'to the verdict of Indian public opinion' when he was being 'treated shabbily' by England, Tilak said, asking the gathering to pass a resolution that 'such a statesman should not be brought before a tribunal'.[15] Jinnah pointed out that Hardinge had said India had been 'bled white' to help the Allies and 'it was India whose help at a most critical moment of the war saved Europe'.[16]

Notably, Tilak pivoted to the question of Britain's broader war approach in order to highlight imperial doublespeak. While Britain was invoking both liberty and democracy, the United States had entered the war in April 1917 and spoke in favour of colonized peoples, and the Russian revolution had taken place in February throwing out the imperial regime (the Bolsheviks would seize control of power in October). In this context, Tilak wrote in the *Kesari* of 18 July, 'Today in this Empire, on the one hand they are talking of granting Home Rule to Ireland and setting all Irish rebels free; the President of the United States declares publicly that the war is started for granting the rights of self-determination to all nations; on the other, the bureaucracy in India tries to gag a learned lady and her associates who work with sincerity and assiduity to further the cause of self-determination in India . . . The fact that the aspirations of Swaraj can no longer be put down by tyranny is made clear by the recent example of Russia.'[17]

Here again, Tilak was demonstrating his mastery of political messaging. He had taken the internment of Besant and her aides and from there zoomed out to the larger question of the urgent need for Home Rule. As far as the war too was concerned, he raised the row over Hardinge's planned indictment only to place it within the bigger frame of the overall conduct of war and the promises and commitment the Raj owed the Indians in the wake of the conflict.

Montagu did some damage control for the Raj immediately, albeit only after Emily Lutyens, the wife of the architect shaping the new imperial capital of New Delhi, asked him to. Emily Lutyens was a friend of Besant's, and she wrote to the new Secretary of State in July, imploring him to release the Irishwoman. Montagu issued the orders for her release in September 'as a gesture of goodwill'.[18]

Montagu also decided to travel to India to see the country he was managing, becoming the first Secretary of State for India to do so. He landed on Bombay's shores on 10 November 1917. At Apollo Bunder, the bald and monocled Montagu read telegrams of welcome for him. Among the senders, he noted in his diary, were '[the rulers of] Bikaner, Alwar, Gwalior, Bannerjea, Tilak (!) and all sorts of associations and leagues'.[19]

The exclamation mark said a lot. Tilak had neither withdrawn nor deferred his movement for Home Rule after Besant's release, arguing that it must be carried on to extract rights from the imperial government. An official government report said of his dominance, 'The capture of the Congress organization by Mrs. Besant and Tilak is complete.

The Moderate Party in the Congress is extinguished. The Congress is completely identified with Home Rule.'[20] Even an arch conservative among the Muslims, Maulana Mohammed Ali of the Muslim League, and his kin had joined the Home Rule League. Montagu wrote in his diary that Besant had written to the viceroy demanding the release of Ali, who had been interned. 'The telegrams that I received from the Moslems are ingeniously worded,' he wrote, anticipating in a way the calls the Muslims would soon make to save the Caliphate or Khilafat. 'They ask me to see that Mohammedans shall not be regarded adversely because they carry out the injunctions of their religion to love all Mohammedans, and then call for the release of this man. I cannot help thinking that is a difficulty we have got into for not trying to shake their faith in the genuine Islamism of the Turk.'[21]

Montagu set up a series of meetings with top Indian leaders in Delhi after he had first met the princely rulers, with many of whom he shared a common interest he'd pursue during his stay in India: *shikar*. His noting in his diary on Sunday, 18 November, after an interaction with Chelmsford that day was: 'I am to see Tilak in a deputation, but not in an interview.'[22] It was a deliberate decision the two biggest officials of the Raj had arrived at. Later, they amended it slightly: while Tilak would meet as part of a delegation, both he and Besant would also be granted one-on-one interviews subsequently.

About Tilak's arrival in Delhi, *The Bombay Chronicle* correspondent wrote, 'Mr. Tilak and party reached . . . amidst thundering ovations, some Mahomedan and Hindu leaders being present. The procession lasted one hour. Thousands are visiting Mr. Tilak's residence every day.'[23] Tilak had only months ago been barred from entering both Delhi and the Punjab. The Delhi commissioner lifted the restriction on his entry when he found out he was on the delegation supposed to meet Montagu. But the Punjab government, led by the imperialist hardliner Michael O'Dwyer, didn't want to annul its order, despite the fact that no matter what route he took to get to Delhi, Tilak would have to pass through Punjab. The Government of India sent a telegram to the Punjab government seeking its nod, and the Punjab government reluctantly granted permission on the condition that Tilak wouldn't take advantage of it and address any meetings or receive deputations. Tilak was told about the condition, and he consented.[24]

On Monday, 26 November, Montagu recorded in his diary, 'Mrs. Besant and the great Tilak came with their Home Rule League.' Just before them, the Congress, the Muslim League, and the Punjab Provincial Congress delegation had seen him with what he called a short and good address. Tilak had been part of the Congress delegation. When Tilak and Besant met the secretary of state after that as leaders of the Home Rule League, on the other hand, they 'read us (Chelmsford sat in on the meeting and on other meetings too) a more extreme and a bitter address, but one which was undoubtedly interesting and good'.[25] After the deputation's meeting, an 'amusing incident' happened, wrote Montagu in his diary, 'Mrs. Besant and Tilak came forward to present to Chelmsford and myself copies of their memorial. Mrs. Besant asked the viceroy if she might put a garland round his neck. He told her "No," and took it in his hands. Tilak did not ask me, but placed the garland round my neck, so that, if it gets out, it will be found that I have been garlanded by the renowned Tilak, who is only a few years out of seven years penal servitude for being, at any rate, indirectly connected by his newspaper writings with the murder of an official.'[26]

The next day, 'after lunch', Montagu noted in his diary, '[W]e saw Tilak, the politician who probably has the greatest influence of any person in India.' He was 'clad in white, with bare feet.' Montagu's observation was that Tilak 'is very extreme. His procession to Delhi to see me was a veritable triumphant one. He was really the author of the Congress League scheme, and although he did not impress me very much in argument, he is a scientific man of great erudition and learning. It was quite obvious that he was not going to be satisfied with anything but what the Congress asks for. "We shall take whatever the Government gives us," he said, "but it will not satisfy us unless it is at least what the Congress asks"'.[27]

On the way back, Tilak had a stopover at Mathura, where he and his associates 'Khaparde, Kelkar, Doctor Sathaye and Velkar' got 'a grand reception'. He was at the height of his popularity, acknowledged all over as the 'Lokmanya', whose appeal went across communities and creeds. His carriage was unhorsed and the procession taken through Mathura's streets, which were 'decorated with arches and Home Rule buntings', and 'the houses and shops presented a festive appearance'. A newspaper reported that 'near the mosque the Mahomedans gave an enthusiastic

ovation', and 'in the evening Mr. Tilak addressed a mass meeting of
ten thousand people'.[28] He had no planned stopover in Agra, from
where the great Shivaji had escaped after more than three months of
imprisonment by the Mughal Emperor Aurangzeb. But on his way to
Bombay, Tilak was 'detained by the Agra public', wrote a paper, 'and taken
in procession to Bharasilal Dharmasala, Rajakimundi. The procession,
which was held by moonlight, passed through thoroughfares with band
and music playing and the city aflame with lights like Dewali. Flowers
were showered along the whole route. The procession lasted four hours,
unprecedented enthusiasm being displayed in the city'. Again Tilak
addressed a mass meeting of over ten thousand people, exhorting them
'to stand firm by the Joint Scheme (Congress–League scheme) and not
be deceived by any other ephemeral substitute schemes.' Indians were
in the thick of the fight, he said. In Jhansi and Gwalior, both places with
a Maratha past and present, the reception was just as enthusiastic.[29]

For the Congress plenary session that December, Tilak succeeded
in having his way fairly easily, something he wasn't used to despite his
vast popular appeal or because of the resistance he faced from intra-
party rivals partly on account of it. Ever since action had been initiated
against Annie Besant, and especially since her release in September, he
had insisted she be picked as president for the session, which was to be
held in Calcutta. Tilak said, 'If we want to prove how keenly we feel
for her, let us elect her president.'[30] His putting his weight behind her
ensured the Irishwoman was chosen. He was backed by Rabindranath
Tagore, among many, though Surendranath Banerjea and some others
were opposed to Besant.[31] Exactly ten years earlier, Tilak had proposed
the name of Lala Lajpat Rai, who had returned after a period of
externment by the British. The Moderates had then foiled his plans.

Along with Besant, Gandhi had acquired tremendous prominence
on the national scene in 1917 with his championing of the cause of the
indigo farmers in Champaran in Bihar. Before the Congress session,
Tilak attended the Gujarat Political Conference held in Godhra under
Gandhi's leadership. The start of the conference was slightly delayed as
Tilak reached late. Apologizing to the attendees, Gandhi said that he
was not responsible for the late start and added in a lighter vein that
they were all asking for Home Rule, and it shouldn't matter to them
if they got it forty-five minutes later. He and Tilak were unanimous

about the promotion of Indian languages, and in keeping with it, Tilak spoke on the occasion in Marathi, his speech translated for the audience smoothly by the fluent-in-Gujarati Khaparde. He said, 'The great claim of the bureaucracy is that it has made India prosperous. I would fain [gladly or willingly] concede it, but the facts are against it.' He rubbished as 'false' the claim of the former Bombay governor Lord Sydenham, who was campaigning aggressively against Indian nationalism and against the Home Rule League in particular as chief of the newly-formed Indo–British Association in London, that India was taking advantage of Britain's troubles during the war to fight for self-rule. Indians had been doing it for more than thirty years, he said, adding, 'All over the world, self-government is on the anvil, and India alone cannot be expected to stand still.'[32]

Gandhi in his own way paid an indirect tribute to Tilak's extraordinarily long fight against the criminal and punishable charge of sedition. Reading the first resolution of the Gujarat conference, which stated that 'We hereby express our fealty to our King-Emperor,' Gandhi dramatically tore it up. 'It would be vulgar to pass such a resolution,' he told the audience. 'So long as we do not rebel, we must be taken as loyal. If any questions are asked as to why no loyalty resolution was brought before the conference, tell them frankly, that it was all Gandhi's doing.'[33]

According to Gandhi's biographer, Tilak was the dominating figure at the Congress's Calcutta session. The turnout was unprecedented: almost 5000 delegates and just as many visitors, including 400 women.[34] Speaking to the attendees, Tilak addressed the lack of clarity in the Montagu declaration which, he knew, was bothering almost all freedom-loving Indians. With a talented editor's and a gifted mass leader's skill for distillation and making stuff effortlessly comprehensible for millions, Tilak said Montagu's declaration could be divided into three parts. One, the imperial government's object was to establish responsible government in India. Two, this responsible government would be given in stages. And three—what these stages would be, and within what period they would come, would be determined by the government. Tilak said he was fine with the first two points, but not with the third. 'We want the stages to be determined by us, and not at the sweet will of the executive,' he noted. He insisted on definite stages and a timeframe for all of it to be fixed in the Act or new legislation to be brought in itself.

As for the still intriguing meaning of responsible government, Tilak offered it himself. It was 'a government where the Executive is entirely responsible to the Legislature, call it Parliament or by any other name.' That legislature 'should be wholly elected,' he said, and trying to push the limits, as he did so often, added that 'even governors and lieutenant-governors must be elected by legislative bodies.'

Many among the masses were still seeking a better definition of Home Rule, and Tilak was dexterously simple about that one too, sidestepping possibly new legal landmines. 'I should be in my own country what an Englishman feels to be in England and in the colonies. The simplest definition is that, and that is the whole of it,' he made plain. 'All those bombastic phrases such as 'partnership in the Empire,' 'terms of equality' etc, mean that I want to be in my country not as outlander but as a master, in the same sense that an Englishman is a master in his own country and in the colonies.'[35]

Just a few months ago, when he had called for passive resistance, he had similarly clarified what was legal and constitutional, and if there was any distinction between the two, at the All-India Committee's meeting at Allahabad. Though he wanted everyone to stay with the limits of both law and constitution, there truly was a difference, Tilak said. So long as law-making was not in Indian hands, 'laws repugnant to justice and morality would be sometimes passed.' Indians 'could not obey them.' Passive resistance, he noted, 'was a means to an end but was not the goal in itself.' It was 'a determination to achieve their goal, and if they were hindered by artificial and unjust legislation and by any unjust combination of circumstances, it was their duty to fight it out. Passive resistance was perfectly constitutional; it did not preach unruliness or illegality, but a fixed determination to reach the goal.'[36]

At the Calcutta session, Tilak also made a personal gesture towards the mother of the Ali brothers Mohammed and Shaukat who had been imprisoned under the Defence of India Act, a notorious legislation brought in in 1915 to arbitrarily lock up anyone who was perceived as a threat to law and order. She was seated on the dais. Tilak read out a resolution calling for the release of her sons and said two things. The first was: 'As their friend and sympathizer, not personal friend but as friend and sympathizer of everyone who is unjustly treated, without distinction of caste, creed or colour, as friend and sympathizer of truth and justice . . . I demand that Messrs. Mohammed and Shaukat Ali be immediately released.' By saying he wasn't a 'personal friend', he was clearly making his basic differences clear. The Ali brothers were Islamic hardliners and believers in pan-Islam. At the same time, he was underlining that he was making an outreach in the interests of Indian unity against colonial repression. 'But let me assure the mother here, on your behalf,' he went on, 'that to become a mother of brave sons far exceeds in importance the title of being a mother only, and . . . all of us have great sympathy with her . . . I pray to God that we may have many more mothers in the country of her type'.[37]

Tilak also emphasized that the Congress should stick to the Lucknow pact which, among other things, spoke of a political arrangement between the Hindus and Muslims until the government, as promised by Montagu, came out with its own new scheme of reforms. When that scheme was revealed, they could think of whether the Lucknow Pact needed amending or not.[38]

An arrangement of sorts had been temporarily reached between the predominantly Hindu Congress and the Muslims. But what of the different castes among the Hindus themselves, and broadly between Brahmans and non-Brahmans? Montagu's announcement created expectations of political representation in the minds of non-Brahmans of Maharashtra, just as they did elsewhere. The non-Brahman movement in the Bombay Presidency, pioneered by Phule's Satyashodhak Samaj, had been principally a Maharashtrian one, with some Kannada-speaking non-Brahmans and almost no Gujaratis.[39] Sometimes united and sometimes divided on the basis of castes themselves, most of the under-represented caste groups in the Deccan had distrusted the Congress. Phule himself had characterized the Poona Sarvajanik Sabha as a 'bhat sabha' and Congress leaders as 'cunning Aryabhat Brahmans', and Tilak's followers' act of threatening to set fire to the pandal hosting the National Social Conference at the 1895 Congress session had alienated the lower castes even more.[40] The Moderates, who termed themselves liberals, had also not covered themselves with glory in this respect. It was they who had started speaking of Tilak as leader of 'the *telis* [oil grinders] and *tambolis* [betel-leaf sellers]', both considered lower castes, and it was meant not as a complimentary remark about his mass appeal but as a negative and nasty comment depicting elite scorn for the masses.[41] Tilak, of course, had thwarted their move by turning the comment to his credit as champion of the common Indians' interests and as mobilizer of the Indian masses for collective political action.

The non-Brahmans in 1917 saw hope in the new proposed set of constitutional reforms. Moreover, an organization of the Maratha sub-caste called the Maratha League had started saying empathically that India did not need Swaraj at all.[42] As non-Brahman anger against both the Brahmans and the Congress, which they saw as an organization representing Brahminical interests, found expression afresh at the Belgaum District Conference held that year, Tilak was asked for his response. While he said he understood the sentiment of the non-Brahmans, he suggested that a lot of the activity of their groups had to do with the British setting them up against the Congress after the Lucknow Pact.

'It is natural that the non-Brahmans should be angry with us,' he said, proceeding to make his allegation and expressing hope in the same breath. 'How could the enemies of the Congress sit still and quietly look on the unity forged at Lucknow between the Hindus and Muslims? We have achieved this by granting special representation to the Muslims. Now the enemies of the Congress have raised up another bogey of disruption. But in one sense I am also happy that the simple-minded non-Brahmans have started demanding certain things for themselves, although out of spite for us at present. This shows a growth of self-confidence. Today the government might concede their demands (such as for community representation on the councils) to sow seeds of disruption among us, but gradually, as the demands go on increasing, government will have to disappoint them and this disappointment will make them join us. If we can prove to the non-Brahmans by example that we are wholly on their side in their demands from the government, I am sure that in times to come their agitation, now based on social inequality, will merge into our struggle. Unless this happens, their movement will peter out in a short time.'[43]

Tilak had said at the Lucknow Congress that he would not mind if only non-Brahmans were elected on the councils; the idea was that a majority of members ought to be Indians instead of foreigners. As caste mobilization to secure non-Brahman rights was renewed in the second half of 1917, Tilak wrote in the *Kesari* that the Brahmans had never asked for all the seats on the councils and if they had got more, it was on account of their education. He thought it was inconceivable that the leaders of the non-Brahmans, who were all educated, would support the despotic colonial system. The non-Brahmans need not be worried about the Congress and the Brahmans, he said by means of reassurance. Describing as 'false' the charge that the Brahmans had put the other castes down by denying them education, Tilak said it was 'doubtful' if the *chaturvarnya* or four-caste system was prevalent 'in its entirety at any time in the past' and 'even if rights of education, sacrifice and gift acceptance were reserved for Brahmans, their extent was very limited'. Education of the kind necessary for daily life and the literacy required for it were within the reach of all, including the Shudras, he claimed, and the only thing they weren't allowed was the learning of the Vedas. He further said that the Brahmans now not only did not obstruct the education of non-Brahmans but they were in fact prepared to assist them. If the government had appointed more Brahmans on the councils, he said, it was only because of their education, so the real distinction was not between Brahmans and non-Brahmans but among the educated and the non-educated, and the educated people of any caste would get opportunities and privileges. Tilak made it clear that he was not in favour of communal representation nationally, yet neither was he opposed to anyone who wished for it.[44]

By theorizing thus, Tilak was attempting to reach out to the non-Brahmans and make common cause with them. It was evident from some of his statements, though, that even if he had travelled some distance from his early days in the direction of social inclusivity, as a man of his times, he hadn't shed his social conservatism.

One very highly-regarded champion of the non-Brahman cause, however, was convinced of Tilak's sincerity. Vitthal Ramji Shinde was a Maratha and a social reformer earlier linked to the Brahmo Samaj and had the reputation of being the founder of the Depressed Classes Mission for the uplift of the so-called Untouchables. In October 1917, he formed the Maratha Rashtriya Sangh in Poona and asked Tilak to address its members the following month as a representative of the Brahman community.[45] Here Tilak, in a bid to assuage concerns that Swaraj would mean a throwback to the old caste hierarchy, said they wanted Swaraj 'not of the old type but on the western pattern'.

He said the British had cemented their rule in India owing to differences between Brahmans and non-Brahmans and if those continued, the country would stay backward even if it obtained Swaraj.[46]

Buoyed by the clauses of the Lucknow pact, many caste organizations had started demanding separate electorates for their groups in anticipation of Montagu's legislation. Shinde, who was famously known as 'Karmaveer', believed separate electorates would be a case of the remedy being deadlier than the disease.[47] He next called Tilak for an All-India Anti-Untouchability Conference he organized in Bombay under the aegis of Baroda ruler Sayajirao Gaekwad on 23 and 24 March 1918. Tilak said he would attend, but in his personal capacity and not as editor of the *Kesari*. Tilak spoke enthusiastically at the conference, saying that he had in 1894 carried the Ganpati idol of a Chambhar (Chamar or cobbler) in his horse carriage for immersion. Here he proclaimed that 'if there is a God that accepts untouchability, I won't recognize such a God', drawing massive applause from all those present. He further said:

There was no basis in the Hindu Shastras for untouchability. Untouchability should not come in the way of the great national work, which required as much manpower as could possibly be mobilized. History told them that on the battlefields, water was carried for drinking in leather pots by the so-called untouchables. The very notion that a certain man was untouchable should be done away with, and everything would follow this. There was equality in the eyes of God for all communities and it was a great sin if anyone asserted that there were any untouchables . . . It was inevitable and urgent that the untouchables and the Depressed should be educated and given equal opportunity for the service of the country and the sacred cause of the Motherland. I was never against this (anti-untouchability) movement and fully sympathized with it.[48]

When the *Kesari* put out a report on Tilak's various meetings between 24 and 27 March, nevertheless, there were details about what he had said in other places but just one line about the Shinde-led conference, saying in faithful reportorial style, 'On Sunday morning, Tilak attended the Anti-Untouchability Conference.'

There was nothing about what he or even others at the conference, including the reformist Baroda ruler, had said. If Shinde had had doubts earlier about what Tilak had meant when he said he was coming not as editor of the *Kesari*, those stood dispelled.[49] Days after the conference, when Shinde went to Sardar Gruha in Bombay to get Tilak's signature on a memorandum for the elimination of untouchability to be signed by members of all castes, Tilak demurred.[50]

When 1918 dawned, Tilak was already half-way through his sixty-second year. He felt old and frail. He had begun to develop great exhaustion after travel and after delivering speeches. Leg pain he had had since his years of incarceration in Mandalay. It still persisted, and of late, it had gotten worse as he had injured one of his legs, and the wound hurt. Public life, politics and the ascent of India towards political liberation were however his great passions, and he'd pursue them relentlessly. In particular, he seriously wanted now to activate his desire to go to England. Not by himself, but as part of a team of Home Rulers that would campaign in London. He was planning this visit for two reasons: the propagation of the idea of Swaraj in the imperial capital, for which Baptista had already proceeded there, and the launch of libel proceedings against Valentine Chirol, the correspondent of *The Times*, London, who had made multiple allegations against Tilak in his book on India. What lent urgency to the idea was the setting up of a group by a coterie of retired Anglo-Indian bureaucrats led by ex-governor of Bombay Lord Sydenham, called the Indo–British Association, which had launched a campaign against Home Rule for India, vowing to carry on as vigorous propaganda as that conducted by Tilak in India. The British Committee of the Congress was doing precious little to counter the group's propaganda, and its paper, called *India*, brought out by the Moderates on British soil, didn't even publish Congress resolutions.[51]

Before the visit could happen, important things intervened, focusing his attention on the war and the reform proposals again. The first was a war conference. Tilak carried out a whirlwind tour of Berar in February and toured Solapur and other places in the southern Marathi-speaking regions in March, chiefly to mobilize funds for the campaign the Home Rulers were planning in England. He was preparing to leave for London when the viceroy called for a three-day war conference in Delhi starting 27 April.

Why was the conference called? The Germans had tied up with the Bolsheviks in Russia and there were fears they would trigger 'a conflagration in Central Asia, Afghanistan and the frontiers of India'.[52] Already Turkish troops had been sent across the Black Sea to Batumi in southwestern Georgia and the Caucasus, entered Azerbaijan, which was then a part of Persia, and were all set to enter Central Asia and Persia.[53] The Empire was alarmed, and the British premier, Lloyd George, had sent a telegram to India's viceroy asking for war efforts to be 'redoubled'.[54]

Inside India, matters weren't as bad as they might have been for the Raj with Turkey's advances. Though Muslim allegiance from within India to Britain's war effort was dictated by interests of faith, the British government had stepped in to pre-empt any trouble when it found Turkey ranged against itself. Both Britain and her allies pledged that Arabia would not be targeted and protection given to Islam's holiest spots by a 'really independent Muslim power' would not be placed in peril.[55] So for the moment at least, there was no danger of the Muslims revolting. What of the Germans? There were some Indian revolutionaries based abroad who sought German assistance during the conflict to free India from the clutches of the British. Some of the revolutionary elements thought they might be able to convince Tilak to be on their side. A revolutionary based in India, V.C. Chidambaram Pillai, met him and had a detailed conversation. Tilak's theory was clear; he didn't mind backing the revolutionaries if he saw a successful outcome. Pillai gave him theories about what might happen, and Tilak heard him patiently but told him at the end that the outcomes he was talking about were unlikely to arise as the situation in Europe was far too complicated for that.[56] Besides, despite the impression sought to be created in certain circles that Tilak wanted Britain to lose the war, he wasn't in favour of the Germans. 'Between the cruel Germans and the English, the latter are nearer to us by habit and inclination. We must help them if they ask for our aid, and if we help, they would be compelled to grant us more political rights in return.'[57]

To the astonishment of all Indians, Tilak's name did not figure on the list of leaders Chelmsford had invited for discussions. Disbelief in his words and actions ran really deep. Annie Besant too wasn't on the list. Gandhi, who got an invite, objected to the exclusion of Tilak and the others and even wired to Tilak asking him to come to Delhi, not knowing that apart from the absence of an invitation, he faced another hurdle: just three months ago, the Delhi government had restricted his entry into the capital once again, and it was in no mood to lift the curbs.[58]

Montagu didn't like Chelmsford's idea of not inviting Tilak. Tilak's biographers in the past have tended to quote only a part of what Montagu wrote in his diary about this in order to bring out only the complimentary part, but Montagu spoke about Tilak's status and his potential to offer assistance of course, but equally about the chance to demolish him totally if he tried to act difficult. Montagu's note for 27 April in his personal diary stated:

> With regard to Tilak, if I were the viceroy I would have had him at Delhi at all costs. He is at the moment probably the most powerful man in India, and he has it in his power, if he chooses, to help materially in War effort. If on the other hand, he attached conditions of a political kind to his offers of help, as, indeed, he would, at such a conference things would be said to him which would forever destroy his influence in India, at least, so I think. If he is not there, it will always be said that we refused to select the most powerful people. Tilak is already saying that in his speeches, and it would have completely taken the wind out of his sails if he had been invited as one of the leaders of Indian opinion. Of course, one can always say: 'No help from such a source', but still, there it is. I read a speech of Tilak's on board ship, and it is quite obvious that he will not accept our report proposals. This seems to me all to the good: he is the leader of the opposition.[59]

Gandhi's objection was nullified by the viceroy, who called him for a personal meeting before the conference and persuaded him to attend.

On 10 June a provincial-level Bombay war conference was held, and Tilak was invited for it by the governor Lord Willingdon. The governor gave the attendees 'a severe sermon' on Home Rule, questioning its 'bona fides'. When Tilak was asked to speak, he wasn't permitted to mention Home Rule at all and had to stop. Jinnah, an Irish friend of India and editor of *The Bombay Chronicle* B.G. Horniman, and Tilak's aides N.C. Kelkar and Dadasaheb Karandikar were similarly interrupted the moment they uttered Home Rule.[60] It was all very humiliating.

Gandhi chaired a public meeting in Bombay to protest against Willingdon's conduct and condemned his 'gratuitous insult to the Home Rulers.'[61] Yet Gandhi was convinced India must plunge into the work of saving the Empire without expecting anything in return. This is where fundamental differences in his approach and that of Tilak became very noticeable.

At the national war conference, Gandhi spoke of the Indian people's aspirations as articulated in the Congress–League pact and added that a lot of the support for the war effort came from the belief and hope that reforms were imminent. However, he noted, 'If I could make my countrymen retrace their steps, I would make them withdraw all the Congress resolutions and not whisper "Home Rule" or "Responsible Government" during the pendency of the war. I would make India offer all her able-bodied sons as a sacrifice to the empire at its critical moment and I know that India, by this very act, would become the most favoured partner in the empire and racial distinctions would become a thing of the past.'[62] Tilak, on the other hand, would not admit of any unconditional support. Not only did he accuse the Raj bureaucracy of making the conference a futile exercise as a result of its unwillingness to let go of its despotic power, but insisted that 'the tide of the world has changed. The question of India's freedom has become a question of world freedom. For the sake of world freedom India must be made free and given Swaraj'. India, he maintained, 'would not come forward to help Britain unless a substantial share of self-government was given to the people.'[63]

The share was deemed not adequately substantial by Tilak when the Montagu–Chelmsford reforms proposals came in July. According to the proposals, the Viceroy's Council was to be replaced by two new bodies, the Legislative Assembly and Council of State, but they would be merely consultative, and provincial legislative councils would have 70 per cent elected members but a two-tier system of government called diarchy would severely curtail their powers, with the governor having control over key departments such as law and order and revenue. Separate electorates would be retained and extended also to 'Sikhs in the Punjab, Indian Christians, Anglo-Indians and even Europeans in other places'.[64]

Tilak described the proposed reforms as a 'sunless dawn', and Annie Besant termed them as 'unworthy of Britain to offer and Indian to accept'.[65] Moderate leaders such as Surendranath Banerjea, Dinshaw Wacha, Chimanlal Setalvad and Narayan Chandavarkar were for wholehearted acceptance of the proposals. Fearing that the Congress would reject the scheme, the Moderates in Bengal led by Banerjea had, surprisingly even before the proposals became public, batted for them and created their own party, the National Liberal League.[66] Anticipating another split in the Congress, Tilak told them there was no point in seceding thus. Considering the sharp differences of opinion, a special session of the Congress was convened in August and September to discuss the matter. Ideally, Tilak wished that the Congress would pass a resolution completely rejecting the proposals 'if we can get it adopted unanimously'.[67] But it looked like the Moderates might just leave, and Tilak thought that a fresh split in the Congress would be disastrous, so he agreed with Besant, who thought like him, and Gokhale's Moderate disciple Srinivasa Sastri, that they shouldn't throw out the proposals altogether. He consented instead to a compromise resolution that the reforms scheme was insupportable 'unless and until it is amended so as to give us full Responsible Government in Provinces and control by compartment in the Imperial [government], so as to bring it as near the Congress scheme as possible.'[68] Sastri wanted to give the government greater latitude, and Tilak accepted his contention that the Congress should agree to keep law, police and justice in the governors' hands for a period of six years.[69] Relieved and hoping that a split had been averted, Tilak said, again playing the role of a realist, 'We were told the Congress was going to reject the whole scheme. I could never understand, and have never understood what it means . . . Fortunately for all, we have been able to place before you a reasoned document, a resolution which combines the wisdom of one party, I may say, the temperament of another party, and if you like to call it – I do not like to call it myself – the rashness of a third party . . . We have tried to satisfy all parties concerned, and a very difficult task has been accomplished.'[70]

By year-end, the Moderates had left the Congress nevertheless. Their exit, and its consequences, were in contrast with what had happened with the Extremists in 1907 and after. The Extremists had been evicted, they hadn't left mostly of their own accord, they had garnered massive support on the outside, and when they had come back with Tilak at the head of their forces, they had quickly assumed control of the organization and dominated it. The Moderates opted out largely on their own owing to their discomfort with the forceful policies of Tilak and his group. After 1918, they formed their own organization, the All-India Liberal Federation, and walked their way into irrelevance. Their Federation was insignificant at best and invisible at worst as India continued her passionate pursuit of freedom in the two remaining years of the Tilak era and the approaching decades of the Gandhian age.[71]

Tilak had in March 1918 decided to take the sea route to England via Colombo. He was sent off with great fanfare by the people of Poona on the 23rd of that month. The famous Marathi playwright and poet Ram Ganesh Gadkari wrote a verse for him, and Vishubua Jog, one of the leading lights of the Warkari sect that took inspiration from the Bhakti saint-poet movement, wrote an *abhang* to send his best wishes. The path to Colombo went through Bombay, so there were meetings to attend there before going ahead. In China Baug, Tilak addressed a meeting meant only for women, and Jinnah presided over a gathering at Girgaum's Shantaram Chawl, which had become a well-known venue for the nationalist caucus.[72] In Madras, the travelling delegation comprising Tilak, B.C. Pal, Khaparde, Karandikar and Kelkar was received by Besant, and the team was taken in a procession from the railway station to Adyar. Religious rites were performed by 500 Brahmans for Tilak at the Parthasarathi temple, and he was taken around the temple 'with the beating of drums, blowing of conches and chanting of mantras'.[73] After addressing a mass meeting of 20,000 people there, Tilak headed for Colombo and was looking forward to boarding the ship when he and his associates were told their passports had been cancelled by the war cabinet of the British government and they couldn't go.

Montagu described the episode in his diary:

The Tilak incident was very characteristic. Passports were issued to him and his friends without reference to me, but in issuing them, it seems to me that the Government were clearly right. Tilak had to go home (Montagu's home, England) to fight the Chirol case; and to stop his expedition at the time that the papers are full of Lord Sydenham's activities would have been a fatal mistake. But, having allowed him to go home, either out of sheer malice or crass stupidity, the Home Department, without reference to the Viceroy, sent home a telegram containing so black a picture of Tilak's antecedents and probable activities that I do not wonder the Home Government were nervous. It seems a little strange, however, that they should have cancelled a passport given by a duly authorized authority without consulting him. However, it was done. I drafted for the Viceroy a telegram of protest, which was ultimately sent, with a request for reconsideration. It has failed; the Home Government refused to let him sail, mainly on the ground that the General Staff will not have it.[74]

If Montagu was secretary of state, why was he routinely complaining in his personal diary and not using his authority to get things done? That was because he was essentially a weak man, unable to stand up to the establishment. Even about the reforms, he said as Churchill and other imperialists came down on him that 'I am not the stuff to carry this sort of thing off'. Chelmsford was worse; he was distant and cold towards the Indians, and just put his head down and worked as an unfeeling colonial administrator. His daughter, Margaret, who was only five years old, put it succinctly: 'My daddy works very hard and my mummy is the viceroy.'[75]

These were the top officials of the colonial regime. What were they going to do for the enslaved Indians?

The British press took prominent notice of the cancelling of Tilak's passport. The *Herald* in London, which was sympathetic towards the subject nations, asked, 'What is there that Mr. Tilak has to tell the people of Britain that the mandarins in Whitehall do not wish us to know? Are the conditions of life so bad in India that the British government dare not allow Indians like Mr. Tilak to come to this country and address meetings?' The same paper published a telegram sent to it by S. Subramania Iyer, Besant and Rangaswami stating 'the Indian people regret the action taken against their most trusted leader'.[76] The pro-imperialist *Times* of London congratulated the British government for having stopped Tilak. In an editorial headlined 'Manufactured Indian Opinion', it accused the Indian nationalists of starting an 'artificial stream of telegrams' from ordinary Indians to

Tilak, which he could show in Britain as 'the force of Indian public opinion' about Home Rule. The editorial stated the passports had been 'quite rightly withdrawn' and pointed out that since Montagu had been in India 'for the greater part of the winter, with the sole object of giving Mr. Tilak and everybody else a full opportunity of expounding their views and aspirations', there was 'no case at this crisis of the war for the distraction' of a Home Rule deputation.[77]

Thinking it was utterly necessary for India's message to go out to the world in the midst of the armed conflict, Tilak, around this time, proposed to Rabindranath Tagore that he should undertake a lecture tour of England and America, for which Tilak would give him a fund of Rs 50,000. Tilak knew fully well that it would be odd to expect Tagore to do the kind of overt political activity he himself was doing, but he understood the nature of what in the twenty-first century is termed as soft power and saw Tagore in the role of freedom-anticipating India's cultural ambassador. Tagore wrote later that 'my surprise was still greater when I was assured that Tilak did not want my help for any propaganda which was his own, that he would be sorry if I followed the path which he himself was pursuing . . . He wanted me to be true to myself and, through my effort to serve humanity, in my own way to serve India. I felt that this proposal from Tilak carried with it the highest honour that I had ever received from my countrymen. I do not know if I was worthy of it, but it revealed to me the greatness of Tilak's personality . . . He had more faith in truth than in method. His ideal of the fulfilment of India's destiny was vast, and therefore it had ample room even for a dreamer of dreams, even for 'music-maker'. He knew that freedom had its diverse aspects, and therefore it could be truly reached if individuals had their full scope to use their special gifts or opening out paths that were diverse in their directions.'[78] Actually, along with a political battle, Tilak was fighting a cultural conflict too, doing his best to demonstrate to the world that India, which the British painted as a dark, uncivilized place, had a rich cultural past and a civilizational, political and societal heritage which made her one of the most ancient centres of knowledge and learning. Not surprising that he thought Tagore could play a vital role in debunking British falsehoods.

Finally in September 1918, Tilak was given permission to go to England. But on one condition—his visit would have to be a private one and he would not involve himself in any political activity. Tilak agreed, under protest,[79] and decided to take along with him his lawyer Dadasaheb Karandikar, Vasukaka Joshi and Madhavrao Joshi's son, who'd be his personal attendant. His aides too had to travel 'on private business', not as delegates.

Tilak had been keeping increasingly unwell of late. That year too, he had travelled a lot in his car for his campaigns. 'People can't possibly realise that I feel so weak,' he said. 'When the moment comes I lecture. But the body is all the while breaking the strain. The lecture over, I retire from the crowds and sleep over my fatigue. Only my will supports me. The body is done up.'[80] But what had to done had to be done. He sailed on the *S.S. Japan* from Bombay on 24 September. The journey was longer than usual as the ship navigators had to consider the peril from enemy submarines. From Port Said, the ship had protection in the form of two submarines, a defence vessel and a few aeroplanes overhead. When it reached Aden, Tilak got a telegram informing him that he had been chosen to be president of the Congress session in December. Of course, he would not be able to attend as he was going to be away. He had bought Western clothes, including a grey Cheviot Chesterfield overcoat to cope with the English winter. He tried them on for the first time on the ship. He would continue to wear his *pagdi* in London, though. Tilak reached Britain's shores on 29 October 1918 and stayed there thirteen months. His base there was a house called 10, Howley Place in Maida Vale which Baptista had rented for Tilak and company.[81] Tilak said soon on arrival that the quarters 'are comfortable. We have six rooms at our disposal. Two on each floor.'[82]

As a faithful vegetarian, Tilak lived on rice, bread, potatoes and vegetables in the British capital and for a while had his food cooked by a Brahman from Telangana. With his health not quite all right and his diabetes troublesome as ever especially with age catching up, he followed, for the most part, a daily routine not very different from the one he maintained back home, though certain changes were inevitable. He woke up by 6 a.m. or latest by 7 a.m. A morning shave was mandatory. In India, someone else did it for him, but here, he had to do it himself, so he used a safety razor in order to avoid nicks and cuts, particularly undesirable for a diabetic whose wounds wouldn't heal quickly. Of late his sight and hearing weren't great, and his walk not as firm as it once used to be with the famous stick tapping its presence everywhere. So he went out mostly for work, eschewing evening social events as much as possible. Traffic in London was dense for an Indian of those times, for India did not boast of so many road vehicles, and one of the aides accompanying him wrote that often, when Tilak wanted to cross the street, he would put his hand up and start moving after the vehicle had come to a halt.[83]

Tilak's first political move in the imperial capital was to give £2000 for the Labour Party's coming election campaign. The Labour leader J. Ramsay MacDonald had earlier criticized the government's decision to block Tilak's visit by cancelling his passport as neither wise nor intelligent, saying Labour could have obtained information about India's claims to self-government from the deputation which would have helped the party discuss the reforms proposals in Parliament and outside.[84] On receiving the funds from Tilak, Labour promised, 'We support the aspirations of the Indian people for freedom. And henceforth our party will afford you every possible assistance.' Though MacDonald became Labour's first prime minister in 1924, the party lost the election immediately following Tilak's visit. Yet it had elected sixty-three MPs, and Tilak said 'it will still be the party in opposition now and as such will be useful to us'.[85] Fortunately, as the war had already ended, the restrictions placed on Tilak's participation in political activities were soon lifted. Through Labour he then distributed vast quantities of Home Rule literature and was also on occasions offered the party platform to speak, once at the Fabian Society meeting at Essex Hall presided over by the playwright George Bernard Shaw.[86] Many Labour MPs also invited Tilak and his aides over for dinner one evening in 1919. Tilak's paper wrote with hope that 'one or two more dinners like this may enlist the full sympathy of the Labour Party in Parliament'.[87]

For the case against Chirol, Tilak engaged the services of a leading and expensive lawyer like John Simon, who later came to India as part of the Simon Commission and is remembered till date for the Indians welcoming him with the slogan 'Simon Go Back'. The hearing in the case began on 29 January 1919, with Justice Darling, with a special jury, getting to know about the passages in Chirol's book *Indian Unrest*, which was 'a revised reprint of his articles in The Times'. Tilak had made the publishers of the book, Macmillan and Co., co-defendants.

The essence of Tilak's argument for libel action was that Valentine Chirol had 'charged him with provoking the Mahomedans to riot by the foundation of "cow protection societies", with urging the Hindus to the use of violence by organizing gymnasia, with levying blackmail for the purposes of political propaganda, and with having been associated with the murder of Indian civil servants.'[88]

While Simon was assisted by E.F. Spence, representing Chirol and the publishers was Edward Carson, who appeared along with Ellis Hume-Williams and Eustace Hills.

Carson cited Tilak's convictions in the past to suggest that he was unreliable and that he had indeed been the unseen hand behind political murders. For example, when the judge asked who had been caught for the murders of Rand and Ayerst in 1897 in which Tilak had been implicated, this is the kind of exchange that happened in the court:

JOHN SIMON: A man was discovered some time afterwards – a man of whom Mr. Tilak knew nothing.
EDWARD CARSON: He was a Brahmin.
JOHN SIMON: I believe that the number of Brahmins in India is about the same as the number of Irishmen in England. (Laughter)[89]

The Tilak versus Carson encounter was the most dramatic part of the proceedings. Cross-examining Tilak, Carson kept up the questions on the Rand murder to paint the plaintiff in a particular light before judge and jury:

CARSON: Was it your opinion that it was the oppression of the administration of Mr. Rand during the plague in Poona that led to his murder?
TILAK: I think that the measures adopted and the harshness adopted led to the murder.
CARSON: Did you say in your newspaper that in the search of the houses great tyranny was practised by the soldiers?
TILAK: I did.
CARSON: Did you say that they entered the temple and brought out women from their houses, broke idols and burnt holy books?
TILAK: I mentioned those facts. They are facts.

CARSON: Did you abuse Mr. Rand to the day of his death?
TILAK: I did not abuse him.
CARSON: Was it your opinion that Mr. Rand was more than a tyrant?
TILAK: I said that the measures were tyrannical.
CARSON: Did you say that he was guilty of callous cruelty?
TILAK: Yes.
CARSON: Yet you say that your writings had nothing to do with his murder?
TILAK: The facts, not my doctrines.

Carson quoted passages from the Kesari in which it was stated that officers were 'terrorizing' people, 'a man went mad through being sent to the segregation camp', and 'pregnant women were caught hold of.' And continued:

CARSON: Didn't you know that British soldiers were every day risking their lives by going into these plague-stricken houses and trying to get rid of this terrible scourge?
TILAK (interjecting): So were we.
CARSON: Did you know that?
TILAK: They did not show the kindness that they should have shown.[90]

Carson also tried to make light of the Tilak side's arguments, as in this instance:

JOHN SIMON: Mr. Tilak is associated with Indian newspapers – two in particular. One of these is in the vernacular and is called Kesari – which meant, "the lion, or King of Beasts." (Laughter)
EDWARD CARLSON: Just, My Lord, like John Bull. (Laughter)
JUSTICE DARLING: I hope that it is not established yet that John Bull is the King of Beasts. (Laughter)[91]

Closing his arguments, Carson asked the jury to consider the material Chirol had at his disposal 'in combating . . . the most wicked doctrines of anarchy.' Carson alleged, 'Mr. Tilak had been organizing a widespread conspiracy to overthrow the British government in India

. . . The jury could realize what it meant to throw out articles in favour of the cult of the bomb, holding up our officials to disrepute, and our soldiers as detestable demons, as men not there to assist in putting down the plague but to take advantage of their misery for the robbing of their houses. It was a horrible story, and might have led to worse results than the murder of a few officials in India.'[92]

At the end of 11 days of trial, Justice Darling summed up for the jury in the evening of 21 February:

> Character, though incorporeal, was none the less a possession . . . The plaintiff's (Tilak's) character was very far from being above reproach, for he had been twice convicted and imprisoned for sedition. Was it an exaggeration to say that the effect of Mr. Tilak's writings was to bring the government under disrepute? It was said that he was only guilty of sedition, but what was worse than sedition except its bedfellow high treason? How long a step was it from articles "seething with sedition" to the overt act which was necessary to constitute high treason? . . . Chapekar (Rand's assassin) justified himself by alleging things about Mr. Rand and the British soldiers which were not true, but which had been alleged in Mr. Tilak's journals. In these circumstances Mr. Tilak reminded him (the judge) of the story in Aesop of the enemy trumpeter who begged the soldier to spare him on the ground that he was a non-combatant. The soldier refused on the ground that without the trumpeter's summons the enemy's soldiers would not have advanced. In the course of his denunciations of Mr. Rand, Mr. Tilak had accused him of segregating persons who were not suffering from plague, and in the witness box he had affirmed the truth of that accusation, alleging that it was borne out by the report of the Plague Commission. That was on the fourth day of the trial. It was now the 11th. The plaintiff and his advisers had all that time to find the passage in the report, but had failed to produce a single line in justification. That was the man who complained that his character had been defamed and who demanded damages.[93]

This was 1897 redux. The jury retired at 5.50 p.m. and after twenty-five minutes returned a verdict in favour of Chirol, with costs to be paid by Tilak.[94] A disappointed Tilak wrote back home that 'all who were present in court felt that but for the biased and impassioned charge of the judge, we should have won'.[95] But the question that really begs to be asked is: What was Tilak thinking, hoping that he'd win a libel case in a court in England on the basis of his political reputation as the Raj's most implacable enemy, convicted in more than one case, for his writings and speeches alone, of 'waging war against the King'?

How financially catastrophic the judgement was for him was made clear by Tilak himself in a letter from London to his favourite nephew, Dhondopant Vidwans. Tilak wrote:

> We shall now have to pay Chirol's cost, unless we appeal and succeed therein, which is very doubtful.
>
> You know that £7,500 were deposited by us in Court. This sum will be lost and I am afraid we shall have to pay something more, how much I cannot say, but certainly not less than £1,500 more. In addition to this I had to pay here £7,100 to our Solicitors for the expense of conducting the case here. Of this sum I had my own cheque for £1,500, and the rest £5,600 I have taken from ___ (unclear in the text). Therefore the whole liability now is over £14,000 . . . Where are all your astrologers who said I would win?[96]

There was much consternation in India about the verdict. *Amrita Bazar Patrika* wrote that 'the foul charges against Mr. Tilak were unfounded, and the result of the trial will only evoke universal sympathy and make him [Tilak] dearer and more beloved'. *Young India* wrote that all government records, public and confidential, were placed at Chirol's disposal, making Tilak face 'the whole bureaucracy of India'. On the other hand, the sympathetic *Herald* of London stated, Tilak was not provided access to a key document he wanted from the government in India to establish his case against Chirol.[97]

Amazingly, after the verdict, a fund was set up by Tilak's admirers in India to help him meet the monetary losses he had suffered, and contributions poured in. People kept urging their fellow citizens to make contributions. A letter writer to *Bombay Chronicle*, for instance, wrote, 'The point is that Lokmanya Tilak is almost ruined from a pecuniary point of view since he had to mortgage all his property and what is worse, even his policy of Rs 10,000.' The letter-writer urged the *Chronicle's* editor to 'treat this point in your paper with your powerful pen, for it will help to a great extent the said fund as it will directly go home to the hearts of all his countrymen'.[98]

The amount eventually collected was over three lakh rupees.[99] Right through his stay in London, however, Tilak wrote in letter after letter back home that the fund should be discontinued and that he did not appreciate it at all as the libel case he had instituted had been a personal one.

Tilak meanwhile determined that he should fix things that could still be prevented from going out of hand. The Delhi Congress session had taken place in December 1918, and the suggestions on suitable improvements to the Montagu scheme made at the earlier special session held in Bombay in Tilak's presence were upheld. Yet the British Congress Committee, Tilak concluded, was in favour of the Montagu scheme, and asked Khaparde, who was in India, to 'see that no money is voted by the Congress' to the committee 'this year'. When a Congress delegation comprising Pal, Vithalbhai Patel, Khaparde, Kelkar and ex-diwan of Mysore V.P. Madhav Rao also arrived in London in May 1919, Tilak succeeded in persuading it to make the British Congress Committee answerable to the Indian National Congress. The Congress also asserted its control over the British committee-run paper *India*. In response, Henry Polak, Gandhi's friend and close aide in his struggle in South Africa, who was editor of *India* at the time, quit. He was temporarily replaced by Tilak's associate Kelkar.[100]

Two Indian delegations were already in London. A third too came in, led by Annie Besant and comprising her aides Jamnadas Dwarkadas, P.K. Telang and B.P. Wadia. Besant was now cut up with the Tilak camp. Though she and Tilak had cooperated, there was also some amount of latent rivalry among them as to who was the No. 1 Home Rule proponent. Her sense of competition, and hurt, came to the fore at the Delhi Congress, where Tilak was absent but his word and ways still seemed to prevail. At this December 1918 Congress, Besant had suggested putting off complete provincial autonomy, backing a suggestion made by Srinivasa Sastri. But Tilak's wing had carried the day, getting all the Bombay Congress session proposals cleared. Khaparde reported to Tilak by mail, 'Mrs. Besant lost all her propositions and was very angry. She threatened to leave and even oppose and join Sastri. We stood firm.'[101] Tilak told Khaparde not to alienate Besant and to also try and convince her to be part of the Congress deputation to England, writing, 'Mrs. Besant would be of greatest use and I think we can settle our differences with her.'[102]

Yet the rift would not heal. Gradually, Besant began to develop bitterness towards both Tilak and Gandhi, the latter the rising star of the Indian national movement. She also openly started backing Montagu's proposals. Montague had already asked, when he had first met her in November 1917, why someone like her had not been cultivated by the Raj establishment. 'She kept her silvery, quiet voice, and really impressed me enormously. If only the Government had kept this old woman on our side! If only she had been well handled from the beginning! If only her vanity had been appealed to!'[103] Besant was tremendously well-liked by the Indian people, but one of the reasons she could not get to the stature of a Tilak or a Gandhi was that for all her famed uncommon eloquence, she did not speak any Indian language, and both Tilak and Gandhi, besides communicating with Indians in their own languages, were advocating Hindi as India's national language and calling for the promotion, protection and propagation of India's myriad tongues.

After the Delhi Congress debacle, Besant entered Montagu's camp fully and rejected the idea of passive resistance. A Congress leader of the time, Pattabi Sitaramayya, who wrote a history of the organization, stated that 'a mystery surrounded the attitude and activities of Mrs. Besant soon after her release'. At one point, Sitaramayya states, both the viceroy and Montagu began to shun her, and when the viceroy told Montagu he'd have to take action against Besant for her speeches, Montagu spoke of her having violated her pledges. 'What these pledges may be, when they were given, and to whom, we do not know!' exclaimed Sitaramayya, adding 'Mrs. Besant was a great believer in the Indo-British connection' and was 'soon feeling out of tune with Government and with the people'.[104]

After she had got her own delegation to England, a meeting of Indians was held under the auspices of her Home Rule League at the Albert Hall in October 1919. Here, the attendees passed a resolution on self-government and self-determination. Besant struck a discordant note, supporting Montagu's scheme 'in unmistakable terms', and

Vithalbhai Patel 'had to contradict her'. The recriminations as a result got so bad that Khaparde then and there nastily referred to her as 'Putana', the female demon known for her attempt on infant Krishna's life by giving him milk from her poisoned breast.[105] Her break from Tilak, nevertheless, had happened much before this unsavoury episode, and she acknowledged as much in a public statement in January 1919 when she noted that 'I regret extremely that his followers have broken off my co-operation with Lok[manya] Tilak. I respect him for his flawless courage, his intense patriotism, and his utter self-abnegation in the cause of the Motherland, and I believe that he and I formed a strong combination, over the disruption of which the enemies of India, though also some of her friends, will rejoice.'[106]

Besant had already distanced herself from Tilak and his aides, and she made her distance from the Congress too particularly obvious during her delegation's stay in England.

And while there were still three separate Indian delegations on British soil, Tilak continued to be the premier political voice of his country in London. A conference was held at the Central Hall in February 1919 to consider the question of post-war India. Addressing it, Tilak referred to the ongoing debate over whether the Montagu reforms were preferable or the Congress-League proposals. Referring to the argument made by proponents of the former that progress should be 'step by step', he remarked that though the Congress-League pact too recognized the point, the Indians desired a good, substantial first step. 'It is the *first* step in these matters that is the most important,' he said. Defending the Indian scheme, he invoked the principle of self-determination, which in this case he referred to as 'the regulation of the steps [towards self-government] by the people, not by the officials'. There were many critics who deemed Indian self-government to be 'undesirable' or 'impossible' owing to 'problems of racial, religious and social diversity'. To them, Tilak said Indians themselves were best qualified to deal with difficulties peculiarly Indian. 'After all,' he remarked, 'we dealt with those problems before the establishment of the British administration, and we can do so again . . . We know our own difficulties best . . . We want reform to come in our own way – that is self-determination.'[107] At the Caxton Hall, Tilak delivered a similar address but seated in a chair. He had sprained his ankle, and his leg, which hurt even otherwise, was hurting more than ever.[108] His statement in front of the Joint Parliamentary Committee headed by Lord Selbourne to discuss the Government of India Bill (Montagu–Chelmsford scheme) was similarly strong. He appeared before the panel as part of the Congress delegation. As soon as Tilak began giving his evidence before the Committee, the ex-Bombay governor Lord Sydenham and now leader of a campaign against Indian Home Rule, left the room in a huff.[109]

On 6 November 1919, Tilak left Britain's shores and returned to India just in time for the Congress, which was held in Amritsar that December. On his way to Amritsar, he got the news that a royal proclamation had been issued granting approval to the Government of India Act of 1919 or the reforms scheme. Among other things, the proclamation announced clemency for political prisoners. Tilak stuck to the middle path he had of late adopted, thanking the British monarch for agreeing to free political prisoners and assuring him of 'responsive co-operation'.[110] What was that term now, his followers wondered. They were confused. It was a term coined by Baptista on the train that he and Tilak were taking to Amritsar, and Tilak was quite taken by it and was happy to use it. Tilak clarified to his followers that they need not worry as he had not changed his views about the Delhi Congress resolution.[111] He was neither totally opposed to the reforms not completely in favour but felt and said, not for the first time, that Indians should take what they were getting and then ask for more so that they'd eventually get 100 per cent of what they wanted. 'We go to Parliament, we ask for a legislation, we get it and we shall make it a basis of further agitation. That is our attitude. We get a bit of what we want; we shall make use of it and always go on agitating for more. That is our duty,' he told the Congress delegates. To dispel any doubts that might have lingered about his stand, he declared, 'Not only do we want full responsible government, but we want it in accordance with the principle of self-determination.'[112] Gandhi was completely in favour of the reforms. When C.R. Das prepared the main resolution essentially saying the Congress was going to stick to its Delhi resolution, Gandhi moved an amendment, stating, 'My amendment means nothing more and nothing less than that we should stare the situation in the face as it exists before the country today and if Tilak Maharaj tells you that we are going to make use of the Reforms Act as he must . . . then I say, be true to yourself, be true to the country and tell the country that you are going to do it.'[113]

Tilak and Gandhi were not totally thinking alike, however. At the Subjects Committee meeting, Tilak joined C.R. Das in pushing for the adoption of a resolution that would call the new Government of India Act 'inadequate, unsatisfactory and disappointing'.[114] There was an exchange between him and Gandhi, because Tilak was on the one hand thanking the monarch for the legislation and in the same breadth calling it disappointing, which to Gandhi seemed odd. One of the attendees, T. Prakasam, later recollected Gandhi telling Tilak that Indian politics must be based on the truth. Tilak replied, 'My friend! Truth has no place in politics.'[115]

It was around this time that Tilak came up with the idea of launching the Democratic Congress Party, 'a party animated by feelings of unswerving loyalty to the Congress and faith in democracy'. It 'proposes to work the Montagu Reforms Act for all it is worth,' he said as he launched it a few months into the new year, and it would work also 'for accelerating the grant of full responsible government, and for this purpose, it will without hesitation offer co-operation or resort to constitutional agitation, whichever may be expedient and best calculated to give effect to the popular will'.[116]

Why should Tilak have felt the need to form such a party, albeit as one under the Congress umbrella? The explanation for this is that Indian politics had changed fundamentally starting in 1918, the year in which he left for England. Deep fissures had developed within the Congress, between the two chief Home Rule Leagues and even within them, and it was all leading to a dissipation of energies and some lack of direction. And while Tilak had been in England, Gandhi had brought forth an extraordinary burst of enthusiasm and energy. Soon after his Champaran and other peasant agitations, the Rowlatt Act was introduced in March 1919, permitting the government to crush any suspected sign of sedition or revolution by arresting anyone without a warrant or a charge. There was an uproar against it, and Gandhi led the nationwide demonstrations, overshadowing all other Indian leaders of the time. In April 1919 came the horror of the Jallianwala Bagh massacre and the overall brutal repression in Punjab under its Lieutenant–Governor Michael O'Dwyer. Gandhi had visited Punjab as part of a Congress committee probing the Punjab brutalities, cementing his reputation as the future leader of the common Indian masses while the biggest mass leader yet, Tilak, was still in England. Tilak apologized to Gandhi that he could not be by his side during the 1919 demonstrations. But by mid-1920, when Gandhi grew totally disillusioned with the working of the new set of reforms and made up his mind to launch a nationwide campaign of non-cooperation, he was in a position to carry it wholly on his shoulders. Just as Tilak had single-handedly carried the Indian national movement on his shoulders for forty long years.

In April 1920, Tilak travelled widely across Sindh, which he visited for the Provincial Conference, holding meetings in Karachi, Hyderabad, Sukkar, Shikarpur and Jacobabad despite his increasingly failing health. From there he attended another conference in Solapur and then the Poona district conference. These back-to-back tours tired him out totally. He was going to turn sixty-four in just a couple of months. Two years previously, he had said he felt he was done and the body wasn't cooperating the way it did earlier. Now the sense of exhaustion was greater, and the diabetes was pronounced. On 22 May, at a massively-attended public meeting in Poona, Tilak was handed a purse of Rs 3 lakh which his followers led by N.C. Kelkar had collected for him.[117] Tilak was overcome with emotion, especially because he had been plainly staring at financial ruin in the aftermath of the Chirol libel case. Days after the Poona meeting, he left for the All-India Congress Committee meeting in Benaras and on the way back visited Jabalpur. This tour further sapped his waning strength.

A little before his sixty-fourth birthday on 23 July, he went to Bombay for some work and stayed at the Sardar Gruha. Here Gandhi, Shaukat Ali and many others came to see him. Before he had come to Bombay, he had had an attack of malaria but had recovered. Some amount of weakness nevertheless remained.

On 20 July, he was feeling slightly better, so when his friend Diwan Chamanlal came to see him at Sardar Gruha, Tilak said they should go on a long drive. Chamanlal sought to dissuade him. It was drizzling, there was a nip in the air, and Tilak had just about recovered from malaria. Tilak insisted, and off they went for a couple of hours, discussing Indian politics all the way.[118]

Tilak was down with a fever soon thereafter, and in a few days, he developed pneumonia. At the start of the last week of July, his daughters came to see him, and albeit feeling very weak and unwell, he joked, 'So you have all gathered again. You are too much in the habit of coming to your parents' house.'[119] He had reason to be satisfied about the family's condition. The daughters were well-settled, the grandchildren were doing fine, and his two surviving sons had grown up and were involved with their higher education. On 29 July, Tilak started showing signs of delirium, once speaking about events in 1818 and saying it was 1918 the other day, and at a different hour speaking as if he were at a public meeting. These were recognizable symptoms of the condition: in delirium, a person can have trouble focusing on a subject or changing subjects, and not know where he is. On 30 July, he had serious trouble speaking, and early past midnight or at 12.40 a.m. on 1 August 1920, he was dead.

His followers asked the government if his last rites could be performed at the Girgaum Chowpatty considering that many people might want to pay their last respects. It was raining when his body was taken out for cremation, but Bombay saw the biggest-ever turnout for a funeral. Lakhs of people had gathered, and if the front end of the funeral procession was at Sardar Gruha where he had breathed his last, the second was at least a couple of kilometres away. All through the funeral procession, Tilak's body was kept in a sitting position, a position that the Hindus reserved only for those who had obtained the highest levels of spiritual enlightenment, the real big yogis. The Indians thought it a fit tribute to him, for they regarded him as a yogi, but not of the usual type. In their view, he was a *karma yogi*—just the way he preferred it.

In the afternoon, when the funeral pyre was lit, Tilak was still resting as a *siddha*, in a sitting position. As the flames went up, shouts of 'Tilak Maharaj Ki Jai!' rent the air. Countless eyes were filled with tears. Amid the tears and the smoke, the flames consumed what the Hindus called 'the mortal coil'. The same day, Gandhi launched his nationwide Non-Cooperation Movement. Before the embers could be extinguished, he picked up the torch of freedom from Tilak. And he walked. One era of India's momentous struggle had ended. Another had begun.

Notes

Introduction

1 *The Myth of the Lokamanya: Tilak and Mass Politics in Maharashtra*, Richard I. Cashman, University of California Press, Berkeley, 1975, p. 3

2 *British Paramountcy and Indian Renaissance, Part 2*, edited by R. C. Majumdar, Bharatiya Vidya Bhavan, Mumbai, 2007, p. 533

3 *Cultural Revolt in a Colonial Society: The Non-Brahman Movement in Western India*, Gail Omvedt, Manohar Publishers, New Delhi (first published in 1976), 2023 edition, p. 205

4 Quoted in Revolutionaries, *The Other Story of How India Won Its Freedom*, Sanjeev Sanyal, Harper Collins India, New Delhi, 2023, p. 40 and pp. 314–315

5 *Lokmanya Tilak Aani Krantikarak*, Y.D. Phadke, Shrividya Prakashan, Pune, 2000, p. 10

6 Ibid

7 Ibid, p. 9

Chapter 1: A Boy Known as 'The Devil' and 'Blunt'

1 *Lokmanya Tilak Yanche Charitra* (Marathi), N.C. Kelkar, published by N.C. Kelkar, Pune, Volume 1, 1923, p. 21; and *Lokmanya Tilak: A Biography*, A.K. Bhagwat and G.P. Pradhan, Jaico, Mumbai, 2016 edition, p. 2

2 Kelkar, Vol. 1, p. 6 and p. 12

3 Ibid, p. 12

4 *Lokmanya* (Marathi), N.R. Phatak, Mauj Prakashan Gruha (first published 1972), 2012 edition, p. 3

5 Kelkar, p. 5–6
6 Ibid, p. 14 and pp. 18–19.
7 Bhagwat and Pradhan, p. 3
8 Kelkar, Vol. 1, p. 25
9 *Lokmanya Tilak: Father of Our Freedom Struggle*, Dhananjay Keer, published by S.B. Kangutkar, Bombay (Mumbai), 1959, p. 12
10 *Lokmanya Tilkanchi Geli Aath Varshe*, A.V. Kulkarni, Induprakash Steam Press, 1909, p. 107
11 Keer (1959 edition), p. 9
12 Kelkar, Vol. 1, p. 28
13 Tilak's eldest son-in-law Vishwanath Gangadhar Ketkar quoted in Phatak, pp. 9–10
14 Ibid
15 Keer, p. 13
16 Keer, p. 13 and Phatak, p. 11
17 Bhagwat and Pradhan, p. 5; Keer, p. 14–15; Kelkar, p. 28–29
18 Phatak, p. 11
19 Ibid
20 Report on the Search for Sanskrit MSS. in the Bombay Presidency, During the Year 1880–81, F. Kielhorn, Government Central Book Depot, Bombay, 1881, pages III–XIV
21 Keer, p. 14
22 A Cambridge Alumni Database, University of Cambridge, accessed at https://venn.lib.cam.ac.uk
23 Keer, p. 14
24 *Shodh: Bal-Gopalancha* (Marathi), Y.D. Phadke, Shrividya Prakashan, Pune, 1977, 2000 edition, pp. 100–105
25 Bhagwat and Pradhan, p. 6
26 Bhagwat and Pradhan, p. 7
27 *Life and Times of Lokamanya Tilak*, N.C. Kelkar (English), translated by D.V. Divekar, 1928, Radha Publications, New Delhi, 2001, p. 54; and Phatak, pp. 13–14
28 Bhagwat and Pradhan, pp. 7–8
29 Ibid, p. 8
30 Kelkar (English), pp. 56–57 and Keer, p. 17
31 Phatak, pp. 15–16

32 Biographical details of Gopal Ganesh Agarkar's early life from Phatak, p. 17–19; Bhagwat and Pradhan, p. 8–9; and *Gopal Ganesh Agarkar: Vyakti Aani Vichar* (Marathi), edited and with an introduction by V.S. Khandekar, Mehta Publishing House, 1945, 2016 edition, p. 6–9

33 Bhagwat and Pradhan, p. 9

34 *Agarkaranshi Olakh* (Marathi), Purushottam Pandurang or P. P. Gokhale, published by Daryanav Ragthunath Kopardekar, Pune, 1945, 1969 edition, p. 32–33

Chapter 2: 'Like Bullocks Whipped Around'

1 Temple's letters of 3 and 9 July 1879 to Lytton quoted in 'The Proper Limits of Agitation: The Crisis of 1879-80 in Bombay Presidency', Richard P. Tucker, *The Journal of Asian Studies*, Vol. 28, No. 2, Feb 1969, pp. 346–347; accessed on Jstor

2 *By-Ways of Bombay*, S. M. Edwardes, D.B. Taraporewala Sons & Co., Bombay, 1912, pp. 95–98

3 *The Proudest Day: India's Long Road to Independence*, Anthony Read and David Fisher, Jonathan Cape, London, 1997, pp. 37–41

4 *Selections from the Minutes and Other Official Writings of the Honourable Mountstuart Elphinstone*, Governor of Bombay, edited by George W. Forrest, Richard Bentley and Son, London, 1884, pp. 4, 39, 65, 260, 262

5 Ibid, p. 60

6 A. Miles and A. Pattle, authors of *The Indian Mutiny* (London, 1885), quoted in the author's note in *The Devil's Wind: Nana Saheb's Story*, Manohar Malgonkar, Hamish Hamilton, London, 1972, pp. I

7 *The Proudest Day*, p. 61

8 Ibid, pp. 61–62

9 Tucker, pp. 341–348

10 *Towards Nationalism: Group Affiliations and the Politics of Public Associations in Nineteenth Century Western India*, J.C. Masselos, Popular Prakashan, Mumbai, 1974, p. 100. Several other details about the Sabha's early days and activities, p. 92–101

11 Ibid, p. 98

12 *Mahadev Govind Ranade: Patriot and Social Servant,* James Kellock, Rupa Publications, New Delhi, 2003, p60

13 *India Conquered: Britain's Raj and The Chaos of Empire,* John Wilson, Simon & Schuster, London, 2016, p. 295

14 Ibid, pp. 295–296

15 Tucker, p. 347

16 Ibid

17 Kelkar (English), p. 63; *East and West,* Sir Edwin Arnold, Longmans, Green and Co., London, 1896, p. 325

18 Ibid

19 *India Revisited,* Sir Edwin Arnold, Kegan Paul, Trench, Trubner & Co. Ltd, London, 1906, p. 73

20 Arnold, *East and West,* p. 331

21 Ibid

22 Kelkar (English), pp. 64–65

23 Ibid, p. 66

24 *The Myth of the Lokamanya,* p. 33 and p. 40; *Western India in the Nineteenth Century,* p. 309–310

25 *The History of the Deccan Education Society,* P.M. Limaye, published by Prof. M.K. Joshi, secretary, Deccan Education Society, Poona, Part II-B, pp. 95–96

26 *Travels in and Dairies of India & Burma,* I. V. Minayeff, translated by Hitendra Sanyal, Eastern Trading Company, Calcutta, 1955, p. 17, pp. 52–54

27 *The Proudest Day,* p. 64

28 'Forerunners of Dadabhai Naoroji's Drain Theory', J.V. Naik, *Economic & Political Weekly,* Nov. 24–30, 2001, Vol. 36, No. 46/47, pp. 4428–4432

29 Letter No. IV by 'A Hindoo,' published in *Bombay Gazette,* 20 August 1841; and J.V. Naik, EPW, Nov. 24–30, 2001, pp. 4428–4432

30 J.V. Naik, EPW, Nov. 24–30, 2001, pp. 4428–4432

31 Descriptions of the Russian's *conversations with students and professors of Deccan College from Travels in and Dairies of India & Burma,* I.V. Minayeff, pp. 49–54 and p. 226

32 Tucker, pp. 347–348

33 *India Conquered: Britain's Raj and The Chaos of Empire*, John
    Wilson, Simon & Schuster, London, 2016, p. 268 and p. 286
34 Ibid, p. 286 and p. 289
35 Ibid, p. 292 and p. 318
36 Minayeff, p. 51 and pp. 223–224
37 'Aamchya Deshachi Stithi' (Marathi) (The state of our nation), one
    of Vishnushastri Chiplunkar's famous essays from Issue No. 77 of
    the *Nibandhmala*, Suvichar Prakashan Mandal, Nagpur, second
    edition, 1945, pp. 4, 13, 17, 22, 26, 27, 29
38 Kelkar (Marathi, Vol. 1), pp. 101–102

Chapter 3: School of Infamous Scribblers

1 Limaye talks about the first reason for the formation of a private
   English school on p. 13 of his *History of the Deccan Society*, and
   the other aims are explicit in V.S. Apte's evidence on 9 September
   1882 before the Education Commission, also quoted in Limaye,
   pp. 38–47
2 Limaye, p. 7
3 Ibid, pp. 8–9
4 'History of Indian Journalism', J. Natarajan, *Part II of the Report
   of the Press Commission*, The Publications Division, Ministry of
   Information and Broadcasting, Government of India, Delhi, 1955,
   p. 80
5 Ibid, p. 85
6 Ibid, 85, and *The Proudest Day*, p. 67
7 Quoted in *Lokmanya* (Marathi), by N.R. Pathak, p. 35
8 *British Paramountcy and Indian Renaissance, Part 1*, Vol IX of
   The History and Culture of the Indian People, edited by R. C.
   Majumdar, Bharatiya Vidya Bhavan, Mumbai (first published in
   1963), 2022 edition, p 155. Details of the entire Satara episode are
   on pp. 145–159
9 Ibid, pp. 965–966
10 More, p. 18
11 Limaye, p. 34 and Matthews, p. 267
12 Quoted in Limaye, pp. 34–35

13 Keer, pp. 29–30; O'Hanlon, p. 288; *History of Indian Journalism*,
    pp. 57–58, 101

14 *History of Indian Journalism*, p. 110

15 O'Hanlon, p. 288

16 Barve's deposition in court quoted in *Bombay Gazette*, 13 March
    1882

17 Barve quoted in *Bombay Gazette*, 10 February 1882

18 Limaye, p. 35

19 Ibid, p. 36

20 *Bombay Gazette*, 10 February 1882

21 *My Thirty Years in India*, Edmund C. Cox, Mills and Boon Ltd,
    London, 1909, p. 63

22 *Bombay Gazette*, 10 February 1882

23 *Shodh Bal-Gopalancha*, Phadke, p. 90

24 Limaye, p. 36

25 *Bombay Gazette*, 13 March 1882

26 Ibid; and Keer, p. 31

27 Barve's deposition quoted in *Bombay Gazette*, 13 March 1882

28 Kesari of 24 January 1882 quoted in *Shodh Bal-Gopalancha*, Phadke,
    p. 92

29 Limaye, p. 37

30 Kelkar (Marathi), Vol. 1, p. 149; and *Shodh Bal-Gopalancha*,
    Phadke, p. 94

31 *Shodh Bal-Gopalancha*, Phadke, pp. 93–94

32 *Bombay Gazette*, 18 July 1882

33 Apology read out in court by M.V. Barve's lawyer, Mr Inverarity,
    quoted in *Bombay Gazette*, 17 July 1882

34 Ibid

35 *Pioneer*, 21 July 1882

36 *Times of India*, 18 July 1882

37 *Dongrichya Turungaat Aamche 101 Divas* (Marathi) (Our 101 Days
    in Dongri Prison), Gopal Ganesh Agarkar, *Sampurna Agarkar*
    (Agarkar's Collected Works), Vol. 2, pp. 220–221. Other details
    about their jail time also from this volume, pp. 218–248

38 *Bombay Gazette*, 18 July 1882; and *Shodh Bal-Gopalancha*, p. 95

39 *Dynan Prakash*, *Subodh Patrika*, *Indian Spectator* and other papers
    quoted in *Shodh Bal-Gopalancha*, Phadke, p. 95

40 *Times of India*, 28 October 1882

41 *Native Opinion* of 29 October 1882 quoted in *Shodh Bal-Gopalancha*, Phadke, p. 97

42 Quoted in the *Times of India*, 31 December 1883

43 Quoted in *Shodh Bal-Gopalancha*, Phadke, p. 98

44 *Amrita Bazar Patrika* quoted in *Times of India*, 18 February 1882

45 *My Thirty Years in India*, Cox, p. 62 and pp. 70–72

Chapter 4: 'Mud of Acrimony and Abuse'

1 Tilak's statement of resignation from the Deccan Education Society, Appendix I of Limaye, p. 18

2 Keer, p. 37

3 *Shodh Bal Gopalancha*, Phadke, pp. 129–130

4 Ibid, pp. 130–131

5 Tilak's statement of resignation from the Deccan Education Society, Appendix I of Limaye, p. 19; and Appendix II of Kelkar (English), p. 549

6 Agarkar's minute on the internal situation in the Deccan Education Society, quoted in Limaye, p. 125

7 *Shodh Bal-Gopalancha*, Phadke, pp. 133–134

8 Tilak's statement of resignation, Appendix I of Limaye, p. 19

9 Ibid, p. 18

10 Ibid, pp. 15–16

11 Agarkar's minute, quoted in Limaye, p. 126

12 Ibid

13 Tilak's resignation, quoted in Limaye, Appendix I, p. 16 and p. 18

14 Ibid, pp. 18–19; Tilak's letter of 23 March 1887 to the Deccan Education Society's secretary quoted in Wolpert, p. 30

15 Quoted in Wolpert, p. 30

16 Agarkar's letter, quoted in Wolpert, p. 30

17 Quoted in *Shodh Bal-Gopalancha*, Phadke, p. 153

18 Ibid, pp. 142–143

19 Ibid, p. 157

20 Agarkar, Phadke, p98

21 *Shodh Bal-Gopalancha*, Phadke, p. 175

22 Ibid, p. 177 and Agarkar, Phadke, p. 98

23 Tilak's letter of 21 December 1888 quoted in Agarkar, Phadke, p. 99

24 Tilak's letter of 22 December 1888 to Trimbakrao Joshi, quoted in Agarkar, Phadke, p. 98

25 Agarkar's letter of 24 December 1888 to Tilak, quoted in Agarkar, Phadke, pp. 99–102 (translation is mine); and quoted in Keer, p. 47

26 Quoted in Wolpert, p. 31

27 Tilak's letter of 24 December 1888 to Agarkar, Ibid, p. 31–32

28 Tilak's letter of 24 December 1888 to Agarkar, quoted in Agarkar, Phadke, p. 103

29 Ibid, p. 104

30 Agarkar's letter of 25 December 1888 to Tilak, quoted in Wolpert, p. 32. While accepting Wolpert's translation on the whole of this paragraph, I have in one place corrected his erroneous translation of the word '*gaadi*', which he takes to be 'the court,' whereas what it actually means is 'the vehicle,' in this case the '*ghoda* gaadi' or horse cart.

31 Tilak's resignation, quoted in Agarkar, Phadke, p. 105

32 His hope for a rapprochement is clear from a letter he wrote on 6 June 1889, soon after his return from his break. In it he stated, 'On the whole the very near danger of a rupture has I hope opened our eyes to the necessity of so guiding our conduct as to avoid unnecessary friction by showing some indulgence to each other.' Quoted in Wolpert, p. 33

33 Tilak's resignation, quoted in Limaye, Appendix I, p. 23

34 Tilak's statement of resignation, Kelkar, pp. 553–554

35 Agarkar, Phadke, pp. 127–128

36 Limaye, p. 119

37 Ibid, p. 120

38 Ibid, pp. 120–121

39 Limaye, Appendix I, p. 25

40 Ibid, Appendix 1, p. 2

41 Ibid, Appendix 1, p. 28

42 Ibid

43 Ibid, p. 3

44 Kelkar (English), pp. 152–153

45 Ibid, p. 157
46 Limaye, Appendix 1, pp. 2–3
47 Ibid, p. 27
48 Ibid

Chapter 5: The Crawford Corruption Scandal

1 *The Arthur Crawford Scandal: Corruption, Governance and Indian Victims*, Michael D. Metelits, Oxford University Press, New Delhi, 2020, pp. 20–21
2 Ibid, p. 22
3 Ibid, p. 3
4 Ibid, p. 2
5 Ibid, p. 3 and p. 5
6 Ibid, p. 5 and p. 7
7 Ibid, p. 64, nn. 52
8 Ibid, p. 26
9 Ibid, p. 60. Several witnesses during the investigation provided accounts of their interaction with Crawford following this pattern.
10 Ibid, p. 126
11 Ibid, p. 46
12 *Times*, London, 19 November 1888 and 11 March 1889
13 *Times*, London, 6 May 1889
14 Ibid
15 Ibid
16 *The Arthur Crawford Scandal*, pp. 85–87
17 Ibid, p. 83 and p. 87
18 Ibid, p. 82
19 Ibid, pp. 78–80
20 Ibid, p. 99
21 *Kesari* editorial of 21 August 1888 in *Samagra Tilak*, Volume 5, p. 727
22 Ibid
23 Ibid, p. 208
24 Ibid, p. 209
25 *Kesari* editorial of 21 August 1888 in *Samagra Tilak*, Volume 5, p. 727

26 Ibid, p. 728
27 Ibid
28 *Kesari* editorial of 21 August 1888, in *Samagra Tilak*, Volume 5, p. 728; and of 2 October 1888, p. 731
29 *Kesari* editorial of 21 August 1888, in *Samagra Tilak*, Volume 5, p729; and of 4 June 1889, p. 747
30 *Kesari* editorial of 23 April 1889, in *Samagra Tilak*, Volume 5, p. 734
31 *The Arthur Crawford Scandal*, p. 179
32 *Kesari* editorial of 7 May 1889, in *Samagra Tilak*, Volume 5, p. 740; and of 21 May 1889, pp. 743–744
33 Tambe's case and his petition to the government given in detail in *The Arthur Crawford Scandal*, pp. 179–185
34 *Kesari* editorial of 7 May 1889, in *Samagra Tilak*, Volume 5, p. 740; and of 21 May 1889, pp. 743–744
35 *Kesari* editorial of 7 May 1889, in *Samagra Tilak*, Volume 5, p. 738
36 *The Arthur Crawford Scandal*, p. 183
37 *Kesari* editorial of 21 May 1889, in *Samagra Tilak*, Volume 5, pp. 741–742
38 Ibid, p. 742
39 *Kesari* editorial of 24 September 1889, in *Samagra Tilak*, Volume 5, pp. 752–753
40 *The Arthur Crawford Scandal*, pp. 195–196
41 *Kesari* editorial of 24 September 1889, in *Samagra Tilak*, Volume 5, pp. 752–753
42 Details of the Poona Sarvajanik Sabha meeting and Tilak's and Gokhale's speeches on the occasion from *The Arthur Crawford Scandal*, pp. 198–204
43 *The Arthur Crawford Scandal*, pp. 7–8

Chapter 6: Faith, Culture and Controversy

1 *Times of India*, 26 June 1885
2 The letter and the editorial comment, *Times of India*, 19 September 1885

3 Rukhmabai's letter of 17 February 1887 to *Times*, London, reproduced in *Times of India*, 3 May 1887; and *Shodh Bal-Gopalancha*, pp. 114–115

4 Ibid

5 'Rukhmabai: Debate Over Woman's Right to Her Person', Sudhir Chandra, *Economic and Political Weekly*, 2 November 1996, p. 2937

6 Ibid, pp. 2937–2938

7 *Missionaries in India*, Arun Shourie, ASA Publications, New Delhi, 1994, p. 61

8 *The Proudest Day*, pp. 40–41

9 *Missionaries in India*, pp. 64–65 and *The Proudest Day*, p. 41

10 Missionaries in India, pp. 67–91

11 Ibid, pp. 92–99

12 'Rukhmabai: Debate Over Woman's Right to Her Person', Sudhir Chandra, *Economic and Political Weekly*, 2 November 1996, p. 2939

13 Ibid

14 Ibid

15 Ibid, p. 2940

16 Ibid

17 Ibid, p. 2942

18 Ibid

19 'Rakmabaicha Khatla (Rukhmabai's case)', Tilak's editorial in *Kesari*, 22 March 1887, *Lokmanya Tilakanche Kesaritil Lekh*, Volume 4, edited by N.C. Kelkar, Kesari-Mahratta Sanstha, 1930, p. 42

20 Ibid

21 Ibid

22 Ibid, pp. 42–43

23 Ibid, p. 43 and p. 45; and the *Kesari* of 5 April 1887 quoted in *Shodh Bal-Gopalancha*, p. 120

24 Tilak's editorial in *Kesari*, 7 June 1887, Ibid, p. 43

25 Rukhmabai, Sudhir Chandra, *EPW*, 2 November 1996, p. 2940

26 Ibid, p. 2941

27 *Shodh Bal-Gopalancha*, p. 123

28 Ibid, pp. 121–122

29 Ibid, p. 177

30 *Kesari* of 28 May 1889, Ibid, pp. 177–178

31 Kosambi, pp. 190–191 and More, p. 52

32 *Times of India*, 13 March 1889

33 Tahmankar, pp. 43–44

34 *Boston Herald* editorial quoted in The Buffalo Commercial, Buffalo (US), 29 August 1889

35 Tahmankar, p. 44

36 Ibid

37 More, p. 52

38 Kosambi, p. 203

39 *Kesari* editorial of 12 January 1904, *Lokmanya Tilakanche Kesaritil Lekh*, Vol 4, p. 378

40 Kosambi, p. 193

41 *Kesari* editorial of 12 January 1904, *Lokmanya Tilakanche Kesaritil Lekh*, Vol 4, p. 378

42 Kosambi, pp. 193–194

43 *Kesari* editorial of 4 October 1887, in *Lokmanya Tilakanche Kesaritil Lekh*, Vol 4, pp. 72–75

44 Ibid

45 Ibid, pp. 75–80

46 Ibid, pp. 77–78

47 Tilak quoted his critics in his *Kesari* editorial of 25 October 1887, *Kesaritil Lekh*, Vol 4, p. 79

48 *Lokmanya Tilak Lekhsangraha*, edited by Tarkathirtha Laxmanshastri Joshi, Sahitya Akademi, New Delhi, 2013, pp. 1–2

49 Kelkar quoted in Phatak, p. 431fn

50 Bapat, Volume 3, p. 315

51 *Sahyadri* (magazine), special issue, August 1945

52 Bapat, Volume 2, p. 28

53 Pathak, p. 434

54 Bapat, Volume 2, p. 27

55 Pathak, p. 435

56 *Lokmanya Tilak Yanchi Geli Aath Varshe*, A.V. Kulkarni, Indu Prakash Steam Press, Mumbai, 1909, p. 8

57 *Sahyadri* (magazine), special issue, August 1945

58 *Sex, Politics and Empire: A Postcolonial Geography*, Richard Philips, Manchester University Press, UK, 2006, p. 65

59 Ibid, p. 75

60 *Kesari* editorial of 12 August 1890, *Kesaritil Lekh*, Vol 4, pp. 86–88

61 Tahmankar, p. 46; and the claim of the orthodox Brahman shastris in Kosambi, p. 183

62 Quoted in Cashman, pp. 56–57

63 Ibid, p. 58

64 Ibid

65 Cashman, pp. 59–62

66 *Kesari*, 12 October 1890, *Kesaritil Lekh*, Vol 4, pp. 99–100

67 Details of the Joshi Hall meeting in *Kesari*, 4 November 1890, *Kesaritil Lekh*, pp. 100–103

68 *Source material for A History of the Freedom Movement in India*, collected from Bombay Government Records, Vol. II, 1885–1920, Government Central Press, Bombay, 1958, Paragraphs 184 and 259 – Political, p. 201

69 *Deccan Herald* report of March 30, 1891, quoted in *Times of India*, 31 March 1891

70 *Times of India*, 27 February 1891

71 *Times of India*, 3 March 1891

72 Quoted in *Tilak and Gokhale*, Wolpert, p. 57

73 *Times of India*, 2 February 1891; and *Tilak and Gokhale*, Wolpert, p. 56

74 *Times of India*, 2 February 1891

75 Agarkar, Phadke, pp. 175–177; and Tahmankar, p. 51

76 More, p. 61

77 Tahmankar, p. 52

78 *Mahadev Govind Ranade*, Kellock, pp. 93–94

79 Phatak, p. 82

80 *Mahadev Govind Ranade*, Kellock, p. 106

81 Quoted in *Tilak and Gokhale*, Wolpert, p. 44

82 Quoted in Wolpert, p. 47

83 Ibid, p. 50–51

84 Cashman, p. 45

85 *Kesari* of 22 November 1892 and 8 Sept 1896, Ibid, p. 46

Chapter 7: One Riot, Two Festivals

1 *Lokmanya Tilak*, Bhagwat and Pradhan, p. 100
2 *The Orion or Researches into the Antiquity of the Vedas*, B.G. Tilak, Mrs Radhabai Atmaram Sagoon, Bookseller and Publisher, 1893, p. 1
3 Ibid, p. iii
4 Different scholars have proposed different dates for the Vedas. The dating of such texts is a highly specialized and highly technical field, of which I have no knowledge.
5 *Bombay Gazette*, 29 July 1893; and *Times of India*, 28 July 1893
6 Cashman, p. 99
7 *Bombay Gazette*, 12 August 1893
8 *Bombay Gazette*, 14 August 1893
9 *Bombay Gazette*, 12 August 1893
10 Cashman, pp. 67–68 and Wolpert, p. 66
11 *Kesari* editorial of 15 August 1893 quoted in *Lokmanya Tilak Lekhsangraha* p. 246
12 Ibid
13 *Lokamanya Tilak: A Biography*, Ram Gopal, Asia Publishing House, Bombay (Mumbai), 1956, pp. 84–85
14 Ibid, pp. 245–246
15 Ibid, pp. 246–299; Cashman, pp. 68–69; and Phatak, p. 87
16 Ibid, p. 247
17 Cashman, p. 69
18 *Kesari* editorial of 15 August 1893, quoted in *Lokmanya Tilak Lekhsangraha*, pp. 247–249
19 *Kesari* editorials of 22 August and 29 August 1893, Ibid, pp. 252–255; and Tahmankar, p. 55
20 Tahmankar, p. 56
21 Wolpert, pp. 66–67
22 Quoted in Cashman, p.78
23 Ibid, p. 83
24 Cashman, p. 92
25 *Bombay Gazette*, 8 November 1894 and *Pioneer*, 9 November 1894
26 Phatak, p. 91
27 Cashman, p. 90 and Phatak, p. 95 and p. 101

28 Phatak, pp. 94–96
29 Bombay Police Abstracts quoted in Cashman, p. 85
30 Ram Gopal, pp. 88–89
31 Phatak, p. 101
32 Ram Gopal, p. 88
33 Phatak, p. 101
34 Ibid, p. 87
35 Ibid, p. 101
36 *Kesari* of 8 September 1896 quoted in Cashman, p. 79
37 *A Book of Bombay*, James Douglas, Government Gazette Steam Press, Bombay, 1883, p. 433
38 *Shivaji and the Indian National Movement*, Anil Samarth, Somaiya Publications Pvt Ltd, Bombay, 1975, p. 8–9
39 *Maratha Historiography*, A.R. Kulkarni, Manohar, New Delhi, 2006, p. 75 and p. 199
40 Ibid, p. 10–11
41 Douglas, p. 433
42 Samarth, p. 16–18 and p. 23
43 Ibid, p. 23; and Ram Gopal, p. 101
44 Ram Gopal, p. 105
45 Cashman, pp. 106–107
46 Samarth, p. 23
47 Ibid, pp. 23–24 and Cashman, p. 105
48 Cashman, p. 105
49 Samarth, p. 24
50 Ibid
51 Phatak, p. 106
52 Ibid, pp. 107–118
53 Ibid
54 Cashman, pp. 63–66
55 Ram Gopal, pp. 103–104
56 Ibid, p. 104
57 Samarth, p. 25
58 Ibid, pp. 25–26
59 Ibid
60 Ibid, pp. 26–27
61 *The Proudest Day*, p. 75

62 Ibid

63 Ibid

64 Details in this passage from *The Proudest Day*, pp. 75–78

Chapter 8: 'Sedition-Monger'

1 *Agarkar*, by Phadke, pp. 222–225

2 Ibid, p. 229

3 Ibid, pp. 227–228

4 Ibid, p. 230

5 Ibid, p. 231

6 Ibid

7 Agarkar, p. 235

8 Ibid, pp. 251–252

9 Ibid, p. 252

10 Ibid, p. 253

11 Kesari editorial of 18 June 1895 quoted in *Samagra Lokmanya Tilak*, Volume 5, pp. 867–871

12 Ibid

13 *Agarkar*, by Phadke, p. 253

14 Wolpert, p. 70

15 Ibid, p. 71; and *Gokhale*, B.R. Nanda, p. 85

16 *Gokhale*, by Nanda, p. 83

17 Ibid, p. 84

18 Ibid, pp. 86–87

19 Ram Gopal, pp. 122–126

20 Tahmankar, p. 69

21 Ibid, p. 70

22 Ibid, p. 69

23 Ibid

24 Ibid, p. 73

25 *Kesari* of 15 December 1896 quoted in Bhagwat and Pradhan, p. 176

26 Tahmankar, p. 71

27 Ibid, p. 72

28 Ibid

29 Ibid, pp. 73–74
30 Ram Gopal, pp. 126–127
31 Phatak, pp. 136–137 and Bhagwat and Pradhan, p. 176
32 *Mahratta* of 21 March 1897 quoted in Ram Gopal, pp. 129–130
33 Ibid
34 Ibid, pp. 131–133
35 *Gokhale*, by Nanda, pp. 102–103
36 Ibid, p. 103
37 The *Kesari* of 9 March 1897 quoted in Bhagwat and Pradhan, p. 179
38 Ibid
39 *Gokhale*, by Nanda, pp. 103–104
40 Ibid, p. 104; and Bhagwat and Pradhan, p. 180
41 *Manchester Guardian*, 2 July 1897
42 *Gokhale*, by Nanda, p. 104
43 Tahmankar, p. 75
44 Phatak, p. 141
45 *Gokhale*, by Nanda, p. 107
46 Ibid, p. 108
47 Ibid
48 *Morning Post*, 25 June 1897
49 Quoted in *Gokhale*, by Nanda, p. 108
50 *Daily Telegraph*, 25 June 1897
51 Quoted in *Gokhale*, by Nanda, p. 109
52 Ibid
53 *Manchester Guardian*, 7 July 1897; and *Kanthasnan Aani Balidan* (Marathi), V.S. Joshi, Raja Prakashan, Mumbai, 1986, pp. 112–113
54 The *Kesari* editorials of 6 July and 13 July 1897 quoted in Ibid, p. 118 and p. 121
55 *Times of India*, 19 June 1897
56 *Times of India*, 25 June 1897
57 Wolpert, p. 129
58 *Times of India*, 25 June 1897
59 *Times of India*, 28 June 1897
60 *Times of India*, 29 June 1897

61 *Times of India*, 30 June 1897

62 Quoted in Pathak, p. 142

63 *Morning Post*, London, 8 July 1897

64 *Guardian*, 7 July 1897 and *Times*, London, 19 July 1897

65 *Times*, London, 23 July 1897

66 *Guardian*, 16 July 1897

67 *Guardian*, 29 July 1897

68 Pathak, pp. 150–151

69 Ibid; and *Guardian*, 29 July 1897

70 Sandhurst's letter to Hamilton of 29 July 1897 quoted in *Lokmanya Tilak Aani Krantikarak* (Marathi), Y D. Phadke, Shrividya Prakashan, Pune, 2000, p. 8

71 The *Guardian*, 29 July 1897

72 Ibid

73 *Badruddin Tyabji*, A. G. Noorani, Publications Division, Government of India, New Delhi, 2009, p. 84

74 *Gokhale*, by Nanda, p. 113; and Phatak, p. 154

75 Tahmankar, pp. 86–87

76 *Indian Political Trials: 1775-1947*, A.G. Noorani, Oxford University Press, New Delhi, 2009, p. 117

77 Samarth, p. 39

78 Ram Gopal, pp. 146–147; Noorani, p. 116; Bhagwat and Pradhan, pp. 182–183; and Samarth, p. 39

79 Samarth, p. 39

80 Ibid, p. 40; and Queen Empress vs Bal Gangadhar Tilak and Keshav Mahadev Bal, The Indian Law Reports, XXII, pp. 114–115

81 Ram Gopal, p. 161

82 Noorani, pp. 117–118

83 Queen Empress vs Bal Gangadhar Tilak and Keshav Mahadev Bal, The Indian Law Reports, XXII, 1898 p. 122

84 Noorani, p. 118

85 Ram Gopal, p. 159

86 Noorani, pp. 119–120; and Ram Gopal, p. 148 and pp. 169–170

87 Ram Gopal, pp. 167–168

88 The Indian Law Reports, XXII, 1898, p. 129

89 Ram Gopal, pp. 175–176

90 Ibid, pp. 141–143
91 Noorani, pp. 119–120
92 Ram Gopal, p. 182
93 Ibid, p. 182–183
94 Ibid, p. 186
95 Bombay government's Report on Native Papers (Confidential) published in the Bombay Presidency, for the week ending 25 September 1897, p. 16
96 *The Hindu*, quoted in the piece https://indianhistorycollective.com/queen-empress-vs-bal-gangadhar-tilak-an-autopsy/
97 Ibid
98 *Native Opinion* of 20 September 1897, quoted in Bombay government's Report on Native Papers, p. 13
99 Ram Gopal, pp. 186–187
100 Tahmankar, p. 88
101 *Kesari* of 21 September 1897 and the Udyogavriddhi of 23 September 1897, quoted in Bombay government's Report on Native Papers, p. 24 and p. 8
102 *Mahratta* of 20 September 1897 quoted in Ibid, p. 23
103 *Kesari* of 21 September 1897 quoted in Ibid, pp. 23–24
104 Ibid, p. 17
105 *Champion* of 19 September 1897 quoted in Ibid, p. 29
106 Quoted in Ram Gopal, pp. 190–191
107 *Rast Goftar* of 19 September 1897 quoted in Ibid, p. 9
108 Ram Gopal, pp. 188–189
109 Noorani, p. 122
110 Keer, p. 130
111 Accounts of Tilak's jail life in 1897 and 1898 from an interview he gave to the *Sudharak* after coming out of prison and from other sources, quoted in Phatak, pp. 169–173; also in Tahmankar, pp. 95–96 and Ram Gopal, pp. 194–196
112 *Scholar Extraordinary: The Life of Friedrich Max Muller*, Nirad C. Chaudhuri, Orient Paperbacks, New Delhi, 1974, p. 343
113 Tahmankar, p. 97
114 Ibid
115 Ram Gopal, p. 199

116 Ibid

117 Phatak, p. 178

118 *Lokmanya Tilak Aani Krantikarak*, Y.D. Phadke, Shrividya Prakashan, Pune, 2000, pp. 7–8; and Wolpert, pp. 90–91

119 Wolpert, p. 92

120 *The Autobiography of Damodar Chapekar*, from the Bombay Police Abstracts of 1910, p. 970, accessed at: https://cultural.maharashtra. gov.in/english/gazetteer/VOL-II/autobiography.pdf

121 Ibid, p. 979 and p. 983

122 Ibid, p. 978 and p. 981

123 Ibid, p. 992

124 Ibid, pp. 994–995

125 *Lokmanya Tilak Aani Krantikarak*, p. 13

126 Details of this entire episode are drawn from *Lokmanya Tilak Aani Krantikarak*, Phadke, and *Tilak and Gokhale*, Wolpert. Phadke, pp. 40–47 and Gokhale, pp. 148–151. They in turn have drawn the details from two specific works: *Vasukaka Joshi va Tyancha Kaal*, T.R. Devagirikar, Pune, 1948 (Devigirikar was manager of Vasukaka Joshi's press and accessed in 1932 his notes which had details of the Nepal plot) and *Deshbhakta Krishnaji Prabhakar urfa Kakasaheb Khadilkar*, K.H. Khadilkar, Pune, 1949).

127 Wolpert, pp. 150–151

Chapter 9: The Raj Goes Fishing

1   *Times of India* quoted in *Daily Record*, Scotland, 22 November 1898

2   *Times of India*, 20 December 1898

3   Ibid

4   *Times of India*, 5 July 1899

5   *Times of India*, 24 November 1899

6   Ibid

7   Ibid

8   Gokhale, by Nanda, p. 121; and Wolpert, p. 129

9   *Times of India*, 16 October 1899

10 Letters of both Sandhurst and Curzon quoted in Gokhale, by Nanda, p. 121

11 Ibid, p. 120
12 Ibid
13 Wolpert, p. 132; and
14 *Nek Naamdar Gokhale*, Govind Talwalkar, Mauj Prakashan Gruha, Mumbai, 2019, p. 291
15 Keer, pp. 145–146; and *Times of India*, 3 January 1898
16 Keer,p153
17 *Sir Pherozeshah Mehta: A Political Biography*, H.P. Mody, Volume II, The Times Press, Bombay, 1921, p. 440
18 Ibid, p439
19 *The Proudest Day*, p. 69
20 *Peace, Poverty and Betrayal: A New History of British India*, p. 56
21 Keer, p. 153
22 Ram Gopal, pp. 200–201
23 Ram Gopal, pp. 204–206
24 Ibid, p. 207
25 Ibid
26 Keer, p. 155 and pp. 165–167
27 Ibid
28 Wolpert, pp. 135–135
29 Cashman, pp. 53–54
30 Wolpert, p. 136
31 Quoted in Shahu Chhatrapati Aani Lokmanya, Y.D. Phadke, Shrividya Prakashan, Pune, first published in 1986, 2018 edition, p. 22
32 Ibid
33 Ibid, pp. 22–42
34 Ibid, pp. 45–46
35 *Memoirs of His Highness Shri Shahu Chhatrapati of Kolhapur*, A.B. Latthe, Vol. 1, The Times Press, Bombay, 1924, p. 196
36 *Shahu Chhatrapati aani Lokmanya*, Phadke, pp. 47–48
37 Ibid, pp. 49–50
38 Ibid, pp. 53–54
39 Tilak's editorials in the *Kesari* of 22 and 29 October 1901, Kesari Vol IV, pp. 316–p323
40 *Memoirs of Shri Shahu Chhatrapati*, Latthe, Vol. 1, pp. 187–188
41 Ibid, p. 195

42 *Cultural Revolt In a Colonial Society: The Non-Brahman Movement in Western India*, Gail Omvedt, Manohar Publishers, New Delhi (first published in 1976), 2023 edition, p. 132

43 Ibid.

44 *Shahu Chhatrapati aani Lokmanya*, pp. 68–70

45 *Kesari*, Vol 4, pp. 322–323

46 Tilak's comment in the *Kesari* of 5 November 1901, *Shahu Chhatrapati aani Lokmanya*, p. 63

47 *Kesari*, Vol 4, pp. 316–323

48 *Shahu Chhatrapati aani Lokmanya*, p. 103

49 Ibid, pp. 81–82

50 *Shahu Chhatrapati aani Lokmanya*, pp. 120–121

51 Tahmankar, p. 102

52 Ibid, pp. 102–103

53 *Shahu Chhatrapati aani Lokmanya*, p. 127

54 Ibid, p. 129

55 Ibid, pp. 129-135 and Tahmankar, p. 103

56 Ibid, pp. 131–133

57 Ibid, p. 136 and Tahmankar, p. 103

58 *Times of India*, 7 April 1902

59 Source Material For a History of the Freedom Movement: Correspondence and Diary of Shrimant G.S. Khaparde (1897 to 1934), Vol. VII, Government of Maharashtra, Bombay, p. 324

60 Tahmankar, p. 104

61 Source Material, Vol. VII, p. 329

62 *Lokmanya Tilkanchi Geli Aath Varshe*, A.V. Kulkarni, p. 8

63 Quoted in Keer, p. 190

64 Source Material, Vol. VII, p. 324

65 Ibid, p. 325

66 Ibid

67 *Times of India*, 6 January 1904

68 *Times of India*, 6 January 1904

69 Report (Confidential) on Native Papers published in the Bombay Presidency for the week ending 5 September 1903, India Office Library and Records, South Asia Open Archives, p. 18

70 Report (Confidential) on Native Papers published in the Madras Presidency for the week ending 5 March 1904, India Office Library and Records, South Asia Open Archive, p. 96

71 Report (Confidential) on Native Papers published in the Bombay Presidency, 1903, p. 19
72 Ibid, pp. 18–19
73 *Times of India*, 6 January 1904
74 Ibid
75 Tahmankar, p. 105
76 *Shahu Chhatrapati aani Lokmanya*, p. 145
77 Report (Confidential) on Indian papers published in the Bombay Presidency for the week ending 24 April 1915, India Office Library and Records, South Asia Open Archive, p. 14
78 Report (Confidential) on Indian papers published in the Bombay Presidency for the week ending 29 July 1916, India Office Library and Records, South Asia Open Archive, p. 12
79 *Lokmanya Tilkanchi Geli Aath Varshe*, A.V. Kulkarni, pp. 2–8
80 Kesari of 4 July 1904 quoted in Wolpert, p. 152
81 Tilak's 4 July 1899 editorial in the *Kesari*, quoted in *Lokmanya Tilak Lekhsangraha*, p. 100–101
82 Ibid, pp. 102–105
83 Dadaji's letter in Vol. 2 of Kelkar (Marathi), quoted in Wolpert, pp. 152–153
84 Ibid
85 Ibid, p. 156

Chapter 10: Curzon 'the Serpent'

1 *Curzon: Imperial Statesman, David Gilmour, Farrar, Straus and Giroux*, New York, 2003, p1; the doggerel composed by his Balliol classmates, p. 30
2 Ibid, p. 135
3 Ibid, p. 165 and *The Proudest Day*, p. 84
4 *Curzon: Imperial Statesman*, pp. 171–172
5 Ibid, p. 168
6 Tilak's editorial of 2 April 1901 quoted in *Kesari, Lokmanya Tilak Lekh Sangraha*, Volume 4, pp. 844–848
7 *Curzon: Imperial Statesman*, David Gilmour, p. 240
8 Ibid
9 Tilak's editorial of 3 January 1903, Ibid, pp. 82–89
10 *The Proudest Day*, pp. 85–86

11 Tilak's editorial of 21 February 1905, *Lokmanya Tilak Lekhsangraha*, p. 120

12 Ibid, p. 119

13 Ibid, p. 121

14 Ibid, p. 124

15 *The Proudest Day*, pp. 86–88

16 Ibid, p. 85

17 *Curzon*, Gilmour, p. 168

18 *The Proudest Day*, p. 87

19 Ibid, p. 89

20 Ibid, p. 88

21 Quoted in Bhagwat and Pradhan, p. 274

22 *Indian Nationalism and the Early Congress*, John R. McLane, Princeton University Press, New Jersey, 1977, p. 171

23 Ibid, p. 143, 150–151, 166–171

24 Ibid, p. 174

25 Tilak's editorial of 15 August 1905 in the *Kesari*, *Lokmanya Tilak Lekhsangraha*, pp. 134–139

26 Ibid

27 *The Proudest Day*, p. 86

28 Tilak's editorial of 29 August 1905 in the *Kesari*, *Lokmanya Tilak Lekhsangraha*, pp. 140–148

29 Tilak's editorial of 22 August 1905 in the *Kesari*, Ibid, pp. 306–311

30 Tilak's editorials of 5 September and 12 December 1905 in the *Kesari*, Ibid, pp. 312–322; and Wolpert, p. 167

31 Tilak's editorial of 27 September and 4 December 1906 in the *Kesari*, Ibid, pp. 361–366

32 Tilak's editorial of 29 January 1907 in the *Kesari*, Ibid, pp. 372–377; and *Struggle For Freedom, The History and Culture of the Indian People*, Volume 11, edited by R.C. Majumdar, Bharatiya Vidya Bhavan, Mumbai, 2022, p. 44

33 *Savarkar: the True Story of the Father of Hindutva*, Vaibhav Purandare, Juggernaut Books, New Delhi, 2019, pp. 59–63

34 Ibid, pp. 63–64

35 *Lokmanya Tilak Darshan*, B.D. Kher, Mehta Publishing House, Pune, 2022, p. 74

36 Ibid
37 *Struggle For Freedom*, Mujumdar, p. 67
38 *Young India: An Interpretation and A History of the Nationalist Movement From Within*, Lajpat Rai, B.W. Huebsch, New York, 1916, pp. 164–166
39 B.D. Kher, pp. 76–77 and Struggle for Freedom, Mujumdar, p. 45
40 Struggle For Freedom, Mujumdar, p. 45
41 B.D. Kher, p. 85
42 Wolpert, p. 172
43 Young India, Lajpat Rai, pp. 159–160
44 Tahmankar, p. 112
45 *Times of India*, 3 and 16 January 1906
46 *Times of India*, 23 January 1906
47 *Struggle for Freedom*, Majumdar, p. 80
48 Wolpert, pp. 176–177
49 Tahmankar, pp. 117–118
50 *Struggle for Freedom*, Majumdar, p. 81
51 Young India, Lajpat Rai, pp. 162–163
52 Khaparde's Correspondence, p. 339
53 *Bal Gangadhar Tilak: His Writings and Speeches*, Ganesh & Co., Madras, 1922, pp. 27–34
54 Ibid
55 Ibid, pp. 35–41

Chapter 11: Split Wide Open

1 The Proudest Day, p. 89
2 Wolpert, p. 174
3 *Struggle for Freedom*, Majumdar, p. 27
4 Ibid, pp. 46–48
5 Bhagwat and Pradhan, p. 285
6 Ibid, p. 286
7 Phatak, p. 247
8 All the information cited on S.G. Deuskar here is from Ajanta Biswas's essay 'Sakharam Ganesh Deuskar and the Swadeshi Movement in Bengal: The Second Identity', *Social Scientist*, March–April 2005, Vol. 33, No. 3/4, pp. 66–73

 9 Khaparde's Correspondence, pp. 344–345
10 Ibid
11 *Times of India*, 7 June 1906
12 *Times of India*, 8 June 1906
13 Wolpert, p. 180
14 *Bal Gangadhar Tilak: His Writings and Speeches*, pp. 42–47
15 Khaparde's Correspondence, pp. 346–347
16 *Bombay Gazette*, 12 June 1906
17 Khaparde's Correspondence, pp. 347–348
18 *Bombay Gazette*, 15 June 1906
19 *Indian Idea of Political Resistance: Aurobindo, Tilak, Gandhi and Ambedkar*, Ashok S. Chousalkar, Ajanta Publications, Delhi, 1990, p. 27
20 *Sri Aurobindo*, M.P. Pandit, Publications Division, Ministry of Information and Broadcasting, Govt of India, New Delhi, 2000, p. 46
21 *Indian Idea of Political Resistance*, p. 29
22 Ibid
23 Tilak's editorial of 10 July 1906 in the *Kesari*, quoted in Bhagwat and Pradhan, p. 297
24 Tahmankar, p. 120
25 Bhagwat and Pradhan, p. 301
26 Ibid
27 Ibid, p302
28 *Times*, London, 2 January 1907
29 Tahmankar, p. 124
30 Tahmankar, pp. 128–129
31 *The New Spirit in India*, Henry W. Nevinson, Harper & Brothers, London and New York, 1908, pp. 16–25
32 Tahmankar, p. 134
33 *Times*, London, 22 October 1907
34 *The Proudest Day*, p. 104
35 *A History of the Indian National Congress*, Volume One, 1885–1918, S.R. Mehrotra, Vikas Publishing House Pvt Ltd, New Delhi, 1995, p. 224
36 Ibid, p. 204

37 Ibid, p. 208
38 Ibid, p. 209
39 Ibid, p. 210
40 Ibid, p. 212
41 Ibid, p. 215
42 Tahmankar, p. 141
43 Mehrotra, p. 226
44 Ibid, pp. 226–227
45 Bhagwat and Pradhan, p. 338 and p. 341
46 Details of the proceedings of the Surat Congress drawn from Mehrotra (who extensively quotes *Guardian* correspondent, Henry Nevinson), pp. 227–231; Bhagwat and Pradhan, pp. 339–345; Wolpert, pp. 210–211; *The Proudest Day*, p. 104; and Majumdar, pp. 88–92
47 *The Proudest Day*, p. 104
48 Ibid

Chapter 12: 'A Diseased Mind'

1 Bhagwat and Pradhan, p. 291
2 Report on the Native Papers for the week ending 21 December 1907, page 38, paragraph 46, Bombay government records, quoted in Source Material For A History of The Freedom Movement in India, Vol II, pp. 252–254
3 Report of H.G. Gell, Bombay police commissioner, to the Secretary, Bombay government, 27 August 1908, where he cites the 15 December 1907 meeting, Ibid, pp. 256–259
4 Ibid, pp. 252–254
5 Report of H.G. Gell, Bombay police commissioner, to the Secretary, Bombay government, 27 August 1908, where he cites the 15 December 1907 meeting, Ibid, pp. 256–259
6 *The Proudest Day*, pp. 103–104
7 Wolpert, p. 216
8 *Struggle For Freedom*, Majumdar, pp. 199–200
9 *Times*, London, 7 May 1908
10 *Daily Telegraph*, 4 May 1908

11 Quoted in *Times*, London, 6 May 1908
12 *Samagra Tilak*, Volume 3, pp. 937–944
13 *Samagra Tilak*, Volume 6, pp. 1032–1050
14 *Karmayogi Lokmanya*, Sadanand More, Shri Gandharv-Ved Prakashan, Pune, 2014, pp. 302–303
15 *Source Material for a History of The Freedom Movement in India*, Vol II, p. 258
16 Ibid, p. 257
17 Ibid, p. 258
18 *The Proudest Day*, p. 93
19 *Trial of Tilak*, p. 40–41
20 Ibid, pp. 41–42
21 Ibid, pp. 42–44
22 *Tilak and Jinnah: Comrades in the Freedom Struggle*, A.G. Noorani, Oxford University Press, Karachi, pp. 5–6
23 *Indian Political Trials*, p. 125
24 *Trial of Tilak*, pp. 50–51
25 Ibid, pp. 54–58
26 Ibid, p. 79
27 *Struggle For Freedom*, p. 109
28 *Trial of Tilak*, pp. 169–171
29 *Trial of Tilak*, pp. 87–182
30 Ibid, pp. 181–182
31 Ibid, p. 182
32 Ibid, p. 188
33 Ibid, p. 218
34 *Indian Political Trials*, p. 125
35 *Trial of Tilak*, p. 228
36 Ibid, p. 229
37 Ibid
38 *Struggle for Freedom*, p. 260
39 Ibid, pp. 261–263
40 *Times, London*, 28 July 1908
41 Keer, pp. 310–311
42 Ibid, p. 268
43 Ibid, pp. 268–269

44 *Lenin The Dictator*, Victor Sebestyen, Weidenfeld & Nicolson, London, 2018, pp. 165–166

45 Inflammable Material in World Politics, Proletary, No. 33, 5 August 1908, published in *Lenin Collected Works, Volume 15*, Progress Publishers, Moscow, 1973, pp. 182–188, accessed here: https://www.marxists.org/archive/lenin/works/1908/jul/23.htm

46 *Daily Telegraph*, 24 July 1908

47 *Observer*, 26 July 1908

48 *Times*, London, 28 July 1908

49 Henry Cotton in the New Age, quoted in *Trial of Tilak*, pp. 429–430

50 *Times*, London, 28 July 1908

51 H.M. Hyndman in *The Times*, London, 27 July 1908

52 Keir Hardie in the *Labour Leader*, quoted in *Trial of Tilak*, p. 434

53 Ibid

54 *Guardian*, 29 July 1908

55 *Scotsman*, quoted in Trial of Tilak, p. 432

56 Ibid, p. 435

57 Ibid, pp. 443–444

58 Ibid, p. 444

59 Ibid, p. 430

60 Ibid, p. 436

61 Ibid, p. 429

62 Ibid, p. 442

Chapter 13: The Prisoner of Mandalay

1 Tilak described the details in a press interview he gave on his return to Pune on 23 June 1914, quoted in Tahmankar, p. 193

2 Ibid, p. 194

3 Ibid pp. 193–195

4 Quoted in Phatak, p. 430

5 Bapat, Volume 1, p. 20

6 Discussion on 'The sentence on Mr. Tilak', in the British House of Commons, 28 July 1908, accessed on Hansard: https://api.

parliament.uk/historic-hansard/commons/1908/jul/28/the-sentence-on-mr-tilak#S4V0193P0_19080728_HOC_185

7 Ibid
8 *Bombay Chronicle*, 17 November 1917
9 Keer, p. 308
10 Bose quoted in Tahmankar, pp. 192–193
11 Vasudeo Kulkarni's account in *Letters of Lokmanya Tilak*, edited by M.D. Vidwans, Kesari Prakashan, Poona, 1966, pp. 5–7
12 Ibid, pp. 7–8
13 Ibid, pp. 22–25
14 Ibid, p. 66
15 Ibid, p. 33
16 Ibid, p. 76
17 Ibid, p. 30
18 Ibid, p. 31
19 Ibid
20 Ibid, p. 32
21 Ibid, p. 37
22 Ibid, p. 41
23 Ibid, p. 36
24 Ibid, p. 8
25 Ibid, pp. 39–40
26 Ibid, p. 53
27 Ibid, p. 55
28 Ibid, p. 57
29 Ibid, p. 23 and *Mandalaycha Rajbandi*, Arvind. V. Gokhale, Rajhans Prakashan, Pune, 2014, pp. 220–221
30 *Letters of Lokmanya Tilak*, p. 63
31 Ibid, pp. 48–49
32 Ibid, p. 64
33 Ibid, p. 53
34 Ibid, p. 74
35 Ibid, p. 76
36 Ibid
37 Ibid, pp. 66–67
38 Ibid, pp. 43–44

39 Ibid, pp. 45–47
40 Ibid, p. 47
41 Tahmankar, p. 196
42 *Letters of Lokmanya Tilak*, p. 26
43 Ibid, pp. 101–103
44 *Sri Bhagvadgita Rahasya or Karma Yoga Shastra*, B.G. Tilak, English translation by B. S. Sukhtankar, published for Tilak Bros by R.B. Tilak, Pune, 1935, pages xxv–xxvi
45 Ibid, pages xvi and xviii
46 Ibid, page xvi
47 Ibid, pages xviii-xix
48 *Letters of Lokmanya Tilak*, p. 111
49 Ibid, p. 53 and pp. 58–59
50 Ibid, pp. 104–108
51 Ibid, p. 109
52 Ibid, pp. 108–109
53 Ibid, p. 122
54 Ibid, pp. 123–124
55 Ibid, pp. 126–127
56 Ibid, p. 129
57 Ibid, p. 131
58 Ibid, p. 133
59 Ibid, p. 131
60 Ibid, pp. 130–132 and p. 136
61 Tahmankar, pp. 199–200
62 *Letters of Lokmanya Tilak*, p. 137
63 Ibid, p. 137
64 Ibid, p. 143
65 Ibid, p. 148
66 Khaparde's Correspondence, p. 380
67 Ibid, p. 382
68 Ibid, p. 384
69 Ibid, pp. 383–384
70 Ibid, p. 385
71 Ibid, p. 386
72 Ibid, p. 384

73 Ibid, p. 382
74 Ibid, 214
75 Ibid, p. 213
76 Ibid, p. 151
77 Ibid, pp. 116–117
78 Ibid, p. 114
79 Ibid, p. 115
80 Ibid, p. 123
81 Ibid, p. 389
82 *Letters of Lokmanya Tilak*, p. 151
83 Tahmankar, pp. 202–203
84 Ibid, p. 203
85 *Letters of Lokmanya Tilak*, p. 170
86 Ibid, pp. 174–176 and p. 179
87 Ibid, p. 177 and p. 182
88 Tahmankar, pp. 197–198
89 Ibid, p. 198
90 Ibid, p. 199 and pp. 206–207; *Bombay Chronicle*, 18 June 1914
91 Ibid, p. 207
92 Ibid, p. 208
93 *Bombay Chronicle*, 18 June 1914
94 Tahmankar, p. 208
95 Ibid, p. 209

Chapter 14: Back Home: Congress, Home Rule and the Lucknow Pact

1 British Secret Official View Regarding Lokmanya Tilak & *Gita Rahasya*, J.V. Naik, Tilak Smarak Trust, Pune, 2005, pp. 64–65
2 Ibid, p. 56 and p. 61
3 Ibid, p. 61
4 *The Struggle For Freedom*, Majumdar, pp. 107–109
5 *Tilak & Gita Rahasya*, p. 59
6 Ibid, pp. 59–60
7 Ibid, p. 60
8 Ibid, p. 57

9   *The Struggle For Freedom*, p. 108

10 *Tilak & Gita Rahasya*, p. 59

11 Ibid, p. 60

12 Ibid, p. 59

13 Ibid, p. 61

14 Ibid

15 Ibid, p. 62

16 Ibid, Appendix XI, p. 145

17 Tahmankar, p. 209

18 *Tilak & Gita Rahasya*, pp. 60–61

19 *Evening Standard*, 27 June 1914

20 *The Proudest Day*, pp. 107–108; and *Peace, Poverty and Betrayal*, pp. 304–305

21 Tilak's statement published in the *Mahratta*, 29 August 1914

22 *Guardian*, 24 September 1914

23 Quoted in *Lokmanya Tilak Aani Krantikarak*, Phadke, p. 120

24 Quoted in *Bombay Chronicle*, 12 October 1914

25 Quoted in *Bombay Chronicle*, 24 October 1914

26 *Bombay Chroncile*, 30 September 1914

27 Ibid

28 Annie Besant and India 1913–1917, Joanne Stafford Mortimer, *Journal of Contemporary History*, Sage, London, Beverly Hills and New Delhi, Vol. 18, 1983, p. 63

29 Ibid, p. 64

30 Ibid, p. 65

31 Wolpert, p. 249

32 Ibid, p. 250

33 Ibid, p. 253

34 Ibid, p. 258

35 Gokhale, Nanda, p. 451

36 Ibid

37 Ibid, pp. 265–266

38 Ibid, p. 453

39 Ibid, p. 266

40 Nanda, pp. 452–453

41 *Bombay Chronicle*, 6 February 1915

42 Wolpert, p. 267
43 Nanda, pp. 455–456
44 Wolpert, p. 270
45 Nanda, p. 456
46 Ibid, p. 457; and Bhagwat and Pradhan, p. 439
47 Bhagwat and Pradhan, p. 439
48 Ibid, p. 445
49 Ibid, p. 446
50 Ibid, pp. 446–447
51 *Bombay Chronicle*, 6 February 1915
52 Nanda, p. 453
53 Ibid, pp. 458–459
54 Ibid, p. 459
55 *Mahatma*, D.G. Tendulkar, Volume I, p. 186
56 Ibid, pp. 187–190
57 *Collected Works of Mahatma Gandhi*, Vol 14,
58 Ibid, p. 195
59 *Karmayogi Lokamanya*, More, pp. 377–378
60 Nanda, p467
61 Bhagwat and Pradhan, p. 448
62 *Lokmanya Tilak and Gita Rahasya*, J.V. Naik, p. 46
63 Ibid, p. 50 and pp. 100–116
64 *Karmayogi Lokmanya*, More, p. 345
65 *Bhagwat and Pradhan*, p. 454
66 *Mahatma*, D.G. Tendulkar, Vol. I, p. 217
67 Bhagwat and Pradhan, pp. 451–454
68 Ibid, pp. 452–455 and p. 459; and Rebels Against the Raj: Western
    Fighters for India's Freedom, Ramachandra Guha, Penguin Allen
    Lane, 2022, p. 30, 31–32
69 Bhagwat and Pradhan, pp. 455–457
70 *Karmyayogi Lokmanya*, pp. 392–393
71 *Lokmanya Tilak: Athvani aani Akhyayika*, Vol 1, pp. 35–37
72 Mahatma, D.G. Tendulkar, Vol. 1, p. 230
73 *Times of India*, 2 May 1916
74 *Times of India*, 12 May 1916

75 *Lokmanya Tilak: Athvani aani Akhyayika*, Vol 1, pp. 35–37

76 *Times of India*, 1 May 1916

77 Bhagwat and Pradhan, pp. 461–462

78 *Times of India*, 24 July 1916

79 *Times of India*, 8 August 1916

80 *Times of India*, 8 and 9 August 1916

81 *Times of India*, 8 August 1916

82 *Times of India*, 8 and 9 August 1916

83 *Times of India*, 15 August 1916

84 *Jinnah and Tilak*, A.G. Noorani, Oxford University Press, Karachi, 2010, P319

85 *Bombay Chronicle*, 9 November 1916

86 *Jinnah and Tilak*, Noorani, p. 344

87 Ibid, pp. 346–347

88 Bhagwat and Pradhan, p. 471

89 *Bombay Chronicle*, 10 November 1916

90 Bhagwat and Pradhan, pp. 472–473

91 *Bombay Chronicle*, 13 November 1916

92 *Karmayogi Lokmanya*, pp. 399–400

93 Quoted in Bhagwat and Pradhan, p. 480

94 *Jinnah of Pakistan*, Stanley Wolpert, p. 42

95 *Mahatma*, D.G. Tendulkar, Vol 1, p. 231

96 *Karmayogi Lokmanya*, More, p. 402

97 *Bombay Chronicle*, 29 December 1916

98 Ibid

99 Ibid

100 *Proudest Day*, pp. 107–108; Mahatma, Vol 1, p. 33; and *Jinnah of Pakistan*, p. 46

101 *Bombay Chronicle*, 29 December 1916

102 *Lokmanya Tilak: Athvani aani Akhyayika*, Vol 2, pp. 535–536

103 *Tilak and Gokhale*, Wolpert, p. 275

104 *Mahatma*, D.G. Tendulkar, Vol 1, p. 234

105 Ibid

106 Ibid

107 Ibid, p. 235

Chapter 15: Towards a Free India

1   Bhagwat and Pradhan, p. 488
2   Ibid, p. 489
3   Ibid, p. 493
4   Ibid, pp. 491–492
5   *The Struggle For Freedom*, Majumdar, p. 255
6   Ibid
7   Bhagwat and Pradhan, p. 493
8   *The Proudest Day*, p. 134
9   *The Struggle For Freedom*, Majumdar, p. 254
10 Ram Gopal, p. 384
11 *Bombay Chronicle*, 11 July 1917
12 *The Proudest Day*, p. 134
13 *Bombay Chronicle*, 17 July 1917
14 The Proudest Day, p. 133
15 *Bombay Chronicle*, 17 July 1917
16 Ibid
17 Bhagwat and Pradhan, pp. 492–493
18 *Rebels Against The Raj*, pp. 41–43
19 *An Indian Diary*, Edwin S. Montagu, William Heinemann Ltd,
    Norwich, 1930, p. 3
20 *The Struggle For Freedom*, Majumdar, p. 256
21 *An Indian Diary*, Montagu, pp. 4–5
22 Ibid, p. 43
23 *Bombay Chronicle*, 27 November 1917
24 *Ram Gopal*, pp. 388–389
25 *An Indian Diary*, Montagu, p. 56
26 Ibid, p. 59
27 Ibid, pp. 61–62
28 *Bombay Chronicle*, 30 November 1917
29 *Bombay Chronicle*, 3 December 1917
30 Bhagwat and Pradhan, p. 498
31 *Mahatma*, Vol 1, D.G. Tendulkar, p. 266
32 Ibid, pp. 265–266
33 Ibid
34 Ibid, p. 266

35 Bhagwat and Pradhan, pp. 511–513

36 Ibid, pp. 501–502

37 Ibid, pp. 513–514

38 *Mahatma*, Vol 1, D.G. Tendulkar, pp. 266–267

39 *Cultural Revolt in a Colonial Society*, p. 200

40 Ibid, p. 203 and p. 205

41 Ibid

42 *Karmayogi Lokmanya*, More, p. 407

43 Bhagwat and Pradhan, pp. 504–505

44 Ibid, pp. 506–508

45 *Cultural Revolt in a Colonial Society*, p. 210; and Bhagwat and Pradhan, p. 506

46 Ibid, p. 506

47 *Shahu Chhatrapati Aani Lokmanya*, p. 282

48 *Bombay Chronicle*, 25 March 1918

49 *Shahu Chhatrapati Aani Lokmanya*, pp. 288–289

50 Bhagwat and Pradhan, p. 530

51 Ram Gopal, pp. 393–394

52 *The Struggle For Freedom*, p. 184

53 Ibid

54 Ibid

55 Ibid

56 Bhagwat and Pradhan, pp. 522–523

57 Ibid, pp. 524–525

58 *Mahatma, Vol 1*, D.G. Tendulkar, p. 277

59 An Indian Diary, Montagu, pp. 373–374

60 Mahatma, Vol 1, D.G. Tendulkar, p280

61 Ibid

62 Ibid, p. 278

63 Bhagwat and Pradhan, p521

64 *The Proudest Day*, p. 137

65 Bhagwat and Pradhan, p. 533 and Ibid, p. 137

66 *The Struggle For Freedom*, pp. 276–277

67 *Tilak and Gokhale*, Wolpert, p. 287

68 Ibid, pp. 288–289

69 Ibid

70 *The Struggle For Freedom*, p. 281
71 Ibid, p. 285
72 *Karmayogi Lokmanya*, More, pp. 409–410
73 *The Struggle For Freedom*, p. 288
74 *An Indian Diary*, Montagu, pp. 345–346
75 *The Proudest Day*, p. 133 and p. 135
76 *Herald*, 13 April 1918
77 *Times*, London, 29 April 1919
78 *Lokmanya Tilak: Athvani Aani Akhyayika*, Vol 2, p. 579
79 *Herald*, UK, 9 November 1918
80 Bhagwat and Pradhan, p. 537
81 Ibid, pp. 537–537 and Wolpert, pp. 283–285
82 Wolpert, p. 284
83 Bhagwat and Pradhan, p. 538
84 *Herald*, 27 April 1918
85 Wolpert, p. 285
86 Ibid
87 Ibid
88 *Times*, London, 30 January 1919
89 *Times*, London, 31 January 1919
90 *Times*, London, 13 February 1919
91 *Times*, London, 30 January 1919
92 *Manchester Evening News*, 17 February 1919
93 *Times*, London, 22 February 1919
94 Ibid
95 Bhagwat and Pradhan, p. 554
96 Bhagwat and Pradhan, pp. 553–554
97 *Guardian*, 19 March 1919 and The Herald, 1 March 1919
98 *Bombay Chronicle*, 18 March 1919
99 Bhagwat and Pradhan, p. 555
100 Wolpert, p. 289
101 Ibid, p. 288
102 Ibid
103 *An Indian Diary*, Montagu, p. 58
104 *History of the Congress*, Pattabhi Sitaramayya, p. 137
105 *History of the Congress*, pp. 175–176

106 *Rebels Against the Raj*, p. 50
107 *Daily Herald*, 8 May 1919
108 Bhagwat and Pradhan, p. 570
109 Ibid, pp. 571–573
110 Wolpert, pp. 290–291
111 Ibid
112 Bhagwat and Pradhan, pp. 582–583
113 Ibid, p. 581
114 Wolpert, p. 291
115 Ibid, p. 291 and Bhagwat and Pradhan, p. 583
116 Bhagwat and Pradhan, pp. 593–594
117 Ibid, p. 587, p. 588, p. 595
118 Ibid, pp. 596–598
119 Ibid, p. 599

Acknowledgements

I would like to say a big 'Thank you!' to:

Premanka Goswami, associate publisher at Penguin Random House India, who believed in this project right from the beginning and made it happen, showing tremendous patience with me as I worked on the manuscript while pursuing my job as a full-time journalist.

The Shree V. Faatak Granth Sangrahalaya in Vile Parle, Mumbai, whose wonderful repository of Tilak's writings in the *Kesari* and *Mahratta* and of reference works on his life and the lives of his contemporaries and associates enabled me to mine all their rich cupboardfuls of volumes.

Vikas Paranjpe, well-known Marathi publisher, who pointed me towards and lent me rare books I would otherwise not have been able to lay my hands on, and who responded to every call I made for help, whether it was for clearing doubts or questions in my mind or discussing issues and controversies related to Tilak's life. Paranjpe's authority on the subject of Tilak's life is complete and he understands nuances so well that every interaction with him about the text was enriching.

The digital library of the Asiatic Society of Bombay, which provided me access to past issues of the *Times of India, Bombay Gazette*, the *Bombay Chronicle* and so many other pro- and anti-Raj newspapers and periodicals of the period.

The British Newspaper Archives, for enabling me to get a comprehensive record of the way newspapers and periodicals in London and the rest of Britain reacted to Tilak's anti-colonial positions.

Rohit Bundelkhandi, who found for me the right scanners for photographs from the archives.

Rachel Rojy and Yash Daiv, who carefully edited the text and helped to improve it by pointing out so many important things; and to Rachel again for shortlisting the photographs.

And last, yet truly always the first, my family: my wife Swapna and son Vikrant, my parents Jagdish and Jyotsna Purandare, my brother Kunal Purandare and sister-in-law Avani, and my two little nephews, Vedant and Vardaan, to whom this book is dedicated.